Why Do You Need This New Edition?

Maintaining its devotion to the examination of the attitudes, gender identities and stereotypes that characterize communication in relationships, *GenderSpeak 5/e* has been thoroughly revised and edited to include the newest research and technology affecting gender communication. This new edition includes the following:

1. Updated **examples of praise and criticism in innovative ad campaigns** that target a female audience have been included to give you the most up-to-date, real-life portrayal of the concepts you study in class.

2. **New information on internet pornography and tips for avoiding these sites** have been added to provide you with the ins and outs of the deceptive techniques of internet pornographers.

3. Discussions on **workplace harassment, women in the American workforce, and the barriers that restrict women in the workplace** give you insight and information for recognizing and avoiding these situations when you begin your career.

4. An increased and updated discussion on **"friends with benefits" and new information on *sexting*** gives you a more theoretical view of these types of relationships and communication styles, and the effects they can have.

5. A concentrated focus in **Chapter 8** on **abuses of power in relationships** through rape/sexual assault and partner violence provides you with necessary information for detection, as well as the **myths and truths surrounding these abuses.**

6. **"Hot Topics"** at the start of each chapter provide you with key issues and **topical chapter outlines that you can use for studying and review. Case studies** provide you with context and real-life examples of the ideas discussed in class.

7. A new section on the **depictions of gay, lesbian, bisexual, and transgender characters in television programming** informs you of recent expansions of such depictions on TV.

PEARSON

Fifth Edition

GenderSpeak

PERSONAL EFFECTIVENESS IN GENDER COMMUNICATION

Diana K. Ivy

Texas A&M University, Corpus Christi

PEARSON

Boston   Columbus Indianapolis   New York   San Francisco
Upper Saddle River   Amsterdam   Cape Town   Dubai   London
Madrid   Milan   Munich   Paris   Montreal   Toronto   Delhi
Mexico City   Sao Paulo   Sydney   Hong Kong
Seoul   Singapore   Taipei   Tokyo

To Important Women
Hazel, Carol, and Karen
DKI

Editor-in-Chief, Communications: Karon Bowers
Assistant Editor: Stephanie Chaisson
Associate Managing Editor: Bayani Mendoza de Leon
Marketing Manager: Blair Tuckman
Manufacturing Buyer: Mary Ann Gloriande
Image Permission Coordinators: Annette Linder/Lee Scher
Photo Researcher: Jennifer Nonenmacher
Project Coordination, Text Design, and Electronic Page Makeup: Laserwords Maine
Art Director, Cover: Nancy Danahy
Senior Cover Design Manager: Nancy Danahy
Printer/Binder/Cover Printer: STP Courier
Cover Images: LAMB/Alamy; Gino's Premium Images/Alamy; Paval Konovalov/Alamy; Kuzma/Alamy; Mittlphoto/Alamy

Credits: page 4, excerpt from Lucy Stone, Suffragist, in her "Disappointment is the Lot of Women" speech of 1855; **page 295,** Why People Stay in Abusive Relationships, © 2008 Corpus Christi Caller-Times. Reprinted with permission.

Library of Congress Cataloging-in-Publication Data

Ivy, Diana K.
  Genderspeak : personal effectiveness in gender communication / Diana K.
Ivy.—5th ed.
    p. cm.
 ISBN-13: 978-0-205-82547-9
 ISBN-10: 0-205-82547-8
1.   Communication—Sex differences. I. Title.
P96.S48I96 2012
302.2081--dc23

                                                          2011034699

Copyright © 2012, 2008 by Pearson Education, Inc.

1 2 3 4 5 6 7 8 9 10—STP-C—14 13 12 11

www.pearsonhighered.com

ISBN-13: 978-0-205-82547-9
ISBN-10:   0-205-82547-8

ABOUT THE AUTHOR

Diana K. Ivy is a professor of Communication at Texas A&M University–Corpus Christi, with specialities in gender, interpersonal, nonverbal, and instructional communication. She received her undergraduate degree in speech communication and theatre from Texas Wesleyan University in her hometown of Fort Worth, Texas. After serving as an administrator at Wesleyan, Ivy pursued graduate education at the University of Oklahoma. She achieved her M.A. and Ph.D. at OU, concentrating on instructional and interpersonal communication. Ivy's first faculty position was as Basic Course Director in the Department of Communication Studies at Texas State University, San Marcos, where she received the Professor of the Year Award from the Nontraditional Student Organization and the departmental Outstanding Teacher Award. She then became Basic Course Director at the Department of Communication at North Carolina State University. At A&M–Corpus Christi, she served as Director of the Women's Center for Education and Service and as Speaker of the Faculty Senate. In 2002, Ivy was named Outstanding Gender Scholar of the Year by the Southern States Communication Association. She is co-author of two other communication textbooks, *Communication: Principles for a Lifetime* and *The Nonverbal Self*, both published by Pearson; author of numerous book chapters, articles, and papers; and a guest contributor to *Cosmopolitan* magazine. Ivy hosts a talk radio show, "Call Me Ivy," for 1440 KEYS radio in Corpus Christi, Texas, with a focus on community issues and communication in relationships.

CONTENTS

PART IV　The Contexts for Our Relationships: Personal Effectiveness in Action

Chapter 8   Power Abuses in Human Relationships   274

Chapter 9   Women and Men in the Workplace: The Challenges of Talking Shop   304

PREFACE

A CHANGING TEXT FOR A RAPIDLY CHANGING WORLD

In just a few short years since the fourth edition of this book was published, much has changed in terms of how college students access information and the ease with which they consume and exchange material digitally. These changes have profound implications for gender communication. Thus, the revision of *GenderSpeak* into its fifth edition wasn't a revision, but an overhaul.

GenderSpeak is written primarily for college undergraduates enrolled in courses that focus on the effects of gender on the communication process; the text is appropriate for upper-division courses as well as more introductory ones. While some prior exposure to basic concepts and theories of interpersonal communication will serve readers well, it's not a prerequisite for understanding the content of this text. Some professors adopt the book (or certain chapters from it) to supplement readings in courses like interpersonal communication and relational communication. Others use the text to supplement assigned readings for master's level seminars in gender communication; it provides graduate students a theoretical foundation, a common language, and a research base for further study.

The book's basic organization remains; the Prologue-plus-ten-chapter organization can easily be covered over the course of a semester or quarter. The Prologue includes contextual and historical information to help students situate the content and realize how far we've come in terms of equality for the sexes. (It also prompts us to ponder how much further we have to go.) Part One, "Communication, Gender, and Effectiveness," contains an overview of the communication process, including an emphasis on the receiver of communication, a discussion of key terminology, and a description of the various components within the personal effectiveness approach.

Part Two, "Influences on Our Choices," encourages readers to explore the many influences that shape their identities, attitudes, expectations, and communication as women and men. This section is based on an assumption that students must first understand what influences them—choices they make about themselves and communication—before they can work to improve their communication skills and relationships. Part Two concludes with a chapter devoted to the influence of mediated communication on sex and gender, including an extensive discussion of pornography.

"Let's Talk: Initiating and Developing Relationships" is the title of Part Three, which begins with an in-depth discussion of language—language used *about* the sexes that influences our perceptions of ourselves and others, as well as language used *between* the sexes in relationships. The focus then shifts to the role of gender communication in the initiation, development, maintenance, and sometimes termination of personal relationships, including online relationships.

After conveying the building blocks of gender communication and relationship development, students proceed to the final section of the text. In Part Four, "The Contexts for Our Relationships: Personal Effectiveness in Action," five chapters explore ways in which gender communication affects and is affected by the following contexts of life situations: friendships (same-sex and cross-sex), intimate or romantic relationships, the workplace, and educational settings. Chapter 8 investigates the "downside" of human relationships—power abuses in the form of sexual assault and partner violence.

GenderSpeak continues in its commitment to the receiver orientation to communication and the personal effectiveness approach to gender communication, but to say that the content was merely revised and updated is an understatement. Granted, authors make that claim often, as they attempt to persuade potential adopters that, indeed, *this revision is really different*. But my contention in offering this fifth edition is that readers will see a book bravely immersed in twenty-first century gender communication, with all its complexities and ramifications.

WHAT'S NEW IN THE FIFTH EDITION

- An expanded discussion in Chapter 2 of the effects of video game portrayals on gender identity development, with new research documenting (a) the presence of more strong female characters in video games; (b) the effects of hypersexualized, objectified, and stereotypical female depiction on children's and adults' attitudes about sex and gender; and (c) a connection between exposure to virtual violence and aggressive attitudes and behavior
- Chapter 3's discussion of the praise and criticism given to innovative ad campaigns targeting a female audience, such as Nike's "Get Real" series and the Dove "Campaign for Real Beauty," and ad campaigns featuring men in offbeat depictions, such as "Old Spice Man"
- A compare-and-contrast exploration of men's and women's portrayals in television, specifically scripted versus reality programming
- A new section on television's inclusion of gay, lesbian, bisexual, and transgender characters in programming, with examples of how such depiction has expanded in recent years
- An updated discussion of the impact of accessible and affordable Internet pornography on consumers of such material, in terms of attitudes about the sexes and relationships between women and men
- Tips for avoiding deceptive techniques Internet pornographers use to lure computer users to pornographic sites
- Updates on sexual content and gender depiction in music videos, in terms of effects on consumers (who can readily access music videos on handheld devices)
- An extensive new section on sex, gender, and new media, including such topics as online gender identity expression through innovations like blogs and avatar creation, virtual versus "real" sexual bodies, and gendered gaming
- A review in Chapter 4 of new studies on marital naming and identity, specifically the often awkward negotiation of who will take whose name in those contexts where it's legal for gays and lesbians to marry
- Information about how "digital natives" (people who've grown up in a digital age and who make little distinction between online and offline lives) view gender communication and achieve relationship satisfaction
- New research on the connection between sexual self-disclosure in intimate relationships, self-esteem of partners, and relationship satisfaction
- Updated information about college students' increasing levels of narcissism, as detected in longitudinal studies, and the resulting impact on their ability to relate empathically to others
- Research findings that suggest male-male online friendships tend to operate differently than face-to-face friendships, particularly in terms of self-disclosure, risk, and intimacy

- A discussion of the unique friendships that often form between straight women and gay men
- New research on unrequited romance, or how friends negotiate one person's failed attempt to turn a friendship into a romantic relationship, so that they can maintain the friendship
- An expanded, updated discussion of an increasingly prevalent form of friendship: "friends with benefits"
- Information about a new approach to relationship development—"frugaling"—which involves more than friendship, but less than dating
- Studies on the impact of mobile phone usage on the relational dialectical tension of autonomy versus connection, with advice about how couples might negotiate the role of texting and talking on cell phones in their relationship development
- College students' preferences for breakup methods, with surprising research showing that the face-to-face conversation is preferred over using technology like text-messaging, IM-ing, or emailing to break up with a relational partner
- New research on gender communication in the post-dissolution relationship (including the "on-again, off-again" romantic relationship)
- Updated research on *sexting*, as well as how relational partners communicate their sexual histories, views about condom use and protection, and preferences for sexual activity
- A concentrated focus in Chapter 8 on two forms of abuses of power in relationships (rape/sexual assault and partner violence), with material on sexual harassment (originally in Chapter 8) streamlined and incorporated within Chapter 9's discussion of workplace harassment
- An expanded discussion of the role of consent in sexual activity and the need for verbal consent rather than nonverbal "vibes"
- Updated statistics regarding partner violence, with new information about same-sex partner abuse
- A discussion of ramifications (for both work life and home life) of the fact that as of 2009, women make up half of the American workforce
- The current status of the "glass ceiling" as well as the "sticky floor" (barriers that keep women in lower paid positions and prevent them from seeking promotion) for women in the American workforce
- Updates on the gender achievement gap among school-aged boys and girls with regard for STEM areas (science, technology, engineering, and mathematics)
- New observations about female and male students, professors' communication, and the "chilly climate" of the college classroom
- New research on *contrapower sexual harassment*, as pertains to students sexually harassing professors, in addition to studies on bullying, incivility, and unwanted sexual attention in college and university settings

PEDAGOGICAL FEATURES

Each chapter includes nine pedagogical features, which serve as aids for instructors and students alike. *Hot Topics* are a means of helping students realize the scope of each chapter. These bulleted phrases serve as topical chapter outlines, which students can use to prepare for exams or to simply check their understanding of chapter content.

Case Studies introduce most chapters, although in Chapter 8 on power abuses, case studies are embedded in the text for the two main topics. In some instances, case studies represent actual events that occurred or emerged from discussions in gender communication classrooms. The case study device is used not only to gain attention from readers as they delve into a new topic, but also to orient or alert the reader to the nature of the discussion that lies ahead.

A popular feature retained and updated in the fifth edition is the *Celebrity Quote*. These fascinating (and sometimes appalling) quotes relate to concepts discussed on the pages. These "pearls of wisdom" come from film and television personalities, athletes, political figures, musicians, and historical figures.

Also updated are chapter-end *Conclusions*, as well as the series of *Discussion Starters* that instructors may use as a means of generating class discussion about chapter content, as actual assignments, or as thought provokers for students to consider on their own time.

Complete *References* to the updated research base cited within the text appear at the end of each chapter. Students may find these references useful as they prepare assignments and/or conduct their own research projects. Instructors may use the references to gather additional material for their own research or to supplement instruction.

The fifth edition also provides updated boxed features entitled *Remember . . .*, which go beyond a simple listing of key terms to provide brief definitions for students' review. These boxes appear intermittently within each chapter as a reminder to students of important concepts they will want to retain.

The *Net Notes* feature was retained, with updated websites related to chapter content. For example, in our discussion of gender and new media in Chapter 3, new information from a website offers tips for avoiding online traps that lure users to porn sites.

Finally, the fifth edition features updated *Hot Button Issue* boxes, where ideas challenge students' thinking related to sex and gender. These boxes often raise controversial issues—not in a way that advocates a particular stance, but that encourages students to think for themselves.

ACKNOWLEDGMENTS

Long-time adopters of *GenderSpeak* will no doubt notice that the fifth edition is single-authored, instead of co-authored with Phil Backlund. After working faithfully and arduously on the multiple editions of this book for over two decades, Phil decided to put his considerable energy into other projects, so the revision to produce this fifth edition of the text was a sole endeavor. No words can adequately convey the gratitude Ivy and Pearson staff feel for Phil's contributions to the original vision of this book, his efforts on subsequent editions, and his continued support and good humor throughout the book's evolution.

This project has certainly been a team effort; thus there are many people to acknowledge and thank. The author wishes to thank the folks I've been privileged to work with at Pearson, including various editors and "queen bee" Karon Bowers, who all offered great assistance, encouragement, and suggestions. Thanks are also extended to the team at Laserwords for their significant contributions in production.

Gratitude goes to colleagues in the field of communication whose advice and encouragement were invaluable throughout the review process over the multiple editions of this text. Reviewers over the years include: Elizabeth Altman, University of Southern California; Janis Andersen, Emerson College; Bernardo Attias, California State University, Northridge; Cynthia Begnal, Pennsylvania State University; Cynthia Berryman-Fink, formerly of University of Cincinnati; Anne E. Boyle, University of Maryland; Diana Carlin, University of Kansas; Dan Cavanaugh, formerly of Texas State University, San Marcos; Sheila A. Cuffy, Indiana–Purdue University, Fort Wayne; Judith Dallinger, Western Illinois University; Marsha D. Dixson, Indiana–Purdue University, Fort Wayne; Rozell R. Duncan, Kent State University; Pamela Dunkin, Southern Oregon State University; Karen Foss, University of Arizona; Marcie Goodman, University of Utah; Trudy Hanson, West Texas A&M University; Jim Hasenauer, California State University, Northridge; Karla Kay Jensen, Texas Tech University; Naomi Johnson, University of North Carolina, Chapel Hill; Meredith Moore, Washburn University; Carol Morgan, Wright State University; Anthony Mulac, University of California, Santa Barbara; Mark P. Orbe, Western Michigan University; Lisa M. Orick-Martinez, Central New Mexico Community College; Jamey A. Piland, Trinity Washington University; Linda M. Pledge, University of Arkansas at Little Rock; Joey W. Pogue, Pittsburg State University; Judith Pratt, California State University, Bakersfield; Pamela Schultz, Alfred University; Robert Smith, University of Tennessee, Martin; Laura Stafford, University of Kentucky; Helen Sterk, Calvin College; Judith Terminin, Gallaudet University; Lynn H. Turner, Marquette University; Melinda S. Woman, Santiago Canyon College; Julia Wood, University of North Carolina, Chapel Hill; Jim Hasenhauer, California State University, Northridge; Lisa M. Orick-Martinez, Central New Mexico Community College; and Melinda S. Womack, Santiago Community College.

Thanks also to colleagues in the Department of Communication at Texas A&M University–Corpus Christi, for their unwavering support and constant praise. Nada Frazier, graduate of Texas A&M University–Corpus Christi, is much appreciated for her contribution to the Prologue. And a very special thanks go to our dear friends and support systems extraordinaire, Steve and Sue Beebe, Texas State University, San Marcos, for their advice, empathy, good humor, and encouragement of a fellow author.

No project for the benefit of college students has probably ever succeeded without the help of college students. Thousands deserve thanks at Texas A&M University–Corpus Christi for being sources of inspiration for the creation and revision of this textbook. Students of gender communication deserve thanks for providing the motivation to write this text and the "fuel" for a good deal of its content.

Finally, families and friends deserve thanks for their listening ears, thought-provoking questions, lively arguments, and persistent belief in this book and its author.

Diana K. Ivy

The Impact of Social Movements on Gender Communication

You Must Know Where You've Been to Know Where You're Going

What question do college students get asked more than any other, especially as they approach graduation? "So, what are you going to do *now?*" Yes, students get asked how things are going, how they like college, and so forth, but the question of future plans is inevitable. That question seems to many people like the "great justifier" for your having gone to college in the first place, the "grand explanation" for why you're doing what you're doing.

As you embark on the journey this book provides, meaning this trip into gender communication as an area of study, you'll be surrounded with topics that make you question the present: What am I doing? How do I talk to people of my same sex and of the opposite sex? Do I have some changes to make? As we all know, so much of how we communicate, how we think and act, and how we form our visions of the future stem from or are related to the past. For example, most of today's female college students can't fathom the notion of being required to have their fathers sign a lease for them to be able to rent an apartment or cosign a loan document to enable the purchase of a car. And yet, even as late as the 1960s in many parts of this country, the law was that a woman had to have either her husband or father cosign important agreements—she didn't have the basic credibility (because she was a woman) or couldn't be trusted to go it alone. It took valiant efforts to change such sexist practices and it will take more valiant efforts to change sexist practices that persist today. To better understand the current status of life for the sexes, we need to first explore the past—how we came to be where we are in this society.

In this prologue, we survey history, examine women's and men's movements, and take a look at some of the individuals who have contributed to social, economic, and political changes that have affected and will continue to affect gender communication. But it is beyond the scope of this prologue to focus on each and every social movement that has had an impact. If we fail to mention individuals or movements you deem significant, we hope you will use the omission as a beginning point for class discussion.

---

*This prologue benefited from the significant contributions of a guest author, Nada Frazier Cano.

LEARNING "HERSTORY"

Regardless of whether you personally embrace feminism, much of what men and women do and enjoy today is the result of actions and advocacies of feminists. Some of you no doubt have grown up taking equality for granted; fortunately, it may be all you have ever known. But it is because of dedicated feminists that many of you are sitting in college classrooms today.

It's impossible to describe every significant feminist in American history. The truth is we simply don't know or don't have information about each significant women's rights and civil rights advocate. Those we do know about are not representative of all who fought to get us where we are today. It's important to remember, especially with respect to women and members of minority groups, that most were considered the property of privileged men. They were not always afforded educational opportunities and often were denied a voice. Those we discuss here somehow made their way into the annals of history, but they are by no means the only ones who made valuable contributions. While history books today are much more inclusive than they've ever been, many would argue they are still "his story," as opposed to "her story." Let's begin by focusing on developments in the realm of education.

Men, Education, and Women—in That Order

When you enter your next class, look around you. Notice the number of university students who once were barred from the education you are receiving today. Who's responsible for education expanding and becoming accessible to everyone?

In Colonial times American women, under the guidance of men, focused on their "helpmeet" role, which centered on economically essential household production (Theriot, 1996, p. 17). In 1778 a Quaker grammar school opened to educate rural mothers responsible for teaching their children (Bernikow, 1997). Emma Hart Willard is often considered the first important female educator in America (Weatherford, 1994). In 1818 Willard appealed to the New York State legislature to allocate taxes for the education of young women, an outlandish concept at the time. Her requests were denied. But she later founded the Troy Female Seminary, which incorporated an unprecedented mathematics and science curriculum that sought to provide women with a comparable education to men's (Lunardini, 1994; Weatherford, 1994).

The first public high school for girls was opened in 1824 in Worcester, Massachusetts, by Quaker Prudence Crandall (Weatherford, 1994). But in 1834 the school was set ablaze and burned to the ground.

In 1837 Mary Lyon founded Mount Holyoke Female Seminary in South Hadley, Massachusetts, which was the first to educate women who were not from the upper class. In 1837 Oberlin College began to admit women students, as did Antioch College in 1853 and Vassar College in 1865 (Bernikow, 1997). Despite these progressive steps, women's equality in education was still a distant goal.

Dr. Edward Clarke, a prestigious Harvard Medical School professor, was vehemently opposed to the formal education of women, claiming higher education harmed not only women but their offspring as well. Doctors who followed Clarke's teachings included S. Weir Mitchell, a then-famous neurologist, who treated Charlotte Perkins Gilman, a commercial artist and writer, and instructed her to "Live as domestic a life as possible. Have but two hours of intellectual life a day. And never touch pen, brush, or pencil as long as you live" (Bernikow, 1997, pp. 153, 154). Gilman defiantly recovered from Mitchell's "cure" and wrote about it in her 1890 short story *The Yellow Wallpaper*, which fictionalized her mental breakdown and contained a radically feminist thesis for the time.

In 1908 New York City teachers, struggling for equal pay for equal work, were forced to resign when they married. School authorities were even known to search the schools for pregnant teachers. Henrietta Rodman, a high school English teacher, quarreled that teachers should be fired for misconduct, but that "marriage is not misconduct." She was suspended when she wrote a letter to the *New York Tribune* protesting the Board of Education's "mother-baiting," and in 1916 went on to form the Teacher's League, later to become the American Federation of Teachers (Bernikow, 1997, p. 148).

The First Wave of Feminism

England's Mary Wollstonecraft is regarded as one of the first feminists. Her book *A Vindication of the Rights of Woman*, which called for women's equality with men, is still widely studied today. Abigail Smith Adams, wife of the second U.S. president, John Adams, and the mother of sixth president, John Quincy Adams, is considered an early feminist as well. She is credited with writing letters in 1776 to her husband while he was at the Continental Congress, prodding him to "remember the ladies" (Lunardini, 1994, p. 16). However, the Constitution originally barred women, African Americans, American Indians, and many poor people from participation. For years after the Constitution was adopted, women were legally subjugated to their husbands. According to the laws in most states, a married woman "literally did not own the clothes on her back"; her husband legally possessed her and everything she earned (Weatherford, 1994, p. 222). Married women could not sign contracts or obtain credit. The first middle-class women employed by the federal government in the Patent Office received paychecks made out to their husbands (Weatherford, 1994).

Women are systematically degraded by receiving the trivial attentions which men think it manly to pay to the sex, when, in fact, men are insultingly supporting their own superiority.
—Mary Wollstonecraft, British feminist

SUFFRAGISTS: THE EARLY EQUALITY SEEKERS   Imagine that as you leave class today you go to vote in the student government elections, only to find that men are allowed to vote but the women on campus are being turned away, arrested and imprisoned for voting. This was what America was like less than 100 years ago. The origins of feminism can be found in antislavery (abolitionist) and temperance campaigns (Humm, 1992; Krolokke & Sorensen, 2006). However, as feminist writer Rachel Fudge (2006) explains, "the centuries-long fight for women's right to vote was not just about ballot-casting, but about securing women's right to participate as full citizens: to hold property, keep their own wages, have guardianship of their children, and, yes, vote" (p. 59).

One of the initial launching grounds for women's organized efforts was in 1837 at the first national antislavery convention in New York. Celebrated female abolitionists at the time included Lucy Stone, Angelina Grimké, Sarah Grimké, Lucretia Mott, Elizabeth Cady Stanton, and Susan B. Anthony. Mott was a delegate at the World Antislavery Convention in London, where women were excluded from participation and forced to sit in the balcony behind a curtain (Greenspan, 1994). After this event Mott's and Stanton's activism for women's equality, particularly their efforts to win women's right to vote, intensified.

On July 19, 1848, the first Women's Rights Convention was held in Seneca Falls, New York, with some 300 women and men attending. Mott and Stanton, along with other early feminists, advocated for social policy changes including equality between husbands and wives and women's suffrage. Stanton wrote the "Declaration of Sentiments," modeled after the Declaration of Independence, which stated, "We hold these truths to be self evident, that all men *and women* are created equal" (Ruth, 2001, p. 460). It further listed eighteen legal grievances and called for major reform in suffrage, marriage, and inheritance laws (Greenspan, 1994).

We want rights. The flour-merchant, the house-builder, and the postman charge us no less on account of our sex; but when we endeavor to earn money to pay all these, then, indeed, we find the difference.

—Lucy Stone, Suffragist, in her "Disappointment Is the Lot of Women" speech of 1855

Varying opinions on issues emerged that led to the establishment of two distinct suffrage organizations, the National Woman Suffrage Association (NWSA) founded by Susan B. Anthony and Elizabeth Cady Stanton, and the American Woman Suffrage Association (AWSA) founded by Lucy Stone (Carver, 1999). (Stone graduated first in her class in 1847 at Oberlin College, but was forced to sit in the audience while a male student read her valedictory speech.) NWSA argued that as long as women were denied their rights, all other issues had to be secondary. The AWSA disagreed with a "radical" nationwide suffrage movement and instead focused on enacting change to individual state constitutions (Lunardini, 1994).

Feminists' discontent intensified in 1870 when the Fifteenth Amendment to the Constitution ensured former male slaves the right to vote, but did not extend that right to women (Lunardini, 1994). As a result, the national election of 1872 was fraught with controversy, even by today's standards. Although she didn't have the legal right to vote, activist Victoria Woodhull, called "Mrs. Satan" by her many opponents, ran for president of the United States (Bernikow, 1997, p. 7). Woodhull's bid for the presidency ended when she was arrested by moral crusader Anthony Comstock for disseminating "obscene" material through the mail, although she was eventually acquitted under First Amendment protections (Lunardini, 1994, p. 92). The material Comstock found obscene was Woodhull's writings that advocated free love, shorter skirts for women, and legalized prostitution. History has tagged Woodhull a "sex radical" suffragist, but her insistence that private issues emerge into public and political debate broadened the reach of the suffrage movement (Frisken, 2000).

The true republic—men, their rights and nothing more; women, their rights and nothing less.

—Susan B. Anthony, Suffragist

Also during the 1872 election, Susan B. Anthony and hundreds of women attempted to vote, knowing that it was against the law (Lunardini, 1994). Anthony was arrested for daring to cast a vote, tried in U.S. District Court, convicted, and ordered to pay a $100 fine (Weatherford, 1994). Anthony was not allowed to speak at her trial, as the law deemed her incompetent to testify because she was a woman. There were other "subversive," but unsuccessful, attempts to vote.

Women continued to fight for the right to vote, but success would not come easily. Suffragists like Alice Paul and Carrie Chapman Catt organized massive rallies and demonstrations, staged boycotts and hunger strikes, destroyed property, chained themselves to public buildings, and carried out other acts of civil disobedience (Krolokke & Sorensen, 2006; Neft & Levine, 1997). Thousands continued to march, the

White House was picketed six days a week, and over a period of two militant years, 500 women were arrested (Bernikow, 1997).

Other notable early feminists were Harriett Tubman and Sojourner Truth. Tubman, an escaped slave, is best known for running the Underground Railroad, but she was also a feminist, a nurse, and a spy for the North during the Civil War (Ventura, 1998). Tubman is credited with leading a raid in 1863 that freed 750 slaves, and she became the first American woman to lead troops into battle in the Civil War (Greenspan, 1994). At the 1851 Women's Rights Convention, Sojourner Truth made one of her marks on history. Truth was the only woman of color in attendance, and amidst the jeers of hostile men she delivered her famous "Ain't I a Woman" speech (Fitch & Mandziuk, 1997; Greenspan, 1994). Truth, a preacher, suffragist, and abolitionist, was born a slave, was sold away from her parents, and was traded numerous times. When she was an adult, her children were sold away from her (Ventura, 1998). Truth dedicated her life to activism against slavery and for segregation and women's rights.

After decades of activism, finally in 1920 the Nineteenth Amendment granting women the right to vote was ratified into law. Many of you probably were unaware of the fact that white women and women of color did not have the right to vote in this country until fifty years after black men (former slaves) were granted their right to vote. Once women obtained the right to vote the public's interest in women's rights waned, and, collectively, feminism lay dormant for years—until World War II changed everything.

Enter "Rosie the Riveter"

World War II sent men off to war and motivated women to enter the workforce to fill industry jobs. More than 6 million women went to work outside the home for the first time, with the majority employed in factory or clerical jobs in war-related industries (Neft & Levine, 1997). "Rosie the Riveter" became a national symbol for women's contributions to the war effort (Colman, 1995). Some employers still refused to hire women, causing the War Department in 1943 to distribute the booklet *You're Going to Employ Women*. Women were hired as welders, electricians, mechanics, police officers, lawyers, statisticians, journalists, and boilermakers. They operated streetcars, taxis, cranes, buses, tractors, and planes.

Job opportunities for women dried up in 1945 when the war ended. Women were terminated in order to ensure jobs for men returning home from the war. Propaganda from government and industry tried to sell women on the idea that it was their patriotic duty to return home and take care of their husbands and children. Many women who attempted to keep their wartime jobs were laid off or forced into lower-paying jobs. Women who wanted or needed employment were encouraged to find traditional women's work as teachers, nurses, or clerical workers. The obvious message to women was that it was their role or duty to focus on husband, children, and home. And for many, home they went and home they stayed (Colman, 1995).

The Civil Rights Movement

Life in Montgomery, Alabama, in 1955 was much different than it is today. Racism was rampant; racist and segregationist rules and practices were the norm. African Americans riding city buses had to enter the front of a bus to pay a fare, and then get off and enter the bus again from the rear door. They were also required to give up their seats if white people were standing (Lunardini, 1994). Rosa Parks, a mild-mannered African American seamstress in her mid-forties, was seated in the first row of the blacks only section when the white section filled up, leaving a white man without a seat (Ventura, 1998). Parks was arrested for failing to follow the bus driver's instructions to surrender her bus seat to the white man (Lunardini, 1994; Ventura, 1998). She was found guilty of the offense but refused to pay her fine and appealed the decision. Both Parks and her husband lost their jobs and received threats to their lives (Ventura, 1998). Within three days of Parks's arrest, Alabama African Americans began a massive bus boycott that continued for a year until Alabama's state and city bus segregation policies were found unconstitutional (Lunardini, 1994).

From this point on, Martin Luther King, Jr., and other civil rights leaders began to vehemently demand overdue civil rights reforms. Women and men fought for racial progress by joining organizations such as the Student Nonviolent Coordinating Committee (SNCC) and Students for a Democratic Society (SDS). Soon Martin Luther King, Jr., Malcolm X, John F. Kennedy, and Robert Kennedy would all be assassinated. Young men would head off to fight the Vietnam War, while others would protest it by proclaiming we should "make love, not war." For many, the 1960s were about change and challenging "the establishment." For some, it was a time of sexual revolution—a revolution with profound impact on relationships and communication between women and men.

The Sexual Revolution

Later chapters in this text explore gender communication in intimate relationships, but again, relevant historical events have had a profound effect on our modern relationships. For example, women have practiced birth control in one form or another throughout history, just not always legally or safely. Obstetrics nurse Margaret Sanger was among the first to make the connection between reproductive rights and women's economic and social equality. She felt that birth control was the key to women's equality (Emerling Bone, 2010). In 1914 Sanger began publishing a journal entitled *Woman Rebel* (Cuklanz, 1995). Even though it contained no specific contraceptive information, it violated laws of the time and led to Sanger's arrest and indictment by an all-male grand jury. By 1938 federal courts altered obscenity laws. Sanger and associates opened a network of 300 birth control clinics nationwide, and in 1942 they established the Birth Control League, which later would become the Planned Parenthood Association (Lunardini, 1994).

In 1960 the Food and Drug Administration approved the manufacture and sale of "the pill" as a new form of contraception, which quickly became the keystone of the so-called sexual revolution (Lunardini, 1994, p. 297). Many people believe that this one innovation in the form of a simple pill helped make the ideas of women's liberation more practical and acceptable to a wider range of American women. In 1965 the Supreme Court ruled that states could not ban the distribution of contraceptives to married people; in 1972 rights were extended to purchase contraceptives without regard to marital status (Weatherford, 1994).

In 2010, much was written about the 50th anniversary of the advent of the birth control pill (Kotz, 2010; Northrup, 2010). The pill is the primary form of contraception in the United States; in 2008, Americans spent over $3.5 billion on birth control pills (Tone, 2010). American studies professor Elaine Tyler May (2010a, 2010b) describes one interesting benefit of this particular form of contraception that could be controlled by women: "Intimate personal relationships changed because women could take the Pill without the approval, participation or even the knowledge of their sexual partners" (2010b, p. 40). In an article for *US News & World Report,* reporter Deborah Kotz (2010) discussed various ways the pill changed lives, with the primary effect being that the pill increased a woman's earning potential. Because women have become better able to control conception, they have worked longer outside the home (many in lucrative careers), have delayed childbearing, and thus, have become more financially secure than women in prepill generations.

The Second Wave of Feminism

In 1953 French writer and philosopher Simone de Beauvoir published *The Second Sex,* which "argued that women—like all human beings—were in essence free but that they had almost always been trapped by particularly inflexible and limiting conditions. Only by means of courageous action and self-assertive creativity could a woman become a completely free person and escape the role of the inferior 'other' that men had constructed for her gender" (McKay, Hill, & Buckler, 1995, p. 1055).

THE SECOND-CLASS STATUS OF WOMEN   Author of several books on women's history, Louise Bernikow (1997) describes the status of U.S. women before 1965:

> Married women could not establish credit in their own names, which meant no credit cards or mortgages or other financial transactions were possible without a husband's agreement. Newspapers carried sex-segregated help-wanted ads. Employers routinely assigned certain jobs to women, others to men, with the women's jobs paying far less. There were few women in law or medical school and few visibly prominent in those professions. Under most state laws, women were routinely not allowed to be administrators of estates. Working women who became pregnant could be fired. An employer who insisted that in order to keep her job, a female employee have sex with him or submit to fondling was not breaking the law. (pp. 43–44)

In 1961 President John F. Kennedy appointed Eleanor Roosevelt to chair the Commission on the Status of Women (Weatherford, 1994). The report from this commission documented discriminatory practices in government, education, and employment and included recommendations for reform. Many states followed suit and identified discriminations at the state level. Hundreds of daily situations exemplified the second-class status of women in our society.

Here's an example. We have it on good authority that some (and we emphasize the word *some*) students (over the age of twenty-one, of course) have been known to frequent an occasional bar or dance club. Today most people would not consider that unusual. However, in the nineteenth and much of the twentieth centuries, women who frequented bars were generally assumed to be prostitutes. Businesses wanting a respectable reputation either banned women or provided a separate ladies' lounge. During World War II millions of women entered bars for the first time to join men in smoking and drinking. In 1948 an unsuccessful lawsuit was filed attempting to overturn legislation that prohibited women from working as bartenders unless their husbands or fathers owned the bar. Some states even maintained legislation into the 1970s that prohibited women from sitting at a bar, rather than at a table (Weatherford, 1994).

At the recommendation of the President's Commission on the Status of Women, Congress passed the Equal Pay Act of 1963, which was the first national legislation for women's employment since the Progressive Era. However, it has proved rather difficult to enforce (Lunardini, 1994). The Civil Rights Act of 1964 prohibited private employers from discriminating on the basis of race, color, religion, national origin, or sex.

THE PROBLEM THAT HAS NO NAME   In 1963 American author Betty Friedan, a Smith College graduate who shortly after graduation married and began raising her family, helped awaken the feminist movement with the publication of her book *The Feminine Mystique*. Friedan wrote of the "problem that has no name," which she described as a vague feeling of discontent and aimlessness (p. 15). Friedan's book helped break the silence on issues such as unequal salaries, limited opportunities, and women's powerlessness in family and society (Lunardini, 1994). Friedan argued that editors of women's magazines, advertising experts, Freudian psychologists, social scientists, and educators "contributed to a romanticization of domesticity she termed 'the feminine mystique'" (Kerber, De Hart, & Dayton, 2010, p. 505). She further asserted that women should help themselves out of their malaise and take positive steps to reassert their identities (Lunardini, 1994). Quickly, Friedan became a celebrity with a mission.

GETTING THEIR ACTS TOGETHER   In 1966 Friedan and twenty-seven other women attending the Washington, D.C., Third National Conference of the Commission on the Status of Women founded the National Organization for Women, commonly referred to as NOW (NOW, 2010). NOW committed to "take action to bring women into full participation in the mainstream of American society . . ." (Friedan, 1963, p. 384). The organization clearly communicated that women were ready for action *now*. NOW's priorities include abortion and reproductive rights, economic justice, ending sex discrimination, lesbian rights, promoting diversity and ending racism, and stopping violence against women.

Other organizations, such as the Women's Equity Action League (WEAL), formed to further women's issues. In 1987 the Feminist Majority was founded to promote "equality for women and men, non-violence, reproductive health, peace, social justice and economic development and to enhance feminist participation in public policy" with a mission to "empower feminists to win equality for women at the decision-making tables of the state, nation, and the world" (Feminist Majority, 2010, p. 1).

MS. GLORIA STEINEM   "Gloria Steinem's name is synonymous with feminism" (Ventura, 1998, p. 160). Steinem is certainly one of the most renowned feminists. She was a leading activist in the early days of NOW, and in 1971 she joined Bella Abzug and

Net Notes

If you are interested in viewing documents produced during the women's liberation movement, check out Duke University's online Archival Collection:

http://scriptorium.lib.duke.edu/wlm

Shirley Chisholm to found the National Women's Political Caucus (Weatherford, 1994). This group encourages women to become involved as officeholders, volunteers, political appointees, convention delegates, judges, and committee members (Lunardini, 1994). Steinem then created *Ms.* magazine, the first mainstream feminist magazine in American history (Ventura, 1997). In 1971 the preview issue of *Ms.* hit the stands, and the initial 300,000 copies were sold out within ten days (Thom, 1997). The *Ms.* Foundation for Women, organized in 1972, further supports the efforts of women and girls to govern their own lives and influence the world around them (*Ms.* Foundation for Women, 2010).

Feminist activists made numerous other groundbreaking accomplishments during the second wave. In 1969 San Diego State University established the first women's studies baccalaureate degree program (Lunardini, 1994). In 1970 the first congressional hearings on sex discrimination in education were held. In 1972 Title IX of the Education Omnibus Act passed, creating penalties for educational institutions for sex discrimination in schools. In 1973 the Supreme Court's *Roe* v. *Wade* decision legalized abortion. In 1975 the Equal Credit Opportunity Act made credit more available to women. That same year the Rhodes Scholarship Foundation, which funded undergraduate study at Oxford University, no longer excluded women from consideration as Rhodes Scholars (Bernikow, 1997). In 1981 Sandra Day O'Connor was appointed the first female justice on the U.S. Supreme Court. In 1983 Sally Ride became the first female astronaut. In 1984 Geraldine Ferraro became the first female vice presidential candidate, as running mate in Walter Mondale's bid for the presidency. Granted, there had been lots of changes, but women still did not have the same, full equal rights as men.

THE EQUAL RIGHTS AMENDMENT (ERA)   Much as gaining the right to vote had brought first-wave feminists together to focus on a common goal, the quest for ratification of the Equal Rights Amendment (ERA) united many second-wave feminists. You may not realize that the ERA was first introduced to Congress in 1923 (Andersen, 2009). For almost fifty years it lay dormant. The 1972 version of the ERA states, "Equality of rights under the law shall not be denied or abridged by the United States or by any State on account of sex" (Kerber, De Hart, & Dayton, 2010, p. 547). By an overwhelming majority, both houses of Congress passed the ERA in 1972. Shortly thereafter, twenty-eight of the needed thirty-eight states had ratified the ERA (Lunardini, 1994). Phyllis Schlafly, a staunchly conservative voice of the time, rallied others in opposition to the ERA, predicting the destruction of the family, among other things. A campaign known as STOP-ERA spread fear that women would be drafted and might have to serve in combat if the ERA passed (Andersen, 2009; Lunardini, 1994). In 1982 the ERA failed, just three states shy of the thirty-eight needed for ratification. In 1983 the amendment was reintroduced in Congress, but its passage is still pending (Kerber, De Hart, & Dayton, 2010). If it had passed, perhaps it wouldn't have taken until the year 1999 for a woman to be named NASA's first female shuttle commander (Dunn, 1999), the year 2001 for women to first pilot combat missions, as they did in the U.S. war on terrorism, and 2010 for Elinor Ostrom to become the first woman to receive the Nobel Prize in economics.

[The fight for the Equal Rights Amendment] is about a socialist, anti-family political movement that encourages women to leave their husbands, kill their children, practice witchcraft, destroy capitalism, and become lesbians.

—Pat Robertson, televangelist & former presidential candidate

No Such Thing as "THE" Feminists

Despite rumors to the contrary, feminism is still alive and well in the United States, as well as internationally; however, it continues to confront misunderstanding and opposition as a movement and philosophy. One way to reduce the perceived power of a movement, such as civil rights or feminism, is to suggest that members of the movement should be one cohesive group, all in agreement, all using the same rhetoric, and all dedicated to the same causes. When it is inevitably discovered that disagreement or diversity exists within the ranks, then the movement can be criticized and the causes ignored, because "they can't even agree among themselves."

There are many "feminisms," meaning different interpretations or approaches to achieving the goal of sexual equality (Bell, 2010; McRobbie, 2009). To attempt to place each and every feminist in a tidy, clearly discernible philosophical box is limiting at best and inaccurate at worst. Yet, there are certain ideologies within different subsets of feminism. Three feminist strands have predominated: liberal, socialist, and radical feminism (Andersen, 2009). *Liberal feminism* has a long history and can be defined as "the theory of individual freedom for women" (Humm, 1992, p. 407). The focus of this feminism is on social and legal reform through policies designed to create equal opportunities for women. *Socialist feminism* contends that patriarchy and capitalism interact to create women's oppression, to further define women as the property of men, and to exploit them for the purposes of profit (Andersen, 2009). And finally, *radical feminism* "argues that women's oppression comes from being categorized as an inferior class on the basis of gender. What makes this feminism radical is that it focuses on the roots of male domination and claims that all forms of oppression are extensions of male supremacy" (Humm, 1992, p. 408). This movement embraces a separatist philosophy of radical lesbian feminism, which promotes a woman-centered world that excludes men.

It is not uncommon for feminist philosophies or viewpoints to blend or overlap at times and for various strands to share members, because, as we've stated, no one guiding perspective can be identified as *the* feminist perspective. But gender inequality has and continues to be an abiding theme within feminism (Lorber, 2005; Valenti, 2007). According to feminist author bell hooks (2000), "Simply put, feminism is a movement to end sexism, sexist exploitation, and oppression" (p. 1).

With the diversity of feminism and the blurring of feminist camp lines, some women felt (and still feel) alienated by the movement. Women who work inside the home and enjoy more traditional family styles often feel that they have little in common with feminists. Some feminists perpetuate the mistrust by not validating those women

Net Notes

The Feminist Majority and the National Organization for Women are viable, activist, and highly visible national and international organizations. Many NOW chapters exist on university campuses. For more information on these organizations, contact:

www.feministmajority.org
www.now.org

who truly want to be traditional housewives and mothers (Lunardini, 1994). While many feminists still vehemently push to further their causes and gain choice, they sometimes are perceived as having violated the feminist golden rule by devaluing the choices of women who follow more traditional paths.

I call myself a feminist. Isn't that what you call someone who fights for women's rights?

—The Dalai Lama

The Third Wave of Feminism

Some critics contend that feminism is dead or "stolen" (Hoff Sommers, 1994) or that we have moved into a "postfeminist" existence because feminism is no longer necessary (Denfeld, 1995; Roiphe, 1993). Others document a feminist movement for the twenty-first century that emerged in the 1990s from women in their twenties and thirties who were proud to call themselves "the third wave" (Tobias, 1997, p. 252). Third-wave feminism draws from the struggles of past waves, but is not a mere extension of a past movement. Third-wave feminists emphasize collective action to effect change and embrace the diversity represented by various feminisms (Heywood & Drake, 1997). They focus on inclusion and multiculturalism and strive to address problems stemming from sexism, racism, social class inequality, and homophobia (Baumgardner & Richards, 2010; Dicker & Piepmeier, 2003; Fixmer & Wood, 2005; Fudge, 2006; Krolokke & Sorensen, 2006; Lotz, 2007; Renzetti & Curran, 2003; Siegel, 2007). A key feature distinguishing third-wave feminism from second-wave is technological innovation that allows feminism a more global reach than past generations were able to accomplish (Whelehan, 2007).

Just as other strains of feminism have had their critics, third-wave feminism has also been scrutinized (Hogeland, 2001; Shugart, 2001; Shugart, Waggoner, & Hallstein, 2001; Woodhull, 2007). Some question the movement's reliance on celebrity and media images and its close association with popular culture, in that some of its icons are television characters, fashion models, musicians, and actors (Dow, 1996; Hunter College Women's Studies Collective, 2005; Shugart et al., 2001). In the foreword to the book *We Don't Need Another Wave,* Lisa Jervis (2006) suggested, "We've reached the end of the wave terminology's usefulness" (p. 14). Although Jervis is a self-avowed third-wave feminist, she believes that the wave metaphor is shorthand that "invites intellectual laziness, an escape hatch from the hard work of distinguishing between core beliefs and a cultural moment" (p. 14).

As we said earlier in this prologue, no matter whether you call yourself a feminist or embrace feminist ideals of any wave, you are now likely to be more aware of the opportunities and freedoms you enjoy that are a direct result of feminists' hard work, determination, and dedication to equality. None of us arrived where we are today without the help and work of others. Finally, let's explore the development of men's movements to see how their contributions continue to affect relationships and communication between women and men.

Net Notes

For more information on third-wave feminism, contact:

feminism.suite101.com
www.thirdwavefoundation.org

WHAT ABOUT "HIS STORY"?

As women's movements have progressed, men's lives have also changed significantly, often as a result of that progress. In Chapter 2, we discuss the fact that many men enjoy privilege based on their biological sex. Privilege, however, varies from man to man, depending on ethnicity, race, social class, age, physical ability, and sexual orientation (Renzetti & Curran, 2003). Men's movements, like women's movements, are not made up of one central group united around a common cause; they reflect a rich diversity of issues and followers. Some movements aren't really considered movements at all, more like efforts to improve the human condition through societal, political, and personal change. As we did for women's movements, we also look at men's movements from a historical standpoint since they have affected and will continue to affect gender communication.

Early Male Supporters of Women's Rights

Historically in the United States, men have benefited from a patriarchally constructed (male-dominated) society. However, there have always been exceptional men who fought societal trends and supported women and their causes. Frederick Douglass, James Mott, and Henry Blackwell openly advocated women's suffrage when it certainly wasn't stylish to do so (Bernikow, 1997). After his passionate speech at the Seneca Falls Convention, antislavery leader Frederick Douglass was maligned in Syracuse newspapers, which first called him a "wimp," then referred to him as an "Aunt Nancy" (Kimmel, 2005, p. 58). James Mott, a Quaker businessperson, cochaired the women's rights meeting at Seneca Falls with his suffragist wife, Lucretia Mott. Persistent women's rights advocate Henry Blackwell helped his wife, Lucy Stone, and daughter, Alice Stone Blackwell, publish *The Woman's Journal* (Bernikow, 1997). In 1910 Columbia philosophy instructor Max Eastman cofounded the Men's League for Woman Suffrage (Kimmel, 2005). While they weren't chaining themselves to fences for women's suffrage, the public support from these men was exceptional for the time.

Effects of the Sexual Revolution on Men

Over time male sex and gender roles have evolved, if not as dramatically or visibly as women's. Author James Doyle (1995) identified three developments that challenged traditional views of the male gender role: technological advances, distrust of established institutions, and the women's movement. As the Industrial Revolution changed our society from an agrarian basis to a technological, service-oriented one, men's role as providers (or "hunters," as they once were in hunter–gatherer cultures) diminished.

In the 1960s and 1970s social conflicts such as the Vietnam War, college campus antiwar protests, the beating of demonstrators at the 1968 Democratic National Convention in Chicago, and the killing of four students at Kent State University turned many against the government (Doyle, 1995). The 1960s saw a convergence of the civil rights movement, the women's movement, the antiwar movement, and the new left movement (Astrachan, 1986). When respect for the traditionally masculine role of soldier declined with America's increasing disillusionment with the military and the government, men experienced a significant shift in role. Along with the women's movement, this shift made it a confusing time to decide just what it meant to be a man. However, some believe that the process of reconsidering sex roles and opening up new avenues of communication between men and women was a very necessary, healthy development.

Men Raised Consciousness Too

We most often think of consciousness-raising as an activity of the women's liberation movement. However, the men's movement (actually more a trend than a movement per se) in the 1970s involved consciousness-raising groups, most often focusing on individual growth as well. These groups "triggered changes in the lives of a few participants, but none excited people to the collective action that affected the whole society, as many women's gatherings did" (Astrachan, 1986, pp. 290–291). Up to the mid-1980s, most men actively participating in men's groups held a single guiding ideology: the elimination of the belief that one sex is superior to the other, or the eradication of sexism (Doyle, 1995). Men considered to be profeminist agreed generally with the feminist critique of patriarchy and organized themselves collectively to change men's behavior and attitudes (Mechling & Mechling, 1994). In 1975 the First National Conference on Men and Masculinity was held in Knoxville, Tennessee. Associations such as the National Organization for Men Against Sexism (originally called the National Organization for Changing Men) were founded during this time (Astrachan, 1986).

Profeminist men (many of whom simply call themselves feminists) are active today (Kimmel, 2005). Sociologist Michael Kimmel (2005) explained, "Profeminist men accept a wary alliance with those groups pressing for social change to embrace diversity and equality for women . . . . Profeminist men believe that men's lives will only be healed when there is full equality for those people who have been traditionally excluded from their full humanity" (pp. 333–334). Groups of profeminists may well be active on your campus. University profeminist men often organize Take Back the Night marches, which are programs that honor survivors of rape and sexual assault; present programs on sexual assault to fraternities, dorms, and athletic teams; and teach and take courses on masculinity (Epstein, 2010; Kimmel, 2005). Perhaps your campus has hosted the "One in Four" program, sponsored by the National Organization of Men's Outreach for Rape Education (NO MORE), a touring educational effort that's teaching college men across the country about sexual assault and how to help sexual assault survivors (National Organization of Men's Outreach for Rape Education, 2010).

Net Notes

For more information regarding masculinity studies and male studies programs on the collegiate level, see the following:

www.malestudies.org
www.men'sstudies.org

Fathers' Movements

Other movements of men, primarily active in the 1960s and 1970s involve fathers' rights in divorce and child custody cases. In Colonial times fathers retained domestic control and defined and supervised their children's development; wives were expected to defer to their husbands (Furstenberg, 1988, as in Skolnick & Skolnick, 2008). Until the middle of the nineteenth century, if "marital disruption" occurred the father was typically awarded custody because fathers "were assumed to maintain control over marital property (of which the children were a part)" (Furstenberg, 1988, p. 224). During this time period women often died in childbirth, leaving their widowed husbands responsible for their children. The children were most often turned over to another woman in the family to raise. With the Industrial Revolution, public and private spheres became more separate—men worked in the outside world and women worked in the home attending to the needs of the children (Doyle, 1995).

By the end of the century women predominantly were awarded custody of their children because women were believed to possess superior parenting skills (Furstenberg, 1988). The courts subsequently adopted a "tender years presumption," meaning that during a child's younger years she or he needed a mother more than a father (Renzetti & Curran, 2003, p. 217). This dramatically shifted custody decisions in favor of mothers and against fathers, a practice that still continues in today's courts. This trend has led many men around the country to challenge the courts for equal custody and parenting rights. Attorney and activist Andrew Kimbrell (1995) asserts that as men promote a national fatherhood policy, it is just as important to change our culture's view of men and fatherhood as it is to change laws and public policy. Support groups and activist organizations have been formed, such as Fathers United for Equal Rights, U.S. Divorce Reform, the Coalition Organized for Parental Equality (COPE), Divorced American Men Unite, and the National Center for Men (Gandy, 2006).

There Are Some "Wild Men" Out There

Another social movement that emerged in the 1980s and 1990s is most often referred to simply as the men's movement, but its more elaborate name is the mythopoetic movement (Barton, 2000). The most noteworthy spokesperson for the mythopoetic movement is author and poet Robert Bly. Bly's 1990 best-selling book *Iron John* utilizes mythology and Grimm's fairy tales to help men find the "community inside the psyche" (p. 227).

Net Notes

Many websites have sprung up in recent years, designed to help fathers gain or retain custody rights of their children. Some sites are nothing more than mere commercials for attorneys, but a few organizations' websites have useful information. Check out:

www.just4dads.org

www.fathersrights.org   (website for the Fathers Rights Foundation, Inc.)

www.dadsrights.org   (website for the organization formerly known as Fathers Rights & Equality Exchange)

This means that men are encouraged to seek out different parts or roles within themselves.

Bly and other advocates of mythopoetics promote men's self-discovery and masculinity through nature and tribal rituals. At retreats called "Wild Man Gatherings," men beat drums, tearfully hug one another, dance in ritualistic circles, smear one another's bodies with mud, and huddle around a campfire howling (Kimbrell, 1995, p. 133; Natharius, 1992). One goal of such gatherings is to encourage men to explore the complicated relationships most have with their fathers, engaging the psychological and emotional wounds left over from childhood. In turn, the hope is that these men will become better fathers to their own children.

We are living at an important and fruitful moment now, for it is clear to men that the images of adult manhood given by the popular culture are worn out; a man can no longer depend on them. By the time a man is thirty-five he knows that the images of the right man, the tough man, the true man which he received in high school do not work in life.

—Robert Bly, author

The Million Man March

On October 16, 1995, an estimated 400,000 men attended the Million Man March on the Federal Mall in Washington, D.C. (*USA Today*, 1996). Organized by the controversial head of the Nation of Islam, Louis Farrakhan, the march was to rally the Black community and strengthen Black families by emphasizing the role of fathers. Farrakhan (1998) described the event as a "Holy Day of Atonement and Reconciliation"; he called for "one million disciplined, committed, and dedicated Black men, from all walks of life in America, to march in Washington, D.C." (p. 1). Emphasizing the need for fathers to bolster Black family life, Farrakhan asserted that "as men, we must recognize and unconditionally atone for the absence, in too many cases, of the Black male as the head of the household, positive role model and building block of our community. We believe that we must atone for, and establish positive solutions to, the abuse and misuse of our women and girls" (p. 1). Similar marches among African American women and rallies for Black youth in Harlem occurred in the decade of the 1990s, with the goal of strengthening African Americans' self-esteem and pride and building community (Bekker, 1997).

Keeping Those Promises

The Promise Keepers, a movement based on fundamental Christian traditions and beliefs, was very influential, yet it lost a great deal of steam at the turn of the century. Bill McCartney, successful University of Colorado head football coach, and his friend Dave Wardell conceived of the organization in 1990 as they were driving to a Fellowship of Christian Athletes dinner (McCartney & Diles, 1995). The two discussed the idea of filling a stadium with Christian men coming together for the purpose of Christian discipleship. Their idea came to fruition, and the first Promise Keepers conference was attended by over 4,000 men in July 1991 (Kellner, 2000).

According to its website, the mission of the Promise Keepers is "to ignite and unite men to become warriors who will change their world through living out the Seven Promises" (Promise Keepers, 2010). The promises these men make are intended to guide them toward Christ, transform them as people, and challenge them to assume active leadership roles within their own families (Dobson et al., 1994; Silverstein, Auerbach, Grieco, & Dunkel, 1999).

Some suggest that the high point for the Promise Keepers movement may have come in 1997, when approximately one million men attended the Stand in the Gap rally in Washington, D.C. Since that time, attendance at rallies has declined, leading to a shift to more arena settings than stadiums and more emphasis on men's groups within local churches (Dooley, 2001). However, the Promise Keepers are still alive and well, with a recent rally focusing on the theme of "Manhood '08: Let the Truth Be Told" (Promise Keepers, 2010).

It will be interesting to track the progress of the several men's movements, including the Promise Keepers, well into the twenty-first century. Will the mythopoetic wild men still be around? Will we see growth in men's (or male) studies programs on college campuses? Will fathers win more custody suits and change the trend in the courts? Will there be more marches on Washington, D.C., in the name of one sex or the other?

GENDER COMMUNICATION: LOOKING FORWARD

Why have we included so much information on women's and men's movements in this prologue? Relevant historical events that shape gender communication are either skimmed over or not taught at most secondary school levels. Even in colleges and universities today, often only students enrolled in specialized courses in women's history are exposed to this important material.

It's important to understand how our current state of gender communication came to be, to realize that there is a historical context for why women and men relate to one another as they do. When you hear feminists discuss disparity in wages between the sexes or men argue for fathers' rights, knowing some of the historical details that preceded the status quo facilitates more effective gender communication. When you embrace racial diversity, it's important to comprehend what people of color have historically encountered. When you participate in intimate relationships and grapple with reproductive issues, it completes your perspective to understand the history of birth control and controversies surrounding reproductive rights. When you hear a statistic cited that less than 40 percent of eligible voters in the United States actually vote these days, perhaps it will make you wonder if suffragists are rolling over in their graves. When you study the theories and effective tools of gender communication we explore in this text, we hope that looking at our past will help you plan your future. After all, that "What will you do next?" question looms.

 References

Andersen, M. (2009). *Thinking about women: Sociological perspectives on sex and gender* (8th ed.). Boston: Pearson/Allyn & Bacon.

Astrachan, A. (1986). *How men feel: Their response to women's demands for equality and power.* Garden City, NY: Anchor Press/Doubleday.

Barton, E. R. (2000). *Mythopoetic perspectives of men's healing work: An anthology for therapists and others.* Santa Barbara, CA: Praeger/Greenwood Press.

Baumgardner, J., & Richards, A. (2010). *Manifesta: Young women, feminism, and the future* (Anv. Rev. Ed.). New York: Farrar, Straus & Giroux.

Bekker, S. (1997, October 26). Sending a message of solidarity: Civil rights issues voiced at Million Woman March. *Corpus Christi Caller Times*, pp. A1, A14.

Bell, E. (2010). Operationalizing feminism: Two challenges for feminist research. *Women and Language, 33,* 97–102.

Bernikow, L. (1997). *The American women's almanac: An inspiring and irreverent women's history.* New York: Berkley.

Bly, R. (1990). *Iron John: A book about men.* Reading, MA: Addison-Wesley.

Carver, M. (1999, October). *Lucy Stone: Apostle for a "New Woman."* Paper presented at the 22nd Conference of the Organization for the Study of Communication, Language, and Gender, Wichita, KS.

Colman, P. (1995). *Rosie the riveter.* New York: Crown.

Cuklanz, L. (1995). Shrill squawk or strategic innovation: A rhetorical reassessment of Margaret Sanger's *Woman Rebel. Communication Quarterly, 43,* 1–19.

Denfeld, R. (1995). *The new Victorians: A young woman's challenge to the old feminist order.* New York: Warner.

Dicker, R., & Piepmeier, A. (2003). Introduction. In R. Dicker & A. Piepmeier (Eds.), *Catching a wave: Reclaiming feminism for the 21st century.* Boston: Northeastern University Press.

Dobson, J., Bright, B., Cole, E., Evans, T., McCartney, B., Palau, L., Phillips, R., & Smalley, G. (1994). *Seven promises of a Promise Keeper.* Colorado Springs: Focus on the Family.

Dooley, T. (2001, September 29). Renewing the promise: Men's group downsizes venues, expands spiritual horizons. *The Houston Chronicle.* [Electronic version].

Dow, B. J. (1996). *Prime-time feminism: Television, media culture, and the Women's Movement since 1970.* Philadelphia: University of Pennsylvania Press.

Doyle, J. (1995). *The male experience* (3rd ed.). Madison, WI: Brown & Benchmark.

Dunn, M. (1999, July 18). Woman will be in charge when Columbia launches this week. *Corpus Christi Caller Times,* pp. A1, A5.

Emerling Bone, J. (2010). When publics collide: Margaret Sanger's argument for birth control and the rhetorical breakdown of barriers. *Women's Studies in Communication, 33,* 16–33.

Epstein, J. (2010, April 8). Male studies vs. men's studies. Retrieved June 27, 2010, from http://www.insidehighered.com

Farrakhan, L. (1998, November 16). Second opinion. *Minister Louis Farrakhan on the Million Man March.* Retrieved from http://users.aol.com/camikem/eyeview/millionman.html

Feminist Majority. (2010). Retrieved June 27, 2010, from http://www.feministmajority.org

Fitch, S. P., & Mandziuk, R. M. (1997). *Sojourner Truth as orator: Wit, story, and song.* Santa Barbara, CA: Greenwood.

Fixmer, N., & Wood, J. T. (2005). The personal is *still* political: Embodied politics in third wave feminism. *Women's Studies in Communication, 28,* 235–257.

Friedan, B. (1963). *The feminine mystique.* New York: Laurel.

Frisken, A. (2000). Sex in politics: Victoria Woodhull as an American public woman, 1870–1876. *Journal of Women's History, 12,* 89–111.

Fudge, R. (2006). Everything you always wanted to know about feminism but were afraid to ask. *Bitch, 31,* 58–67.

Furstenberg, F. F., Jr. (1988). Good dad—bad dads: Two faces of fatherhood. In A. Cherlin (Ed.), *The changing American family.* New York: Urban Institute Press.

Gandy, K. (2006, Summer). Viewpoint: Father's rights . . . and wrongs. *National NOW Times,* p. 4.

Greenspan, K. (1994). *The timetables of women's history: A chronology of the most important people and events in women's history.* New York: Simon & Schuster.

Heywood, L., & Drake, J. (1997). *Third wave agenda: Being feminist, doing feminism.* Minneapolis: University of Minnesota Press.

Hoff Sommers, C. (1994). *Who stole feminism? How women have betrayed women.* New York: Simon & Schuster.

Hogeland, L. M. (2001). Against generational thinking, or, some things that "third wave" feminism isn't. *Women's Studies in Communication, 24,* 107–121.

hooks, b. (2000). *Feminism is for everybody: Passionate politics.* Cambridge, MA: South End Press.

Humm, M. (Ed.). (1992). *Modern feminisms: Political, literary, cultural.* New York: Columbia University Press.

Hunter College Women's Studies Collective. (2005). *Women's realities, women's choices: An introduction to women's studies.* New York: Oxford University Press.

Jervis, L. (2006). Foreword: Goodbye to feminism's generational divide. In M. Berger (Ed.), *We don't need another wave: Dispatches from the next generation of feminists* (pp. 13–18). Emeryville, CA: Seal Press.

Kellner, M. A. (2000). Keeping their promises. *Christianity Today, 44,* 21.

Kerber, L., De Hart, J., & Dayton, C. H. (2010). *Women's America: Refocusing the past* (7th ed.). New York: Oxford University Press.

Kimbrell, A. (1995). *The masculine mystique: The politics of masculinity.* New York: Ballantine.

Kimmel, M. S. (2005). *Manhood in America: A cultural history* (2nd ed.). New York: Oxford University Press.

Kotz, D. (2010, May 7). Birth control pill turns 50: 7 ways it changed lives. Retrieved May 7, 2010, from http://www.usnews.com

Krolokke, C., & Sorensen, A. S. (2006). *Gender communication: Theory and analyses.* Thousand Oaks, CA: Sage.

Lorber, J. (2009). *Gender inequality: Feminist theories and politics* (4th ed.). New York: Oxford University Press.

Lotz, A. D. (2007). Theorising the intermezzo: The contributions of postfeminism and third wave feminism. In S. Gillis, G. Howie, & R. Munford (Eds.), *Third wave feminism: A critical exploration* (pp. 71–85). New York: Palgrave/Macmillan.

Lunardini, C. (1994). *What every American should know about women's history.* Holbrook, MA: Bob Adams.

McCartney, B., & Diles, D. (1995). *From ashes to glory.* Nashville: Thomas Nelson.

McKay, J., Hill, B., & Buckler, J. (1995). *A history of western society, volume II: From absolutism to the present* (5th ed.). Boston: Houghton Mifflin.

McRobbie, A. (2009). *The aftermath of feminism: Gender, culture and social change.* Los Angeles: Sage.

Mechling, E., & Mechling, J. (1994). The Jung and the restless: The mythopoetic men's movement. *Southern Communication Journal, 59,* 97–111.

Ms. Foundation for Women. (2010). Retrieved June 27, 2010, from http://www.ms.foundation.org

Natharius, D. (1992, October). *From the hazards of being male to fire in the belly: Are men finally getting it and, if so, what are they getting?* Paper presented at the meeting of the Speech Communication Association, Chicago, IL.

National Organization for Women (NOW). (2010). Retrieved June 27, 2010, from http://www.now.org

National Organization of Men's Outreach for Rape Education. (2010). Retrieved June 27, 2010, from http://www.nomorerape.org

Neft, N., & Levine, A. (1997). *Where women stand: An international report on the status of women in 140 countries, 1997–1998.* New York: Random House.

Northrup, C. (2010). The pill turns 50: Taking stock. Retrieved May 8, 2010, from http://www.thehuffingtonpost.com

Promise Keepers. (2010). Retrieved June 27, 2010, from http://www.promisekeepers.org

Renzetti, C., & Curran, D. (2003). *Women, men and society* (5th ed.). Boston: Allyn & Bacon.

Roiphe, K. (1993). *The morning after: Sex, fear, and feminism on campus.* Boston: Little, Brown.

Ruth, S. (2001). *Issues in feminism: An introduction to women's studies* (5th ed.). Mountain View, CA: Mayfield.

Shugart, H. A. (2001). Isn't it ironic?: The intersection of third-wave feminism and generation X. *Women's Studies in Communication, 24,* 131–168.

Shugart, H. A., Waggoner, C. E., & Hallstein, D. L. O. (2001). Mediating third-wave feminism: Appropriation as postmodern media practice. *Critical Studies in Media Communication, 18,* 194–210.

Siegel, D. (2007). *Sisterhood interrupted: From radical women to grrls gone wild.* New York: Palgrave/Macmillan.

Silverstein, L. B., Auerbach, C. F., Grieco, L., & Dunkel, F. (1999). Do Promise Keepers dream of feminist sheep? *Sex Roles, 40,* 665–688.

Skolnick, A., & Skolnick, J. (2008). *Family in transition* (15th ed.). New York: Longman.

Theriot, N. (1996). *Mothers and daughters in nineteenth-century America: The biosocial construction of femininity.* Lexington: University of Kentucky Press.

Thom, M. (1997). *Inside Ms.: 25 years of the magazine and the feminist movement.* New York: Henry Holt.

Tobias, S. (1997). *Faces of feminism: An activist's reflections on the women's movement.* Boulder, CO: Westview.

Tone, A. (2010). Birth control pill turns 50 on Mother's Day. Retrieved May 12, 2010, from http://www.examiner.com

Tyler May, E. (2010a, May 7). 50 years on the pill. *The Chronicle Review,* B4–B5.

Tyler May, E. (2010b, Spring). The pill turns 50. *Ms.,* 40.

USA Today. (1996, February 16). Washington's great gatherings. *USA Today.* [Electronic version]. Retrieved from http://www.usatoday.com

Valenti, J. (2007). *Full frontal feminism: A young woman's guide to why feminism matters.* Berkeley, CA: Seal Press.

Ventura, V. (1998). *Sheroes: Bold, brash, and absolutely unabashed superwomen.* Berkeley, CA: Conari.

Weatherford, D. (1994). *American women's history: An A to Z of people, organizations, issues, and events.* New York: Prentice Hall.

Whelehan, I. (2007). Foreword. In S. Gillis, G. Howie, & R. Munford (Eds.), *Third wave feminism: A critical exploration* (pp. xv–xx). New York: Palgrave/Macmillan.

Woodhull, W. (2007). Global feminisms, transnational political economies, third world cultural production. In S. Gillis, G. Howie, & R. Munford (Eds.), *Third wave feminism: A critical exploration* (pp. 156–167). New York: Palgrave/Macmillan.

HOT TOPICS

▶ What gender communication is and why you are studying it

▶ Meanings for such terms as *sex, gender, identity, androgyny, sexual orientation, heterosexism, homophobia,* and *transgender*

▶ What feminism and sexism mean today

▶ How to communicate from a receiver orientation

▶ What it means to be personally effective in communication with women and men

▶ How values are associated with gender communication that leads to successful and satisfying relationships

Talking the Talk and Walking the Walk
Becoming a Better Gender Communicator

WHAT IS GENDER COMMUNICATION?

Societal issues continue to perplex women and men, whether they involve situations of professional communication between coworkers, confusion over interpersonal signals, competing messages of homemaker versus careerism, or verbal exchanges that result in violence. One thing is for certain: Communication between women and men is a popular topic of conversation, study, and research—more now than ever, it seems. But is this popular topic all there is to the term *gender communication?* What all is encompassed by the term? Just what *is* this topic you're going to read about and study?

First you need to understand that we're putting the words *gender* and *communication* together to form a modern label for an ancient phenomenon. Gender communication is a unique, fascinating subset of a larger phenomenon known as communication. From our perspective, not all communication is gender communication.

Here's a simple way to understand this perspective of gender communication: **Gender communication is communication *about* and *between* men and women.** The first part of the statement—the "about" aspect—involves how the sexes are discussed, referred to, or depicted, both verbally and nonverbally. The second part of the sentence—the "between" aspect—is the interpersonal dimension of gender communication, and it's a bit harder to understand.

We believe that communication becomes *gendered* when sex or gender overtly begins to influence your choices—choices of what you say and how you relate to others. For example, two students could be talking about a project for class. The students could be both male, both female, or of opposite sexes. The sex composition of the communicators doesn't matter in a judgment of whether gender communication is going on. Thus far, the conversation about the class project doesn't necessarily involve gender communication. But what happens if the conversation topic shifts to a discussion of political issues especially relevant to women, opinions regarding parenting responsibilities, or who the interactants are dating? For these topics, the awareness of one's own sex, the other person's sex, or both may come into play; thus gender communication is occurring. Notice that we said "may come into play," because the topic doesn't always dictate whether gender communication is occurring. When sex or gender becomes an overt factor in your communication, when you become conscious of your own or another person's sex or gender, then gender communication is operating.

However, some scholars believe that gender is an all-encompassing designation, that it is so pervasive a characteristic of a person that communication cannot escape the effects of gender. In this view, all communication is gendered (Spender, 1985; Thorne, Kramarae, & Henley, 1983; Wilson Schaef, 1981). These viewpoints—our more restricted approach to gender communication and the more pervasive perspective—aren't necessarily contradictory, meaning that you can study gender communication and operate from both perspectives.

WHY STUDY GENDER COMMUNICATION?

Gender communication is . . .

- *Provocative:* Gender communication is **provocative** because we're all interested in how we're perceived, how we communicate with others, and how others respond to us. Of special interest is communication with members of the other sex, mainly because we can't experience the other sex firsthand; we can't "walk in each other's shoes" (physically speaking). We're also interested in the potential rewards that may result from effective gender communication.
- *Popularized:* Have you read those books that claim the sexes are from different planets or different cultures? Gender communication is a hot topic in our culture, evidenced by the many viral videos, books, TV shows, websites, films, and songs devoted to the topic. You're likely to be more aware of pop culture's treatment of gender, so we offer a balance by reviewing research findings on the subject.
- *Pervasive:* Gender communication is **pervasive,** meaning that interaction with women and men occurs 24/7. The sheer number of contacts we have with members of the other sex heightens interest in the effects of sex and gender on communication. When those contacts affect us in profound ways, such as in social or work relationships, we realize the need for improved understanding of gender communication.
- *Problematic:* Saying that gender communication is **problematic** doesn't mean that all gender communication centers around problems, but that it is complicated. Communication itself is complex; it's not a simple process that can be accomplished just because we're human beings who learned language at some early age or because we've been talking all our lives. When you add sex and gender (like other forms of human diversity) to the mix, you expand the complexity because now there is more than one way of looking at or talking about something.
- *Unpredictable:* Gender communication is **unpredictable** in that societal norms, rules, and roles have changed dramatically and continue to change. For example, our students talk about their difficulties with seemingly simple rituals, such as heterosexual dating etiquette. Female students reveal their own inconsistency, in that they want a guy to treat them to a night out, but they also like offering to pay for themselves. Male students explain that a guy doesn't know if paying for everything

on a date will cause him to be viewed as old-fashioned or simply courteous by today's "modern" woman. Will his date interpret such actions as controlling, as disrespecting a woman's right to contribute to the economics of a date? How should a guy respond if his date offers to pay? If he accepts, will he be viewed as cheap or as liberated, viewing his date as an equal who is capable of paying her own way? Even the simplest things can become complicated. In this context and others, lessons learned while growing up come into conflict with changes in society, leaving confusion about what is appropriate behavior.

That's where we come in—your textbook author and your instructor. We not only summarize research-based and popularized information in this text and this course you're taking, but also provide practical suggestions about how to apply the knowledge to your life's experiences. We want you to not only *know* the information, but also be able to *use* the information to improve your communication skills and enhance your relationships.

GENDER JARGON

Many gender-related terms are assigned different meanings, primarily by the media. Your own experience also may give you meanings that differ from textbook terminology. So to reduce the potential for confusion, here we offer you some common gender communication terms and their most commonly used meanings. Becoming more skilled in your communication with men and women begins with the use of current, sensitive, accurate language.

Is It Sex or Is It Gender?

You've probably already heard the terms *sex* and *gender* used interchangeably. For the sake of clarity, we use them in this text with exclusive meanings, even though some people think the terms are interchangeable. For our purposes, the term *sex* means the biological/physiological characteristics that make us female or male. At some points in this text we use the term *sex* to refer to sexual activity between men and women, but it will be clear to you whether the term is meant as a categorization of persons or an activity.

The term used most often in this text (even in the title) is *gender*. Most narrowly, gender refers to psychological and emotional characteristics of individuals. You may understand these characteristics to be masculine, feminine, or androgynous (a combination of both feminine and masculine traits). But gender encompasses more than this. According to gender scholars Perry and Ballard-Reisch (2004), gender refers to "how one is socialized to behave in relation to one's sex" (p. 18). Defined broadly, the term *gender* not only includes personality traits, but also involves psychological makeup; attitudes, beliefs, and values; sexual orientation; and gender identity (defined later).

> *I can't stand people that can't stand one of the sexes. We've only got two. Why would you dislike one of them?*
> —**Drew Barrymore, actor**

Gender is socially and culturally constructed, meaning that one's femaleness or maleness is much more extensive than the fact of being born anatomically female or male (Andersen & Hysock, 2010; LaFrance, Paluck, & Brescoll, 2004; Lunceford, 2010; Marecek, Crawford, & Popp, 2004). What is *attached* or *related* to that anatomy is taught to you through your culture, virtually from the time you are born. Culture, with its evolving customs, rules, and expectations for behavior, has the power to affect your perception of gender. For example, if you were raised in the Middle East, your views regarding the status and role of women in society would be quite different than if you were raised in the United States. Perhaps you grew up with strict rules for appropriate male–female behavior, such as "men ask women out on dates; women do not call men for dates." When you encounter members of other cultures (or your own culture, for that matter) who do not adhere to clearly drawn gender lines or who operate from rules different than your own, the notable difference may reinforce your original conception of gender or cause it to change.

In studying communication about and between women and men, it is helpful to use the term *sex* as a biological determination and *gender* as something that is culturally constructed. Sex is binary: There are only two choices. However, many choices exist when it comes to gender. Thus, you'll see references in this text to the "opposite or other sex," meaning a comparison between female and male. If you understand the notion of gender as a broad-based, multifaceted concept, then you understand why there is no such thing as an "opposite gender."

Viewing gender as culturally constructed allows one to change or reconstruct gender. This is a powerful idea. For example, the way you see the gender of "male, masculine" or "female, feminine" is not the way you *have* to see it. You can learn to see it differently and more broadly if you discover new information. This is discussed more thoroughly in Chapter 2; but for now, consider these examples: What if a guy discovers that "being a man" doesn't mean that he has to be strong and emotionally nonexpressive? He might decide that he's tired of always being the strong one, that he'd rather express his emotions and get some help instead. A woman might realize that her ability to climb the ladder of professional success is stronger than her nurturing instinct, so she chooses a career over motherhood as her primary life's work. Might these discoveries alter one's vision of gender? Possibly, but these people don't merely replace one stereotypical trait with another; they expand their options and find new ways of seeing themselves in relation to others. That's one of the goals of this text—to give you different ways of seeing things, including gender.

Biological sex suggests several things about how women and men communicate and are communicated with, but biology isn't destiny, and that's the powerful potential of studying gender communication. A person's sex isn't easily changed, but a person's conception of gender is far more open to change and development.

Gender Identity, Androgyny, and Sexual Orientation

In this text, we use the term *gender identity* as a subset of gender to refer to the way you view yourself—how you see yourself relative to stereotypically feminine or masculine traits. As gender scholars Andersen and Hysock (2010) explain it, "gender identity is an individual's specific definition of self, based on that person's understanding of what it means to be a man or a woman" (p. 2).

Many people are more comfortable viewing themselves as androgynous, meaning that they possess and blend traits typically associated with one sex or the other. *Androgyny* is a term made popular by gender scholar Sandra Bem (1974); the term is derived

Remember . . .

Gender Communication: Communication about and between women and men

Sex: Biological designation of being female or male

Gender: Cultural construction that includes biological sex (male or female), psychological characteristics (femininity, masculinity, androgyny), attitudes about the sexes, and sexual orientation

from the Greek *andros,* meaning man, and *gyne,* meaning woman. Androgynous women aren't necessarily masculine or sexless; likewise, androgynous men aren't necessarily effeminate, gay, or asexual. This form of gender identity simply involves a blending of sex-associated traits, rather than an adherence only to those traits associated with femininity or masculinity (Lippa, 2005).

Another component of gender is your general perception of appropriate roles for women and men in the society of which you are a member. Your gender identity thus encompasses not only your vision of self, but also your vision of the roles or functions for human beings within a given culture. While your gender identity is affected by your sex and your gender, it is within your control to change this identity. But what about a remaining element within the broad-based view of gender—an element that, in the view of many, you have no control over?

To use the term *sexual preference* to designate a person as heterosexual, homosexual, or bisexual is to use outdated terminology. The word *preference* implies that a person *chooses* his or her sexuality, that a person can make a conscious decision about sexuality. The prevailing view is that one's *sexual orientation,* that is, to whom one is sexually attracted or with whom one has sexual relations, is a characteristic of a person, not a person's choice (Perry & Ballard-Reisch, 2004). Many members of the gay and lesbian community in this country and abroad contend that they were born gay, not shaped into homosexuality by life's experiences or societal factors. Whatever your view of choice or no choice, being inclusive, sensitive, and contemporary in language usage requires referring to a person's sexuality as an orientation, not a preference.

Discriminatory attitudes and behavior that communicate the belief that heterosexuality is superior to homosexuality or bisexuality are termed *heterosexist* (Griffin, 1998). Often this form of discrimination manifests itself by omission, rather than by commission—it's not what you say, it's the assumption you communicate by what you leave out or don't say. The following question will illustrate what we mean here: Have you ever heard an instructor use a real or hypothetical example involving homosexuals to illustrate or clarify a principle or concept in a class? Even today, in a world that is more enlightened about different forms of sexuality, when instructors casually provide an example depicting dating behaviors of a homosexual couple, for instance, the reactions of students across the room may be such that the example can't continue. Students often seem so taken aback by such a reference as "John and Bob out on a first date" that the lesson, the point of the example, becomes lost. Has this happened at your institution? An instructor's choice to use—primarily, if not exclusively—examples of heterosexual interaction to clarify information about human communication, as well as students' protestations at merely raising an example involving homosexual individuals, may represent heterosexism of omission (Heinz, 2002). Instances of more obvious, concrete discrimination against anything not heterosexual represents heterosexism of commission.

As if terms for sex and gender weren't confusing enough, along come *metrosexual,* a media-generated term for heterosexual men who are more concerned with their appearance than the stereotypical straight man (Coad, 2008; Flocker, 2003; Mullen, 2003). As one magazine article explains, *"metrosexual* is a term for the evenly moisturized, sensitive— but straight!—guy" (Endelman, 2003, p. 17).

Some confusion surrounds the term *homophobia* (Kantor, 2009). We have found three usages of this term:

1. Homophobia can refer to a general fear of persons who are homosexual in sexual orientation.
2. The term may also describe the fear of being labeled a homosexual.
3. Within homosexual communities, homophobia may be used to mean behavior or attitudes that indicate a self-hatred or severe loss of self-esteem. In these cases, the homosexual individual, out of anger or hatred for her or his orientation, acts or thinks in ways that direct this anger onto the self.

A final term warrants attention in this section—persons describing themselves as *transgender.* You may be unfamiliar with this term, but more and more is being written and discussed about this form of identity (Girshick & Green, 2009; Herman, 2009; Lorber, 2009; Lorber & Moore, 2010; Valentine, 2007). First, don't make the mistake of confusing this term with others, like *transvestitism* (cross-dressing), *hermaphroditism* or *intersexuality* (persons born with both male and female genitalia), or *transsexualism* (being biologically one sex, but identifying psychologically with the other, often resulting in the altering of one's biological sex through medical methods). Gender scholars Ekins and King (1997) offer this distinction: Transvestite and transsexual "identities were/are hidden identities. The male transsexual and the male transvestite in public seek to pass as women—not to be read as a transsexual or transvestite. In contrast, the transgender identity breaks down the gender dichotomy by mixing and matching its characteristics in any combination. It is also a more open identity in that transgenderists are perceived as neither male nor female" (p. 341). Gender scholar Carla Golden (2009) suggests: "'Trans' means *across* or *beyond,* and thus transgender means that which moves across or beyond gender (as it is defined by the culture). As applied to people, it refers to someone who moves across or beyond gender boundaries" (p. 22).

As author of *Transgender Warriors,* Leslie Feinberg (1997) explains, "[transgender identity involves] the right of each individual to express their gender in any way they choose, whether feminine, androgynous, masculine, or any point on the spectrum between. And that includes the right to gender ambiguity and gender contradiction." Transgender persons strive to challenge the patriarchal, traditional idea of gender, in essence, taking the gender-as-constructed notion to its fullest. For example, Lennard Davis (2000) writes about a conversation with his son who explained that he was transgender. He didn't mean that he was homosexual or desirous of a sex change operation, but simply that he didn't want to comply with the boundaries of binary sex (only two

Hot Button Issue

"Gender Blurring"

Ah, the good old days when men were men and women were women, and you knew the difference. But were those days really that good? While we may sometimes yearn for simpler times, a time when navigating the gender and relationship waters was less complicated, was it really preferable to what we have now? In this day and age, images of a man, a woman, maleness, and femaleness are more blurred than in the past. Might that be seen as a good thing? Is it a welcome freedom for individuals to create their own genders, released from the confines of societal definitions for how they're supposed to behave, feel, and express themselves?

---

choices) or societal confines of gender. He wanted to be free to dress as he pleased, express himself as he wanted, and associate with whom he pleased, not necessarily in line with what was expected from a biological male.

As we said, we're all learning about what is meant by the term *transgender*. But for now, try to understand it as an identity that seeks to cross genders, to transcend the limitations and expectations of sex and gender, in order to construct a personal and unique form of gender.

Feminism (The "F-Word") and Sexism

When you first saw the term *feminism* in the title of this section, what thoughts or images came to mind? In the prologue to this book, we overviewed feminism from its historical

Remember . . .

Gender Identity: View of the self relative to feminine or masculine traits, as well as one's vision of the roles or functions for people within a given culture

Androgyny: Blending of masculine and feminine personality traits

Sexual Orientation: To whom one is sexually attracted or with whom one has sexual relations

Heterosexism: Discriminatory attitudes and behavior that communicate the belief that heterosexuality is superior to homosexuality or bisexuality

Homophobia: General fear of homosexual persons, a fear of being labeled a homosexual, and/or a homosexual's behavior or attitudes that indicate self-hatred or severe loss of self-esteem

Transgender: Unique gender identity not confined by traditional notions of masculinity or femininity

perspective, starting with the first wave (suffrage), then the second wave (beginning with women's liberation movement), and the more recent third wave of feminism. For our purposes in this chapter, it's illuminating to find out what people, especially college students, know and think about feminism these days.

The term *feminist* was referred to as the new "F-word" by a communication colleague, although you may have seen or heard this reference in recent years (DeFrancisco, 1992). When students in gender communication classes are asked, "Do you believe that women and men should receive equal opportunities and treatment in all facets of life?" they reply with a confident, hearty affirmative. When asked, "Are you a feminist?" the response is much more convoluted, with the most prevalent response being, "Well, no, I wouldn't call myself a feminist." Research suggests that although people may believe in equality, which is the basic tenet of feminism, many do not consider themselves feminists and do not want to be called this F-word (Basden Arnold, 2000; Collins, 2010; Dahl Crossley, 2010; Fudge, 2006; Martin & Sullivan, 2010; McIntosh, 2000; Olson et al., 2008).

Why does feminism conjure up visions, among men *and* women, of angry, radical, bra-burning, man-hating, humorless, masculine women storming out of the National Organization for Women (NOW) headquarters to try to gain superiority over men? These negative connotations in large part come from selective images the media transmitted (and continues to transmit) to the mass audience (hooks, 2000; Valenti, 2007). For example, did you know that there are no documented accounts of actual bra-burning episodes among "women's libbers" in the late 1960s? Only one incident was remotely connected—a protest of the 1968 Miss America pageant in which protesters threw their bras into a trash can! Yet the bra-burning image of feminists persists.

One of the strongest feminist voices of our time is bell hooks; in her book *Feminism Is for Everybody* (2000), hooks describes another attempt in history to discredit or marginalize the feminist movement: "Embedded in the portrayal of feminists as man-hating was the assumption that all feminists were lesbians. Appealing to homophobia, mass media intensified anti-feminist sentiment among men" (p. 68). We still see evidence of this today, when students reveal that they associate feminism with lesbianism, assuming that all feminists are homosexual and, in turn, man-hating. Let's clear up

Hot Button Issue

"Don't Call Me a Feminist!"

We realize that most of you reading this material are likely get a negative mental image when you hear reference made to "feminism." Yet in our experience with college students, once they understand the basic tenets of the feminist movement, they find themselves in agreement. Is there a better term, one that is less divisive or negative? One that would rally people around the issues rather than turn them off?

the confusion: First, not all feminists are female; second, not all female feminists are lesbians; and finally, we don't know of any lesbian feminists who hate men.

In the most basic sense, a feminist is a person—male or female—who believes in equality, especially sex and gender equality. hooks (2000) calls for people to "come closer to feminism," citing her favorite definition of the term: "Feminism is a movement to end sexism, sexist exploitation, and oppression" (p. 1). Authors of *Manifesta: Young Women, Feminism, and the Future*, Baumgardner and Richards (2010) describe feminism as being "the movement for social, political, and economic equality of men and women. Feminism means that women have the right to enough information to make informed choices about their lives" (p. 56).

Discriminatory practices or attitudes are referred to as *sexist*, typically pertaining to the treatment of women. But the term *sexism* simply means the denigration of one sex and the exaltation of the other, or, stated another way, the valuing of one sex over the other. Thus, sexism does not refer exclusively to devaluing women, just as racism does not refer exclusively to the denigration of one specific race in preference for another. Given this definition of sexism, there can be no such thing as "reverse sexism," even though some have used this term in specific reference to the discriminatory treatment of men.

> *I've always had large agendas. It makes me go, baby. I'm driven. I don't like inequities. Don't like to see people hurt. If I were on the tour today and a guy wasn't getting a good deal, I'd be fighting for him, too. You just want each person to have equal opportunity in everything they do.*
>
> **—Billie Jean King, activist/former professional tennis player**

Sexism continues to be a topic of interest to researchers (Cralley & Ruscher, 2005; Dardenne, Dumont, & Bollier, 2007; Kim, 2008; Leaper & Van, 2008). Scholars conducting one study of sexism found that female college students who had experienced sexism were more likely to confront the perpetrator of that sexism if they self-identified as feminists, if the sexist perpetrator was familiar to them or of equal status (meaning, perceived as a peer), and if the sexist event involved comments rather than unwanted sexual attention (Ayres, Friedman, & Leaper, 2009).

Perhaps you believe that our society isn't male dominated or that sexism is okay because "that's just the way it is." Maybe you feel that no opportunities have been denied either sex or that neither sex has endured particular suffering during your lifetime. But stop and think for a moment, not only on a personal level but also on a global one. Which sex is still the most underrepresented among decision makers, such as political leaders and judges, and among highly paid corporate executives (Ragins, Townsend, & Mattis, 2006)? For the first time in American history, women make up half

Remember . . .

Feminism: Movement or philosophy based on a belief in sex and gender equality

Sexism: Denigration of one sex and the exaltation of the other; valuing one sex over the other

the workforce, yet they still earn, on average, 77 cents to the man's dollar (Boushey, 2009; How We're Doing, 2009; U.S. Census Bureau, 2008). Conversely, which parent is most often denied child custody in divorce proceedings, simply because of that parent's sex? Perhaps you haven't yet seen any overt instances of sex discrimination in your personal life. But what about missed opportunities—those jobs, benefits and rewards, or relationships that did not come your way merely because someone held a limited view of which sex is best suited for a certain circumstance?

Today, individuals have many options when it comes to gender communication and behavior. This relatively recent development stems from changing roles, a wider, more tolerant view of what is considered appropriate behavior, and increased opportunities for both men and women. Many of the changes in societal expectations, opportunities, and relational patterns resulted (and continue to result) from the work of feminists and their supporters.

COMMUNICATION: A COMPLEX HUMAN PROCESS

Communication is a word that you hear a lot, especially since technology has become so sophisticated that we can easily and quickly interact around the world. As the channels for communicating have expanded, so have the meanings of the term *communication*. In fact, two communication theorists back in the 1970s isolated 126 definitions of communication (Dance & Larson, 1976). For our purposes, here's a fairly basic perspective of communication.

Human communication isn't static; it's an ongoing and dynamic process of sending and receiving messages for the purpose of sharing meaning. To accomplish this purpose, people use both *verbal* and *nonverbal* communication (including body movement, physical appearance, facial expression, touch, and tone of voice). Communication flows back and forth simultaneously, both verbally and nonverbally, between *sender* and *receiver* (Beebe, Beebe, & Ivy, 2013; DeVito, 2008).

Becoming Receiver Oriented in Your Communication

While the roles of sender and receiver in the communication process are both important, we believe the receiver's interpretation of the sender's message makes the difference between shared meaning and misunderstanding. Thus, the approach we advocate is termed the *receiver orientation to communication*. What the sender *intends* to convey is important, but it is less important than what the receiver *thinks is being conveyed*, or how the receiver interprets the message. You may clearly understand your intentions in what you say, but a listener may take your message in a different way than you originally intended. The result of not taking a receiver orientation can sound like this: "What do you MEAN, I'm late in calling you?! I said I'd call you AROUND five o'clock. Six-thirty IS around five o'clock!" In an instance like this, obviously the sender intended something different than the receiver's interpretation. Taking a receiver orientation—stopping to think about how your message will be understood by a listener *before* you say it—can greatly enhance your skill as a communicator.

When one is misunderstood, a typical response is to think that the receiver is at fault for not understanding the message. This reaction becomes particularly relevant to gender communication when you consider how often women report that they don't understand men because they don't react like women. And men get frustrated with women when they don't communicate or interpret communication like men. Here's our proposition to you:

> If people would spend more time figuring out how a listener will best hear, accept, understand, and retain a message and less time figuring out how they want to say something to please themselves, then their communication with others would vastly improve.

This sounds like the "golden rule of communication," doesn't it? Do you currently communicate from this perspective, even though you didn't know what to call it? Think of it this way: If you talk, but no one is there to listen or receive what you say, has communication occurred? Some will say yes; at the very least the sender has communicated with the self. But others will argue that without a listener, communication does not occur, making the receiver the most necessary link for the communication process to work. Again, this is part of the receiver orientation to communication.

If communication breaks down (as it seems to regularly), whose fault is it? Rarely is it completely the sender's fault for breakdowns. Sometimes the best forethought, insight, experience, and skill applied to a situation still lead to misunderstanding on the part of a receiver. But, in a receiver-oriented view of communication, the sender is responsible for communicating in a manner that will be most easily understood by the receiver; the receiver's responsibility is to attempt to understand the intent of the sender. Communication researchers Beebe, Beebe, and Ivy (2013) frame the receiver orientation as a skill of adaptation, a critical skill to develop as an effective communicator. They explain, "When you adapt a message, you make choices about how best to formulate it and respond to someone to achieve your communication goals. Adapting involves appropriately editing and shaping your responses so that others accurately understand your messages and so that you achieve your goal without coercing or using false information or other unethical methods" (p. 22).

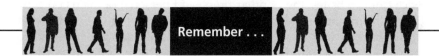

Remember . . .

Communication: Ongoing and dynamic process of sending and receiving messages for the purpose of sharing meaning

Verbal Communication: Sending and receiving of messages, in the form of words, so as to create shared meaning

Nonverbal Communication: Sending and receiving of messages without words, such as the use of body movement, eye contact, and facial expression, so as to create shared meaning

Sender: Initiator or source of a message

Receiver: Listener or recipient of a message

Receiver Orientation to Communication: Approach to communication that places more emphasis on a receiver's interpretation of a message than on a sender's intentions in communicating

Considering in advance how a receiver will interpret your message will go a long way toward improving your skills as a communicator. This stance is especially critical for gender communication, which is highly complex. It's advisable in every situation to focus on the receiver of your message *before, during,* and *after* you communicate.

THE PERSONAL EFFECTIVENESS APPROACH TO GENDER COMMUNICATION

Have you ever had difficulty communicating with someone of the other sex? Of course; everyone has. Have you ever wished that you were better at gender communication? What does "better" mean? Here are a few male students' questions and concerns:

> "In a conversation with a woman, when a problem's solved, why does the woman still want to continue the conversation?"

> "My wife says that men don't listen. I think that women listen too much."

> "In a serious situation, do women prefer that guys get emotional and all upset, or not show emotion, stuff it inside, and deal with it on their own?"

From female students, we receive questions like these:

> "When guys say, 'I'll call you,' what do they really mean?"

> "Why is it that men find it so difficult to say what they mean if emotions are involved? Are they afraid of what other men will say? Or do they feel they'll be viewed as less of a man?"

> "Guys usually want sex from women. So, after a woman goes to bed with a man, why does he act like he no longer respects her?"

Advice from websites, the popular press, and personal opinions on gender communication problems are prevalent. Here's a different point of view—the *personal effectiveness approach.* Becoming "better" at gender communication depends on becoming a more personally effective communicator. Personal effectiveness begins with knowledge and a perception of yourself and your own tendencies, extends to your understanding of the "rules" of society and the communication process, plus judgments that other people make about you. Let's examine these components one at a time.

Personal Effectiveness: Your Own Perception

At various times, you may have looked at how some people communicate and thought, "They're good at this; I wish I was that good." Then you probably looked at others and thought, "They need some help." No one can be effective *all* of the time, but each of us can be effective *more* of the time. The following four elements work together to help you be more effective more of the time.

- *Repertoire.* You've been communicating for a number of years and have developed communication behaviors that feel natural to you. Some ways of communicating work most of the time, some don't, and sometimes you may not know which to use. But few of us want to be the kind of person who always communicates or responds a certain way—like a "default mode"—no matter whom we're dealing with or what situation we're in. That's taking a comfortable pattern or behavior too far for most of us, and it can quickly land us in a communicative and relational rut. One of the goals of personal effectiveness is to expand the range of behaviors or repertoire at your disposal, to enlarge your communicative "bag of tricks" from which to choose when you confront various communication situations so that you're not locked into some predictable pattern.

• *Selection.* Once you've expanded your repertoire, you need to know which behavior to choose. In subsequent chapters, we talk about selecting the most appropriate behavior for various circumstances. For now, just realize that the selection depends on an analysis of your goals, the other person's goals, and the situation.

• *Skill.* To be personally effective, you also need the skill to perform a behavior so that another person accepts it and responds positively. We spend a good deal of time in this text discussing this skills element of personal effectiveness, as it applies to various situations you may encounter. We also encourage you to observe others, to ask questions of your instructor and classmates to find out how they deal with certain situations, and then to develop and practice your communication skills to enhance your view of yourself and your relationships.

• *Evaluation.* This element involves your ability to judge your own success. You need to be able to assess whether your efforts have been effective in the way that you wanted them to be and to use this information to adapt your behavior the next time. If you don't evaluate, you won't know what to change; you might continue to make the same mistake over and over.

Personal Effectiveness: Others' Perceptions

People interact with each other and make judgments about effectiveness all the time. You've probably been involved in conversations with people and then walked away thinking, "So much for *that*" or "What a head case." Other conversations leave you positively impressed. The point here is that only part of a judgment of effectiveness comes from the viewpoint of the communicator; the remainder rests with the person who receives the communication.

One fundamental aspect of becoming more personally effective is to increase the number of times you're positively regarded or evaluated by others. Let's say that you have observed someone else interacting in an effective way with a member of the other sex, and you wish to emulate this behavior. For example, one of your friends is especially skilled in first conversations—the exchange that occurs when people first meet. You'd like to get better at this kind of communication, so you add your friend's behavior to your "bag of tricks" (*repertoire*) and try it out in a subsequent encounter (*selection*). In a way you're practicing new communication *skills* on others. The last step is to *evaluate* the results of this experiment. When you do this, it's wise to go further than just your own reactions or judgments of effectiveness; you'll want to seek honest feedback from others.

Personal Effectiveness: Approach to communication that begins with knowledge of self, extends to an understanding of societal rules and expectations, and includes the development of greater control over one's communication behavior

Repertoire: Range of communicative behaviors from which to choose in social situations

Selection: Ability to choose appropriate communication for any given situation

Skill: Ability to enact selected communication behaviors to achieve desired results

Evaluation: Reflecting on one's communication and seeking feedback from others, so as to improve in future situations

Our point in presenting the personal effectiveness approach to gender communication to you is that you may experience some change while taking this course and reading this text. We don't suggest that you merely learn to "figure people out" only to get more of what you want. We *do* suggest that you develop yourself, that you change your behaviors for the better. If you want to be more personally effective, you may need to communicate differently than you do now. You'll want to further develop your ability to analyze what is going on and to communicate in a way that is beneficial for you and those you encounter. As a result, you'll find your communication with both men and women more satisfying.

VALUES TO GUIDE YOUR CHOICES

Not making wise choices has probably gotten a lot of us into trouble. How do you make wise choices in gender communication? An assessment of your personal values, with regard for human beings and relationships, can be useful. Here are some values relevant to gender communication to serve as useful guides for you as you enhance your communication ability and personal effectiveness.

Value 1: Equalizing Power

Some relationships function successfully with an uneven distribution of power (e.g., parent–child, mentor–protégé, employer–employee), although abuses of power exist within these relationships. However, when an imbalance of power isn't necessarily societally induced or an appropriate expectation for a relationship, such as in marriage, dating and romantic relationships, work relationships, or friendships, an ideal or goal to work toward is an even distribution of power or control. Empowerment—power *to* rather than power *over*—involves a shared approach to power or control that capitalizes on the strengths of each relational partner (Darlington & Mulvaney, 2002; Kuhn, 2008; Schiff, 2009).

Value 2: Talking to Make It Better

We profoundly believe in the power of communication to help solve the problems we face. You've probably all heard or read news reports of people who have difficulty verbally expressing anger and frustration and who wind up using physical violence as a means of solving problems. Granted, not all problems can be solved through communication; but in most situations, talking it over is absolutely critical to personal effectiveness in relationships.

Value 3: Believing in Freedom of Choice

When we talk about becoming more personally effective and developing more successful relationships, we include the possibility that you will influence or persuade someone else. With that possibility comes more responsibility. A value we hold central to this process is the freedom of the other person to choose his or her own line of action. People often manipulate the emotions of their partners to get what they want, which restricts the partner's freedom to choose. While the information in this text may help you become more persuasive in your relationships, you should use these skills in a manner that respects the right of each person to choose her or his own response to persuasive attempts.

Value 4: Being Open-Minded and Willing to Change

Have you ever talked with people who are completely closed-minded? It's frustrating, and frequently we have a reaction like, "Oh, what's the use? They'll never change their minds anyway, so there's no point in even talking." That's not a desirable reaction if the goal is effective communication. In connection with Value 3, a basic dimension of personal effectiveness is the belief on the part of other people that we are open to influence and change. In a relationship, the more each person believes that the other person can be influenced, the more they are both likely to communicate.

Value 5: Treating Another Person as an Individual

Stereotyping is hard to avoid. Can you imagine starting from scratch with every person you meet, meaning that you can't use past experiences to clue you as to what to expect? In some ways, stereotypes help reduce our uncertainty and increase our ability to predict what will happen. But sometimes those stereotypes seriously limit the range of possibilities (Ridgeway, 2010).

Get even more specific: In your relationships, should you stereotype women and men based on their sex? We suggest not—not just because there are so many differences between people, but because no one likes to be treated as a stereotype. A man doesn't like to be told that he is just another unfeeling, inexpressive guy. No woman likes to be told that "all women are too emotional." In the first place, we are all different, and our differences need to be recognized and celebrated. Second, actions based on stereotypes do nothing to advance relationships. And third, stereotypes can negatively affect someone's self-esteem. When possible, treat people as individuals, not categories.

Conclusion

In this opening chapter, we offered a definition of gender communication and described it as provocative, popularized, pervasive, problematic, and unpredictable. We also explained key terms so that you would more fully understand the gender jargon used in the remainder of this textbook. We explored the communication process from a receiver orientation and introduced the personal effectiveness approach to gender communication. As we stated, one goal of this text is to help you develop greater personal effectiveness so that you understand more of what is happening when women and men communicate. This process begins with a fuller awareness and understanding of your own communication behavior, so that you can better predict the potential impact of your communication on other people. If you can do that, you will be better at selecting the best option from your repertoire of communication behaviors and enacting that option with skill. Finally, we want to develop your ability to evaluate your communication with others and to explain why things worked out the way they did, because these steps are critical to personal effectiveness as a communicator.

Discussion Starters

1. Think about how roles have changed for men and women in our society. What kinds of roles did your parents model for you when you were growing up? What kinds of attitudes have you developed about appropriate roles for women and men in our society? Will you assume different roles than your same-sex parent as you continue to mature?

2. What comes to mind when you hear the term *women's liberation movement*? What comes to mind when you hear the term *feminism*? Do you consider yourself a feminist? Why or why not?

3. Think of something you consider to be really sexist. It could be a policy or practice, or something that you saw, read, or heard. What was your reaction to this sexist stimulus at the time? What is your reaction now? If your reactions are different, why are they different?

4. Recall a situation in which your interpretation of a message (as the receiver) did not match a person's intentions (as the sender). It could be something simple such as a miscommunication over the time or place where you were supposed to meet someone, or it could be something more serious, such as misunderstanding an instructor's explanation of an upcoming assignment. Analyze that situation: Was it a same-sex or mixed-sex conversation? What do you think the sender of the message intended to communicate? How did you, as the receiver, interpret the message? What was said or done during the conversation that was the primary cause of misunderstanding? How was the situation resolved? Using a receiver orientation to communication, what could the sender in the conversation have done to make the situation better? How could you, as the receiver, have reduced the potential for misunderstanding?

5. How are your values reflected in your communication? Consider the five values presented in

this chapter. Which of these values are already consistent with yours? Which ones represent new ideas for you? Are there values that you would add to our list?

References

Andersen, M. L., & Hysock, D. (2010). The social construction of gender. In B. Hutchinson (Ed.), *Annual editions: Gender 10/11* (pp. 2–5). New York: McGraw-Hill.

Ayres, M. M., Friedman, C. K., & Leaper, C. (2009). Individual and situational factors related to young women's likelihood of confronting sexism in their everyday lives. *Sex Roles, 61,* 449–462.

Basden Arnold, L. (2000). "What is a feminist?" Students' descriptions. *Women & Language, 23,* 8–18.

Baumgardner, J., & Richards, A. (2010). *Manifesta: Young women, feminism, and the future* (Anv. Rev. Ed.). New York: Farrar, Straus, & Giroux.

Beebe, S. A., Beebe, S. J., & Ivy, D. K. (2013). *Communication: Principles for a lifetime* (5th ed.) Boston: Pearson/Allyn & Bacon.

Bem, S. L. (1974). The measurement of psychological androgyny. *Journal of Consulting and Clinical Psychology, 42,* 155–162.

Boushey, H. (2009). The new breadwinners. In *The Shriver report: A study by Maria Shriver and the Center for American Progress.* Retrieved October 28, 2009, from http://awomansnation.com

Coad, D. (2008). *The metrosexual: Gender, sexuality, and sports.* New York: State University of New York Press.

Collins, G. (2010, May). The "F" word. *O: The Oprah Winfrey Magazine, 228,* 230.

Cralley, E. L., & Ruscher, J. B. (2005). Lady, girl, or woman: Sexism and cognitive busyness predict use of gender-biased nouns. *Journal of Language and Social Psychology, 24,* 300–314.

Dahl Crossley, A. (2010). "When it suits me, I'm a feminist": International students negotiating feminist representations. *Women's Studies International Forum, 33,* 125–133.

Dance, F. E. X., & Larson, C. E. (1976). *The functions of human communication.* New York: Holt, Rinehart, & Winston.

Dardenne, B., Dumont, M., & Bollier, T. (2007). Insidious dangers of benevolent sexism: Consequences for women's performance. *Journal of Personality and Social Psychology, 93,* 764–779.

Darlington, P. S. E., & Mulvaney, B. M. (2002). Gender, rhetoric, and power: Toward a model of reciprocal empowerment. *Women's Studies in Communication, 25,* 139–172.

Davis, L. J. (2000, March 24). Gaining a daughter: A father's transgendered tale. *The Chronicle of Higher Education,* pp. B4–B6.

DeFrancisco, V. (1992, March). *Position statement: How can feminist scholars create a feminist future in the academic environment?* Paper presented at the Tenth Annual Conference on Research in Gender and Communication, Roanoke, VA.

Devito, J. A. (2008). *The interpersonal communication book* (12th ed.). Boston: Allyn & Bacon.

Ekins, R., & King, D. (1997). Blending genders: Contributions to the emerging field of transgender studies. *The International Journal of Transgenderism, 1.* [Excerpt derived from Paul, E. L. (2002). *Taking sides: Clashing views on controversial issues in sex and gender* (2nd ed., pp. 340–347). New York: McGraw-Hill/Dushkin.]

Endelman, M. (2003, November 21). Man handle. *Entertainment Weekly,* 17.

Feinberg, L. (1997). *Transgender warriors: Making history from Joan of Arc to Dennis Rodman.* Boston: Beacon.

Flocker, M. (2003). *The metrosexual guide to style: A handbook for the modern man.* Cambridge, MA: DeCapo.

Fudge, R. (2006). Everything you always wanted to know about feminism but were afraid to ask. *Bitch, 31,* 58–67.

Girshick, L. B., & Green, J. (2009). *Transgender voices: Beyond women and men*. Lebanon, NH: University Press of New England.

Golden, C. (2009). The intersexed and the trans-gendered: Rethinking sex/gender. In J. W. White (Ed.), *Taking sides: Clashing views in gender* (4th ed., pp. 22–29). New York: McGraw-Hill.

Griffin, G. (1998). Understanding heterosexism—the subtle continuum of homophobia. *Women & Language, 21*, 33–39.

Heinz, B. (2002). Enga(y)ging the discipline: Sexual minorities and communication studies. *Communication Education, 51*, 95–104.

Herman, J. (2009). *Transgender explained for those who are not*. Bloomington, IN: AuthorHouse.

hooks, b. (2000). *Feminism is for everybody: Passionate politics*. Cambridge, MA: South End.

How we're doing. (2009, Fall). *Ms.*, 11.

Kantor, M. (2009). *Homophobia: The state of sexual bigotry today* (2nd ed.). Santa Barbara, CA: Praeger.

Kim, J. (2008). Let's talk about sex(ism). *Columbia Journalism Review, 47*, 12–14.

Kuhn, R. (2008). *Self-empowerment 101: Re-enchantment with our own capacity for empowering ourselves and others*. Charleston, SC: BookSurge Publishing.

LaFrance, M., Paluck, E. L., & Brescoll, V. (2004). Sex changes: A current perspective on the psychology of gender. In A. H. Eagly, A. E. Beall, & R. J. Sternberg (Eds.), *The psychology of gender* (2nd ed., pp. 328–344). New York: Guilford.

Leaper, C., & Van, S. R. (2008). Masculinity ideology, covert sexism, and perceived gender typicality in relation to young men's academic motivation and choices in college. *Psychology of Men and Masculinity, 9*, 139–153.

Lippa, R. A. (2005). *Gender, nature, and nurture* (2nd ed.). London: Psychology Press.

Lorber, J. (2009). *Gender inequality: Feminist theories and politics* (4th ed.). Los Angeles: Roxbury.

Lorber, J., & Moore, L. J. (2010). *Gendered bodies: Feminist perspectives* (2nd ed.). New York: Oxford University Press.

Lunceford, B. (2010). Clothes make the person? Performing gender through fashion. *Communication Teacher, 24*, 63–68.

Marecek, J., Crawford, M., & Popp, D. (2004). On the construction of gender, sex, and sexualities. In A. H. Eagly, A. E. Beall, & R. J. Sternberg (Eds.), *The psychology of gender* (2nd ed., pp. 192–216). New York: Guilford.

Martin, C. E., & Sullivan, J. C. (2010). *Click: When we knew we were feminists*. Berkeley, CA: Seal Press.

McIntosh, T. (2000, Winter). Fear of the f-word. *Bust*, 38–39.

Mullen, J. (2003, July 25). Hot sheet. *Entertainment Weekly*, 12.

Olson, L. N., Coffelt, T. A., Berlin Ray, E., Rudd, J., Botta, R., Ray, G., & Kopfman, J. E. (2008). "I'm all for equal rights, but don't call me a feminist": Identity dilemmas in young adults' discursive representations of being a feminist. *Women's Studies in Communication, 31*, 104–132.

Perry, L. A. M., & Ballard-Reisch, D. (2004). There's a rainbow in the closet: On the importance of developing a common language for "sex" and "gender." In P. M. Backlund & M. R. Williams (Eds.), *Readings in gender communication* (pp. 17–34). Belmont, CA: Thomson/ Wadsworth.

Ragins, B. R., Townsend, B., & Mattis, M. (2006). Gender gap in the executive suite: CEOs and female executives report on breaking the glass ceiling. In P. J. Dubeck & D. Dunn (Eds.), *Workplace/women's place: An anthology* (pp. 95–109). Los Angeles: Roxbury.

Ridgeway, C. L. (2010). Framed before we know it: How gender shapes social relations. In B. Hutchinson (Ed.), *Annual editions: Gender 10/11* (pp. 6–12). New York: McGraw-Hill.

Schiff, S. (2009, September). 31 ways of looking at power. *O: The Oprah Winfrey Magazine*, 181–197.

Spender, D. (1985). *Man made language* (2nd ed.). London: Routledge & Kegan Paul.

Thorne, B., Kramarae, C., & Henley, N. (1983). Language, gender, and society: Opening a second decade of research. In B. Thorne, C. Kramarae, & N. Henley (Eds.), *Language, gender, and society* (pp. 7–24). Rowley, MA: Newbury.

U.S. Census Bureau. (2008). Income, poverty and health insurance in the United States: 2008. Available: http://www.census.gov/hhes/ www/income/incomestats.html

Valenti, J. (2007). *Full frontal feminism: A young woman's guide to why feminism matters.* Berkeley, CA: Seal Press.

Valentine, D. (2007). *Imagining transgender: An ethnography of a category.* Durham, NC: Duke University Press.

Wilson Schaef, A. (1981). *Women's reality: An emerging female system in the white male society.* Minneapolis: Winston.

HOT TOPICS

- Sex and gender identity development
- Effects of gender identity on communication
- Changing definitions of masculinity and femininity
- How social interpretations of biological sex differences affect gender identity development
- Social and psychological theories of gender identity development
- Gender transcendence, androgyny, and the expanded communication repertoire
- Effects of socialization (e.g., families, clothes, toys, peers, and schools) on gender identity development
- Culture and its impact on gender identity development
- Intersections of identity—how different aspects of identity interact
- Intercultural gender communication—how culture and gender affect communication

Becoming a Woman, Becoming a Man, and Becoming a Person

Biological, Social, and Cultural Influences on Gender Identity Development

CHAPTER **2**

Case Study

Am I Masculine? Am I Feminine? What's That Mean, Anyway?

When you read or hear the words *masculine* and *feminine,* what comes to mind? What were your early lessons about femininity and masculinity? Did you grow up hearing "Act like a lady!" or "Buck up little soldier; boys don't cry!"? Did masculine and feminine stereotypes affect your thinking, or were you raised with "outside the box" views of what it meant to be feminine or masculine? Are your current views on the subject in line with earlier thinking, or have you changed your vision as you've grown up and matured?

Your earliest teachings and thoughts about what it means to be a girl, boy, man, and woman are powerful. Remnants of those early lessons about masculinity and femininity stay with us, try as hard as we may to undo early lessons we learned about women, men, and how they're supposed to behave. Your views of appropriate feminine and masculine behavior, as well as what you've learned about androgyny, affect how you communicate and develop relationships with members of your own sex, as well as the opposite sex. Those views arise from and continue to be shaped by your culture and experiences. That's the subject of this chapter.

I n Chapter 1, we made the point that we are born with a biological sex, but our gender is socially constructed. We each develop our own identity as a woman or man within our cultural context. This chapter explores factors that influence our identity development and our communication. We begin with a description of the importance of self-identity and the role gender plays in identity development, then move on to three major influences on that identity development—biology, society, and culture. We conclude with an examination of what happens when these factors intersect.

To what degree can we control or influence these factors? Are we designed to be a certain way, or is our identity more open to change? As you read the information that follows, think about these five questions:

1. What do you think has the most influence on your identity as a woman or man?
2. To what extent is your biological sex (being male or female) a part of your identity?
3. What is the most important aspect of who you are?
4. How does your culture define sex roles for men and women?
5. How do you communicate your identity to others?

HOW YOU DEVELOP YOUR IDENTITY

How do you come to understand who you are? Your *identity* is the sum total of the answers to the question "Who am I?" An interesting exercise to try some time is to write down on a sheet of paper twenty answers to that question. For some students, twenty answers come easily; for others, it's a more difficult task. If you do the exercise, you're likely to find such responses as son/daughter, brother/sister, student, friend, and employee. You might also include a sex identifier such as male/female or man/woman, because your sex is very much a part of your identity. Here's another interesting twist: If you're Caucasian, you likely didn't list that as one of your identifying characteristics. However, if you belong to a non-White culture, you probably did list your cultural or ethnic identity. Check this with your classmates. This interesting phenomenon points to the fact that sex is only one facet (and sometimes not the most important one) of who people are as individuals.

Fundamentals of Identity

Let's first review some basics about how identity develops in general. A good place to start is with the long-enduring question of nature versus nurture: Do people behave the way they do because they were born that way, or because they were socialized and educated to be that way? This question has been debated for years, and you probably have an opinion about it. But it doesn't have to be an either-or question. Identity is actually the product of the fusion of your genetically determined tendencies and your culturally determined socialization. In other words, identity is created through the combination of your biology and your external social environment.

This view leads to two important points regarding identity: First, no two identities are the same. This may seem like a completely obvious statement, but it has significant implications for communication. We can't ever assume that two people—whether they're from the same sex, the same group, or the same culture—will act or see the world in precisely the same way. Similarities will exist of course, but so will differences. Second, identities aren't fixed. Since identities are created through the interaction of the individual and the environment, and since both change and evolve over time, an individual's identity also is malleable and can be altered.

Identity Development and Communication

In this chapter, we can't review all the ways in which a person's identity develops, but we can discuss a few salient points that are helpful. First, social groups (e.g., family, schoolmates, friends, culture) shape cultural identities. These groups might be based on sex, ethnicity, sexual orientation, social class, religion, nationality, or other factors. All serve to shape the person you're becoming. In addition, different parts of your identity are formed at different times. For example, *sex identity,* defined as identity related to your biological properties of being either female or male, appears to come early, between one and three years of age (Martin & Nakayama, 2010). During this stage, boys and girls begin to identify themselves as belonging to one sex or the other, but we emphasize the word *begin* because the process of identifying with a particular sex takes time to develop. Sex identity is a subset of *gender identity,* just as your biological sex is a subset of your psychological, social, and cultural gender—a distinction we made in Chapter 1. Gender identity is more complex than mere biology; it includes how you see yourself in terms of sexuality or sexual orientation, how you relate to culturally defined notions of masculinity and femininity, and your views about appropriate roles for men and women in society.

The second relevant point regarding identity development is that it occurs through communication. Identities are negotiated, cocreated, reinforced, and challenged through communication (Hecht, Ribeault, & Collier, 1993). As you communicate who you think you are to other people and they respond to your identity presentation, they come to form judgments about you. This process has been called *avowal* and *ascription* (Martin & Nakayama, 2010). *Avowal* is the identity you portray to others. *Ascription* is the process by which others attribute characteristics and identities back to you.

A third aspect concerns the fact that you learn multiple roles as part of your identity. In various contexts, different parts of your identity come to the fore. For example, in a college classroom, your student identity may be the most obvious. But in a bar or club, your sexual orientation might be the most obvious. The point is that the self you present (avow) to the world can vary widely from context to context, and you communicate differently based on which part of your identity is at the forefront.

At times, different parts of your identity come into conflict with other parts of your identity, increasing the level of difficulty in communication. For example, a male student might try to follow the stereotypical role of being a man (e.g., "Don't ask for help or you'll appear weak"), which could conflict with his role as a student ("I have no idea what's going on in class!"). Or a woman might want to assertively confront a coworker in a meeting, but that conflicts with her notion that "women are supposed to defer to others."

Last, identity is a bridge between your interior and your exterior (Martin & Nakayama, 2010). Your interior mind consists of the sum total of your attitudes, values, and beliefs—all the things you think are true, right, and worthwhile; your exterior involves your experiences with other people and the environment within which you operate. These aspects of identity guide and even govern how you see the world and, consequently, how you communicate with people in it. Your identity helps you answer three great existential questions: "Who am I? What am I doing here? Who are all these other people?" As an individual, you might think about the ways your identity influences your communication with others, and whether your communication treats equitably people who have very different identities. Your identity provides a means of interpreting reality and a perspective for understanding the social world, including the definition of other identities. How you define a group, social class, or sex will subsequently govern how you will act toward that group. Defining men or women in a certain way will significantly govern your communication behavior toward members of either sex. This perspective is critical if you want to understand why you communicate in particular ways to men, women, or members of other identity classifications.

Your interaction with others is shaped and judged by how well you perform your identity. Just as your identity affects how you see others and communicate with them, so other people's identities govern how they communicate with you. Interaction is smooth when someone accepts your offered identity and you accept hers or his. But frequently conflicts arise when differences exist between who you think you are and who others think you are. For example, an assertive American female college student on a study-abroad program in the Middle East may not have her opinion readily accepted by men with whom she interacts. This is likely to conflict with her view of herself as a person who has the right to speak her mind. Her avowed identity wasn't confirmed in these circumstances; in fact, it was most likely challenged. The interesting question for her becomes, how much should she change her identity to get along in that part of the world? There are no easy answers to that question. Understanding your own identity and how it is shaped by culture and gender is important to understanding how you communicate. Being open to and accepting of others' avowed identities is critical to developing successful relationships. Thus, issues of identity are particularly important to understanding gender communication and becoming more personally effective in its use.

Masculine and Feminine Identity Revisited

As we consider degrees of similarity and difference within sex and gender identity, we must consider the basic concepts of masculinity and femininity. By now, we hope you accept the idea that gender is a social construct based in interaction and that definitions of femininity and masculinity can and do change according to the needs of the society that created the definition. For example, when American society was organized more closely around agriculture, the differences between masculinity and femininity were less distinct (Rudman & Glick, 2008). Both women and men assumed responsibility for the family and for economic survival. Since the husband's work was in the same physical location as that of the wife (or very close to it), the two were much more interdependent. This interdependence created a sense of shared and relatively equal responsibility for the family. However, when factories emerged and men began to work outside the home, the concept of separate gender identities expanded greatly. Men's working environment and separateness led to an impersonal, public, and utilitarian attitude. Women remained at home and became more directly associated with the personal, the private, the nurturing, and the emotional. References to women as weak and decorative, inferior, negative, and trivial emerged at that time.

What is most beautiful in virile men is something feminine; what is most beautiful in feminine women is something masculine.

—Susan Sontag, author

As society changed, so did conceptions of femininity and masculinity. Qualities that had been important to women in agricultural life such as ambition, strength, and decisiveness slowly faded from the feminine gender identity. Qualities important to men in agricultural society such as emotionality, nurturance, and interdependence (essential to family life) likewise diminished from the masculine gender identity. As women were confined to the private domain, femininity was redefined as nurturing, relational, and caring for others, first described by Bakan (1966, as in Rudman & Glick, 2008) as a communal fundamental modality. As men became more removed from the home, masculinity was redefined to include independence, aggressiveness, self-control, and achievement, described by Bakan as an agentic fundamental modality. These conceptions of masculinity and femininity became so prevalent that they became stereotypes. To *stereotype* is to presume that someone is like members of a particular group, rather than an individual.

Social psychologist Douglas Kenrick and his colleagues suggest, "Stereotyping is a cognitively inexpensive way of understanding others: By presuming that people are like other members of their groups, we avoid the effortful process of learning about them as individuals" (Kenrick, Neuberg, & Cialdini, 2005, p. 399). In American culture, the stereotypical woman is soft-spoken (when she speaks at all), emotional, subjective, self-effacing by reflecting uncertainty and humbleness, and compliant through submissiveness. Femininity results in warm and continued relationships with men, a sense of maternity, interest in caring for children, and the capacity to work productively and continuously in female occupations. For the women reading this, is this true for you? These descriptions imply that women be heterosexual, which in turn requires women to focus on their attractiveness to men.

The stereotypical American man is an ineffective listener, emotionally inexpressive, categorical and certain in his language use, and dominating in discussions. Psychologist Joseph Pleck (1981) suggests that one or more of the following conveys masculinity in our society:

1. Displaying success or high status in one's social group
2. Exhibiting a manly air of toughness, confidence, and self-reliance
3. Demonstrating aggression, violence, and daring
4. Avoiding anything associated with femininity

These descriptions require men to organize themselves and society in a competitive, hierarchical manner. Competition is driven by a goal of individual achievement, and it requires participants to show a degree of emotional insensitivity to others' pain or losses. This stereotype leaves little room for relationships.

The societal conditions that gave rise to the current stereotypical definitions of masculinity and femininity occurred more than a hundred years ago, and these conditions have changed a great deal in the past three decades. Yet the definitions themselves have been slower to change. Riesman (1990) notes that the "institutionalized roles of husband and wife continue to provide a blueprint for marriage, situating men's work primarily in the public sphere and women's in the private sphere" (p. 51). Femininity remains linked to the home, family, emotional expressiveness, and caring for others. Masculinity continues to focus on the public areas of work and is associated with power and dominance, emotional reserve, and productivity (Wood, 1994).

Have you ever been talked to or treated a certain way, merely because of your sex? Can you recall a situation when someone sized you up because you were a woman or a man, and then talked to you based on a stereotype of your sex? Here are some common examples. People assume that because men tend to have more muscle mass than women, all men can lift all kinds of heavy things. They often get called on to help people move, help rearrange bulky furniture, or lift heavy boxes and objects. Many men have strained their backs or, worse, developed hernias and detached retinas from all of the lifting they are "supposed" to be able to do. Why assume that a guy always has the strength or, for that matter, *wants* to do physical labor?

And for the women, have you ever taken your car to a service center for repairs and been treated by the mechanic as though you don't speak English? (Yes, men are treated this way too, but there seems to be some expectation that men can understand cars better than women.) People who don't know you may assume a lot about you, simply because of your sex.

THE CHANGING FACE OF MASCULINITY Men get a great deal of advice on how to be men. American men's magazines such as *Men's Health, Details, Maxim,* and *Men's Fitness* focus on self-improvement and include topics such as diet and exercise tips, relationship columns, sex advice, health updates, and information on how be more masculine. Men's magazines are catching up to what women's magazines have been doing for years. The danger, as author Ann Dobosz (1997) points out, is that the focus on "shaving creams, sexual performance, and well-toned abs may create a men's culture as warped and obsessive as women's mass culture" (p. 91). Is that what we want?

Views of what is masculine and what masculinity actually means continue to change (Beynon, 2002; Connell, 1995, 2000; Connell & Messerschmidt, 2005; DeVisser, 2010; Janssen, 2008; Schrock & Schwalbe, 2009; Tragos, 2009). Scholars across multiple academic disciplines explore what it means to be male and masculine, with regard for sex and gender identity (Addis, Mansfield, & Syzdek, 2010; Harris, 2010; Paechter, 2006; Soulliere, 2006; Ward, Merriwether, & Caruthers, 2006). Research on boyhood is on the rise (Bartlett, 2009); university courses of study with such labels as Masculinity Studies and Male Studies are increasingly popular on college campuses (Adams & Savran, 2002; Kegan Gardiner, 2002; McCarry, 2007; Traister, 2000).

One of the most prolific scholars to write about masculinity is sociologist Michael Kimmel (2005, 2009; Kimmel, Hearn, & Connell, 2004; Kimmel & Messner, 2009). In one of his earlier works on the subject, *Changing Men,* Kimmel (1987) explained, "As women's studies has radically revised the traditional academic canon, men's studies seeks to use that revision as the basis for its exploration of men and masculinity" (p. 10). Men's studies "attempts to treat masculinity not as the normative referent against which standards are assessed but as a problematic gender construct" (p. 10).

Author Michael Segell (1996) argues for the utility of certain traditional aspects of masculinity such as fearlessness and the ability to mask emotions, take risks, and be aggressive. According to Segell, aggression and dominance (male characteristics), not sensitivity and submissiveness (female characteristics), contribute to superior self-esteem in both men and women. But author Cooper Thompson (1992) maintains that, taken to an extreme, masculinity promotes violence. Thompson notes that high school boys use the word *fag* as the most humiliating put-down. If a boy is called a fag, it means that he is perceived as weak or timid and therefore not masculine enough for his peers. Enormous pressure is placed on the boy to fight back; not being tough at these moments only proves the allegation. Thompson believes that boys must learn different patterns of behavior because the cost of being masculine is high, in that toughness leads to increased chances of stress, physical injury, and early death.

One interesting difference between masculinity and femininity is that masculinity seems to be something that must be "attained." Masculinity, in much of the world, is earned and achieved rather than merely socially prescribed (Majors & Billson, 1992). This is reflected in the common exhortation, "Be a man!" One rarely hears women say to each other, "Be a woman!" with the underlying message of "you aren't there yet, so get there!" The words "be a man" come with a long list of socially prescribed role behaviors that men in training must work up to. Consequently, manhood can be revoked. A man may hear, "You are no longer a man" if he loses his job, is unable to provide for his family, cannot stand up to an aggressor, or experiences some other culturally determined criteria. This kind of communication can be damaging to both identity and self-esteem.

THE CHANGING FACE OF FEMININITY   Cultural definitions of femininity have a history of negative characteristics, reviewed earlier in this chapter. Has this changed? One study examined meanings for feminine and femininity throughout the twentieth century (Greene, 1997). The author concluded that although times have changed and definitions have moved from the negative to a celebration of the feminine, the cultural belief in distinct sexes makes it likely that future meanings of femininity will still be influenced by biological roots. In similar research Lueptow, Garovich, and Lueptow (1995) compared gender stereotypes held by over 3,600 college students over a seventeen-year period—from 1974 to 1991. Contrary to predictions and despite dramatic changes in sex roles and attitudes during this time period, perceptions of sex-typed personality traits not only stayed stable but slightly increased. However, other studies offer evidence that perceptions, particularly about femininity, have changed somewhat and in a positive direction (Dummer, 2007; Holmes & Schnurr, 2006; Kehily & Nayak, 2008; Kelly, Pomerantz, & Currie, 2006). Views of what it means to be feminine continue to change, from self-definitions to ideas about body image, athleticism, clothing, and nonconformity, such that a wider range of behaviors, attitudes, and choices may be viewed as feminine in this day and time (Mean & Kassing, 2008).

One significant factor affecting the evolution of what it means to be feminine involves the increasing number of women, particularly young women, who participate in sports (Flanagan, Baker, Fortin, & Tinsley, 2006). While equality with male athletes clearly has not been achieved, gains have been made. According to the Women's Sports Foundation (2010), women who play sports enjoy greater physical and emotional health, are less likely to engage in a host of risky health behaviors (e.g., drug use, smoking, drinking), and have fewer incidences of breast cancer and osteoporosis later in life than nonparticipants. Betsey Stevenson (2007, 2010), business professor at the Wharton School at the University of Pennsylvania, conducted studies on the advantages of sports participation for girls and women. Her studies show that girls who participate in high school sports are more likely to achieve higher levels of education and have greater earning potential and enhanced employment opportunities than those who don't engage in athletics. Girls develop skills playing sports that translate into advantages later in life, like enhanced communication skills, the ability to work well with others, competitiveness, assertiveness, and self-discipline. In general, sports participation by boys and girls affects the likelihood of becoming a productive member of society (O'Brien, 2010).

Most people simply cannot live up to the ideal or the stereotypical images of masculinity and femininity. The frustration and disillusionment that may set in when the ideal is not reached can have lasting effects on the individual's self-esteem. The more one consciously learns about options in defining and living out one's feminine and masculine identity, the easier it is to select a definition that fits one's own personality, needs, and goals.

Remember . . .

Identity: Sum total of answers to the question "Who am I?"

Sex Identity: Subset of gender identity; identity related to biological properties of being female or male

Gender Identity: More complex than mere biology; includes the view of self in terms of sexuality or sexual orientation, how one relates to culturally defined notions of masculinity and femininity, and one's views about appropriate roles for men and women in society

Avowal: Self-identity communicated to others

Ascription: Process by which people attribute characteristics and identities to other people

Stereotype: Presumption that someone is like members of a group, rather than an individual

THE EFFECTS OF SOCIAL INTERPRETATIONS OF BIOLOGICAL SEX ON IDENTITY

Biological differences between men and women continue to be hot topics these days. Some people believe that because biological differences between women and men are natural and uniquely human, they are something to be appreciated, not downplayed or resented. These biological properties "make the world go 'round," so why be concerned about them? Why focus on similarities? Others believe that biological sex differences are fairly insignificant; the real issue is the social interpretation of those differences. For example, communication scholar Peter Andersen (1998) supports the notion that biology isn't destiny, suggesting that "a thorough review of the evidence on sex differences reveals that they are a function of culture, biology, and their interaction" (p. 98).

In more recent work, Andersen (2006) provides an interesting starting point in the consideration of sex differences. Based on the work of communication pioneer Ray Birdwhistell, Andersen describes three levels of differences. The first is primary sexual characteristics that relate to basic reproductive functions and behaviors such as the production of sperm, eggs, and the ability to lactate. These are the most obvious of differences between men and women, and are the ones least amenable to change. As Andersen points out, even sex change operations do not give the patient the ability to produce eggs or sperm. The second level of difference is the indirect result of these reproductive roles, such as the amount of body hair one has, one's muscle mass, and certain behaviors that research suggests are biologically based, such as a female's apparent higher degree of nonverbal sensitivity and a male's advantage in navigation and spatial visualization. The third level consists of those patterns of social behaviors that are learned, culturally based, and situationally produced.

Andersen makes it clear that our behavior, including communication behavior, stems from all three levels. As noted, the primary level is the most resistant to change, and these reproductive differences will likely always be with us. Of particular interest are the other two layers, especially the third level. At these two levels, are men and women completely different? Or is there some similarity and overlap?

Communication scholar Kathryn Dindia wrote an interesting article titled *Men Are from North Dakota, Women Are from South Dakota* (2006), a takeoff on a popular book that came out about a decade ago (something about Mars and Venus?). After a review of research on communication and psychological variables (Andersen's third layer), Dindia concluded that sex differences in these areas are, on the average, small. She suggests, "The average woman is not that much different from the average man . . . approximately 85 percent of women and men overlap across various psychological variables, whereas approximately 15 percent of men and women do not overlap" (pp. 10–11). Dindia states, "Scholars as well as laypeople are not justified in labeling women and men as different, at least insofar as psychological variables and communication variables are concerned" (pp. 10–11).

For a number of years, gender researcher Janet Shibley Hyde (2005, 2006; Peterson & Shibley Hyde, 2010) has advanced a supposition known as the Gender Similarities Hypothesis. This hypothesis holds that women and men are more alike than they are different. This hypothesis does not state that men and women are similar in every psychological dimension; Hyde notes that some differences are moderate while others are large in magnitude. Examples include sex differences in smiling, emotional expressiveness, sensitivity to nonverbal cues, and attitudes about casual sex. But the commonalities outweigh the differences.

While this chapter will inform you about some biological sex differences, those differences are neither our central focus nor critical to our approach to gender communication. We don't want to make too much out of biological differences because we've seen that they sometimes become a cop-out. ("That's just the way we *are*.") This view implies that somehow biology gives us permission to behave in a certain way—even if that way is discriminatory or inappropriate. For many of us who study gender communication, this is not a workable stance. Ever heard the phrase, "biology isn't destiny"? So while we want to explore the biology, we are most interested in how identity development and communication are affected by the social translations of that biology.

"Innies" and "Outies": Anatomical Differences and Social Interpretations

Some of the biological findings described in this section may be quite familiar to you, while some may surprise you. We challenge you to think about the social interpretations of the biology in ways that you might not have thought of before now. Think also about how those interpretations affect your identity as a man or woman, as well as how they influence they way you communicate.

SEXUAL ORGANS   The human fetus starts to form internal female or external male genitalia at around three or four months into development (Crawford & Unger, 2004). Think for a moment about the consequences of that simple differentiation of genitalia. Consider the interesting parallel between the sexes' genitalia and their roles in society. For centuries the male penis has been viewed as a symbol of virility—an external, outward sign of men's strength and their ability to assert themselves in the world. In contrast, the internal genitalia of women is paralleled with the more passive, submissive profiles that women have traditionally assumed—profiles endorsed by men, and often, society in general. The social interpretations of women's sexual organs identify them as reactors, receivers, followers, and beneficiaries of men's decisions.

The male is by nature superior, and the female inferior; the one rules, and the other is ruled. The lower sort are by nature slaves, and it is better for them as for all inferiors that they should be under the rule of a master.

—Aristotle, Greek philosopher

Maybe you've never considered these parallels before; maybe your reaction to these ideas is: "The world has changed; these depictions of women and men are past history, so why draw the parallel to sexuality?" If that's what you're thinking, then congratulate yourself. We agree that, for many people, these profiles no longer apply and thus the biological parallel doesn't apply either. But at times you may be painfully reminded that within many institutions in society—business, education, political arenas—more than mere echoes of this "historical" view of women and men still exist.

REPRODUCTIVE FUNCTIONS   While the sexual organs represent the more obvious anatomical sex differences, perhaps the most profound difference rests in the sexes' *reproductive functions*. What makes the sexes so different in this regard is the woman's capacity to carry a developing fetus for nine months, give birth, and nurse an infant—something that a man cannot do. These tasks have long been protected, even to the extent that turn-of-the-century medical information warned women against too much thinking or exercise so as not to divert blood away from their reproductive systems (Borisoff & Merrill, 1998; McLoughlin, Shryer, Goode, & McAuliffe, 1988). The reproductive capabilities of men and women have more profound social translations than any other biological property or function.

To better explain that last statement, allow us to re-create a segment of a rather lively discussion that occurred at a gathering of some friends. We were talking about biological sex differences when one of the men commented that sex differences exist in their current form because of centuries of *hunter–gatherer cultures.* These were societies in which the men combed the land, hunted the food, and protected their families from danger, while the women had the birthing and child-rearing duties and developed tools to gather and carry the food. This separation of labor formed the basis of a social structure that worked very well; thus it continued into modern times, in the opinion of our friend at the party. But more important than a mere anthropological lesson, the point in this explanation of sex differences is that because of simple biology, whole societal structures were set in place. Did you ever think that so much might rest on the capacity to reproduce? This is a prime example of what we mean by biological factors contributing to a wide range of social norms and expectations.

Medical knowledge and technology have progressed to the point that women, in particular, can benefit from alternatives to their own biology—alternatives that continue to change our social structure. Although still able to carry and give birth to babies, women now have several methods of preventing conception. In 2010, the birth control pill turned 50, meaning that this simple but effective means of contraception has now been available to women for 50 years in the United States (Kotz, 2010; Northrup, 2010). Some hold the view that the development, accessibility, and affordability of "the pill" contributed more than other events or discoveries in altering male–female dynamics in recent U.S. history (Tyler May, 2010a, 2010b, 2010c). In addition, if women do become pregnant, they don't necessarily have to be the biologically designated, primary caregivers once the baby is born. Many women choose to return to work (or have to work because of economic constraints) or pursue other endeavors. More men are now single parents, and in two-parent families, some fathers choose to take time off from their jobs after a baby's birth or even quit their jobs to care for their children (Aasen, 2009; Boushey, 2009; Brott, 2008; Brott & Ash, 2004; Coontz, 2009; Gray & Anderson, 2010; O'Leary & Kornbluh, 2009; Painter, 2010; Simmons, 2009; U.S. Census Bureau, 2009; Winter & Pauwels, 2006). These choices affect how the sexes view each other, as well as how they communicate.

Do social backlashes still emerge against women who don't follow the more traditional path of motherhood? Have you heard criticism leveled at women who choose not to have children or who return to their careers while their babies are still quite young? If a man chose not to father any children or not to become the primary caregiver for a newborn because it would disrupt his career goals, do you think that he would receive as much criticism as a woman who makes the same choice? In sum, even though it isn't as unusual to see women returning to work after giving birth and men choosing to be primary child-caregivers, statistics indicate that this profile of family is still much more an aberration than the norm (Johnson, 2005).

THE MEASURE OF STRENGTH   When the subject of biological sex differences is introduced, students are quick to comment about issues surrounding *physical strength* and endurance. Heightened by events in America's campaign against terrorism and other military conflicts, such topics as biological attributes of male and female soldiers, differing fitness standards, and women in frontline combat generate provocative discussions (Cergol, 2010; Hanafin, 2010; Holland, 2006; Neary, 2010). A common theme in these discussions is whether women, whose bodies are higher in fat and lower in muscle in comparison to men's, have the strength and endurance necessary for combat or other sustained military action. Some people contend that if women are able to endure childbirth, they ought to be able to handle combat. However, *National Review* reporter Elaine Donnelly (2010) contends that "Women on average do not have the physical capability to lift a fully loaded male soldier who has been wounded under fire, in order to save his life. Even average-sized men have that capability; no one should have to die because women do not."

> *Strong women leave big hickeys.*
> —*Madonna, performer*

Besides men's higher concentrations of muscle, four other factors give men more natural strength than women: (1) a greater oxygen-carrying capacity, (2) a lower resting heart rate, (3) higher blood pressure, and (4) more efficient methods of recovering from physical exertion (Stockard & Johnson, 1980). Because of these characteristics, men have long been thought of as the stronger sex, women the weaker sex. But let's take a closer look at determinations of strength.

Strength is defined in Webster's dictionary as force, invulnerability, or the capacity for exertion and endurance. If you examine strength from a vulnerability or endurance angle, then the sex-typed strength argument breaks down a bit. Research documents six differences between males and females:

1. Male fetuses experience many more developmental difficulties and birth defects, average an hour longer to deliver, and have a higher death rate than female fetuses.
2. For the top fifteen leading causes of death in the United States, men have higher death rates than women.
3. Women outlive men by an average of five years.
4. Men do not tend to see themselves as ill or susceptible to disease or injury, when they actually are more susceptible.

5. Men generally drive more recklessly than women, accounting for three out of every four traffic fatalities.

6. In some sports requiring extreme levels of endurance (such as ultramarathons and dogsled racing), women have been catching up to and surpassing men (Crowther, 2001; Schmid, 2005; *Science Daily*, 2007; Shephard & Astrand, 2000; Stibich, 2008; Tirrito, 2010; TrafficSTATS, 2010).

Could it be that the notion of male strength has more to do with social interpretations than biological fact? The answer to that question is no, if you equate strength with higher muscle mass, but yes, if you equate strength with vulnerability and endurance. Most often a determination of strength depends on the individual, not the sex. We've all seen some women who were stronger (in terms of muscle strength) than some men and vice versa. But it's quite fascinating when you realize how many social expectations and stereotypes are steeped in the basic biology.

On the one hand, we'll never experience childbirth. On the other hand, we can open all our own jars.
—*Bruce Willis, actor*

Social Interpretations of "Raging" Hormones

When people think about or comment on biological differences between the sexes, most often those differences are attributed to hormones (Jacklin, 1989). However, as hormonal studies become more frequent and utilize more sophisticated methods, they produce inconsistent results, though some do show the effect of hormones on behavior. Some of the complexity stems from not knowing where genetics leave off and environment begins.

For the sake of simplicity, here we've chosen to explore those hormones most associated with masculinity (androgens, more specifically, testosterone) and femininity (estrogen). We've pared some complex information down to three key elements: hormonal

Hot Button Issue

"Women in the Military"

For some people, the presence of women in the American armed forces is still a hot button issue. Even though women have served in the military for decades, debate continues over the roles they should play, whether they should have equal access to all military situations (including ground combat and male-dominated ships at sea), and differing standards for physical ability. Is this a hot button issue for you, one for which you hold strong opinions?

From time to time, talk emerges across the nation about reinstating the draft, given the strain currently placed on the all-volunteer U.S. military forces stationed around the world. If a draft were to be reinstated, should women and men alike be eligible for the draft? If members of both sexes can volunteer for military service, shouldn't both sexes be included equally in a draft? What would the national debate about this issue sound like? What sex-based expectations and stereotypes do you anticipate would emerge in such a discussion?

effects on nurturance, aggression, and cycles. These functions are the most distinctive for the sexes and have the most significant social interpretations.

NURTURANCE   Stereotypically, *nurturance* is associated with women's mothering roles, but it is defined as the "giving of aid and comfort to others" (Maccoby & Jacklin, 1974, pp. 214–215). Research by Anke Ehrhardt determined a relationship between female hormones and the inclination to nurture. Ehrhardt and colleagues (1980, 1984) examined young girls who had been prenatally "masculinized" by receiving large doses of androgens (male hormones) from drugs prescribed for their mothers. These subjects rarely fantasized or daydreamed about marriage and pregnancy, nor did they show much interest in caring for small children. They more often gave career a higher priority than marriage in discussions of future plans, generally liked to play and associate with boys more than girls, and were more likely to exhibit high levels of physical energy. These studies and other evidence led researchers to link hormones and nurturance.

But many researchers argue that the ability to nurture goes beyond biology. Sex role researchers Stockard and Johnson (1980) caution that "hormonal influence helps prompt the appearance of and interest in nurturing behavior, but social situations and interactions also exert an influence, making it possible for males as well as females to nurture" (p. 137). Such experiences as participation in childbirth, early contact between parents and infants, and even whether one has younger siblings may affect one's ability to nurture. Psychologists Crawford and Unger (2004) suggest that a "nurturing person-ality" can be developed simply when adults are put into nurturing roles (p. 320). Given this information, why does society tend to readily associate femininity with the ability to nurture and comfort, as though men were incapable of doing so? Granted, the association between motherhood and nurturance is deeply ingrained in our culture and the identity of "mother" is central in most of our lives; thus, it is a reasonable connection. But does it have to be the only connection?

If a man finds that he has a stronger or equally strong nurturing tendency as his wife or partner, should his masculinity be threatened? Think about why, until only recently, mothers were almost always awarded custody of children in divorce proceed-ings, regardless of which parent was actually the better nurturer. Conversely, if a woman isn't particularly fond of children and isn't at all interested in motherhood, does this mean that she has a hormonal deficit or that she is somehow less feminine than women who want to nurture children? It's easy to see how hormonal functioning can lead to labels and stereotypes for the sexes—labels that affect our opportunities and influence our choices in communication.

AGGRESSION   Aggressive behavior may be learned, but research indicates that hor-mones influence *aggression,* defined as the stereotypically male trait of asserting or inflict-ing force (Lippa, 2002; Snowbeck, 2001). Aggressiveness has been long viewed as a male characteristic related to androgens (primarily testosterone), while passivity has been related to the female system's lack of androgens (Maccoby & Jacklin, 1980). However, professor of medical science Anne Fausto-Sterling (1992) discovered that many stud-ies attempting to link male aggression and testosterone levels produced contradictory results, meaning that the relationship between hormones and aggression was question-able. So researchers continue their attempts to better understand this relationship.

Why do we still tend to associate masculinity with aggressive behavior, femininity with passive behavior? Could it again be the case that judgments about aggression and the sexes have more to do with social influences than biological fact? Think about the messages that lots of little boys receive from their mothers and fathers, siblings, peers, and the media. In addition to those messages about strength that we discussed in an earlier section, boys are warned not to "act like a sissy" and chastised for anything resembling feminine behavior. You see fathers, uncles, and older brothers teaching young boys to stick up for themselves, to develop aggressive attitudes by playing contact sports, and not to "throw like a girl." Granted, things are changing and not all families raise their male children in this manner, but the notion of the male as aggressor is still around.

Many men are not particularly proud of the legacy of aggression. In fact, they're working hard to turn this legacy around because the expectation that they will be constantly strong and aggressive constitutes a burden they'd rather not carry. They seek alternatives to expected behavior and resent the implication that being a "real man" means being aggressive, competitive, emotionally aloof or detached, and in control all the time.

Now consider the sexual flip side of aggression. How do most people react when women exhibit assertive or aggressive behavior? Unfortunately, many people react negatively, as though a woman who expresses this stereotypically masculine trait is experiencing a hormonal imbalance or simply behaving inappropriately. Occasionally, off-base, derogatory insinuations about sexual orientation are made. Some men are threatened or put off by aggressive women, because they don't welcome another context for competition. Also, some women are put off by unexpected, aggressive behavior in other women. For example, if a female manager were to argue aggressively with her coworkers or boss, interrupt the verbal contributions of colleagues, or aggressively strive to achieve a promotion, think about whether she would be viewed through the same lens as a man behaving similarly.

What about aggression and sports? Acting out aggression on the football field, in the hockey arena, or in the boxing ring is encouraged, expected, and rewarded in men. But, as more women's sports gain prominence and respectability, how do people view athletic aggression by females? Is this one of very few arenas in which female aggression is rewarded? Does it look the same and is it received as well as aggression by male athletes?

> *My male roommate and I mixed up our nicotine and testosterone patches. He got cranky and hungry. I got a raise and a corner office.*
>
> *—Karen Ripley, comedian*

Most people encourage verbal and physical aggression by women in the sporting context, as long as that aggression isn't aimed at male competitors. Maybe you think that statement is harsh, but even in this day and age, how many sports allow direct, physical competition between women and men? Apart from the occasional anomaly—such as the famous 1973 "Battle of the Sexes" tennis match between Billy Jean King and Bobby Riggs, successful NASCAR driver Danica Patrick, and female golfers who occasionally qualify to compete on the PGA tour (which is, to date, an all-male organization)—few women are given the opportunity to compete against men in either professional or collegiate sports. No contact sports on these levels, such as football, basketball, soccer, rugby, wrestling, or hockey, place the sexes in direct competition with each other. Neither do many noncontact sports, with the exception of mixed doubles matches in tennis and some endurance races. Perhaps a continued rise in popularity of women's sports, to the degree that they become more commonplace instead of exceptions to the rule, will affect people's stereotypical notions about aggression.

CYCLES   When we think of biological cycles, we typically associate them with women's biology in general and with premenstrual syndrome (PMS) in particular. Three decades ago, the medical profession largely chalked up women's menstrual discomfort to hypochondria. When enough research documented women's reports of menstrual problems over time, the medical community declared PMS a disease (Richmond-Abbott, 1992). Some scholars believe that labeling PMS a disease has added credibility to the condition, but it has also reinforced an old stereotype (Caplan, 2008). Dramatic accounts of outlandish, overemotional, even violent behavior, as well as exaggerated images of women unable to meet their responsibilities have been attributed to PMS. There's even a T-shirt with the message, "I Have PMS and ESP. That Makes Me a Bitch Who Knows It All." In their book on women's psychology, Crawford and Unger (2004) state: "The notion that their reproductive cycle makes women vulnerable to psychological problems serves to limit women—to define them as dangerous and deviant and to exclude them from a role in society equal to that of men" (p. 490). At the same time that diagnosing the condition legitimized women's complaints and brought folklore into reality, it gave society more impetus to question women's abilities.

The question (loaded with stereotypes) that still persists today about this issue is, "Would you want the hand of a woman with PMS on the button to detonate a nuclear bomb?" (Kleiman, 1992, p. 2E). This question implies that women are such victims of their own biology that they could not possibly be relied on in critical situations. What is most interesting here is that the same argument could be made about men's levels of testosterone and aggressive behavior. Do men's hormonal functioning and bent toward aggression better equip them to handle conflict? If that statement seems comical to you, it's likely because that kind of argument is hardly ever made. While society is quick to link female hormonal functioning with debilitation, the same cannot be said for men.

But what about the notion of a male biological cycle? The male cycle is more than a mere notion, according to research. Tracking back a bit, researchers in the mid-1970s began to investigate male hormonal functioning as evidence of a male cycle. Ramey (1976) found that men displayed regular variations in emotions over each twenty-four-hour period within a six-week time frame. Ramey also detected a thirty-day cycle for men's hormonal functioning. During these cycles, men's physical strength, emotionality, and intellectual functioning were affected. Doreen Kimura (1987), in internationally noted research, identified a tentative link between seasons of the year and men's cognitive functioning. According to Kimura, in the spring, when testosterone levels are lower, men's mathematical and analytic skills are enhanced. These abilities decrease in the fall when testosterone levels are higher. The popular press picked up on this research, having fun comparing women's monthly periods to what it called men's seasonal "commas" (Kleiman, 1992, p. 1E). Other researchers have investigated the possibility of male menopause, noting a link between depleted testosterone levels and depression (Fischman, 2001).

What if, a few years from now, evidence overwhelmingly documents the existence of a male cycle? What would be the social reaction to such news? Do you think that jobs, opportunities, responsibilities, and social roles would change to reflect this biological "instability" in men? How would men's identities be altered? Could this change communication between women and men in some way? We don't know the answers to these

Hot Button Issue

"A Male Period"

This is one of those topics that makes men feel squeamish while women want to laugh. When broaching this subject with students in gender communication classes, invariably one or more of the women will describe how she swears her boyfriend or husband has some sort of hormonal cycle, something akin to the female menstrual cycle. While there's no physical manifestation of the cycle, these men seem to go through regular, predictable periods of irritability, sensitivity, and depression. The female students suggest that if their men were to be tested at those times, a lowered level of testosterone and other male hormones would probably be detected. If you are female and reading this, do you agree with our female students? If you are male and reading this, do you see evidence of a cycle in yourself, or do you think this is completely nuts?

questions, but if this scenario becomes reality, it's likely that the social interpretations of the biology will be far more interesting than the biology itself.

Mind over Matter: Are Men's and Women's Brains Really Different?

Information regarding sex differences and brain functioning has caused more than mild controversy. As one researcher suggests, "This is a politically charged area of research because the stakes are high for the more and less cognitively able" (Paul, 2002, p. 93). Brain functions are extremely complex, tied into hormonal functioning, affected by environmental and social factors, and related to cognitive abilities (Halpern, 2000; Mithers, 2009; Wade, 2007). In the 1990s as well as the first decade of the twenty-first century, many books were published on the subject of how differently male and female brains function (Blum, 1998; Fisher, 2009; Legato & Tucker, 2006; Moir & Jessel, 1992). Perhaps the two most prominent (or at least, most popularized) books, *The Female Brain* and *The Male Brain,* were authored by Louann Brizendine (2007, 2010), but her findings and observations aren't without controversy. Critics suggest that Brizendine's conclusions are overly dichotomizing and divisive, leading to unhelpful sex stereotyping and notions of biology-as-destiny that aren't useful. This is not meant to be an introductory physiology lesson, so we review only the primary research findings, emphasizing their social interpretations.

BRAIN FUNCTIONING   Some researchers report sex differences in brain size, glucose metabolism counts, and cerebral blood flow (Gur et al., 1982; Gur et al., 1995; Halpern, 2000). But others conclude that studies in this area actually show minimal differences (indicating that the sexes' brains are actually more similar than different) and are used primarily to engender divisiveness (Bleier, 1984; Gibbons, 1991; Tavris, 1992). Prolific gender scholar Celeste Condit contends that a good deal of research on sex differences and the brain is biased in its assumptions and faulty in its methods, constituting a form of "bad science" (1996, p. 87).

Research has shown that the brain has two hemispheres that house various human capabilities. The left hemisphere is primarily responsible for the production of language, while the right hemisphere manages spatial ability. It has long been thought—and many still contend—that men perform better on tests of spatial skills while women excel on tests of verbal ability, as a result of hormonal and brain functioning (Kimura, 2000). Author Simon Baron-Cohen (2004) states succinctly on the first page of his book, *The Essential Difference: Male and Female Brains and the Truth about Autism,* that "the female brain is predominantly hard-wired for empathy. The male brain is predominantly hard-wired for understanding and building systems" (p. 1). Since most of the social interpretations of the information on brain functioning relate to cognitive ability, let's explore this area before considering those interpretations.

COGNITIVE ABILITY   A consistent pattern emerged over two decades of conducting research on gifted girls and boys: Boys outscored girls on the math portions of the SAT (Benbow & Stanley, 1980). This finding led to the conclusion that male dominance in math was related to hemispheric specialization in the brain, that is, that the right hemisphere was more fully developed in men than in women (Pinker, 2005). However, social scientists on the nurture side of the nature/nurture argument have other explanations for sex differences in cognitive functioning, insisting that social and environmental factors affect the picture (Spelke, 2005). These researchers have found that since boys are expected to excel in math, they are encouraged and coached by parents and teachers, while attitudes and anxiety about the difficulty of math inhibit girls' achievement (Baenninger & Newcombe, 1995; Eccles, 1989; Linn & Petersen, 1986).

> *It was a very cool thing to be a smart girl, as opposed to some other, different kind. And I think that made a great deal of difference to me growing up.*
>
> *—Supreme Court Justice Elena Kagan, 4th woman appointed to the U.S. Supreme Court*

Concerning verbal ability, the general opinion for decades was that females outperformed males in such capacities as language acquisition, vocabulary, spelling, writing, and verbal expressiveness. But again, research has produced findings to the contrary. Researchers now believe that, if there once was a gap in verbal abilities and math and spatial abilities between the sexes due to brain differences and hormonal functioning, this gap has all but disappeared (Corbett, Hill, & St. Rose, 2008; Crawford & Unger, 2004; Hill, Corbett, & St. Rose, 2010; Mortenson, 2008). If the human brain hasn't changed, then what explains the sexes performing more similarly in specific areas than in times past?

One explanation relates to changing times and changing parents. More parents have backed off of the old stereotypes, believing now that female and male children can do anything, given encouragement, support, and education. Another explanation regards educational systems. If teachers demonstrate sex bias in their instruction, these biases have ways of becoming eventualities. Teachers who refrain from sex-biased behaviors are helping students to maximize their potential, regardless of expectations for their sex. Educational institutions that offer and encourage mathematical and spatial curricula for all children help to enhance these abilities. In sum, societal shifts are affecting students' visions of what they can accomplish, and the gender gap in cognitive ability is narrowing.

Remember . . .

Reproductive Functions: Sexes' differing abilities to conceive, carry, give birth to, and nurture offspring

Hunter–Gatherer Cultures: Ancient societies in which men's and women's roles were distinguished according to who provided food, protected the family from danger, and birthed and reared children

Physical Strength: Societally derived judgment based on physical characteristics such as muscle mass, vulnerability, and endurance

Nurturance: Stereotypically female trait of giving aid and comfort to others

Aggression: Stereotypically male trait of asserting or inflicting force

THE EFFECTS OF SOCIAL INFLUENCES ON PSYCHOLOGICAL GENDER IDENTITY

In the previous section of this chapter we talked about biological sex differences; note that here we switch the focus to psychological variables or gender identity. As we noted earlier, gender is culturally based and socially constructed out of psychological characteristics; it also contains such things as attitudes and beliefs, sexual orientation, and perceptions of appropriate roles for women and men in society.

Learning to Be Girls and Boys

The development of gender understanding in young children is fascinating because children sometimes believe gender to be changeable (Devor, 1992). (Ah, the wisdom of children.) They see gender not as being based on anatomy, but as a role that can be changed much like changing a hairstyle. As children start to understand themselves as individuals separate from others, they begin to understand that others see them and respond to them as people of a particular sex. Theories have been generated to explain this identity development process or how one becomes "gendered." We summarize some of the more prominent theories, then explore the connection between gender identity and gender communication.

SOCIAL LEARNING THEORY   Social psychologists Walter Mischel (1966) and Albert Bandura (1971, 1986) are noted for their research on social learning theory as an explanation for human development. This theory suggests that children learn gender-related behavior from their social contacts, primarily their parents and peers. Children model the thoughts, emotions, and actions of others. This role modeling has a powerful effect on how children see themselves, how they form gender identities.

A related practice involves a sort of trial-and-error method. Parents, teachers, peers, and other agents of socialization reward some behaviors in little girls and boys; the same behaviors enacted by the opposite sex are punished. As children continue to receive positive and negative responses to their behaviors, they generalize to other situations and come to develop identities as girls or boys (Lippa, 2002; Peach, 1998).

One problem with this theory is the suggestion that children develop according to gender stereotypes; some theories consider this idea a limited or confining view of human development. For example, what if a little girl rejects stereotypical girlish behavior because she likes the status or acceptance she sees little boys receiving? She might be labeled a tomboy, perhaps gaining her some acceptance, but also occasional ridicule. If she patterns her behavior after same-sex models, it is possible that she will not receive the respect, power, and status that she wants. If a little boy is surrounded predominantly by models of the other sex, like his mother and most of his preschool and elementary school teachers, what happens if he closely follows their behavior? These examples illustrate what some consider to be a weakness in the theory—its emphasis on gender stereotypes as guides for behavior and identity development.

However, we know that our sense of identity is affected by how we imitate or learn from our parents. Think about whom you modeled your behavior after; was it your mom or your dad, or was it both? Did you pattern more after a same-sex parent or an opposite-sex parent? Maybe an important model for you when you were growing up was a sibling, a grandparent, or some other significant person. Maybe you didn't grow up with two parents. As our culture continues to diversify, the number of single-parent families is growing. If you've experienced this family profile, what effect do you think the focus on one parent had on your notions about gender?

COGNITIVE DEVELOPMENT THEORY   One of the more prominent gender identity theories results primarily from the work of Lawrence Kohlberg. According to Kohlberg (1966), as children's minds mature, they gain an understanding of gender roles and self-identity without external reinforcement (in contrast to the suggestions of social learning theory). Kohlberg's theory essentially is that children socialize themselves into feminine or masculine identities via progress through four stages of mental ability. In stage 1, very young children are beginning to recognize sex distinctions, but they cannot attach a sex identity to a person. They are likely to say such things as "Daddy is a girl." In stage 2, children learn their own sexual identity, as well as how to identify other people's sex correctly (Ruble, Balaban, & Cooper, 1981). In stage 3, children learn that there are "ground rules" for sex roles, or guidelines for sex-typed appropriate behavior, that stem from one's culture. Children become motivated to behave in accordance with those rules, persuading others to conform, too. For example, most girls want to wear ruffly, "girly" clothing, and boys are appalled at the thought of playing with dolls. At this point, children begin to value and imitate those behaviors associated with their own sex, more so than behaviors associated with the other sex.

This progress continues into stage 4, when children separate their identities from those of their primary caregivers (typically their mothers). For boys, the importance of their father's identity and behavior is compounded. But because female children cannot separate themselves from the mother's female identity, they remain at stage 3, unlike their male counterparts who progress through all four stages. In essence, a girl's development is stunted because her sex identity is the same as her mother's. Can you anticipate any problems with this theory? A major criticism of this theory has to do with its use of a male model of development that is then generalized to all humans. The model suggests that girls' development is somehow less complete or advanced than boys'.

GENDER SCHEMA THEORY   Gender schema theory, primarily advanced by psychologist Sandra Bem (1983), states that once a child learns an appropriate cultural definition of gender, this definition becomes the key structure around which all other information is organized. A schema is a cognitive structure that helps us interpret the world. In cultures that adhere closely to traditional gender differentiation, gender schemas are likely to be complex and elaborate. Before a schema can be formulated and gender-related information can be viewed through it, the child must be old enough to identify gender accurately. When a girl learns that cultural prescriptions for femininity include politeness and kindness, she incorporates these traits into her emerging schema and begins to behave in a polite and kind way. Gender schemas provide prescriptions for how to behave and can strongly influence a child's sense of self-esteem.

As children develop a gender schema, they increasingly use it as an organizing perspective. A schema related to a child's own sex appears to develop first, and it becomes more complex and detailed than schemas for the other sex. Using his or her own schema, a child takes in new information, plans activities, and chooses roles. The development of and subsequent adherence to gender schemas may help us understand why it is so difficult to dislodge gender-stereotypical thinking.

GILLIGAN'S GENDER IDENTITY DEVELOPMENT THEORY   Carol Gilligan (1982) challenged human development theorists in her groundbreaking book *In a Different Voice: Psychological Theory and Women's Development.* Gilligan's theory expands previous views of human development to account for both female and male paths to gender identity. In a nutshell (which does not do justice to this theory), the core of identity development rests within the mother–child relationship. The female child connects and finds gender identity with the mother, but the male child must find identity by separating himself from this female caregiver. Thus—unlike male development, which stresses separation and independence—female identity revolves around interconnectedness and relationship.

Gilligan's theory offers insight into how men and women function. But Gilligan's critics claim that the theory focuses too heavily on female development, and that it implies an advantage for females who can identify with a same-sex caregiver, while merely drawing occasional comparisons to how the process works for males. How, then, does one make sense of all these theories? Does a "best" theory of gender identity exist?

While the theories we've reviewed significantly contribute to our understanding, they tend to dichotomize, focusing heavily on maleness and femaleness. This focus depletes the broader concept of gender, relegating it to an either-or discussion of sex. Another problem is that each theory tends to focus primarily on childhood development or how children discover gender and corresponding social expectations. What we believe to be more interesting for our discussion of gender communication is a model that begins with how we experience gender as children, but shifts to how we progress or transcend that experience later in life. A theory of transcendence offers real insight into how adults negotiate and renegotiate their gender identities, over time, given experiences and education.

GENDER TRANSCENDENCE AND ANDROGYNY   Several researchers have developed, expanded, and refined a theory of gender identity development called *gender transcendence.*

Our discussion begins with the notable contributions of psychologist Joseph Pleck, in a comparison between traditional sex-role identity development theory and gender transcendence.

In traditional views of development, the term sex role is defined as "the psychological traits and the social responsibilities that individuals have and feel are appropriate for them because they are male or female" (Pleck, 1977, p. 182). The emphasis here is on the two designations—masculine and feminine. Masculinity involves instrumental or task-oriented competence and includes such traits as assertiveness, self-expansion, self-protection, and a general orientation of self *against* the world. Femininity is viewed as expressive or relationship-oriented competence, with corresponding traits that include nurturance and concern for others, emphasis on relationships and the expression of feelings, and a general orientation of self *within* the world (Eccles, 1987).

Critics of traditional views of development believe that the prevailing theories perpetuate the dichotomy between males and females and limit individuals' options regarding identity. Gender transcendence theory responds to this criticism. Within transcendence theory, Pleck (1975) envisions a three-stage sequence of gender identity development. The first two stages resemble Kohlberg's (1966) cognitive development model. However, stage 3 represents the point where transcendence theory departs from the more traditional theories. Stage 3 occurs when individuals experience difficulty because the rules of behavior no longer seem to make sense or because they begin to suspect that they possess both expressive (feminine) and instrumental (masculine) abilities.

At this point, individuals may "transcend" their understanding of the norms and expectations of gender to develop "psychological androgyny in accordance with their inner needs and temperaments" (Pleck, 1975, p. 172). (As we discussed in Chapter 1, transgender persons may have accomplished gender transcendence, in that they have moved past traditional role definitions and no longer rely on those definitions when determining their own behavior or assessing the behavior of others.) Communication researcher Harold Barrett (1998) describes the shift in emphasis from biological sex to psychological gender this way: "The emphasis now is less on determination of role by sex—male versus female—and more on awareness of gender plurality in an individual's nature" (p. 83). The notion of "gender plurality" is another way of conceiving of gender transcendence.

Like other theories of gender identity development, transcendence theory begins with a discussion of child development. However, it emphasizes adolescence as a period when traditional definitions of what is male and female are likely to be challenged for the first time. The theory then tracks into adult development, as changing values, social

Net Notes

It's inappropriate to equate transgenderism with transvestitism or transsexualism, although there is some overlap between these forms of identity. For an interesting website on transgenderism, try **www.susans.org**, the official website for Susan's Place, which offers a wide variety of transgender resources, including chat rooms, links to other sites, and reading suggestions.

pressures, education, and life events (e.g., marriage, new jobs, parenting, retirement) cause adults to reevaluate their gender identities. Transcendence, then, may occur in adolescence and adulthood; however, not everyone experiences it. Some people continue throughout adulthood to adhere to traditional roles and definitions of what is female and male, and they manage this quite successfully.

Androgyny, which we discussed briefly in Chapter 1, is related to this notion of gender transcendence. Androgyny is more understandable if you envision a continuum with masculinity placed toward one end, femininity toward the other end, and androgyny in the middle. You don't lose masculine traits or behaviors if you are androgynous, or somehow become masculine if you move away from the feminine pole. Androgyny is an intermix of the feminine and the masculine. Some androgynous individuals may have more masculine traits than feminine, and vice versa.

If I'm androgynous, I'd say I lean towards macho-androgynous.
—John Travolta, actor

Perhaps a diagram will clarify the idea of androgyny further (see Figure 2.1). At the top are two bell curves labeled "masculinity" and "femininity." If you adopt a traditional view of sex roles, you fall under one of these two curves depending on your sex. In the middle, you see that the bell curves have merged somewhat, so that their overlap represents androgyny. As individuals continue to challenge traditional sex-typed roles and to experience gender transcendence, they widen their identities to include male and female traits and behaviors. Over time, the androgynous identity continues to widen, as depicted in the expanded androgynous area at the bottom.

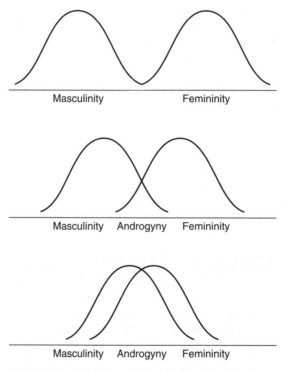

FIGURE 2.1 Continuum of Gender Transcendence

While their identity expands, gender-transcended individuals' repertoire of communication behavior also has the capacity to expand. This should sound familiar, since it is fundamental to the personal effectiveness approach to gender communication. In Chapter 1, we explained how effective individuals develop a wider range of communication behaviors from which to choose, know how to analyze a situation and select the best behaviors from their repertoire, enact those behaviors, and evaluate the results. Because the process of gender transcendence causes an individual to incorporate feminine and masculine traits into a unique blend, that individual is more likely to choose to behave in ways that aren't confined by traditional, stereotypical notions of how men and women are *supposed* to behave. For example, an androgynous male may be more likely than a masculine type of male to talk about and openly express his emotions because he does not buy into the notion that revealing emotions is "unmanly." Androgynous individuals, in general, are adaptive to situations and comfortable with communicative options—options that become extremely helpful in the complicated realm of gender communication (Johnson, Murphy, Zewdie, & Reichard, 2008; Kada, Brunner, & Maier, 2009; Pickard Leszczynski, 2009; Sidelinger, Frisby, & McMullen, 2009).

Another advantage of an androgynous orientation involves how you see and respond to others—an important component of the receiver orientation to communication. In enacting this orientation, you will more easily accept people for what makes them unique. Because androgynous individuals have expanded views of sex roles and corresponding behavior, they tend to be more generally accepting and less judgmental of others whose behavior deviates from social expectations for the sexes.

What is your reaction to the theory of gender transcendence and the concept of androgyny? Some of you may be thinking that the theory reduces the importance of masculinity or femininity, that it waters down unique, important properties of being female or male. If you have these thoughts, you're not alone. The idea is to view androgyny as you would a glass that is half full, rather than half empty. Rather than taking away from the distinctiveness of the sexes, androgyny is an identity that recognizes and celebrates the best qualities of masculine and the feminine—a way of making these qualities *human,* rather than options for one sex but not the other.

We've made the case for gender transcendence and androgyny, but of course there are some cautions regarding this information. First, while we believe that androgyny and repertoire expansion fit together logically, we don't mean to suggest that the *only* way to expand the communication repertoire is to adopt an androgynous gender identity. A person who aligns himself or herself with a traditionally feminine or masculine gender identity may still expand the communication repertoire. In many situations, this individual may behave appropriately and be viewed as an effective communicator. It's important to keep in mind that, while we consider an androgynous person more likely to develop a greater repertoire than a traditionally sex-typed person, this is just a trend, not a hard and fast rule.

The second caution is sort of a reverse of the first. We don't mean to insinuate that *all* androgynous people are *automatically* effective communicators in *all* situations, just because they embody masculine and feminine traits and behaviors. As you are becoming aware, there are neither easy answers nor "quick fixes" in gender communication. We believe that gender transcendence broadens your approach and enhances your repertoire and that it's a desirable position from which to communicate with others, but it offers no guarantees.

Remember . . .

Gender Identity Development: Theory about how one develops one's gender, with regard to feminine traits, masculine traits, or a blend of both

Social Learning Theory: Theory about how children learn gender-related behavior from social contacts, primarily parents and peers

Cognitive Development Theory: Theory about how children socialize themselves into feminine or masculine identities as they progress through various stages of mental ability

Gender Schema Theory: Theory about how children learn appropriate cultural definitions of gender, which become key structures around which all other information is organized

Gilligan's Gender Identity Theory: Theory suggesting that the core of gender identity development rests within the mother–child relationship; involves the development of connectedness in girls and autonomy in boys

Gender Transcendence: Rejection of traditional gender identities (masculine or feminine); integration of feminine and masculine selves into a self-defined gender identity

Androgyny: Intermix or blending of feminine and masculine traits

SOCIALIZATION AND GENDER IDENTITY DEVELOPMENT

The process of developing gender identity involves acquiring information about cultural norms and roles for men and women (a social function), then adjusting one's view of self, one's role in society, and one's behavior in response to those norms (a psychological function). Some prefer to call this *socialization,* defined as the process through which individuals learn their culture, develop their potential, and become functioning members of society (Lindsey & Christy, 1997; Martin & Ruble, 2004). The primary vehicle for socialization is communication. Socialization occurs throughout the life cycle and includes gender identity development as only one facet. For our purposes in this discussion, focusing on gender identity within the larger framework of socialization helps us understand how we come to develop our sense of self, our own vision of appropriate roles and behavior for women and men, and our patterns in gender communication.

The Family as a Primary Socializing Agent

Our society is never finished socializing us, and the family is by far the most significant agent of socialization (Owen Blakemore & Hill, 2007). Family communication scholar Virginia Satir (1972, 1988) views family as a place where "peoplemaking" occurs. This is a useful perspective because families do create people, not just children. The family context (including the communication within it) continues to shape and mold an adult throughout her or his life. The family has the ability to influence the gender identities of the people it makes by reinforcing the status quo or by offering a broader view of how to be a boy or girl, man or woman (Haddock, Zimmerman, & Lyness, 2003).

    Gender differences in the treatment of female and male children begins *before* birth. While parents indicate that their first priority is to have a healthy baby, preferences for one sex over the other are prevalent. Across the globe, most couples prefer male over female children, especially in a first or only child—a finding that has not changed much since the 1930s (Grayling, 2005; Jain, Missmer, Gupta, & Hornstein, 2005; Shannon, 2003; Stein, 2004; Wiseman, 2002). In some countries, this preference results in the under-reporting of female births, female infanticide, neglect of female infants, abortion of female fetuses, and many abuses as underground overseas adoption services flourish (Oomman & Ganatra, 2002). Adding to concerns about sex preferencing are technological developments that offer a high rate of success in choosing the sex of a child. One technique, Microsort, is a procedure that helps couples conceive a baby of their preferred sex 65 to 90 percent of the time (Joyce, 1999).

After the birth of a child, the family maintains the major responsibility for socializing the child during the critical years of life, even when other socializing influences exist. In the family, the child gains a sense of self, learns language, and begins to understand norms of interaction with parents, siblings, and significant others. Research over multiple decades has explored sex-typing of babies. In studies using infants of similar weight, length, and health, both parents described sons as big, tough, strong, firm, and alert, while daughters were cheerful, gentle, delicate, soft, and awkward (Rubin, Provensano, & Luria, 1974; Stern & Karraker, 1989).

Sex-typed socialization continues as children grow and mature (Rudman & Glick, 2008). Research indicates that fathers are significantly more likely than mothers to differentiate between their sons and daughters and to encourage more traditional sex-specific behavior in their sons (Fagot & Leinbach, 1995; Hardesty, Wenk, & Morgan, 1995; Kane, 2006; Raley & Bianchi, 2006). Parents tend to engage in more physical, rough play with sons (Lindsey & Mize, 2001; Ross & Taylor, 1989), to maintain closer physical proximity to daughters (Bronstein, 1988), and to believe that girls need more help than boys (Snow, Jacklin, & Maccoby, 1983). Girls are encouraged to participate in activities that keep them close to their homes and families, while boys are provided more opportunities for play and other activities away from home and independent of adult supervision, a finding that holds in both Western and non-Western cultures (Erwin, 1992). Finally, one study found that assertiveness in daughters was viewed less positively than assertiveness in sons, while appropriate interpersonal communication skills were viewed more favorably in daughters than in sons (Leaper, Anderson, & Sanders, 1998).

Secondary Agents of Socialization

Because of parents' influence on children's understanding of gender, some modern parents are trying a nongendered approach. They are giving children gender-neutral toys, games, and books in efforts to avoid the more traditional items that often perpetuate stereotypes, like Barbie, G.I. Joe, and traditional fairy tales (Messner, 2000; Morgan, 1993). In this section, we address the socializing effects of clothing, toys, peer relationships, and teachers as role models. The media have a significant impact on children's gender identity development too—a topic that we'll save for Chapter 3. For now, think about those things you played with as a child and those relationships in the neighborhood or at school that had the greatest effect on your gender identity development.

CLOTHES AND TOYS   After birth, the first things acquired for an infant are clothes and toys. When the sex of a baby is not known, friends and family members try to buy sex-neutral gifts, like yellow receiving blankets or green bibs. Color-coded and sex-typed clothing of infants and young children is still quite prevalent (Fagot, Rodgers, & Leinbach, 2000; Koller, 2008).

Along with clothing, toys and play are powerful forces of socialization (Libby, 2008; Messner, 2000). For girls, probably the most popular and influential toy of all time is the Barbie doll. Would it surprise you to know that you can now purchase a tattooed Barbie? A new version of Barbie now comes with a tattoo on her arm and a "tramp stamp" on her lower back (*NBC Nightly News,* 2009). (Parents can relax, however; the tattoos are stick-ons that can be removed.) Barbie and her variations introduced across the years continue to be the subject of much research and discussion, in terms of the doll's impact on young girls, how they see themselves, and how they develop notions of femininity and attractiveness (Barnett & Rivers, 2005; Jacobs & Shaw, 2000; Kluger, 2000; Kuther & McDonald, 2004). Years ago, the male counterpart to Barbie was G.I. Joe. That series of "action figures" (certainly not dolls) set the model for a range of action figures targeted to boys. These figures emphasize ruggedness, adventure, and large muscles, and in many ways are as unrealistic for boys as Barbies are for girls. In fact, research has shown that gendered toys are linked to lower self-esteem and eating disorders in children (Grogan & Richards, 2002; Kenway & Bullen, 2001). Helga Dittmar (2010), psychology professor at the University of Sussex, published a book about consumer culture, in which she links the hugely popular Barbie and G.I. Joe dolls and their physiques to eating disorders and hypermuscularity for boys. Dittmar explains that "the ubiquitous Barbie doll, marketed at girls, is so thin that her waist is 39% smaller than that of anorexic patients, whereas boys are targeted with action figures whose muscularity has increased to such an extent that it often exceeds that of bodybuilders" (p. 13).

Toys for girls encourage domesticity, interpersonal closeness, and social orientation, whereas boys receive not only more categories of toys, but also toys that are more complex and expensive, and that foster self-reliance, problem solving, and fantasy (Owen Blakemore & Centers, 2005). Boys' toys tend to be rated higher in sociability, competitiveness, aggressiveness, and constructiveness, whereas girls' toys are rated higher in creativity, manipulability, nurturance, and attractiveness (Owen Blakemore & Centers, 2005).

Some scholars believe that children construct a great deal of their sense of gender through play (Messner, 2000). Much of children's play has shifted from outdoors to indoors, with the rapidly increasing popularity and accessibility of video games. According to the National Purchase Diary (NPD Group), a marketing research company that tracks consumer and retail trends in North America, children are now introduced to video games at younger ages than in years past; 82 percent of children ages 2 through 17 reported being active video gamers (NPD Group, 2009a, 2009b). The amount of time American children spend playing video games has also risen dramatically in recent years (NPD Group, 2007, 2008, 2009b, 2010). Researchers continue to explore how video games and their depictions of male and female characters shape children's views of sex and gender. As you might imagine, research results are quite mixed on this front. Even though video games have been around for decades, they've changed a great deal; thus, their impact on children and adults continues to generate research interest.

It's beyond the scope of this chapter to review the large volume of publications devoted to video gaming socialization effects; we examine this topic more in depth in Chapter 3 on media. But for our purposes here, a few studies deserve mention, even if the results are contradictory. One of the earliest threads of research on video games explored whether exposure to violent games led to enhanced violent or aggressive behavior in children (Zorrilla, 2010). For every study suggesting that exposure to virtual violence, especially the victimization of girls and women, affects aggressive attitudes and enhances aggressive behavior in real life (Carnagey & Anderson, 2005; Eastin, 2006; Konijn, Nije Bijvank, & Bushman, 2007; Norris, 2004; Shibuya, Sakamoto, Ihori, & Yukawa, 2008; Williams, Consalvo, Caplan, & Yee, 2009), there's an equally well-executed study saying "video games don't kill people, people kill people," in essence, a "don't blame the messenger" type of finding (Blake, 2008; Brenick, Henning, Killen, O'Connor, & Collins, 2007; Ferguson, 2007; Williams & Skoric, 2005).

Several books and studies document a male dominance in terms of numbers of male characters in leading roles, as well as dominant, aggressive personalities and behaviors of those characters, and sexualized, marginalized depictions of female characters (Behm-Morawitz & Mastro, 2009; Cassell & Jenkins, 2000; Dill & Thill, 2007; Ivory, 2006; Miller & Summers, 2007). But other research notes a significant increase in strong female characters in recent years, spurred by the popularity of the Lara Croft character, which some view as empowering to young girls and women who play such games (Bertozzi & Lee, 2007; Herbst, 2005; Jansz & Martis, 2007; Kafai, Heeter, Denner, & Sun, 2008). Kacie Glenn (2008), in her review of books on video gaming and its evolving effects on players, describes how the video game "tug of war between girl power and girliness is becoming less important than it once was, not only to female players, but to the industry" (p. B20). She quotes the editorial team of one book who suggests that "there has been a noticeable shift from pink or purple games to a more-complex approach to gender" (Kafai et al., 2008, as in Glenn, 2008, p. B20).

Studies continue to examine hypersexualized images of female characters in video games for their effects on players, especially on children's and adults' thoughts about sex and gender in general, and the objectification of females in specific (Fox & Bailenson, 2009; Yao, Mahood, & Linz, 2010). Other research has explored the impact of video game play and exposure to stereotypically drawn characters on such variables as tolerance of sexual harassment, adherence to myths about rape and sexual assault, and attitudes about body image (Dill, Brown, & Collins, 2008; Martins, Williams, Harrison, & Ratan, 2009; Ogletree & Drake, 2007). Research on these topics and other variables related to video gaming and gender will no doubt be prolific in coming years, as the inventiveness and popularity of video gaming continues.

PEERS AND SCHOOL   As children get older, they are gradually introduced into the world outside the family. Parents' gender expectations at home become extended into the child's social world. Parents initiate the first relationships for their children and for the first few years of life, children prefer playing with children of a similar age, sex unspecified. Oftentimes this is related to proximity, meaning that we tend to play with other kids from our neighborhood or building since they're close by and handy. The sex of the child doesn't matter much, until we start school—then our preference for playmates changes quickly. Activities and games in schools tend to be strongly related to gender roles and are powerful agents of socialization (Lindsey & Christy, 1997).

Schools have a major responsibility for ensuring that children are educated in the ways of society, but many accomplish this task in a manner that perpetuates gender stereotypes (Lindsey, 2005; Lindsey & Christy, 1997). Schools are generally set up for competitive, independent work in which initiative is valued, which are generally seen as masculine values. While schools may offer cooperative learning activities with shared participation, they still stress individual achievement. How often were you graded as a group in school? Schools' and teachers' differential treatment of the sexes is explored more in depth in Chapter 10.

GENDER AND CULTURE

All cultures differentiate between female and male behavior, though not in the same ways. Ancient Greek and Roman views of men and women mirror some of the current gender stereotypes. For example, women were assumed to be naturally emotional and nurturing. Men were assumed to be naturally rational and strong. These beliefs formed the basis of the patriarchal (male-dominated) system (Learner, 1986). Once this dominance was established largely on the basis of sex, it lasted for over 2,500 years and was incorporated into most, but not all, cultures. Let us first consider culture, in general, before turning to the role that sex and gender play in culture.

Culture Considered

Defining *culture* is as problematic as defining gender or communication. According to one definition, culture is "a learned system of knowledge, behavior, attitudes, beliefs, values, and norms that is shared by a group of people and shaped from one generation to the next" (Smith, 1966). Culture includes such elements as history, religion, values, social organization, and language. Anthropologist William Haviland (2002) states "in humans, it is culture that sets the limits on behavior and guides it along predictable paths" (p. 26). Culture essentially tells us who we are and what we should do. Culture strongly influences a person's behavior, including communication behavior. Another anthropologist, Edward T. Hall (1976), suggests that communication and culture are inseparable, in that you can't talk about one without the other.

Cultural expert Claude Levi-Strauss (2004) suggests that humans are represented by two sexes and a handful of races, but literally thousands of cultures. Cultural patterns, including sex and gender roles, reflect far too much diversity to be explained by biology or any other internal, hardwired mechanism. To understand sex and gender roles, you must begin with the notion that roles are arbitrarily constructed by the cultures in which they reside (Cooper, Calloway-Thomas, & Simonds, 2007). It is difficult, if not impossible, to understand your own role without at least having some understanding of your culture.

Dutch anthropologist Geert Hofstede (1980, 1991) believes that culture is the "mental software" that helps us understand our world. He and his colleagues developed four fundamental dimensions of culture, or ways to understand cultures: individualism/collectivism, power distribution, uncertainty avoidance, and masculinity/femininity. Of most interest to our discussion is the dimension of masculinity/femininity.

Hofstede (1998) identifies cultures as existing on a continuum from masculine to feminine. He describes *masculine cultures* as societies in which men are supposed to be assertive, tough, and focused on material success, while women are supposed to be modest, tender, and concerned with the quality of life. In *feminine cultures*, both women and men are supposed to be modest, tender, and concerned with the quality of life. In one line of research, Hofstede and Hofstede (2005) rated seventy-four countries on a scale called the Masculinity Index, which measures masculine values such as assertiveness, performance, and competitiveness, and how much these values prevail over typically feminine values. Results showed that the five most masculine nations were Slovakia, Japan, Hungary, Austria, and Venezuela. The most feminine countries were the four Scandinavian countries—Denmark, the Netherlands, Norway, and Sweden, with Slovenia and Costa Rica close behind. The United States ranked nineteenth on the Masculinity Index, meaning that our culture adheres more closely to prescribed sex roles than many other countries in the world (Hofstede & Hofstede, 2005). However, Hofstede is careful to point out that his conclusions about cultural characteristics are not absolute; his results represent tendencies, not explicit or clear-cut differences.

In masculine cultures, both women and men express a strong preference for distinct and separate masculine and feminine roles. But in most feminine cultures, no difference exists between the responses of women and men; both indicate a preference for a tender and nurturing value system. People in masculine cultures tend to be less permissive, more formal, and more structured than people in feminine cultures, and they conduct business in a more aggressive style, viewing meetings as opportunities to express themselves and to sell ideas. People in feminine cultures tend to prefer shorter working hours to higher salaries, and meetings are viewed as opportunities for cooperative consensus building (Hofstede, 1998; Hofstede & Hofstede, 2005).

Is One Culture Better Than Another?

The question of value placed on a culture is difficult, because your view of what is better or worse is shaped by your culture of origin (the culture in which you grew up). We caution students not to judge other cultures as "weird," "wrong," or "inferior" simply because the values other cultures' members hold about men's and women's roles, for example, differ from values held by citizens of the United States. Looking at other cultures through an American lens, you might believe that women face many inequities compared with the status and luxuries many men in those cultures receive. And you would be correct, from an American perspective. But to take the next step, to condemn other cultures because ancient practices and cultural traditions may favor men and disfavor women will not help you develop a more sensitive communication style when interacting with members of those other cultures. As hard as it sounds, it's important to adopt an attitude of tolerance, if not acceptance, of other cultural values and the people who hold them, even if those values seriously contrast with how you were raised and what you believe to be right, wrong, true, false, good, and bad.

Brief examples will help illustrate this point: The status of women tends to be profoundly different within Islamic versus Christian cultures. As daily news accounts of American women and men in the military, politics, corporations, and the media operating in Middle Eastern countries bear witness, sex roles and acceptable behavior for men and women in many of these countries are vastly different from what we are used to in the United States. In Saudi Arabia, for example, women cannot even speak the name of a husband's friend; to do so would be inappropriate, because it would suggest a degree of intimacy (Areibi, 1994). Individuals within both Islam and Christianity continue to debate whether women are empowered or disadvantaged by such sex-based practices. Such powerful cultural norms can cross borders and influence women who have settled elsewhere.

Are cultural practices necessarily wrong because they reflect different values than most Americans hold? Our point here is that it's difficult to examine how the sexes are viewed and the cultural practices that constrain their behavior around the world without overlaying American values onto the picture. But we caution you about just that: To better understand how women and men relate to one another within a given culture, it's preferable to withhold judgment so that you thoroughly understand the cultural values and practices within the context of any given culture, and so that you can better communicate with members of other cultural groups. As renowned psychotherapist Carl Rogers used to say, "acceptance must precede change" (1961, p. 19).

So we now know that culture is a major influence on sex and gender identity, and that it's one of a number of factors that influence who we are, what we value, and how we communicate. What happens when culture and other factors intersect or blend? How is identity affected?

When Aspects of Identity Intersect

Internal identity conflicts (and some external ones too) are frequently caused by the intersection or overlapping of different parts of your identity. When different segments of your identity bump up against one another, you experience *intersectionality*. The conceptual origins of intersectionality emanated from the work of sociologist W. E. B. DuBois. In his influential book *The Souls of Black Folks* (1903/2004), DuBois described the intersection of race, class, and nation to explain the situation facing Black people at the time. According to sociologist Patricia Collins (2000), "DuBois saw race, class, and nation not primarily as personal identity categories but as social hierarchies that shaped African American access to status, property, and power" (p. 42). Collins' interpretation of DuBois asserts that culture, race, gender, and economic class are not merely personal identifiers, but aspects of identity that mark or even control how people interact in society at large. For example, DuBois contended that Black women carried a special burden—not only were they Black, poor, and second-class citizens, but they were female as well. The ways in which these identity characteristics interact provide keen insights into human behavior.

> *Sex and race, because they are easy and visible differences, have been the primary ways of organizing human beings into superior and inferior groups. . . . We are talking about a society in which there will be no roles other than those chosen or those earned.*
>
> —*Gloria Steinem, author/ political activist*

Collins (1998) probed more specifically the relationship between race, class, and gender, contending that gender identities are not the same across racial groups and social classes. White women, Black women, Hispanic women, and Asian women, among others in the United States, do not have the same or even similar gender identities. Collins believes that we must examine how the meaning of gender is constructed within the context of race and class, not separately as a construct unto itself. Doing so allows a complex web of understanding and social relationships to emerge. Moreover, Collins suggests that, to further our understanding of the human condition, we must move beyond race, class, and gender to encompass additional categories, such as nationality, sexuality, ethnicity, age, and religion.

Many young people of color struggle with identity intersections. The dominant American culture may suggest one path for them, their parents' culture suggests another path, and social class may pull them in yet another direction. Japanese American Rona Tamiko Halualani (2006) describes her experience learning sex and gender roles in a mixed Japanese and Hawaiian home, in which her grandparents wanted her to be a traditional Japanese woman, but her parents wanted her to be a strong, independent woman. Her story reflects the difficulty some individuals face when significant people (e.g., parents, grandparents, friends, spouses) have different expectations about how someone should enact her or his gender role. Halualani realized that "gender norms and roles are always up for negotiation and reconfiguration, though often this is done subtly and indirectly. . . . We can share our gendered/cultural experiences with others, and we can negotiate what 'gender/culture' means in our specific relationships and at specific times in our lives" (p. 107).

Regarding the intersection of race and gender, communication scholars Jackson and Dangerfield (2003) examined Black masculinity in the United States, which, in many ways, differs significantly from White masculinity. Jackson and Dangerfield point out that Black men are frequently seen as violent, sexual, and incompetent. They suggest, "Black masculine identity development is impossible without acknowledging and countering the stereotypes that threaten the survival of Black masculinity" (p. 125). They suggest that people (particularly Caucasians) need to realize that ascribed sex and gender roles vary widely from culture to culture, sometimes to the detriment of members of nondominant cultures. Second, conceptions of masculinity (and femininity) are not monolithic, meaning that if you try to force all members of a particular culture and gender into a specific role definition, you damage both the role definition and the person judged.

Intercultural Gender Communication

Intercultural communication has been defined by Samovar and Porter (2009) as "involv[ing] interaction between people whose cultural perceptions and symbol systems are distinct enough to alter the communication event" (p. 12). The last part of this definition is similar to the view of gender communication we've articulated in this text. Recall from Chapter 1 that gender communication occurs when sex or gender begins to influence the choices of what you say and how you relate to others. It follows, then, that *intercultural gender communication* occurs when both culture *and* gender significantly influence what you say or how you relate to another person.

Intercultural gender communication combines two of the most powerful aspects of identity into one phenomenon. No wonder communication problems exist in this area. Communication scholar Becky Mulvaney (2004) explains that we can view men and women as essentially coming from different cultures (not planets). If we view culture as a set of values, expectations, and behaviors that are socialized into a person, then we can see that men and women often appear to come from different cultures. In addition, Mulvaney suggests that women and men differ in the way they view the world, how they use language, and how they express themselves nonverbally. These differences can negatively affect communication.

In the United States, we obviously have a variety of *co-cultures* (cultural groups within a larger culture); notions of masculinity and femininity are not consistent across those co-cultures. However, much of the mainstream media only portrays and reinforces a White, middle-class view of sex and gender roles (MacKinnon, 2003). Perhaps even more unfortunately, a majority of research in gender communication and articles

Remember . . .

Socialization: Process through which individuals learn their culture, develop their potential, and become functioning members of society

Culture: A learned system of knowledge, behavior, attitudes, beliefs, values, and norms that is shared by a group of people and shaped from one generation to the next

Masculine Cultures: Cultures in which men are supposed to be assertive, tough, and focused on material success, while women are supposed to be modest, tender, and concerned with the quality of life

Feminine Cultures: Cultures in which both women and men are supposed to be modest, tender, and concerned with the quality of life

Intersectionality: When identity variables such as gender, race/ethnicity, and class collide

Intercultural Communication: Interaction between people whose cultural perceptions and symbol systems are distinct enough to alter the communication event

Intercultural Gender Communication: When culture and gender significantly influence what you say or how you relate to another person

Co-culture: A cultural group within a larger culture

in popular magazines do not consider cultural differences as a factor, nor do they specifically limit the results or advice to a specific co-culture. For example, many men and women of color look at popular magazines, such as *Cosmopolitan* and *Maxim,* and wonder, "Where am I in this?"

We know we've tossed a great many ideas your way in this chapter on sex and gender identity development, but we trust that you'll iron out the information and find a way to make sense out of it and apply it to your life. We leave you with an interesting exercise to try, one that encapsulates what we've been talking about in this chapter: Pick someone—anyone. It could be a classmate, a dorm or apartment roommate, family member, or relational partner. Write down the factors of that person's identity you perceive to be primary, meaning those aspects of his or her identity that rise up in importance (from your perspective). What factors did you list? Gender? Race or ethnicity? Religion? Social class? Educational level? Sexual orientation? What came to mind first? Did you think of one primary factor and then allow that factor to overshadow others? Or could you only see the whole person, not separate facets? After you've generated the list, ask the person to do the same thing about herself or himself, independently of your list. Then share lists and check for agreement. Significant discrepancies might mean that the person views himself or herself quite differently than others do. It might be that the person just isn't very good at self-presentation, or perhaps she or he extends only certain parts of the personality to you, saving others aspects for other people. Perhaps you focused on one part of the person's identity to the exclusion of other parts. Why might this have happened? This exercise will likely make you closer to the other person, or at least know him or her better, so choose your person with that in mind. The exercise can be extended by delving into a discussion of how people handle conflicts between various aspects of their identity, particularly as relates to the enactment of sex and gender roles.

Conclusion

Learning to be a woman or man is both interesting and problematic. This section of the text is about influences on your choices; this chapter examined factors that influence your sex and gender identity development. What it means to be masculine and feminine in today's modern society changes—it seems like almost every day. It's important to factor in your personality attributes, experiences, and culture as you shape your view of yourself and others as masculine, feminine, and androgynous human beings.

Biological influences discussed in this chapter affect your view of self. Social and cultural influences, as well as your own attitudes about appropriate roles for others to assume in society, shape your view of self. Out of these biological, social, and cultural influences, you form a psychological response—your gender identity—which is expressed in your communication with others. Sex and gender are not the only, and sometimes not the most important, aspects of a person's identity. Knowing and attending to the intersections of various dimensions of

one's own identity and others' identities can do much to enhance your communication.

Developing personal effectiveness in gender communication starts with introspection—with a long, hard look at yourself in terms of your sex and your gender identity. As you learn more about the effects of gender on the communication process, your identity may begin to change. Or you may become more comfortable with your current view of self, so that it solidifies. We challenge you to answer the following questions for yourself, either after reading this chapter or this text, or after taking a course in gender communication: What is your current gender identity? What aspects of your biology most affect this identity? What social and cultural influences most shaped your identity? How does your communication (particularly with members of the opposite sex) clue people as to your gender identity? What other factors of identity (e.g., race, class, religion) intersect with your sex and gender, to create your full identity? How can you become more personally effective in communicating who you are to others?

Discussion Starters

1. On a sheet of paper, list ten of the most common adjectives describing women; then list ten for men. Discuss in class whether these adjectives reflect stereotypes or "real" traits. Have people's stereotypes of the sexes changed? In what ways? What does it mean now, in the twenty-first century, to be feminine? masculine?

2. Think about the reproductive capabilities of women. What if someday science and technology were to progress to the point where men could carry a fetus and give birth? It sounds

crazy now, but what if they could someday? Would they still be "men"? After all, what is the real definition of a man? a woman?

3. Of the various agents of socialization discussed in this chapter—family, clothes, toys, peers, and school—which do you think has had the greatest impact on your gender identity? If, for example, the greatest influence on you was your family, do you adhere to stereotypical masculine or feminine traits learned in your family, or has your identity transcended gender?

4. Have you had the opportunity to communicate with someone of the other sex who was from a different culture? What similarities or differences did you notice between that person and opposite-sex members of your own culture? If there were some awkward moments in the conversation, would you attribute them to sex differences or cultural differences?

5. Consider the intersections of various aspects of your identity and how those aspects are viewed. Have you had internal conflicts over how to communicate your identity? If so, how did you work them out? Have you experienced conflicts about your own gender identity versus how someone significant to you views your identity? If so, how did you resolve that conflict?

 References

Aasen, E. (2009, July 26). Daddy's new job. *The Dallas Morning News*, pp. 1A, 16A.

Adams, R., & Savran, D. (Eds.) (2002). *The masculinity studies reader*. London: Wiley-Blackwell.

Addis, M. E., Mansfield, A. K., & Syzdek, M. R. (2010). Is "masculinity" a problem?: Framing the effects of gendered social learning in men. *Psychology of Men and Masculinity, 11*, 77–90.

Andersen, P. A. (1998). Researching sex differences within sex similarities: The evolutionary consequences of reproductive differences. In D. J. Canary & K. Dindia (Eds.), *Sex differences and similarities in communication* (pp. 83–100). Mahwah, NJ: Erlbaum.

Andersen, P. A. (2006). The evolution of biological sex differences in communication. In K. Dindia & D. J. Canary (Eds.), *Sex differences and similarities in communication* (2nd ed., pp. 117–136). Mahwah, NJ: Erlbaum.

Areibi, S. (1994). *Women and words in Saudi Arabia: Politics of literary discourse*. New York: Columbia University Press.

Baenninger, M. A., & Newcombe, N. (1995). Environmental input to the development of sex-related differences in spatial and mathematical ability. *Learning and Individual Differences, 7*. [Excerpt derived from Paul, E. L. (2002). *Taking sides: Clashing views on controversial issues in sex and gender* (2nd ed., pp. 97–107). New York: McGraw-Hill/Dushkin.]

Bandura, A. (1971). Social-learning theory of identificatory processes. In D. A. Goslin (Ed.), *Handbook of socialization theory and research*. Chicago: Rand McNally.

Bandura, A. (1986). *Social foundations of thought and action: A social cognitive theory*. Englewood Cliffs, NJ: Prentice Hall.

Barnett, R. C., & Rivers, C. (2005). *Same difference: How gender myths are hurting our relationships, our children, and our jobs*. New York: Basic Books.

Baron-Cohen, S. (2004). *The essential difference: Male and female brains and the truth about autism*. New York: Basic Books.

Barrett, H. (1998). *Maintaining the self in communication*. Incline Village, NV: Alpha & Omega.

Bartlett, T. (2009, November 27). The puzzle of boys. *The Chronicle of Higher Education*, pp. B7–B9.

Behm-Morawitz, E., & Mastro, D. (2009). The effects of the sexualization of female video game characters on gender stereotyping and female self-concept. *Sex Roles, 61*, 808–823.

Bem, S. L. (1983). Gender schema theory and its implications for child development: Raising gender-aschematic children in a gender-schematic society. *Signs, 8*, 598–616.

Benbow, C. P., & Stanley, J. C. (1980). Sex differences in mathematical ability: Fact or artifact? *Science, 210*, 1262–1264.

Bertozzi, E., & Lee, S. (2007). Not just fun and games: Digital play, gender, and attitudes towards technology. *Women's Studies in Communication, 30*, 179–204.

Beynon, J. (2002). *Masculinities and culture*. Buckingham, UK: Open University Press.

Blake, B. (2008, June 27). Go ahead, steal my car. *The Chronicle Review*, pp. B6–B7.

Bleier, R. (1984). *Science and gender: A critique of biology and its theories on women*. New York: Pergamon.

Blum, D. (1998). *Sex on the brain: The biological differences between men and women*. New York: Penguin Books.

Borisoff, D., & Merrill, L. (1998). *The power to communicate: Gender differences as barriers* (3rd ed.). Prospect Heights, IL: Waveland.

Boushey, H. (2009). The new breadwinners. In H. Boushey & A. O'Leary (Eds.), *The Shriver report: A woman's nation changes everything.* Washington, DC: Center for American Progress.

Brenick, A., Henning, A., Killen, M., O'Connor, A., & Collins, M. (2007). Social evaluations of stereotypic images in video games. *Youth and Society, 38,* 395–419.

Brizendine, L. (2007). *The female brain.* New York: Broadway.

Brizendine, L. (2010). *The male brain: A breakthrough understanding of how men and boys think.* New York: Broadway.

Bronstein, P. (1988). Father-child interaction: Implications for gender role socialization. In P. Bronstein & C. P. Cowan (Eds.), *Fatherhood today: Men's changing role in the family* (pp. 107–126). New York: Wiley.

Brott, A. A. (2008). *Fathering your child from the crib to the classroom* (2nd ed.). New York: Abbeville Press.

Brott, A. A., & Ash, J. (2004). *Father knows best: The expectant father, facts, tips, and advice for dads-to-be.* New York: Abbeville Press.

Caplan, P. J. (2008, Summer). Pathologizing your period. *Ms.,* 63–64.

Carnagey, N., & Anderson, C. (2005). The effects of reward and punishment in violent video games on aggressive affect, cognition, and behavior. *Psychological Science, 16,* 882–889.

Cassell, J., & Jenkins, H. (Eds.) (2000). *From Barbie to Mortal Kombat.* Cambridge, MA: MIT Press.

Cergol, G. (2010, March 11). Women in combat: What's the impact? Retrieved August 11, 2010, from http://www.nbcnewyork.com

Collins, P. H. (1998). On book exhibits and new complexities: Reflections on sociology as science. *Contemporary Sociology, 27,* 7–11.

Collins, P. H. (2000). Gender, black feminism, and black political economy. *The Annals of the American Academy of Political & Social Science, 568,* 41–53.

Condit, C. (1996). How bad science stays that way: Brain sex, demarcation, and the status of truth in the rhetoric of science. *Rhetoric Society Quarterly, 26,* 83–109.

Connell, R. L. (1995). *Masculinities.* Sydney: Allen & Unwin.

Connell, R. L. (2000). *The men and the boys.* St. Leonards, New South Wales: Allen & Unwin.

Connell, R. L., & Messerschmidt, J. W. (2005). Hegemonic masculinity: Rethinking the concept. *Gender and Society, 19,* 829–859.

Coontz, S. (2009). Sharing the load: Quality marriages today depend on couples sharing domestic work. In H. Boushey & A. O'Leary (Eds.), *The Shriver report: A woman's nation changes everything.* Washington, DC: Center for American Progress.

Cooper, P. J., Calloway-Thomas, C., & Simonds, C. J. (Eds.) (2007). *Intercultural communication: A text with readings.* Boston: Pearson/Allyn & Bacon.

Corbett, C., Hill, C., & St. Rose, A. (2008). *Where the girls are: The facts about gender equity in education.* Washington, DC: American Association of University Women.

Crawford, M., & Unger, R. (2004). *Women and gender: A feminist psychology* (4th ed.). New York: McGraw-Hill.

Crowther, G. (2001). Gender and endurance performance. Retrieved August 11, 2010, from http://faculty.washington.edu

DeVisser, R. O. (2010). I'm not a very manly man: Qualitative insights into young men's masculine subjectivity. In B. Hutchinson (Ed.), *Annual editions: Gender 10/11* (pp. 39–41). Boston: McGraw-Hill.

Devor, H. (1992). Becoming members of society: Learning the social meanings of gender. In M. Schaum & C. Flanagan (Eds.), *Gender images: Readings for composition* (pp. 23–33). Boston: Houghton Mifflin.

Dill, K. E., Brown, B. P., & Collins, M. A. (2008). Effects of exposure to sex-stereotyped game characters on tolerance of sexual harassment. *Journal of Experimental Social Psychology, 44,* 1402–1408.

Dill, K. E., & Thill, K. P. (2007). Video game characters and the socialization of gender roles: Young people's perceptions mirror sexist media depictions. *Sex Roles, 57,* 851–864.

Dindia, K. (2006). Men are from North Dakota, women are from South Dakota. In K. Dindia & D. J. Canary (Eds.), *Sex differences and similarities in communication* (2nd ed., pp. 3–21). Mahwah, NJ: Erlbaum.

Dittmar, H. (2010). *Consumer culture, identity and well-being: The search for the "good life" and the "body perfect."* London: Psychology Press.

Dobosz, A. M. (1997, November–December). Thicker thighs by Thanksgiving. *Media,* 89–91.

Donnelly, E. (2010, February 16). Women in combat, ctd. Retrieved August 11, 2010, from http://www.nationalreview.com

DuBois, W. E. B. (1903/2004). *The souls of black folks*. Boulder, CO: Paradigm Publishers. (Original work published in 1903)

Dummer, S. (2007, November). *Naughty or nice?: Myths of femininity and the experience of girlhood*. Paper presented at the meeting of the National Communication Association, Chicago, IL.

Eastin, M. (2006). Video game violence and the female game player: Self- and opponent-gender effects on presence and aggressive thoughts. *Human Communication Research, 32*, 351–372.

Eccles, J. S. (1987). Adolescence: Gateway to gender-role transcendence. In D. B. Carter (Ed.), *Current conceptions of sex roles and sex typing* (pp. 225–241). New York: Praeger.

Eccles, J. S. (1989). Bringing young women to math and science. In M. Crawford & M. Gentry (Eds.), *Gender and thought: Psychological perspectives* (pp. 36–58). New York: Springer.

Ehrhardt, A. A. (1984). Gender differences: A biosocial perspective. In T. B. Sonderegger (Ed.), *Psychology and gender* (pp. 37–57). Lincoln: University of Nebraska Press.

Ehrhardt, A. A., & Meyer-Behlburg, H. (1980). Prenatal sex hormones and the developing brain: Effects on psycho-sexual differentiation and cognitive functions. *Annual Progress in Child Psychology & Child Development*, 177–191.

Erwin, P. (1992). *Friendship and peer relations in children*. Chichester, UK: Wiley.

Fagot, B., & Leinbach, M. D. (1995). Gender knowledge in egalitarian and traditional families. *Sex Roles, 32*, 523–526.

Fagot, B. L., Rodgers, C. S., & Leinbach, M. D. (2000). Theories of gender socialization. In T. Eckes & H. Trautner (Eds.), *The developmental social psychology of gender* (pp. 65–89). Mahwah, NJ: Erlbaum.

Fausto-Sterling, A. (1992). *Myths of gender: Biological theories about women and men* (2nd ed.). New York: Basic Books.

Ferguson, C. (2007). The good, the bad, and the ugly: A meta-analytic review of positive and negative effects of violent video games. *Psychiatric Quarterly, 78*, 309–316.

Fischman, J. (2001, July 30). Do men experience menopause? *U.S. News & World Report*, 47.

Fisher, H. E. (2009). *Why him? Why her?: Finding real love by understanding your personality type*. New York: Henry Holt and Co.

Flanagan, K. E., Baker, C. I., Fortin, M., & Tinsley, D. V. (2006). The effect of gender opportunity in sports on the priorities and aspirations of young athletes. *The Sports Journal, 9*. Retrieved August 22, 2006, from http://www.thesportjournal.org

Fox, J., & Bailenson, J. N. (2009). Virtual virgins and vamps: The effects of exposure to female characters' sexualized appearance and gaze in an immersive virtual environment. *Sex Roles, 61*, 147–157.

Gibbons, A. (1991). The brain as "sexual organ." *Science, 253*, 957–959.

Gilligan, C. (1982). *In a different voice: Psychological theory and women's development*. Cambridge, MA: Harvard University Press.

Glenn, K. (2008, October 3). She's got game. *The Chronicle Review*, p. B20.

Gray, P. B., & Anderson, K. G. (2010, May 14). Darwin's daddies. *The Chronicle Review*, pp. B12–B14.

Grayling, A. C. (2005, April 9). The power to choose. *New Scientist*, 17.

Greene, S. (1997). Psychology and the re-evaluation of the feminine. *Irish Journal of Psychology, 18*, 367–385.

Grogan, S., & Richards, H. (2002). Body image: Focus groups with boys and men. *Men & Masculinity, 4*, 219–232.

Gur, R. C., Gur, R. E., Obrist, W. D., Hungerbuhler, J. P., Younkin, D., Rosen, A. D., Skolnick, B. E., & Reivich, M. (1982). Sex and handedness differences in cerebral blood flow during rest and cognitive activity. *Science, 217*, 659–661.

Gur, R. C., Mozley, L. H., Mozley, P. D., Resnick, S. M., Karp, J. S., Alavi, A., Arnold, S. E., & Gur, R. E. (1995). Sex differences in regional cerebral glucose metabolism during a resting state. *Science, 267*, 528–531.

Haddock, S. A., Zimmerman, T. S., & Lyness, K. P. (2003). Changing gender norms: Transitional dilemmas. In F. Walsh (Ed.), *Normal family processes: Growing diversity and complexity* (3rd ed., pp. 301–336). New York: Guilford.

Hall, E. T. (1976). *Beyond culture*. Garden City, NY: Doubleday.

Halpern, D. (2000). *Sex differences in cognitive abilities* (3rd ed.). Mahwah, NJ: Erlbaum.

Halualani, R. T. (2006). "This is the way things are!": Making sense of gender roles in cultures. In M. W. Lustig & J. Koester (Eds.), *Among us: Essays on identity, belonging, and intercultural competence* (2nd ed., pp. 104–108). Boston: Pearson.

Hanafin, R. L. (2010, March 1). Department of Defense lifting ban on women in combat but not gays. Retrieved August 11, 2010, from http://www.veteranstoday.com

Hardesty, C., Wenk, D., & Morgan, C. S. (1995). Paternal involvement and the development of gender expectations in sons and daughters. *Youth & Society, 267,* 283–297.

Harris, F., III. (2010). College men's meanings of masculinities and contextual influences: Toward a conceptual model. *Journal of College Student Development, 51,* 297–319.

Haviland, W. A. (2002). *Cultural anthropology* (10th ed.). Belmont, CA: Wadsworth.

Hecht, M. L., Ribeault, S. A., & Collier, M. J. (1993). *African American communication: Ethnic identity and cultural interpretation.* Newbury Park, CA: Sage.

Herbst, C. (2005). Shock and awe: Virtual females and the sexing of war. *Feminist Media Studies, 5,* 311–324.

Hill, C., Corbett, C., & St. Rose, A. (2010). *Why so few? Women in science, technology, engineering, and mathematics: Executive summary.* Washington, DC: American Association of University Women.

Hofstede, G. H. (1980). *Culture's consequences: International differences in work-related values.* Beverly Hills, CA: Sage.

Hofstede, G. H. (1991). *Cultures and organizations: Software of the mind.* London: McGraw-Hill.

Hofstede, G. H. (Ed.). (1998). *Masculinity and femininity: The taboo dimension of national cultures.* Thousand Oaks, CA: Sage.

Hofstede, G. H., & Hofstede, G. J. (2005). *Cultures and organizations: Software of the mind* (2nd ed.). New York: McGraw-Hill.

Holland, S. L. (2006). The dangers of playing dress-up: Popular representations of Jessica Lynch and the controversy regarding women in combat. *Quarterly Journal of Speech, 92,* 27–50.

Holmes, J., & Schnurr, S. (2006). "Doing femininity" at work: More than just relational practice. *Journal of Sociolinguistics, 10,* 31–51.

Ivory, J. D. (2006). Still a man's game: Gender representation in online reviews of video games. *Mass Communication and Society, 9,* 103–114.

Jacklin, C. N. (1989). Female and male: Issues of gender. *The American Psychologist, 44,* 127–134.

Jackson, R. L., & Dangerfield, C. L. (2003). Defining black masculinity as cultural property: Toward an identity negotiation paradigm. In L. A. Samovar & R. E. Porter (Eds.), *Intercultural communication: A reader* (10th ed., pp. 120–131). Belmont, CA: Wadsworth.

Jacobs, A. J., & Shaw, J. (2000). Legend of the doll. *Entertainment Weekly, 16.*

Jain, T., Missmer, S. A., Gupta, R. S., & Hornstein, M. D. (2005). Preimplantation sex selection demand and preferences in an infertility population. *Fertility and Sterility, 83,* 649–658.

Janssen, D. F. (2008). *International guide to literature on masculinity.* Harrison, TN: Men's Studies Press.

Jansz, J., & Martis, R. G. (2007). The Lara phenomenon: Powerful female characters in video games. *Sex Roles, 56,* 141–148.

Johnson, J. O. (2005, October). Who's minding the kids? Child care arrangements. *Household Economic Studies,* U.S. Census Bureau. Retrieved August 16, 2006, from http://www.census.gov

Johnson, S. K., Murphy, S. E., Zewdie, S., & Reichard, R. J. (2008). The strong, sensitive type: Effects of gender stereotypes and leadership prototypes on the evaluation of male and female leaders. *Organizational Behavior and Human Decision Processes, 106,* 39–60.

Joyce, C. (1999, May 14–16). Special delivery: Science is perfecting a way to select the sex of your next child. *USA Weekend,* 6–7.

Kada, O., Brunner, E., & Maier, M. (2009). Do male nurses suffer more? Focusing masculinity, femininity, sense of coherence, and work strain. *Journal of Men's Health, 6,* 247.

Kafai, Y. B., Heeter, C., Denner, J., & Sun, J. Y. (Eds.) (2008). *Beyond Barbie and Mortal Kombat: New perspectives on gender and gaming.* Cambridge, MA: MIT Press.

Kane, E. W. (2006). "No way my boys are going to be like that!" Parents' responses to children's gender nonconformity. *Gender & Society, 20,* 149–176.

Kegan Gardiner, J. (Ed.) (2002). *Masculinity studies and feminist theory: New directions.* New York: Columbia University Press.

Kehily, M. J., & Nayak, A. (2008). Global femininities: Consumption, culture, and the significance of place. *Discourse: Studies in the Cultural Politics of Education, 29,* 325–342.

Kelly, D. M., Pomerantz, S., & Currie, D. H. (2006). "No boundaries?" Girls' interactive, online learning about femininities. *Youth and Society, 38,* 3–28.

Kenrick, D. T., Neuberg, S. L., & Cialdini, R. B. (2005). *Social psychology: Unraveling the mystery* (3rd ed.). Boston: Allyn & Bacon.

Kenway, J., & Bullen, E. (2001). *Consuming children: Education, entertainment, and advertising.* Buckingham, UK: Open University.

Kimmel, M. S. (1987). *Changing men: New directions in research on men and masculinity.* Newbury Park, CA: Sage.

Kimmel, M. S. (2005). *Manhood in America: A cultural history.* New York: Oxford University Press.

Kimmel, M. S. (2009). *Guyland: The perilous world where boys become men.* New York: Harper Paperbacks.

Kimmel, M. S., Hearn, J. R., & Connell, R. W. (Eds.) (2004). *Handbook of studies on men and masculinities.* Thousand Oaks, CA: Sage.

Kimmel, M. S., & Messner, M. A. (2009). *Men's lives* (8th ed.). Boston: Pearson/Allyn & Bacon.

Kimura, D. (1987). Are men's and women's brains really different? *Canadian Psychology, 28,* 133–147.

Kimura, D. (2000). *Sex and cognition.* Boston: MIT Press. [Excerpt derived from Paul, E. L. (2002). *Taking sides: Clashing views on controversial issues in sex and gender* (2nd ed., pp. 94–96). New York: McGraw-Hill/Dushkin.]

Kleiman, C. (1992, January 23). Males and their raging hormones. *Raleigh News and Observer,* pp. 1E, 2E.

Kluger, B. (2000, May 7). Kids can learn about Washington at Politicians R Us. *New York Times News Service,* as in *Corpus Christi Caller Times,* pp. A24, A25.

Kohlberg, L. (1966). A cognitive-developmental analysis of children's sex-role concepts and attitudes. In E. E. Maccoby (Ed.), *The development of sex differences* (pp. 82–173). Stanford, CA: Stanford University Press.

Koller, V. (2008). "Not just a colour": Pink as a gender and sexuality marker in visual communication. *Visual Communication, 7,* 395–423.

Konijn, E. A., Nije Bijvank, M., & Bushman, B. J. (2007). I wish I were a warrior: The role of wishful identification in the effects of violent video games on aggression in adolescent boys. *Developmental Psychology, 43,* 1038–1044.

Kotz, D. (2010, May 7). Birth control pill turns 50: 7 ways it changed lives. Retrieved May 12, 2010, from http://usnews.com

Kuther, T. L., & McDonald, E. (2004). Early adolescents' experiences with and views of Barbie. *Adolescence, 39,* 39–51.

Learner, G. (1986). *The creation of patriarchy.* New York: Oxford University Press.

Leaper, C., Anderson, K., & Sanders, P. (1998). Moderators of gender effects on parents' talk to their children: A meta-analysis. *Developmental Psychology, 34,* 3–27.

Legato, M. J., & Tucker, L. (2006). *Why men never remember and women never forget.* New York: Rodale Books.

Levi-Strauss, C. (2004). Gender differences in communication: An intercultural experience. In F. Jandt (Ed.), *Intercultural communication: A global reader* (pp. 221–229). Thousand Oaks, CA: Sage.

Libby, L. (2008, December 11). Boy, oh boy. It's tough being a girl at Christmas. *Corpus Christi Caller Times.* Retrieved December 11, 2008, from http://www.caller.com

Lindsey, E. W., & Mize, J. (2001). Contextual differences in parent-child play: Implications for children's gender role development. *Sex Roles, 44,* 155–176.

Lindsey, L. L. (2005). *Gender roles: A sociological perspective* (4th ed.). Upper Saddle River, NJ: Pearson/Prentice Hall.

Lindsey, L. L., & Christy, S. (1997). *Gender roles: A sociological perspective* (3rd ed.). Upper Saddle River, NJ: Prentice Hall.

Linn, M. C., & Petersen, A. C. (1986). A meta-analysis of gender differences in spatial ability: Implications for mathematics and science achievement. In J. S. Hyde & M. C. Linn (Eds.), *The psychology of gender: Advances through meta-analysis* (pp. 67–101). Baltimore: Johns Hopkins University Press.

Lippa, R. A. (2002). *Gender, nature, and nurture.* Mahwah, NJ: Erlbaum.

Lueptow, L. B., Garovich, L., & Lueptow, M. B. (1995). The persistence of gender stereotypes in the face of changing sex roles: Evidence contrary to the sociocultural model. *Ethology & Sociobiology, 16,* 509–530.

Maccoby, E. E., & Jacklin, C. (1974). *The psychology of sex differences.* Stanford, CA: Stanford University Press.

Maccoby, E. E., & Jacklin, C. (1980). Sex differences in aggression: A rejoinder and reprise. *Child Development, 5,* 964–980.

MacKinnon, K. (2003). *Representing men: Maleness and masculinity in the media.* New York: Arnold.

Majors, R., & Billson, J. (1992). *Cool pose: The dilemmas of black manhood in America.* New York: Lexington.

Martin, C. L., & Ruble, D. (2004). Children's search for gender cues: Cognitive perspectives on gender development. *Current Directions in Psychological Science, 13,* 67–70.

Martin, J. N., & Nakayama, T. K. (2010). *Experiencing intercultural communication* (4th ed.). New York: McGraw-Hill.

Martins, N., Williams, D. C., Harrison, K., & Ratan, R. A. (2009). A content analysis of female body imagery in video games. *Sex Roles, 61,* 824–836.

McCarry, M. (2007). Masculinity studies and male violence: Critique or collusion? *Women's Studies International Forum, 30,* 404–415.

McLoughlin, M., Shryer, T. L., Goode, E. E., & McAuliffe, K. (1988, August 8). Men vs. women. *U.S. News & World Report,* 50–56.

Mean, L. J., & Kassing, J. W. (2008). "I would just like to be known as an athlete": Managing hegemony, femininity, and heterosexuality in female sport. *Western Journal of Communication, 72,* 126–144.

Messner, M. A. (2000). Barbie girls versus sea monsters: Children constructing gender. *Gender & Society, 14,* 765–784.

Miller, M. K., & Summers, A. (2007). Gender differences in video game characters' roles, appearances, and attire as portrayed in video game magazines. *Sex Roles, 57,* 733–742.

Mischel, W. (1966). A social learning view of sex differences in behavior. In E. E. Maccoby (Ed.), *The development of sex differences* (pp. 56–81). Stanford, CA: Stanford University Press.

Mithers, C. (2009, August). Terra incognita: The male brain. *O: The Oprah Winfrey Magazine,* 95.

Moir, A., & Jessel, D. (1992). *Brain sex: The real differences between men and women.* Surrey, UK: Delta Publishing.

Morgan, R. (1993, November/December). Raising sons: We know our dreams for our daughters; what about our sons? *Ms.,* 36–41.

Mortenson, T. G. (2008, June 6). Where the boys were: Women outnumber them in colleges and the work force, and too many men are failing to keep up. *The Chronicle of Higher Education,* p. A31.

Mulvaney, B. M. (2004). Gender differences in communication: An intercultural experience. In F. Jandt (Ed.), *Intercultural communication: A global reader* (pp. 3–8). Thousand Oaks, CA: Sage.

NBC Nightly News. (2009, April 30). New Barbie has tattoos. [Television broadcast.]

Neary, L. (2010, March 1). Ending ban on women in combat is long overdue. Retrieved August 11, 2010, from http://www.npr.org

Norris, K. (2004). Gender stereotypes, aggression, and computer games: An online survey of women. *CyberPsychology and Behavior, 76,* 714–727.

Northrup, C. (2010, April 22). The pill turns 50: Taking stock. Retrieved May 12, 2010, from http://www.thehuffingtonpost.com

NPD Group. (2007, October 16). Amount of time kids spend playing video games is on the rise. Retrieved August 13, 2010, from http://www.npd.com

NPD Group. (2008, September 23). Young girls say they are spending more time on entertainment related activities this year than they did in 2007. Retrieved August 13, 2010, from http://www.npd.com

NPD Group. (2009a, May 20). More Americans play video games than go out to the movies. Retrieved August 13, 2010, from http://www.npd.com

NPD Group. (2009b, December 2). Among American kids ages 2–17, 82 percent report they are gamers. Retrieved August 13, 2010, from http://www.npd.com

NPD Group. (2010, March 2). Research shows average number of hours per week spent on online gaming has grown by 10% since 2009. Retrieved August 13, 2010, from http://www.npd.com

O'Brien, K. (2010, August 1). She shoots, she scores! What sports actually do for girls—and for all of us. *The Boston Globe.* Retrieved August 11, 2010, from http://www.boston.com/bostonglobe

Ogletree, S., & Drake, R. (2007). College students' video game participation and perceptions: Gender differences and implications. *Sex Roles, 56,* 537–542.

O'Leary, A., & Kornbluh, K. (2009). Family friendly for all families. In H. Boushey & A. O'Leary (Eds.), *The Shriver report: A woman's nation changes everything.* Washington, DC: Center for American Progress.

Oomman, N., & Ganatra, B. R. (2002). Sex selection: The systematic elimination of girls. *Reproductive Health Matters, 10,* 184–188.

Owen Blakemore, J. E., & Centers, R. E. (2005). Characteristics of boys' and girls' toys. *Sex Roles, 53,* 619–634.

Owen Blakemore, J. E., & Hill, C. A. (2007). The Child Gender Socialization Scale: A measure to compare traditional and feminist parents. *Sex Roles, 58,* 192–207.

Paechter, C. (2006). Masculine femininities/feminine masculinities: Power, identities, and gender. *Gender and Education, 18,* 253–263.

Painter, K. (2010, June 14). New dads can be a cautious lot. *USA Today,* p. 4D.

Paul, E. L. (Ed.). (2002). *Taking sides: Clashing views on controversial issues in sex and gender* (2nd ed.). New York: McGraw-Hill/Dushkin.

Peach, L. J. (1998). Women in culture: Introduction. In L. J. Peach (Ed.), *Women in culture: A women's studies anthology* (pp. 1–12). Malden, MA: Blackwell.

Peterson, J. L., & Shibley Hyde, J. (2010). A meta-analytic review of research on gender differences in sexuality, 1993–2007. *Psychological Bulletin, 136,* 21–38.

Pickard Leszczynski, J. (2009). A state conceptualization: Are individuals' masculine and feminine personality traits situationally influenced? *Personality and Individual Differences, 47,* 157–162.

Pinker, S. (2005, May 16). The science of gender and science: Pinker vs. Spelke. *The Edge.*

Pleck, J. H. (1975). Masculinity-femininity: Current and alternative paradigms. *Sex Roles, 1,* 161–178.

Pleck, J. H. (1977). The psychology of sex roles: Traditional and new views. In L. A. Cater, A. F. Scott, & W. Martyna (Eds.), *Women and men: Changing roles, relationships, and perceptions* (pp. 181–199). New York: Praeger.

Pleck, J. H. (1981). *The myth of masculinity.* Cambridge, MA: MIT Press.

Raley, S., & Bianchi, S. (2006). Sons, daughters, and family processes: Does gender of children matter? *Annual Review of Sociology, 16,* 401–422.

Ramey, E. (1976). Men's cycles (They have them too you know). In A. Kaplan & J. Bean (Eds.), *Beyond sex-role stereotypes.* Boston: Little, Brown.

Richmond-Abbott, M. (1992). *Masculine and feminine: Gender roles over the life cycle* (2nd ed.). New York: McGraw-Hill.

Riesman, C. (1990). *Divorce talk: Women and men make sense of personal relationships.* New Brunswick, NJ: Princeton University Press.

Rogers, C. R. (1961). *On becoming a person.* Boston: Houghton Mifflin.

Ross, H., & Taylor, H. (1989). Do boys prefer daddy or his physical style of play? *Sex Roles, 20,* 23–31.

Rubin, J. Z., Provensano, F., & Luria, Z. (1974). The eye of the beholder: Parents' views on sex of newborns. *American Journal of Orthopsychiatry, 44,* 312–319.

Ruble, D. N., Balaban, T., & Cooper, J. (1981). Gender constancy and the effects of sex-typed televised toy commercials. *Child Development, 52,* 667–673.

Rudman, L. A., & Glick, P. (2008). *The social psychology of gender: How power and intimacy shape gender relations.* New York: Guilford.

Samovar, L. A., & Porter, R. E. (2009). *Communication between cultures* (7th ed.). Belmont, CA: Thomson/Wadsworth.

Satir, V. (1972). *Peoplemaking.* Palo Alto, CA: Science and Behavior.

Satir, V. (1988). *The new peoplemaking.* Mountain View, CA: Science and Behavior.

Schmid, R. E. (2005, March 1). US life expectancy up to 77.6 years; gender gap narrows. Retrieved August 11, 2010, from http://www.bostonglobe.com

Schrock, D., & Schwalbe, M. (2009). Men, masculinity, and manhood acts. *Annual Review of Sociology, 35,* 277–295.

Science Daily. (2007, January 7). Age, gender major factors in severity of auto-accident injuries. Retrieved August 11, 2010, from http://www.sciencedaily.com

Segell, M. (1996, October). The second coming of the alpha male. *Esquire,* 12–17.

Shannon, T. (2003). *Reproductive technologies: A reader.* Lanham, MD: Rowman & Littlefield.

Shephard, R. J., & Astrand, P.-O. (Eds.) (2000). *Endurance in sport* (2nd ed.). London: Blackwell Science.

Shibley Hyde, J. (2005). The gender similarities hypothesis. *American Psychologist, 60,* 581–582.

Shibley Hyde, J. (2006). Epilogue. In K. Dindia & D. J. Canary (Eds.), *Sex differences and similarities in communication* (2nd ed., pp. 413–418). Mahwah, NJ: Erlbaum.

Shibuya, A., Sakamoto, A., Ihori, N., & Yukawa, S. (2008). The effects of the presence and contexts of video game violence on children: A longitudinal study in Japan. *Simulation and Gaming, 39,* 528–539.

Sidelinger, R. J., Frisby, B. N., & McMullen, A. L. (2009). The decision to forgive: Sex, gender, and the likelihood to forgive partner transgressions. *Communication Studies, 60,* 164–179.

Simmons, J. (2009). Genders full of question marks. In H. Boushey & A. O'Leary (Eds.), *The Shriver report: A woman's nation changes everything.* Washington, DC: Center for American Progress.

Smith, A. G. (Ed.). (1966). *Communication and culture.* New York: Holt, Rinehart & Winston.

Snow, M. E., Jacklin, C. N., & Maccoby, E. E. (1983). Sex-of-child differences in father-child interactions at one year of age. *Child Development, 54,* 227–232.

Snowbeck, C. (2001, September 9). The many moods of testosterone. *Pittsburgh Post-Gazette,* as in *Corpus Christi Caller Times,* p. C7.

Soulliere, D. M. (2006). Wrestling with masculinity: Messages about manhood in the WWE. *Sex Roles, 55,* 1–11.

Spelke, E. (2005, May 16). The science of gender and science: Pinker vs. Spelke. *The Edge.*

Stein, R. (2004, December 14). A boy for you, a girl for me: Technology allows choice. *Washington Post,* p. A1.

Stern, M., & Karraker, K. H. (1989). Sex stereotyping in infants: A review of gender labeling studies. *Sex Roles, 20,* 501–522.

Stevenson, B. (2007). Title IX and the evolution of high school sports. *Contemporary Economic Policy, 25,* 486–506.

Stevenson, B. (2010). Beyond the classroom: Using Title IX to measure the return to high school sports. *Review of Economics and Statistics, 92,* 284–337.

Stibich, M. (2008, June 4). Why do women live longer than men? Retrieved August 11, 2010, from http://longevity.about.com

Stockard, J., & Johnson, M. (1980). *Sex roles.* Englewood Cliffs, NJ: Prentice Hall.

Tavris, C. (1992). *The mismeasure of woman.* New York: Simon & Schuster.

Thompson, C. (1992). A new vision of masculinity. In M. Schaum & C. Flanagan (Eds.), *Gender images: Readings for composition* (pp. 77–83). Boston: Houghton Mifflin.

Tirrito, S. J. (2010). Women as endurance athletes: What you need to know. Retrieved August 11, 2010, from http://www.coachtroy.com

TrafficSTATS. (2010). Motorists get improved risk information. Retrieved August 11, 2010, from http://www.cmu.edu

Tragos, P. (2009). Monster masculinity: Honey, I'll be in the garage reasserting my manhood. *The Journal of Popular Culture, 42,* 541–553.

Traister, B. (2000). Academic Viagra: The rise of American masculinity studies. *American Quarterly, 52,* 274–304.

Tyler May, E. (2010a, May 7). 50 years on the pill. *The Chronicle Review,* pp. B4–B5.

Tyler May, E. (2010b, Spring). The pill turns 50. *Ms.,* 40.

Tyler May, E. (2010c). *America and the pill: A history of promise, peril, and liberation.* New York: Basic Books.

U.S. Census Bureau. (2009). Retrieved June 14, 2010, from http://www.census.gov

Wade, N. (2007, April 10). Pas de deux of sexuality is written in the genes. *New York Times,* pp. D1, D6.

Ward, L. M., Merriwether, A., & Caruthers, A. (2006). Breasts are for men: Media, masculinity ideologies, and men's beliefs about women's bodies. *Sex Roles, 55,* 703–714.

Williams, D., Consalvo, M., Caplan, S., & Yee, N. (2009). Looking for gender: Gender roles and behaviors among online gamers. *Journal of Communication, 59,* 700–725.

Williams, D., & Skoric, M. (2005). Internet fantasy violence: A test of aggression in an online game. *Communication Monographs, 72,* 217–233.

Winter, J., & Pauwels, A. (2006). Men staying at home looking after their children: Feminist linguistic reform and social change. *International Journal of Applied Linguistics, 16,* 16–36.

Wiseman, P. (2002, June 19). China thrown off balance as boys outnumber girls. *USA Today.* Retrieved August 13, 2010, from http://www.usatoday.com

Women's Sports Foundation. (2010). New study links early athletic participation with success later in life. Retrieved August 11, 2010, from http://www.womenssportsfoundation.org

Wood, J. T. (1994). Engendered identities: Shaping voice and mind through gender. In D. R. Vocate (Ed.), *Intrapersonal communication: Different voices, different minds* (pp. 145–168). Hillsdale, NJ: Erlbaum.

Yao, M. A., Mahood, C., & Linz, D. (2010). Sexual priming, gender stereotyping, and likelihood to sexually harass: Examining the cognitive effects of playing a sexually-explicit video game. *Sex Roles, 62,* 77–88.

Zorrilla, M. (2010). *Video games and gender: Game representation, gender effects, differences in play, and player representation.* Unpublished undergraduate thesis, Central Washington University, Ellensburg, WA.

HOT TOPICS

- Theories of media effects on consumers
- The impact of stereotypical depictions of women and men in advertisements on attitudes about the sexes
- Gendered messages in scripted and reality television programming
- Gender bending in film and how men's and women's film roles impact viewers
- The pervasive influence of pornography and the effects of its consumption on women's and men's attitudes and relationships
- Song lyrics and music video portrayals of the sexes
- Gender and new media, specifically online identity, disembodiment, and gaming

Pictures, Porn, and Pop
Gender and Media

CHAPTER 3

Case Study

A Day in Two Lives:
Rey and His Dad

It's 6:30 a.m., the clock radio alarm goes off, and a couple of people on a morning talk-radio show are chatting away. Rey's dad shuts off the alarm, rolls out of bed, and begins his morning routine. Over his usual bowl of cereal, he unfolds the local newspaper and *The Wall Street Journal* that arrived at his doorstep, reading stock indexes with interest and making a mental note to check stocks again later in the day. While shaving, he uses the remote to turn on his TV and tunes to the Weather Channel for a quick check of the local forecast, then switches to a cable news source for the latest headlines. He finishes breakfast, then pulls his daily planner out of his briefcase to review his schedule. Before leaving the house, he checks his old but reliable VCR to make sure it will correctly record the network nightly news as well as a few of his favorite TV programs. It could be a long day at work today, so better to record the shows than risk missing them.

On the drive to work, Rey's dad tunes in his car radio and checks back with the talk show. It's the same old blah, blah, blah, so he decides he'd rather listen to a favorite CD to put him in a better frame of mind for work. He knows a stack of faxes that came through overnight await him on his desk, plus there'll be mounds of e-mails to wade through. When he arrives at the office, his secretary is on the phone, so he swings by the central mailboxes and picks up his mail, including notes of phone calls he should return, some interoffice memos, and a couple of magazines he subscribes to. When he gets to his desk, the light on his office phone is blinking, indicating that he has voice mail messages. He picks up the phone and dials in his code to start listening to the messages while at the same time firing up his computer. The computer comes to life; he logs on to the Internet, and an e-mail icon and a voice saying, "You've

(continued)

Case Study (*continued*)

got mail," greet him. Rey's dad reads his interoffice messages first, thinking he'll check his other e-mail accounts later—postings to a listserv he subscribes to, as well as messages from colleagues, family members, and friends across the country. Hopefully just before lunch he'll remember to check stocks via the Internet. If he doesn't have time for this, there's always the evening newspaper waiting at his door when he gets home. He'd love to knock off early today to catch the newest action film, but there's just too much to do. Too much going on, too many things and people to deal with, too little time.

It's 7:30 a.m., Rey's alarm on his cell phone rings, and he shuts it off, pulling it out of where it's been charging overnight. Rey begins his morning routine which involves a bowl of cereal and his smartphone. On his phone, he logs on to the Internet, checks local newspaper headlines, stock reports in *The Wall Street Journal,* and the forecast via Weather Underground. While shaving, he listens to a podcast of Jon Stewart's *The Daily Show,* which he couldn't watch on his DVR last night because he was too tired.

He finishes breakfast while responding to a friend's play on "Words With Friends," updates his Facebook status, checks postings from friends on LinkedIn, tweets a clever message about his busy day via Twitter, then scans the calendar function on his phone, noting his schedule for the day. He meant to spend some time this morning with his virtual friends through their avatars on Second Life, but there's no time for that now. He rushes out the door, realizing that he didn't set his DVR, but knows he can program it from his phone, catch his favorite shows via Primetime On Demand within a day or two, or see re-broadcasts on Hulu or network websites. If those options aren't convenient, DVDs of TV shows are usually out within a few months; he can catch up by watching them (or the latest Netflix arrival) on his iPad.

On the drive to work, Rey plugs the address of a potential new client into his car's GPS, sees that the location is out of the way, and makes a mental note to check out the address another time. At a red light, he sees an interesting piece of property that he might like to check into later, so he snaps a picture of it with his phone. His Bluetooth car phone is synched with his cell, so he can talk on the phone hands-free when he drives; he gets a quick call from a buddy and confirms a racquetball match for after work. The DVD player in his car starts up where he left off with a movie he wanted to watch, but traffic is too crazy for that today. He punches the dashboard computer in his car to hear a favorite CD instead.

He has time for a Starbucks, checking a few e-mails and texts on his phone while in line at the drive-thru. No time to answer them now; he texts his secretary that he'll be at the office within 10 minutes. She texts him back immediately, saying that his first meeting (a group conference via Skype, the company's webcam provider) has been pushed back a half hour, so he pulls over in a parking lot and replies to a few of the more urgent texts. He no longer has a fax machine or an office phone system; all e-mails, voice mails, and text messages go to his phone, but, having had a couple of close calls with texting while driving, he tries to avoid it as much as possible.

When he arrives at the office and gets to his desk, he takes his computer out of sleep mode and begins working on his current project. His work is occasionally interrupted by a "bling" sound that indicates a new e-mail message or a prepro-grammed stock update has arrived in his inbox. He routes all e-mails—interoffice and other accounts—through his phone, but keeps an e-mail system on his computer, just for extra convenience. Some e-mail replies, especially those going to potential clients, are better typed on his computer keyboard than texted on his phone. Rey sighs a deep sigh; he likes what he does, but, despite all the technology that should help him do his job faster and more efficiently, it seems there's just always more work to do than hours to do it in. Rey thinks: If only my smartphone was smart enough to give me a shave.

Sometimes Rey thinks that he'd like to escape all the technology and sit on an island somewhere, staring off into the deep blue sea. Sometimes there's just too much going on, too many things and people to deal with, too little time. But then he laughs at himself, realizing that he wouldn't get a strong enough wireless signal on that island to download anything. He'd probably be bored stupid!

Rey and Rey's dad are both on time to work at 8:30 a.m.; both work very long days. Whose routine would you rather have? Is Rey's day better than his dad's, mainly because of how he uses media and technology? Does technology make you more efficient or just add more to your day? How much of your day is spent interact-ing with media and technology, versus interacting with people, face to face?

How much media and technology do you consume each day? What influence do they have on you? What messages about the sexes are communicated via the media you consume? That's the topic of this chapter. But before we go further, let's define some terminology so we're all on the same page.

You've probably heard or read the term *mass communication,* which refers to "com-munication accomplished through a mediated message that is sent to many people at the same time" (Beebe, Beebe, & Ivy, 2013, p. 25). Radio and TV broadcasts are forms of mass communication. But more commonly now you hear the term "media," which seems to be a catchall for everything from broadcasts to film to viral videos on YouTube or Hulu to newspapers, magazines, and other print forms of media that you can access a variety of ways. It's beyond our scope in this book to debate exactly what's media and what's not. If we take into account more traditional forms of mediated messages (e.g., TV ads, song lyrics, music videos), as well as technologically-assisted media (e.g., YouTube, Facebook, smartphones), perhaps the best, all-encompassing term is *mediated communication.* This term refers to "any communication that is carried out using some channel other than those used in face-to-face communication" (Beebe, Beebe, & Ivy, 2013, p. 13). This term is prefer-able to *computer-mediated communication* (CMC), which refers to communication facilitated through the use of a computer. Not all technological innovations we use to communicate today are computer-driven; smartphones and iPads aren't computers (not *yet,* anyway).

In the remaining chapters of this book, we discuss gender, sex, and the impact of technological innovation on how we communicate with each other and form relation-ships. But for now, just remember that our focus in these early chapters is on gender communication *about* men and women, not *between* them. Some of the more traditional forms of media are our focus in this chapter because the ways people are communicated *about* in our culture affects communication *between* people.

THE POWER OF MEDIATED COMMUNICATION: EFFECTS ON OUR LIVES

Perhaps no other force influences our daily lives more than media. Parents are hugely important, teachers have significant impact, friends affect us in profound ways but, over time, media may have the strongest effect of all. Consider how often you compare real life—work, family, relationships—to how these things are depicted in various media. It's common to hear someone refer to something on TV, such as, "I don't trust that guy I went out with last night; he reminds me of that guy on (insert show here)" or "I feel like I've stepped into a sad country-and-western tune." Media are highly influential in how they communicate messages about women and men.

A Bombardment of Media

Your modern existence is jammed full of mediated communication every sunrise to sunset, but just how are you affected by it? You are literally bombarded with media every day, and the effects of this bombardment are dramatic (Chia & Gunther, 2006; Harris, 2011; Strasburger, 2005; Ziegler, 2007).

As a college-educated person, you are probably an above-average critical consumer of media, meaning that you consciously select mediated messages to take in and to filter out. However, a great deal of mediated information is absorbed unconsciously, even by the most critical of consumers. Few of us have time in our busy lives to focus concentrated attention on all the mediated messages we receive in a typical day and make conscious decisions about their effects. This critical thinking process becomes a skill we use less often as we take in more and more mediated information. Just how this absorption affects us has been the subject of a good deal of attention among media researchers.

Best & Wittiest—Kevin Siers/Distributed by North America Syndicate.

Approaches to Studying the Effects of Media Consumption

In the 1970s, media scholar Gaye Tuchman (1979) described an explosion of media research, as mass media grew exponentially during the years between World War II and the beginning of the 1980s. Several research approaches and theories emerged at that time and since then, in an attempt to explain how media affect consumers.

HYPODERMIC NEEDLE OR DIRECT-EFFECTS THEORY   This early theory viewed the mass audience as passively and directly consuming mediated messages. The imagery was that of a hypodermic needle that injected mass communication directly into the veins of its noncritical consumers (Campbell, Martin, & Fabos, 2011). This theory offered an inadequate, overly simplistic explanation of media effects because it ignored how other factors might influence the process, but it was a start.

MINIMAL-EFFECTS MODEL   With increasing sophistication in social scientific techniques came dissatisfaction with direct-effects theory. Media theorists began to argue that consumers were only minimally affected by mediated messages, and that they selectively exposed themselves to media messages and selectively retained those messages that reinforced or were consistent with behaviors, attitudes, and values they already held. This theory suggested that consumers were less at the power of persuasive media than previously thought (Campbell et al., 2011).

USES AND GRATIFICATIONS THEORY   Media expert John Vivian (2011) describes the uses and gratifications approach as a theory that no longer viewed mass audiences as passive sponges, but rather as active users of media. The theory describes how consumers are motivated to use various media and what gains, rewards, or gratifications they receive from such consumption. Researchers have employed uses and gratifications theory to better understand such things as the gratification people derive from watching reality TV programs (Barton, 2009) or using MP3 players (Zeng, 2011); social media, like comparisons of Facebook to Instant Messaging (Quan-Haase & Young, 2010); perceptions of political candidates' profiles on MySpace (Ancu & Cozma, 2009); and consumers' evaluations of commercial websites in other countries (Mahmoud, Klimsa, & Auter, 2010).

AGENDA-SETTING RESEARCH   The seeds of this research approach date back to the 1920s and the early work of Walter Lippmann, who suggested that media "create pictures in our heads" (as in Campbell et al., 2011, p. 524). A contemporary of Lippmann's, Robert Park, proposed that the media do not merely report, reflect, or dramatize what is important in society, media actually guide what we think is important (Vivian, 2011). The media generate awareness of issues; thus, media may not be dictating attitudes or stances on issues, but they have the power to affect what we think *about*. In essence, viewers may allow a media outlet to set an agenda for what should be most important to them (Douglas, 2009; Heaton & Wilson, 1995).

CULTIVATION THEORY   This theory suggests that media consumption "'cultivates' in us a distorted perception of the world we live in, making it seem more like television portrays it, than it is in real life" (Bittner, 1995, p. 465). The media blur reality and fantasy, what life is really like and how it is represented on television and in movies, magazine ads, romance novels, and so on. Media scholar George Gerbner and various colleagues are among the most prominent researchers to develop cultivation theory to better understand the relationship between the social reality of violence and crime and media's depiction of it (Gerbner, 2003; Gerbner, Gross, Morgan, & Signorielli, 1980; Signorielli & Morgan, 1990). Gerbner, who began his investigations of television violence in the late 1960s, contends that a typical American child will see 32,000 on-screen murders before she or he turns eighteen (as in Vivian, 2011). Cultivation theory suggests, for example, that some children who see violent mediated images will expect that they can repeat those acts of violence in their lives, without consequences or harm to others. One need only check recent newspaper headlines to see evidence of this theory in action, as children have harmed and, in some instances, killed other children by replicating wrestling moves or other violent acts, believing that the victim will spring back up or be unharmed by their actions (Levine & Carlsson-Paige, 2003; Potter, 2003). As another example of research from a cultivation perspective, information technology scholars Chia and Gunther (2006) examined the cultivation effect of different types of media on students' perceptions of their peers' sexual behavior.

CULTURAL STUDIES APPROACHES   Just as minimal-effects research approaches developed in reaction to earlier techniques, cultural studies approaches to understanding media effects developed out of a reaction to what was perceived to be too much data gathering, number crunching, and trend charting in social scientific research. Cultural studies approaches are more interpretive and intuitive; researchers "try to understand how media and culture are tied to the actual patterns of communication in daily life" (Campbell et al., 2011, p. 527). Everyday cultural symbols, as found in print and visual media, are analyzed for their power to make meaning, to create and communicate reality, and to help people understand their daily existence (Kellner, 2011). Researchers are particularly interested in issues of race, gender, class, and sexuality, and the inequities therein. As an example of this approach to media effects research, cultural studies scholars have examined television shows' depictions of families in which social class and ethnicity are emphasized (Butsch, 2011; Esposito, 2011; Lipsitz, 2011).

ADVERTISING: SELLING A PRODUCT OR SELLING SEXISM?

Advertising is a huge and pervasive industry. While we used to think of advertisements merely as interruptions in our favorite TV programs or radio broadcasts, or as filler in magazines, advertisers are getting craftier and more desperate to get their products and services into our view. Ads come through unprompted on websites and your phone, play in your ear when you're on hold, precede movies you see in theatres, introduce the DVDs you rent or purchase, and appear as product placements in TV programs and films, such as when a character is depicted typing on a particular brand of computer or drinking a name-brand beer (deGregorio & Sung, 2010; Scott & Craig-Lees, 2010; Wiles & Danielova, 2009). Ads are digitized to appear behind the batter's box or in the middle of a football field, and the images and products change as you watch the televised sporting event. If you're attending a major sporting event, you'll see ads on the blimp flying overhead. Ads clutter websites, line the walls of buses and subways, and provide often unwanted "color" on your road trip, in the form of billboards. Estimates indicate that by the time you are 65, you will have been exposed to two million TV ads; over 3,000 ads *each day* will come your way—each wanting to persuade you and separate you from your money (Schwartz, 2005).

Remember . . .

Mass Communication: Communication accomplished through a mediated message that is sent to many people at the same time

Mediated Communication: Communication that is carried out using some channel other than those used in face-to-face communication

Computer-Mediated Communication (CMC): Communication conveyed via computer, rather than through the use of other technology or through face-to-face conversation

Hypodermic Needle/Direct-Effects Theory: Early media effects theory that proposed the mass audience passively and directly consumed mediated messages

Minimal-Effects Theory: Suggestion that consumers are only minimally affected by mediated messages, that consumers selectively expose themselves to media messages and selectively retain those that reinforce or are consistent with behaviors, attitudes, and values they already hold

Uses and Gratifications Theory: Theory that describes how consumers are motivated to use various media and what gains, rewards, or gratifications they receive from such consumption

Agenda-Setting Theory: Proposition that viewers allow media outlets to set an agenda for what should be most important to them

Cultivation Theory: Theory that media cultivate distortions in consumers, that media blur the lines between reality and fantasy

Cultural Studies Approaches: Interpretive and intuitive approaches to studying media effects; explorations of how media and culture reflect patterns in daily life

Advertising has a powerful effect that goes well beyond the purpose of selling products to consumers; it affects our culture and our views (Cortese, 2008). A great deal of research has been conducted on the ways women and men are depicted in print and electronic advertisements, as well as the messages these ads communicate to media consumers. A good deal of these depictions evoke stereotypes. Media researchers Wells, Moriarity, and Burnett (2005) explain that *stereotyping* "involves presenting a group of people in an unvarying pattern that lacks individuality and often reflects popular misconceptions" (p. 49). Let's look at some of the various stereotypical portrayals of the sexes in ads, including a few exceptions, and then consider the overall effects on consumers.

Babes in Bras: Female Depiction in Advertising

Groundbreaking programmatic research by marketing professors Alice Courtney and Thomas Whipple (1974, 1980, 1983, 1985) forms the basis for the claim that advertising has a major impact on individuals' views of gender. From the compiled results of numerous studies, Courtney and Whipple produced a list of trends and female *gender stereotypes* prevalent in advertising; researchers expounded on their work, discovering more female stereotypes in ads (Artz, Munger, & Purdy, 1999; Browne, 1998; Lin, 1997; Simonton, 1995). Unfortunately, the abundance of recent

I would close down all those teenage magazines that encourage young girls to diet. The influence of all those magazines on girls as young as 13 is horrific.

—Penelope Cruz, actor

research confirms that little has changed in terms of gender stereotyping in ads (Arima, 2003; Baker, 2005; Bennett, 2008; Ganahl, Prinsen, & Netzley, 2003; Lindner, 2004; Hentges, Bartsch, & Meier, 2007; Monk-Turner, Kouts, Parris, & Webb, 2007; Tanner-Smith, Williams, & Nichols, 2006; Yoder, Christopher, & Holmes, 2008). One study of ads for technological innovations (in this case, smartphones) found prevalent sex-based stereotypes invoked to sell the product (Doring & Poschl, 2006). Read the following list and see if you have any stereotypes to add.

1. Fewer depictions of women, in general, than men
2. Women in isolation, particularly from other women
3. Women depicted as sex objects, often in sleepwear, underwear, and lingerie more than in professional clothing
4. Young girls and women portrayed as passive and in need of help and protection by men
5. Women as kitchen and bathroom product representatives
6. Women appearing more than men in ads for personal hygiene products
7. An abundance of women serving men and boys
8. Medical ads depicting male physicians interacting with hysterical female hypochondriacs
9. Women more often depicted in family- and home-oriented roles than in business roles
10. Young housewives shown performing household duties, whereas older men act as product representatives who give advice to housewives
11. Women portrayed as decorative, nonfunctioning entities incapable of making important decisions
12. Women depicted as being obsessed with physical attractiveness
13. Fewer depictions of older women than older men
14. Fewer depictions of minority women than minority men
15. Fewer women than men advertising expensive luxury products
16. Few women depicted actively engaged in sports
17. Ads overtly critical of feminist rights and issues
18. Women's body parts, especially genitalia, featured in ads, rather than the whole body
19. Frequent decapitated images of women, meaning women often pictured only from the mouth or neck downward (as though they don't have brains)
20. Women in bondage depictions, such as being embedded in inanimate objects or bound with tape, fabric, or rope

Perhaps some of you are familiar with the work of Jean Kilbourne, particularly her educational films. Her first, *Killing Us Softly*, was released in 1979, and Kilbourne continues to produce research and films that support her assertion that advertising presents women almost exclusively in one of two roles: housewife or sex object. In the most recent film in the series, *Killing Us Softly 4* (Kilbourne, 2010a), Kilbourne's examples include women's bodies turned into things (like beer bottles) and thin, tall, long-legged mannequin-like women with perfect skin and no signs of aging.

Kilbourne (2010b) has countless examples of how ruthlessly and fiercely advertisers have clung to their use of sexualized, often demoralized images of women to sell all kinds of products. She commented about the status of today's sexist advertising, in response to a *Ms.* magazine article on the hit TV show, *Mad Men.* (If you haven't checked out the show, watch it to get a fascinating glimpse into the American advertising industry in the 1960s. Seeing how women in business were treated during this period of our history will make you glad you live in the twenty-first century.) Kilbourne explains:

> We no longer see ads with demented housewives pathologically obsessed with cleanliness, and current ads feature many more women in the workplace and some (not enough) men caring for their children and doing domestic chores without screwing them up. In many ways, however, things have gotten worse. The ideal image of beauty is more tyrannical than ever. Not satisfied with ever-thinner models, advertisers can now use Photoshop to alter the human body freakishly. Women of color are generally portrayed as beautiful only if they have light skin, straight hair, Caucasian features and thin bodies. Advertising is relentlessly heterosexist. (p. 34)

Kilbourne describes another double standard in today's advertising—one regarding age. Men's portrayals in ads have an "aging gracefully" dimension to them, meaning that advertisements often portray men as handsome when they're young, rugged when they reach middle age, and able-bodied and even distinguished in their elder years. In contrast, most ads display only young women unless the ads are for products or services for middle aged and elderly women, sending a strong message to women that they'd better stay young looking if they're going to be relevant in our society.

As Kilbourne (2010b) mentioned, women of color fare poorly in ads, both in the quantity of depictions and the quality of the roles (Bramlett-Solomon, 2001; Brooks & Hebert, 2006). According to author Gail Baker Woods (1995), "When they are seen, black women are often portrayed as 'jive'-talking, sassy 'sisters' or overweight, wise-cracking, church-going women" (p. 28). Hispanic, Asian American, and Native American women are less represented in ads than African American women, who are less represented than white women. When women of color appear in ads, often they are expected to conform to standards of white beauty (Cortese, 2008; Mueller, 2011; Wilson & Gutierrez, 2003). A particularly disturbing trend is for ads, primarily aimed at a male audience, to depict adult women as sexy little girls; research is beginning to explore a connection between enjoyment of such ads and beliefs about child sexual abuse (Machia & Lamb, 2009).

However, although an abundance of current research findings show perpetual female stereotyping in ads, one study detected a slight shift over time. Business scholars Mager and Helgeson (2011) conducted a content analysis of portrayals of women and men in American magazine advertisements over a 50-year period. In their analysis of nearly 8,000 portrayals in some 3,200 ads, they found that "magazine advertising showed a trend toward objective role portrayals of women fairly equal to men" (p. 238). They didn't see evidence of Courtney and Whipple's finding that women are primarily depicted in the home, nor that women in ads appear as though they don't do important things or make critical decisions. Mager and Helgeson credit the feminist movement and the pressure feminists exerted over the advertising industry for the changes, suggesting that "arguments presented by the feminist movement may have been too compelling for the U.S. culture to ignore, resulting in objective differences in role portrayals from those of the prefeminist (traditional) era" (p. 250).

Ads did persist in their portrayals of women as dependent and in need of protection by men; their depiction as sexual objects for the pleasure of men, rather than as whole and capable people, actually increased over the 50-year span. Given statistics that show that the American workforce is now 50/50 in terms of female and male workers, and that 40 percent of breadwinners in American homes are women, it looks like the advertising industry is trying to catch up with women's changing lives (Boushey, 2009).

Some manufacturers have changed their approach to advertising products for female consumers—the operant word being *some*. In the 1990s, Nike developed a series of ads along with a "Get Real" slogan that attempted to endorse feminist ideals and depict more realistic female body types, while promoting health and fitness (through the use of Nike products, of course). On the surface the ads looked innovative and promising, but they received criticism because the women in the photos for the ads were all white, young, and slim, even though they were of somewhat different body shapes.

The Dove "Campaign for Real Beauty," launched in September of 2004 (by the makers of Dove soap and other products), represented another departure from how women were typically depicted in ads. The print ads showed average American women of different body shapes, ages, and ethnicities who didn't weigh what models weigh; in some ads women wore underwear that real women wear, not the sexy lingerie some men fantasize about women wearing. In one version of the ads, women who did not possess "perfect" bodies posed nude individually—discreetly nude (meaning more private parts were masked by body positioning). These ads (including enlarged images attached to buildings in Times Square) starred "real women with real bodies and real curves" in an attempt to "make more women feel beautiful every day—celebrating diversity and real women by challenging contemporary stereotypical views of beauty" (Cortese, 2008, p. 68). The Dove campaign sparked other efforts around the country, including projects to help girls develop better body image and self-esteem.

However, the Dove campaign was not without its critics (Duffy, 2010; Givhan, 2005). The main criticism related to the product the campaign was designed to sell—slimming body cream! As media scholar Rosalind Gill (2007) explains, "The irony of selling creams to slim and firm the body on the back of a campaign for real beauty was not missed by everyone" (p. 88). Another criticism surrounded the fact that the women in the ads were in relatively good shape; none were extremely thin, none were significantly overweight, none were physically disabled, so how "real" was "real"?

Some companies have made serious, laudable, relatively successful attempts to communicate to female consumers that they understand them and find them important—but these companies are the exception, not the rule. When men and women appear together in ads, women still are too often portrayed less than fully clothed and in sexy, flirtatious, and vulnerable ways. We don't see sexism lurking at every turn, but we do worry about the prevalence of sexual images of women being used to sell all kinds of products—especially products geared to men.

ADVERTISING'S EFFECTS ON WOMEN   Sexist and stereotypical ad portrayals have severe negative effects on women (Aubrey, 2007; Durham, 2009a; Harper & Tiggemann, 2007; Levine & Murnen, 2009; Stankiewicz & Rosselli, 2008; Zimmerman & Dahlberg, 2008). Kilbourne (1998) states: "A woman is conditioned to view her face as a mask and her body as an object, as *things* separate from and more important than her real self, constantly in need of alteration, improvement, and disguise. She is made to feel dissatisfied with and ashamed of herself, whether she tries to achieve 'the look' or not. Objectified constantly by others, she learns to objectify herself" (p. 129). Studies continue to reveal our culture's obsession with women's thinness and beauty, as reflected in advertising

(Chambers & Alexander, 2007; Cortese, 2008; Gill, 2011; Raiten-D'Antonio, 2010; Wykes & Gunter, 2005). The results are consistent and overwhelming:

1. Women receive many times more advertising messages about thinness and body shape than men.
2. The volume of these ads in prominent magazines and on television is staggering.
3. The trend toward severe thinness is inescapable in ads, creating an ever-widening gap between the weight of an average American woman and the ideal.
4. Thin female models are perceived to be more attractive than average weight or overweight models in ads.
5. The majority of African American models, including supermodels Tyra Banks and Naomi Campbell, are slim, although the thinness standard isn't as extreme among black women as for other racial and ethnic groups.
6. The pressure to be thin is not as great for men as for women, as evidenced by the higher number of average weight and overweight male models in ads, in comparison to females.
7. Young women's images of their bodies become distorted when they are presented with images of ideal body shape. (Many simply believe that they cannot be thin enough, and they suffer poor health and self-esteem loss trying to achieve the media's unreal perfect body.)
8. The term *heroin chic* was coined late in the 1990s to describe the gaunt, unhealthy look of many top fashion models. Kate Moss was the poster child for this look.

We've all heard the phrase "sex sells," but women's sex *really* sells, as ads prove time and time again. Many of us have grown weary of women's bodies and sexuality being used in every possible way to draw a viewer's or reader's attention and sell a product—*any* product.

MIXED SIGNALS CREATE CONFUSION   People are confused by images in the media; at times, this confusion has consequences for their relationships and communication. Many men wonder if women want to be treated as equals and professionals, as traditional helpmates and caregivers, or as sex kittens, because the media readily provide continuous, seemingly acceptable images of each.

One source of confusion is the cover pictures on women's magazines and the contradictory headlines describing the magazine's contents. Extremely thin female models, their breasts squeezed into outfits to create cleavage, appear on the covers—opposite headings such as "How to Get Your Boss to Take You Seriously." In ads found in various print sources, the images of women create a paradox that is only compounded by reading the copy accompanying the ad (Jackson, 1991; Kuczynski, 2000). For example, an ad meant to depict a typical day in the life of a professional career woman shows her dressed in a business suit with briefcase in hand, but the copy says she'd really like to be anywhere but at work; she's on the job, but actually thinking of her man.

Probably the best, and most insidious, example of mixed-signal advertising has been perpetrated by the makers of Virginia Slims cigarettes, whose ads first emerged during the heyday of the women's liberation movement. The early television and print ads were done in sepia tones, to look like old-fashioned movie reels or still photographs. In the TV ads, a male voice-over described how some women in history got into trouble for being rebellious and smoking. These ads then cut to modern-day images of women, accompanied by the motto (originally sung) "You've come a long way, baby, to get where you got to today!" The point was to illustrate how women's status had improved in American society because women were finally allowed to smoke.

Ads in the 80s and 90s depicted women doing fun, active things (as active as you could be with a cigarette in your hand), while employing the language of liberation. Tobacco ad campaigns have been criticized by healthcare officials, media critics, political activists, and feminists outraged by the fact that tobacco companies make mild attempts to show concern over health issues, all the while packaging their products as though they epitomize liberation, adventure, youthfulness, and machismo (Morrison, Krugman, & Park, 2008; Murphy-Hoefer, Hyland, & Rivard, 2010; Smith & Malone, 2003). In point of fact, their products actually enslave and age people.

Studs in Suits: Male Depiction in Advertising

Just as there are female stereotypes in advertising, male stereotypes appear as well (Katz, 2011; MacKinnon, 2003). More research has been conducted on women's depictions, but several studies provide interesting revelations about men in advertisements.

CORPORATE SUCCESS, GREAT DAD, AND ANGRY GUY   Studies in the 1980s showed that men were typically portrayed in ads as dominant, successful professionals in business settings or engaged in fun activities in settings away from home (Courtney & Whipple, 1983). They were still portrayed this way in 1990s ads, but a new trend depicted men involved in domestic tasks such as taking care of children, preparing family meals, and doing household chores (Craig, 1992; Richmond-Abbott, 1992). In addition, men were more often presented as sex objects and in decorative, nonfunctional roles that had no relation to the product being sold (Lin, 1997).

While some think ads depicting men as sex objects are realistic and humorous, others see them as male-bashing. A Hyundai ad from a few years ago was particularly memorable, if for no other reasons than its blatant role reversal and sexual innuendo—and the fact that it was hugely successful. In the ad, two women critique men who get out of fancy sports cars, saying that one "must be compensating for a shortcoming." When a man arrives in a sensible Hyundai, one woman says to the other, admiringly, "I wonder what he's got under *his* hood." Researcher Philip Patterson (1996) identified this trend, terming such ads *power babe commercials* in which "women enjoy the upper hand over men" (p. 93). He is critical of two prominent stereotypes of men in advertising, what he calls *Rambo* and *Himbo depictions:* "The image of men in advertising is either that of a 'Rambo,' solo conqueror of all he sees, or a 'Himbo,' a male bimbo" (p. 94). These stereotypical, overdrawn images of men persist today.

Another trend emerged in late 1990s advertising and has expanded in this new century—"angry guy" portrayals. Media scholar Jackson Katz (2011) describes a trend toward depictions of violent white males in advertising for a wide range of products. Katz detects recurring themes in magazine advertising: "The angry, aggressive, white, working-class male as antiauthority rebel; violence as genetically programmed male behavior; the use of military and sports symbolism to enhance the masculine identification and appeal of products; and the association of muscularity with ideal masculinity" (p. 263). He cites examples such as white rap artist Eminem, who epitomizes the angry white male with attitude, shown most often scowling, overly serious, or in violent poses. Other common depictions include men in uniforms with their weapons or gear—both military and sporting.

A few years ago, we got a letter from a professor whose class used this textbook and found an omission in the media chapter. They didn't see a list of male stereotypes that corresponded to Courtney and Whipple's list of depictions of women. So the class created one, and we think it's well worth reprinting. According to Lynn Wells' students at Saddleback College in Mission Viejo, California (to whom we're grateful), male depictions in ads include the following:

1. Stud Cowboy, like the Marlboro Man
2. Jock, who can perform in all sports
3. Handyman, who can fix anything
4. Young and hip, as in sports drinks ads
5. Handsome ladies' man, as in beer commercials
6. Kind and grandfatherly, as in insurance ads
7. Professional, knowledgeable
8. Couch potato man
9. Blue-collar worker, sometimes seen as a sex symbol
10. Androgynous, as in Calvin Klein ads
11. Romantic, drink coffee man
12. Fonzie type, Joe Cool
13. Helpless, as in the "Got Milk" commercials
14. Just a kid, who needs a woman to save him

Because Mager and Helgeson's (2011) research we cited earlier found some subtle shifts in women's depictions in magazine ads over the last 50 years, let's revisit this study for what can be learned about men's depictions. Although women still appear in sexually suggestive poses in ads with more frequency, men appearing in such poses is on the rise, alluding to an increasing sexualization of men in advertising.

Mager and Helgeson also studied ads that display only body parts, rather than the entire figure of a person; for many years it's been quite typical for women to appear in what's commonly termed *decapitation ads,* where their bodies are shown, but not their heads. Sometimes only limbs or other limited sections of women's bodies are depicted, emphasizing their sexuality or vulnerability. Media scholar Anthony Cortese (2008) terms these "body chopping" or *dismemberment ads,* where bodies are hacked apart or body parts are shown immersed in or emerging from inanimate objects (p. 42). Interestingly enough, male decapitation or dismemberment ads didn't increase over the 50-year-period Mager and Helgeson examined; perhaps the American public is still squeamish about seeing a man's genital area highlighted in an ad or his head cut off, such that the focus is on his body. Perhaps advertisers don't believe such a depiction will sell a product, whereas focusing on women's breasts or crotches and depicting them headless (sending a message that a woman's body is more important than her brain) are still perceived as effective ad techniques.

One final result is interesting: Mager and Helgeson found that, while depictions of men in executive roles still occurred more frequently than such depictions of women, the rate of occurrence decreased over time. In the past, men were often shown in dominant positions, as authorities, alongside women who received their instruction. This dynamic is less obvious in today's ads. The research didn't specify what role depictions were starting to replace the portrayal of men as business executives and leaders, but it's a safe bet that depictions have broadened to show men more often in varying roles, such as parents, spouses, average citizens, and so forth.

Hot Button Issue

"Old Spice Man, the Man Your Man Could Smell Like"

We realize that the "Old Spice Man" TV ads could be long gone from the airways and the Internet by the time you read this chapter, but the ads have caused a stir and they're worth discussing. (You'll probably be able to find them on YouTube for many years to come.)

The day after the 2010 Super Bowl, Old Spice (a long-standing men's aftershave brand) debuted its "Old Spice Man" in the form of Isaiah Mustafa, a deep-voiced, well-toned, usually shirtless or towel-clad, light-skinned African American male (and former NFL player) who looks to be in his late twenties or early thirties. The first ads were inexpensive to create, as ads go, but received such acclaim and exposure that a series of them were developed and launched through all sorts of media, including viral video (Neff, 2010a, 2010b). From most people's perspectives, the ads are hilarious, depicting Old Spice Man riding a horse backwards, appearing out of a pile of sand (guitar in tow, puppies inside guitar), or stepping out of the shower with chain saw in hand. In each ad, he generally looks perfect because, of course, he uses Old Spice body wash. (Even though you can't smell him through your TV set, computer, or smartphone, you just *know* he smells great—that's part of the power of the ads.) Some ads encourage men to "Smell like a man, man," whereas the ads aimed at female consumers suggest that the Old Spice Man is "the man your man could smell like" if only he'd "stop using lady-scented body wash." Part of the comedic effect of the ads is the pretense that Old Spice Man is a "man's man," shaming other men into trying to smell better and have better hygiene; some believe he represents hypermasculinity, while others view the ads as parody, in some ways mocking masculinity and encouraging women to take charge and buy the products they want their men to use.

No matter your take on the ads, the campaign's success is undeniable. Old Spice body wash sales increased 55 percent in the three-month period after the ads debuted; however, some believe the increase was the result of a two-for-one coupon the company offered during the same time period. According to entrepreneur and author Gary Vaynerchuk (2011), the ads are evidence of what he calls a "Thank You Economy," one in which corporations should rely less on traditional marketing blizzards to improve sales and more on personal, customer-driven approaches using social media and innovative techniques, like the Old Spice campaign employed so effectively. He cites cutting-edge techniques such as Old Spice making effective use of Twitter and Facebook, asking consumers to submit questions to Old Spice Man as part of a contest. People voted for their favorite questions, and then "Old Spice Man" responded online to winners' questions. Millions of people have viewed the ads on TV and online.

What do you think of the ads? Do they reinforce male stereotypes or make fun of them? Do they represent a smart departure from traditional ad campaigns, or just the latest retreads of ads we've seen for years, ones that exploit sexuality to sell a product?

ADVERTISING'S EFFECTS ON MEN   Most people prefer not to relate to men as though they were stereotypes. But it's hard not to wonder if men actually want such treatment, given that so many macho images of men still pervade many forms of media, from magazine ads depicting rugged men in their pickup trucks to infomercials pushing the latest exercise equipment (Gentry & Harrison, 2010).

If you're a male reader, what's your reaction to an ad in which a scantily clad man is depicted as a sex object, as some would argue Calvin Klein, Versace, and other magazine ads do? Or how about the now-infamous Diet Coke ad from the early 1990s, in which a hunky, sweaty construction worker removed his shirt and downed a Diet Coke to the delight of the women working next door, who watched the clocks for their "Diet Coke break"? For our male readers, do you notice male-objectifying ads more or in a different way than, for example, Victoria's Secret lingerie ads, which began appearing on television in the late 1990s? Do these ads make you feel badly about yourself in comparison to some stud women swoon over? Or do you find them refreshing and realistic because men are shown as sexy and women show their "appreciation"?

Some scholars believe that men are now the targets of an all-out assault on self-esteem, mainly because the market for assaulting women's self-esteem—which forces them to buy products and services ranging from simple beauty remedies to full-scale plastic surgery—is saturated, profits maxed out (Lin, 1997). We continue to see a significant increase in ads showing barely clothed men with perfect bodies, skin, hair, and teeth, touting the products and services that can get men that way (Feasey, 2009). These ads encourage men to think of themselves as sex objects (Dobosz, 1997). *Washington Monthly* magazine editor Michelle Cottle (2003) admits to a guilty pleasure in reading *Men's Health* magazine. In her article entitled, "Turning Boys into Girls," Cottle describes a trend she sees in men's advertising:

> *Men's Health* . . . and a handful of others like it, are leveling the playing field in a way that *Ms.* can only dream of. With page after page of bulging biceps and Gillette jaws, robust hairlines and silken skin . . . *Men's Health* is on its way to making the male species as insane, insecure, and irrational about physical appearance as any *Cosmo* girl. (p. 68)

Even more perplexing are the increasing number of ads for "sexual enhancement products," such as Viagra and Cialis. One particularly bizarre TV ad that ran in the early 2000s featured Mike Ditka (renowned macho man and former coach of the Chicago Bears), who encouraged men to "get back in the game"—meaning the game of having sex. The warnings that tend to come with such ads—the suggestion that men taking the drug and maintaining an erection for more than four hours should go to an emergency room—are especially jarring. More recently, former Dallas Cowboys coach Jimmy Johnson appeared in a TV ad, touting the wonders of Extenz, a male enhancement pill. (What's up with former NFL coaches and penis products?)

You may find you've become so desensitized to sexually objectifying ads—of both men and women—that you hardly notice them anymore. Since sexually objectifying female ads don't seem to be going away, do you think it's a form of equality to sexually objectify men in ads? Do ads like these develop or increase in men an irrational concern with appearance, image, and sex appeal?

LESSONS FROM THE SMALL SCREEN: TELEVISION AND GENDER

Ninety-nine percent of American households contain at least one television set; most have more than one set (Vivian, 2011). Recording—primarily through the use of *black box technologies,* such as TiVo and DVR services that often come with local cable providers—has

Remember . . .

Stereotype: Recurring media depiction that places people into narrowly defined categories

Gender Stereotypes: Recurring depictions of men and women that place them into narrowly defined roles

Heroin Chic: Term coined for the gaunt, unhealthy look of some top fashion models

Power Babe Commercials: Ads that depict women objectifying or enjoying the upper hand over men

Rambo Depiction: Male stereotype in advertising, in which a man is depicted as a conquering hero

Himbo Depiction: Male stereotype in advertising, in which a man is depicted as a bumbling idiot or fool—a male bimbo

Decapitation Ads: Ads in which people's bodies are shown, but without heads or with their heads cut out of the picture

Dismemberment Ads: Ads in which only people's limbs or sections of their bodies are shown

greatly expanded television's impact. Approximately 36 million American homes now contain DVRs, which shows a shift from VCRs and even DVD players (Rice, 2009). These technologies allow consumers to record and watch cable and network programming when convenient—a practice known as *time shifting*. Since we can now watch TV shows on our computers, iPads, and phones, it seems reasonable that television's depiction of the sexes will continue to have an impact on the viewing audience (Lotz, 2006, 2008).

Television: Mirroring Reality or Creating It?

Television is a rapidly changing industry; it's likely that some of the TV shows we refer to in this chapter will be off the air when you read this material. But one thing will remain—a chicken-or-egg argument about whether the media merely reflect what is happening in society or actually create the issues and trends that then become relevant in society. Perhaps it's a bit of both.

On the "media reflect reality" side, one could argue that the economic pressures and changing lifestyles of young professionals in the twenty-first century are reflected in various network and cable programs. On the other hand, many researchers support the "media drive or create culture" view, believing that television actually expands viewers' range of behaviors. Probably the best example of this view was the hit series *Seinfeld*, which media scholars believe at once expanded language and created a whole new way of relating to friends, jobs, parents, lovers, and life in general (Stark, 2000a). Yet another school of media thought contends that television programming, for the most part, neither reflects nor creates reality; rather, its exaggerated portrayals and overly dramatized situations (including the drama that emerges in "reality" programs) are nowhere near the realities of most people's lives. (Maybe any of *The Real Housewives* series are good examples of this perspective?) In this view, TV programs and other forms of media serve purely as escapism and entertainment for consumers, as uses and gratifications theory suggests.

While it's beyond our focus in this book to delve deeply into the effects of television viewing on children and adolescents, research continues to show that TV has a lot of power to shape girls' and boys' visions of themselves and their notions about how men and women behave (Ata, Ludden, & Lally, 2006; Aubrey & Harrison, 2004; Douglas, 2010a, 2010b; Hust, Brown, & L'Engle, 2008; McCabe & Ricciardelli, 2005; Strasburger, 2005; Tiggemann, 2005; Tolman, Kim, Schooler, & Sorsoli, 2007; Ziegler, 2007). Whether as an adult you tend to relate more to traditional portrayals or to groundbreaking characterizations of the sexes, one implication is that our communication with relational partners, as well as attitudes about gender and behavior in relationships, is influenced, in varying degrees, by TV programming.

One way we used to "slay the beast" of discussion about men's and women's TV portrayals was to contrast prime-time versus daytime television. Now, with the greater availability of viewing TV programs through new technology, we can time shift and watch just about anything just about anytime we want. The distinctions between day and night aren't as relevant. To help focus our discussion, let's think of prime-time programming as more of the first-run shows, network and cable, that air primarily in the evening, many of which are replayed all hours of the day and night.

> *I find television very educational. Every time someone switches it on I go into another room and read a good book.*
> —*Groucho Marx,*
> *actor/comedian*

A further distinction and clarification: To talk intelligently about women's and men's portrayals on television these days, you can't just think in terms of scripted TV shows, like sitcoms and dramas. With the meteoric rise in popularity of reality TV, how the sexes are represented on these shows is fascinating to examine as well.

Men in Prime-Time Television

Have men's depictions in prime-time TV changed much in recent years? Would it surprise you to know that the answer to that question is "not much"? Interestingly, although the methods of producing, delivering, and consuming TV programming have changed dramatically, research shows that male depictions have not changed all that much. Sure, images of macho, Marlboro-type men have diminished, but that trend has been occurring for a few decades now.

Media scholar Marvin Moore (1992) surveyed family depictions in American prime-time television from 1947 to 1990 and found that 94 percent of families in the programs were white and two-thirds involved the traditional profile of a married couple, with or without children. Media scholars since that time have found that little has changed: Sitcoms and dramas are still primarily about white, young to middle-aged, middle-class America, with male roles outnumbering female roles (Butsch, 2011; Elasmar, Hasegawa, & Brain, 1999; Harwood & Anderson, 2002). These shows are also highly *heteronormative*, meaning that they present heterosexuality as the norm or predominant form of human relations (Kim et al., 2007). Research shows that men on TV are still primarily portrayed in work-related roles, whereas female characters "continue to inhabit interpersonal roles involved with romance, family, and friends" (Lauzen, Dozier, & Horan, 2008, p. 200).

In 2010, *Entertainment Weekly* magazine published its ten best TV shows of the year; five shows featured male leads (*Breaking Bad, Mad Men, Justified, Friday Night Lights,* and *Men of a Certain Age*). The remaining shows featured mixed-sex casts (*Modern Family, Fringe*) or were female-dominated (*The Good Wife, 30 Rock, Parks and Recreation*; Tucker, 2010). (As an aside, the worst series of the year on the list predominantly featured women, including *Kate Plus 8, Losing It With Jillian,* and *America's Got Talent,* primarily because of the presence of Sharon Osbourne as one of the judges.) Let's examine some of the more prominent characterizations of men in scripted programs, then explore some trends in reality programming.

SCRIPTED MEN   A kinder, gentler heterosexual male character took prominence in the 1990s and 2000s in prime-time TV, which some deemed a "feminized" version of men (Beynon, 2004; MacKinnon, 2003). These male characters weren't buffoons or wimps, but likable, masculine men who struggled to understand themselves, communicate with the women in their lives, and be better parents. The multifaceted depictions of male roles proved popular with male and female viewers alike, but the trend mostly reflected an effort to reach women viewers because women constituted (and still do) the majority of prime-time television viewers, as well as the primary shoppers for households. (Never underestimate the power of the dollar to control even such things as TV characters.)

At the same time, another trend emerged—one that media scholar Robert Hanke (1998) termed the *mock-macho sitcom.* These shows addressed "white, middle class, middle-aged men's anxieties about a feminized ideal for manhood they may not want to live up to, as well as changes in work and family that continue to dissolve separate gender spheres . . ." (p. 76). These male characters mocked machismo while preserving masculinity, in that they simultaneously presented "male comic television actors who ridicule their own lack of self-knowledge" and men who were "objects of laughter" (p. 76). Predominant in sitcoms, these depictions reflected a main male character who was typically a devoted husband and father and an equal partner to his wife, but who often goofed up and admitted he didn't understand women (Stark, 2000a). This characterization was termed the *playful patriarch* and could be found in such sitcoms as *Home Improvement* and *Roseanne* (Traube, 1992). We still see these portrayals in current scripted television programming (Walsh, Fursich, & Jefferson, 2008). Could the male characters in today's *The Big Bang Theory* be younger, geekier extensions of this kinder, gentler male character on prime-time TV? Could the overweight, bumbling-in-love character of police officer Mike in the sitcom *Mike & Molly* fit the description?

And then you have the exceptions to the trend: Enter Charlie Sheen. We're hoping that at the time this book lands in your hands, Charlie Sheen's highly publicized meltdown and subsequent firing from the highest rated comedy show on television in 2010–2011, *Two and a Half Men,* will be a distant memory. But it's hard to refute that the concept for the show was fascinating: two brothers (one womanizing cad, one nerdy but well-meaning divorcee), both involved in raising the nephew/son—the "half man." Part of what made the premise interesting was the hypermasculine Charlie Sheen character juxtaposed against the more moral Jon Cryer character, both playing a role in the development of the adolescent boy (Hatfield, 2010).

Another break-from-the-norm scripted show that has garnered positive reviews and audience interest is TNT's *Men of a Certain Age,* which we mentioned earlier as being one of *Entertainment Weekly*'s top-ranked shows in 2010. Three middle-aged friends support each other as they work through divorce, domineering father figures, professional development (or lack thereof), midlife crises, parenting challenges, and self-image problems (Steinberg, 2011). An interesting element that sets this show apart from others is the fact that one of the three friends is African American, portrayed by actor Andre

Braugher. Yes, black and white friends have coexisted peacefully on the small screen for years, but the difference here is that Braugher's character is depicted as equal to the other two white lead characters, rather than being the occasionally seen buddy, eccentric neighbor, or coworker (Miller, 2010).

One show that we predict will be off the air by the time this book goes to print, but that still deserves brief mention is MTV's scripted drama, *Skins,* which debuted in 2011 (Stack, 2011). Derivative of a British series of the same name, *Skins* depicts the sex-and-drug-filled lives of a group of nine teenagers, some of whom are in the throes of discovering their sexual identities. The "edginess" of the show has been taken to task by the watchdog group the Parents Television Council, and *Skins* has lost sponsors and viewers since its debut. It might be a stretch to call the portrayals of male characters on this show "groundbreaking," but are they realistic depictions of young male angst in a complicated twenty-first century? Is the realism too realistic for American audiences?

"REAL" MEN   We put the word *real* in quotes because we want to use the term loosely. We're certainly not the first to suggest that reality television programming is anything *but* real, even though it purports to be and sells itself as such. Much of reality's "real" moments are scripted, rehearsed, shot, re-shot, and highly edited to create a desired effect (Pozner, 2010a; Skeggs & Wood, 2008). Critics, as well as proponents, of reality TV are everywhere, offering all kinds of contentions about this form of "guilty pleasure," "manipulated reality," or "constructed fiction" and its effects on our culture (Andrejevic, 2003; Dubrofsky, 2006; Funt, 2009; Moorti & Ross, 2004; Ouellette & Hay, 2008; Pozner, 2010b). But we cannot escape one reality: Reality TV is not a fad; it is a force unto itself in television programming around the world, not just in the United States.

Some reality TV shows revolve predominantly around men (e.g., *Cops, Dog the Bounty Hunter, Deadliest Catch*) and some around women (e.g., *The Real Housewives of* [insert city here], *Say Yes to the Dress, What Not to Wear*); many are ensemble-based (the oldest of modern reality shows, MTV's *The Real World; Survivor; Top Chef; The Bachelor/ Bachelorette* series; *American Idol; The Apprentice*) (Bierly, 2011; Jordan, 2011; Kinnick & Parton, 2005). Some shows focus on family life—the roles of husband and wife, interactions with children, and occasional complications from extended family members (e.g., *Supernanny, Wife Swap, Extreme Makeover: Home Edition*) (Ferguson, 2010; Palmer, 2011).

In terms of how reality TV viewers process these shows, in particular dating shows, a study of college students revealed that most subjects (men and women alike) were occasional or frequent viewers of at least one of these shows (Zurbriggen & Morgan, 2006). Members of both sexes revealed that they viewed the shows primarily for pure entertainment value, but male participants reported a "learning motive," meaning they watched the shows to learn something about dating and women. Students who viewed more of these shows also tended to endorse a sexual double standard (meaning they held different expectations of men and women), to believe that men are more highly sex driven than women, to heavily emphasize physical appearance in dating, and to view dating as a "game" (p. 1).

Interestingly enough, the men of reality TV aren't often the subject of research; much more research has been conducted on how women are depicted and how they behave, with considerable heteronormative focus on the interplay between female and male personalities. (Does this mean that reality TV is becoming the province of women?) Recent studies have focused on two trends regarding male depiction in reality TV: dating shows and shows depicting fatherhood.

Media scholar Dana Cloud (2010) describes reality dating shows as an "irony bribe," meaning that viewers can see the programs as both "'real' and 'not-real,' and therefore worth viewing and worthless at the same time" (p. 413). Viewers can participate in the fantasy of romance while voyeuristically standing apart or outside the fantasy, not taking it seriously. (Sometimes this effect is referred to as the ultimate fly-on-the-wall phenomenon.) Cloud uses Brad Womack's first appearance on *The Bachelor* as a case in point; Womack's first attempt didn't end in an engagement with one of the contestants, unlike his second appearance on the show, which culminated in an engagement. In *The Bachelor*, men *act* while women *appear*, according to Cloud; the bachelor has his pick among a bevy of young, attractive women (which Cloud calls the "harem") who clamor for his attention and compete to be his final selection. Men are actors, women are reactors. The power dynamic is apparent, in that the bachelor gets to choose, whereas "the women's role is that of supplicant, waiting passively for the redemption of romance" (p. 420).

Of course, when a woman takes the lead, as in seasons of *The Bachelorette,* the roles are reversed, with a bachelorette as chooser and a group of men as chosen (or rejected). But the power dynamics don't seem to be parallel, meaning the power of public rejection by the bachelorette seems somehow different than when the bachelor dismisses the women. Perhaps the difference lies in the postrejection confessionals—the brief self-disclosures by rejected contestants as they exit the house or ride off in the backseat of a limo. Rejected female contestants tend to be very emotional, with tears and declarations of themselves as "losers." In contrast, rejected male contestants' speeches tend toward demonstrations of anger and protestations of bravado (as in, "she doesn't know what she's missing"), with only a very few "what's wrong with me" speeches.

A second trend in male depiction in reality TV surrounds men's roles as fathers, with research focusing specifically on black fatherhood post-*The Cosby Show.* Media scholar Debra Smith (2008) examined the intersections of race, class, and sex in her analysis of two reality TV shows: *Run's House* and *Snoop Dogg's Father Hood.* Smith contends that *Cosby* supplanted negative media representations of black families with an image of an upper-middle-class family whose culture and values served to "dignify Blackness on television" (p. 393). In *Run's House,* Joseph Simmons (formerly of the rap group Run-DMC) is a successful East Coast rapper, so successful that he is "housebound," meaning that his professional accomplishments afford him plenty of time at home with his family (Smith, 2008, p. 399). One of the driving forces in the show is Simmons' efforts to combat absent fatherhood among black families by role modeling how a strong father figure should behave. Snoop Dogg's presence in the Broadus family is portrayed more blatantly (and some would argue, more crudely) than Simmons', as Snoop's success as a West Coast rapper is displayed in possessions, the people he knows and entertains in his home, and the time he chooses to spend with his children rather than working on his career.

In contrast to many scripted TV shows, the success of the male leads on these reality TV shows is illustrated by the fruits of their labor, rather than how they behave in professional contexts. As she concludes her analysis, Smith explains, "This examination of Black fathers in reality television confirms, contradicts, and challenges images of Black fathers that exist in our culture" (p. 407). A good deal of research continues to examine the intersections of race, gender, and class in reality TV programming (Bell-Jordan, 2008; Boylorn, 2008; Brooks & Hebert, 2006; Dubrofsky & Hardy, 2008; Hopson, 2008; Orbe, 2008; Squires, 2008).

Women in Prime-Time Television

In the 1970s, media scholar Gayle Tuchman and colleagues described women's presence on prime-time television as a "symbolic annihilation" (Tuchman, Daniels, & Benet, 1978). Several studies examining trends in women's portrayals in prime-time television programming offer evidence that the annihilation is far from over (Lindsey, 2003). As we alluded to previously in our discussion of men on television, male roles outnumber female roles on TV, and women are still primarily portrayed interpersonally, meaning in connection to other people, rather than their work or social/political issues (Butsch, 2011; Harwood & Anderson, 2002; Lauzen, Dozier, & Horan, 2008).

SCRIPTED WOMEN   Media scholars have explored women's roles in prime-time television for several decades, noting various trends. We referred to Marvin Moore's (1992) analysis of television families in the 1980s in the earlier section on men and prime-time TV; Moore was critical of how women were portrayed during this time period. While TV programs depicted men in nontraditional roles, communicating that men had the freedom to choose different paths for themselves without societal sanctions, women's changing roles in society were largely ignored. The reality was that huge numbers of women entered the workforce during the 80s, but televised representations of them were few and far between. Moore cited *The Cosby Show*'s Claire Huxtable as an example; at the time, this show was the most successful sitcom of the decade. Claire Huxtable was a successful lawyer, but rarely mentioned her job or was depicted in legal settings.

Greenberg and Collette (1997) examined thirty years worth of TV programming, noting women's underrepresentation, traditional depictions (e.g., wives and mothers), and general youthfulness. Olson and Douglas (1997) analyzed the top ten most popular prime-time American sitcoms over a forty-year span and found that both the quantity and quality of women's roles in these programs declined. Signorielli and Bacue (1999) conducted a similar study, focusing on TV dramas airing during the period from 1967 through 1998. They found that although women's presence in prime-time programming increased over time, women were still greatly underrepresented compared to their numbers in the U.S. population, were depicted as younger than their male counterparts, and appeared more in sitcoms than dramas, which was a disadvantage, given that dramas garner more respect and are taken more seriously by the viewing public. Signorielli and Bacue (1999) found one departure from earlier studies: In the more recent years under investigation, more women were presented as employed outside the home, in more prestigious occupations, and more frequently in traditionally male jobs (e.g., law enforcement, medicine) than in the past.

Research also examined how the few contemporary working female characters on TV dealt with the tension between their personal and professional lives—the "juggling" issue (Douglas, 1995b; Dow, 1996; Vande Berg & Streckfuss, 1992). Studies found that although many female characters were depicted as having both successful careers and personal lives, plot lines centered around their love lives (meaning their men; Japp, 1991; Steenland, 1995). One notable example from this period of research is the still-popular show, *Desperate Housewives*, which offers depictions of working women more focused on their personal lives and intrigue on Wisteria Lane than their careers (Hill, 2010; Merskin, 2011; Sharp, 2011). Although the tension between personal and professional constitutes a reality for many contemporary women (even more so today), the relational elements in female TV characters' lives receive more emphasis, sending a message that no matter how professional or successful a woman becomes, what matters most, what really makes a woman acceptable or unacceptable in American consciousness, is her relationship with a man.

Some breakthrough roles emerged for women on television during this time. Although action–adventure television remains a male-dominated form of entertainment, action–adventure roles for women increased, through the vehicle of such shows as *Star Trek: Voyager, Xena: Warrior Princess, Buffy the Vampire Slayer,* and *Alias* (Kim, 1995; Signorielli & Bacue, 1999). Sitcom characters like Roseanne Connor and Murphy Brown broke new ground for women, challenging the social norms of femininity and addressing the "juggling" aspect in a new way (Douglas, 1995a; Krolokke & Sorenson, 2006; Morrison, 2006; Rowe, 1990).

But probably no other women's TV depictions represented breakthroughs like the four female characters of *Sex and the City* (Gerhard, 2011; Schwartz, 2009). Scholars and media critics view this show as an example of mixed-signal TV programming (Baxter, 2009; Lorie, 2011; Paglia, 2008). On the one hand, viewers got strong messages of women's liberation—that it's fine (even preferable) to be single and sexually active, even experimental; to have and raise a baby on your own (or choose not to have children); to break up with men who aren't right for you instead of feeling pressure to marry; and to divorce if you're unhappy (Soll, 2008). On the other hand, the four central characters focused more on their romances than their careers or other aspects of their lives—again, a throwback to a more conventional depiction of women. Although friendship was the primary focus of the show, the almost constant subject of conversation and plot lines was men—how to get them, what to do with them, whether or not to keep them, and when it was time to move on to the next one. By the time the first full-length *Sex and the City* movie came out, all four characters were in committed heterosexual relationships, albeit in various stages of success.

The point is not that men aren't important to women, but the constant heteronormativity and the message reinforced about men's importance in women's lives doesn't seem to be in balance with how successful men are portrayed on prime-time TV shows. What one might conclude from this analysis is that what counts most in a woman's life is her relationship to a man, whereas what counts in a man's life is how successful his career is. Is that the current reality, both on television and in our society?

Media scholar Susan Douglas (2009), writing about women's television portrayals for *The Shriver Report* (which we reference several times in this book), suggests the following "profound contradictions between image and reality currently facing us":

1. Women's occupations on television that bear scant resemblance to the jobs women actually hold;
2. Successful, attractive women journalists in front of the camera that masks how vastly outnumbered women are by men as experts and pundits;
3. The hype of the non-trend of mothers "opting out" of the workplace rather than the real lives of mothers as breadwinners;
4. Young women in America portrayed as shallow, cat-fighting sex objects obsessed with their appearances and shopping;
5. The dismissive coverage of powerful, successful women versus their real achievements;
6. The denigration of feminism—which is a movement important to the well-being of men, women, and children—as somehow irrelevant to the realities of the workplace and family life in the twenty-first century. (p. 2)

Douglas is critical of the gap between what girls and women see in the media and how the vast majority of them live their lives. This gap is important to consider and attempt to rectify, because media don't simply mirror reality: As Douglas points out, "Media are funhouse mirrors that magnify certain kinds of people, values, attitudes, and issues, while minimizing others or even rendering them invisible" (p. 3).

However, other research refutes the trends Douglas critiques. Media scholars Shanahan, Signorielli, and Morgan (2008) examined prime-time TV programming over a three-decade period and reported significant changes in how women were portrayed. They found that, over time, women's presence on TV increased, they were more likely to be portrayed in traditionally male professions, and the number of married women portrayed approached that of male characters (whereas the trend used to be that most male characters were married, whereas most female characters were single).

Media scholar Nancy Signorielli, whose work in the 1990s we referenced earlier, continues to study TV roles for women, but through a lens of race and ethnicity (Signorielli, 2009a, 2009b). In a content analysis of prime-time TV broadcasts that aired in the decade of the 2000s, Signorielli (2009b) found an increase in the number of white characters and a decrease in black and Hispanic characters. She also found that although black characters' representation paralleled black Americans' numbers in the population, their media representation was one of segregation and isolation, especially for black women. Signorielli concluded that "prime time network broadcast programs at the end of this decade were less racially representative of the U.S. population than they were at the beginning of the decade" (p. 323).

Signorielli (2009a) also studied prime-time network TV shows airing between 1997 and 2006 for their depictions of the sexes and races in various occupations. She found a high level of segregation in the programs, meaning few programs depicted racial diversity and parity within their casts. Only one in five characters were people of color. When factoring sex and race together, black women fared the poorest, appearing less frequently and in mostly racially segregated programs, leading Signorielli again to conclude that black women were isolated in prime-time TV programming. In terms of occupations, professionalism, and prestige, black female characters fared poorly; black women workers held the least prestige in their jobs and were the group least likely to be depicted as professionals. Perhaps new programs slated for the fall of 2011 will help make up some of this ground. Three network shows will premier with African American actresses in lead roles: Angela Bassett in ABC's police drama *Identity,* Taraji P. Henson in CBS's drama *Person of Interest,* and Kerry Washington as a powerful publicist in ABC's *Damage Control* (Armstrong & Jensen, 2011). (It remains to see if these programs will survive on air by the time you're reading this page.)

"REAL" WOMEN   Let's begin this discussion by focusing on one of the older, yet still popular, forms of reality (or unscripted) TV programming: the talk show. Because there are between twenty and thirty nationally syndicated talk shows on the air in any given year in the United States, the impact of these shows cannot be denied (Cragin, 2010; Peck, 2006; Wood, 2009). Although talk show audiences were and are still dominated by women viewers, particularly daytime shows, the male audience has grown steadily since the 1990s (Albiniak, 2010; Henson & Parameswaran, 2008; Shattuc, 2004). Some suggest that this growth relates to the inclusion (and encouragement) of more conflict and controversy on such programs as *The Jerry Springer Show* and *Maury;* actually, the trend may have more to do with recession-induced unemployment rates for men and the rise in stay-at-home fathers.

The original modern TV talk show, *The Phil Donahue Show*, revolutionized by *The Oprah Winfrey Show* (and others), provided a platform for discussions of social issues; some would argue that these shows, and daytime talk shows in general, are more about women's issues than social issues (Heaton & Wilson, 1995; Shattuc, 1997; Stark, 2000b). Feminist media critic Roseann Mandziuk (1991) studied daytime TV talk shows, discovering that the intimacy of the topics, discussion, and revelations from guests, hosts, and audience members parallels a cultural feminine stereotype of women as sensitive, nurturing, relational, and responsive. In addition, Mandziuk exposed an agenda-setting function, concluding that such shows actually instruct women as to what they should worry about. Topics like "the husband who likes to wear his wife's lingerie" or "the girl who flirts with her sister's boyfriend" trivialize the more critical issues facing contemporary women. A greater problem ensues when the larger, general public "ghettoizes" important issues (e.g., equal pay, reproductive rights, sexual harassment, child care) by labeling them women's issues rather than societal or human issues. Treatments of the bigger issues may get suppressed in favor of topics that appeal to a wider base of audience.

But TV talk shows have morphed over time; they may still be primarily the province of women, but their scope has broadened and their reach has extended. Few will doubt the power of Oprah Winfrey (and the industry that she has become) to transform many people's lives, especially women's lives. In 2011, as Ms. Winfrey exited her long-running talk show, she debuted OWN (The Oprah Winfrey Network), her "own" cable television network which offers a wide range of television programming, including talk shows. Helen Wood (2009), author of *Talking with Television,* suggests that many viewers don't just absorb TV talk shows, they personalize and interact with them, talking back to their TVs while watching. This more active approach to television viewership creates a heightened familiarity as well as a faux intimacy with shows, guests, and hosts. In the case of *Ellen,* audience members get to dance with Ellen DeGeneres as she weaves through the crowd; no doubt many at-home viewers also dance and develop a sense that Ellen is a trusted friend (Moore, 2011; Skerski, 2007).

No matter your television viewing preferences or habits, it's doubtful that TV talk shows will go away anytime soon, mainly because they are way cheaper to produce than other formats. Whether you prefer *The View*, its newer competitor *The Talk*, or quirky cable programs like *Chelsea Lately* and *The Joy Behar Show,* the way women are depicted on these programs, how social issues get discussed, and how women and men respond to the programs will remain a subject of fascination in American culture and for scholars.

A whole host of reality TV programs beyond the talk show communicate images of women in our society. From dating shows, cooking demonstrations, model competitions, and portrayals of rampaging brides and dramatic housewives to MTV's offerings about teen pregnancy (*16 and Pregnant* and *Teen Mom*), "reality" is everywhere (Armstrong, 2010; Dubrofsky, 2009; Givhan, 2009). Whether you're a fan or a critic of reality TV, unless you've been living under a rock, you've probably seen a few shows, whether on live TV, a DVR recording, or a clip on your computer, electronic tablet, or smartphone. What kinds of messages are communicated *about* women via reality TV?

We explored reality TV a few pages back when we focused on men's depictions; it's probably not surprising for you to learn that a great deal of research has explored women and reality TV. One trend in this research is the inspection of reality TV shows that focus on women's bodies and attractiveness, including cosmetic surgery makeover shows (Banet-Weiser & Portwood-Stacer, 2006; Hasinoff, 2008; Marwick, 2010; Nabi, 2009; Stern, 2009; Tait, 2011).

Communication scholar Carolyn Davis (2008) examined perceptions of reality TV personalities, specifically contestants across several seasons of *Survivor.* Although four trends or categories emerged for male contestants, only one emerged for the women—what Davis termed "Beauty and the Beast" (p. 14). Subjects' perceptions of the women on *Survivor* focused mainly around their appearance and level of physical strength. On the "beauty" end of the scale, female contestants who were perceived as highly physically attractive were also perceived to be highly feminine, passive, and emotional; they were the ones who cried the most on the show. On the "beast" side of the equation, these women tended to be the older cast members who were perceived as masculine, less physically attractive, and more rugged looking, but who were deemed capable of performing well in challenges and surviving rough conditions. Few female contestants fell between these two polar characterizations, from the perspectives of participants in the study. These results represent a trend in perceptions of TV personalities (and, many would argue, in real life in our culture): Women are judged more harshly for their looks and attractiveness than men, whereas their intelligence or other factors are diminished.

> *When you are one of two girls who have really big breasts and a great hot body with six other women who aren't, you can say that is a handicap.*
>
> **—Jeff Probst, host of Survivor**

Other media scholars critique the fact that women on reality TV programs often use their sexuality and flirtatiousness to accomplish their goals, whether the goal is landing a fiancé (as on *The Bachelor*), winning lots of money (as on *The Amazing Race* and many other shows), or having a major event go as planned, where one is the center of attention (enter *Bridezillas*). From one viewpoint, the women in such a show as WEtv's *Bridezillas* represent a combination of femininity and control (Engstrom, 2009); from another view, they represent an unfortunate gender stereotype (Brown, 2005; Egley Waggoner, 2004). Is using whatever skills and talents you possess to achieve a desired outcome an example of being empowered to succeed, even if manipulation, deception, and narcissism emerge along the way? Is such an approach merely strategy and competitiveness, or is it a throwback to a gender stereotype—using "feminine wiles" to trick others, to outpower them?

In Chapter 1 we defined *empowerment* as power *to* rather than power *over;* it refers to a shared approach to power or control that capitalizes on the strengths of people. How empowering is reality TV for women? Researchers Cato and Dillman Carpentier (2010) explored that issue, but looked at empowerment from more of a third-wave feminist perspective that focuses more on individual choice than a social movement for the good of all women. (For a review of third-wave feminism, we refer you to the Prologue of this book.) In their study, college-aged women who held positive attitudes about reality TV embraced a form of sexual empowerment, which the authors describe as feeling good about one's sexual self and one's ability to make sexual choices, no matter what those choices are. Subjects also endorsed stereotypical roles for women in society, relating sexuality with hyperfemininity, and reported being more sexually permissive. In a nutshell, this study showed that the more favorable a woman is toward reality TV and the more she embraces notions of sexual empowerment, the more sexually permissive she tends to be, which, in turn, affects her preferences for certain reality TV shows (like *The Girls Next Door*, a show of focus in the study).

So we leave you with a mixed bag regarding reality TV programming and what it communicates about women in American culture. This genre is changing, but not going away—there's no doubt about that. Whether future depictions of men and women in reality TV will reflect what's going on in the culture, will adhere to someone's view of how the sexes should behave (the "someone" here being the people making money off the shows), or will encourage social change (i.e., be liberating from sex-role stereotypes), we'll all have to wait and see.

TV and GLBT

One final trend in TV programming warrants brief discussion before we move on to discuss other forms of media. Depending on your belief system, you may or may not welcome this trend, but it shows no signs of reversing. Whether the TV programs are scripted or reality, daytime or prime-time, the inclusion of gays, lesbians, bisexuals, and transgenders (GLBTs) is more frequent, their portrayals generally more positive and a great deal more open than in times past. Remember from Chapter 1 that sexual orientation is a subset of gender; here we talk about gender portrayals in media, specifically television, rather than biological sex.

When do you suspect that the first gay male character appeared in American television programming? 1960s? 1980s? It will likely surprise you to learn that the first "queer" character was a wrestler named Gorgeous George, who was one of the biggest media stars of the 1940s (Capsuto, 2000). We put that term *queer* in quotes because that's how Gorgeous George was referred to in our source and back in the time period when he was popular. Scholars in recent years have reclaimed the term, using it in a nonpejorative sense and generating an area of scholarship known as queer studies (Avila-Saavedra, 2009; Meyer & Kelley, 2004).

Stephen Tropiano (2002), author of *The Prime Time Closet*, provides a chronology of major milestones in television's depictions of gays and lesbians. The first major sitcom to address the subject of homosexuality was *All in the Family* in 1971, when the Neanderthal lead character of Archie Bunker learned that his buddy, a former pro football player, was gay. The first gay recurring cast member of a TV show was played by Billy Crystal on *Soap*; Crystal's character wanted a sex change operation so he could live openly with his closeted lover, who was also a pro football player. (Do we detect a trend?) Before the first episode of *Soap* aired (but after Crystal's story line was made public), the ABC network received 30,000 letters demanding cancellation.

Another television milestone that received much scholarly and popular attention occurred in 1997, when Ellen DeGeneres' character on the sitcom *Ellen* disclosed she was gay, as well as on the cover of *Time* magazine—Ellen came out both as Ellen Morgan on the show and as herself (Dow, 2001; Hubert, 2003; Moore, 2011; Reed, 2005, 2011; Shugart, 2001; Sloop, 2006). Prior to that time, gay, lesbian, and bisexual identities were implied, portrayed by secondary or ensemble characters, or depicted in ways that suggested sexuality, but without blatantly showing homosexual affection. (Transgender characters were virtually nonexistent, save the poorly drawn, overly dramatized cross-dresser on the occasional cop show.) For example, the popular drama *Melrose Place* included a central gay male character who lived at the apartment unit on Melrose. One of the most risqué scenes (for that period of television history) was when the character neared his male date for a kiss, then the camera cut away, leaving the audience to surmise that the kiss was delivered in shadows. One of the most popular prime-time dramas of the 1980s was *thirtysomething*, which broadcast a controversial scene of two bare-chested men sharing a bed, having a conversation after sex. The drama survived, even after losing $1.5 million in ad revenues after the episode aired (Tropiano, 2002). Yet another significant development was the 1998 premier of *Will & Grace,* a sitcom deemed groundbreaking for its depiction of a close friendship between a gay man and a straight woman, plus the contrasting personalities of the two central gay male characters, Will and Jack (Battles & Hilton-Morrow, 2002; Hart, 2003; Linneman, 2008; Shugart, 2003).

Fast-forward into the 2000s to witness a proliferation (some call it an explosion) of TV programming featuring gay and lesbian characters, plotlines, and issues, primarily on cable TV, such as Showtime's *Queer as Folk* and *The L Word* and Bravo's *Queer Eye for the Straight Guy.* The two dramas garnered much scholarly and popular press attention during their runs, perhaps because their inclusion on a pay cable channel's lineup granted them liberties and an openness not seen on network television. *Queer as Folk,* derived from a successful British series of the same name, focused primarily on a group of young, white male friends, their lovers, and a lesbian couple in a committed relationship who were friends with the men (Noble, 2007; Porfido, 2011).

Receiving even more notoriety than *Queer as Folk* after its debut in 2004, *The L Word* was praised for its portrayal of lesbian relationships (Aaron, 2006; Wolfe & Roripaugh, 2006). One writer for *Ms.* magazine explained: "*The L Word* broke new ground in its focus on women who love women, who live with and orient their intimate and daily lives around women. Yes, there are men on *The L Word,* and there are heterosexual relationships, but they are never the center of the action or dialogue for very long" (Renshaw, 2009, p. 59). The show was criticized for its lack of ethnic diversity and its cast of beautiful, thin, highly fashionable women (Dove-Viebahn, 2011). In the lesbian community, the women of *The L Word* were considered "femmes" as opposed to more masculine lesbian women whom many believed should have been represented on the show as well (Farr & Degroult, 2008; Pratt, 2011).

Reality TV shows have included lesbian, gay, and, on occasion, bisexual and transgender cast members for some time, such as openly gay Richard Hatch, winner of the first season of *Survivor,* and Adam Lambert (who didn't fully out himself as a gay man until after his season of *American Idol* concluded; Wypijewski, 2009). But many argue that it was the "Fab Five" of *Queer Eye* who broke the doors wide open for nonheterosexual presence in reality TV (Clarkson, 2005; Pullen, 2007; Streitmatter, 2009). Similarly to responses to scripted shows featuring nonheterosexuals, *Queer Eye* was both acclaimed and denounced. On the pro side, the show received kudos for deepening the culture's understanding of sexual and gender identity and for how positively gay and straight men related to each other (Gallagher, 2004; Hart, 2004; Weiss, 2005; Westerfelhaus & Lacroix, 2006). On the con side, the show received criticism for what some deemed stereotypical depictions of gay men as fashion-, design-, and etiquette-obsessed, as well as for conveying condescending attitudes toward straight men who desperately needed their makeover help (Pearson & Reich, 2004; Sender, 2006; Westerfelhaus & Lacroix, 2006).

We are likely still in a transitional period in terms of LGBT portrayals on television, with research on the subject producing mixed results in terms of effects on the viewing public (Calzo & Ward, 2009; Fisher, Hill, Grube, & Gruber, 2007; Ivory, Gibson, & Ivory, 2009). In the decade of the 2000s, gays, lesbians, and bisexuals were depicted on TV less frequently than they are now, but with more emphasis on their sexuality, meaning that plot lines and descriptions highlighted the fact that these characters' sexuality was something other than hetero (Fisher et al., 2007). It seems like now, the majority of casts

Remember . . .

Black Box Technology: Technology that expands the time frame in which a viewer can record a show, such as TiVo and DVRs

Time-Shifting: Using media technology to record and watch television programming when convenient

Heteronormative: Presenting heterosexuality as the norm or predominant form of human relations

Mock-Macho Sitcom: Television situation comedy with a central theme of mocking or making fun of a middle-aged man's anxieties

Playful Patriarch: Male leading character in a sitcom who is typically a devoted husband and father, but who often goofs up and admits he doesn't understand women

on TV (reality or scripted) includes a gay couple (such as *Modern Family*), or lesbian, gay, bisexual, or transgender characters (such as *The Good Wife,* with the bisexual investigator, Kalinda; *Glee,* with Kurt and Blaine's and Santana and Britney's relationships; and *Family Guy,* which depicted a character who had undergone gender reassignment; Armstrong, 2011; Dove-Viebahn, 2010; Stransky, 2010).

LESSONS FROM THE BIG SCREEN: FILM AND GENDER

Here's an interesting exercise: Imagine that you had to put together a time capsule, a snapshot of American life that represented your time on Earth, something that future generations would stumble upon and use to better understand their heritage. No doubt you'd turn to media to help you fill the capsule; no doubt you'd include some movies. The question is: Which movies would you include and why? Going even further, if only three movies would fit in the capsule, which three would you make sure got in? Would you include films from different genres, such as a western, a romance, and a horror movie? Would you include a classic like *Casablanca*, a sci-fi film like *Star Wars*, or a movie that depicts your version of typical American life? What would your choices say to future generations about your view of the sexes?

Gender in the Movies

Film has the power to communicate gender roles. It may not be blatant messages about roles women and men play in society or about how we communicate in relationships; the more subtle messages that we see and hear repeatedly are more likely to sink in on some level and affect us. On the most basic level, if a subject is dramatized on the big screen, it's there for a reason; it has to be important, right? The potential effect on children is even greater, evidenced by the significant impact of Disney films on kids (Artz, 2011; Bell, Haas, & Sells, 2008; Davis, 2005, 2007; Gilliam & Wooden, 2008; King, 2010; Towbin, Haddock, Zimmerman, Lund, & Tanner, 2004).

One phenomenon in film that stirs up a good deal of talk and controversy, not surprisingly, has to do with gender. Before we begin discussing that topic, here are a few questions for you to think about: Have you seen any movies that affected how you interact with members of the opposite sex, at work or in your social or family life? Was there a memorable movie that changed your views about women's and men's roles or that changed one of your relationships? Do you think "chick flicks" are just for girls, while action films are for guys?

ONE FOR THE CAPSULE   One memorable, outlook-altering movie is *Tootsie,* a film that to this day conjures up confused but pleasant thoughts about gender roles. If you haven't seen this movie, rent it, but until then, here's a synopsis of the plot: Dustin Hoffman plays Michael, an actor who desperately wants work, but whose opportunities are limited because of his reputation as being difficult. When his agent tells Michael that no one will hire him, Michael sets out to prove him wrong by auditioning for a role on a popular soap opera. The twist is that the role is for a woman, so Michael auditions in drag as an actress named Dorothy Michaels. After landing the part, Michael encounters a number of sticky situations because of his hidden identity. The stickiest situation arises when Michael realizes that he's falling for Julie, another actress on the soap, played in the movie by Jessica Lange. As Michael (via Dorothy) becomes good friends with Julie, he is confronted with how to admit the deception and still have a chance with Julie.

One amazing aspect of this movie is how Dustin Hoffman's portrayal of Dorothy, through the character of Michael, becomes real to viewers, so real that when Michael reveals his true identity in one of the final scenes, audiences are sad because they are going to miss Dorothy. Another fascinating aspect of this movie was that it fulfilled a fantasy for many people—walking in the opposite sex's shoes, seeing how they are treated, and getting to know an attractive member of the opposite sex without the hang-ups and pressures that often accompany romantic relationships. It was also intriguing to think about the opportunity of putting one's newfound insight into the opposite sex to work in a relationship. As Michael explained to Julie in the last scene of the movie, "I was a better man with you, as a woman, than I ever was as a man. I've just got to learn to do it without the dress."

The film *Tootsie* frames the rest of our discussion nicely, because it exemplifies the theme of *gender bending,* a term referring to media depictions in which characters' actions belie or contradict what is expected of members of their sex (Benshoff & Griffin, 2009; Daughton, 2010; Gatewood, 2001). But our use of this term is not limited only to people who have masqueraded in films as members of the opposite sex. The example of *Tootsie* serves to start our thinking, but gender bending doesn't necessarily mean actors in drag.

BUDDIES ON A DEAD-END ROAD   *Thelma & Louise* was a groundbreaking gender-bending film on many counts; it was an open-road, buddy film, but with female instead of male buddies (Glenn, 1992; Welsch, 2001). One of the most laudable effects of this film was that it sparked a great deal of discussion. In fact, it still sparks discussion. Although the film opened in May of 1991, people still talk about it, and media critics and scholars still write about it.

Female audiences for this movie had complex emotions and varied reactions (Cooper, 2000). Some cheered what they perceived to be payback, especially in a scene with a piggish trucker and his rig. At the same time, many felt odd to be applauding revenge. Besides the dominant images and "radical" behaviors of the female leads, male characters in *Thelma & Louise* were portrayed in an atypical fashion for the movies.

These portrayals led to claims of male bashing, based on contentions that the male characters were unrealistic and exaggerated, particularly because they were repeatedly vanquished by the two women.

What messages about women and men did audiences get from this movie? Some people came away thinking that women were winning some kind of war against male oppression and retaliating against unacceptable male behavior in like fashion. This is a gender-bender message taken to an extreme. However, while believing that the movie made a significant statement about relationships between men and women in the 90s, some film scholars contend that *Thelma & Louise* was not a triumphant women's rights movie. They point out that the film depicts the desperation of women in modern times—women who counter the powerlessness they feel with some very isolated, extreme actions, but who, in the long run, are still out of power in a patriarchal system (Cook, 2007; Fournier, 2006; Sturken, 2008).

GENDER BENDING, "CHICK FLICKS," AND OTHER TRENDS IN FILM   A few movies have followed in *Thelma & Louise*'s blazing trail, one being *The Brave One*, which some suggest was gender bending because of the vigilante, hero–villain role that actress Jodie Foster played (Sisco King, 2010). Other examples include *Baby Mama*, specifically Amy Poehler's portrayal of a mannish, crude character; *Mr. and Mrs. Smith*, in which Angelina Jolie played an assassin; and *Million Dollar Baby*, with Hilary Swank as a boxer (Schwarzbaum, 2008).

Would you consider *Brokeback Mountain* gender bending? Film scholars and critics are mixed on this front. Some argue yes, because of the complexity related to sexual orientation the male lead characters in the film grappled with, while others contend that labeling a film gender bending simply because of the presence of nonheterosexual characters and the depiction of the challenges they often experience is homophobic (Leung, 2008; Needham, 2009; Patterson, 2008; Spohrer, 2009). Reviewing the definition of gender bending, being attracted to a member of one's same sex and struggling with what that means isn't stepping outside what is expected for one's sex—it's a matter of sexual orientation, not biological sex.

Although we really detest the term "chick flicks," many use this term to refer to a film genre that tends to appeal more to heterosexual women than other segments of American society. Perhaps movies like the *Twilight* series, *Eat Pray Love*, and romantic comedies like *Date Night* and *Bridesmaids* fit the bill because of their emphasis on romantic relationships. But popular film critic Lisa Schwarzbaum (who both loves and hates chick flicks) contends that "Guys are the new girls," suggesting that "All they need is love, but all they get is heartache. Men have revived romantic comedies by embracing their feminine sides" (Schwarzbaum, 2008, p. 48; 2009). She cites such films as *The 40-Year-Old Virgin, Juno, Enchanted, Knocked Up*, and *Forgetting Sarah Marshall* in which male film characters exhibit feminine virtues, unafraid of emotional display. Schwarzbaum (2008) believes that "These men behaving softly (but still manfully) are no accidents of nature or of the seasonal movie release calendar. They're diplomats of unisex appeal in the latest Hollywood campaign to keep romantic comedies viable—and profitable" (pp. 48–49).

History documents the power of the media to sweep change through a culture. Will other gender-bending films that are bound to explore these issues continue to make a significant impact? Who can predict? In any case, gender-bending movies challenge us to think further and deeper, and in ways that may be new to us. They challenge us to take inventory of our attitudes and expectations about women and men. They ask us to reconsider how we communicate with one another and how we derive pleasure out of our relationships.

THE COMMUNICATIVE POWER OF PORNOGRAPHY

We usually don't begin our coverage on a topic with a disclaimer or apology, but this subject is different—*really* different. Pornography is a topic that continues to generate a great deal of research and writing, and there is no way we can do justice to that body of information in a short section within this chapter on media. Many books, articles, websites, and blogs offer insightful analyses of the pervasiveness of pornography in modern existence, its effects on how women and men are viewed in our culture, and its impact on everyday relationships. All we offer here is a snapshot—a highly condensed introduction to the topic—just to get you thinking about pornography, perhaps in a way you haven't before.

Multiple Definitions of Pornography: The Beginnings of Controversy

A specific, universally agreed-upon legal definition of pornography doesn't exist. In legal contexts, *obscenity* is the term used, but not all pornographic material meets the legal standard of obscenity (deGrazia, 1992; Tedford, 2001). Sometimes the term *erotica* is confused with pornography, although erotica pertains to material that portrays sex as an equal activity involving mutual sensual pleasure, not activity involving power or subordination (Crawford & Unger, 2004; Steinem, 1983). Strictly speaking, erotic material isn't pornographic, but material that some deem pornographic may also contain erotica. (We told you this was a complicated topic.) Scholars have offered descriptions of what the term *pornography* might encompass, even tracing the term to its linguistic roots:

> Numerous attempts have been made to define pornography and to distinguish it from what some consider its more acceptable form—"erotica." The word pornography comes from the Greek "writings of prostitutes" (*porno* = prostitute and *graphein* = to write). In recent definitions, material has been classified as pornography when the producer's intent is to elicit erotic responses from the consumer, when it sexually arouses the consumer, or when women characters are degraded or demeaned.... (Malamuth & Billings, 1984, pp. 117–118)

Malamuth and Billings (1984) go on to explain that the main difference between material deemed erotic versus pornographic relates to power aspects of sexual relations. If power is depicted as unequal between subjects in the material, then it can be considered por-nographic; if power is portrayed relatively equally, the material may be deemed simply erotic, not pornographic. Sometimes these distinctions seem arbitrary.

Catherine MacKinnon and the late Andrea Dworkin have been prominent activists on a variety of feminist fronts, especially through their writings about the serious negative effects of pornographic images on women's lives and American culture in general. MacKinnon and Dworkin made one of the most tangible contributions to the anti-pornography effort to date by trying to get an anti-pornography ordinance passed in Minnesota in the 1980s. The definition of pornography in this bill was written from the standpoint of women's

Erotica is pornography I am willing to publicy admit I like.
—Spider Robinson, sci-fi author

victimization, which is understandable given that more women than men are victimized in pornography. MacKinnon and Dworkin's definition is as follows:

> "Pornography" means the graphic sexually explicit subordination of women through pictures and/or words...that also includes one or more of the following: (1) Women are presented dehumanized as sexual objects, things, or commodities. (2) Women are presented as sexual objects who enjoy humiliation or pain...(3) Women are presented in postures or positions of sexual submission...(4) Women's body parts...are exhibited such that women are reduced to those parts. (5) Women are presented being penetrated by objects or animals. (6) Women are presented in scenarios of degradation, humiliation, injury, or torture...(as in Gillespie et al., 1994, p. 44)

MacKinnon and Dworkin contended that their definition also pertained to electronic materials containing pornographic images in the various categories, lest we think their definition covered only traditional media like magazines, films, books, and so forth. They also explained that, while their categories specifically mentioned women as subordinated through pornography, men, children, and transsexual individuals could be substituted in the language of their definition.

Representing another viewpoint is Nadine Strossen, author of the book *Defending Pornography: Free Speech, Sex, and the Fight for Women's Rights* (2000), and one of the most outspoken critics of anti-pornography efforts. In Strossen's view, "Pornography is a vague term. In short, it is sexual expression that is meant to, or does, provoke sexual arousal or desire" (p. 18). She goes on to critique others' definitions: "In recent times, the word 'pornography' has assumed such negative connotations that it tends to be used as an epithet to describe—and condemn—whatever sexually oriented expression the person using it dislikes. As one wit put it, 'What turns *me* on is erotica, but what turns *you* on is pornography!'" (p. 18). In her book, Strossen differentiates between pornography that is destructive and degrading and that which is merely sexually arousing. She still considers the latter pornography, but acceptable pornography.

In their 2009 book, *The Porning of America,* authors Carmine Sarracino and Kevin Scott discuss the complexities of pornography: "Porn is not one thing. Porn is not a single color, but a whole spectrum. Therefore, its influences on the culture are similarly varied and complex" (p. xiii). They explain their view that some pornography is definitely bad, such as child pornography; other porn they describe as "toxic waste," in reference to some very dark and violent pornography that has begun to emerge on the Internet (p. xiii). But they also suggest that amateur home videos, for example, are a more benign form of porn that American culture readily consumes, possibly with little harmful consequence.

Types of Readily Accessible Pornography

Other terms are important to discuss before going further. *Hard-core pornography* depicts or describes intercourse and/or other sexual practices (e.g., oral sex, anal sex). In *soft-core pornography,* such acts are implied but not fully or explicitly acted out on a screen or displayed on a page. However, Pamela Paul (2005), author of *Pornified: How Pornography Is Damaging Our Lives, Our Relationships, and Our Families,* contends that hard-core/soft-core distinctions are no longer relevant or particularly descriptive. In the casual world we live in where pornographic images are readily available and easily accessible and the repercussions of consuming pornography are mild, if not nonexistent, the old categorical distinctions are meaningless. Moreover, many people who consume porn nowadays do so without much explanation, embarrassment, or need for secrecy. Although people in past generations thought it wasn't nice to look at "dirty pictures," Paul suggests, "Today, pornography is so seamlessly integrated into popular culture that embarrassment or surreptitiousness is no longer part of the equation" (p. 4).

We've found two other terms that appear in research on pornography: The type of amateur porn Sarracino and Scott, as well as other scholars, discuss—real people shown having sex in real locations—has been termed *realcore* (Messina, as in Attwood, 2011). Another form of pornography is *gonzo* porn—cheaply made movies that offer no plotlines (even bad ones), but that simply string sexual scenes together (Dines & Jensen, 2004).

In the next few paragraphs, we present divergent viewpoints on pornography. But before doing so, we have some questions for you to consider: Before you dismiss or downplay this discussion because you don't believe yourself to be a consumer of pornography, think again. If you adopt a broad definition of pornography as material that provokes sexual desire, then what can be considered pornographic takes on a much wider frame (Mayer, 2005). For example, some consider the *Girls Gone Wild* videos and the reality TV show *The Girls Next Door* pornographic (Boyle, 2011; Pitcher, 2006). What about *Playboy* and *Penthouse* magazines? Are these publications somehow in a different, more acceptable category than *Hustler* magazine? If the depictions in *Playboy* are sexually arousing, then do they qualify as pornographic? How about the swimsuit issue of *Sports Illustrated?* (Uh-oh, we've just tread on some *really* sacred ground.) Believe it or not, there is considerable opinion that the swimsuit issue actually is soft-core porn, just packaged in a sports magazine to make it appear more socially acceptable (Davis, 1997; Hopper, 2011). If you deem something pornographic because it contains images that exploit, objectify, and denigrate, then advertising images we see every day in *Time, Vogue,* and *Esquire* could be considered pornographic (Caputi, 2011). What about the stripping and dancing in so-called "gentleman's" clubs? Is this erotic, but not pornographic, even though it may be sexually arousing to the viewers?

We continue to go through this exact process as we struggle in our own minds as to what should and should not be considered pornographic. Just because something might be pornographic, is it necessarily harmful, degrading, and dangerous for society? Does pornography serve some useful purpose? Concerned adults must deal with these questions and others about pornography carefully and thoughtfully. Sexually explicit, arousing material is all around us and available for our consumption any hour of the day, especially on the Internet (Cronin & Davenport, 2010; Familysafemedia.com, 2011; Flood, 2009; Jensen, 2007; Paul & Shim, 2008; Sabina, Wolak, & Finkelhor, 2008). What you consume, what you believe consenting adults have the right to consume, and what adults should protect children from consuming are very important decisions each individual should make.

Multiple Camps for a Complex Issue

As we've said, there are different ways of looking at the issue of pornography. One thing to remember is that the two main camps we discuss below aren't really opposing sides of the issue. You can be in more than one camp regarding pornography. The two main groups—anti-pornography and anti-censorship—both talk about pornography, but in very different ways. The anti-pornography people do not consider themselves pro-censorship; the anti-censorship people do not consider themselves pro-pornography.

VOICES FROM THE ANTI-PORNOGRAPHY CAMP   Dworkin (1986), in an address before the Attorney General's Commission on Pornography, stated the following (be forewarned about the language and graphic descriptions):

> In this country where I live, every year millions and millions of pictures are being made of women with our legs spread. We are called beaver, we are called pussy, our genitals are tied up, they are pasted, makeup is put on them to make them pop out of a page at a male viewer. Millions and millions of pictures are made of us in postures of submission and sexual access so that our vaginas are exposed for penetration, our anuses are exposed for penetration, our throats are used as if they are genitals for penetration. In this country where I live as a citizen real rapes are on film and are being sold in the marketplace. And the major motif of pornography as a form of entertainment is that women are raped and violated and humiliated until we discover that we like it and at that point we ask for more. (p. 277)

As anti-porn as Dworkin was, don't get the idea that she was in favor of censorship; she and MacKinnon believed that the pornography issue really had nothing to do with censorship—it had to do with respect (Dworkin, 2000). As Dworkin explained, "The mindset has to change. It's not a question of looking at a magazine and censoring the content. It's a matter of looking at the social reality, the subordination of women necessary to create the magazine, and the way that the magazine is then used in the world against women" (as in Gillespie et al., 1994, pp. 37, 38). Law professor and author Mari Matsuda commented "We need to get away from male-centered notions of free speech. We should say that pornography, sexual harassment, racist speech, gay-bashing, anti-Semitic speech—speech that assaults and excludes—is not the same as the forms of speech deserving protection. Why is it that pornography, which undermines women's equality, is singled out for absolute protection?" (as in Pornography, 1994, p. 42).

Anti-pornography proponents argue that not only does porn degrade women, reinforcing sexist attitudes in cultures around the world, but also consuming porn has other deleterious effects (American Psychological Association, 2007). Most studies continue to find more male involvement with and positive responses to pornography than female, across age groups and ethnicities (Allen, Emmers-Sommer, D'Alessio, Timmerman, Hanzal, & Korus, 2007; Kolehmainen, 2010; Paul & Shim, 2008; Wallmyr, 2006). For adolescents, media images have the power to communicate what is acceptable human behavior; repeated exposure to violent and degrading pornographic material warps a child's view of normal functioning in adult relationships (Durham, 2009b; Flood, 2009; Hunter, Figueredo, & Malamuth, 2009; Peterson & Hyde, 2010; Sabina et al., 2008; Villani, 2001).

Pornographic materials that depict male aggression and female degradation, but stop short of physical violence, have been found to arouse male viewers (Glascock, 2005). Compared to their female counterparts, male adolescents exposed to sexually explicit material online perceived that the images were realistic and reported more positive, permissive attitudes about recreational sex (i.e., viewing sex as a game and for personal gratification rather than to foster a relationship; Peter & Valkenburg, 2006, 2008, 2010). In a longitudinal study of adolescents as they matured into adulthood, female and male subjects who were exposed to pornography early on in their lives were more sexist in their gender role attitudes and more likely to have sexual experiences (primarily oral sex and intercourse) earlier than subjects who were not exposed to pornography at early ages. In addition, male subjects were more permissive in their attitudes about sexual activity and more likely to sexually harass women later in life (Brown & L'Engle, 2009). Another study found a similar connection between pornography exposure, specifically viewing X-rated movies and having Internet access at home, and younger ages of reported sexual activity (Kraus & Russell, 2008).

VOICES FROM THE ANTI-CENSORSHIP CAMP   Strossen (2000) describes herself as a feminist who is "dedicated to securing equal rights for women and to combating women's continuing second-class citizenship in our society," but she "strongly opposes any effort to censor sexual expression" (p. 14). She and other activists believe that if you suppress women's sexuality, you actually oppress them. Strossen describes the position of many members of the anti-censorship camp: "We are as committed as any other feminists to eradicating violence and discrimination against women. But we believe that suppressing sexual words and images will not advance these crucial causes. To the contrary, we are convinced that censoring sexual expression actually would do more harm than good to women's rights and safety" (p. 14). While we would not put Malamuth and his colleagues (1984, 2000) in the anti-censorship camp, they acknowledge other perspectives: "Some of those who see pornography as sexual communication interpret its function in light of consumers' needs. Accordingly, pornography affects only the realm of fantasy or provides desirable information often lacking in many people's sex education" (Malamuth & Billings, 1984, p. 118).

Those who take a more positive view of pornography talk about how watching porn with a committed partner can spice up your love life, getting you past your "pornophobic" tendencies (Chupack, 2007, p. 294). Amanda Maddox, project coordinator for the University of Denver's Center for Marital and Family Studies, suggested to staff writers for *Women's Health* magazine that "Couples who view sexy movies together are more dedicated to each other and more sexually satisfied than those who watch them alone" (XXX marks the spot, 2010, p. 40). (Do you think there's a difference between "sexy movies" and pornography?)

Other voices from the anti-censorship camp raise the issue of the relationship between pornography consumption and tendencies toward violence, especially rape and sexual assault. Such proponents argue that although porn availability and consumption is up in the United States, rates of sexual violence have decreased or remained stagnant, as found in Department of Justice statistics indicating that sexual violence has decreased over the past 25 years (D'Amato, 2009; Diamond, 2009). Others refute such claims (Bergen, 2000; Malamuth, Addison, & Koss, 2000). Department of Justice statistics exclude the rape of children under age 12 and, more to the point, such statistics are based on *reported* acts of violence (Reisman, 2009). One of the most underreported crimes in America is rape.

Complicating the picture are different responses to and views of pornography held by men and women. Although we stated earlier that men still tend to be more frequent consumers of pornography than women, one study examined men's and women's perceptions of the opposite sex's reactions to porn (Reid, Byrne, Brundidge, Shoham, & Marlow, 2007). Men in the study perceived "the average woman" as being more "repulsed and offended" by pornography than they, themselves, were; they also perceived that they, themselves, were more "aroused and excited" by pornography than the average woman. Results for female subjects in the study paralleled findings for men: Women perceived the "average man" as being more "aroused and excited" by porn, whereas they viewed themselves as being more "repulsed and offended" than the average man. In other words, the study confirmed "women as repulsed by porn" and "men as aroused by porn" stereotypes, from the viewpoints of both women and men (Reid et al., 2007, p. 143).

WHERE TO PUT UP YOUR TENT   If you're having trouble deciding which camp to align yourself with, you're not alone. Elements of both positions have merit, we realize. There are well-known, outspoken feminists who adopt what could be perceived as a middle position. One such person is Marilyn French, author of eight books including *The War Against Women* (1992). In a *Ms.* magazine discussion, French admitted that she viewed the Dworkin-MacKinnon ordinance against pornography as a form of censorship.

Third-wave feminist authors Jaclyn Friedman and Jessica Valenti (2008), in their book about female sexual power and a world without rape, discuss how "feminist pornography" (erotic imagery that doesn't degrade women) can actually help people who have experienced sexual violence. The authors explain that "pornography can be a less risky way for survivors to reintroduce sexuality into their lives before they are ready to do so with another person" (pp. 111–112). Moreover, "Feminist pornography . . . provides viewers with actors of diverse sizes and shapes and examples of people using safer-sex methods" (p. 112). And finally, Friedman and Valenti have a message for previous generations of feminists: "If the second-wave feminists that comprise the leadership of many rape crisis centers truly advocate for a world in which women are in control of their sexuality, it may be worthwhile for them to take a look at some of this work and evolve their arguments beyond the anti-pornography stance that is so often the dominant message within the movement now" (p. 112).

The Crux of the Matter: Pornography Is Personal

We have two purposes in presenting this material on pornography to you: first, to help you better understand the complexities of the issue through a discussion of diverse viewpoints; and second, to challenge you to think about the impact of pornography in your own life. The barrage of sexual images we consume daily—in song lyrics and music videos (as we explore in the next section of this chapter), television and film images, advertisements in magazines and newspapers, images in comic books, cartoon strips, and cyberspace—simply *have* to have some effect. Mediated messages really *do* affect how we believe we are supposed to behave toward one another, what we expect from each other in relationships (both platonic and romantic), how we communicate our desires and needs (especially in sexual situations), and how much respect we develop for ourselves and others.

Here's an example to make this stance more concrete; you might think it an extreme case, but it involves a male student, just like someone sitting in one of your classes. A few years back one of the TV news magazine shows did a story on a pornography users' support group, a group of about thirty or so male students at Duke University that began as a small group of guys in a campus dorm having regular informal discussions about

Net Notes

Deceptive Techniques and Internet Porn

Jerry Ropelato (2003), contributor to the Family Safe Media website, in an article entitled "Tricks Pornographers Play," describes deceptive techniques now prevalent on the Internet, designed to lure computer users to pornographic sites. Here are some of the more common techniques. (For more information on pornography, statistics about porn use, and detrimental effects on families, check out **www.familysafemedia.com**.)

Deceptive Techniques

- Porn-napping: Pornographers purchase expired domain names when the original owners forget or don't renew them; unsuspecting Internet users get redirected to porn sites.
- Cyber-squatting: Pornographers purchase domain names for legitimate topics or entities, then alter them in a way typically unnoticed by Internet users. People search for sites innocently, but then get directed to porn sites instead. (Example whitehouse.gov versus whitehouse.com)
- Doorway scams: Pornographers have discovered how to carefully design websites so that they get picked up by popular search engines; the content is designed around nonpornographic themes, which places them high on a search engine's list.
- Misspellings: Pornographers buy up misspelled, trendy domain names that typically generate high traffic on the Internet. (Example: googlle.com, which sent people to an Asian porn site until it got shut down)
- Advertising: Pornographers create fake system errors; when users respond to error messages, they get redirected to porn sites. Other website features such as message alert boxes and false forms dupe users into clicking on buttons that activate porn sites.

Ropelato also mentions entrapment, meaning ways your computer can become altered or marked after you make any of the mistakes above and get lured into a porn site. He warns us to be careful about file sharing and downloading, because these are becoming more prevalent mechanisms for exposing Internet consumers to unexpected pornography.

---

sex and the effects of pornography on their lives. The camera taped one of the weekly discussions, and the men's revelations were startlingly honest. One student's admission was particularly painful and memorable: He described a sexual encounter with a woman he was very interested in. They'd been out a couple of times but had not yet had sex. He was highly attracted to the woman and wanted to be intimate with her, but when the opportunity to have sex with her arrived, to his embarrassment he was unable to get an erection. He then explained how he enabled himself to function in the situation by imagining the woman beneath him as a pornographic image of a woman from a magazine. When he shut his eyes, tuned out the real person he was with, and vividly imagined the graphic magazine picture, only then did he become aroused. He was not only worried that this signaled his sexual future—that he was doomed to a life of being aroused not by real people, but by mediated images—but also mortified at the impersonal way he behaved with the woman. He couldn't continue the relationship after this experience and had had no other sexual encounters at the time the group met.

Remember . . .

Gender Bending: Media depiction in which a character's actions belie or contradict what is expected for members of her or his sex

Obscenity: Legal term used in reference to pornographic material

Erotica: Material that portrays sex as an equal activity involving mutual sensual pleasure, not activity involving power or subordination

Pornography: Material produced with an intent to elicit erotic responses from a consumer, to sexually arouse a consumer, to degrade or demean women characters in a sexual manner, or to portray unequal power in sexual activity

Hard-Core Pornography: Material that depicts or describes intercourse and/or other sexual practices

Soft-Core Pornography: Material in which sexual acts are implied but not fully or explicitly acted out or portrayed

Realcore: Form of pornography depicting real people having sex in real locations

Gonzo Pornography: Cheaply made pornographic movies that offer no plotlines but simply string sexual scenes together

What's your reaction to this story? Do you know people who seem to be more comfortable with pornography than with real lovers? We worry about how pornographic images harm women and men, how they keep women "in their place," as sexualized commodities to be purchased and used for gratification, and how they add to the pressure men feel to be sexual performers. But we also worry about people like the former Duke students who might now be considered sex addicts. We wonder how some men can say that they respect their wives when they regularly frequent strip clubs or adult film houses, become aroused by the dancers or images, and then come home wanting to have sex with their wives. What's the role of pornography in these men's lives? And we cannot help but believe that the enormous problem of violence, such as date rape and sexual assault, that occurs between people in romantic situations is connected to the all-pervasive, ready-and-waiting-for-your-consumption pornography.

WE COULD MAKE BEAUTIFUL MUSIC TOGETHER . . .

Music is a powerful force in our culture; its influence pervades our existence. In this section of the chapter, we examine how song lyrics and music videos communicate images of men and women.

From Pop to Rock to Rap to Hip-Hop to Country: The Women and Men of Song Lyrics

Sometimes when you listen to a song you want to concentrate on the lyrics; you attend to the words from a more critical standpoint. But other times you simply like the rhythm, beat, and musical performance, so you tune out the lyrics. Have you ever read the lyrics to a particular song and said to yourself, "Oh *that's* what they're saying"? That's much easier to do nowadays, with full transcripts of words often accompanying CDs and easily found on the Internet. Sometimes, however, you find yourself humming or singing along with a song on the radio or on a favorite CD when you suddenly realize what the words really are. You become acutely aware that what you're singing with or listening to isn't something you'd like to repeat in *any* company, especially mixed company.

Just about as many different ways to process music exist as there are delivery systems for it and people who listen to it. The repetition of songs (particularly ones with hypnotic "hooks") throughout a typical radio day or on CDs, iPods, and MP3 playlists reinforces lyrics deeply into listeners' psyches. Music, specifically song lyrics depicting the sexes and relationships, have more impact on you than you probably realize (Frisby, 2010; Timmerman, Allen, Jorgensen, Herrett-Skjellum, Kramer, & Ryan, 2008). Researchers have found that listening to sexually suggestive song lyrics affects how subjects evaluate the looks and sex appeal of potential romantic partners (Dillman Carpentier, Knobloch-Westerwick, & Blumhoff, 2007).

Studies have also found a connection between listening to sexually explicit and degrading song lyrics and permissive attitudes toward premarital sex, negative attitudes toward women, distorted perceptions of peers' sexual activities, and becoming sexually active at early ages (Brown, L'Engle, Pardun, Guo, Kenneavy, & Jackson, 2006; Fischer & Greitemeyer, 2006; Martino, Collins, Elliott, Strachman, Kanouse, & Berry, 2006; Pardun, L'Engle, & Brown, 2005; Primack, Gold, Schwarz, & Dalton, 2008). So what do song lyrics communicate specifically about women and men?

GENDER TRENDS IN LYRICS   Research over the past few decades has found some interesting trends in terms of gender and song lyrics. In the 1970s, scholars Freudiger and Almquist (1978) examined images and gender-role depictions of men and women in song lyrics of three genres of popular music. They reviewed the top fifty hits on the *Billboard* country, soul, and easy listening charts and found, first, that women were more the focus of song lyrics than men across all three music genres. Second, women were rarely criticized and were most often positively portrayed in these lyrics, but they were described primarily in stereotypes of submissiveness, supportiveness, and dependency. In contrast, when men were mentioned in lyrics—especially songs written from a female perspective—they were portrayed in a more negative and critical light, especially in country lyrics. Men's depictions reflected stereotypical traits of aggression, consistency, action, and confidence.

In the 1980s, studies identified stereotypical portrayals of women in American popular music, portrayals that are still prevalent today. Communication scholars Butruille and Taylor (1987) detected "three recurring images of women: The Ideal Woman/Madonna/Saint, the evil or fickle Witch/Sinner/Whore, and the victim (often dead)" (p. 180). Some of these images date back to early religious customs and beliefs about the sinful versus virginal nature of woman. As communication researcher Janet Wyman (1993) suggests, "The virgin/whore dichotomy is destructive to women not only because it polarizes, and thus limits their sexual identity, but because neither category is particularly flattering. The virgin/whore dichotomy stifles the social power of women since both the virgin and the whore are powerless positions" (pp. 6–7). Interestingly enough, one explanation for the popularity of the late Tejano singer Selena was her ability to combine saint and sinner, meaning that she presented a sexual, sensual image through dress and demeanor along with a "good girl" quality and a strong connection to family (Willis & Gonzalez, 1997).

One trend in the 1990s involved female artists' lyrics that described difficult choices, abusive situations, and destructive relationships (Maxwell, 2001; Perry, 2003; Sellnow, 1999). While some scholars contended that women's music was just as focused on romantic relationships as it always was, others believed that women's bold representations of brutality and degradation they experienced in relationships communicated an unprecedented honesty.

Women are really empow-ering themselves in politics and in every facet of life now. Music tends to represent what's going on with youth, and the youth of America felt really frustrated a few years ago, and you had these angry alterna-bands. Now you have a lot of females who are step-ping up to represent women in America or women in the world, becoming role models for young girls.

—Sheryl Crow, singer/ songwriter

In terms of trends for song lyrics and depictions of the sexes in this new century, a good deal of the research focuses on imagery in rap and hip-hop music, which we discuss in the next section. Researchers have examined other trends, such as masculine identity as affected by the lyrics of heavy metal music (Rafalovich, 2006); lyrics of breakout country stars, like Gretchen Wilson, and what their non-norm personas contribute (Horn, 2009); and the intersections of gender and race in themes of current song lyrics (Bragg & McFarland, 2007; Brooks & Hebert, 2011; Henry, West, & Jackson, 2010; Molina Guzman & Valdivia, 2004).

Unfortunately, at times it feels like we're regressing to an earlier age in our country's development: A study of "The Hot 100" list of pop songs on the Billboard Chart found evidence of the following themes in song lyrics: men and power over women; sex as a top priority for males; objectification of women; sexual violence against women; women being defined by having a man; and women not valuing themselves (Bretthauer, Schindler Zimmerman, & Banning, 2006). The primary audience for this music is adolescents; American youth listen to music between one and a half and two and a half hours each day—a rate that only increases with age (Roberts, Foehr, & Rideout, 2003). Given research that documents that adolescents are significantly impacted by the music they consume, the themes in current song lyrics are more than disturbing.

SEX AND DEGRADATION IN SONGS   Pop culture scholars in the 1980s asserted that rock music provided the most derogatory, sexist images of women among all forms of popular music (Harding & Nett, 1984). However, in the view of many, rap and hip-hop music have overtaken rock as the most misogynistic (i.e., woman-hating) forms (Adams & Fuller, 2006; Glassner, 2005; Squires, Kohn-Wood, Chavous, & Carter, 2006; Tyree, 2009; Utley, 2010; Weitzer & Kubrin, 2009). Although some rap and hip-hop artists focus on racial and political issues and attempt to show positive images of relationships in their music (Azikwe, 2011; Chaney, 2009; Corrigan, 2009; Santa Cruz Bell & Avant-Mier, 2009; Utley & Menzies, 2009), other artists are notorious for their depictions of men as all-powerful aggressors and women as virtual sex slaves (Jeffries, 2009; Natalle & Flippen, 2004; Rose, 2011; Shugart & Egley Waggoner, 2005). Lyrics penned and performed by the controversial Eminem have contributed to the view that rap and hip-hop music are inherently anti-woman (Martin & Yep, 2004; Stephens, 2005).

Freelance music critic Jeff Niesel (1997) offers a helpful distinction that keeps all rap and hip-hop music from being labeled woman-hating. He distinguishes alternative rap from gangsta rap:

When I first started listening to rap music in the early 1990s, I found that the gender paradigms…were often alienating and presented views of women with which I could not identify. Shortly afterward, I realized that there was an alternative to gangsta rap. These artists, by blurring the boundaries between male and female and between black and white, they suggested that for political activism to be truly successful, coalitions must be built across the lines that divide people.…For "alternative" rappers, rap music had the most potential of any music to inspire social change…(pp. 240–241)

Niesel contends that alternative rap is more inclusive of women than gangsta rap, thus it has a more feminist bend. Do you agree with Niesel in his belief that rap music (or today's more modern version, hip-hop) has more potential to change our society than any other form of music? Do you even think of music as holding the potential to alter society, or is it just art or merely for our enjoyment?

It's interesting to consider what effects song lyrics have on your perceptions or expectations of members of your same sex and the opposite sex. If you can easily remember the lyrics to a popular song (as opposed to formulas for your math exam), it's clear that they're permeating your consciousness on some level. So while we might not regulate our relationships according to what we hear depicted in song lyrics, those lyrics do affect all of us in some way.

Sex Kittens and He-Men in Music Videos

What happens when visual images in music videos reinforce the messages of song lyrics? What happens when they contradict images we have in our heads, based on just listening to the lyrics? Many people report in research that when they listen to a song after having seen the video for the song, their interpretation of the lyrics is significantly affected; the video's visual images dominate the imagination (Jhally, 2003; Williams, 2007).

Music video doesn't get talked about much these days or researched as much as in past decades. After MTV went on the air in 1981 and quickly infiltrated American households, the music video industry skyrocketed (Vivian, 2011). One writer for *Entertainment Weekly* magazine described how MTV's introduction of the reality TV show *The Real World* in 1992 signaled the demise of music video, mainly because the ratings overwhelmingly favored programming rather than videos (Stransky, 2011). But music videos, whether delivered through TV sets or on computers and smartphones through the wonders of the Internet, still have power to impact our culture and communicate messages about women and men (Greenblatt, 2004). Case in point, consider Lady Gaga's digital dominance in popular culture: Gaga's singles have received over 321 million plays on MySpace; her provocative, cutting-edge videos (like "Telephone" with Beyoncé), are easily and inexpensively downloaded onto a smartphone, defy categorization, and offer paradoxical portrayals of femininity (Borisoff & Chesebro, 2011). In 2011, *Forbes* magazine replaced Oprah Winfrey with Lady Gaga as the "World's Most Powerful Celebrity."

In a study of the portrayal of violence, sex, and substance use in music video, media scholar Stacy Smith (2005) found less violence than expected in music videos airing on MTV, with more violence depicted in rap than rock videos. However, she also found more sexual content than expected, leading her to conclude that sexual activity is more "a staple in music videos than violence" (p. 92). Such sexual content makes an impression on adolescents, who are among the heaviest consumers of music video in the United States (Martino et al., 2006). Studies have found a consistent connection between the early onset of adolescents becoming sexually active, their sexual risk-taking (e.g., multiple partners, sex without protection), permissive attitudes toward sex, and acceptance of sex-role stereotypes and their viewing of sexually charged music videos (Pardun et al., 2005; Ward, Hansbrough, & Walker, 2005; Zhang, Miller, & Harrison, 2008).

The results for college students' consumption of music videos isn't that different. In their study of music video viewers' acceptance of the objectification of women in media, sexual permissiveness, gender attitudes, and rape myth acceptance, media scholars Kistler and Lee (2010) found the following: (1) Men who watched highly sexual hip-hop music videos held a more positive view of the objectification of women; (2) they also revealed more stereotypical views of men and women; and (3) they demonstrated more acceptance of rape myths (e.g., women secretly want to be raped, it's not rape if the woman is drunk) than women in the study, as well as men who watched music videos containing no or low levels of sexual content. College women in the study were not similarly affected by exposure to sexually charged music videos. What are the ramifications of such findings? Kistler and Lee concluded:

> The most disturbing finding is the significant effect of exposure on male participants' acceptance of rape myths. Men in the highly sexual hip-hop videos were portrayed as powerful, sexually assertive, and as having a fair degree of sexual prowess, whereas the women were portrayed as sexually available, scantily clad, and often preening over the men. This might have served as a cue to male participants that sexual coercion is more acceptable and that women exist for the entertainment and sexual fulfillment of men. (p. 83)

GENDER AND RACE IN MUSIC VIDEO   Although music video has been praised for its innovativeness, it has also been criticized for its stereotypical depictions of relationships between women and men and between people of different racial groups (Railton & Watson, 2005; Richardson, 2007). In fact, not too long after music video was introduced into the United States (having first emerged in Europe in the 1970s), researchers began to investigate the extent of gender and ethnic stereotyping in music videos (Peterson, 1987; Seidman, 1992; Sherman & Dominick, 1986).

In 1980s music videos, women were predominantly depicted as decorations and sex objects; female artists most often portrayed themselves in seductive clothing and situations in their videos, with Tina Turner and Madonna heading up this list (Vincent, 1989). Media specialists Brown and Campbell (1986) assessed race and sex differences in music videos airing on MTV and *Video Soul,* a program broadcast by the Black Entertainment Television cable channel. Their research revealed that Black and White women were significantly less often portrayed in professional settings in comparison to men of these races, a finding corroborated by subsequent research (Seidman, 1992; White, 2000). Brown and Campbell concluded, "White men, primarily by virtue of their greater numbers, are the center of attention and power and are more often aggressive and hostile than helpful and cooperative. Women and blacks are rarely important enough to be a part of the foreground" (p. 104).

Hot Button Issue

"Do You Love Love the Way You Lie?"

Many people have viewed the video for *Love the Way You Lie,* featuring Eminem and Rihanna; if you haven't seen this video, check it out on YouTube (just be prepared for some of the language in the song). People have different interpretations of this video, some believing that it was Rihanna's way to offer commentary on the abuse she experienced in her relationship with Chris Brown. Others are more critical, believing it's just more of the sex, violence, and angst typical of Eminem's music and videos.

Still others think it sends a powerful message in its depiction of the cycle couples in violent, abusive relationships go through—the repetitive push-pull of passion, violence, remorse, forgiveness, reconciliation, and so forth that some intimate partners experience. As Adela Garcia (2011), community educator for The Women's Shelter of South Texas, explains, "The violence carries an ensuing, desperate need to put out the fires of the explosion. This breeds the desire for a quick fix to smother the burn. The 'passion' from the violent episode is then channeled into a sexual encounter, completing the quick burning cycle. All in all, passion becomes a way out, a way to disguise and cope with the violence" (p. 10). One of the most interesting scenes in the video is when the couple enacting the volatile relationship move from room to room in a house, revealing changes in their emotions and how they relate to each other as they go.

Emotions can be confusing, and they can surprise us with how they emerge when we least expect it in our relationships, especially in those intimate, high-priority relationships. But, no matter some objectionable or gritty content (especially for feminists who take Eminem and other popular musicians to task regularly), here's an example of a music video that has the ability to teach us about the complexities of relationships—the destruction, passion, and confusion that typically characterize abusive relationships. Music video may be past its heyday, but it still has instructive power and the potential to offer provocative commentary on society.

Research in the 1990s found little evidence of increased equity in music videos. An analysis of forty music videos regularly broadcast on MTV produced the following results:

- Men appeared in videos twice as often as women.
- Men were significantly more aggressive and dominant in their behavior than women.
- Women were highly sexual as well as subservient in their behavior.
- Women were often targets of explicit and aggressive sexual advances (Sommers-Flanagan, Sommers-Flanagan, & Davis, 1993).

Another study of the 100 most popular MTV videos of the early 90s produced more bad news for women (Gow, 1996). In these videos, five times as many men as women held lead roles. Women most often appeared performing their music for the camera or dancing while lip-synching a song, suggesting that, in contrast to men's musical talents, women's appearance, sexiness, and physical talents were more important or emphasized. Perhaps you have seen the documentary film *Dreamworlds 3: Desire/Sex/Power in*

Music Video, by Sut Jhally (2007), which explores music video's hypersexualized images of women. In many videos, especially rock videos, women appear as mere sex objects designed to please men—as "legs in high heels" according to Jhally.

On a more positive note, a study of country music video showed a progression in the way female country music stars were depicted in the 1990s (Andsager & Roe, 1999). Even though male country artists outnumbered female country artists by three to one and female artists did not receive the same status as their male counterparts, music videos by female artists portrayed women more progressively and less stereotypically. In contrast, music videos by male country artists continued to include many of the same old female stereotypes as in past decades.

What's the story today? Images of men and women in music videos are a "mixed bag," in sort of a one-step-forward, two-steps-back way. Media scholar Imani Perry (2003) found that sexually objectifying and degrading images of women were prevalent in hip-hop videos at the turn of the new century. However, she also saw evidence of a change or progression, particularly in black women's depictions in videos produced by African American female artists, such as Mary J. Blige, Beyoncé, Missy Elliott, Erykah Badu, Alicia Keys, and India Arie. Although many women's images in videos were still sexual, Perry distinguished between presenting oneself as a sexual *object,* there for the pleasure of others, versus a sexual *subject,* a sexual human being worthy of respect. Similarly, research by media scholar Murali Balaji (2010) documents black women's attempts to reclaim and redefine black womanhood through the performance of music video.

Several studies published in the early part of this new century show that videos featuring African Americans are significantly more likely to portray sexual content, with women appearing in provocative clothing and as sexual objects dominated by men, than videos produced by and featuring white men and women (Conrad, Dixon, & Zhang, 2009; James, 2008; Railton & Watson, 2005; Turner, 2010). These perpetual images of black women in all sort of media have led author Patricia Hill Collins (2004) to conclude that "the sexualized Black woman has become an icon in hip-hop culture" (p. 126).

Music video is still a prevalent form of media, particularly in the lives of young people. However, it's not as pervasive or intrusive into your day as music that you hear on the radio as you're driving to class or to work, or that you carry with you every hour of the day. Turning on the television and tuning in to music videos implies more conscious choice and action than merely listening to background music. But think for a moment about the whole effect—the very powerful effect of combining visual images

Net Notes

Here's a hip-hop music website that focuses on the cultural contributions of female artists:
www.b-gyrl.com The site is primarily about music, but it also offers links to articles on authors, activists, and entrepreneurs who are trying to effect social change.

And in case you don't have a friend who keeps his or her finger on the pulse of the newest music around, here's a helpful website that tips you off to new bands worth checking out, with free MP3s and newsletters:
myspoonful.com

with musical sound, a beat, and lyrics. Whether you actually watch every second of the average three-minute music video or really attend to the lyrics in a song, you still receive the message. Somewhere your brain is processing the information, sometimes on a conscious level, but most times on a subconscious level.

Do you think that taking in so many stereotypical, sexist messages has some effect on you? We encourage you to think about how the music you listen to and videos you watch (if you watch them) affect your view of self, your attitudes about sex roles in society, the expectations you form (especially of members of the opposite sex), and your gender communication within relationships.

SEX, GENDER, AND NEW MEDIA

Just what the heck do we mean by new media? Is new media the same thing as digital media? As electronic media? Is social networking part of new media? Let's just answer these questions with a big ole' confused, "We're not sure." We cobbled together some definitions to come up with the following: *New media* refers to electronic, interactive forms of media, especially mass media, typically combined with computers and considered experimental.

As soon as we start talking about what's new, it's no longer new. Media scholar Mia Consalvo (2006) explains that "The term *new media* is ambiguous and relative—what was new in the early 1990s . . . became mundane and accepted within a decade and was quickly replaced by newer media" (p. 355). In his collection of articles on "digital cultures," "new media cultures," "Internet cultures," and "cybercultures," media scholar Pramod Nayar (2010) describes new media this way: "[The] terrain is varied, complex, and shifting. Cybercultures is a notoriously difficult and slippery 'discipline' to theorize for the simple reason that it is arguably the fastest-growing set of practices in contemporary times" (p. ix).

In our discussion of gender and new media, we draw from Consalvo's categories and themes as well as Nayar's edited volume, with supplements from other research, to help us place some parameters on a topic too elusive, changeable, and vast to conquer. We ask your indulgence here, gentle readers, as we broach this subject rather narrowly, despite the breadth of the topic at hand.

Although social networking is a form of new media (to many people's thinking), we've made mention of social networking many other places in this book. Here we choose to cover a few underrepresented topics related to new or digital media, including online identity development, disembodiment, and gender in virtual gaming communities. Indulge us as we choose to ignore some obvious intersections, such as how people develop online identities through their use of Facebook or how Twitter followers and viral video fans can become virtual communities.

Online Identity and Gender

In the 1990s, feminists and gender scholars believed that the Internet would afford people the ability to surpass the limitations of their physical or bodily identities; thus, one's gender identity would become less a factor than in other communicative contexts, like the development of face-to-face relationships. However, studies quickly refuted these assumptions as researchers came to view online outlets, such as newsgroups, listservs, web pages, and computer games, as gendered (Consalvo, 2006).

Theorists then began viewing new media as a place for identity exploration, such as when people create onscreen identities in terms of gender, sexuality, race, class, and so on, that differ from their offscreen identities (Stone, 1996; Turkle, 1995; van Zoonen, 2002). People could explore aspects of their identity through anonymously-generated, gender-neutral (or unidentified) *blogs* (short for web logs, diarylike entries that people share over the Internet) and web pages (Barlow, 2007; Stern, 2004). The anonymity and privacy that Internet usage could afford encouraged gender identity expression; you could blog as *anybody*. In response to the wave of identity exploration that ensued, gender scholars critiqued such a cavalier approach, mainly because when people experimented with gender and sexuality online, some of the same, tired stereotypes emerged and were reinforced. Sexism is in our culture; why would we presume that it wouldn't exist in our cyberculture as well?

Contemporary scholars like Sherry Turkle (2011), author of *Alone Together;* Naomi Baron (2008), who wrote *Always On;* and others point to such virtual sites as World of Warcraft and *Second Life* (very popular with college students) as provocative outlets for identity exploration (Brookey & Cannon, 2011; Nakamura, 2011). In many ways, virtual reality is just the newest form of fantasy, like escaping into novels, films, or soap operas where most everyone is young, beautiful, able-bodied, rich, successful, and in love. It's a way to step outside one's life and "play at being other" (Turkle, 2011, p. 159). The themes are the same, but the technological innovations make the experience different.

Research into gendered identity and new media continues to this day, with studies emerging on such topics as the following:

- The link between women's use of mobile phones and the development of an independent identity and control over one's life (Doring & Poschl, 2006);
- Identity exploration via *moblogs* (blogs that can be uploaded from mobile phones) (Doring & Gundolf, 2010);
- Website designs that foster community for women (Kennedy, 2000; Mitra, 2010);
- Internet usage that affords marginalized groups a voice in personal as well as political matters (Harcourt, 2000).

Even with this flurry of activity, a larger, more cohesive thread or theory uniting the research has yet to emerge.

Disembodiment: Virtual Versus "Real" Bodies

Disembodiment means divesting of or being freed from bodily or physical form. Initially, virtual reality (or cyberspace) looked like it was going to offer people a "disembodied space," meaning a place where participants could work, play, become educated, and generally live in a way that separated them from the confines of their physical bodies (Consalvo, 2006, p. 359). However, theorists began to argue that just because people chose to function in virtual reality part of the time in their lives, such usage didn't actually eliminate people's bodies; it didn't disengage or separate them from their bodies as it was purported to do (Balsamo, 1996; Kramarae, 1995). Gender scholars contended that virtual reality "privileged sight over other senses, encouraged a masculine view of the world, and perpetuated a mind/body split that falsely believed gender would become irrelevant" (Consalvo, 2006, p. 359).

Researchers studying web pages and blogs found that, rather than freeing one from one's body, bodies are often described and talked about online, thus making them real and central rather than representational or nonfactors (Currier, 2010; Herring, Kouper, Scheidt, & Wright, 2004; Stern, 2002, 2004). Other scholars have found that designs of digital characters and *avatars* (graphical embodiments or personifications that represent people) in video games and virtual communities (like *Second Life*) often invoke gender stereotypes, especially feminine stereotypes, which can affect how online players and users relate to the characters (Ensslin & Muse, 2011; Lim & Reeves, 2009; Nowak, Hamilton, & Hammon, 2009; Nowak & Rauh, 2005; Palomares & Lee, 2010). One example is the Lara Croft video game character who represents a masculine standard of the ideal female body type—beautiful, slender, and shapely (Giresunlu, 2009; Mikula, 2003).

As Consalvo (2006) explains, "The body is not so easily left behind" (p. 359). Even as we create new personae or online extensions of ourselves, our creations are affected by ideal images of men and women we see evidenced in media every day. We see strong, tall, nonbalding, athletic (typically well-endowed) male bodies that represent a cultural ideal for men and shapely, buxom female bodies with great skin, long legs, perfect rear ends, and no body fat, many of whom are portrayed as overtly sexual in skimpy, provocative clothing designed to show off their physical assets, which they may or may not allow men to enjoy. The heteronormativity of many of these online sites is substantial, with the "queering" of online communities still a relatively new phenomenon (Boler, 2010; Brookey & Cannon, 2011; Bryson, 2004; Enteen, 2009; Friedman, 2010; Nip, 2004).

Gendered Gaming

Researchers have studied digital game usage and design in general, as well as in terms of gender factors (Ensslin & Muse, 2011; Juul, 2010; Mortensen, 2010). (Because avatars are often a part of video/computer games, we recognize some overlap in this section with the last theme of disembodiment.) In studies, gender emerges as a significant factor in understanding people's approaches to game play (Nakamura, 2011; Sanbonmatsu, 2011; Taylor, 2003). For this section, we could certainly explore some of the more widely-criticized, incendiary games for their sexist elements—those that serve as fodder for media figures and critics, like *Grand Theft Auto* and various "FPRs" or "first-person shooter" games, like the newly released *L.A. Noire* (Royse, Lee, Baasanjav, Hopson, & Consalvo, 2010, p. 410). But we're going with a more nuanced approach, choosing to highlight one fascinating study of female gamers.

New media scholars Royse, Lee, Baasanjav, Hopson, and Consalvo (2010) conducted individual and focus group interviews with a group of female college students of various levels of gaming expertise to understand "how women described their electronic gaming experiences and how they constructed their own perspectives about gaming culture" (p. 411). Three groups emerged, based on play time: nongamers didn't play at all; moderate gamers spent one to two hours a week playing video/computer games; and power gamers played from three to more than 10 hours a week.

Computer games don't affect kids, I mean if Pac Man affected us as kids, we'd all be running around in darkened rooms, munching pills and listening to repetitive music.
—Marcus Brigstocke,
English comedian
and radio personality

The power gamers integrated gaming into their lives; thus they were the most comfortable with gaming technology and themes. They revealed their level of integration not just by how frequently they played, but also by how easily they used the technology and talked about their enjoyment of various types of games. They reported using games to fulfill certain desires, like being competitive and excelling into mastery of a game. These findings parallel Taylor's (2003), in that many women enjoy game combat because it allows them to challenge gender norms and act on their feelings of aggression without repercussion. Power gamers often chose character representations for themselves that outsiders might view as unfortunate, harmful feminine stereotypes, but the gamers reported that such avatar selection enhanced their pleasure of playing the game. They preferred their avatars to reflect strength as well as sexiness, at the same time being careful to retain markers of femininity, such as retaining long fingernails while gripping rocket launchers and blowing virtual competitors away.

Royse et al. (2010) suggest, "We are presented with a paradox of sorts—the gamer who embodies 'femininity,' while performing 'masculinity'" (p. 414). Power gamers acknowledged the hypersexualization of some female images in games, as well as the sexism some male players exhibited online, but their enjoyment of computer games was connected to choice, mastery, and control. For some power gamers, their avatars represented who they'd like to be or wished they were in their offline lives—their better selves.

As to the moderate gamers in Royse et al.'s (2010) study, these women mentioned control as a factor, but it was more about using a game to control their circumstances or environment. Gaming was a coping mechanism, a distraction or escape from everyday life for these users. The authors explain, "Gaming offers . . . a vehicle used to escape momentarily the gendered role of life's caretaker; here, distraction can be seen as a means of self-control, a way to cope with the demands of women's daily lives" (p. 416). The moderate female gamers in this study also drew a distinction between the games they played and those they presumed men played, those they perceived as violent and fantasy based. Their gaming intent wasn't necessarily to defeat opponents; the form of competitiveness they preferred was beating the game itself or making the right moves to solve a problem or puzzle. Moderate gamers in this study didn't perceive avatars as empowering for women; they viewed them as simply characters, not embodiments of unfulfilled identity.

For the most part, nongamers in this study were critical of gamers (deeming them "interpersonally inept") and games, viewing them as an antisocial activity and a waste of time (p. 419). They expressed concerns about the sexualized and violent content of many games, but acknowledged that these qualities were problems in other forms of media as well. They viewed themselves as traditionally female—grounded in the real world, secure in their priorities—in opposition to men who were more frequent users of computer games and less feminine women who aggressively played the games.

As a result of their research into this phenomenon, Royse et al. (2010) call for a "technologies of the gendered self" approach to further inquiry, which helps us understand how people "negotiate game play, gender expectations and roles in relation to technology use" (p. 421). This perspective factors gender into the way people design and interface with all sorts of new media, to help us better understand this relatively new frontier for communication that will no doubt play an increasingly important role in our lives.

Remember . . .

New Media: Electronic, interactive forms of media, especially mass media, typically combined with computers and considered experimental

Blogs: Short for web logs, diarylike entries that people share over the Internet

Moblogs: Blogs that can be uploaded from mobile phones

Disembodiment: Divesting of or being freed from bodily or physical form

Conclusion

You may not feel you have reached media expert status, but we suspect that you know more about the forms of media that surround you every day than you did before you read this chapter. When you think about the many media outlets and methods that have the potential to influence you, it's almost overwhelming. But rather than feeling overwhelmed by media influence, your knowledge can empower you to better understand the effects of media messages about gender. We hope that you not only have an increased knowledge about mediated communication, but that you are able to more critically assess the role media—traditional and new forms—play in your life. That critical assessment enables you to make thoughtful choices about just how much you will allow the media to affect you.

Think about whether you have some standards for romantic relationships and where those standards came from. Do your expectations reflect romance as portrayed in movies or between characters on television? If you were to describe someone's relationship or use it as an example, would you mention a couple from real life or would you compare it to how virtual couples behave in *Second Life?* Now that you're more aware of the wide range of mediated images that could be considered pornographic, do you think any of those readily accessible images have affected your expectations about relationships?

When you're feeling down, are there certain songs and musical artists that either help you feel your pain more fully or that help raise your spirits? Have you ever watched TV characters go through some trauma, such as the death of a loved one, an angry exchange between friends, or the breakup of an important relationship, and then later used how the characters talked about the experience in your own life events? We encourage you to take more opportunities to consciously decipher media influence, particularly in reference to gender communication. The more you understand what's influencing you, the more ready you'll be to dive into new relationships or strengthen your existing ones.

Discussion Starters

1. When your favorite magazine arrives at your door or when you decide to buy the newest edition of it at the store, don't plunge into it right away. Try this exercise first: Thumb through the magazine, paying special attention to the advertisements. How many ads depict members of your same sex? How many depict members of the opposite sex?

2. What's your favorite prime-time television show? Think of several reasons why this show is your favorite. Do your reasons have more to do with the characters, the setting or scenery, the plot lines, or something else? Now think about a prime-time television show that you watched and just hated. What was so irritating about that show? Are there any gender issues affecting your decision about most and least favorite TV shows?

3. Have your views on pornography changed at all as a result of the information in this chapter? Think about the different definitions of pornography and then think about media you consume—magazine ads, TV shows, films, music videos, and online material. How much could be classified as pornographic? What role, if any, has pornography played in your developing understanding of gender?

4. Assess your music collection. Whom do you listen to—predominantly artists of the same sex as you or of the opposite sex? If there's a pattern, why do you think the pattern exists? Then pick one CD and play the cut on it that you are the least familiar with. Listen carefully and try to take in every word of the lyric. Did you hear anything for the first time?

5. Have you experimented with computer games where you create an avatar, such as in *Second Life*? If so, did you generate an avatar that resembles you in "real" life, or did you choose to alter your identity in some way? How do you think gender identity exploration in online settings affects your view of sex and gender in other aspects of life?

 ## References

Aaron, M. (2006). New queer cable? *The L Word*, the small screen, and the bigger picture. In K. Akass, J. McCabe, & S. Warn (Eds.), *Reading* The L Word: *Outing contemporary television* (pp. 33–42). London: I. B. Tauris.

Adams, T. M., & Fuller, D. B. (2006). The words have changed but the ideology remains the same: Misogynistic lyrics in rap music. *Journal of Black Studies, 36,* 938–957.

Albiniak, P. (2010). What women want to watch. *Broadcasting and Cable, 140,* 21.

Allen, M., Emmers-Sommer, T. M., D'Alessio, D., Timmerman, L., Hanzal, A., & Korus, J. (2007). The connection between the physiological and psychological reactions to sexually explicit materials: A literature summary using meta-analysis. *Communication Monographs, 74,* 541–560.

American Psychological Association. (2007). *Report of the APA Task Force on the Sexualization of Girls.* Washington, DC: Author. Retrieved March 28, 2011, from http://www.apa.org

Ancu, M., & Cozma, R. (2009). MySpace politics: Uses and gratifications of befriending candidates. *Journal of Broadcasting & Electronic Media, 53,* 567–583.

Andrejevic, M. (2003). *Reality TV: The work of being watched.* Lanham, MD: Rowman & Littlefield.

Andsager, J. L., & Roe, K. (1999). Country music video in country's Year of the Woman. *Journal of Communication, 49,* 69–82.

Arima, A. (2003). Gender stereotypes in Japanese television advertisements. *Sex Roles, 49,* 81–80.

Armstrong, J. (2010, November 29). *16 and Pregnant* delivers big. *Entertainment Weekly, 49.*

Armstrong, J. (2011, January 28). Gay teens on TV. *Entertainment Weekly, 34–41.*

Armstrong, J., & Jensen, J. (2011, March 18). Fall TV gets some much-needed diversity. *Entertainment Weekly, 22.*

Artz, L. (2011). Monarchs, monsters, and multiculturalism: Disney's menu for global hierarchy. In G. Dines & J. M. Humez (Eds.), *Gender, race, and class in media: A critical reader* (3rd ed., pp. 383–388). Los Angeles: Sage.

Artz, N., Munger, J., & Purdy, W. (1999). Gender issues in advertising language. *Women & Language, 22,* 20–26.

Ata, R., Ludden, A. B., & Lally, M. M. (2006). The effects of gender and family, friend, and media influences on eating behaviors and body image during adolescence. *Journal of Youth Adolescence, 36,* 1024–1037.

Attwood, F. (2011). No money shot? Commerce, pornography, and new sex taste cultures. In G. Dines & J. M. Humez (Eds.), *Gender, race, and class in media: A critical reader* (3rd ed., pp. 283–292). Los Angeles: Sage.

Aubrey, J. S. (2007). The impact of sexually objectifying media exposure on negative body emotions and sexual self-perceptions: Investigating the mediating role of body self-consciousness. *Mass Communication and Society, 10,* 1–23.

Aubrey, J. S., & Harrison, K. (2004). The gender-role content of children's favorite television programs and its links to their gender-related perceptions. *Media Psychology, 6,* 111–146.

Avila-Saavedra, G. (2009). Nothing queer about queer television: Televised construction of gay masculinities. *Media, Culture, and Society, 31,* 5–21.

Azikwe, M. D. (2011). More than baby mamas: Black mothers and hip-hop feminism. In G. Dines & J. M. Humez (Eds.), *Gender, race, and class in media: A critical reader* (3rd ed., pp. 137–143). Los Angeles: Sage.

Baker, C. N. (2005). Images of women's sexuality in advertisements: A content analysis of black- and white-oriented women's and men's magazines. *Sex Roles, 52,* 13–27.

Baker Woods, G. (1995). *Advertising and marketing to the new majority.* Belmont, CA: Wadsworth.

Balaji, M. (2010). Vixen resistin': Redefining black womanhood in hip-hop music videos. *Journal of Black Studies, 41,* 5–20.

Balsamo, A. (1996). *Technologies of the gendered body: Reading cyborg women.* Durham, NC: Duke University Press.

Banet-Weiser, S., & Portwood-Stacer, L. (2006). "I just want to be me again!" Beauty pageants, reality television and post-feminism. *Feminist Theory, 7,* 255–272.

Barlow, A. J. (2007). *Blogging America: The new public sphere.* Santa Barbara, CA: Praeger.

Baron, N. (2008). *Always on: Language in an online and mobile world.* New York: Oxford University Press.

Barton, K. M. (2009). Reality television programming and diverging gratifications: The influence of content on gratifications obtained. *Journal of Broadcasting & Electronic Media, 53,* 460–476.

Battles, K., & Hilton-Morrow, W. (2002). Gay characters in conventional spaces: *Will & Grace* and the situation comedy genre. *Critical Studies in Media Communication, 19,* 87–105.

Baxter, J. (2009). Constructions of active womanhood and new femininities: From a feminist linguistic perspective, is *Sex and the City* a modernist or a post-modernist TV text? *Women & Language, 32,* 91–98.

Beebe, S. A., Beebe, S. J., & Ivy, D. K. (2013). *Communication: Principles for a lifetime* (5th ed.). Boston: Pearson/Allyn & Bacon.

Bell, E., Haas, L., & Sells, L. (Eds.) (2008). *From mouse to mermaid: The politics of film, gender, and culture.* Bloomington: Indiana University Press.

Bell-Jordan, K. E. (2008). *Black.White.* and a *Survivor of The Real World:* Constructions of race on reality TV. *Critical Studies in Media Communication, 25,* 353–372.

Bennett, L. (2008, Spring). Feminist Super Bowl AdWatch finds few women, but plenty of demeaning stereotypes. *National NOW Foundation Times,* p. 11.

Benshoff, H. M., & Griffin, S. (2009). *America on film: Representing race, class, gender, and sexuality at the movies* (2nd ed.). New York: Wiley-Blackwell.

Bergen, R. K. (2000). Exploring the connection between pornography and sexual violence. *Violence & Victims, 15,* 227–234.

Beynon, J. (2004). The commercialization of masculinities: From the "new man" to the "new lad." In C. Carter & L. Steiner (Eds.), *Critical readings: Media and gender* (pp. 198–217). Maidenhead, Berkshire, UK: Open University Press.

Bierly, M. (2011, March 18). The *Cops* effect. *Entertainment Weekly,* 10.

Bittner, J. R. (1995). *Mass communication: An introduction* (6th ed.). Englewood Cliffs, NJ: Prentice Hall.

Boler, M. (2010). Hypes, hopes, and actualities: New digital Cartesianism and bodies in cyberspace. In P. K. Nayar (Ed.), *The new media and cybercultures anthology* (pp. 185–208). Malden, MA: Wiley-Blackwell.

Borisoff, D. J., & Chesebro, J. W. (2011). *Communicating power and gender.* Long Grove, IL: Waveland.

Boushey, H. (2009). Women breadwinners, men unemployed. In H. Boushey & A. O'Leary (Eds.), *The Shriver report: A woman's nation changes everything.* Washington, DC: Center for American Progress.

Boyle, K. (2011). "That's so fun": Selling pornography for men to women in *The Girls Next Door.* In G. Dines & J. M. Humez (Eds.), *Gender, race, and class in media: A critical reader* (3rd ed., pp. 293–300). Los Angeles: Sage.

Boylorn, R. M. (2008). As seen on TV: An autoethnographic reflection on race and reality television. *Critical Studies in Media Communication, 25,* 413–433.

Bragg, B., & McFarland, P. (2007). The erotic and pornographic in Chicana rap. *Meridians: Feminism, Race, Transnationalism, 7,* 1–21.

Bramlett-Solomon, S. (2001, October). *Rarely there but redefining beauty? Black women in fashion magazine ads.* Paper presented at the meeting of the Organization for the Study of Communication, Language, and Gender, San Diego, CA.

Bretthauer, B., Schindler Zimmerman, T., & Banning, J. H. (2006). A feminist analysis of popular music: Power over, objectification of, and violence against women. *Journal of Feminist Family Therapy, 18,* 29–51.

Brookey, R. A., & Cannon, K. L. (2011). Sex lives in *Second Life.* In G. Dines & J. M. Humez (Eds.), *Gender, race, and class in media: A critical reader* (3rd ed., pp. 571–581). Los Angeles: Sage.

Brooks, D. E., & Hebert, L. P. (2006). Gender, race, and media representation. In B. Dow & J. T. Wood (Eds.), *The Sage handbook of gender and communication* (pp. 297–317). Thousand Oaks, CA: Sage.

Brown, J. D., & Campbell, K. (1986). Race and gender in music videos: The same beat but a different drummer. *Journal of Communication, 36,* 94–106.

Brown, J. D., & L'Engle, L. K. (2009). X-rated: Sexual attitudes and behaviors associated with U.S. early adolescents' exposure to sexually explicit media. *Communication Research, 36,* 129–151.

Brown, J. D., L'Engle, L. K., Pardun, C. J., Guo, G., Kenneavy, K., & Jackson, C. (2006). Sexy media matter: Exposure to sexual content in music, movies, television, and magazines predicts black and white adolescents' sexual behavior. *Pediatrics, 117,* 1018–1027.

Brown, L. S. (2005). Outwit, outlast, out-flirt? The women of reality TV. In E. Cole & J. Henderson Daniel (Eds.), *Featuring females: Feminist analyses of media* (pp. 71–83). Washington, DC: American Psychological Association.

Browne, B. A. (1998). Gender stereotypes in advertising on children's television in the 1990s: A cross-national analysis. *Journal of Advertising, 27,* 83–96.

Bryson, M. (2004). When Jill jacks in: Queer women and the net. *Feminist Media Studies, 4,* 239–254.

Butruille, S. G., & Taylor, A. (1987). Women in American popular song. In L. P. Stewart & S. Ting-Toomey (Eds.), *Communication, gender, and sex roles in diverse interaction contexts* (pp. 179–188). Norwood, NJ: Ablex.

Butsch, R. (2011). Ralph, Fred, Archie, Homer, and the king of Queens: Why television keeps re-creating the male working-class buffoon. In G. Dines & J. M. Humez (Eds.), *Gender, race, and class in media: A critical reader* (3rd ed., pp. 101–109). Los Angeles: Sage.

Calzo, J. P., & Ward, L. M. (2009). Contributions of parents, peers, and media to attitudes toward homosexuality: Investigating sex and ethnic differences. *Journal of Homosexuality, 56,* 1101–1116.

Campbell, R., Martin, C. R., & Fabos, B. (2003). *Media and culture: An introduction to mass communication* (updated 3rd ed.). Boston: Bedford/St. Martin's.

Campbell, R., Martin, C. R., & Fabos, B. (2011). *Media and culture: An introduction to mass communication* (7th ed.). Boston: Bedford/St. Martin's.

Capsuto, S. (2000). *Alternate channels: The uncensored story of gay and lesbian images on radio and television, 1930 to the present.* New York: Ballantine Books.

Caputi, J. (2011). Everyday pornography. In G. Dines & J. M. Humez (Eds.), *Gender, race, and class in media: A critical reader* (3rd ed., pp. 311–320). Los Angeles: Sage.

Cato, M., & Dillman Carpentier, F. R. (2010). Conceptualizations of female empowerment and enjoyment of sexualized characters in reality television. *Mass Communication and Society, 13,* 270–288.

Chambers, K. L., & Alexander, S. M. (2007). Media literacy as an educational method for addressing college women's body image issues. *Education, 127,* 490–497.

Chaney, C. (2009). Trapped in the closet: Understanding contemporary relationships in the African-American hip hop community. *Women & Language, 32,* 59–67.

Chia, S. C., & Gunther, A. C. (2006). How media contribute to misperceptions of social norms about sex. *Mass Communication and Society, 9,* 301–320.

Chupack, C. (2007, October). Live your best love life! *O: The Oprah Winfrey Magazine,* 294.

Clarkson, J. (2005). Contesting masculinity's makeover: *Queer Eye,* consumer masculinity, and "straight-acting" gays. *Journal of Communication Inquiry, 29,* 235–255.

Cloud, D. (2010). The irony bribe and reality television: Investment and detachment in *The Bachelor. Critical Studies in Media Communication, 27,* 413–437.

Conrad, K., Dixon, T., & Zhang, Y. (2009). Controversial rap themes, gender portrayals and skin tone distortion: A content analysis of rap music videos. *Journal of Broadcasting & Electronic Media, 53,* 134–156.

Consalvo, M. (2006). Gender and new media. In B. J. Dow & J. T. Wood (Eds.), *The Sage handbook of gender and communication* (pp. 355–369). Thousand Oaks, CA: Sage.

Cook, B. (Ed.) (2007). *Thelma and Louise live!: The cultural afterlife of an American film.* Austin: University of Texas Press.

Cooper, B. (2000). "Chick flicks" as feminist texts: The appropriation of the male gaze in *Thelma & Louise. Women's Studies in Communication, 23,* 277–306.

Corrigan, L. M. (2009). Sacrifice, love, and resistance: The hip hop legacy of Assata Shakur. *Women & Language, 32*, 2–13.

Cortese, A. J. (2008). *Provocateur: Images of women and minorities in advertising* (3rd ed.). Lanham, MD: Rowman & Littlefield.

Cottle, M. (2003). Turning boys into girls. In A. Alexander & J. Hanson (Eds.), *Taking sides: Clashing views on controversial issues in mass media and society* (7th ed., pp. 68–74). Guilford, CT: McGraw-Hill/Dushkin.

Courtney, A. E., & Whipple, T. W. (1974). Women in TV commercials. *Journal of Communication, 24*, 110–118.

Courtney, A. E., & Whipple, T. W. (1983). *Sex stereotyping in advertising.* Lexington, MA: Lexington.

Cragin, B. (2010). Beyond the feminine: Intersectionality and hybridity in talk shows. *Women's Studies in Communication, 33*, 154–172.

Craig, R. S. (1992, October). *Selling masculinities, selling femininities: Multiple genders and the economics of television.* Paper presented at the meeting of the Speech Communication Association, Chicago, IL.

Crawford, M., & Unger, R. (2004). *Women and gender: A feminist psychology* (4th ed.). New York: McGraw-Hill.

Cronin, B., & Davenport, E. (2010). E-rogenous zones: Positioning pornography in the digital economy. In P. K. Nayar (Ed.), *The new media and cybercultures anthology* (pp. 284–306). Malden, MA: Wiley-Blackwell.

Currier, D. (2010). Assembling bodies in cyberspace: Technologies, bodies, and sexual difference. In P. K. Nayar (Ed.), *The new media and cybercultures anthology* (pp. 254–267). Malden, MA: Wiley-Blackwell.

D'Amato, A. (2009). Porn up, rape down. In J. W. White (Ed.), *Taking sides: Clashing views in gender* (4th ed., pp. 164–167). Boston: McGraw-Hill.

Daughton, S. M. (2010). "Cursed with self-awareness": Gender-bending, subversion, and irony in *Bull Durham. Women's Studies in Communication, 33*, 96–118.

Davis, A. M. (2005). The "dark prince" and dream women: Walt Disney and mid twentieth century American feminism. *Historical Journal of Film, 25*, 213–230.

Davis, A. M. (2007). *Good girls and wicked witches: Women in Disney's feature animation.* New Barnet, Herts, UK: John Libbey Publishing.

Davis, C. (2008, May). *The gender factor of "Survivor": A Q method.* Paper presented at the meeting of the International Communication Association, Montreal, Canada.

Davis, L. R. (1997). *The swimsuit issue and sport: Hegemonic masculinity in* Sports Illustrated. Albany: State University of New York Press.

deGrazia, E. (1992). *Girls lean back everywhere: The law of obscenity and the assault on genius.* New York: Random House.

deGregorio, F., & Sung, Y. (2010). Understanding attitudes toward and behaviors in response to product placement. *Journal of Advertising, 39*, 83–96.

Diamond, M. (2009). Pornography, public acceptance and sex-related crime. *International Journal of Law and Psychiatry, 32*, 304–314.

Dillman Carpentier, F., Knobloch-Westerwick, S., & Blumhoff, A. (2007). Naughty versus nice: Suggestive pop music influences on perceptions of potential romantic partners. *Media Psychology, 9*, 1–7.

Dines, G., & Jensen, R. (2004). Pornography and media: Toward a more critical analysis. In M. S. Kimmel & R. F. Plante (Eds.), *Sexualities: Identities, behaviors, and society* (pp. 369–380). New York: Oxford University Press.

Dobosz, A. M. (1997, November–December). Thicker thighs by Thanksgiving. *Ms.,* 89–91.

Doring, N., & Gundolf, A. (2010). Your life in snapshots: Mobile weblogs. In P. K. Nayar (Ed.), *The new media and cybercultures anthology* (pp. 515–525). Malden, MA: Wiley-Blackwell.

Doring, N., & Poschl, S. (2006). Images of men and women in mobile phone advertisements: A content analysis of advertisements for mobile communication systems in selected popular magazines. *Sex Roles, 55*, 173–185.

Douglas, S. J. (1995a). Sitcom women: We've come a long way. Maybe. *Ms.,* 76–80.

Douglas, S. J. (1995b). *Where the girls are: Growing up female with the mass media.* New York: Random House.

Douglas, S. J. (2000). Signs of intelligent life on TV. In S. Maasik & J. Solomon (Eds.), *Signs of life in the U.S.A.: Readings on popular culture for writers* (pp. 260–264). Boston: Bedford/St. Martin's.

Douglas, S. J. (2009). Where have you gone, Roseanne Barr? In H. Boushey & A. O'Leary (Eds.), *The Shriver report: A woman's nation changes everything.* Washington, DC: Center for American Progress.

Douglas, S. J. (2010a). *Enlightened sexism: The seductive message that feminism's work is done.* New York: Times Books.

Douglas, S. J. (2010b). *The rise of enlightened sexism: How pop culture took us from girl power to girls gone wild.* New York: St. Martin's Griffin.

Dove-Viebahn, A. (2010, Spring). Stand by your man? *The Good Wife* defies gender—and genre—norms. *Ms.,* 47–48.

Dove-Viebahn, A. (2011). Fashionably femme: Lesbian visibility, style, and politics in *The L Word.* In T. Peele (Ed.), *Queer popular culture: Literature, media, film, and television* (pp. 71–84). New York: Palgrave Macmillan.

Dow, B. J. (1996). *Prime-time feminism: Television, media culture, and the Women's Movement since 1970.* Philadelphia: University of Pennsylvania Press.

Dow, B. J. (2001). Ellen, television, and the politics of gay and lesbian visibility. *Critical Studies in Media Communication, 18,* 123–140.

Dubrofsky, R. E. (2006). *The Bachelor:* Whiteness in the harem. *Critical Studies in Media Communication, 23,* 39–56.

Dubrofsky, R. E. (2009). Fallen women in reality TV. *Feminist Media Studies, 9,* 353–368.

Dubrofsky, R. E., & Hardy, A. (2008). Performing race in *Flavor of Love* and *The Bachelor. Critical Studies in Media Communication, 25,* 373–392.

Duffy, B. E. (2010). Empowerment through endorsement? Polysemic meaning in Dove's user-generated advertising. *Communication, Culture, and Critique, 3,* 26–43.

Durham, M. G. (2009a). *The Lolita effect: The media sexualization of young girls and five keys to fixing it.* New York: The Overlook Press.

Durham, M. G. (2009b, January 9). X-rated America. *The Chronicle of Higher Education,* pp. B14–B15.

Dworkin, A. (1986). Pornography is a civil rights issue. In A. Dworkin (Ed., 1993), *Letters from a war zone.* Brooklyn, NY: Lawrence Hill.

Dworkin, A. (2000). Against the male flood: Censorship, pornography, and equality. In D. Cornell (Ed.), *Feminism & pornography* (pp. 19–38). New York: Oxford University Press.

Egley Waggoner, C. (2004). Disciplining female sexuality in *Survivor. Feminist Media Studies, 4,* 217–220.

Elasmar, M., Hasegawa, K., & Brain, M. (1999). The portrayal of women in U.S. prime-time television. *Journal of Broadcasting & Electronic Media, 44,* 20–34.

Engstrom, E. (2009). Creation of a new "empowered" female identity in WEtv's *Bridezillas. Media Report to Women, 37,* 6–12.

Ensslin, A., & Muse, E. (Eds.) (2011). *Creating second lives: Community, identity, and spatiality as constructions of the virtual.* New York: Routledge.

Enteen, J. B. (2009). *Virtual English: Queer Internets and digital creolization.* New York: Routledge.

Esposito, J. (2011). What does race have to do with *Ugly Betty?* An analysis of privilege and postracial(?) representations on a television sitcom. In G. Dines & J. M. Humez (Eds.), *Gender, race, and class in media: A critical reader* (3rd ed., pp. 95–99). Los Angeles: Sage.

Familysafemedia.com. (2011). Pornography statistics. Retrieved March 27, 2011, from http://familysafemedia.com

Farr, D., & Degroult, N. (2008). Understand the queer world of the l-esbian body: Using *Queer as Folk* and *The L Word* to address the construction of the lesbian body. *Journal of Lesbian Studies, 12,* 423–434.

Feasey, R. (2009). Spray more, get more: Masculinity, television advertising, and the Lynx effect. *Journal of Gender Studies, 18,* 357–368.

Ferguson, G. (2010). The family on reality television: Who's shaming whom? *Television and New Media, 11,* 87–104.

Fischer, P., & Greitemeyer, T. (2006). Music and aggression: The impact of sexual-aggressive song lyrics on aggression-related thoughts, emotions, and behavior toward the same and the opposite sex. *Personality and Social Psychology Bulletin, 32,* 1165–1176.

Fisher, D. A., Hill, D. L., Grube, J. W., & Gruber, E. L. (2007). Gay, lesbian, and bisexual content on television: A quantitative analysis across two seasons. *Journal of Homosexuality, 52,* 167–188.

Flood, M. (2009). The harms of pornography exposure among children and young people. *Child Abuse Review, 18,* 384–400.

Fournier, G. (2006). *Thelma and Louise and women in Hollywood.* Jefferson, NC: McFarland.

French, M. (1992). *The war against women.* New York: Summit.

Freudiger, P., & Almquist, E. M. (1978). Male and female roles in the lyrics of three genres of contemporary music. *Sex Roles, 4,* 51–65.

Friedman, E. J. (2010). Lesbians in [cyber]space: The politics of the Internet in Latin American on- and off-line communities. In P. K. Nayar

(Ed.), *The new media and cybercultures anthology* (pp. 268–283). Malden, MA: Wiley-Blackwell.

Friedman, J., & Valenti, J. (2008). *Yes means yes: Visions of female sexual power and a world without rape.* Berkeley, CA: Seal Press.

Frisby, C. M. (2010). Sticks 'n' stones may break my bones, but words they hurt like hell: Derogatory words in popular songs. *Media Report to Women, 38,* 12–18.

Funt, P. (2009, December 23). Reality TV is simply a microcosm of our society. *USA Today,* p. 15A.

Gallagher, M. (2004). *Queer Eye* for the heterosexual couple. *Feminist Media Studies, 4,* 223–225.

Ganahl, D., Prinsen, T. J., & Netzley, S. B. (2003). A content analysis of prime-time commercials: A contextual framework of gender representation. *Sex Roles, 49,* 545–551.

Garcia, A. (2011, First Quarter). Exploring the burn: A critical look at *Love the Way You Lie. Making the difference: A publication of The Women's Shelter of South Texas,* pp. 10–11.

Gatewood, F. (2001). She-devils on wheels: Women, motorcycles, and movies. In M. Pomerance (Ed.), *Ladies and gentlemen, boys and girls: Gender in film at the end of the twentieth century* (pp. 203–216). New York: State University of New York Press.

Gentry, J., & Harrison, R. (2010). Is advertising a barrier to male movement toward gender change? *Marketing Theory, 10,* 74–96.

Gerbner, G. (2003). Television violence at a time of turmoil and terror. In G. Dines & J. M. Humez (Eds.), *Gender, race, and class in media: A critical reader* (2nd ed., pp. 339–348). Thousand Oaks, CA: Sage.

Gerbner, G., Gross, L., Morgan, M., & Signorielli, N. (1980). The "mainstreaming" of America: Violence profile no. 11. *Journal of Communication, 30,* 10–29.

Gerhard, J. (2011). *Sex and the City:* Carrie Bradshaw's queer postfeminism. In G. Dines & J. M. Humez (Eds.), *Gender, race, and class in media: A critical reader* (3rd ed., pp. 75–79). Los Angeles: Sage.

Gill, R. (2007). *Gender and the media.* Cambridge, UK: Polity Press.

Gill, R. (2011). Supersexualize me! Advertising and the "midriffs." In G. Dines & J. M. Humez (Eds.), *Gender, race, and class in media: A critical reader* (3rd ed., pp. 255–260). Los Angeles: Sage.

Gillespie, M. A., Dworkin, A., Shange, N., Ramos, N., & French, M. (1994, January–February). Where do we stand on pornography? *Ms.,* 33–41.

Gilliam, K., & Wooden, S. R. (2008). Post-princess models of gender: The new man in Disney/Pixar. *Journal of Popular Film and Television, 36,* 2–8.

Giresunlu, L. (2009). Cyborg goddesses: The mainframe revisited. *At the Interface/Probing the Boundaries, 56,* 157–187.

Givhan, R. (2005, August 19). Sorry, Dove: Bigger isn't necessarily better. Retrieved March 13, 2011, from http://www.washingtonpost.com

Givhan, R. (2009, April 12). "Housewives" function best on dysfunction. Retrieved December 1, 2010, from http://www.washingtonpost.com

Glascock, J. (2005). Degrading content and character sex: Accounting for men and women's differential reactions to pornography. *Communication Reports, 18,* 43–53.

Glassner, B. (2005). Black men: How to perpetuate prejudice without really trying. In M. B. Zinn, P. Hondagneu-Sotelo, & M. A. Messner (Eds.), *Gender through the prism of difference* (3rd ed., pp. 489–496). New York: Oxford University Press.

Glenn, R. J. III. (1992, November). *Echoes of feminism on the big screen: A fantasy theme analysis of "Thelma and Louise."* Paper presented at the meeting of the Speech Communication Association, Chicago, IL.

Gow, J. (1996). Reconsidering gender roles on MTV: Depictions in the most popular music videos of the early 1990s. *Communication Reports, 9,* 151–161.

Greenblatt, L. (2004, November 12). College rocks: Hot, influential MTVU is putting the music back into TV—finally! *Entertainment Weekly,* 21.

Hanke, R. (1998). The "mock-macho" situation comedy: Hegemonic masculinity and its reiteration. *Western Journal of Communication, 62,* 74–93.

Harcourt, W. (2000). The personal and the political: Women using the Internet. *CyberPsychology and Behavior, 3,* 693–697.

Harding, D., & Nett, E. (1984). Women and rock music. *Atlantis, 10,* 60–77.

Harper, B., & Tiggemann, M. (2007). The effect of thin ideal media images on women's self-objectification, mood, and body image. *Sex Roles, 58,* 649–657.

Harris, M. (2011, March 4). Taking multitasking to task. *Entertainment Weekly,* 29.

Hart, K.-P. R. (2003). Representing gay men on American television. In G. Dines & J. M. Humez (Eds.), *Gender, race, and class in media: A critical reader* (2nd ed., pp. 507–607). Thousand Oaks, CA: Sage.

Hart, K.-P. R. (2004). We're here, we're queer—and we're better than you: The representational superiority of gay men to heterosexuals on *Queer Eye for the Straight Guy*. *Journal of Men's Studies, 12,* 241–253.

Harwood, J., & Anderson, K. (2002). The presence and portrayal of social groups on prime-time television. *Communication Reports, 15,* 81–97.

Hasinoff, A. A. (2008). Fashioning race for the free market on *America's Next Top Model*. *Critical Studies in Media Communication, 25,* 324–343.

Hatfield, E. F. (2010). "What it means to be a man": Examining hegemonic masculinity in *Two and a Half Men*. *Communication, Culture, and Critique, 3,* 526–548.

Heaton, J. A., & Wilson, N. L. (1995, September/October). Tuning in to trouble. *Ms.,* 44–51.

Henry, W. J., West, N. M., & Jackson, A. (2010). Hip-hop's influence on the identity development of black female college students: A literature review. *Journal of College Student Development, 51,* 237–251.

Henson, L., & Parameswaran, R. E. (2008). Getting real with "tell it like it is" talk therapy: Hegemonic masculinity and the *Dr. Phil Show*. *Communication, Culture, and Critique, 1,* 287–310.

Hentges, B. A., Bartsch, R. B., & Meier, J. A. (2007). Gender representation in commercials as a function of target audience age. *Communication Research Reports, 24,* 55–62.

Herring, S. C., Kouper, I., Scheidt, L. A., & Wright, E. (2004). Women and children last: The discursive construction of weblogs. In L. Gurak, S. Antonijevic, L. Johnson, C. Ratliff, & J. Reyman (Eds.), *Into the blogosphere: Rhetoric, community, and culture of weblogs*. Retrieved March 31, 2011, from http://blog.lib.umn.edu

Hill, L. (2010). Gender and genre: Situating *Desperate Housewives*. *Journal of Popular Film and Television, 38,* 162–169.

Hill Collins, P. (2004). *Black sexual politics: African Americans, gender, and the new racism*. New York: Routledge.

Hopper, D. (2011, February 15). *Sports Illustrated* swimsuit issue keeps getting closer to porn without being porn. Retrieved March 27, 2011, from http://www.bestweekever.tv

Hopson, M. C. (2008). "Now watch me dance": Responding to critical observations, constructions, and performances of race on reality television. *Critical Studies in Media Communication, 25,* 441–446.

Horn, A. (2009). "Keepin' it country": What makes the lyrics of Gretchen Wilson hard? *Popular Music and Society, 32,* 461–473.

Hubert, S. J. (2003). What's wrong with this picture? The politics of Ellen's coming out party. In G. Dines & J. M. Humez (Eds.), *Gender, race, and class in media: A critical reader* (2nd ed., pp. 608–612). Thousand Oaks, CA: Sage.

Hunter, J. A., Figueredo, A. J., & Malamuth, N. M. (2009). Developmental pathways into social and sexual deviance. *Journal of Family Violence, 25,* 141–148.

Hust, S. J. T., Brown, J. D., & L'Engle, K. L. (2008). Boys will be boys and girls better be prepared: An analysis of the rare sexual health messages in young adolescents' media. *Mass Communication and Society, 11,* 3–23.

Ivory, A. H., Gibson, R., & Ivory, J. D. (2009). Gendered relationships on television: Portrayals of same-sex and heterosexual couples. *Mass Communication and Society, 12,* 170–192.

Jackson, K. (1991, September 14). Have you come a long way, baby? *Dallas Morning News*, pp. 1C, 3C.

James, R. (2008). "Robo-diva R&B": Aesthetics, politics, and black female robots in contemporary popular music. *Journal of Popular Music Studies, 20,* 402–423.

Japp, P. M. (1991). Gender and work in the 1980s: Television's working women as displaced persons. *Women's Studies in Communication, 14,* 49–74.

Jeffries, M. P. (2009). Can a thug (get some) love? Sex, romance, and the definition of a hip hop "thug." *Women & Language, 32,* 35–41.

Jensen, R. (2007). *Getting off: Pornography and the end of masculinity*. Cambridge, MA: South End Press.

Jhally, S. (2003). Image-based culture: Advertising and popular culture. In G. Dines & J. M. Humez (Eds.), *Gender, race, and class in media: A critical reader* (2nd ed., pp. 249–257). Thousand Oaks, CA: Sage.

Jhally, S. (Producer/Director). (2007). *Dreamworlds 3: Desire/sex/power in music video* [Motion picture]. United States: Media Education Foundation.

Jordan, C. (2011). Marketing "reality" to the world: *Survivor*, post-Fordism, and reality television. In G. Dines & J. M. Humez (Eds.), *Gender, race, and class in media: A critical reader* (3rd ed., pp. 459–465). Los Angeles: Sage.

Juul, J. (2010). Games telling stories: A brief note on games and narratives. In P. K. Nayar (Ed.), *The new media and cybercultures anthology* (pp. 382–393). Malden, MA: Wiley-Blackwell.

Katz, J. (2011). Advertising and the construction of violent white masculinity. In G. Dines & J. M. Humez (Eds.), *Gender, race, and class in media: A critical reader* (3rd ed., pp. 261–269). Los Angeles: Sage.

Kellner, D. (2011). Cultural studies, multiculturalism, and media culture. In G. Dines & J. M. Humez (Eds.), *Gender, race, and class in media: A critical reader* (3rd ed., pp. 7–18). Los Angeles: Sage.

Kennedy, T. L. M. (2000). An exploratory study of feminist experiences in cyberspace. *CyberPsychology and Behavior, 3*, 707–719.

Kilbourne, J. (1998). Beauty and the beast of advertising. In L. J. Peach (Ed.), *Women in culture: A women's studies anthology* (pp. 127–131). Malden, MA: Blackwell.

Kilbourne, J. (1999). *Can't buy my love: How advertising changes the way we think and feel.* New York: Touchstone.

Kilbourne, J. (Writer). (2010a). *Killing us softly 4* [Motion picture]. United States: Media Education Foundation.

Kilbourne, J. (2010b, Summer). Sexist advertising, then & now. *Ms.*, 34–35.

Kim, A. (1995, January 20). Star trip: A new "Trek," a new network, a new captain—and (red alert!) she's a woman. *Entertainment Weekly*, 14–20.

Kim, J. L., Sorsoli, C. L., Collins, K., Zylbergold, B. A., Schooler, D., & Tolman, D. L. (2007). From sex to sexuality: Exposing the heterosexual script on primetime network television. *Journal of Sex Research, 44*, 145–157.

King, C. (2010). *Animating difference: Race, gender, and sexuality in contemporary films for children.* Lanham, MD: Rowman & Littlefield.

Kinnick, K. N., & Parton, S. R. (2005). Workplace communication: What *The Apprentice* teaches about communication skills. *Business Communication Quarterly, 68*, 429–456.

Kistler, M. E., & Lee, M. J. (2010). Does exposure to sexual hip-hop music videos influence the sexual attitudes of college students? *Mass Communication and Society, 13*, 67–86.

Kolehmainen, M. (2010). Normalizing and gendering affects. *Feminist Media Studies, 10*, 179–194.

Kramarae, C. (1995). A backstage critique of virtual reality. In S. Jones (Ed.), *Cybersociety: Computer-mediated communication and community* (pp. 36–56). Thousand Oaks, CA: Sage.

Kraus, S. W., & Russell, B. (2008). Early sexual experiences: The role of Internet access and sexually explicit material. *CyberPsychology and Behavior, 11*, 162–168.

Krolokke, C., & Sorensen, A. S. (2006). *Gender communication theories & analyses: From silence to performance.* Thousand Oaks, CA: Sage.

Kuczynski, A. (2000, March 5). Selling it all: "Red hot sex" and a stellar tuna casserole. *New York Times* News Service, as in the *Corpus Christi Caller Times*, p. A25.

Lauzen, M. M., Dozier, D. M., & Horan, N. (2008). Constructing gender stereotypes through social roles in prime-time television. *Journal of Broadcasting & Electronic Media, 52*, 200–214.

Leung, W. (2008). So queer yet so straight: Ang Lee's *The Wedding Banquet* and *Brokeback Mountain*. *Journal of Film and Video, 60*, 23–42.

Levine, D. E., Carlsson-Paige, N. (2003). The Mighty Morphin Power Rangers: Teachers voice concern. In G. Dines & J. M. Humez (Eds.), *Gender, race, and class in media: A critical reader* (2nd ed., pp. 359–366). Thousand Oaks, CA: Sage.

Levine, M. P., & Murnen, S. K. (2009). Everybody knows that mass media are a cause of eating disorders: A critical review of evidence for a causal link between media, negative body image, and disordered eating in females. *Journal of Social and Clinical Psychology, 28*, 9–42.

Lim, S., & Reeves, B. (2009). Being in the game: Effects of avatar choice and point of view on psychophysiological responses during play. *Media Psychology, 12*, 348–370.

Lin, C. A. (1997). Beefcake versus cheesecake in the 1990s: Sexist portrayals of both genders in television commercials. *Howard Journal of Communications, 8*, 237–249.

Lindner, K. (2004). Images of women in general interest and fashion magazine advertisements from 1955 to 2002. *Sex Roles, 51*, 409–421.

Lindsey, K. (2003). In their prime: Women in nighttime drama. In G. Dines & J. M. Humez (Eds.), *Gender, race, and class in media: A critical reader* (2nd ed., pp. 625–632). Thousand Oaks, CA: Sage.

Linneman, T. J. (2008). How do you solve a problem like Will Truman? The feminization of gay masculinities on *Will & Grace*. *Men and Masculinities, 10*, 583–603.

Lipsitz, G. (2011). The meaning of memory: Family, class, and ethnicity in early network television programs. In G. Dines & J. M. Humez (Eds.), *Gender, race, and class in media: A critical reader* (3rd ed., pp. 25–32). Los Angeles: Sage.

Lorie, A. F. (2011). Forbidden fruit or conventional apple pie? A look at *Sex and the City's* reversal of the female gender. *Media, Culture, and Society, 33,* 35–51.

Lotz, A. D. (2006). *Redesigning women: Television after the network era.* Champaign: University of Illinois Press.

Lotz, A. D. (2008). *The television will be revolutionized.* New York: New York University Press.

Machia, M., & Lamb, S. (2009). Sexualized innocence: Effects of magazine ads portraying adult women as sexy little girls. *Journal of Media Psychology, 21,* 15–24.

MacKinnon, K. (2003). *Representing men: Maleness and masculinity in the media.* New York: Arnold.

Mager, J., & Helgeson, J. G. (2011). Fifty years of advertising images: Some changing perspectives on role portrayals along with enduring consistencies. *Sex Roles, 64,* 238–252.

Mahmoud, A. E.-B., Klimsa, P., & Auter, P. J. (2010). Uses and gratifications of commercial websites in Egypt: Towards a new model. *Journal of Arab and Muslim Media Research, 3,* 99–120.

Malamuth, N. M., Addison, T., & Koss, M. (2000). Pornography and sexual aggression: Are there reliable effects and can we understand them? *Annual Review of Sex Research, 11,* 26–91.

Malamuth, N. M., & Billings, V. (1984). Why pornography? Models of functions and effects. *Journal of Communication, 34,* 117–129.

Mandziuk, R. (1991, February). *Cementing her sphere: Daytime talk and the television world of women.* Paper presented at the meeting of the Western States Communication Association, Phoenix, AZ.

Martin, J. B., & Yep, G. Y. (2004). Eminem in mainstream public discourse: Whiteness and the appropriate of Black masculinity. In R. A. Lind (Ed.), *Race/gender/media: Considering diversity across audiences, content, and producers* (pp. 228–235). Boston: Pearson.

Martino, S. C., Collins, R. L., Elliott, M. N., Strachman, A., Kanouse, D. E., & Berry, S. H. (2006). Exposure to degrading versus nondegrading music lyrics and sexual behavior among youth. *Pediatrics, 118,* 430–441.

Marwick, A. (2010). There's a beautiful girl under all of this: Performing hegemonic femininity in

reality television. *Critical Studies in Media Communication, 27,* 251–266.

Maxwell, J. P. (2001). The perception of relationship violence in the lyrics of a song. *Journal of Interpersonal Violence, 16,* 640–661.

Mayer, V. (2005). Soft-core in TV time: The political economy of a "cultural trend." *Critical Studies in Media Communication, 22,* 302–320.

McCabe, M. P., & Ricciardelli, L. A. (2005). A prospective study of pressures from parents, peers, and the media on extreme weight change behaviors among adolescent boys and girls. *Behaviour Research and Therapy, 43,* 653–668.

Merskin, D. (2011). Perpetuation of the hot-Latina stereotype in *Desperate Housewives*. In G. Dines & J. M. Humez (Eds.), *Gender, race, and class in media: A critical reader* (3rd ed., pp. 327–334). Los Angeles: Sage.

Meyer, M. D. E., & Kelley, J. M. (2004). Queering the eye? The politics of gay white men and gender (in)visibility. *Feminist Media Studies, 4,* 214–217.

Mikula, M. (2003). Gender and videogames: The political valency of Lara Croft. *Continuum: Journal of Media and Cultural Studies, 17,* 79–87.

Miller, P. (2010). TNT makes small step, portrays black man as friend, not sidekick. *Advertising Age, 81,* 14.

Mitra, A. (2010). Voices of the marginalized on the Internet: Examples from a website for women of South Asia. In P. K. Nayar (Ed.), *The new media and cybercultures anthology* (pp. 166–182). Malden, MA: Wiley-Blackwell.

Molina Guzman, I., & Valdivia, A. (2004). Brain, brow, and booty: Latina iconicity in U.S. popular culture. *Communication Review, 7,* 205–221.

Monk-Turner, E., Kouts, T., Parris, K., & Webb, C. (2007). Gender role stereotyping in advertisements on three radio stations: Does musical genre make a difference? *Journal of Gender Studies, 16,* 173–182.

Moore, C. (2011). Resisting, reiterating, and dancing through: The swinging closet doors of Ellen DeGeneres's televised personalities. In G. Dines & J. M. Humez (Eds.), *Gender, race, and class in media: A critical reader* (3rd ed., pp. 531–540). Los Angeles: Sage.

Moore, M. L. (1992). The family as portrayed on prime-time television, 1947–1990: Structure and characteristics. *Sex Roles, 26,* 41–61.

Moorti, S., & Ross, K. (2004). Reality television: Fairy tale or feminist nightmare? *Feminist Media Studies, 4,* 211–214.

Morrison, M. A., Krugman, D. M., & Park, P. (2008). Under the radar: Smokeless tobacco advertising in magazines with substantial youth readership. *American Journal of Public Health, 98,* 543–548.

Morrison, M. F. (2006, Anniversary). Mary go round: What happened to TV's independent women? *Bitch,* 77–79; 110.

Mortensen, T. E. (2010). WoW is the new MUD: Social gaming from text to video. In P. K. Nayar (Ed.), *The new media and cybercultures anthology* (pp. 394–407). Malden, MA: Wiley-Blackwell.

Mueller, B. (2011). Reaching African American consumers: African American shopping behavior. In G. Dines & J. M. Humez (Eds.), *Gender, race, and class in media: A critical reader* (3rd ed., pp. 213–219). Los Angeles: Sage.

Murphy-Hoefer, R., Hyland, A., & Rivard, C. (2010). The influence of tobacco countermarketing ads on college students' knowledge, attitudes, and beliefs. *Journal of American College Health, 58,* 373–381.

Nabi, R. L. (2009). Cosmetic surgery makeover programs and intentions to undergo cosmetic enhancements: A consideration of three models of media effects. *Human Communication Research, 35,* 1–27.

Nakamura, L. (2011). "Don't hate the player, hate the game": The racialization of labor in *World of Warcraft.* In G. Dines & J. M. Humez (Eds.), *Gender, race, and class in media: A critical reader* (3rd ed., pp. 563–569). Los Angeles: Sage.

Natalle, E. J., & Flippen, J. L. (2004). Urban music: Gendered language in rapping. In P. M. Backlund & M. R. Williams (Eds.), *Readings in gender communication* (pp. 140–149). Belmont, CA: Thomson/Wadsworth.

Nayar, P. (Ed.) (2010). *The new media and cybercultures anthology.* Malden, MA: Wiley-Blackwell.

Needham, G. (2009). *Brokeback Mountain: American indies.* Edinburgh, Scotland: Edinburgh University Press.

Neff, J. (2010a). Meet the man your man could smell like. *Advertising Age, 81,* 2–3.

Neff, J. (2010b). Cracking the viral code: Look at your ads. Now look at Old Spice. *Advertising Age, 81,* 16–17.

Niesel, J. (1997). Hip-hop matters: Rewriting the sexual politics of rap music. In L. Heywood & J. Drake (Eds.), *Third wave agenda: Being feminist, doing feminism* (pp. 239–253). Minneapolis: University of Minnesota Press.

Nip, J. (2004). The relationship between online and offline communities: The case of the Queer Sisters. *Media, Culture, and Society, 26,* 409–428.

Noble, B. (2007). Queer as box: Boi spectators and boy culture on Showtime's *Queer as Folk.* In M. L. Johnson (Ed.), *Third-wave feminism and television: Jane puts it in a box* (pp. 147–165). London: I. B. Tauris.

Nowak, K. L., Hamilton, M. A., & Hammond, C. C. (2009). The effects of image features on judgments of homophily, credibility, and intention to use as avatars in future interactions. *Media Psychology, 12,* 50–76.

Nowak, K. L., & Rauh, C. (2005). The influence of avatar on online perceptions of anthropomorphism, androgyny, credibility, homophily, and attraction. *Journal of Computer-Mediated Communication, 11,* 153–178.

Olson, B., & Douglas, W. (1997). The family on television: An evaluation of gender roles in situation comedy. *Sex Roles, 36,* 409–427.

Orbe, M. P. (2008). Representations of race in reality TV: Watch and discuss. *Critical Studies in Media Communication, 25,* 345–352.

Ouellette, L., & Hay, J. (2008). *Better living through reality TV: Television and post-welfare citizenship.* New York: Wiley-Blackwell.

Paglia, C. (2008, May 23). In defense of the working girl. *Entertainment Weekly,* 69.

Palmer, G. (2011). *Extreme Makeover: Home Edition:* An American fairy tale. In G. Dines & J. M. Humez (Eds.), *Gender, race, and class in media: A critical reader* (3rd ed., pp. 37–43). Los Angeles: Sage.

Palomares, N. A., & Lee, E.-J. (2010). Virtual gender identity: The linguistic assimilation to gendered avatars in computer-mediated communication. *Journal of Language and Social Psychology, 29,* 5–23.

Pardun, C. J., L'Engle, L. K., & Brown, J. D. (2005). Linking exposure to outcomes: Early adolescents' consumption of sexual content in six media. *Mass Communication Sociology, 8,* 75–91.

Patterson, E. (2008). *On Brokeback Mountain: Meditations about masculinity, fear, and love in the story and the film.* Lanham, MD: Lexington Books.

Patterson, P. (1996). Rambos and Himbos: Stereotypical images of men in advertising. In P. Lester (Ed.), *Images that injure* (pp. 93–96). Westport, CT: Praeger.

Paul, B., & Shim, J. W. (2008). Gender, sexual affect, and motivations for Internet pornography use. *International Journal of Sexual Health, 20*, 187–199.

Paul, P. (2005). *Pornified: How pornography is damaging our lives, our relationships, and our families.* New York: Henry Holt and Company.

Pearson, K., & Reich, N. M. (2004). *Queer Eye* fairy tale: Changing the world one manicure at a time. *Feminist Media Studies, 4*, 229–231.

Peck, J. (2006). TV talk shows as therapeutic discourse: The ideological labor of the televised talking cure. *Communication Theory, 5*, 58–81.

Perry, I. (2003). Who(se) am I? The identity and image of women in hip-hop. In G. Dines & J. M. Humez (Eds.), *Gender, race, and class in media: A critical reader* (2nd ed., pp. 136–148). Thousand Oaks, CA: Sage.

Peter, J., & Valkenburg, P. M. (2006). Adolescents' exposure to sexually explicit online material and recreational attitudes toward sex. *Journal of Communication, 56*, 639–660.

Peter, J., & Valkenburg, P. M. (2008). Adolescents' exposure to sexually explicit Internet material and sexual preoccupancy: A three-wave panel study. *Media Psychology, 11*, 207–234.

Peter, J., & Valkenburg, P. M. (2010). Processes underlying the effects of adolescents' use of sexually explicit Internet material: The role of perceived realism. *Communication Research, 37*, 375–399.

Peterson, E. E. (1987). Media consumption and girls who want to have fun. *Critical Studies in Mass Communication, 4*, 37–50.

Peterson, J. L., & Hyde, J. S. (2010). A meta-analytic review of research on gender differences in sexuality, 1993–2007. *Psychological Bulletin, 136*, 21–38.

Pitcher, K. C. (2006). The staging of agency in *Girls Gone Wild. Critical Studies in Media Communication, 23*, 200–218.

Porfido, G. (2011). *Queer as Folk* and the spectacularization of gender identity. In T. Peele (Ed.), *Queer popular culture: Literature, media, film, and television* (pp. 57–70). New York: Palgrave Macmillan.

Potter, W. J. (2003). On media violence. In A. Alexander & J. Hanson (Eds.), *Taking sides: Clashing views on controversial issues in mass media and society* (7th ed., pp. 34–46). Guilford, CT: McGraw-Hill/Dushkin.

Pozner, J. L. (2005, Fall). Dove's "real beauty" backlash. *Bitch*, 15.

Pozner, J. L. (2010a). Creating the illusion of popular demand. *Extra!, 23*, 14–15.

Pozner, J. L. (2010b). *Reality bites back: The troubling truth about guilty pleasure TV.* Berkeley, CA: Seal Press.

Pratt, M. (2011). "This is the way we live . . . and love!" Feeding on and still hungering for lesbian representation in *The L Word*. In G. Dines & J. M. Humez (Eds.), *Gender, race, and class in media: A critical reader* (3rd ed., pp. 341–348). Los Angeles: Sage.

Primack, B. A., Gold, M. A., Schwarz, E. B., & Dalton, M. A. (2008). Degrading and nondegrading sex in popular music: A content analysis. *Public Health Reports, 123*, 593–600.

Pullen, C. (2007). *Documenting gay men: Identity and performance in reality television and documentary film.* Jefferson, NC: McFarland.

Quan-Haase, A., & Young, A. L. (2010). Uses and gratifications of social media: A comparison of Facebook and Instant Messaging. *Bulletin of Science, Technology, and Society, 30*, 350–361.

Rafalovich, A. (2006). Broken and becoming godsized: Contemporary metal music and masculine individualism. *Symbolic Interaction, 29*, 19–32.

Railton, D., & Watson, P. (2005). Naughty girls and red blooded women: Representations of female heterosexuality in music video. *Feminist Media Studies, 5*, 51–63.

Raiten-D'Antonio, T. (2010). *Ugly as sin: The truth about how we look and finding freedom from self-hatred.* Deerfield Beach, FL: Health Communications Inc.

Reed, J. (2005). Ellen Degeneres: Public lesbian number one. *Feminist Media Studies, 5*, 23–36.

Reed, J. (2011). The 3 phases of Ellen: From queer to gay to postgay. In T. Peele (Ed.), *Queer popular culture: Literature, media, film, and television.* New York: Palgrave Macmillan.

Reid, S. A., Byrne, S., Brundidge, J. S., Shoham, M. D., & Marlow, M. L. (2007). A critical test of self-enhancement, exposure, and self-categorization explanations for first- and third-person perceptions. *Human Communication Research, 33*, 143–162.

Reisman, J. (2009). Pornography's link to rape. In J. W. White (Ed.), *Taking sides: Clashing views in gender* (4th ed., pp. 169–170). Boston: McGraw-Hill.

Renshaw, S. (2009, Winter). The F word on *The L Word. Ms.*, 59.

Rice, L. (2009, June 19). Look who's talking too! *Entertainment Weekly*, 37.

Richardson, E. (2007). "She was workin' like foreal": Critical literacy and discourse practices of African American females in the age of hip hop. *Discourse and Society, 18,* 789–809.

Richmond-Abbott, M. (1992). *Masculine and feminine: Gender roles over the life cycle* (2nd ed.). New York: McGraw-Hill.

Roberts, D. F., Foehr, U. G., & Rideout, V. (2003). *Generation M: Media in the lives of 8–18 year olds.* Menlo Park, CA: Henry J. Kaiser Foundation.

Ropelato, J. (2003). Tricks pornographers play. Retrieved March 29, 2011, from http://www.familysafemedia.com

Rose, T. (2011). "There are bitches and hoes." In G. Dines & J. M. Humez (Eds.), *Gender, race, and class in media: A critical reader* (3rd ed., pp. 321–325). Los Angeles: Sage.

Rowe, K. (1990). Roseanne: Unruly woman as domestic goddess. *Screen, 31,* 408–419.

Royse, P., Lee, J., Baasanjav, U., Hopson, M., & Consalvo, M. (2010). Women and games: Technologies of the gendered self. In P. K. Nayar (Ed.), *The new media and cybercultures anthology* (pp. 408–424). Malden, MA: Wiley-Blackwell.

Sabina, C., Wolak, J., & Finkelhor, D. (2008). Rapid communication: The nature and dynamics of Internet pornography exposure for youth. *CyberPsychology and Behavior, 11,* 691–693.

Sanbonmatsu, J. (2011). Video games and machine dreams of domination. In G. Dines & J. M. Humez (Eds.), *Gender, race, and class in media: A critical reader* (3rd ed., pp. 427–436). Los Angeles: Sage.

Santa Cruz Bell, J., & Avant-Mier, R. (2009). What's love got to do with it? Analyzing the discourse of hip hop love through rap balladry, 1987 and 2007. *Women & Language, 32,* 42–49.

Sarracino, C., & Scott, K. M. (2009). *The porning of America: The rise of porn culture, what it means, and where we go from here.* New York: Beacon Press.

Schwartz, B. (2005). *The paradox of choice: Why more is less.* New York: Harper Perennial.

Schwartz, M. (2009, December 11). Sarah Jessica Parker and the women of *Sex and the City. Entertainment Weekly*, 55.

Schwarzbaum, L. (2008, May 16). Guys are the new girls. *Entertainment Weekly*, 48–49.

Schwarzbaum, L. (2009, February 20). Why I love chick flicks and why I hate them. *Entertainment Weekly*, 39–41.

Scott, J., & Craig-Lees, M. (2010). Audience engagement and its effects on product placement recognition. *Journal of Promotion Management, 16,* 39–58.

Seidman, S. A. (1992). An investigation of sex-role stereotyping in music videos. *Journal of Broadcasting & Electronic Media, 36,* 209–216.

Sellnow, D. D. (1999). Music as persuasion: Refuting hegemonic masculinity in "He Thinks He'll Keep Her." *Women's Studies in Communication, 22,* 66–84.

Sender, K. (2006). Queens for a day: *Queer Eye for the Straight Guy* and the neoliberal project. *Critical Studies in Media Communication, 23,* 131–151.

Shanahan, J., Signorielli, N., & Morgan, M. (2008, May). *Television and sex roles 30 years hence: A retrospective and current look from a cultural indicators perspective.* Paper presented at the meeting of the International Communication Association, Montreal, Canada.

Sharp, S. (2011). Disciplining the housewife in *Desperate Housewives* and domestic reality television. In G. Dines & J. M. Humez (Eds.), *Gender, race, and class in media: A critical reader* (3rd ed., pp. 481–486). Los Angeles: Sage.

Shattuc, J. (1997). *The talking cure: TV talk shows and women.* New York: Routledge.

Shattuc, J. (2004). Freud vs. women: The popularization of therapy on daytime talk shows. In C. Carter & L. Steiner (Eds.), *Critical readings: Media and gender* (pp. 307–327). Maidenhead, Berkshire, UK: Open University Press.

Sherman, B. L., & Dominick, J. R. (1986). Violence and sex in music videos: TV and rock and roll. *Journal of Communication, 36,* 79–93.

Shugart, H. A. (2001). Parody as subversive performance: Denaturalizing gender and reconstituting desire in *Ellen. Text & Performance Quarterly, 21,* 93–113.

Shugart, H. A. (2003). Reinventing privilege: The new (gay) man in contemporary popular media. *Critical Studies in Media Communication, 20,* 67–91.

Shugart, H. A., & Egley Waggoner, C. (2005). A bit much: Spectacle as discursive resistance. *Feminist Media Studies, 5,* 65–81.

Signorielli, N. (2009a). Race and sex in prime time: A look at occupations and occupational prestige. *Mass Communication and Society, 12,* 332–352.

Signorielli, N. (2009b). Minorities' representation in prime time: 2000 to 2008. *Communication Research Reports, 26,* 323–336.

Signorielli, N., & Bacue, A. (1999). Recognition and respect: A content analysis of prime-time television characters across three decades. *Sex Roles, 40,* 527–544.

Signorielli, N., & Morgan, M. (1990). *Cultivation analysis: New directions in media effects research.* Newbury Park, CA: Sage.

Simonton, A. J. (1995). Women for sale. In C. M. Lont (Ed.), *Women and media: Content, careers, criticism* (pp. 143–164). Belmont, CA: Wadsworth.

Sisco King, C. (2010). The man inside: Trauma, gender, and the nation in *The Brave One. Critical Studies in Media Communication, 27,* 111–130.

Skeggs, B., & Wood, H. (2008). The labour of transformation and circuits of value "around" reality television. *Continuum: Journal of Media and Cultural Studies, 22,* 559–572.

Skerski, J. (2007). From prime-time to daytime: The domestication of Ellen DeGeneres. *Communication and Critical/Cultural Studies, 4,* 363–381.

Sloop, J. M. (2006). Critical studies in gender/sexuality and media. In B. J. Dow & J. T. Wood (Eds.), *The Sage handbook of gender and communication* (pp. 319–333). Thousand Oaks, CA: Sage.

Smith, D. C. (2008). Critiquing reality-based televisual black fatherhood: A critical analysis of *Run's House* and *Snoop Dogg's Father Hood. Critical Studies in Media Communication, 25,* 393–412.

Smith, E. A., & Malone, R. E. (2003). The outing of Philip Morris: Advertising to gay men. *American Journal of Public Health, 93,* 988–993.

Smith, S. L. (2005). From Dr. Dre to *Dismissed:* Assessing violence, sex, and substance use on MTV. *Critical Studies in Media Communication, 22,* 89–98.

Soll, L. (2008, May 23). In her shoes. *Entertainment Weekly,* 69.

Sommers-Flanagan, R., Sommers-Flanagan, J., & Davis, B. (1993). What's happening on music television? A gender role content analysis. *Sex Roles, 28,* 745–753.

Spohrer, E. (2009). Not a gay cowboy movie? *Journal of Popular Film and Television, 37,* 26–33.

Squires, C. R. (2008). Race and reality TV: Tryin' to make it real—but real compared to what? *Critical Studies in Media Communication, 25,* 434–440.

Squires, C. R., Kohn-Wood, L. P., Chavous, T., & Carter, P. L. (2006). Evaluating agency and responsibility in gendered violence: African American youth talk about violence and hip hop. *Sex Roles, 55,* 725–737.

Stack, T. (2011, February 18). News & notes: More drama for MTV. *Entertainment Weekly,* 22–24.

Stankiewicz, J. M., & Rosselli, F. (2008). Women as sex objects and victims in print advertisements. *Sex Roles, 58,* 579–589.

Stark, S. (2000a). A tale of two sitcoms. In S. Maasik & J. Solomon (Eds.), *Signs of life in the U.S.A.: Readings on popular culture for writers* (pp. 236–241). Boston: Bedford/St. Martin's.

Stark, S. (2000b). *The Oprah Winfrey Show* and the talk-show furor. In S. Maasik & J. Solomon (Eds.), *Signs of life in the U.S.A.: Readings on popular culture for writers* (pp. 241–248). Boston: Bedford/St. Martin's.

Steenland, S. (1995). Content analysis of the image of women on television. In C. M. Lont (Ed.), *Women and media: Content, careers, criticism* (pp. 179–189). Belmont, CA: Wadsworth.

Steinberg, B. (2011). Chevy takes on ambitious role in TNT's "Men" program. *Advertising Age, 82,* 3–22.

Steinem, G. (1983). Erotica vs. pornography. In G. Steinem (Ed.), *Outrageous acts and everyday rebellions* (pp. 219–230). New York: Holt, Rinehart & Winston.

Steinem, G. (1990, July–August). Sex, lies, and advertising. As reprinted in the spring 2002 issue of *Ms.,* 60–64.

Stephens, V. (2005). Pop goes the rapper: A close reading of Eminem's genderphobia. *Popular Music, 24,* 21–36.

Stern, D. M. (2009). Consuming the fractured female: Lessons from MTV's *The Real World. Communication Review, 12,* 50–77.

Stern, S. (2002). Virtually speaking: Girls' self-disclosure on the WWW. *Women's Studies in Communication, 25,* 223–253.

Stern, S. (2004). Expressions of identity online: Prominent features and gender differences in adolescents' World Wide Web home pages. *Journal of Broadcasting & Electronic Media, 48,* 218–243.

Stone, A. R. (1996). *The war of desire and technology at the close of the mechanical age.* Cambridge: MIT Press.

Stransky, T. (2010, Year-end special). 2010 breakout TV stars. *Entertainment Weekly,* 103–105.

Stransky, T. (2011, March 18). Apologizing for *The Real World. Entertainment Weekly,* 63.

Strasburger, V. C. (2005). Adolescents, sex, and the media: Ooooo, baby, baby—a Q & A. *Adolescent Medicine Clinics, 16,* 269–288.

Streitmatter, R. (2009). *From "perverts" to "Fab Five": The media's changing depiction of gay men and lesbians.* New York: Routledge.

Strossen, N. (2000). *Defending pornography: Free speech, sex, and the fight for women's rights.* New York: New York University Press.

Sturken, M. (2008). *Thelma and Louise.* London: British Film Institute.

Tait, S. (2011). Television and the domestication of cosmetic surgery. In G. Dines & J. M. Humez (Eds.), *Gender, race, and class in media: A critical reader* (3rd ed., pp. 509–517). Los Angeles: Sage.

Tanner-Smith, E. E., Williams, D. T., & Nichols, D. (2006). Selling sex to radio program directors: A content analysis of *Radio & Records* magazine. *Sex Roles, 54,* 675–686.

Taylor, T. L. (2003). Multiple pleasures: Women and online gaming. *Convergence, 9,* 21–46.

Tedford, T. L. (2009). *Freedom of speech in the United States* (6th ed.). New York: Strata.

Tiggemann, M. (2005). Television and adolescent body image: The role of program content and viewing motivation. *Journal of Social and Clinical Psychology, 24,* 361–381.

Timmerman, L. M., Allen, M., Jorgensen, J., Herrett-Skjellum, J., Kramer, M. R., & Ryan, D. J. (2008). A review and meta-analysis examining the relationships of music content with sex, race, priming, and attitudes. *Communication Quarterly, 56,* 303–324.

Tolman, D. L., Kim, J. L., Schooler, D., & Sorsoli, C. L. (2007). Rethinking the associations between television viewing and adolescent sexuality development: Bringing gender into focus. *Journal of Adolescent Health, 40,* 9–16.

Towbin, M. A., Haddock, S. A., Zimmerman, T. S., Lund, L. K., & Tanner, L. R. (2004). Images of gender, race, age, and sexual orientation in Disney feature-length animated films. *Journal of Feminist Female Therapy, 15,* 19–44.

Traube, E. (1992). *Dreaming identities: Class, gender, and generation in 1980s Hollywood movies.* Boulder, CO: Westview.

Tropiano, S. (2002). *The prime time closet: A history of gays and lesbians on television.* Milwaukee: Applause Books.

Tuchman, G. (1979). Women's depiction by the mass media. *Signs, 4,* 528–542.

Tuchman, G., Daniels, A. K., & Benet, J. (Eds.). (1978). *Hearth and home: Images of women in the mass media.* New York: Oxford University Press.

Tucker, K. (2010, Year-end special). TV: The best shows of the year. *Entertainment Weekly,* 93–97.

Turkle, S. (1995). *Life on the screen: Identity in the age of the Internet.* New York: Touchstone.

Turkle, S. (2011). *Alone together: Why we expect more from technology and less from each other.* New York: Basic Books.

Turner, J. S. (2010). Sex and the spectacle of music videos: An examination of the portrayal of race and sexuality in music videos. *Sex Roles, 64,* 173–191.

Tyree, T. C. M. (2009). Lovin'momma and hatin' on baby mama: A comparison of misogynistic and stereotypical representations in songs about rappers' mothers and baby mamas. *Women & Language, 32,* 50–58.

Utley, E. A. (2010). "I used to love him": Exploring the miseducation about black love and sex. *Critical Studies in Media Communication, 27,* 291–308.

Utley, E. A., & Menzies, A. L. (2009). Show some love: Youth responses to "Kiss Me Thru the Phone." *Women & Language, 32,* 68–77.

van Zoonen, L. (2002). Gendering the Internet: Claims, controversies, and cultures. *European Journal of Communication, 17,* 5–23.

Vande Berg, L. R., & Streckfuss, D. (1992). Prime-time television's portrayal of women and the world of work: A demographic profile. *Journal of Broadcasting & Electronic Media, 36,* 195–208.

Vaynerchuk, G. (2011, March 3). Old Spice Man marketing, redux: What went right—and what did not. Retrieved March 11, 2011 from http://www.fastcompany.com

Villani, S. (2001). Impact of media on children and adolescents: A 10-year review of the research. *Journal of the American Academy of Child and Adolescent Psychiatry, 40*, 392–401.

Vincent, R.C. (1989). Clio's consciousness raised? Portrayal of women in rock videos, re-examined. *Journalism Quarterly, 66*, 155–160.

Vivian, J. (2011). *The media of mass communication* (10th ed.). Boston: Allyn & Bacon.

Wallmyr, G. (2006). Young people, pornography, and sexuality: Sources and attitudes. *The Journal of School Nursing, 22*, 290–295.

Walsh, K. R., Fursich, E., & Jefferson, B. S. (2008). Beauty and the patriarchal beast: Gender role portrayals in sitcoms featuring mismatched couples. *Journal of Popular Film and Television, 36*, 123–132.

Ward, L. M., Hansbrough, E., & Walker, E. (2005). Contributions of music video exposure to black adolescents' gender and sexual schemas. *Journal of Adolescent Research, 20*, 143–166.

Weiss, D. (2005). Constructing the queer "I": Performativity, citationality, and desire in *Queer Eye for the Straight Guy. Popular Communication, 3*, 73–95.

Weitzer, R., & Kubrin, C. E. (2009). Misogyny in rap music: A content analysis of prevalence and meanings. *Men and Masculinities, 12*, 3–29.

Wells, W. D., Moriarty, S., & Burnett, J. (2005). *Advertising principles and practice* (7th ed.). New York: Prentice Hall.

Welsch, J. R. (2001). "Let's keep goin'!" On the road with Louise and Thelma. In M. Pomerance (Ed.), *Ladies and gentlemen, boys and girls: Gender in film at the end of the twentieth century* (pp. 249–266). Albany, NY: State University of New York Press.

Westerfelhaus, R., & Lacroix, C. (2006). Seeing "straight" through *Queer Eye:* Exposing the strategic rhetoric of heteronormativity in a mediated ritual of gay rebellion. *Critical Studies in Media Communication, 23*, 426–444.

Whipple, T. W., & Courtney, A. E. (1980). How to portray women in TV commercials. *Journal of Advertising Research, 20*, 53–59.

Whipple, T. W., & Courtney, A. E. (1985). Female role portrayals in advertising and communication effectiveness: A review. *Journal of Advertising, 14*, 4–8.

White, L. A. (2000, November). *A re-investigation of sex-role stereotyping in MTV music videos.* Paper presented at the meeting of the National Communication Association, Seattle, WA.

Wiles, M. A., & Danielova, A. (2009). The worth of product placement in successful films: An event study analysis. *Journal of Marketing, 73*, 44–63.

Williams, L. (2007, May). *Music lyrics versus music videos: The importance of platform in assessing exposure to sexual content.* Paper presented at the meeting of the International Communication Association, San Francisco, CA.

Willis, J., & Gonzalez, A. (1997). Reconceptualizing gender through intercultural dialogue: The case of the Tex-Mex Madonna. *Women & Language, 20*, 9–12.

Wilson, C. G., & Gutierrez, F. (2003). Advertising and people of color. In G. Dines & J. M. Humez (Eds.), *Gender, race, and class in media: A critical reader* (2nd ed., pp. 283–292). Thousand Oaks, CA: Sage.

Wood, H. (2009). *Talking with television: Women, talk shows, and modern self-reflexivity.* Champaign: University of Illinois Press.

Wolfe, S. J., & Roripaugh, L. A. (2006). The (in)visible lesbian: Anxieties of representation in *The L Word.* In K. Akass, J. McCabe, & S. Warn (Eds.), *Reading* The L Word: *Outing contemporary television* (pp. 43–54). London: I. B. Tauris.

Wykes, M., & Gunter, B. (2005). *The media and body image: If looks could kill.* London: Sage.

Wyman, J. M. (1993, November). *The virgin/whore dichotomy of sexual powerlessness: Vampire bitches, brides, and victims in Bram Stoker's Dracula.* Paper presented at the meeting of the Speech Communication Association, Miami, FL.

Wypijewski, J. (2009, June 15). Return of the fabulous. *The Nation,* 7–8.

XXX marks the spot. (2010, May). *Women's Health,* 40.

Yoder, J. D., Christopher, J., & Holmes, J. D. (2008). Are television commercials still achievement scripts for women? *Psychology of Women Quarterly, 32*, 303–311.

Zeng, L. (2011). More than audio on the go: Uses and gratifications of MP3 players. *Communication Research Reports, 28*, 97–108.

Zhang, Y., Miller, L. E., & Harrison, K. (2008). The relationship between exposure to sexual music videos and young adults' sexual attitudes. *Journal of Broadcasting & Electronic Media, 52,* 368–386.

Ziegler, S. G. (2007). The (mis)education of Generation M. *Learning, Media, & Technology, 32,* 69–81.

Zimmerman, A., & Dahlberg, J. (2008). The sexual objectification of women in advertising: A contemporary cultural perspective *Journal of Advertising Research, 48,* 71–79.

Zurbriggen, E. L., & Morgan, E. M. (2006). Who wants to marry a millionaire? Reality dating television programs, attitudes toward sex, and sexual behaviors. *Sex Roles, 54,* 1–17.

HOT TOPICS

▶ The power of choosing and using language
▶ Language, sexist language, and the interrelationship between language and thought
▶ Reasons for using nonsexist language
▶ Forms of sexist language, such as man-linked terms and generic pronouns
▶ Sexual language and what it communicates about men and women

▶ Linguistic practices that reflect bias, such as married names and titles for women and men
▶ The relational and content axiom of communication (the functions of conversation)
▶ Vocal properties and linguistic constructions that communicate tentativeness
▶ Ways that men and women manage conversation

Part III Let's Talk:
Initiating and Developing
Relationships

CHAPTER 4

Choosing and Using Gendered Language

Case Study

Go Team!

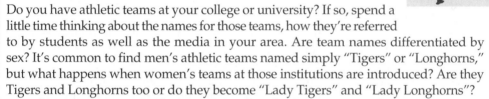

Do you have athletic teams at your college or university? If so, spend a little time thinking about the names for those teams, how they're referred to by students as well as the media in your area. Are team names differentiated by sex? It's common to find men's athletic teams named simply "Tigers" or "Longhorns," but what happens when women's teams at those institutions are introduced? Are they Tigers and Longhorns too or do they become "Lady Tigers" and "Lady Longhorns"?

At many institutions, the latter is exactly what happens, so is that a sexist practice or just a matter of which came first? Would it surprise you to know that there's research on this topic? Sociologist Faye Linda Wachs (2006) extended previous decades' research on this subject (Eitzen & Baca Zinn, 1989, 1993; Nuessel, 1994; Ode, 1999; Taylor, 2006; Ward, 2004) by studying the "male universal" norm in the sports world. Wachs concluded that "women's teams are often marked with feminized nicknames, while male teams hold the general mascot name (i.e., Lady Gamecocks, Wildkittens, Lady Lions). Though this practice is decreasing over time, it remains a barrier to equality for women's sports" (p. 45). Wachs points out that even major tournaments contain differentiated (some would argue, sexist) uses of language. In collegiate basketball, the men's tournament is simply the NCAA tournament, whereas the women's counterpart event is marked by the term "women's" or "ladies'." Many other examples exist, be they names for events, teams, or sports associations like the Professional Golfers Association (PGA) and the Ladies Professional Golfers Association (LPGA).

Other research investigated the extent of the problem among collegiate athletic teams in the South, finding that seven out of ten schools used some form of gender marking for their women's teams; 61 percent of schools in the study used the

(continued)

Case Study (*continued*)

term "lady" to distinguish women's teams from men's. None used
the marker "gentleman" as an adjective for the men's team names
(Fabrizio Pelak, 2008). Research has shown that women's athleticism
is stronger at schools with nonsexist (non–gender-marked) team names and that more
women are likely to serve in coaching positions at such schools (Ward, 2004). Language
is, indeed, powerful.

Your book author works at a university that bucked the trend when it launched
its Division 1 NCAA athletics program in the mid 1990s. The university's mascot
is the Islanders, but sincere efforts were made, in both written materials as well as
conversationally, to call teams "Islander Women" and "Islander Men." When local
radio and TV sports reporters mistakenly refer to the "Lady Isles," people e-mail and
call the stations to correct the usage, so successfully has the nonsexist language usage
been ingrained into the community.

What are your thoughts about this naming business? Much ado about nothing
or a tradition that needs to be exposed and changed?

H ave you ever thought about language—how yours originated and how it has
changed and evolved over time? (We assume that the language you used in middle
school is not the same language you're using today, as a college student.) Why are
some people so protective of language and resistant to attempts to update it, as though
the words they used were a central part of their identities? Sometimes it seems that we
hold onto language just like we hold onto old, worn-out luggage.

This chapter offers an in-depth examination of language because *the language we
choose to use reveals to others who we are.* Language and gender scholar Julia Penelope
(1990) put it this way: "What we say *is* who we are" (p. 202). We put language under a
microscope in this chapter, because as much as some people discount its importance, the
language you choose to use is your primary tool of communication, your primary method
of communicating who you are to others, of becoming known by them (McConnell-Ginet,
2010). That puts language at the center of what most of us find incredibly important.

CHOOSING YOUR LANGUAGE

Choosing and *using* aspects in the chapter title refer to our view of using language by
choice. Many people use language out of habit—they talk the way they've always talked,
simply because they've always talked that way. These people rarely think about the
influence of language on their view of self, their relationships, and their communication.
After reading this chapter, maybe you won't be one of these people.

This chapter scrutinizes language in order to examine its powerful influences on
communication. We explore language in two ways, which also parallel our definition
of gender communication: communication *about* and *between* women and men. We first
focus on how language treats us, how it is used to communicate *about* the sexes. The latter
part of the chapter explores language from the *between* standpoint, how gender affects
our choice of language as we communicate with others.

Students sometimes suggest that, rather than wasting time talking about language, we should concentrate on issues that have more serious consequences on people's lives—such as equal pay for equal work and reproductive and family rights. We agree that equal opportunity, wage gaps, and other political and economic issues affecting the sexes are extremely important. But politics and economics aren't the focus of this text; gender communication *is*. Think about it this way: If language is at the very base of our culture, and if that language is flawed or biased, then that flawed, biased language is what we use to communicate about so-called bigger issues. Language is not a neutral container of thoughts and content, but it shapes thinking and content much like a bottle holds and shapes its content. Why not address the container (language) and how it shapes the issues?

LANGUAGE: A POWERFUL HUMAN TOOL

What Is Language? What Is Sexist Language?

A *language* is a system of symbols (words or vocabulary) governed by rules (grammar) and patterns (syntax) common to a community of people (Beebe, Beebe, & Ivy, 2013). Authors Graddol and Swann (1989) suggest that language is both personal and social, that it is a "vehicle of our internal thoughts" as well as a "public resource" (pp. 4–5). Our thoughts take form when they are translated into language, but sometimes language is inadequate to truly express (it may even distort) our thoughts or, particularly, our emotions. Have you ever seen or felt something that you just could not put into words?

Language has power because it allows us to make sense out of reality, but that power can also be constraining. If you don't have a word for something, can you think about it? Have you ever considered that maybe your thinking might be limited by your language? A whole host of "realities" may exist that you have never thought of because there are no words within your language to describe them.

> *We die. That may be the meaning of life. But we do language. That may be the measure of our lives.*
>
> —*Toni Morrison, author*

Two researchers who investigated this notion were Edward Sapir and his student Benjamin Lee Whorf. They developed what has come to be called the *Sapir–Whorf Hypothesis,* which suggests an interrelationship between language and thought. Whorf (1956) hypothesized that "the forms of a person's thoughts are controlled by inexorable laws of pattern of which he [she] is unconscious" (p. 252). In this view, human thought is so rooted in language that language may actually control (or at least influence) what you can think about.

Thus, language is a powerful tool in two ways: It affects how you think, shaping your reality; and it allows you to verbally communicate what you think and feel, to convey who you are to others. In the discussion of terminology in Chapter 1, we defined *sexism* as attitudes, behavior, or both that denigrate one sex to the exaltation of the other. It follows, then, that *sexist language* is verbal communication that conveys those differential attitudes or behaviors. Not surprisingly, research documents a connection between people's attitudes toward the sexes and their language usage (Parks & Roberton, 2005, 2008). One study found that people who hold sexist attitudes tend to use sexist language, both in their written communication and in their conversation (Cralley & Ruscher, 2005).

Net Notes

We all could use a little vocabulary expansion—whether for speaking or writing. We found a few useful websites that focus on language:

http://www.yourdictionary.com This extensive website offers dictionaries in many languages, a thesaurus, word-of-the-day, and specialized dictionaries.

http://www.vocabulary.com This site allows users to paste any text or url into a search area to make the text a hyperlink, which leads to a dictionary definition.

http://www.wordsmyth.net A weekly theme and related vocabulary are provided.

http://www.word-detective.com This online version of a newspaper column addresses readers' questions about words and language.

http://www.wordspy.com This site is self-described as "the word lover's guide to new words."

http://wordnik.com This website provides "everything you want to know" about words, related words, nontraditional definitions, related images, statistics, and audio pronunciations.

http://www.wordsmith.org You can sign up for A.Word.A.Day on this site, which also offers anagramming and other tidbits of information about language.

http://www.dictionary.com If you seek a definition for a word, type the word in at this site, and it will provide several definitions from multiple reputable dictionaries, so that you can compare meanings. The site will also translate words, phrases, or an entire web page from one major European language (including English) into another.

Much of what research has exposed as sexist language reflects women's traditional lower status and the male-dominated nature of our society. In fact, some scholars contend that English and similar languages cause women to be a *muted group* (Ardener, 2005; Kramarae, 1981, 2005). Communication scholar Cheris Kramarae (1981), who first generated muted group theory, explains:

> Women (and members of other subordinate groups) are not as free or as able as men are to say what they wish, when and where they wish, because the words and the norms for their use have been formulated by the dominant group, men. So women cannot as easily or as directly articulate their experiences as men can. Women's perceptions differ from those of men because women's subordination means they experience life differently. However, the words and norms for speaking are not generated from or fitted to women's experiences. Women are thus "muted." (p. 1)

Communication scholar Robert Hopper (2003) offers a distinction between what he terms "soft core" and "hard core" sexist language. One example comes from an organizational setting, in which an employee might make the following derogatory statements:

"This broad lacks the balls to be a manager."

"I'm not sure this little lady is management material."

Both messages convey the same basic meaning, and few would deny that the first statement reflects blatant or hard-core sexism, with its overt reference to male body parts. The second statement, through the use of the reference "this little lady," is less obvious, but still carries a demeaning or patronizing tone and uses language that can put a professional woman "in her place." Hopper terms the latter kind of reference soft-core sexism, which he views as more problematic than hard-core sexism because the language is more subtle. Someone pointing out the sexism in the second statement might be called "picky" or "oversensitive," thus it's even more difficult to critique this form of language and make attempts to change it. Soft-core sexist language is no less sexist than hard-core, and its continued use reveals and sustains sexist views.

The intent in this chapter is to explore the English language, wonderful and flawed as it is—not to blame anyone, not to suggest that men use language purposefully to oppress women, and not to make readers feel defensive about how they use language. We all inherited a male-dominated language, but it's not some mystical entitity that can't be studied or changed. Granted, some people use sexist language more out of habit or laziness than with an intent to be sexist. Because of this tendency, sexist language is sometimes referred to as gender-exclusive language and contrasted with gender-inclusive language, which is preferred in both written and oral discourse.

Language may control some people, but it need not control you. Think of language as something that has tremendous influence on us, but remember that we can *choose* how to use it and how to influence *it*.

WHY USE NONSEXIST LANGUAGE?

Inventorying your language and making some changes takes work, but the benefits you'll experience can be considerable. Below are a few reasons for incorporating nonsexist language into your communication repertoire.

Reason 1: Nonsexist Language Demonstrates Sensitivity

Sensitivity seems like an obvious reason for using nonsexist language, but it may be more obvious in spirit than in practice. While you may have a basic philosophy that variations among people are worthy of respect, you may communicate in a manner that contradicts your philosophy—either out of ignorance (you just didn't know any better) or out of nonchalance (thinking that sexist communication is "no big deal"). Maybe you simply feel that subtle forms of sexist language that have developed into habits will take too much time and effort to change. But remember that spoken and written communication are ways of extending yourself into the world, of getting to know others and being known by them. If you want to present yourself as a caring, sensitive individual who believes in a basic system of fairness for everyone, doesn't it seem logical for your language to reflect that desire?

Reason 2: Nonsexist Language Reflects Nonsexist Attitudes

Even though we aren't sure about the exact relationship between language and thought, it's clear that a relationship exists. So if you communicate in a sexist manner—whether you're aware that a particular usage is sexist and regardless of your intentions—it's possible that you hold some form of sexist attitudes (Swim, Mallett, & Stangor, 2004). That conclusion may seem pretty strong, but if thoughts are indeed influenced by language and if language affects the quality of thought, then sexist language may be linked to sexist thoughts. Stop and think for a moment: Can you safely say that your communication, both oral and written, is free from sexist language? The tougher question is: If your communication contains some sexist usages, could someone claim that you have sexist attitudes?

Reason 3: Nonsexist Language Is Basic to the Receiver Orientation to Communication

Hardly any other topic we discuss in this text pertains more to the principles of receiver orientation to communication (explained in Chapter 1) than the topic of sexist language. Simply put, if a listener perceives your language to be sexist, then from a receiver orientation to communication, that's a legitimate judgment—one you need to think about. For example, if you say, "If a person is in trouble, he should feel confident calling on a policeman for help," a listener may interpret your use of male language as sexist because it might insinuate (1) that only men are persons, and (2) that only men are police officers. You may not mean anything sexist or demeaning in your message, but if your message is interpreted by a listener as sexist, you can't erase it, can you? The communication is *out there*, and undoing it or convincing a listener that you meant otherwise takes ten times as long as if you'd applied a little forethought before speaking.

Reason 4: Nonsexist Language Is Contemporary

One set of goals within higher education is that upon graduation, students will be able to think, write, and converse in a manner befitting a highly educated person. Using outdated, sexist language undermines that goal. The reality we all share is that the roles women and men can fulfill have changed a great deal. Because changes are likely to keep occurring, language should evolve to reflect current society. We encourage you to inventory your spoken and written language in efforts to exorcise the sexism, if you haven't done so already, so that you'll be viewed as an educated individual.

Reason 5: Nonsexist Language Strengthens Expression

Another benefit of nonsexist language usage is an enhanced writing style (Maggio 1988, 1992). Some students believe that nonsexist language is cumbersome, that it "junks up" one's speaking and writing with a bunch of extra words, just to include everybody. However, once they learn and begin to practice simple methods of avoiding sexist, exclusive means of expression, they readily admit that it does make their communication more clear and dynamic.

Remember . . .

Language: System of symbols (words or vocabulary) governed by rules (grammar) and patterns (syntax) common to a community of people

Sapir–Whorf Hypothesis: Supposition about the interrelationship between language and thought

Sexist Language: Verbal communication that conveys differential attitudes or behaviors with regard to the sexes; language that demonstrates that one sex is valued over the other

SEXIST LANGUAGE: FORMS, PRACTICES, AND ALTERNATIVES

This section is divided into two main areas: *forms* of sexist language and sexist *practices* that involve language. The first area has to do with language that is sexist in and of itself. In the second area, it's not the words themselves that are sexist but the traditions inherent in how we use language.

Forms of Sexist Language

MAN-MADE EVERYTHING   Words or phrases that include *man,* as though these terms should operate as generics to stand for all persons, are referred to as man-linked terminology—a form of sexist language that has diminished but not disappeared (Miller, Swift, & Maggio, 1997; Steinem, 1995). Anyone told you to "man up" lately? The term *man* or its derivative *mankind* in reference to all persons creates ambiguity and confusion when one doesn't know whether the term refers to a set of male persons or to all persons in general.

Originally, *man* was derived from a truly generic form, similar to the term *human.* Contrary to popular belief, the term *woman* did not derive from the term *man,* nor did *female* derive from *male* (Hardman, 1999). The terms for female-men (*wifmann*) and male-men (*wermann*) developed when the culture decided that it needed differentiating terms for the sexes (McConnell-Ginet, 1980). Maggio's (1988) dictionary of gender-free terminology provides Greek, Latin, and Old English terms for human, woman, and man. In Greek, the terms are *anthropos, gyne,* and *aner;* in Latin, *homo, femina,* and *vir;* and in Old English, *man, female,* and *wer* (pp. 176–177). *Wer* fell out of use, and *man* came to mean *men.* The problem is that *man* should be a designation only for *male* persons, not *all* persons. Masculine mental images arise when the term *man* is used. Again, not only does this term exclude women, but it reinforces the male-as-standard problem.

Even though the word *human* contains *man,* it is derived from the Latin *homo,* meaning all persons. The term *human* does not connote masculine-only imagery like the term *man* does (Graddol & Swann, 1989; Maggio, 1988). Man-linked terms include expressions such as *man the phones* or *manned space flight* as well as numerous words that have *man* attached to or embedded within them (e.g., *repairman*), which convert the term into a role, position, or action that an individual can assume or make (Palczewski, 1998). Unfortunately, people see the masculine part of the term and form perceptions that the word describes something masculine only.

Alternatives to *man* (e.g., *people, persons, individuals*), the simplest being *human* (and its derivatives *human being, humanity,* and *humankind*), have become more commonplace in everyday language usage. Many man-linked terms can be "nonsexed" by simply substituting *person* for the word *man; chairman* becomes *chairperson, spokesman* becomes *spokesperson,* and so forth. Other terms require more creativity, such as *postman* becoming *mail carrier, spaceman* becoming *astronaut,* etc. Most people are used to the *-person* version of terms now, but when this innovation was first introduced into the language, many people assumed that using the *-person* version of a word signaled a female person in that role or position rather than a generic reference (Aldrich, 1985).

ANTIMALE BIAS IN LANGUAGE   Language scholar Eugene August (1992) describes three forms of antimale language in English: gender-exclusive language, gender-restrictive language, and language that evokes negative stereotypes of males. First, August explores the equating of *mother* and *parent*, suggesting that the terms are often used interchangeably, whereas the term *noncustodial parent* is almost always synonymous with *father*. He suggests that males are also excluded from terms describing victims, such as the expressions *wife abuse* and *innocent women and children*. This language implies that males cannot be victims of violence, rape, and abuse. This is clearly not the case, and our language is beginning to reflect that fact. For example, *spousal abuse* or *partner abuse* reflects the reality that either spouse or partner could be the abused party.

The second category, gender-restrictive language, refers to language that limits men to a social role. August's examples include language that strongly suggests to boys the role they are to play and chastises them if they stray from that role or don't perform as expected (e.g., *sissy, mama's boy, take it like a man,* and *impotent*). In the final category, August claims that "negative stereotyping is embedded in the language, sometimes it resides in people's assumptions about males . . ." (p. 137). As evidence of this tendency, August cites terms linked to crime and evil, such as *murderer, mugger, suspect,* and *rapist*—terms he contends evoke male stereotypes that are "insulting, dehumanizing, and potentially dangerous" (p. 132). In reference to the term *rape,* August discusses the fact that the majority of rapes are committed by males on female victims; however, the bias comes in with the assumption of a female victim, ignoring rapes perpetrated against men in our culture.

THE PERPETUAL PRONOUN PROBLEM   Think about what you were taught regarding pronouns. If you were taught that the masculine pronoun *he* (and its derivatives *his, him,* and *himself*) was perfectly acceptable as a generic term for all persons, both female and male, then you got an outdated lesson. Research from the 1970s to the present provides convincing evidence that the generic *he* isn't generic at all; it's masculine and conjures up masculine images (Clason, 2006; Conkright, Flannagan, & Dykes, 2000; Gabriel, 2008; Gastil, 1990; Gygax, Gabriel, Sarrasin, Oakhill, & Garnham, 2009; Hamilton, 1988; He, 2010; Krolokke & Sorenson, 2006; Lee, 2007; Moulton, Robinson, & Elias, 1978; Romaine, 1999; Stinger & Hopper, 1998). As Hopper (2003) points out, if the choice is made to say *he* not in reference to a specific man, two meanings for the word are created: a male individual and a person of undetermined sex. The listener's job then is to figure out which meaning is intended. Why give the listener that task? Why not make it clear?

One of the most illuminating early studies on this topic was conducted by gender psychologist Wendy Martyna (1978), who investigated college students' use of pronouns by asking them to complete sentence fragments, both orally and in writing. The students were required to provide pronouns to refer to sex-indefinite nouns, as in the statement, "Before a judge can give a final ruling, _____." Fragments depicting typically male occupations or roles included such terms as *doctor, lawyer, engineer,* and *judge;* feminine referents included *nurse, librarian, teacher,* and *babysitter;* neutral fragments used such nouns as *person, individual,* and *student.* The participants also were asked to reveal what particular image or idea came to mind as they chose a certain pronoun to complete a sentence.

In a nutshell, college students in Martyna's research continually read sex into the subjects of sentence fragments and responded with sex-specific pronouns. The nurses, librarians, teachers, and babysitters were predominantly *she,* while the doctors, lawyers, engineers, and judges were *he.* The neutral subjects most often received the pronoun *they.* If the pronoun *he* had truly been a term indicating all persons, then *he* would have been the pronoun of choice no matter what role the sentence depicted. In conjunction with their choices of pronouns, students reported sex-stereotyped images that came to mind when they read the fragments.

If you think that Martyna's study is so dated that the results couldn't apply to more modern-day college students, think again. At two universities, a group of researchers repeated and extended Martyna's study, hoping to find that contemporary college students were attuned to the problem of sexist pronouns (Ivy, Bullis-Moore, Norvell, Backlund, & Javidi, 1995). On the contrary, the results were virtually the same. For terms such as *lawyer, judge,* and *engineer,* students responded predominantly with masculine pronouns and imagery, while *nurses, librarians,* and *babysitters* were female. Martyna's and the other study's results underscore the fact that people (at least in American culture) can hardly function without knowing the sex of a person. If they aren't told the sex of a person, they generally assign one based on stereotypes.

Besides the fact that generic masculine pronouns aren't really generic, other negative consequences of using this form of exclusive language have emerged from research. Studies show that exclusive pronoun usage (1) places undue emphasis on men over women; (2) maintains sex-biased perceptions; (3) shapes people's attitudes about careers that are appropriate for one sex but not the other; (4) causes some women to believe that certain jobs and roles aren't attainable; and (5) contributes to the belief that men deserve more status in society than women do (Briere & Lanktree, 1983; Brooks, 1983; Burkette & Warhol, 2009; Gygax et al., 2009; Ivy, 1986; Stericker, 1981; Stinger & Hopper, 1998).

THE PRONOUN SOLUTION   Does a pronoun exist that can stand for everyone? Some scholars have attempted to introduce new words, or *neologisms,* into the language primarily for the purpose of inclusivity. Such neologisms as *gen, tey, co, herm,* and *heris* are interesting, but they haven't had success in being adopted into common usage.

If you want to refer to one person—*any* person of either sex—the most clear, grammatical, nonsexist way to do that is to use either *she or he, he/she,* or *s/he* (Kennedy, 1992). Other ways to avoid excluding any portion of the population in your communication are to omit a pronoun altogether, either rewording a message or substituting an article (*a, an,* or *the*) for the pronoun; to use *you* or variations of the indefinite pronoun *one;* or to use the plural pronoun *they.* Using a plural pronoun in a singular sense is becoming more common and acceptable, both in written and oral forms (Madson & Shoda, 2006). You often hear people talk about one individual, but use plural pronouns like *they, them,* and *theirs* instead of making an effort to identify the sex of the referent. The cause may relate more to laziness or a tendency to revert to shorthand, meaning an easier way to communicate than having to choose the appropriate pronoun, but it may also be a sign of a trend to "desex" one's language. One study examined uses of the gender-neutral, plural third-person pronoun *they* in students' writing (Strahan, 2008). Results indicated that students used *they* frequently when they were unsure of the sex of a person they were writing about and, more interesting, when the sex of the referent didn't matter— when it wasn't important to the meaning they were trying to convey. Other innovations include alternating female-only and male-only pronouns, particularly in written discourse; however, initial responses to such approaches have been neutral to negative (Madson & Shoda, 2006).

THE LADY DOCTOR AND THE MALE NURSE   A subtle form of sexist language, called *marking,* involves placing a sex-identifying adjective in front of a noun to designate the reference as somehow different or deviant from the norm (DeFrancisco & Palczewski, 2007; West, 1998). Examples of this practice include *woman* or *lady doctor, male secretary, female boss, female soldier,* and *lady lawyer.* As more men and women enter in greater numbers into fields typically dominated by members of their opposite sex, some of these references are disappearing from accepted usage. (However, one such reference readily comes to mind in the form of Ben Stiller's character of Greg Fokker objecting to being ridiculed as a *male nurse* in both "Fokker" movies). Though some things are changing, sex-marked language continues to be limiting, discriminatory, and unnecessary. (We refer you to the opening case study of this chapter, for a discussion of how sex marking occurs in reference to sports teams.) Why does one need to point out the sex of a doctor, lawyer, or boss? The implication is that one incarnation of a role or position is the norm, whereas the opposite sex in that role or position is an aberration or "not normal." Such language can have an isolating effect on the person who is "not the norm." Think how odd it would be to say "the male lawyer" or "the female nurse."

HOW'S TRIX?   We have the eleventh-century French language to thank for many suffixes like *-ette, -ess, -enne,* and *-trix* used frequently in English to form a feminine version of a generic or masculine term, such as in *bachelor/bachelorette* and *governor/governess.* Over time, these terms have proved problematic because, first, they often connote smallness, such as in reference to inanimate objects like *booklets* and *kitchenettes* (Holmes, 2001). Second, researchers have deemed it a subtle sexist practice to attach suffixes to a male form of a word to establish a female form (He, 2010; Miller, Swift, & Maggio, 1997). The suffix "perpetuates the notion that the male is the norm and the female is a subset, a deviation, a secondary classification. In other words, men are 'the real thing' and women are sort of like them" (Maggio, 1988, p. 178). Does it really matter if the person waiting on a table at a restaurant is female or male? Does someone who is admired need to be called a *hero* or a *heroine?* Such terminology makes a person's sex too important, revealing a need to know the sex to determine how to behave or what to expect. Linguist Janet Holmes (2001) contends that suffixes are "widely perceived as trivializing women's occupations, undermining their professional status" (p. 117).

How can sexist suffixes be avoided? You can simply use the original term and omit the suffix. If there is a legitimate reason for specifying sex, a pronoun can be used, as in "The actor was performing her monologue beautifully, when someone's cell phone rang in the theatre." (Creators of the hit TV show *The Bachelor/The Bachelorette* will no doubt disagree.)

SPEAKING OF A HIGHER POWER . . .   Saying that the topic of sexism in religious language is "sticky" is a major understatement. It's not our intent here to uproot anyone's religious beliefs, but merely to provide food for thought.

People continue to debate the potential sexism in biblical language, as well as litany (what gets read or spoken in worship services; Bryant, 2008; Clason, 2006). In their book about language and the sexes, Miller and Swift (1991) explain that within the Judeo-Christian tradition, religious scholars for centuries have insisted that the translation of such an abstract concept as a deity into language need not involve a designation of sex. According to these researchers, "the symbolization of a male God must not be taken to mean that God really is 'male.' In fact, it must be understood that God has no sex at all" (p. 64). To one dean of the Harvard Divinity School, masculine language about God is "a cultural and linguistic accident" (Stendahl, as in Miller & Swift, 1991, p. 67). As one rabbi put it, "I think of God as an undefinable being; to talk about God in gender terms, we're talking in terms we can understand and not in terms of what God is really like" (Ezring, as in Leardi, 1997, p. H1).

The problem, at least for religions relying on biblical teachings, is that translations of scriptures from the ancient Hebrew language into Old English rendered masculine images of deity, reflecting the culture of male superiority (Kramarae, 1981; Schmitt, 1992). Thus, the literature is dominated by the pronoun *he* and such terms as *father* and *kingdom*. Linguistic scholars contend that much of the original female imagery was lost in modern translation or was omitted from consideration by the canonizers of the Bible (Miller & Swift, 1991; Spender, 1985). This point received resurgent attention when the book and movie *The DaVinci Code* came out. The Old Testament says that humans were created in God's image—both male and female. It's interesting, then, that we have come to connect masculinity with most religious images and terms. Also interesting, as August (1992) contends, is the "masculinization of evil," the fact that male pronouns and images are most often associated with Satan, such as a reference to the *Father of Lies*. August says, "Few theologians talk about Satan and her legions" (p. 139).

Are you uncomfortable enough at this point in your reading to say to yourself, "Come on now; you're messing with religion. Enough is enough"? That's understandable, because religion is a deeply personal thing. It's something that a lot of us grew up with; thus, its images and teachings are so ingrained that we don't often question them or stop to consider where some of the traditions originated. However, questioning the language of religion doesn't mean that one is questioning his or her faith.

A few religions have begun to lessen male dominance in their communication. Scholars Jones and Mills (2001) explain: "Judaism has been unprecedented in its efforts to include women in a traditionally patriarchal religion. Over the past thirty years the language of ancient rituals and ceremonies, sacred to the faith, have been altered and re-written to include women . . ." (p. 58). In some Christian sects, the masculinity *and* femininity of God are beginning to receive equal emphasis, as in one version of the Apostles' Creed which begins with "I believe in God the Father and Mother almighty, maker

Hot Button Issue

"Stay Out of Scripture?"

Our discussion of sexism in religious language may raise some hairs on the back of your neck, because religion, to many of us, is something deeply felt and rooted in tradition. Many people feel that changing the language in current translations of the Bible is akin to (or worse than) altering Shakespeare. If you are a person within the Christian tradition, which is grounded in biblical teachings, do you feel your faith or your ability to worship would be shaken if more female language or gender-neutral terms appeared in the Bible? Would you trip over such language or see it as a welcome change? Is it political correctness gone amok, or an opportunity for more people to relate to biblical teachings?

of heaven and earth." In January of 2002, publishers of a leading version of the Bible in the United States, the New International Version (NIV), announced that they would begin producing editions that contained more inclusive language (Gorski, 2002). Not all references to *men* were changed to *people,* nor were male references to God removed. What changed was that sex-specific language was altered when it was evident that the original text didn't intend any sex. For example, some references to *sons* were changed to *children* and *brothers* into *brothers and sisters.* Then in 2006, controversy arose again when publishers of a gender-inclusive Bible translation, *Today's New International Version,* were criticized by evangelical Christian groups who contended that the version was a feminist-driven effort to undermine Christian theology (Clason, 2006). These kinds of reforms are interesting and increasing in number, but they are unnerving to many people.

REDUCED TO A BODY PART   Language about sexuality profoundly affects how women and men perceive the sexes, as well as how they communicate with one another. Most of us know that reducing a human being to his or her sexuality is a degrading practice that can be personally devastating.

Although research in the twenty-first century continues to explore sexual language usage (Braun & Kitzinger, 2001a, 2001b; Butler, 2004; Motschenbacher, 2009), we defer to the important work of linguist Robert Baker in the 1980s, who was interested in conceptions of women in American culture. Although men also are described in sexualized terms, significantly more sexual terms identify women than men. For example, one study uncovered 220 terms for sexually promiscuous women and only twenty-two terms for sexually promiscuous men (Stanley, 1977). Baker (1981) contends that the following five categories of terms are recognized as "more or less interchangeable with 'woman'" (p. 167):

1. Neutral terms, such as *lady, gal,* and *girl*
2. Animal terms
3. Words that describe playthings or toys, such as *babe, baby, doll,* and *cuddly*
4. Clothing terms, such as *skirt* or *hem*
5. A whole range of sexual terms

In reference to Baker's category 5, think of how many terms exist in our language that are based on anatomy, but that may be used to describe the whole person. Over the years of teaching gender communication on the college level, students have been asked to participate in a "mature exercise," in which they provide current sexual terms—the language of their generation, even if they themselves rarely use such language. It's been interesting to see the shifts over the years, as well as the "creative" additions that inevitably make their contributions to the lexicon. Again, pardon the adult nature of this material, but here are some terms that describe women's anatomy or sexual behavior, many of which are interchangeable with the word *woman: vajayjay* (thanks to the TV show *Grey's Anatomy*), *coozie, coochie, vag, snatch, twat, pussy, beaver, cherry, a piece, box, easy, some* (as in "getting some"), *slut, whore* (or *ho*), and a *screw, hookup,* or *lay.* Here's some male sexual lingo, again generated by research as well as college students: *wiener, dingle, schlong, peter, wanker, sausage, prick, cock, male member, dick, willy, tallywacker, johnson, dingdong, tool,* and a *screw, hookup,* or *lay.* Obviously, there are more terms than these, but we leave those to your imagination rather than putting them in print.

My mother never saw the irony in calling me a son-of-a-bitch.

—Jack Nicholson, actor

Anthropologist Michael Moffat (1989) studied university dormitory residents' use of language and found that one-third of young men in the study, in conversations with other men, consistently referred to women as "chicks, broads, and sluts," reflecting what Moffat termed a "locker-room style" of communication about women (p. 183). More recently, Hopper (2003) analyzed the speech patterns of dozens of men as they commented on women; he concluded that the degree of objectification and references to body parts was startling. Now, we know that both men and women are capable of using sexually demeaning terminology. In fact, Hopper determined that women frequently call or refer to other women in sexually objectifying terms, but primarily they use terms that imply sexual promiscuity (e.g., *slut, ho, easy*). However, in his research, members of both sexes rarely talked about men in sexually degrading terms. Do you agree that conceiving of and communicating about a person in sexual terms is demeaning and sexist?

Two other studies examined college students' use and perceptions of sexual language (Murnen, 2000). In the first study, male and female students were asked to self-report the kinds of sexual language they used to describe others. Results showed that men were much more likely than women in the study to use (a) sexually degrading terms in reference to opposite-sex genitalia, and (b) highly aggressive terms to refer to sexual intercourse. In a follow-up study, subjects listened to either two men or two women conversing about having sex with someone they'd just met the night before. Both male and female speakers who used degrading sexual language were evaluated negatively by the listeners; however, in highly degrading conversations, the object of the degradation was judged as less intelligent and less moral than those persons who were spoken of in more respectful terms. The researcher concluded that use of sexual language is affected by gender and that one's attitudes toward members of the opposite sex, as well as about sexual activity, are revealed by one's choice of language.

Another form of sexual language describes sexual activity, with an emphasis on verbs and their effect on the roles women and men assume sexually. Baker's synonyms for sexual intercourse, as generated by his students in the early 1980s, include *screwed, laid, had, did it, banged, slept with, humped,* and *made love to.* Feminist theorist Deborah Cameron (1985, 2009) adds the verb *poked* to the list. Author Jonathan Green (1999) offers

Hot Button Issue

"Dirty Words"

We realize that many of you don't use the language we discuss (so bluntly) in this section of the chapter. But perhaps you've found yourself using language you wouldn't ordinarily use—only in specific situations, like when you were really down over being dumped from an important relationship or when you've been frustrated or mad. You probably know people who do use this kind of language, even if you don't use it yourself. How have your reacted when you've heard friends or acquaintances equate people with their sexual organs or body parts? Should language be an emotional release for people? Stated another way, is there a place and time for foul or degrading language? Does it depend on who's around to hear you?

Remember . . .

Man-Linked Terminology: Use of words or phrases that include man in them as generics to stand for all persons

Antimale Bias: Language use that excludes men, restricts the roles for and perceptions of men, and evokes negative stereotypes of men

Generic Pronoun: Use of a masculine pronoun as a term to stand for all persons

Neologism: New word introduced into a language

Marking: Placing a sex-identifying adjective in front of a noun to designate the reference as somehow different or deviant from the norm

Feminine Suffix: Adding a suffix to a male term to form a female term

such metaphorical language for intercourse as *jumped someone's bones* or *bod, bumped uglies, gave a tumble,* and *knocked boots.* Local students have generously contributed their own linguistic examples to the mix, including *hooked up with, got some from, got some play, made* (someone), *did the deed with, porked, boned, boinked, did the horizontal polka* (or *mambo*) *with, took,* and even *mated.*

According to Baker, the sexism in sexual descriptions comes from the placement of subjects that precede some of the verbs and the objects that follow them. Sentences like "Dick screwed Jane" and "Dick banged Jane" describe men as the doers of sexual activity, while women are almost always the recipients. When a female subject of a sentence appears, the verb form changes into a passive rather than an active construction, as in "Jane was screwed by Dick" and "Jane was banged by Dick"—the woman is still the recipient (pp. 175–176). Baker labels "inadequate" the argument that the linguistic tendency to describe males as active and females as passive reflects the fact that men's genitalia are external and women's genitalia are internal. If active sexual roles in women were the norm or more accepted, then Baker contends that the verb *to engulf* would be in common usage. Cameron (1985) proposes that the term *penetration* as a synonym for the sexual act suggests male origins; if a woman had set the term, it might have been *enclosure.*

Students of the twenty-first century believe that the dichotomy of male-active, female-passive sexuality is changing, as is the corresponding language. They offer a few active constructions for women's sexual behavior (largely related to women being on top in heterosexual intercourse, such as in the language *to ride*). Interesting changes will continue to take place in the sexual arena, linguistically speaking.

Sexist Linguistic Practices

THE NAME GAME   Talk about something that has changed, only to seem like it's changing . . . back. What's your view of the whole married name issue, meaning whether someone should change his or her last name when getting married? Many of us believe that our names are an integral part of our identity. The long-standing practice of wives taking husbands' surnames isn't necessarily sexist; what is sexist is the expectation that a married heterosexual woman is supposed to or must take her husband's last name. For some women, assuming a husband's surname is something they've looked forward to all their lives. For others, this custom identifies the woman as property, which actually is the historic intent behind the practice.

Throughout a good deal of the twentieth century, American states required married women to assume their husbands' names in order to participate in such civic activities as voting (Emens, 2007). Romantic movies from the 1940s and 50s contained scenes depicting women dreamily writing out "Mrs. John Smith" in their diaries, just to get the feel of how the new moniker would look in writing or sound when said aloud.

Then came the 1960s and 70s, laws were overturned, and many married women began calling themselves *Ms.* instead of *Mrs.* (a topic for a subsequent section) and retaining their maiden names (Arichi, 1999; Emens, 2007; Goldin & Shim, 2004; Hopper, 2003). (Interesting when you think about it, that there's really no such thing as a "maiden" name because most women's maiden or birth names are their fathers' last names.) Alternative naming practices became more prevalent during this period of time, such as keeping one's maiden name, adding the husband's last name to the maiden name (having a two-word or hyphenated last name), or coming up with a completely new hybrid last name for both spouses to adopt (often a difficult-to-pronounce "creative combo" that signaled one's resistance to authority and status as a free thinker; Foss, Edson, & Linde, 2000; Johnson & Scheuble, 1995; Tracy, 2002). Such practices were suspect in traditional social circles. Andy Rooney, commentator for CBS' *Sixty Minutes,* was quoted as saying that "women who keep their own names are less apt to keep their husbands."

Move forward into the 1990s and now the twenty-first century and it seems as though the pendulum has swung back to the traditionalism of earlier generations. Fewer heterosexual women now retain their maiden names once married than in the past (Boxer & Gritsenko, 2005; Brightman, 1994; Kopelman, Fossen, Paraskevas, Lawter, & Prottas, 2009; Scheuble, Klingemann, & Johnson, 2000). Fewer couples choose to hyphenate; occasionally, wives may add their husbands' last name to their maiden name, but rarely do husbands follow suit. She may become Mary Smith Jones, but rarely does he become John Smith Jones; he's just John Jones. Married women who changed their names received warnings from academic sources as well as the popular press about a loss of identity and self-esteem, but research did not detect any difference in self-esteem levels among women who kept their birth names, adopted their husbands' surnames, hyphenated, or used the two-name approach (Stafford & Kline, 1996). Do current naming trends signal a loss of identity for women, a lackadaisical surrender of women's quest for independence, or do you believe our culture has simply evolved past the need for such decision making? Perhaps the "name game" now is more about expedience and a need to keep things simple, rather than some strategic decision, political statement, or symbol of identity.

Of all the couples your book's author is acquainted with, only one couple chose to legally use the two-name approach, what they call a "family" name. Like many other couples, the decision was prompted by the birth of their first child. When they first got married, he stayed Grady Blount and she became Kit Price Blount. A few years later, they made the conscious decision to create a family name they and their children would all use, so the whole family became Price Blount(s). (Grady tells a funny story about how legal officials thought he was joking or "off his rocker" when he submitted paperwork for his name change.)

Another interesting, related trend has emerged in American culture that research has begun to study, a practice termed *situational naming*. Sociologists Scheuble and Johnson (2005) surveyed 600 married women about their naming practices and found that 12 percent of subjects reported situational last name use. In family situations wives tended to use their husbands' last name only, but in professional situations they preferred a hyphenated version, one that communicated a sense of independence associated with their professional rather than their personal life. The decision to use last names situationally was associated with being employed full time versus part time, having achieved higher levels of educational attainment, and having been at an older age when first married. Similar studies found that marital age, feminist attitudes, level of career commitment, professional stature, concerns of ancestry, and value placed on motherhood were factors that affected women's decisions about married names (Hoffnung, 2006; Laskowski, 2010).

Perhaps the most high-profile "naming" situation surrounds Hillary Clinton versus Hillary Rodham Clinton. Press sources document that Secretary of State Clinton reportedly dropped Rodham from public common usage at two key moments in her history: when her husband ran for and served as governor of Arkansas, and when she ran for president (John, 2007). Although her advisors insisted to the press that these name changes weren't strategic, the decision making was interesting, given statistics showing that 95 percent of married heterosexual women in America from the 1960s through the 1990s chose to adopt their husbands' last names (Scheuble, et al., 2000). Was the linguistic decision made for simplicity's sake because a shorter name fits more neatly on a bumper sticker? (Most campaign stickers and posters simply said "Hillary," which was enough to get the point across.) Or was it indeed strategic, as a means of aligning with larger numbers of women, perhaps more traditional women?

One final topic warrants discussion in this section: How do lesbian and gay couples handle the last name issue in those states where same-sex marriage or civil unions are legal? Do same-sex partners struggle with such decisions the way some heterosexual couples do? Is there any expectation that one partner or the other will change her or his last name, or is the trend for each partner to keep their birth name? This is an underresearched topic, at least at present; perhaps so many issues surrounding same-sex marriage rise to a greater level of importance than the name dilemma, with the result being that this just isn't on the radar for many gay and lesbian couples (Lannutti, 2008).

However, let us bring two studies of interest to your attention. A small Internet survey was conducted by Suter and Oswald in 2003; they found that lesbian respondents in same-sex committed relationships held varying views of marital naming. Although some believed that changing one or the other partner's last name to a commonly shared family name was a strategy to secure external recognition and acceptance of one's status as a family, others preferred no name change as a means of preserving each partner's individual identity. The researchers expected that any sort of name change would be associated with and announced publicly at couples' marriage or commitment ceremonies, but surprisingly, more often name changing was ritualized and celebrated on other special occasions for the couples, such as partners' birthdays or intimate dinner parties with friends.

A more recent study explored the question of "Who would take whose name?" among gay and lesbian married couples (in states with legal same-sex marriage) and committed couples (in states that recognize legal commitment, but not marriage; Clarke, Burns, & Burgoyne, 2008). Researchers found that, out of 30 people interviewed for the study, only one reported changing her last name when her relationship became formalized. Others reported being open to some future name change, but most did not have immediate plans for any name changing or development of a common family name. The question of name changing was a relatively new one for gay/lesbian interviewees, who can turn to few if any societal conventions for assistance or guidance on the matter. Most participants in the study did not want to give up their names entirely, so most considered a hyphenated version with their partner as a potential compromise. One interesting reason cited for not wanting any sort of name change was a resistance to heteronormativity; in other words, why change names when that's what straight people do? If more states legalize same-sex unions, it will be interesting to see how gay and lesbian couples grapple with linguistic choices that reflect and affect their relationships.

When I got married my feminist friends went mad. One sniffed, "Are you going to take your husband's name?" I said, "No, because I don't think 'Dave' suits me very much."
—Jo Brand,
British comedian

EUPHEMISMS AND METAPHORS   The English language contains a great many expressions about the sexes that go seemingly unnoticed, but that form subtly sexist patterns. These expressions are usually in the form of *metaphors* or *euphemisms*—more comfortable substitutes for other terms (Cralley & Ruscher, 2005; Hegstrom & McCarl-Nielsen, 2002; McGlone, Beck, & Pfiester, 2006). One of the most influential authors on the topic of euphemistic language is Robin Lakoff, whose research from the 1970s continues to have impact today. Lakoff (1975) explored euphemisms for the word *woman,* such as *lady* and *girl,* and their connotations. While many people think of *lady* as a term of respect that puts a woman on a pedestal, to some it suggests negative qualities such as being frail, scatterbrained, sugary sweet, demure, flatterable, and sexually repressed. To illustrate, substitute *ladies* for *women* in the following organizations' titles: the National Organization for Women, the Black Women's Community Development Foundation, and the Harvard Committee on the Status of Women (Lindsey, 2005). In this context, the term *ladies* minimizes the seriousness of the group.

Connotations of the word *girl* have changed a great deal in recent years, as has its spelling in the media (*grrrl*) (Siegel, 2007). Many adult women in the 70s and 80s reported feeling patronized and disrespected when referred to as *girls.* The term connoted childishness, innocence, and immaturity—and most women don't want to be thought of in those terms. However, today more positive meanings for *girl* have emerged (especially for women in their teens and 20s). Many positive efforts and projects across the country continue to use *grrrl*-language as a means of enhancing young girls' self-esteem and sense that they're not powerless in the world (Aragon, 2008; Radway, 2009; Riordan, 2001).

Some euphemistic confusion exists in the fact that there's no acceptable female equivalent term for *guy.* When males are called *guys,* females are called *girls,* rather than *gals* or *women.* Think about what would happen if you were to say to a group of men, "Good morning, boys!" It would most likely be interpreted as a condescending euphemism for men. The most appropriate terms to use depend on the context in which you find yourself.

A PARALLEL UNIVERSE   *Symmetry* or *parallelism* in language refers to the use of gender-fair terms in referring to the sexes. Terms can be asymmetrical and sexist in three ways. The first involves words that may appear parallel, but in actuality are not parallel (or equal). An example that seems to be on its rightful way out is the statement, "I now pronounce you man and wife" (Miller, Swift, & Maggio, 1997). If you don't see anything wrong with this last statement, look closer. The man is still a man, but the woman is now a wife, with the connotation that she is relegated to that one role while he maintains a complete identity. How different would the connotation be if the traditional statement were, "I now pronounce you woman and husband"?

A second type of asymmetry relates to terms originally constructed as parallel whose meanings have changed with common usage and time, so that the feminine form has a negative connotation (DeFrancisco & Palczewski, 2007; Romaine, 1999). Examples include *governor/governess, master/mistress, sir/madam,* and *bachelor/spinster* or *old maid.* A man who governs is a *governor,* but a *governess* has come to mean a woman who takes care of someone else's children. You can certainly see the gap between meanings in the second and third examples—*mistress* and *madam* have taken on negative, sexual connotations while the masculine forms still imply power and authority. The last example is dramatic—as men grow older and stay single, they remain *bachelors* while women degenerate into *spinsters* and *old maids.*

The third type of asymmetry involves acceptable words, but their use is unacceptable because it alters the equality (Lakoff, 1975; Maggio, 1988). Examples can be readily found in media, such as in July of 2009 when a newsperson for CNN reported that three American tourists had been taken hostage in Iran for straying over the border; the reporter clarified that "three people have been taken hostage—one is a woman." You often hear nonparallel usage in reference to soldiers killed in conflicts around the world, when special note is made of female military casualties or prisoners. The language depicts men as the norm and women as the aberrations. Is a hostage or casualty situation made worse because one of the people is female? The message sent is this: The presence of men in these situations is a given or the rule; the presence of women deserves extra attention and language because they are exceptions to the rule. This kind of attention is limiting and unnecessary; the language makes women outsiders.

OUT OF ORDER   Have you heard the traditional saying "ladies first"? While some people still operate by this standard in things like opening doors, the "ladies first" pattern isn't predominant in the language. When you put language under the microscope, you find that male terms are almost always communicated first and female terms second, as in the following: his and hers; boys and girls; men and women; men, women, and children; male and female; husband and wife; Mr. and Mrs. Smith; the duke and duchess of Windsor; king and queen; the president and first lady; brothers and sisters. Three exceptions include the traditional greeting, "ladies and gentlemen," references to the "bride and groom," and a mention of someone's parents, as in "How are your mom and dad doing?" Putting the masculine term first gives precedence to men and implies that women were derived from men or are secondary to them (Amare, 2006; Frank & Treichler, 1989). The simple suggestion here is that you try to alternate which term you say or write first when you use these constructions in communication. If you're sharp you've noticed that, in this text, for every "women and men" and "she or he," a "men and women" and "he or she" appears. It's a small correction in your language and few may notice, but it will make your communication more gender-sensitive.

TITLES AND SALUTATIONS   The accepted male title *Mr.* doesn't reflect a man's marital status. Mr. Joe Schmoe can be single, married, divorced, or widowed. The titles for women include *Miss, Mrs.,* and *Ms.,* which have been called *nubility titles,* derived from the term *nubile,* which means sexually attractive or marriageable (Romaine, 1999). What differentiates *Miss* from *Mrs.* is marital status, but this is only a fairly recent usage. Until the nineteenth century, the two terms merely distinguished female children and young women from older, more mature women (Spender, 1985). History isn't clear about why the function of the titles changed, but some scholars link it to the beginning of the Industrial Revolution, when women began working outside the home. Supposedly, working obscured a woman's tie to the home, so the titles provided clarity (Miller & Swift, 1991). Because of the patriarchal nature of language, people deemed it necessary to be able to identify whether a woman was married, though it was not necessary to know a man's relationship to a woman.

To counter this practice, women began to use the neologism *Ms.* a few decades ago, although the term has existed as a title of courtesy since the 1940s (Miller & Swift, 1991). People of both sexes resisted the use of *Ms.* when it first came on the scene, claiming that it was hard to pronounce. But is it any harder to pronounce than *Mrs.* or *Mr.?* Some women today choose not to use the title because they believe it links them with feminists, a connection they consider undesirable. Others use *Ms.* just exactly for that reason—its link with feminism—and to establish their identity apart from men (Atkins-Sayre, 2005; Fuller, 2005; Kuhn, 2007). A common misconception is that *Ms.* is a title referring exclusively to divorced women (Chivero, 2009).

Regarding written salutations and greetings, for many years the standard salutation in a letter to someone you did not know (and did not know the sex of) was "Dear Sir" or "Gentlemen." If you only knew the last name of a person in an address or if the first name did not reveal the sex of the person, the default salutation was "Dear Mr. So-and-So." But that sexist practice is changing because of questions about why the masculine form should stand for all people. The terms *Sirs* and *Gentlemen* no more include women than the pronoun *he* or the term *mankind.*

What are your nonsexist options for salutations? Sometimes a simple phone call or e-mail to the organization you want to contact will enable you to specify a greeting. An easier way to fix this problem is to use terms that don't imply sex, such as: (Dear) Officers, Staff Member, Managers, Director, and the like. It may seem awkward the first time you use terminology like this; if it's more comfortable for you to use a sex-identified term, use inclusive references such as *Ms./Mr.* or *Sir or Madam.* Other alternatives include omitting a salutation altogether, opting for an opening line that says "Greetings!" or "Hello!" or structuring a letter more like a memo, beginning with "Regarding Your Memo of 9/7" or "TO: Friends of the Library" (Maggio, 1988, p. 184). We caution against using the trite "To Whom It May Concern"; your letter may end up in the trash simply because "no one was concerned."

> *Could you do me a favor? Could you say "senator" instead of "ma'am"? I worked so hard to get that title.*
>
> *—Senator Barbara Boxer, to an Army Brigadier General during a Senate hearing*

USING LANGUAGE: ONCE YOU CHOOSE IT, HOW DO YOU USE IT?

Now that you understand what we mean by choice in language, here comes the real challenge: the actual usage of language in everyday interactions with others. We now move on to the *between* aspect of language—communication *between* the sexes, not *about* them.

Remember . . .

Euphemism: More comfortable term that substitutes for another term

Metaphor: Use of language to draw a comparison; the nonliteral application of language to an object or action

Symmetrical or Parallel Language: Use of language that represents the sexes in a balanced and fair manner

Order of Terms: Language usage that alternates which sex appears or is said first

Titles: Designations such as *Mr.* or *Ms.* before a person's name

Salutations: Letter or memo greetings that often contain sexist, exclusively male language

An Axiom of Communication

Three communication scholars—Watzlawick, Beavin, and Jackson (1967)—developed a set of *axioms*, or basic rules, about how human communication operates. They proposed, as one axiom, that "Every communication has a content and a relationship aspect such that the latter classifies the former and is therefore a metacommunication" (p. 54). The *content* aspect of communication is what is actually said or the information imparted from one communicator to another. The *relational* aspect of the message is termed *metacommunication* (communication about communication) because it tells the receiver how the message should be interpreted and communicates something about the nature of the relationship between the interactants.

A simple "hello" to someone in a warm tone of voice conveys a sense of friendship and familiarity, whereas a hollow, perfunctory tone may indicate a more formal and impersonal relationship. Tone of voice, in this case, serves as metacommunication; that is, it indicates how the message should be interpreted and gives clues about the relationship. The content element is generally conveyed through verbal communication, whereas the relational element primarily takes the form of nonverbal communication.

Even the simplest exchange has a relational and a content dimension. If a complete stranger walked toward you on the sidewalk, made eye contact, and said "Hi, how's it going?" you might reply with some minimal greeting like "Okay, thanks." But if someone you knew was walking down the hallway at school and extended the same greeting, although you might answer the same way, your response would probably sound and look different from your response to the stranger. In both interactions, the content of the message is a basic greeting, but the relational aspects signal a difference in relationship.

Women, Men, and the Relational versus Content Approach to Communication

On the basis of Watzlawick, Beavin, and Jackson's axiom, we suggest that a fundamental difference exists in what many women and men believe to be the function or purpose of communication. (Granted, this is a generalization, and there are exceptions.) Specifically, men tend to approach conversation more with the intent of imparting information (content aspect) than to convey cues about the relationship (relational aspect). In contrast, women tend to view conversation as functioning more as an indication of relationship than as a mechanism for imparting information. This doesn't mean that every time a man speaks, he's conveying information only; on the contrary, *every* message carries content and relational meanings. Nor does it mean that women only communicate relationally, without ever exchanging any real information. What it does mean is that men may use communication primarily for information exchange rather than for relationship development. Male friendships more often develop out of *doing*, rather than *talking*. Women like to *do* as well as *talk*, but their relationships with other women are more often maintained via conversation than by doing things together. This represents a fundamental sex difference before women and men even meet, and it may set us up for conflict when we communicate.

Here are some real-life examples to illustrate this supposition—what we term the *relational versus content approach to communication.* A friend explained that a man she'd been seeing gave her the "silent treatment" one evening at her house. She asked him a couple of times if anything was wrong and he politely replied "No," but he continued to be quiet. In frustration, she finally accused him of holding something back; she assumed he didn't care about her or they'd be talking. His response was that he just didn't have anything to say, but that obviously he must care about her because "After all, I'm *here* aren't I?" A student recalled a recent argument he'd had with his girlfriend: "We'd been talking about something that happened a few nights before and it led to an argument. When I felt that I'd explained my side of the story sufficiently and that we'd argued enough, I simply said, 'There's nothing more to say. End of discussion.' This made her furious and I couldn't figure out why. She wanted to continue talking about the incident, my side of it, her side of it, what the argument meant about our relationship, and I just wanted the conversation *over.*"

These examples illustrate men's and women's different views of the uses or functions of conversation. Research on communication motives sheds some light here, as we attempt to better understand *why* people communicate, not just *how* (Fowler, 2009; Myers, Martin, & Mottet, 2002; Punyanunt-Carter, 2009). Rubin, Perse, and Barbato (1988) examined the communication motives of over 500 people ranging in age from twelve to ninety-one. Results of this study indicated a significant sex difference, in that female subjects reported being "more likely to talk to others for pleasure, to express affection, to seek inclusion, and to relax," whereas male subjects reported a desire to control situations and people rather than express affection or seek inclusion (p. 621).

Sociolinguist Deborah Tannen's (1986, 1990) research supports the content/relational distinction as well. She terms a female style of communication *rapport-talk,* described as a "way of establishing connections and negotiating relationships" (1990, p. 77). A male style can be termed *report-talk,* "primarily a means to preserve independence and negotiate and maintain status. This is done by exhibiting knowledge and skill, and by holding center stage through verbal performance such as story-telling, joking, or imparting information" (1990, p. 77).

Many times women want to talk just to reinforce the fact that a relationship exists and that the relationship is important. What is actually being said is usually less important than the fact that a conversation is taking place. Conversely, men generally approach conversation from a functional standpoint. A conversation functions as a means of exchanging information or content, not as some reinforcement of the relationship.

© Universal Press Syndicate.

No wonder men often think that women talk on and on about nothing. No wonder women often think that men's relationships (and sometimes, men themselves) are superficial. What's going on here? It's not that women are insecure chatterboxes who have nothing better to do than carry on long, pointless conversations because they need relational reinforcement. And it's not that men are relationally aloof clods who don't need relationship reinforcement or can't manage even a simple conversation to save their souls. What's going on here is that, in general, women and men use communication for different purposes.

What's Preferable—Relational or Content Communication?

Neither the relational nor the content approach is necessarily preferable. Remember that every message—no matter how brief or trivial—has both content and relational elements. The difference seems to lie in a person's view of the function or purpose of a given message. Watzlawick, Beavin, and Jackson (1967) believed that healthy relationships evidenced a balance of content and relational aspects. To them, a "sick" relationship could be characterized by communication that focuses too heavily on the relational dimension, such that even the simplest messages become interpreted as statements about the relationship. Likewise, relationships in which communication degenerates into mere information exchange could also be termed "sick" (p. 53).

Throughout this text we encourage you to expand your choices of behavior into a more fully developed repertoire of communicative options. An understanding of male and female approaches to talk is illuminating, but an important goal is to develop an integrated or balanced approach derived from the best attributes of both. Such an approach recognizes that certain times, situations, and people require different kinds of communication. Skill is involved in determining which communicative approach—relational or content—is better, given the dictates of the situation. In this manner, men could strengthen their male friendships through conversation rather than relying primarily on action or shared activities. Such conversation would provide good experience that could carry over into their relationships with women. Likewise, more women could realize that in many of their relationships with men, talk may not be the primary way to develop the relationship. Women might become more comfortable in approaching conversation with men more on the basis of content, rather than expecting the conversation to reveal how men feel about them or how men view the relationship. The ideal would be to respond to each other in the most effective manner possible, unencumbered by what is expected or stereotypical for each sex.

Axiom of Communication: Basic rules or lawlike statements about how human communication operates

Relational Approach: View that communication functions primarily to establish and develop relationships between interactants

Content Approach: View that communication functions primarily for information exchange between interactants

Metacommunication: Communication about communication

Rapport-Talk: Tannen's term for a female style of communicating, based on the motivation of establishing connections between people

Report-Talk: Tannen's term for a male style of communicating, based on the motivation of preserving independence and gaining and maintaining status

LANGUAGE USAGE BETWEEN WOMEN AND MEN

This final section of the chapter examines ways in which language is used in communication *between* women and men—*how* we communicate. Some studies have documented linguistic sex differences (Cohen, 2009; Erlandson, 2005; Tannen, 1995) profound enough to form *genderlects,* defined as "speech that contains features that mark it as stereotypically masculine or feminine" (Hoar, 1992, p. 127). In general, female speech patterns have been viewed as being weaker, more passive, and less commanding of respect, in comparison with male styles. But other research has produced different results regarding linguistic sex patterns, with male and female styles often being indistinguishable (Brownlaw, Rosamond, & Parker, 2003). In various studies conducted by Anthony Mulac and his associates, subjects frequently incorrectly identified the sex of a speaker, based on written transcripts of casual conversation, as well as discussions in problem-solving groups (Mulac, 1998; Mulac, Bradac, & Gibbons, 2001; Mulac, Wiemann, Widenmann, & Gibson, 1988).

While Mulac discovered more similarities than differences in women's and men's speaking styles, he isolated some consistent male language features, which include references to quantity; judgmental adjectives (e.g., "Reading can be such a drag"); elliptical or abbreviated sentences, like "Great picture"; directives (commands); locatives (such as "in the background"); and "I" references. Female language features include intensive adverbs (such as use of the term *really*), references to emotions, dependent clauses (instead of full sentences), sentence-initial adverbials (such as use of the word *actually* to begin a sentence), longer sentences, uncertainty verbs (e.g., "It seems to be . . ."), negations (using negative terms such as *not*), hedges (e.g., "It's kind of . . ."), and questions (Mulac, Bradac, & Palomares, 2003).

An overdrawn, media-hyped linguistic sex difference garnered a lot of attention in the latter part of the 2000s; the focus was on who talked more—men or women. The ancient, enduring stereotype is that women *way* outtalk men, but does research bear this out? The controversy was launched when Louann Brizendine, author of *The Female Brain* (2006) and *The Male Brain* (2010), claimed that women use 20,000 words on average per day, whereas men only average 7,000 a day. The implication was either that women were verbose or men were reticent. Whichever interpretation you prefer, the purported difference was dramatic.

All sorts of personalities and pundits quoted the "facts," including Jordan's Queen Rania in a speech in support of International Women's Day. The problem was, the numbers didn't add up. Researchers at different institutions around the country studied the phenomenon, concluding that no such sex differences in sheer volumes of speaking were scientifically documented (Do Women Really, 2010; Newman, Groom, Handelman, & Pennebaker, 2008; Stipe, 2010). Seasoned public speaking coaches estimate that the average English (American) speaker talks at a rate of about 125 words per minute (around 2 words per second). Speaking 20,000 words at that rate would take 160 minutes total—about 2.6 hours in a 24-hour day. That equates to 10 minutes per hour in a 16-hour day, meaning that the average woman is silent for 50 minutes each hour (excluding 8 hours of sleep). When you do the math for the men's statistics, the average man speaks only 56 minutes in an entire 16-hour day, or 3.5 minutes each hour. Does that seem accurate to you? Does that match your experience? Here's one of those times when getting the facts—doing just a bit of research—helped counter a sex-based, Mars vs. Venus stereotype.

Vocal Properties and Linguistic Constructions

Vocal properties are aspects of the production of sound related to the physiological voice-producing mechanism in humans. *Linguistic constructions* reflect speech patterns or habits; they are communicative choices people make.

HOW LOW CAN YOU GO?   The *pitch* of a human voice can be defined as the highness or lowness of a particular sound due to air causing the vocal chords to vibrate (Karpf 2006). Physiological structures related to voice production, as well as hormones, allow women to produce higher-pitched sounds, while men produce lower-pitched sounds (Kooijman, Thomas, Graamans, & deJong, 2007; Krolokke & Sorensen, 2006; Tracy, 2002). But scholarly evidence suggests that differences may have more to do with social interpretations than with physiology alone. Research indicates that women and men have equal abilities to produce high pitches, but that men have been socialized not to use the higher pitches for fear of sounding feminine (Ivy & Wahl, 2009; Viscovich et al., 2003).

In comparison to the low tones that most men are able to produce, the so-called high-pitched female whine has drawn long-standing societal criticism (McConnell-Ginet, 2010); this has led to, as Cameron (1985) puts it, "a widespread prejudice against women's voices" (p. 54). In a patriarchal society such as ours, men's lower-pitched voices are deemed more credible and persuasive than women's. Gender scholar Nancy Hoar (1992) suggests, "Women who aspire to influential positions are often advised to cultivate lower-pitched voices, voices that communicate authority" (p. 130). Examples of this are readily found at radio stations and on network and cable news shows, in which the women who serve as anchors, as well as those who report or offer commentary, tend to have (or develop) lower-pitched voices than women in the general population. For women who want to be perceived as more credible, a slightly lower voice will move in that direction.

Men with higher-pitched voices are often ridiculed for being effeminate. Their "feminine" voices detract from their credibility and dynamism, unless another physical or personality attribute somehow overpowers or contradicts that judgment. (Mike Tyson, former heavyweight boxing champion, is one example of this.)

INDICATIONS OF TENTATIVENESS   A great deal of research shows that women are far more *tentative* in their communication than men, and this tentativeness can reduce the power of women's messages, making them appear uncertain, insecure, incompetent, powerless, and less likely to be taken seriously (Carli, 1990; McConnell-Ginet, 2010). However, other studies suggest that factors such as culture, status and position in society, the goal or intent of the communicator, and the nature of the group in which communication occurs (same-sex or mixed-sex) have much more impact than sex on stylistic variations (Aries, 2006; Eckert & McConnell-Ginet, 2003; Mulac et al., 2001).

One vocal property that indicates tentativeness is *intonation,* described by sociolinguist Sally McConnell-Ginet (1983) as "the tune to which we set the text of our talk" (p. 70). Research is contradictory as to whether rising intonation (typically associated with asking questions) is more indicative of a female style or a sex-based stereotype. Another tentativeness indicator is the *tag question,* as in "This is a really beautiful day, don't you think?" The primary function of the tag question is to seek agreement or a response from a listener (Blankenship & Craig, 2007). Lakoff (1975) believed that tag questions serve as an "apology for making an assertion at all" (p. 54). She attributed the use of tag questions to a general lack of assertiveness or confidence about what one is saying, more indicative of the female style than the male style. Some research supports a connection between women's style and the use of tag questions (Carli, 1990; Zimmerman & West, 1975), but other research finds no evidence that tag questions occur more in female speech than in male speech, nor that tag questions necessarily function to indicate uncertainty or tentativeness (Holmes, 1990; Roger & Nesshoever, 1987).

Qualifiers, hedges, and *disclaimers* are other linguistic constructions generally interpreted as indicating tentativeness and stereotypically associated with women's speech. *Qualifiers* include *well, you know, kind of, sort of, really, perhaps, possibly, maybe,* and *of course. Hedging* devices include such terms as *I think (believe, feel), I guess, I mean,* and *I wonder* (Holmes, 1990; Winn & Rubin, 2001). *Disclaimers* are typically longer forms of hedges that act as prefaces or defense mechanisms when one is unsure or doubtful of what one is about to say (Beach & Dunning, 1982; Hewitt & Stokes, 1975). Disclaimers generally weaken or soften the effect of a message. Examples of disclaimers (like ones we often hear students say) include "I know this is a dumb question, but . . ." and "I may be wrong here, but I think that . . ."

Linguists assert that sex-typed interpretations of tentativeness must be made within the given context in which the communication occurs (Mulac et al., 2001; Ragan, 1989). Holmes (1990) discovered, for example, that men and women were equally as likely to use tentative linguistic devices, depending on the needs or mandates of the particular situation. Cameron (1985) found that male subjects exhibited tentative communication when placed in certain roles, such as facilitators of group interaction.

An overabundance of tentative forms of expression in one's communication can be interpreted as a sign of uncertainty and insecurity. But tentative language may also indicate politeness (Watts, 2003) and may have positive, facilitative uses; these kinds of expressions need not be identified with one sex or the other. For example, a manager holding a high-status position within an organization might use disclaimers or hedges in attempts to even out a status differential, foster a sense of camaraderie among staff members, and show herself or himself as open to employees' suggestions and ideas.

MANAGING TO CONVERSE   Have you ever considered how conversation is organized or "managed"? *Conversation management* involves several variables, but one interesting vein of research surrounds indicators of conversational dominance.

Conversation typically occurs in *turns*, meaning that one speaker takes a turn, then another, and so on, such that interaction is socially organized (Sacks, Schegloff, & Jefferson, 1978). Sociologists West and Zimmerman have conducted significant research into how turn taking is accomplished. When people take turns talking, they may experience *overlaps*, defined as "simultaneous speech initiated by a next speaker just as a current speaker arrives at a possible turn-transition place" and *interruptions*, which are "deeper intrusions into the internal structure of the speaker's utterance" (West & Zimmerman, 1983, pp. 103–104). Interruptions and overlaps have been interpreted as indicating disrespect, restricting a speaker's rights, serving as devices to control a topic, and revealing an attitude of dominance and authority (Guerrero & Floyd, 2006; Weiss & Fisher, 1998). Overlaps are considered less egregious than interruptions because overlapping someone's speech may be seen as supportive—as trying to reinforce or dovetail off of someone's idea. Interruptions more often indicate dominance and power play because they cut off the speaker in midstream and suggest that the interrupter's comment is somehow more important or insightful.

In the most widely cited study of adult conversations, Zimmerman and West (1975) found few overlaps and interruptions within same-sex interactions. However, in cross-sex conversations, more interruptions occurred than overlaps, and 96 percent of the interruptions were made by males. Other early research revealed definite evidence of male conversational dominance in terms of initiating topics, working to maintain conversation around those topics, talking more often and for longer durations, offering minimal responses to women's comments, and using more declaratives than questions (Edelsky, 1981; Fishman, 1983).

However, later studies have explored beyond sex effects to examine the complexity of dominance in such contexts as face-to-face interaction, same-sex and mixed-sex dyads and groups, marital dyads, and electronic conversations. Researchers now suggest that many nonverbal, contextual, and cultural factors, such as perceptions of power and status, seating arrangements, and sex-typed topics, affect judgments of dominant or powerless styles (Aries, 2006; Guerrero & Floyd, 2006).

News talk shows on television, such as MSNBC's *Hardball* and Fox News' *The O'Reilly Factor,* are prime opportunities to observe conversation management (or, many times, mismanagement). The displays of vocal dominance and competitiveness among male and female hosts and guests is fascinating in these forums. The more seasoned guests have learned techniques to control the topics they respond to and raise with hosts, hold their turns at talk longer, and minimize interruptions from other guests or the host. Take a break some time from all that studying you do every night and tune in to one of these programs. See if you detect the elements we describe, as well as other linguistic and vocal devices that are used to manage conversation.

Remember . . .

Genderlects: Language containing specific, consistent features that mark it as stereotypically masculine or feminine

Vocal Properties: Aspects of the production of sound related to the physiological voice-producing mechanism in humans

Linguistic Constructions: Speech patterns or habits; communicative choices people make

Pitch: Highness or lowness of a particular sound due to air causing the vocal chords to vibrate

Tentativeness: Forms of language, typically used by women, that indicate hesitation or speculation and that can make them appear uncertain, insecure, incompetent, powerless, and less likely to be taken seriously

Intonation: Use of pitch that creates a pattern or that sends a specific message, such as a rising pitch to indicate a question

Tag Question: Linguistic construction related to tentativeness, which involves adding a brief question onto the end of a statement

Qualifier, Hedge, and Disclaimer: Linguistic constructions related to tentativeness, which preface or accompany a message so as to soften its impact or deflect attention away from the statement

Conversation Management: How a conversation is organized or conducted in a series of turns

Overlap: Linguistic construction typically associated with conversational dominance, in which one person begins speaking just as another person finishes speaking

Interruption: Linguistic construction typically associated with conversational dominance, in which one speaker intrudes into the comments of another speaker

 Conclusion

In this chapter on language, we've explored some influences existing in your world that profoundly affect your gender communication. You first need to understand how you are influenced before you can choose to lessen or negate the influence. This chapter has given you more than a few things to think about, because when you put something under a microscope, you see it in a whole new way. We have tossed a lot at you for one main reason—so that you won't use language by default or habit but instead *choose* to use language that accurately reflects who you are and how you think.

This chapter has challenged you to consider more fully how communication is used to talk *about* the sexes, as well as why and how communication occurs *between* them. We first explored the nature of language and some reasons for using nonsexist language; then we reviewed several forms and practices related to sexist language usage, as well as nonsexist alternatives. Regarding communication *between* the sexes, we examined relational and content approaches to determine whether the sexes view communication as serving different functions or purposes. We then focused on vocal properties and linguistic constructions that continue to be studied for what they reveal about the sexes and how we communicate. As we said in the introduction to this chapter, the goal of this chapter was to focus on language and its important role in gender communication, to offer ways that you can expand your linguistic options, and to challenge you to *choose* and *use* language in a more inclusive and unbiased way in order to enhance your personal effectiveness in gender communication and your relationships.

Discussion Starters

1. What were you taught in middle school or high school about sexist language? If you received no such instruction, why do you think this information wasn't included in your education? Have you been taught anything in college English classes about sexist language?

2. Sexism in religious language is one of the more difficult topics to explore and discuss. For some people, it's an affront to put the language used to convey their deeply personal religious beliefs under the microscope. What are your views on this subject?

3. Think of two people—a woman and a man—whose communication styles most closely (or stereotypically) correspond to the relational and content approaches presented in this chapter. What are the most marked aspects of each person's communication that make them stand out in your mind as examples?

4. In light of the information in this chapter on conversation management, assess your own style of communication. Are you more likely to be interrupted or to interrupt someone else? How do you respond to others' overlaps and interruptions? Do you have a lot of tag questions, qualifiers, hedges, and disclaimers in your communication? Think about classroom communication: Do you find yourself saying things like, "This might be a dumb question, but . . ." or "I could be wrong, but . . ."? If so, what effect do these disclaimers have on how you're perceived?

References

Aldrich, P. G. (1985, December). Skirting sexism. *Nation's Business*, 34–35.

Amare, N. (2006). Finding Dickinson: Linguistic sexism and inconsistent indexing in *Masterplots. Women & Language, 29,* 37–42.

Aragon, J. (2008). The lady revolution in the age of technology. *International Journal of Media and Cultural Politics, 4,* 71–85.

Ardener, S. (2005). Muted groups: The genesis of an idea and its praxis. *Women & Language, 28,* 50–54.

Arichi, M. (1999). Is it radical? Women's right to keep their own surnames after marriage. *Women's Studies International Forum, 22,* 411–415.

Aries, E. (2006). Sex differences in interaction: A reexamination. In K. Dindia & D. J. Canary (Eds.), *Sex differences and similarities in communication* (2nd ed., pp. 19–34). Mahwah, NJ: Erlbaum.

Atkins-Sayre, W. (2005). Naming women: The emergence of "Ms." as a liberatory title. *Women & Language, 28,* 8–16.

August, E. R. (1992). Real men don't: Anti-male bias in English. In M. Schaum & C. Flanagan (Eds.), *Gender images: Readings for composition* (pp. 131–141). Boston: Houghton Mifflin.

Baker, R. (1981). "Pricks" and "chicks": A plea for "persons." In M. Vetterling-Braggin (Ed.),

Sexist language: A modern philosophical analysis (pp. 161–182). New York: Rowman & Littlefield.

Beach, W. A., & Dunning, D. G. (1982). Pre-indexing and conversational organization. *Quarterly Journal of Speech, 67,* 170–185.

Beebe, S. A., Beebe, S. J., & Ivy, D. K. (2013). *Communication: Principles for a lifetime* (5th ed.). Boston: Pearson/Allyn & Bacon.

Blankenship, K. L., & Craig, T. Y. (2007). Language and persuasion: Tag questions as powerless speech or as interpreted in context. *Journal of Experimental Social Psychology, 43,* 112–118.

Boxer, D., & Gritsenko, E. (2005). Women and surnames across cultures: Reconstituting identity in marriage. *Women & Language, 28,* 1–11.

Braun, V., & Kitzinger, C. (2001a). "Snatch," "hole," or "honey-pot"? Semantic categories and the problem of nonspecificity in female genital slang. *Journal of Sex Research, 38,* 146–158.

Braun, V., & Kitzinger, C. (2001b). Telling it straight? Dictionary definitions of women's genitals. *Journal of Sociolinguistics, 5,* 214–232.

Briere, J., & Lanktree, C. (1983). Sex-role related effects of sex bias in language. *Sex Roles, 9,* 625–632.

Brightman, J. (1994). Why Hillary chooses Rodham Clinton. *American Demographics, 16,* 9–11.

Brizendine, L. (2006). *The female brain.* New York: Broadway.

Brizendine, L. (2010). *The male brain.* New York: Broadway.

Brooks, L. (1983). Sexist language in occupational information: Does it make a difference? *Journal of Vocational Behavior, 23,* 227–232.

Brownlaw, S., Rosamond, J. A., & Parker, J. A. (2003). Gender-linked linguistic behavior in television interviews. *Sex Roles, 49,* 121–132.

Bryant, C. J. (2008). Concerns of faith inclusive language: Will it solve the problems? *Language in India, 8,* 2.

Burkette, A., & Warhol, T. (2009). "The bush was no place for a woman": Personal pronouns and gender stereotypes. *Women & Language, 32,* 70–76.

Butler, J. (2004). *Undoing gender.* London: Routledge.

Cameron, D. (1992). *Feminism and linguistic theory* (2nd ed.). New York: Palgrave/Macmillan.

Cameron, D. (2009). *The myth of Mars and Venus: Do men and women really speak different languages?* New York: Oxford University Press.

Carli, L. L. (1990). Gender, language, and influence. *Journal of Personality and Social Psychology, 59,* 941–951.

Chivero, E. (2009). Perceptions of "Ms." as title of address among Shona-English bilinguals in Harare. *NAWA: Journal of Language and Communication, 3,* 174–186.

Clarke, V., Burns, M., & Burgoyne, C. (2008). "Who would take whose name?" Accounts of naming practices in same-sex relationships. *Journal of Community & Applied Social Psychology, 18,* 420–439.

Clason, M. A. (2006). Feminism, generic "he," and the *TNIV* Bible translation debate. *Critical Discourse Studies, 3,* 23–35.

Cohen, S. J. (2009). Gender differences in speech temporal patterns detected using lagged co-occurrence text-analysis of personal narratives. *Journal of Psycholinguistic Research, 38,* 111–127.

Conkright, L., Flannagan, D., & Dykes, J. (2000). Effects of pronoun type and gender role consistency on children's recall and interpretation of stories. *Sex Roles, 43,* 481–499.

Cralley, E. L., & Ruscher, J. B. (2005). Lady, girl, or woman: Sexism and cognitive busyness predict use of gender-biased nouns. *Journal of Language and Social Psychology, 24,* 300–314.

DeFrancisco, V. P., & Palczewski, C. H. (2007). *Communicating gender diversity: A critical approach.* Los Angeles: Sage.

Do women really talk more than men? (2010). Retrieved February 3, 2010, from http://www.amazingwomenrock.com.

Eckert, P., & McConnell-Ginet, S. (2003). *Language and gender.* New York: Cambridge University Press.

Edelsky, C. (1981). Who's got the floor? *Language in Society, 10,* 383–421.

Eitzen, D. S., & Baca Zinn, M. (1989). The de-athleticization of women: The naming and gender marking of collegiate sport teams. *Sociology of Sport Journal, 6,* 362–370.

Eitzen, D. S., & Baca Zinn, M. (1993). The sexist naming of collegiate athletic teams and resistance to change. *Journal of Sport and Social Issues, 17,* 34–41.

Emens, E. F. (2007). Changing name changing: Framing rules and the future of marital names. *University of Chicago Law Review, 74,* 761–863.

Erlandson, K. (2005). Gender differences in language use. *Communication Teacher, 19,* 116–120.

Fabrizio Pelak, C. (2008). The relationship between sexist naming practices and athletic opportunities at colleges and universities in the southern United States. *Sociology of Education, 81,* 189–213.

Fishman, P. M. (1983). Interaction: The work women do. In B. Thorne, C. Kramarae, & N. Henley (Eds.), *Language, gender, and society* (pp. 89– 101). Rowley, MA: Newbury.

Foss, K., Edson, B., & Linde, J. (2000). What's in a name? Negotiating decisions about marital names. In D. O. Braithwaite & J. T. Wood (Eds.), *Case studies in interpersonal communication* (pp. 18–25). Belmont, CA: Wadsworth.

Fowler, C. (2009). Motivations for sibling communication across the lifespan. *Communication Quarterly, 57,* 51–66.

Frank, F. W., & Treichler, P. A. (1989). *Language, gender, and professional writing: Theoretical approaches and guidelines for non-sexist usage.* New York: Modern Language Association.

Fuller, J. M. (2005). The uses and meanings of the female title *Ms. American Speech, 80,* 180–206.

Gabriel, U. (2008). Language policies and in-group favoritism: The malleability of the interpretation of generically intended masculine forms. *Social Psychology, 39,* 103–107.

Gastil, J. (1990). Generic pronouns and sexist language: The oxymoronic character of masculine generics. *Sex Roles, 23,* 629–641.

Goldin, C., & Shim, M. (2004). Making a name: Women's surnames at marriage and beyond. *Journal of Economic Perspectives, 18,* 143–160.

Gorski, E. (2002, February 3). Christian leaders debate new gender-neutral Bible translation. Knight Ridder Newspapers, as in *Corpus Christi Caller Times.*

Graddol, D., & Swann, J. (1989). *Gender voices.* Cambridge, MA: Basil Blackwell.

Green, J. (1999). *The big book of filth.* London: Cassell.

Guerrero, L. K., & Floyd, K. (2006). *Nonverbal communication in close relationships.* Mahwah, NJ: Erlbaum.

Gygax, P., Gabriel, U., Sarrasin, O., Oakhill, J., & Garnham, A. (2009). Some grammatical rules are more difficult than others: The case of the generic interpretation of the masculine. *European Journal of Psychology of Education, 24,* 235–246.

Hamilton, L. C. (1988). Using masculine generics: Does generic "he" increase male bias in the user's imagery? *Sex Roles, 19,* 785–799.

Hardman, M. J. (1999). Why we should say "women and men" until it doesn't matter any more. *Women & Language, 22,* 1–2.

He, G. (2010). An analysis of sexism in English. *Journal of Language Teaching and Research, 1,* 332–335.

Hegstrom, J. L., & McCarl-Nielsen, J. (2002). Gender and metaphor: Descriptions of familiar persons. *Discourse Processes, 33,* 219–234.

Hewitt, J. P., & Stokes, R. (1975). Disclaimers. *American Sociological Review, 40,* 1–11.

Hoar, N. (1992). Genderlect, powerlect, and politeness. In L. A. M. Perry, L. H. Turner, & H. M. Sterk (Eds.), *Constructing and reconstructing gender: The links among communication, language, and gender* (pp. 127–136). Albany: State University of New York Press.

Hoffnung, M. (2006). What's in a name? Marital name choice revisited. *Sex Roles, 55,* 817–825.

Holmes, J. (1990). Hedges and boosters in women's and men's speech. *Language & Communication, 10,* 185–205.

Holmes, J. (2001). A corpus based view of gender in New Zealand English. In M. Hellinger & H. Bussmann (Eds.), *Gender across languages: Volume 1: The linguistic representation of women and men* (pp. 115–133). Philadelphia: John Benjamins Publishing Company.

Hopper, R. (2003). *Gendering talk.* East Lansing: Michigan State University Press.

Ivy, D. K. (1986, February). *Who's the boss?: He, he/she, or they?* Paper presented at the meeting of the Western Speech Communication Association, Tucson, AZ.

Ivy, D. K., Bullis-Moore, L., Norvell, K., Backlund, P., & Javidi, M. (1995). The lawyer, the babysitter, and the student: Inclusive language usage and instruction. *Women & Language, 18,* 13–21.

Ivy, D. K., & Wahl, S. T. (2009). *The nonverbal self: Communication for a lifetime.* Boston: Pearson/Allyn & Bacon.

John, L. (2007, April 30). Hillary Clinton drops "Rodham" from name. Retrieved July 2, 2010, from http://www.associatedcontent.com.

Johnson, D. R., & Scheuble, L. K. (1995). Women's marital naming in two generations: A national study. *Journal of Marriage and the Family, 57,* 724–732.

Jones, K. T., & Mills, R. (2001). The rhetoric of heteroglossia of Jewish feminism: A paradox confronted. *Women & Language, 24,* 58–64.

Karpf, A. (2006). *The human voice: How this extraordinary instrument reveals essential clues about who we are.* New York: Bloomsbury.

Kennedy, D. (1992). Review essay: She or he in textbooks. *Women & Language, 15,* 46–49.

Kooijman, P. G. C., Thomas, G., Graamans, K., & deJong, F. I. C. R. S. (2007). Psychosocial impact of the teacher's voice throughout the career. *Journal of Voice, 21,* 316–324.

Kopelman, R. E., Fossen, R. J. S-V., Paraskevas, E., Lawter, L., & Prottas, D. J. (2009). The bride is keeping her name: A 35-year retrospective analysis of trends and correlates. *Social Behavior and Personality: An International Journal, 37,* 687–700.

Kramarae, C. (1981). *Women and men speaking.* Rowley, MA: Newbury.

Kramarae, C. (2005). Muted group theory and communication: Asking dangerous questions. *Women & Language, 28,* 55–61.

Krolokke, C., & Sorensen, A. S. (2006). *Gender communication theories & analyses: From silence to performance.* Thousand Oaks, CA: Sage.

Kuhn, E. D. (2007). Rethinking Ms. *Women & Language, 30,* 4.

Lakoff, R. (1975). *Language and woman's place.* New York: Harper & Row.

Lannutti, P. (2008, May). *Tying the knot? Couples' deliberations regarding legally recognized same-sex marriage.* Paper presented at the meeting of the International Communication Association, Montreal, Canada.

Laskowski, K. A. (2010). Women's post-marital name retention and the communication of identity. *Names: A Journal of Onomastics, 58,* 75–89.

Leardi, J. (1997, September 28). Is God male or female? For some, issue of God and gender is subject to debate. *Corpus Christi Caller Times,* pp. H1, H3.

Lee, J. F. K. (2007). Acceptability of sexist language among young people in Hong Kong. *Sex Roles, 56,* 285–295.

Lindsey, L. (2005). *Gender roles: A sociological perspective* (4th ed.). Upper Saddle River, NJ: Pearson/Prentice Hall.

Madson, L., & Shoda, J. (2006). Alternating between masculine and feminine pronouns: Does essay topic affect readers' perceptions? *Sex Roles, 54,* 275–285.

Maggio, R. (1988). *The nonsexist word finder: A dictionary of gender-free usage.* Boston: Beacon.

Maggio, R. (1992). *The bias-free word finder: A dictionary of nondiscriminatory language.* Boston: Beacon.

Martyna, W. (1978). What does "he" mean? Use of the generic masculine. *Journal of Communication, 28,* 131–138.

McConnell-Ginet, S. (1980). Linguistics and the feminist challenge. In S. McConnell-Ginet, R. Borker, & N. Furman (Eds.), *Women and language in literature and society* (pp. 3–25). New York: Praeger.

McConnell-Ginet, S. (1983). Intonation in a man's world. In B. Thorne, C. Kramarae, & N. Henley (Eds.), *Language, gender, and society* (pp. 69–88). Rowley, MA: Newbury.

McConnell-Ginet, S. (2010). *Making meanings, making lives: Gender, sexuality, and linguistic practice.* New York: Oxford University Press.

McGlone, M. S., Beck, G., & Pfiester, A. (2006). Contamination and camouflage in euphemisms. *Communication Monographs, 73,* 261–282.

Miller, C., & Swift, K. (1988). *The handbook of nonsexist writing* (2nd ed.). New York: Harper & Row.

Miller, C., & Swift, K. (1991). *Words and women: New language in new times.* New York: HarperCollins.

Miller, C., Swift, K., & Maggio, R. (1997, September–October). Liberating language. *Ms.,* 50–54.

Moffat, M. (1989). *Coming of age in New Jersey.* New Brunswick, NJ: Rutgers University Press.

Motschenbacher, H. (2009). Speaking the gendered body: The performative construction of commercial femininities and masculinities via body-part vocabulary. *Language in Society, 38,* 1–22.

Moulton, J., Robinson, G. M., & Elias, C. (1978). Sex bias in language use: "Neutral" pronouns that aren't. *American Psychologist, 33,* 1032–1036.

Mulac, A. (1998). The gender-linked language effect: Do language differences really make a difference? In D. J. Canary & K. Dindia (Eds.), *Sex differences and similarities in communication* (pp. 127–155). Mahwah, NJ: Erlbaum.

Mulac, A., Bradac, J. J., & Gibbons, P. (2001). Empirical support for the gender-as-culture hypothesis: An intercultural analysis of male/female language differences. *Human Communication Research, 27,* 121–152.

Mulac, A., Bradac, J. J., & Palomares, N. (2003, May). *A general process model of the gender-linked language effect: Antecedents for and consequences of language used by men and women.* Paper presented at the meeting of the International Communication Association, San Diego, CA.

Mulac, A., Wiemann, J. M., Widenmann, S. J., & Gibson, T. W. (1988). Male/female language differences and effects in same-sex and mixed sex dyads: The gender-linked language effect. *Communication Monographs, 55*, 315–335.

Murnen, S. K. (2000). Gender and the use of sexually degrading language. *Psychology of Women Quarterly, 24*, 319–327.

Myers, S. A., Martin, M. M., & Mottet, T. P. (2002). Students' motives for communicating with their instructors: Considering instructor socio-communicative style, student socio-communicative orientation, and student gender. *Communication Education, 51*, 121–133.

Newman, M., Groom, C. J., Handelman, L. D., & Pennebaker, J. W. (2008). Gender differences in language use: An analysis of 14,000 text samples. *Discourse Processes, 45*, 211–236.

Nuessel, F. (1994). Objectionable sport team designation. *Names: A Journal of Onomastics, 42*, 101–119.

Ode, K. (1999, June 6). "Hey, lady; you'll have to leave now": It's long past time to dump the term as a nickname for female athletic teams. *Minnesota Star-Tribune*, p. 67.

Palczewski, C. H. (1998). "Tak[e] the helm," man the ship . . . and I forgot my bikini! Unraveling why woman is not considered a verb. *Women & Language, 21*, 1–8.

Parks, J. B., & Roberton, M. A. (2005). Explaining age and gender effects on attitudes toward sexist language. *Journal of Language and Social Psychology, 24*, 401–411.

Parks, J. B., & Roberton, M. A. (2008). Generation gaps in attitudes toward sexist/nonsexist language. *Journal of Language and Social Psychology, 27*, 276–283.

Penelope, J. (1990). *Speaking freely: Unlearning the lies of the fathers' tongues.* New York: Pergamon.

Punyanunt-Carter, N. M. (2009). Understanding communication motives. *Texas Speech Communication Journal, 34*, 42–43.

Radway, J. (2009, May). *Girls, zines, and the limits of the body.* Paper presented at the meeting of the International Communication Association, Chicago, IL.

Ragan, S. L. (1989). Communication between the sexes: A consideration of sex differences in adult communication. In J. F. Nussbaum (Ed.),

Life-span communication: Normative processes (pp. 179–193). Hillsdale, NJ: Erlbaum.

Riordan, E. (2001). Commodified agents and empowered girls: Consuming and producing feminism. *Journal of Communication Inquiry, 25*, 279–297.

Roger, D., & Nesshoever, W. (1987). Individual differences in dyadic conversational strategies: A further study. *British Journal of Social Psychology, 26*, 247–255.

Romaine, S. (1999). *Communicating gender.* Mahwah, NJ: Erlbaum.

Rubin, R. B., Perse, E. M., & Barbato, C. A. (1988). Conceptualization and measurement of interpersonal communication motives. *Human Communication Research, 14*, 602–628.

Sacks, H., Schegloff, E. A., & Jefferson, G. (1978). A simple systematic for the organization of turn taking for conversation. In J. Schenkein (Ed.), *Studies in the organization of conversational interaction* (pp. 7–55). New York: Academic.

Scheuble, L. K., & Johnson, D. R. (2005). Married women's situational use of last names: An empirical study. *Sex Roles, 53*, 143–151.

Scheuble, L. K., Klingemann, K., & Johnson, D. R. (2000). Trends in women's marital name choices: 1966–1996. *Names: A Journal of Onomastics, 48*, 105–114.

Schmitt, J. J. (1992). God's wife: Some gender reflections on the Bible and biblical interpretation. In L. A. M. Perry, L. H. Turner, & H. M. Sterk (Eds.), *Constructing and reconstructing gender: The links among communication, language, and gender* (pp. 269–281). Albany: State University of New York Press.

Siegel, D. (2007). *Sisterhood, interrupted: From radical women to grrls gone wild.* New York: Palgrave/Macmillan.

Spender, D. (1985). *Man made language* (2nd ed.). London: Routledge & Kegan Paul.

Stafford, L., & Kline, S. L. (1996). Married women's name choices and sense of self. *Communication Reports, 9*, 85–92.

Stanley, J. P. (1977). Paradigmatic woman: The prostitute. In D. L. Shores (Ed.), *Papers in language variation.* Birmingham: University of Alabama Press.

Steinem, G. (1995, September–October). Words and change. *Ms.*, 93–96.

Stericker, A. (1981). Does this "he or she" business really make a difference? The effect of masculine pronouns as generics on job attitudes. *Sex Roles, 7,* 637–641.

Stinger, J. L., & Hopper, R. (1998). Generic *he* in conversation? *Quarterly Journal of Speech, 84,* 209–221.

Stipe, B. (2010). Why can't he hear what you're saying? Retrieved February 3, 2010, from http:// lifestyle.msn.com/relationship.

Strahan, T. (2008). "They" in Australian English: Non-gender-specific or specifically non-gendered? *Australian Journal of Linguistics, 28,* 17–29.

Suter, E. A., & Oswald, R. F. (2003). Do lesbians change their last names in the context of a committed relationship? *Journal of Lesbian Studies, 7,* 71–83.

Swim, J. K., Mallett, R., & Stangor, C. (2004). Understanding subtle sexism: Detection and use of sexist language. *Sex Roles, 51,* 117–128.

Tannen, D. (1986). *That's not what I meant!* London: Dent.

Tannen, D. (1990). *You just don't understand.* New York: William Morrow.

Tannen, D. (1995). *Talking 9 to 5: Women and men at work.* New York: Harper.

Taylor, A. (2006). Women, sport, and media, redux. *Women & Language, 29,* 1–2.

Tracy, K. (2002). *Everyday talk: Building and reflecting identities.* New York: Guilford.

Viscovich, N., Borod, J., Pihan, H., Peery, S., Brickman, A. M., & Tabert, M. (2003). Acoustical analysis of posed prosodic expressions: Effects of emotion and sex. *Perceptual and Motor Skills, 96,* 759–777.

Wachs, F. L. (2006). "Throw like a girl" doesn't mean what it used to: Research on gender, language, and power. In L. K. Fuller (Ed.), *Sports, rhetoric, and gender: Historical perspectives and media representations* (pp. 43–52). New York: Palgrave/Macmillan.

Ward, R. E., Jr. (2004). Are doors being opened for the "ladies" of college sports? A covariance analysis. *Sex Roles, 51,* 697–708.

Watts, R. J. (2003). *Politeness.* Cambridge, UK: Cambridge University Press.

Watzlawick, P., Beavin, J. H., & Jackson, D. D. (1967). *Pragmatics of human communication.* New York: Norton.

Weiss, E. H., & Fisher, B. (1998). Should we teach women to interrupt? Cultural variables in management communication courses. *Women in Management Review, 13,* 37–44.

West, C. (1998). When the doctor is a "lady": Power, status and gender in physician-patient encounters. In J. Coates (Ed.), *Language and gender: A reader* (pp. 396–412). Malden, MA: Blackwell.

West, C., & Zimmerman, D. H. (1983). Small insults: A study of interruptions in cross-sex conversations between unacquainted persons. In B. Thorne, C. Kramarae, & N. Henley (Eds.), *Language, gender, and society* (pp. 102–117). Rowley, MA: Newbury.

Whorf, B. L. (1956). Science and linguistics. In J. B. Carroll (Ed.), *Language, thought, and reality.* Cambridge: Massachusetts Institute of Technology Press.

Winn, L. L., & Rubin, D. L. (2001). Enacting gender identity in written discourse: Responding to gender role bidding in personal ads. *Journal of Language & Social Psychology, 20,* 393–418.

Zimmerman, D. H., & West, C. (1975). Sex roles, interruptions and silences in conversation. In B. Thorne & N. Henley (Eds.), *Language and sex: Difference and dominance* (pp. 105–129). Rowley, MA: Newbury.

HOT TOPICS

▶ The role of information in the choosing and being chosen process

▶ Barriers or roadblocks to relational success

▶ The ups and downs of initiating relationships online

▶ The role of attraction, physical appearance, proximity, and similarity in relationship initiation

▶ Strategies to reduce uncertainty about potential relationships

▶ Initial contact, first conversations, and flirting

▶ How sex differences in communication skills such as self-disclosure, empathy, listening, and nonverbal expressiveness and sensitivity influence relationship development

Gender and Relationships
Developing Potential into Reality

CHAPTER 5

Case Study

Choosing and Being Chosen

Open up any website, even ones devoted to "hard news," turn on a TV news program, or tune into your favorite talk radio station, and you'll likely hear something that used to be relegated to the tabloid newspapers and gossip outlets: news of the latest celeb hookup or breakup. Much as we might protest to the contrary, American culture is saturated with information about "all things celeb." From Jennifer and (insert male name here) breaking up to "Brangelina" having babies to the latest coupling and uncoupling, if Americans didn't have an appetite for this stuff, we wouldn't hear about it. Maybe you consider yourself immune to celebrity hype, but the line between hard news and cultural gossip is disappearing, making it harder to get the information we seek and avoid what doesn't interest us.

What topic seems to grab people's interest more than others? Relationships and all the human tragedies and triumphs that go with them. (And this isn't a "woman thing," lest you think we are directing this to female readers only. In our experience, men are just as likely as women to gossip and be interested in information about other people and their relationships, much as they may deny it.) Did Ryan and Scarlet make the right choice in ending their marriage because they were in love with other people? Because they worked so much they never saw each other? Let's bring the discussion down to a more local level—have you seen your friends making good or bad relational choices lately? What about *your* choices?

Maybe you believe that relational circumstances are more about fate, destiny, or dumb luck than choice; maybe you should think again. In this chapter, we challenge you to look at your own relationships—family, coworkers, bosses, friends, acquaintances,

(continued)

Case Study (*continued*)

dates, romantic partners—in terms of *choice*. What choices do you make every day in regard to the people you come into contact with— the people regularly in your life, as well as occasional acquaintances? Which people did you choose to have a relationship with, versus those who chose you? How do you choose to manage those relationships through communication and shared activities? Are certain channels of communication appropriate or preferred for some of those relationships, but not for others? (Like to text your friends, but not your mother?) When people choose to end a relationship, does it really end, or do people so greatly imprint on our hearts and minds that there's no such thing as an ending?

For most of us, relationships are what brings us life's greatest satisfaction. Probably more than anything else in life, relationships bring us our highest highs and, sad to say, our lowest lows. This chapter examines the bases of relationship choices and the forms of communication that facilitate those choices. Rather than hoping or believing that if you wait long enough or experiment enough, the perfect friend, dating partner, or mate will find his or her way to you, this chapter suggests a more proactive (rather than reactive) strategy. Relationship initiation and development are based on *choice*—*choosing* and *being chosen*. You clearly can't have close, personal relationships with everyone, so you must choose. On the flip side, it is very flattering to be chosen and can be very painful not to be.

BETTER INFORMATION = BETTER CHOICES

In talking with students about the relationship choice process or who chooses whom and why, it seems to come down to one thing: not physical appearance, not opposites attract, but *information*. Most of the time, people choose people they *know the most about*. And what is the source of this information? *Communication*. The information you gather may be based on verbal or nonverbal, conscious or unconscious, or intentional or unintentional communication. The better and more complete your information, the better your choices. Initiating relationships depends more on information gathered through the communication process than on any other factor, even physical appearance (no matter what the media and the fashion industry would have you believe).

The basic process works like this: You observe, you communicate, you evaluate, you make choices, you act. And other people are looking at you, doing exactly the same thing. How relationships develop and change and who takes responsibility for these tasks are questions many students have pondered, yet most are not fully aware of the information they use to make their choices or send to others to help them make their choices. Understanding how the process works and, more importantly, understanding how women and men deal with relational issues are critical.

It is our choices that show what we really are, far more than our abilities.

—*J. K. Rowling, from* **Harry Potter and the Chamber of Secrets**

At various stages in a developing relationship, you will make decisions about the future of the relationship. These instances may be seen as *choice points*. Imagine that you have a superficial friendship with someone at work. However, you think the person is interesting and decide a more personal friendship might be possible. By making that decision, you have exercised some control over the direction of the relationship. You've decided to accelerate the rate of change and move the relationship from one level to another. Each of us has faced decisions such as whether to turn an acquaintance into a friend, a friendship into something deeper, or a romantic relationship back to a friendship (good luck). Choice points such as these occur frequently, and the decisions that arise from them have an obvious impact on the quality of a relationship.

Before going further into this chapter, let's clarify our use of the terms *relationship* and *relational partner*. There are all kinds of relationships, and the word *relationship* is widely used. When using the word *relationship* in gender communication classes, students typically think of dating or romantic relationships rather than other kinds. We discuss in this chapter some elements that pertain more to dating or romantic relationships. But there are many concepts and research findings that apply to relationships in general—all kinds of relationships. When we use the term *relational partner*, it does not necessarily suggest a romantic relationship; nor does it imply the same permanence implied by the term *marital partner*. It is simply a means of identifying the two people in a relationship.

RELATIONSHIP ROADBLOCKS

Sometimes relationships work very well; other times, they just don't go well at all. Before exploring aspects of gender communication that enhance relationship initiation and maintenance, let's examine eight common barriers to healthy, satisfying relationships.

Roadblock 1: High Expectations

Websites, movies, television shows, and romance novels often set us up for unrealistic expectations when it comes to relationships, especially romantic ones. The media frequently depict attractive, glamorous people engaged in fun, seemingly worry-free, highly physical romantic relationships. The media rarely show these relationships six months or a year later, as they have developed over time, nor do they usually depict the work necessary to make relationships successful. We may fantasize about the perfect mate, but we know that nobody's perfect. So sometimes when we set unrealistically high expectations for others and our relationships, we really set ourselves up for a fall.

Roadblock 2: This Should Be Easy

We're sure you realize by now that communication isn't a natural thing you can do successfully just because you've been communicating all your life. So, why do we sometimes think it ought to be so easy to just relax and talk to someone? Why do we sometimes get a case of the "Bozos" when attraction and nervousness get the better of us and the wrong things come out of our mouths or we can't say anything at all? Communication in relationships is a challenge, whether we're in those initial stages or later on as relationships develop. Effective communication isn't easy and the more you have riding on the success of your relationship, the more difficult communication seems to be. Hopefully, with a better understanding of gender communication and more practice to develop your relational skills, your "Bozo" moments will be fewer.

Roadblock 3: Fear of Failure

This is the reverse of Roadblock 2: The fear of failing at relationships so stymies some people that they don't even try to make friends, much less date. The person they talk to the most is their dog. Failure is part of the relational process, however painful it might be. And, even though it's a cliché, we do learn from failure.

Roadblock 4: If I Just Relax, a Good Relationship Will Find Me

It doesn't matter whether your partner is the same sex or the opposite sex, all of it is tough.
—Lynda Bird Johnson, eldest daughter of President Lyndon B. Johnson

Even though we believe in a proactive approach to relationships, there are those rare times when things just happen. You aren't thinking about dating anyone, you don't expect to meet someone wonderful, and—bingo—Ms. or Mr. Incredible comes into the picture. There's no outguessing this process, but you may be setting yourself up for some lonely times if you merely wait and expect friendship or romance to find you. A proactive, balanced approach of introspection, planning, patience, communication skill development, and maybe a bit of faith is likely to generate better results than just waiting for something to happen.

Roadblock 5: Weighed Down by Baggage

No one arrives at a new relationship with a clean slate; we all carry our past experiences with us into new situations and relationships. Some of us have troubled pasts—maybe our parents' relationship wasn't the best role model for how we want to relate to others, or we've been burned in past relationships, making us fearful or hesitant about new ones. But here's a key question: Are those just experiences or are they "baggage"? Most of us view baggage as a negative, something that weighs us down, something we have to overcome in a new relationship or circumstance. Perhaps we should reframe our view of our baggage to see our past experiences, choices, and outcomes as lessons learned, as a road map of our relational history—one that informs the next situation and enables us make better choices. We definitely aren't "doomed" to repeat the past.

Roadblock 6: It's Got to Happen Now!

As Carrie Fisher wrote in *Postcards from the Edge*, "Instant gratification takes too long." Some people express a desire to have a remote control for relationships, so they can zip and zap, getting what they want when they want it. Probably all of us could use a bigger dose of patience in our relationships. Solid, successful relationships of all kinds take time to nurture and develop. Wanting too much too soon (and sometimes getting it) can be a big problem. Not taking adequate time to nurture a relationship can sabotage a potentially wonderful connection before it's had its chance.

Roadblock 7: Giving Up Too Much Just to Have a Dating Relationship

University residence advisors describe a problem that they see regularly, the fact that some students (more often female than male) are too willing to compromise themselves sexually or in other ways in order to get a dating relationship started or keep one going. Are women more prone than men to want dating or romantic relationships, or is this just a stereotype? Women often feel a tension between the traditional message that they

Remember . . .

Choice Points: Moments in a relationship when you make decisions about the future of the relationship

Relationship: Any type of partnering between two people, e.g., friendships, workplace connections, romantic or committed partnerings

Relational Partners: Term to identify the two people in any type of relationship

should have a man in their lives and the modern messages of careerism and autonomy. Sometimes this desire for acceptance causes people to do things they really don't want to do. No one should have to bend to pressure or be motivated by the desire to impress another person or to achieve some form of social status.

Roadblock 8: Looking Over Someone's Shoulder

Diving into a relationship, especially a romantic one, is a leap of faith for most of us. Some people deny themselves good relationships because they think something (someone) better will come along. They'll look you in the eye at the beginning of a conversation, but soon start scanning the area for something more interesting or attractive. (We mean this concretely, as well as metaphorically.) They don't want to commit to working on a relationship because of the fear of wasted energy, a fear that they'll miss out on something better, someone more right for them, someone who they believe can give them more self-esteem, rewards, or status. People do this with friendships sometimes too—holding off developing a friendship because they think they deserve a "higher class" of friend or that having higher-status friends will garner them more respect, inclusion, perks, and so forth. The "Is there something better" question is deadly for relationships and can leave you alone, friendless and dateless. People tend not to like comparisons, both to real or imagined other people.

STAGE 1: IS THERE A RELATIONSHIP GOLD MINE OUT THERE? PROSPECTING AND BEING A PROSPECT

Initiating relationships is a process similar to prospecting for gold. Like a prospector, you are looking for something that will add value to your life (if not actually make you rich!). Like a prospector, you go out into the "field" and examine "samples" for possible value to you. If a sample (person) looks interesting, you can examine him or her more closely. There is (at least) one big difference—while you are examining prospects, they could be examining you. You are a prospect as well as a prospector.

Prospecting—whether for gold or for a relationship—is an active process. This is very different than the wait-for-something-to-happen belief epitomized by the expression, "If it's meant to be, it will be." The proactive approach presented here puts you in charge of your relational life; you neither wait for something to happen nor blame something or someone if it doesn't happen. Did you ever see the bumper sticker, "So many men, so little time?" In your lifetime, you have the potential to initiate and develop hundreds of relationships. Whether you entered college right out of high school or started your college career later in life, college is a prime time for experiencing various kinds of relationships, and it presents numerous opportunities for relationship initiation.

Seeing and Being Seen

The first part of stage 1 in relationship development, normally, is seeing others and being seen. Information gathered through observations guides your first choices, but when men and women go prospecting, what do they look for? What features catch the eye and spark the imagination? Research suggests that we form impressions and make judgments about people in the first 10 seconds of meeting them (Burch, 2001). What kind of impression do you make when someone first meets you?

We like to ask our male and female students what they look for in potential dating partners; their responses are amazingly similar. Both sexes seem to look for people who are physically appealing (but not so exceptionally gorgeous that they are unapproachable), who look nice (usually that means nonthreatening, well-groomed, etc.), who show an appropriate degree of self-confidence, who smile a lot and have a good sense of humor, who aren't too afraid or too macho to show interest, and who will impress their parents and friends. It's interesting that this list doesn't usually contain comments about being "Joe Stud" or looking like a Victoria's Secret model.

Not Being Seen: Prospecting Online

Obviously, seeing a person is not the only way a relationship can begin. Not only has the Internet vastly increased opportunities for relationship development, it's also had an impact on our understanding of relationships (Gibbs, Ellison, & Heino, 2006; Hardey, 2004; Yurchisin, Watchravesringkan, & McCabe, 2005).

During the first decade of this new century over 70 percent of people living in the United States reported actively using the Internet (Baron, 2008). Maybe that figure sounds low to you (because college students are heavy Internet users), but, in comparison, only 40 percent of Europeans reported actively using the Internet during the same time frame. Younger people—those whom scholar Marc Prensky (2001) calls "digital natives"—have grown up in a digital age and are so comfortable with technology that they make little distinction between their online and offline lives (Palfrey & Gasser, 2008). Personal web pages, blogs, and social networking sites such as Facebook, Twitter, and LinkedIn provide opportunities for people to connect without first (or ever) meeting face to face (Barnes, 2008; Grill, 2011). And we don't have to tell you, beloved college students, that most of you interface with these social networking sites from your smartphones. You don't have to have seen the 2010 movie *The Social Network* to agree with media experts who suggest that social media is a "revolution in the way we communicate" (Hoffman, as in Chirinos, 2010, p. 1B).

Research on electronically mediated relationships has determined that many people find these forms of relationships just as satisfying as face-to-face relationships (Tidwell & Walther, 2002). Some of the advantages of developing relationships online include the availability of people who seek companionship; the ability to learn basic information about people (for example, someone's status and photos on Facebook) before revealing anything about oneself or choosing to meet in person; getting to know someone through lower-risk means like texts or e-mail exchanges before deciding to choose more risky contact, like a face-to-face conversation; the ease of contacting someone (versus the dreaded task of asking for a phone number); the protection of one's identity; an enlarged pool of available companions not hindered by physical geography; and the lesser expense compared to what face-to-face dating costs nowadays (West & Turner, 2011).

Interestingly, some research appears to indicate that sex differences diminish in electronically mediated communication. One study found that women were at less of a disadvantage in online communication than in face-to-face communication and could be more participative and direct (McConnell, 1997). Other research determined that, besides reducing the importance of physical traits, online communication increases the significance of rapport and similarity and allows more freedom from gender role constraints (Cooper & Sportolari, 1997; Gibbs et al., 2006).

One of the most interesting aspects of Internet communication is the possibility for identity alteration and gender bending (Herring & Martinson 2004; Yurchisin et al., 2005). It is possible for people to take on totally different identities online, to present themselves as a member of the opposite sex, and to "walk on the wild side" in relative safety. Thus you may never know exactly with whom you are communicating; you and the other person may both be experimenting.

Being Attracted to a Prospect

Just what is attraction? According to students, it can be "lust," "a sort of chemistry between you and another person," "wanting to have sexual intercourse with another person," "liking someone—not just physically, but for personality traits." You can see from these responses that some people use the term *attraction* to apply to platonic friendships, in which one person is attracted to another on a nonphysical, nonsexual basis, whereas others associate attraction with sexual interest. *Attraction* has been defined as a motivational state that causes someone to think, feel, and behave in a positive manner toward another person (Berscheid, 1985). More specifically, *sexual attraction* could be considered more of an "animal attraction"—being drawn to another person because you want to have sexual contact with her or him. You may or may not actually fulfill that desire, but the attraction is felt nonetheless. For our purposes in this chapter, let's use a broader interpretation of the term attraction: *interpersonal attraction* is the degree to which you desire to form and possibly maintain an interpersonal relationship with another person (Beebe, Beebe, & Ivy, 2013). That relationship might be a same-sex or cross-sex friendship, a coworker relationship, a romantic relationship (nonsexual), or a sexual relationship.

Net Notes

Not sure what you're attracted to, in terms of developing a relationship? Maybe you're attracted to certain qualities of a person, only to find that sort of person isn't right for you over the long haul. Maybe you're not interested in the "long haul" right now, but you'd like some guidance when it comes to attraction. Would it surprise you to know that all sorts of quizzes are available at websites, designed to help you narrow down what you're attracted to and interested in? Sites like **quizplz.com** and **gotoquiz.com** offer batteries of questions to help you better understand your likes and dislikes when it comes to attracting a potential date or long-term partner.

ATTRACTIVE TERRITORY AHEAD   Some of us are just drawn to people because they're cool, they seem different from us, or they're interesting for a variety of reasons. (Remember, we're talking about all kinds of attraction here, not just romantic or sexual.) Sometimes we're drawn to people simply because they're drawn to us, and we find that flattering.

One concept integral to attraction is *proximity*, which relates to the space around you and the physical distance between you and someone else, the amount of time you spend physically near that person, how easily you can gain access to her or him, and how physical closeness affects the relationship. Research shows you are more likely to be attracted to someone if you perceive that there are opportunities to spend time with that person (Guerrero, Andersen, & Afifi, 2011; Kenrick, Neuberg, & Cialdini, 2005; Knapp & Hall, 2010). Sometimes, we may choose to create proximity by generating opportunities to connect with someone we find attractive. For example, we may join the same club or gym we know the attractive other is a member of, or just happen to be in the hallway when a certain someone's class lets out. Relational partners or friends who were once in close physical proximity but who experience geographical separation know firsthand the challenges that nonproximity to a partner can create (Dainton & Aylor, 2001; Rhodes, 2002; Sahlstein, 2006; Stafford, Merolla, & Castle, 2006).

But once again, here's where technological advancements affect how we relate to others, because *everyone's close in cyberspace.* What we mean is that we can now communicate across the globe with such ease and speed that we can act on our attraction and develop a feeling of closeness that has nothing to do with geography or the physical realm. You may become attracted to people, for a variety of purposes, by reading their blogs, coming into contact with them through e-mail at work, or being "introduced" as a friend of a friend through Facebook. You may find their ideas interesting, their sense of humor engaging, or their intellect compelling, and your attraction begins and possibly grows the more you learn about them. Or, in the case of relationships that were once physically close but circumstances have separated the partners, such as military families in which one or more family members are geographically separated, being able to communicate through e-mail, text messaging, and web cam applications such as Skype may keep the attraction alive, so to speak.

CHECKING OUT THE PROSPECTS   One prospecting strategy for gathering information about other people is to observe them. You look at others; they look at you. You check out each other's physical appearance. Are the sexes different, in terms of how much importance they place on physical appearance as a determinant of attraction? As odd as it sounds, both men and women begin by seeking signals of physical health (Li, Bailey, Kenrick, & Linsenmeier, 2002). Some research suggests that members of both sexes also emphasize physical appearance as a factor in attraction (Geary, Vigil, & Byrd-Craven, 2004). However, positive social interactions with others may enhance our perceptions of their physical attractiveness (Albada, Knapp, & Theune, 2002). Have you ever talked with someone and then thought, "Did you just get cuter or *what*?" A great conversation may increase and even generate attraction in the first place. Of course, this works in the reverse too. Ever talk to people you thought were "hotties," only to have that perception altered when they opened their mouths?

Another interesting point regarding attraction is that you may see someone you deem physically attractive but remain unattracted to that person. We are not necessarily attracted to people who have a pleasing appearance. Haven't you ever seen someone who was beautiful, but he or she just didn't stir you in any way? Social psychological research in the 1970s produced a fascinating observation of human behavior that has stood the test of time and has come to be known as the *matching hypothesis* (Bar-Tal & Saxe, 1976). This research indicates that while you may appreciate the appearance of someone who is stunningly good looking, you usually have relationships (and partnerships) with people you feel are similar in physical attractiveness to you. An average-looking heterosexual man may appreciate the physical appearance of a very good-looking woman, but he is more likely to be attracted to, date, and even marry a woman he believes is at a level of attractiveness similar to his own.

LIKING PEOPLE WHO ARE LIKE YOU   Perhaps you have heard the cliché, "Opposites attract." Some people may be interested in others who are radically different from them—differences can be intriguing. But often these relationships don't last because as the initial intrigue fades, the differences become obstacles, sometimes insurmountable ones. The differences can be quite exciting at the beginning of the relationship, but may present major issues later on. In the article, "From Appealing to Appalling: Disenchant-ment with a Romantic Partner," sociologist David Felmee (2001) describes the five most common traits that can evolve from "appealing to appalling." These include nice to pas-sive, strong to stubborn, funny to flaky, outgoing to over the top, and caring to clingy. These terms describe similar behaviors, but different labels.

Most of us prefer *similarity* over difference in relationships. Research indicates that under most circumstances, you will generally be more interested in someone whose upbringing, attitudes, beliefs, and values are more similar to yours than differ-ent (Jones, Pelham, Carvallo, & Mirenberg, 2004; Kenrick, Neuberg, & Cialdini, 2005; Morry, 2005; Waldron & Applegate, 1998). Social psychologists Berscheid and Reis (1998) put it aptly: "The most basic principle of attraction is familiarity. As opposed to the unfamiliar, familiar people usually are judged to be safe and unlikely to cause harm"(p. 205).

How do you turn this information into a strategy—both for choosing and being chosen? It's a good idea to place yourself in the company of people who are similar to you and to learn to what extent those similarities exist. For example, if you think that bar or club scenes are great opportunities for socializing with fun people, you are more likely to find someone with similar attitudes if you look for them in a bar or club than elsewhere. If your religious values are such that you believe attending church is impor-tant, then your chances of finding someone with similar values and beliefs are greater in a church setting than other places.

Strategies for Gaining Information

As you perceive other people and begin to learn about them, understanding the role of information in this process may be helpful. Communication researchers have developed a theory of *uncertainty reduction*. Some situations, like meeting new people or forging new levels of relationships with people we already know, generate a degree of uncertainty for most of us. In an effort to reduce our uncertainty and make ourselves more comfortable, we respond by seeking information (Berger & Calabrese, 1975; Berger & Douglas, 1981; Douglas, 1990). Reducing uncertainty by gaining information enables *choice*—the choice you will make about whether to proceed with someone, as well as the choice someone else will make about you.

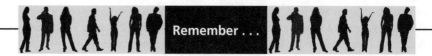

Remember . . .

Attraction: Motivational state that causes someone to think, feel, and behave in a positive manner toward another person

Sexual Attraction: Feeling drawn to another person because you want to have sexual contact with her or him

Interpersonal Attraction: Degree to which you desire to form and possibly maintain an interpersonal relationship with another person

Proximity: Space (territory) around you; physical and psychological distance between you and others

Matching Hypothesis: Tendency to form relationships, particularly romantic relationships, with persons you feel are similar in physical attractiveness to you

Similarity: Tendency to be more interested in someone whose upbringing, attitudes, beliefs, and values are more similar to yours than different

Three general strategies emerge for reducing uncertainty, all of which are based on information. The strategies are progressive, meaning that people usually start with the first and progress through the other two. Anywhere along the line, however, you can choose to break off the search for information if you deem it too risky or if you discover something that leads you to think the relationship will not be rewarding. First, people engage in *passive strategies*—observing people, most of the time without them knowing it. A common passive strategy for this "wired" society we live in is the Google search; most people "google" someone's name to find out more before deciding if further interaction is warranted or desirable. We might also search for someone on Facebook, Twitter, or other social media sites to learn more about her or him before instigating any form of more assertive communication. In our offline world, if we're thinking about making friends with someone, we may watch to see who that person hangs out with and what he or she does. The more observations we make, the more we know and the more our uncertainty is reduced.

The second category, *active strategies,* requires more action than observation and typically involves a third party or another indirect means of gaining information. In an online setting, an active strategy might be to be part of a listserv (a community or group of online e-mailers) and simply read a person's postings rather than e-mail directly with them. (In the chatrooms of old, this tendency to read others' exchanges rather than entering an online conversation was termed "lurking.") If your university professor uses an online classroom delivery system like WebCT or Blackboard, you might read postings of classmates. You might not be direct friends with someone on Facebook, but you read messages that friends of friends send. These aren't passive strategies, but they don't represent direct communication with the person of interest either. As another example, you might "follow" someone on Twitter, reading his or her postings, but not post a message back or directly to the person you're following. Again, this is an active strategy to gain information and reduce uncertainty about a person, but the strategy falls just shy of direct communication.

Remember . . .

Uncertainty Reduction: People's responses to low predictability and high uncertainty about other people and circumstances

Passive Strategy: Uncertainty reduction strategy of gaining information by observing people, but not directly communicating

Active Strategy: Uncertainty reduction strategy that involves a third party or other indirect means of gaining information

Interactive Strategy: Uncertainty reduction strategy that engages the interested party directly in communication, either one-on-one or in a group, to gain more information

The most obvious tactic is to ask other people about someone—what the person is like, what he or she does, if the person is involved with someone at the time, and so on. As another active strategy, although it sounds a bit manipulative, people sometimes stage situations to gain information about how another person responds. Relationship experts Guerrero, Andersen, and Afifi (2011) recount an example from one of their female students. The student wrote a note asking to get together, signed it "a secret female admirer," and placed it on her boyfriend's car. The student wanted to know if her boyfriend would tell her of such a letter and whether he would meet the admirer. As it turns out, the boyfriend never mentioned the letter to the girlfriend, but neither did he make the "rendezvous."

The most direct method to reduce uncertainty is an *interactive strategy*, one that involves asking the "object of one's affection" direct questions or engaging her or him in conversation, one-on-one, in a group, or in some sort of mediated format. This strategy takes self-confidence and nerve for most of us, but it seems to be the most reliable, straightforward, and time-efficient method of getting information.

STAGE 2: ENGAGING THE PROSPECT—CONVERSATIONS

No clear-cut line exists between the first and second stages; they merely have some identifying characteristics. Stage 2 consists of the opening interactions of a relationship. Each person has made the initial choice in favor of the other person and has indicated a willingness to begin to interact and learn about the other. In this stage, people expend a good deal of energy trying to get the other person to think well of them. Here are a few strategies that help accomplish that goal.

Digging In and Discovering More

Most decisions about whether to act further on one's attraction are made in the first few minutes of a conversation, so a lot rides on that first encounter. Your interest—and we use the word *interest* as an extension of attraction—now demands that you verbally communicate. What are the best ways to begin and develop an effective conversation?

CONVERSATION STARTERS   Conversations have to start somewhere, and there has to be an opening verbalization. Everyone laughs at the old pickup lines of the 1960s and 1970s, lines like "What's your sign?" "Haven't I seen you somewhere before?" and "What's a nice girl like you doing in a place like this?" While those lines are pretty laughable, the advice given to men regarding "picking up women" has become increasingly sophisticated—and sometimes troubling. For example, a book called *The Game: Penetrating the Secret Society of Pickup Artists* (Strauss, 2005) is devoted to giving advice to men on how to pick up as many women as possible. The goal is not a long-standing, loving relationship, but as many short-term relationships as a man can generate.

Reducing effective communication down to a gimmick and packaged opening lines is obviously inconsistent with the principles underlying the receiver orientation to communication because it generally ignores the process of adapting one's communication to the receiver of the message and treating the receiver as a person, not an object. So why would someone use a line? Sometimes it's simply easier—people who might be nervous sometimes resort to trite beginnings just to get the ball rolling. For these reasons, we grant that lines or conversational openers may be useful at times, but not necessarily as efforts to pick up or hit on someone. Conversational beginnings that reflect a thoughtful, sincere attempt at interaction can serve as icebreakers between you and someone you're interested in. Perhaps you've observed something about the other person that you can comment on, such as a book the person is carrying that might lead into a conversation about college classes, or a T-shirt the person is wearing from a place you've visited or a favorite sports team.

As a means of getting to know someone or getting a potential relationship off the ground, most of us resort to the good old-fashioned question-and-answer sequence, where we ask an easy, innocuous question, which is followed by an equally easy response, like asking where people are from, what their hobbies are, and so forth. This back-and-forth exchange of information is typical of the initiating stage of relationship development (Knapp & Vangelisti, 2009). Research continues to show that initiating conversations in the early stages of relationships is perceived as an equally appropriate activity for men and women in American culture (Kankiewicz, 2007; Kleinke, Meeker, & Staneski, 1986; Smith, 2006). Try to keep questions and answers light and simple in the beginning; you don't want to "grill" someone or make them feel like they're on a stressful job interview, being barraged by questions.

Daniel Menaker (2010), author of *A Good Talk: The Story and Skill of Conversation*, believes that neither person in a face-to-face encounter should initiate conversation by talking about themselves or the other person; instead, Menaker suggests that a third subject, a third person, or object should start the conversation. He offers an example of when he was doing a crossword puzzle and someone noticed and commented on it, which started a conversation in an easy, nonthreatening, nonintrusive way. Menaker explains that this is why people so often strike up conversation by discussing the weather, as an "attempt at neutrality" (p. 121). Talking about the weather suggests commonality and isn't an invasion of privacy; such topics can offer a simple test case of conversation to see if something more between conversants is possible or desirable.

ASKING GREAT QUESTIONS   If you wonder what makes a good conversationalist, the best answer we can provide is this: Learn to ask great questions. Notice we said "great" questions, not just questions. A great question is, first, tailored as much as possible to the recipient of the question. Unlike a job interview in which an interviewer may bombard an applicant with as many questions as time allows, a social encounter requires a kinder, gentler approach. Use whatever you can observe from the person and the situation to help you formulate questions that will draw the other person out. Basic informational questions (e.g., "Where are you from?" "What do you do for a living?") help break the ice, but "yes–no" questions that can be answered with a single word don't extend a conversation. Also, avoid questions that might be perceived as too personal.

The second skill that helps develop conversational ability relates to listening. Many people go through the motions of asking questions, but they don't really listen to the answers. They may find themselves repeating questions they've already asked, embarrassing themselves and turning off the person they're trying to impress. It's important to listen intently when someone responds to your question, then pose a follow-up question that shows you're really listening and interested—not a statement that takes the focus away from the other person. Although some people become uncomfortable talking about themselves or their views, most of us enjoy the attention and feel like genuine interest is being shown.

Studies have found that more women than men ask questions to generate conversation in social situations (Coates, 2005; Lindsey & Zakahi, 1996, 2006). But we all need to develop and hone our conversational skills so that one person isn't responsible for getting a conversation off the ground and keeping it going. The skill of asking great questions doesn't happen like magic or overnight—time, maturity, and experience will help you improve your conversational ability.

The Art and Skill of Flirting

Is it typical of you to be unaware that someone really does like you? How do you detect that someone is interested in you, either on a friendship or romantic level? How do you show your interest in another person? Are you likely to reveal your interest through nonverbal means first, rather than coming right out and declaring undying love and affection? What exactly does it mean to flirt?

Flirting is a popular term for a long-standing phenomenon: showing attraction to and interest in another person (Metts, 2006). We suggest caution here, however, because not all flirting is an indication of interest (Egland, Spitzberg, & Zormeier, 1996). Researchers have found that "people may flirt because they see it as innocent fun, they want to make a third party jealous, they want to develop their social skills, or they are trying to persuade someone to do something for them" (Guerrero et al., 2011, p. 191).

No matter what type of relationship is being initiated, most of us usually convey our interest in others nonverbally, rather than strolling up to someone and saying, "I find you interesting" (Beres, Herold, & Maitland, 2004; Hall, Cody, Jackson, & Flesh, 2008). One study conducted in singles bars detected fifty-two (!) nonverbal cues that heterosexual women use to signal their interest in men. At the top of this list of cues were smiling, surveying a room with the eyes, and increased physical proximity (Moore, 1985). People are also more likely to preen; they may adjust their clothing, fidget with their hair, and alter their posture in the presence of an attractive person (Daly, Hogg, Sacks, Smith, & Zimring, 1999; Grammer, Knuck, & Magnusson, 1998; Scheflen, 1965). Ethologist Irensus Eibl-Eibesfeldt (1975) filmed women's flirtatious behavior in both industrialized cultures and hunter–gatherer cultures around the world. She found a common sequence of behaviors that can easily be observed at any nightclub. The sequence

Hot Button Issue

"Flirting Is a Tricky Business"

You've lived a few number of years now, so we don't have to tell you that flirting is a tricky business. Some suggest that, heterosexually speaking, it's a woman's job to flirt and a man's job to pick up on that flirtation and choose to do or not do something about it. But it's not really that simple, is it?

We call flirting a hot button issue to make this point: One person's flirtation is another person's sexual harassment. These days, you have to be very careful when you show romantic interest in another person. Since Americans' working lives take up increasingly significant amounts of time, it would follow that many people now find their social and romantic outlets through coworkers (Work & Family Facts & Statistics, 2010). But developing a romantic relationship with a colleague is a delicate endeavor, particularly if the colleague is your boss, you are his or her boss, or status differences exist for other reasons. Flirting at the office might seem perfectly harmless to you, but the more important point is if the object of your flirtation sees it as harmless, too.

Books on professional behavior will warn you to stay away from romantic entanglements at the office—period—no matter if both of you are on the same status level within the organization. We understand this suggestion, but realize that sometimes office liaisons just happen—and they can lead to wonderful relationships. We know of many colleagues who met their spouses at work or through professional circles. But the books' advice on flirting at the office is sound: Be very, very careful with any kind of public demonstrations of interest. You never know who's looking and how that behavior may come back to haunt you. Apply caution to cyberflirting with colleagues and clients as well (Whitty, 2004; Whitty & Carr, 2003).

Remember that for most of us as employees, we don't own the computer systems, office phones, or cell phones that are given to us by the companies we work for. The company owns these devices and all the messages we deliver and receive on them, so a simple flirtatious e-mail with a coworker in the next cubicle is the property of the company and could legally be read by your boss! Are flirtatious texts or e-mails the kind of communication you want your boss connecting to you?

---

begins with eye contact, a quick smile, and an eyebrow flash, followed by dropping and turning the head, and concluding with a sidelong glance. While these nonverbal cues were detected in research over four decades ago, these same behaviors can be seen in social settings today.

Communication scholars Trost and Alberts (1998, 2006) provide a fascinating discussion of heterosexual courtship, flirting, and sex differences, which they explain from a biological or evolutionary perspective. While the details of their argument would take us beyond the scope of our current discussion, these researchers do provide evidence from a body of work on the topic, and their conclusions are illuminating. The general conclusion from studies is that women are more dominant or in control of the flirting process than men. Specifically, research is consistent in four findings: (1) women are more skilled at encoding and decoding flirtatious nonverbal behaviors; (2) women exhibit a wide variety of flirting behaviors that are used to signal their interest to men they desire to attract; (3) women have a widely developed repertoire of rejection strategies; and (4) women who exhibit flirtatious behaviors typically will be approached by men. Recent research supports these findings (Hall et al., 2008).

Think about how flirtation actually seems to work in real life. As we suggested earlier, in the section on attraction, women typically initiate the process of "seeing and being seen" by nonverbally signaling their interest in a man. For decades, nonverbal communication research has determined that women tend to give off more nonverbal cues and decipher the cues of others with more accuracy than men (Knapp & Hall, 2010). Typically, if a woman is attracted and interested in a man, she will show that interest nonverbally, leaving it to the man to pick up on her cues, decipher them as indications of interest, and make a decision to approach or not approach (Arliss, 2001). (This puts a lot of pressure on the man!) While men do most of the physical approaching to initiate an encounter, men usually approach only after a woman has indicated nonverbally that the approach is welcome (Henningsen, Braz, & Davies, 2008). Granted, flirting doesn't always work this way. Some women tease and give off miscues of interest (Kowalski, 1993); men sometimes misread cues (Abbey, 1982, 1987, 1991; Abbey, Zawacki, & Buck, 2005; Henningsen, 2004; Koeppel, Montagne, O'Hair, & Cody, 1999). Men may not reciprocate women's interest, and women are certainly capable of charging right up to men and declaring their interest verbally. But these research findings are illuminating; ponder them and then see if they match your experience.

Once you've put yourself out there so as to see and be seen, you've been attracted and attractive, you've flirted, you've opened a conversation— perhaps with some scintillating, prepared lines or well-thought-out questions—you've listened to responses to your questions, and you've followed up those responses with other questions or comments. Now what? If those first conversations were successful enough to make you feel there is real potential with someone, congratulations! Now you have more work to do.

A study in the Washing-ton Post *says that women have better verbal skills than men. I just want to say to the authors of that study: Duh.*
—Conan O'Brien, television talk show host

STAGE 3: DEVELOPING THE CLAIM AND ESTABLISHING THE RELATIONSHIP

As a relationship develops, a judgment of *communicative competence* (meaning how effectively and appropriately one communicates) appears to outweigh other factors, such as appearance or similarity, in determinations of success in initiating relationships, as well as overall relationship satisfaction (McEwan & Guerrero, 2010; Miczo, Segrin, & Alspach, 2001). Thus it is important to work to establish effective communication behaviors and patterns if you want a relationship to succeed—any kind of relationship. If we asked men and women, "What types of communication are most critical to relational success," would they generate similar lists? A few forms of communication have been studied a great deal in our discipline, as well as in related disciplines; they tend to show up on both women's and men's lists as being critical to relationships, so we review these in the pages that follow.

Opening a New Vein: Intimacy and Self-Disclosure

We use a couple of important terms in the heading of this section. First, *intimacy* is something most people long for in relationships—whether they are family relationships, friendships, or romantic relationships. What exactly is intimacy? Relationship experts Harvey and Weber (2002) provide such descriptions as bonding, closeness, and emotional connection, all based on sharing personal, private information and experiences over time. Our particular favorite definition comes from couples therapist Jeffrey Fine (2001): "To be intimate is to be totally transparent, emotionally naked in front of another who is equally transparent. You want to see into the other's heart. What people should mean when they say *intimacy* is in-to-me-see" (p. 225). Granted, different kinds of relationships will have different levels of intimacy, but it appears that some level of intimacy is a goal of most relationships.

You probably know by now that it's hard to make effective decisions or act effectively toward another person without accurate and useful information. The most common means of actively sharing information to develop intimacy is known as *self-disclosure*, originally researched by psychologist Sidney Jourard (1971). Jourard suggests that self-disclosure occurs when we voluntarily provide information to others that they wouldn't learn if we didn't tell them. For example, your height and weight are generally noticeable aspects of your being, but your exact height and (especially) weight will most likely not be known by someone unless you choose to tell them. Research suggests that closeness and satisfaction in relationships of all types are closely tied to the level and quality of disclosure (Afifi & Steuber, 2009; Derlega, Winstead, & Greene, 2008; Dindia, 2002).

Some of our thinking about the sexes and self-disclosure is based on stereotypes, but the stereotypes have been supported by research. Consistent findings over a few decades indicate that women like to and tend to self-disclose more than men, especially about their relationships, and they take more risks in disclosure by relating sensitive feelings and personal problems (Burleson, 2003; Dindia, 2002; Shaffer, Pegalis, & Bazzini, 1996). Not only do women tend to disclose more than men, women are much more often the recipient of others' disclosures (Aries, 2006; Petronio, Martin, & Littlefield, 1984).

Jourard (1971) addressed male–male disclosure (or the lack of it) and the consequences to men's physical health in a book chapter entitled, "The Lethal Aspects of the Male Role." He suggested that men who have difficulty expressing their thoughts and feelings also have higher levels of stress-related diseases compared to men who are able to disclose more fully. Other research supports this finding, noting that male role stress has not significantly declined since Jourard's work was published (Copenhaver & Eisler, 1996). For many men, expressing their thoughts and feelings suggests weakness and vulnerability, as though one gives up power and control by revealing oneself. In personal relationships, however, a balance between power and disclosure facilitates the development of satisfying friendships, romantic relationships, marriages, and coworker relationships.

Let's stop and think about these sex differences for a moment. Does disclosure need to be expressed in words? Perhaps men disclose themselves through what they *do* in relationships; perhaps they seek and express intimacy more nonverbally than verbally. Research has called into question earlier findings on the sexes and disclosure, and the stereotypes that may accompany them (Borisoff, 2001; Galvin & Bylund, 2001; Reis, 1998). For example, Wood and Inman (1993) make a case for considering joint activities (basketball, watching sports together, etc.) as a path to closeness in male friendships. While women's friendships with other women more often develop and deepen through communication, particularly self-disclosure, rather than shared experiences, we should not make the judgment that men's relationships with other men are superficial because they involve more *doing* than *talking.* We need to avoid measuring intimacy or relationship satisfaction with a feminine yardstick. However, men should not use this argument as a reason to avoid appropriate disclosure.

One final topic related to self-disclosure warrants brief mention here, although we discuss it more fully in Chapter 7, where we explore gender communication in romantic or intimate relationships. For many of us, disclosing our opinions or attitudes is one thing; disclosing our sexual desires, preferences, fears, and experiences is another (Peterson, 2011). Why do many of us find it difficult to talk about sex with our sex partners? We may banter about sex in the locker room with members of our same sex or "dish" with girlfriends over happy hour about a sexual conquest or a fantasy. But when it comes down to having open, frank conversations with a sexual partner about the sexual activity we're having (or not having) in our relationship, we often find ourselves at a loss for words, embarrassed to even address the subject, or inept in our communication, stumbling until we simply give up.

It probably won't surprise you to know that research has examined the connection between sexual self-disclosure and relationship satisfaction (Badr & Carmack Taylor, 2009; Faulkner & Lannutti, 2010; Litzinger & Gordon, 2005). People who have higher levels of self-esteem, specifically in terms of their view of themselves sexually, tend to be more sexually disclosive and assertive, as well as more satisfied with the sexual activity they experience in their relationships (Menard & Offman, 2009). When people report reciprocal self-disclosure in general in their relationships, they also report engaging in more sexual disclosure (Byers & Demmons, 1999). This means that if you talk more openly about a range of topics to your partner and your partner reciprocates, you're more likely to talk about your sex life as well. Byers and Demmons' (1999) findings on sex differences parallel studies on general self-disclosure: Women tend to sexually self-disclose more than men; however, the disclosure by both parties tends not to be as full or complete as it is for nonsexual topics. Partners (women in particular) will disclose about sexuality to a degree, but report not feeling comfortable disclosing as fully as they might about other, less-intimate or less-risky topics (Byers & Demmons, 1999). Research also shows that the more sexual disclosure in a relationship, the more satisfied the partners are with their relationship and the communication within it (Holmberg & Blair, 2009; LaFrance, 2010; MacNeil & Byers, 2005).

The Big "E": Empathy

Understanding and responding effectively to another person is critical to long-term relational success. You probably value people who seem to understand you, and you probably want to increase contact with them.

Empathy has been called one of the "hallmarks of supportive relationships," and yet it remains a difficult concept to define (Beebe, Beebe, & Ivy, 2013, p. 78). To empathize means that you try to understand and feel what another person is feeling; you try to step into the shoes of the other person, to experience as closely as you can what she or he is experiencing.

Research underscores the power of empathy to enhance the quality of close relationships (Clark, 2010; Devoldre, Davis, Verhofstadt, & Buysse, 2010; Hakansson &

Montgomery, 2003; Trout, 2009). Empathy is a concept and a skill that allows a person to express understanding and concern for another person, but many times empathy goes beyond understanding to actually feeling or achieving the emotional state that the other party feels. Even if you haven't gone through exactly what another person is experiencing, you can still relate to that person's emotion; empathy matches emotion to emotion, *not* experience to experience. For example, you may not yet have experienced the death of a parent, but if one of your friends loses a parent, you can relate to your friend's sadness and fear, if not to the actual experience itself.

Can empathy be taught, or do some people just have "natural" empathy, while others of us only watch and wish we could respond this way? Some people are more empathic than others. But it remains to be seen whether they have an "empathy gene,"

I view that quality of empathy, of understanding and identifying with people's hopes and struggles, as an essential ingredient for arriving at just decisions and outcomes. We need somebody on the court with the empathy to recognize what it's like to be a young, teenaged mom, the empathy to understand what it's like to be poor or African American, or disabled or gay or old. And that's the criteria by which I'm going to be selecting my judges.

—President Barack Obama, before selecting Sonia Sotomayor and Elena Kagan as Supreme Court Justices

learned this behavior at an early age so they're more comfortable extending empathy than others, or simply tend to or choose to respond with empathy more often, thus reinforcing their skill over time through experiences with others. Empathy definitely can be a communication skill taught and learned, just like we can learn to become better listeners or public speakers (Barone et al., 2005). The ability to correctly infer a partner's thoughts and feelings and to respond appropriately and supportively is critical to the success of all sorts of relationships, especially long-term, intimate relationships.

Beebe, Beebe, and Ivy (2013) offer the following suggestions for developing and demonstrating empathy: First, stop focusing on yourself, your messages, and your thoughts; focus instead on the messages of the other person. Next, pay attention to nonverbal cues as you try to understand the other person's emotions. Then concentrate and listen to what the other person is telling you; imagine how you would feel if you were in her or his situation. Finally, ask appropriate questions and, when suitable, paraphrase the other person's communication to demonstrate your understanding of the situation and how the person feels about it. We don't mean to offer here an exact formula for empathy; we simply offer some tried-and-true ways to communicate.

Notice that we didn't include "give helpful advice" in our list. Many people believe, incorrectly, that the way to show empathy is to offer advice, to suggest something someone can do to respond to or improve a situation (Harvey & Weber, 2002; Johnson, 2011). They bypass empathy altogether and try to move the person into action, typically before that person is ready. When people need empathy, they don't need advice (although advice may come later). Remember that empathy meets people at their emotional level. It doesn't talk them out of what they are feeling, distract them from their emotions or the situation, move them to act, or downplay events with a "Well, it'll all blow over soon."

How do women and men show empathy in relationships? The stereotype suggests that women are more empathic than men; however, research has found mixed results regarding differences, according to both gender and sex. Some research has found no significant differences between the sexes' empathic ability (Graham & Ickes, 1997), whereas other studies have found women more empathic than men (Reis, 1998; Staats, Long, Manulik, & Kelley, 2006; Toussaint & Webb, 2005). Fong and Borders (1985) focused on gender rather than sex as related to empathy, finding that androgynous individuals were more empathic, regardless of sex. Perhaps this is another one of those situations where talking is emphasized over doing. Perhaps men show empathy by just being there—being present and in the moment with someone—whereas women express empathy more though conversation.

One's cultural background plays a role, too, in that members of different cultures grow up learning and witnessing their role models' approaches to expressing emotions and responses to others' emotional displays, according to what's considered appropriate for a given cultural group. Thus, expressions of empathy are culturally rooted (Cassels, Chan, Chung, & Birch, 2010).

A final, troubling trend regarding empathy warrants brief mention: A three-decade analysis of 72 studies of American college students showed a decline in empathy over the last 40 years, as measured by various scientific instruments and surveys (O'Brien, Hsing, & Konrath, 2010). The greatest decline occurred during the first decade of the twenty-first century. These results parallel a general research trend of today's college students reporting significantly more narcissism and competitiveness than previous generations. Researchers suggest a couple of factors that may contribute to the trend: (1) an increased exposure to media, especially violent video games, which can lead people to be increasingly numb to the pain of others; and (2) a hypercompetitive social and professional environment, one that encourages getting ahead rather than feeling empathy for the plight of others.

No matter the trends, we will continue to stress the importance of learning and enhancing one's empathy skills as a critical component of successful relationships. The ability to feel and express empathy is a fundamental skill to add to your communication repertoire or to exercise more fully.

Are You Listening?

Although many factors come into play during relationship development, one seems to make the most difference: listening. Researchers have estimated that more than 70 percent of adults' waking time is spent in some act of communication. On average, 30 percent of one's communicative energy is engaged in speaking, while 45 percent is spent listening (Galvin & Cooper, 2006). As we explained earlier in our section on asking great questions, being deemed a successful conversationalist lies more in your listening skill than your speaking skill. Effective listening and appropriate responding are critical skills in relationship development and success (Halone & Pecchioni, 2001; Harris & Sherblom, 2011).

Listening to a woman is almost as bad as losing to one. There are only three things that women are better at than men: cleaning, cooking, and having sex.

—Charles Barkley, former NBA star

Have you ever said something to someone whose lack of response made you feel like you were completely invisible? Or maybe the person responded with her or his own ideas, never acknowledging yours (zero empathy). On a more positive note, have you ever found yourself talking more and about more personal things to someone, only to stop and wonder how you got to that depth in the conversation? In both the positive and the negative circumstances, the quality of

Net Notes

Now that you've read more about empathy, are you wondering just how empathic you really are? Although we don't suggest that any one questionnaire or survey gives a complete picture, you can try a few online quizzes, like the ones we list here, and get a sense of where you stack up, empathy-wise:

glennrowe.net/empathyquotient

chatterbean.com/love-sex-quizzes/empathic

complimentquotient.com

the listening most likely brought about the result. Since we are major proponents of the receiver orientation to communication, it's no surprise that we believe listening ability more significantly affects the direction of a relationship than speaking ability.

Evidence suggests that men and women can be equally good listeners, but they may listen differently or for different purposes (Kirtley Johnston, Weaver, Watson, & Barker, 2000; Pearce, Johnson, & Barker, 2003; Sargent & Weaver, 2003; Tannen, 1990). Here's a chart that summarizes key research findings on listening styles and the sexes.

Listening Styles and the Sexes

	Female Style	Male Style
Differences in attending to information	• Tends to search for the relationships among separate pieces of information	• Tends to look for a new structure or organizational pattern
	• Tends to identify individual facts and other isolated pieces of information	• Tends to listen for the "big picture" and seek the major points being communicated
Differences in listening goals	• More likely to listen to new information to gain new understanding and insights	• More likely to listen to new information to solve a problem
	• Tends to use information to develop relationships with listening partners	• Tends to listen to reach a conclusion; shows less concern about relationship cues and more concern about using the information gained
Differences in attending to nonverbal cues	• Tends to emphasize meaning communicated through nonverbal cues	• Tends to emphasize the meaning of words and information exchanged
	• Typically uses more eye contact with the other person when listening	• Typically uses less eye contact with the other person when listening

Adapted with permission from Beebe, S. A., Beebe, S. J., & Ivy, D. K. (2013). *Communication: Principles for a lifetime* (5th ed.). Boston: Pearson/Allyn & Bacon.

In expanding their repertoire of communication behaviors, the sexes can learn from each other's listening tendencies and unlearn some habits and sex-typed conditioning. While listening to support a speaker is an admirable approach, women can expand their listening ability to more thoroughly track facts and comprehend information, rather than reading into a conversation more than the facts or trying to "take the emotional temperature" of the other person (Beebe, Beebe, & Ivy, 2013). Men can demonstrate more active listening by using more nonverbal signals like head nodding and eye contact and by offering vocal cues such as "uh-huh," "Tell me more," and "How did you feel about that?" These *back-channel cues* reinforce and draw out more information from a speaker (Guerrero et al., 2011; Knapp & Hall, 2010). Research shows that women tend to offer more nonverbal signals of interest in a conversation than men (Aries, 2006). For example, there's a concept in nonverbal communication research known as the *visual dominance ratio*, which is the amount of eye contact one makes while speaking versus while listening (Knapp & Hall, 2010). Men tend to look more at others when they are speaking, then look elsewhere when others are speaking, which can be interpreted as a sign that one has lost interest or isn't listening. Again, expanding one's range of behavior—in this case, different listening patterns—can do much to enhance gender communication effectiveness.

Remember...

Conversation Starters: Use of opening lines or questions to get a conversation off the ground

Flirting: Means of showing attraction to and interest in another person

Communicative Competence: How effectively and appropriately one communicates

Intimacy: Sharing personal, private information and experiences over time for the purposes of bonding, developing closeness, and forming an emotional connection

Self-Disclosure: Voluntarily providing information to others that they wouldn't learn if you didn't tell them

Empathy: Understanding and feeling what another person is feeling

Back-Channel Cues: Vocalizations such as "uh-huh" and "yeah," which indicate listening and can reinforce and draw out more information from a speaker

Visual Dominance Ratio: Amount of eye contact one makes while speaking versus while listening

Those All-Important Nonverbal Communication Skills

An integral component of the receiver orientation to communication, as well as one of the most useful skills in demonstrating empathy and effective listening, is the development of your ability to nonverbally communicate effectively and appropriately. Effective nonverbal encoding and decoding skills are directly linked to relationship satisfaction (Miczo, Segrin, & Allspach, 2001). *Nonverbal communication* is message exchange without words, such as the way you use pitch variation and tone of voice to convey sarcasm, your facial expressions, walk, stance, and so forth. We explore this important topic in two parts, but the skills are interrelated.

EXPRESSING YOURSELF NONVERBALLY *Nonverbal expressiveness* pertains to the nonverbal communication you express to others, knowingly or unknowingly. It's not enough just to develop your "gift of gab"; you need to work on expressing yourself appropriately through nonverbal cues, because nonverbal communication facilitates relationship initiation, development, and maintenance.

A set of nonverbal cues critical in relationships has been termed by Albert Mehrabian (1970) as nonverbal *immediacy*. These are behaviors that indicate liking or a positive regard for another person. Just as immediacy behaviors generate a positive feeling between people who are meeting for the first time and beginning to know one another, conveying positive feelings toward another person is important at all points in a relationship (Andersen, Guerrero, & Jones, 2006; Ivy & Wahl, 2009). Generally, as one person in a relationship uses more immediate and direct nonverbal communication, the other person feels support and is more likely to value the interaction and the relationship.

Would it surprise you to learn that women tend to use more immediate nonverbal communication than men? We suspect not, since you probably know by now that women's behaviors, both verbal and nonverbal, tend to emphasize their connection to and affiliation with others. Immediacy behaviors displayed frequently by women include forward lean, direct body orientation (meaning that they tend to face people directly when engaged in conversation), closer proximity, head nodding, smiling, more animated facial expression, more variation in vocal expression, and increased touching (Guerrero & Floyd, 2006; Hall, 2006; Hall, Carney, & Murphy, 2002; Hess, Adams, Grammer, & Kleck, 2009; LaFrance, Hecht, & Levy Paluck, 2003; Richmond, McCroskey, & Hickson, 2008; Viscovich et al., 2003). Again, it's not that women value relationships more than men, but that women more actively communicate the importance of relationships by utilizing nonverbal channels to adapt to their partner, accommodate his or her nonverbal style, and display greater nonverbal expressiveness (Burgoon & Hoobler, 2002; Knapp & Hall, 2010).

Nonverbal research has found that men tend to display indirect nonverbal cues. They tend to talk at angles to each other and look less directly at each other, maintain a turned out body position, use more nonverbal signals of power, and are generally less nonverbally immediate in conversations, even with people they really like (Ivy & Wahl, 2009). One explanation for these sex-based trends relates to the differing status of women and men in a patriarchal society, such as ours. Men's nonverbal tendencies may relate to their general higher status in society, because higher status persons exhibit many of the same nonimmediate traits ascribed to men (e.g., less direct body orientation, backward rather than forward lean, less eye contact, less touch). Women, who still

Net Notes

The Center for Nonverbal Studies has produced *The Nonverbal Dictionary*, found at **center-for-nonverbal-studies.org**, a guide to help you more accurately decipher nonverbal cues. Entries provide examples, descriptions, and possible meanings for a range of nonverbal behaviors.

typically hold less status in society than men, are more likely to afford a higher status person more personal space, to make more eye contact than is directed at them, and to do more head nodding and smiling than a higher status individual (Henley, 2001; Knapp & Hall, 2010).

Becoming more nonverbally expressive doesn't come naturally for many of us; we have to learn what skills work and when to use them, and then practice their use. With enough practice and positive reinforcement from others, your nonverbal expressiveness can become a more natural element of your communication repertoire.

BECOMING MORE SENSITIVE TO OTHERS' NONVERBAL COMMUNICATION   *Nonverbal sensitivity* refers to our ability to detect and accurately interpret nonverbal cues from others. Some people may be more naturally sensitive and adept at reading nonverbal cues, but like we said for nonverbal expressiveness, most of us have to work at it. Let us extend a caution here: No one can become a perfect interpreter of others' nonverbal communication. While we encourage you to deepen your understanding of nonverbal communication and develop greater skill in interpreting the meanings behind others' nonverbal actions, realize that nonverbal communication is complex, rooted in culture and context, and very individualized (Beebe, Beebe, & Ivy, 2013).

> *When the eyes say one thing, and the tongue another, a practiced man relies on the language of the first.*
> *—Ralph Waldo Emerson, poet/essayist/philosopher*

We want to help you catch more clues about others, but don't assume that your read on someone is necessarily correct.

Surprise, surprise—research for several decades shows that women tend to be better decoders of others' nonverbal cues than men (Baron-Cohen, Wheelwright, Hill, Raste, & Plumb, 2001; Hall, 2006; Scherer, Banse, & Wallbott, 2001; Vogt & Colvin, 2003). Some scholars contend that this ability may have to do with female socialization, in that females are conditioned, almost from birth, to be attentive and sensitive to others' needs and feelings (Lippa, 2006). Another explanation is similar to one posited for sex differences and immediacy cues: women's general lower status in society and history of oppression have caused women to develop nonverbal decoding skills for basic survival (Henley, 2001).

As we've said before, becoming more adept at interpreting nonverbal cues is a skill that takes time and practice to develop. Spending some time watching other people and comparing their use of nonverbal cues to your own might cause you to become more self-aware, as well as more astute in reading people's nonverbals. For the male readers, do you think it would improve your relationships if you were more nonverbally expressive and sensitive? For female readers, might it be a good idea to think about how you would react to a man who uses a higher degree of immediacy cues than average? At what

Remember . . .

Nonverbal Communication: Message exchange without words
Nonverbal Expressiveness: Nonverbal communication you give off to others, knowingly or unknowingly
Immediacy: Behaviors that indicate liking or a positive regard for another person
Nonverbal Sensitivity: Ability to detect and accurately interpret nonverbal cues of others

point, if any, might the use of these cues surprise you or make you uncomfortable? Do women really want men to develop nonverbal communication skills, or do they prefer keeping that "edge" or advantage for themselves?

Effective use of the four skills just discussed—self-disclosure, empathy, listening, and nonverbal expressiveness and sensitivity—will likely lead to greater feelings of closeness and less psychological distance between partners in a relationship. When choice points arise that cause you to make decisions about a relationship, these basic communication skills can do much to help you implement effective choices.

Conclusion

The topics explored in this chapter represent a significant challenge for most of us—the challenge of turning relationship potential into reality. The relationships that come into your life can change you in powerful and significant ways. Friendships, workplace relationships, romantic relationships, and committed partnerings all have a significant impact on you. This chapter has explored the other side of that process—your influence on relationship initiation and development through the choices you make. A consistent theme in this text has been the acquisition of awareness—awareness of how various factors (e.g., biology, sociology, media, and language) influence you and your choices;

awareness of how you can gain control over or manage those influences; and, in this chapter, awareness of how choices may influence your relationships.

Becoming more personally effective in initiating and creating the type of relationships you desire is a worthwhile, important goal. In this chapter, we began with a view of relationship development as "prospecting" and followed through with thoughts on finding prospects, testing a prospect, and developing a "claim." Understanding the skills associated with moving a relationship from one level to another and understanding women's and men's tendencies in such changes can give you greater insight into how positive change might be brought about. It can also keep you from getting the relationship "shaft."

The final section of this text connects these concepts to some specific contexts in your life—friendships, romance, work, and education. Effective gender communication in these contexts involves applying the concepts described in the chapters you have just read.

Discussion Starters

1. Think about the role of information in the initiation of relationships. What information do you use to make decisions about people when initiating a friendship? Do you need different kinds of information when initiating a dating relationship than a friendship with someone? What information about yourself as a potential relational partner do you think is most important? What's the most important information to learn about someone else as a potential partner?

2. Some people believe that the initiation of a dating or romantic relationship should be men's work. Do you think women should be able to initiate dating relationships in the same ways men can? If you believe they can, and you are a heterosexual woman, have you ever initiated a relationship with a man? If you are a man who has been "chosen" by a woman, how did you feel when she initiated a relationship with you?

3. Do you know men who disclose more than the typical amount of personal information? What are some reactions to these men? Is the reaction the same or different than the reaction a woman gets when she discloses more than is expected?

4. In your experience, how do people signal that they want to change the level of a relationship? Do men use different signals than women? Are the signals usually nonverbal in nature? Do people ever say to you, "I'd like to change our relationship"? Have you ever said that to someone? If so, what was the result?

References

Abbey, A. (1982). Sex differences in attributions for friendly behavior: Do males misperceive females' friendliness? *Journal of Personality and Social Psychology, 42*, 830–838.

Abbey, A. (1987). Misperception of friendly behavior as sexual interest: A survey of naturally occurring incidents. *Psychology of Women Quarterly, 11*, 173–194.

Abbey, A. (1991). Misperception as an antecedent of acquaintance rape: A consequence of ambiguity in communication between men and women. In A. Parrot & L. Bechhofer (Eds.), *Acquaintance rape: The hidden crime* (pp. 96–111). New York: Wiley.

Abbey, A., Zawacki, T., & Buck, P. O. (2005). The effects of past sexual assault perpetration and alcohol consumption on reactions to women's mixed signals. *Journal of Social and Clinical Psychology, 25*, 129–157.

Afifi, T., & Steuber, K. (2009). The Revelation Risk Model (RRM): Factors that predict the revelation of secrets and the strategies used to reveal them. *Communication Monographs, 76*, 144–176.

Albada, K. F., Knapp, M. L., & Theune, K. E. (2002). Interaction appearance theory: Changing perceptions of physical attractiveness through social interaction. *Communication Theory, 12*, 8–40.

Andersen, P. A., Guerrero, L. K., & Jones, S. M. (2006). Nonverbal behavior in intimate interactions and intimate relationships. In V. Manusov & M. L. Patterson (Eds.), *The Sage handbook of nonverbal communication* (pp. 259–277). Thousand Oaks, CA: Sage.

Aries, E. (2006). Sex differences in interaction: A reexamination. In K. Dindia & D. J. Canary (Eds.), *Sex differences and similarities in communication* (2nd ed., pp. 21–37). Mahwah, NJ: Erlbaum.

Arliss, L. P. (2001). When myths endure and realities change: Communication in romantic relationships. In L. P. Arliss & D. J. Borisoff (Eds.), *Women and men communicating: Challenges and changes* (2nd ed., pp. 115–131). Prospect Heights, IL: Waveland.

Badr, H., & Carmack Taylor, C. L. (2009). Sexual dysfunction and spousal communication in couples coping with prostate cancer. *Psycho-Oncology, 18*, 735–746.

Bar-Tal, D., & Saxe, L. (1976). Perceptions of similarity and dissimilarity of attractive couples and individuals. *Journal of Personality and Social Psychology, 33*, 772–781.

Barnes, S. B. (2008). Understanding social media from the media ecological perspective. In E. A. Konijn, S. Utz, M. Tanis, & S. B. Barnes (Eds.), *Mediated interpersonal communication* (pp. 14–33). New York: Routledge.

Baron, N. S. (2008). *Always on: Language in an online and mobile world.* New York: Oxford University Press.

Baron-Cohen, S., Wheelwright, S., Hill, J., Raste, Y., & Plumb, I. (2001). The "Reading the Mind in the Eyes" Test Revised Version: A study with normal adults, and adults with Asperger syndrome or high-functioning autism. *Journal of Child Psychology and Psychiatry, 42*, 241–251.

Barone, D. F., Hutchings, P. S., Kimmel, H. J., Traub, H. L., Cooper, J. T., & Marshall, C. M. (2005). Increasing empathic accuracy through practice and feedback in a clinical interviewing course. *Journal of Social and Clinical Psychology, 24*, 156–171.

Beebe, S. A., Beebe, S. J., & Ivy, D. K. (2013). *Communication: Principles for a lifetime* (5th ed.). Boston: Pearson/Allyn & Bacon.

Beres, M. A., Herold, E., & Maitland, S. B. (2004). Sexual consent behaviors in same-sex relationships. *Journal of Sexual Behavior, 33*, 475–486.

Berger, C. R., & Calabrese, R. J. (1975). Some explorations in initial interaction and beyond. Toward a developmental theory of interpersonal communication. *Human Communication Research, 1*, 99–112.

Berger, C. R., & Douglas, W. (1981). Studies in interpersonal epistemology III. Anticipated interaction, self-monitoring, and observational context selection. *Communication Monographs, 48*, 183–196.

Berscheid, E. (1985). Interpersonal attraction. In G. Lindzey & E. Aronson (Eds.), *Handbook of social psychology* (3rd ed.). New York: Random House.

Berscheid, E., & Reis, H. T. (1998). Attraction and close relationships. In D. T. Gilbert, S. T. Fiske, & G. Lindzey (Eds.), *The handbook of social psychology* (4th ed., vol. 2, pp. 93–281). New York: McGraw-Hill.

Borisoff, D. E. (2001). The effect of gender on establishing and maintaining intimate relationships. In L. P. Arliss & D. E. Borisoff (Eds.), *Women and men communicating: Challenges and changes* (2nd ed., pp. 15–31). Prospect Heights, IL: Waveland.

Burch, P. (2001, July 15). Silent judgment: Experts say you have 10 seconds to project your true image. Scripps Howard News Service, as in *Corpus Christi Caller Times*, pp. C4, C5.

Burgoon, J., & Hoobler, G. D. (2002). Nonverbal signals. In M. L. Knapp & J. Daly (Eds.), *Handbook of interpersonal communication* (3rd ed., pp. 240–299). Thousand Oaks, CA: Sage.

Burleson, B. R. (2003). The experience and effects of emotional support: What the study of cultural and gender differences can tell us about close relationships, emotion, and interpersonal communication. *Personal Relationships, 10*, 1–23.

Byers, E. S., & Demmons, S. (1999). Sexual satisfaction and sexual self-disclosure within dating relationships. *Journal of Sex Research, 36*, 180–189.

Cassels, T. G., Chan, S., Chung, W., & Birch, S. A. J. (2010). The role of culture in affective empathy: Cultural and bicultural differences. *Journal of Cognition and Culture, 10*, 309–326.

Chirinos, F. S. (2010, September 12). Social networks generate waves in city. *Corpus Christi Caller Times*, pp. 1B–2B.

Clark, A. J. (2010). Empathy and sympathy: Therapeutic distinctions in counseling. *Journal of Mental Health Counseling, 32*, 95–101.

Coates, J. (2005). *Women, men, and language: A sociolinguistic account of gender differences in language* (3rd ed.). New York: Longman.

Cooper, A., & Sportolari, L. (1997). Romance in cyberspace: Understanding online attraction. *Journal of Sex Education & Therapy, 22*, 7–14.

Copenhaver, M. N., & Eisler, R. M. (1996). Masculine gender role stress: A perspective on men's health. In P. M. Kato & T. Mann (Eds.), *Handbook of diversity issues in health psychology* (pp. 219–235). New York: Plenum.

Dainton, M., & Aylor, B. (2001). A relational uncertainty analysis of jealousy, trust, and maintenance in long-distance versus geographically close relationships. *Communication Quarterly, 49*, 172–188.

Daly, J. A., Hogg, E., Sacks, D., Smith, M., & Zimring, L. (1999). Sex and relationship affect social self-grooming. In L. K. Guerrero, J. DeVito, & M. L. Hecht (Eds.), *The nonverbal communication reader: Classic and contemporary readings* (2nd ed., pp. 56–61). Prospect Heights, IL: Waveland.

Derlega, V. J., Winstead, B. A., & Greene, K. (2008). Self-disclosure and starting a close relationship. In S. Sprecher, A. Wenzel, & J. Harvey (Eds.), *Handbook of relationship initiation* (pp. 153–194). New York: Psychology Press.

Devoldre, I., Davis, M. H., Verhofstadt, L. L., & Buysse, A. (2010). Empathy and social support provision in couples: Social support and the need to study the underlying processes. *Journal of Psychology, 144*, 259–284.

Dindia, K. (2002). Self-disclosure research: Knowledge through meta-analysis. In M. Allen, R. W. Preiss, B. M. Gayle, & N. A. Burrell (Eds.), *Interpersonal communication research: Advances through meta-analysis* (pp. 169–185). Mahwah, NJ: Erlbaum.

Douglas, W. (1990). Uncertainty, information-seeking, and liking during initial interaction. *Western Journal of Speech Communication, 54*, 66–81.

Egland, K. I., Spitzberg, B. H., & Zormeier, M. M. (1996). Flirtation and conversational competence in cross-sex platonic and romantic relationships. *Communication Reports, 9*, 105–118.

Eibl-Eibesfeldt, I. (1975). *Ethology: The biology of behavior* (2nd ed.). New York: Holt, Rinehart, & Winston.

Faulkner, S. L., & Lannutti, P. J. (2010). Examining the content and outcomes of young adults' satisfying and unsatisfying conversations about sex. *Qualitative Health Research, 20*, 375–385.

Felmee, D. H. (2001). From appealing to appalling: Disenchantment with a romantic partner. *Sociological Perspectives, 44*, 263–280.

Fine, J. (2001, October). Intimacy. *O: The Oprah Winfrey Magazine*, 225.

Fong, M. L., & Borders, L. D. (1985). Effects of sex role orientation and gender on counseling skills training. *Journal of Counseling Psychology, 32*, 104–110.

Galvin, K. M., & Bylund, C. (2001). First marriage families: Gender and communication. In L. P. Arliss & D. E. Borisoff (Eds.), *Women and men communicating: Challenges and changes* (2nd ed., pp. 132–148). Prospect Heights, IL: Waveland.

Galvin, K. M., & Cooper, P. (Eds.) (2006). *Making connections: Readings in relational communication* (4th ed.). Los Angeles: Roxbury.

Geary, D. C., Vigil, J., & Byrd-Craven, J. (2004). The evolution of human mate choice. [Electronic version] *Journal of Sex Research, 41*, 27–43.

Gibbs, J. L., Ellison, N. B., & Heino, R. D. (2006). Self-presentation in online personals: The role of anticipated future interaction, self-disclosure, and perceived success in Internet dating. *Communication Research, 33*, 152–177.

Graham, T., & Ickes, W. (1997). When women's intuition isn't greater than men's. In W. Ickes (Ed.), *Empathic accuracy* (pp. 117–143). New York: Guilford.

Grammer, K., Knuck, K. B., & Magnusson, M. S. (1998). The courtship dance: Patterns of nonverbal synchronization in opposite sex encounters. *Journal of Nonverbal Behavior, 22*, 3–25.

Grill, B. D. (2011). From Telex to Twitter: Relational communication skills for a wireless world. In K. M. Galvin (Ed.), *Making connections: Readings in relational communication* (5th ed., pp. 89–96). New York: Oxford University Press.

Guerrero, L. K., Andersen, P. A., & Afifi, W. A. (2011). *Close encounters: Communicating in relationships* (5th ed.). Los Angeles: Sage.

Guerrero, L. K., & Floyd, K. (2006). *Nonverbal communication in close relationships*. Mahwah, NJ: Erlbaum.

Hakansson, J., & Montgomery, H. (2003). Empathy as an interpersonal phenomenon. *Journal of Social & Personal Relationships, 20,* 267–284.

Hall, J. A. (2006). Women's and men's nonverbal communication: Similarities, differences, stereotypes, and origins. In V. Manusov & M. L. Patterson (Eds.), *The Sage handbook of nonverbal communication* (pp. 201–218). Thousand Oaks, CA: Sage.

Hall, J. A., Carney, D. R., & Murphy, N. A. (2002). Gender differences in smiling. In M. H. Abel (Ed.), *An empirical reflection on the smile: Mellen studies in psychology* (Vol. 4, pp. 155–185). Lewiston, NY: Edwin Mellen.

Hall, J., Cody, M., Jackson, G., & Flesh, J. (2008, May). *Beauty and the flirt: Attractiveness and approaches to relationship initiation.* Paper presented at the meeting of the International Communication Association, Montreal, Canada.

Halone, K. K., & Pecchioni, L. L. (2001). Relational listening: A grounded theoretical model. *Communication Reports, 14,* 59–71.

Hardey, M. (2004). Mediated relationships: Authenticity and the possibility of romance. *Information, Communication & Society, 7,* 207–222.

Harris, T. E., & Sherblom, J. C. (2011). Listening and feedback: The other half of communication. In K. M. Galvin (Ed.), *Making connections: Readings in relational communication* (5th ed., pp. 61–76). New York: Oxford University Press.

Harvey, J. H., & Weber, A. L. (2002). *Odyssey of the heart: Close relationships in the 21st century* (2nd ed.). Mahwah, NJ: Erlbaum.

Henley, N. M. (2001). Body politics. In A. Branaman (Ed.), *Self and society: Blackwell readers in sociology* (pp. 288–297). Malden, MA: Blackwell.

Henningsen, D. D. (2004). Flirting with meaning: An examination of miscommunication in flirting interactions. *Sex Roles, 50,* 481–489.

Henningsen, D. D., Braz, M., & Davies, E. (2008). Why do we flirt? *Journal of Business Communication, 45,* 483–502.

Herring, S. C., & Martinson, A. (2004). Assessing gender authenticity in computer-mediated language use: Evidence from an identity game. *Journal of Language and Social Psychology, 23,* 424–446.

Hess, U., Adams, R. B., Jr., Grammer, K., & Kleck, R. E. (2009). Face gender and emotion expression: Are angry women more like men? *Journal of Vision, 9,* 1–8.

Holmberg, D., & Blair, K. L. (2009). Sexual desire, communication, satisfaction, and preferences of men and women in same-sex versus mixed-sex relationships. *Journal of Sex Research, 46,* 57–66.

Ivy, D. K., & Wahl, S. T. (2009). *The nonverbal self: Communication for a lifetime.* Boston: Pearson/Allyn & Bacon.

Johnson, D. (2011). Helpful listening and responding. In K. M. Galvin (Ed.), *Making connections: Readings in relational communication* (5th ed., pp. 70–76). New York: Oxford University Press.

Jones, J. T., Pelham, B. W., Carvallo, M., & Mirenberg, M. C. (2004). How do I love thee? Let me count the Js: Implicit egotism and interpersonal attraction. *Journal of Personality and Social Psychology, 87,* 665–683.

Jourard, S. (1971). *The transparent self.* Princeton, NJ: Van Nostrand.

Kankiewicz, K. (2007, May 10). 50 questions you haven't already asked your date. Retrieved February 7, 2011, from http://www.suite101.com.

Kenrick, D. T., Neuberg, S. L., & Cialdini, R. B. (2005). *Social psychology: Unraveling the mystery* (3rd ed.). Boston: Allyn & Bacon.

Kirtley Johnston, M., Weaver, J. B., III, Watson, K. W., & Barker, L. B. (2000). Listening styles: Biological or psychological differences? *International Journal of Listening, 14,* 32–46.

Kleinke, C. L., Meeker, F. B., & Staneski, R. A. (1986). Preference for opening lines: Comparing ratings by men and women. *Sex Roles, 15,* 585–600.

Knapp, M. L., & Hall, J. A. (2010). *Nonverbal communication in human interaction* (7th ed.). Belmont, CA: Wadsworth.

Knapp, M. L., & Vangelisti, A. L. (2009). *Interpersonal communication and human relationships* (6th ed.). Boston: Pearson/Allyn & Bacon.

Koeppel, L. B., Montagne, Y., O'Hair, D., & Cody, M. J. (1999). Friendly? Flirting? Wrong? In L. K. Guerrero, J. DeVito, & M. L. Hecht (Eds.), *The nonverbal communication reader* (2nd ed., pp. 290–297). Prospect Heights, IL: Waveland.

Kowalski, R. M. (1993). Inferring sexual interest from behavioral cues: Effects of gender and sexually relevant attitudes. *Sex Roles, 29,* 13–35.

LaFrance, B. H. (2010). Predicting sexual satisfaction in interpersonal relationships. *Southern Communication Journal, 75,* 195–214.

LaFrance, M., Hecht, M. A., & Levy Paluck, E. (2003). The contingent smile: A meta-analysis of sex differences in smiling. *Psychological Bulletin, 129,* 305–334.

Li, N. P., Bailey, J. M., Kenrick, D. T., & Linsenmeier, J. A. (2002). The necessities and luxuries of mate preferences: Testing the tradeoffs. *Journal of Personality and Social Psychology, 82,* 947–955.

Lindsey, A. E., & Zakahi, W. R. (1996). Women who tell and men who ask: Perceptions of men and women departing from gender stereotypes during initial interaction. *Sex Roles, 34,* 767–786.

Lindsey, A. E., & Zakahi, W. R. (2006). Perceptions of men and women departing from conversational sex role stereotypes. In K. Dindia & D. J. Canary (Eds.), *Sex differences and similarities in communication* (2nd ed., pp. 281–298). Mahwah, NJ: Erlbaum.

Lippa, R. A. (2006). *Gender, nature, and nurture* (2nd ed.). Mahwah, NJ: Erlbaum.

Litzinger, S., & Gordon, K. C. (2005). Exploring relationships among communication, sexual satisfaction, and marital satisfaction. *Journal of Sex and Marital Therapy, 31,* 409–424.

MacNeil, S., & Byers, E. S. (2005). Dyadic assessment of sexual self-disclosure and sexual satisfaction in heterosexual dating couples. *Journal of Social & Personal Relationships, 22,* 169–181.

McConnell, D. (1997). Interaction patterns of mixed sex groups in educational computer conferences. *Gender and Education, 9,* 345–363.

McEwan, B., & Guerrero, L. K. (2010). Freshmen engagement through communication: Predicting friendship formation strategies and perceived availability of network resources from

communication skills. *Communication Studies, 61,* 445–463.

Mehrabian, A. (1970). A semantic space for nonverbal behavior. *Journal of Counseling and Clinical Psychology, 35,* 248–257.

Menaker, D. (2010, January). How to break the ice. *O: The Oprah Winfrey Magazine,* 121.

Menard, A. D., & Offman, A. (2009). The interrelationships between sexual self-esteem, sexual assertiveness, and sexual satisfaction. *Canadian Journal of Human Sexuality, 18,* 35–45.

Metts, S. (2006). Gendered communication in dating relationships. In B. J. Dow & J. T. Wood (Eds.), *The Sage handbook of gender and communication* (pp. 25–40). Thousand Oaks, CA: Sage.

Miczo, N., Segrin, C., & Allspach, L. E. (2001). Relationship between nonverbal sensitivity, encoding, and relational satisfaction. *Communication Reports, 14,* 39–48.

Moore, M. M. (1985). Nonverbal courtship patterns in women: Context and consequences. *Ethology and Sociobiology, 6,* 237–247.

Morry, M. M. (2005). Relationship satisfaction as a predictor of similarity ratings: A test of the attraction-similarity hypothesis. *Journal of Social and Personal Relationships, 22,* 561–584.

O'Brien, E. H., Hsing, C., & Konrath, S. (2010, May). *Changes in dispositional empathy over time in American college students.* Paper presented at the meeting of the Association for Psychological Science, Boston, MA.

Palfrey, J., & Gasser, U. (2008). *Born digital.* New York: Basic Books.

Pearce, C. G., Johnson, I. W., & Barker, R. T. (2003). Assessment of the Listening Styles Inventory. *Journal of Business and Technical Communication, 17,* 84–113.

Peterson, V. V. (2011). *Sex, ethics, and communication.* San Diego, CA: Cognella.

Petronio, S., Martin, J., & Littlefield, R. (1984). Prerequisite conditions for self-disclosing: A gender issue. *Communication Monographs, 51,* 268–272.

Prensky, M. (2001). Digital natives, digital immigrants. *On the Horizon, 9.* Retrieved October 2, 2010, from http://www.twitchspeed.com

Reis, H. T. (1998). Gender differences in intimacy and related behaviors: Context and process. In D. J. Canary & K. Dindia (Eds.), *Sex differences and similarities in communication* (pp. 203–231). Mahwah, NJ: Erlbaum.

Rhodes, A. R. (2002). Long-distance relationships in dual-career commuter couples: A review of counseling issues. *The Family Journal: Counseling and Therapy for Couples and Families, 10,* 398–404.

Richmond, V. P., McCroskey, J. C., & Hickson, M. L. III. (2008). *Nonverbal behavior in interpersonal relations* (6th ed.). Boston: Allyn & Bacon.

Sahlstein, E. (2006). Making plans: Praxis strategies for negotiating uncertainty-certainty in long-distance relationships. *Western Journal of Communication, 70,* 147–165.

Sargent, S. L., & Weaver, J. B., III. (2003). Listening styles: Sex differences in perceptions of self and others. *International Journal of Listening, 17,* 5–18.

Scheflen, A. E. (1965). Quasi-courtship behavior in psychotherapy. *Psychiatry, 27,* 245–257.

Scherer, K. R., Banse, R., & Wallbott, H. G. (2001). Emotion inferences from vocal expression correlate across languages and cultures. *Journal of Cross-Cultural Psychology, 32,* 76–92.

Shaffer, D. R., Pegalis, L. J., & Bazzini, D. G. (1996). When boy meets girl (revisited): Gender, gender-role orientation, and prospect of future interaction as determinants of self-disclosure among same- and opposite-sex acquaintances. *Personality and Social Psychology Bulletin, 22,* 495–506.

Smith, T. J. (2006, March 2). 100 dating conversation starters. Retrieved February 7, 2011, from http://www.searchwarp.com

Staats, S., Long, L., Manulik, K., & Kelley, P. (2006). Situated empathy: Variations associated with target gender across situations. *Social Behavior and Personality, 34,* 431–441.

Stafford, L., Merolla, A. J., & Castle, J. D. (2006). When long-distance dating partners become geographically close. *Journal of Social & Personal Relationships, 23,* 901–919.

Strauss, N. (2005). *The game: Penetrating the secret society of pickup artists.* New York: Regan.

Tannen, D. (1990). *You just don't understand: Women and men in conversation.* New York: William Morrow.

Tidwell, L. C., & Walther, J. B. (2002). Computer-mediated communication effects on disclosure,

impressions, and interpersonal evaluations: Getting to know one another a bit at a time. *Human Communication Research, 28,* 317–348.

Toussaint, L., & Webb, J. R. (2005). Gender differences in the relationship between empathy and forgiveness. *Journal of Social Psychology, 145,* 673–685.

Trost, M. R., & Alberts, J. K. (1998). An evolutionary view on understanding sex effects in communicating attraction. In D. Canary & K. Dindia (Eds.), *Sex, gender, and communication: Similarities and differences* (pp. 233–255). Mahwah, NJ: Erlbaum.

Trost, M. R., & Alberts, J. K. (2006). How men and women communicate attraction: An evolutionary view. In K. Dindia & D. J. Canary (Eds.), *Sex differences and similarities in communication* (2nd ed., pp. 317–336). Mahwah, NJ: Erlbaum.

Trout, J. D. (2009). *The empathy gap: Building bridges to the good life and the good society.* New York: Viking.

Viscovich, N., Borod, J., Pihan, H., Peery, S., Brickman, A. M., & Tabert, M. (2003). Acoustical analysis of posed prosodic expressions: Effects of emotion and sex. *Perceptual and Motor Skills, 96,* 759–777.

Vogt, D., & Colvin, C. R. (2003). Interpersonal orientation and the accuracy of personality judgments. *Journal of Personality, 71,* 267–295.

Waldron, V. R., & Applegate, J. L. (1998). Similarity in the use of person-centered tactics: Effects on social attraction and persuasiveness in dyadic verbal disagreements. *Communication Reports, 11,* 155–165.

West, R., & Turner, L. H. (2011). Technology and interpersonal communication. In K. M. Galvin (Ed.), *Making connections: Readings in relational communication* (5th ed., pp. 379–386). New York: Oxford University Press.

Whitty, M. T. (2004). Cyber-flirting: An examination of men's and women's flirting behaviour both offline and on the Internet. *Behaviour Change, 21,* 115–126.

Whitty, M. T., & Carr, A. N. (2003). Cyberspace as potential space: Considering the web as a playground to cyber-flirt. *Human Relations, 56,* 869–891.

Wood, J. T., & Inman, C. C. (1993). In a different mode: Masculine styles of communicating closeness. *Journal of Applied Communication Research, 21*, 279–295.

Work and family facts and statistics. (2010). Retrieved July 5, 2010, from http://www.aflcio.org/issues/factsstats/

Yurchisin, J., Watchravesringkan, K., & McCabe, D. B. (2005). An exploration of identity recreation in the context of Internet dating. *Social Behavior and Personality, 33*, 735–750.

Part IV The Contexts for Our Relationships:
Personal Effectiveness in Action

CHAPTER 6

Gender Communication "Just Among Friends"

Case Study

When "Friend" Became a Verb

"To friend" or "not to friend"—that is the question. . . . Whether or not you're on Facebook, you now know that the word *friend* (long known as a simple noun) has now become a verb, as in "to friend someone." That's the premise behind the gigantic social networking site Facebook—friends finding and "friending" friends.

Do you have Facebook or online friends whom you've never met in person? How did you become friends if you've never met? Did you "meet" them on Facebook through friends of friends or by searching for people in your local area or who share your interests? Did you find them through the now outdated, outmoded MySpace or some other social media outlet? Are you friends with your Twitter followers or are those people just followers, not friends? What about more restrictive social networks, such as LinkedIn—are relationships in those networks somehow different than ones established through wider-reaching social media? What if someone sends you a friend request and you don't want to be friends back—any guilt involved in ignoring their request? Do you create levels of intimacy within your social networks, meaning that certain information you will only "share" with certain friends, not your entire online network?

More questions: Are your online friends just as meaningful and "real" to you as friends you keep up with through other means, such as face-to-face conversations, text messaging, or phone conversations? (Or the rapidly disappearing, old-fashioned written letter? Who writes letters anymore?) How is your communication different with online friends versus the people you hang around with at school or work?

Now throw sex and gender into the mix: Do you have more same-sex or opposite-sex online friends? Does that mixture of people mirror your face-to-face

(continued)

Case Study (*continued*)

circles of friends? Does it matter? Do you communicate differently to your male versus female friends online? Face to face? These questions are exhausting.

Because the nature of friendship, how friendships get established and maintained, and the role of communication within friendship have changed as our society (and the world) has changed due to the explosion of technology, it's important from time to time to take a moment, breathe, and ponder your friendships. Think back to the playground when you were in elementary school, how you developed friendships with neighborhood kids or through activities like summer sports, or kids you met at camp. Consider how many of those people are in your Facebook friends circle today. Think about whether you prefer the way friendships can develop now, as the world opens itself to us via technology, or if you miss the quaint ways you used to find a buddy when you were a kid. The goal is for this chapter to give you pause and encourage you to think about many of these questions, as we explore one of the most meaningful, important connections we can make with people in our lives.

In this chapter we explore friendship, in general, because friendships are among our most important, life-sustaining relationships. Specifically, we examine communication that leads to increased personal effectiveness in the contexts of same-sex and cross-sex friendship. As we've said throughout the text, members of both sexes can expand their repertoire of communication behaviors to become more effective in gender communication. A widened range of behaviors, an orientation to the receiver (the friend), and enhanced personal effectiveness can all lead to greater satisfaction, fewer conflicts, and deeper, longer-lasting friendships.

A SINGLE SOUL IN TWO BODIES

Aristotle defined a friend as "a single soul who resides in two bodies." More modern definitions are a bit less poetic. Ellen Goodman and Patricia O'Brien (2000), who are friends and coauthors of a book on women's friendships entitled *I Know Just What You Mean,* ask: "What's a friend? If the Eskimos have twenty-six different words for snow, Americans have only one word commonly used to describe everyone from acquaintances to intimates. It is a word we have to qualify with adjectives: school friends, work friends, old friends, casual friends, good friends" (p. 18). Friendships are a unique class of relationships. Author Jan Yager (1999) coined the term "friendshifts," referring to the ways friendships change as people go from one life stage to another (p. 4). Yager suggests "friendship is crucial for school-age children or for singles who are between romantic relationships. However, friends count for even the happiest couples: friendship affirms and validates in a more distinctive way than even the most positive romantic or blood tie. It is now known that friendship is vital *throughout* life" (p. 6).

Learning to Be Friends

For many adults, cross-sex friendships are very rewarding, but our early patterns as boys and girls do not encourage the formation of cross-sex friendships; we have to learn how to develop friendships later in life with members of the opposite sex. Sex segregation in friendship shows up around three years of age in children (Crawford & Unger, 2004; Maccoby, 1998). While interesting theories abound about genetics, "hardwiring," and psychosocial development related to this pattern, it's clear that society extends its influence in teaching children how to be friends.

Gender scholar Suzanne Romaine (1999) suggests that we only have to look to schools for the roots of sex segregation. While neighborhood kids may play together, when these same kids are at school they are categorized first by age, then by sex. Children have to line up to go from the classroom to the restroom, cafeteria, auditorium, and so forth, and they frequently form separate lines for boys and girls. Granted, the sex separation for toilet use has a basis in reality, in that most schools separate facilities for females and males. But Romaine explains that this too marks school as a different context for children because in a typical home, toilets aren't sex segregated. Further sex segregation occurs on playgrounds when students engage in team sports. School athletic activities (particularly in high school) are, almost exclusively, sex segregated. In addition, children who say that they play in mixed-sex groups in their neighborhoods ignore opposite-sex playmates at school, out of a concern about being teased (Thorne, 1994). These simple traditions within schools help set up a dichotomizing, segregating pattern that affects one's choice of friends, one's understanding of people of the opposite sex, and one's behavior with same- and cross-sex friends.

Research shows that, beginning about age seven, boys form extended friendship networks with other boys while girls tend to cluster into exclusive same-sex friendship dyads (Rawlins, 2001). In those dyads, girls acquire the social skills of communicating their feelings and being nurturing. In contrast, boys learn to follow rules and get along with groups of people. To varying degrees, these tendencies remain into adulthood. One explanation that may seem simple, but that has received considerable research attention, relates to similarity: We tend to gravitate toward and develop friendships with people we perceive to be similar to ourselves, more so than to those we perceive to be different from us (Fehr, 2008; Foster, 2005; Gifford-Smith & Brownell, 2003; Pinel, Long, Landau, Alexander, & Pyszczynksi, 2006; Rushton & Bons, 2005). Biological sex is one form of basic similarity.

Social scientist John Reisman (1990) examined communication in friendship through the formative years, with particular attention to self-disclosure. In Chapter 5, self-disclosure was defined as voluntarily providing information to others that they wouldn't learn if you didn't tell them. As opposed to earlier years, when children disclose almost exclusively with members of their same sex, Reisman found that male adolescents disclose about the same amount of information with friends of either sex, but female adolescents exhibit less self-disclosure with boys than with other girls. This behavior

A friend will tell you she saw your old boyfriend—and he's a priest. A friend will lie about your home permanent and threaten to kill anyone who tries to come into a room where you are trying on bathing suits. But, most of all, a friend will not make every minute of every day count and foul it up for the rest of us.

—Erma Bombeck, columnist/author

changes again, as people leave their teen years. Young female adults generate similar levels of disclosure with both males and females, while males express higher levels of self-disclosure with members of the opposite sex than their same sex. The latter finding is consistent with a good deal of research demonstrating that women receive other people's disclosures more often than men (Aries, 2006; Perry, Turner, & Sterk, 1992).

During childhood and adolescence, we tend to be drawn to same-sex more than cross-sex friends, but this tendency shifts as we age and mature. It's interesting to explore the unique properties of each type of friendship, as well as the communication that sustains them. We begin that exploration by considering same-sex friends.

COMMUNICATION IN SAME-SEX FRIENDSHIPS: FROM BUTCH AND SUNDANCE TO THELMA AND LOUISE

To many people's thinking, same-sex friendships require less work to maintain than cross-sex friendships. Same-sex friendships do not, for the most part, experience the same tensions as cross-sex friendships, such as romance versus friendship, sexuality, jealousy, emotional intensity, and how others perceive the relationship. Another assumption about same-sex friendships is that friends are equals; power dynamics that may play a role in cross-sex friendships are absent or less of a factor. In one study of power and friendship quality, both women and men rated equal-power friendships as more emotionally close, satisfying, enjoyable, disclosing, and rewarding than unequal-power friendships (Veniegas & Peplau, 1997).

Male–Male Friendship: Functions and Characteristics

Friendships between men have evolved, just like many other types of relationships. Although once a subject of popular culture's ridicule, like beer commercials making fun of "male bonding," men's friendships have been studied in terms of their significance, the communication or shared experiences that launch such connections, and what's necessary to sustain them (Bentall, 2004; Nardi, 1992; Rawlins, 2009; Way, 2011). Author of *Buddy System: Understanding Men's Friendships* Geoffrey Greif (2008) talks of men's friendships this way: "It is important to men's survival that they figure out friendships and improve them if they are unfulfilling. Men do not live as long as women. Friendships, where help is given and received, can be one way of helping men communicate their needs better. If men can improve the number and quality of their friendships, they may live longer and healthier lives" (p. 18).

WHY MEN FORM FRIENDSHIPS   For male readers, why do you form friendships with other men? If you follow the typical pattern, you form them so that you have *something to do* and *someone to do it with.* For many men, male friends are important but replaceable; men tend to have more numerous but less intimate same-sex friendships than women (Greif, 2008). Research has shown that while men and women typically have similar numbers of friends and spend similar amounts of time with friends, men's friendships with other men tend to serve different purposes than women's friendships with other women (Bentall, 2004).

First, men often form friendships through groups because it satisfies a need to belong to something or to other people. These group friendships may form through participation on teams, memberships in clubs and fraternities, involvement with work or study groups, and so forth. Boys' friendships tend to emerge from larger networks in which they learn to follow rules and get along with all kinds of people, even people they don't like (Bate & Bowker, 1997). These organized friendships center on group activities and give men a sense of belonging (Strikwerda & May, 1992). For centuries, men have used group belongingness as a source of power and connection. Historically male-dominated religious ceremonies, initiation rituals inherent in such organizations as fraternities and civic groups, and male-only discussions (like might occur as locker-room conversations, for example) have an air of secrecy about them, and a code of correct behavior that controls access to these groups and marks women as outsiders (Spain, 1992).

Another motivation many men have for forming friendships with other men is to further their own achievement; this sounds manipulative and self-serving, but think about it further. Psychologist Suzanna Rose (1985) suggests that since men control much of the power and rewards in American society, men value friendships with other men more than with women because they can attain more social and economic rewards from other men. In the business world, if a man cannot help you get ahead, the possibility of a friendship may decrease—not disappear necessarily, but decrease.

Your friends love you anyway.
—Dave Barry,
columnist/author

In some instances, male friendships form out of conflict. While we tend to think of conflict as separating people, it can also be quite cathartic and can clear the air toward greater understanding and feelings of closeness. Conflict experienced by people on the same side—be it in war situations, sporting events, or interpersonal disagreements—can generate significant closeness as well.

"DOING" VERSUS "TALKING"   In the preceding paragraph, we mentioned "doing" rather than "talking" as a characteristic of men's friendships. In fact, the activity-orientation of men's friendships is one of its primary characteristics. Many men's friendships begin with, are sustained by, and sometimes dissolve over doing things together and sharing (or enduring) experiences (Brehm, 2001; Rawlins, 2001). Through shared experiences and activities, men develop feelings of closeness and express their commonality with male friends. Think of the war stories or fishing tales that your father, uncle, or grandfather tells. Men do talk with their friends, and they may value talk as much as women friends do, but the content of that talk may differ from women's, in that it tends to focus around the activities that men share, not their feelings about those activities or one another (Greif, 2008; Martin, 1997). As author and psychologist Helen Fisher (2009) explains, "Men often regard intimacy as working or playing side-by-side. Sure, they might discuss a bad week at work, even troubles in their love lives. But rarely do they share their secret dreams and darkest fears. (When they do, they often use 'joke speak,' camouflaging their feelings with humor.)" (p. 138).

Researchers Bruess and Pearson (1997) extended the analysis of "doing" versus "talking" by conducting a study of friendship rituals. Rituals are repeated events such as a "guys' night out," which one group in the study described as a night of barbecuing steaks, smoking cigars, and watching boxing on television. For men, rituals tend

© GEC Inc./Dist. by United Feature Syndicate, Inc.

to be important because they create a familiar, structured pattern to a friendship that reduces uncertainty and in some situations, facilitates a friendship without the need for a great deal of conversation. As it turns out, this may not be a disadvantage. Another study found that people were likely to choose, and be satisfied with, individuals who have similar levels of communication skills. Low-skill pairs were just as satisfied as high-skill pairs; the key was that the levels of communication skills matched (Burleson & Samter, 1996).

As you are no doubt aware, women generally base their friendships less on shared activities than on conversation and an exchange of thoughts and feelings (Brehm, 2001). We will say more about female–female friendships in a subsequent section, but you should be aware of the contrast here. For male readers, think about your own friendships with other men; for female readers, think about friendships between men you know. Were most of these male friendships initiated through an activity, such as a sport, drinking beer, hunting, playing video games, or the like? Do male friends spend most of their friendship time engaged in these kinds of activities? Do friendships sometimes end because the friends lose interest in the activity that bonded them together?

INTIMACY IN MALE–MALE FRIENDSHIP   Feelings of closeness are important in any friendship, and the expression of closeness between men has changed (Rawlins, 1992; 2009). In Chapter 5, we defined intimacy as bonding, closeness, and emotional connection, based on sharing personal, private information and experiences over time. We offered Jeffrey Fine's (2001) version of intimacy, as "in-to-me-see" (p. 225). Intimacy is something most people long for in their relationships (Beck, 2006, 2007; Sanderson, Keiter, Miles, & Yopyk, 2007). But is intimacy actually the goal in male–male friendship?

Gender scholars Strikwerda and May (1992) suggest that "men in America are clearly stymied in pursuing intimacy with other males because of fears involving their sexuality, especially culturally inbred homophobia. The taboo against males touching, except in firm public handshake, continues these teenage prohibitions" (p. 118). Many of the men in our classes admit that they have difficulty with intimacy, especially when it is operationalized in the form of hugging or otherwise expressing or verbalizing affection for a male friend or family member. Psychologists Bank and Hansford (2000) ascribe the source of this difficulty to male homophobia and emotional constraint. In this perspective, men pose a constant and relentless threat to each other, so that throughout men's lives, they fear being exposed or unmasked as feminine. These fears produce a very narrow bandwidth of acceptable behavior for men in their friendships, and it takes a conscious decision to move beyond this constraint. In their research regarding affection in nonromantic relationships, Floyd and Morman (1997) found that in situations or relationships in which one's motive for affection might be misunderstood, such as male friendships, the parties are more reluctant to express affection because they run the risk of being rejected, teased or made fun of, and seen as odd.

Regarding male intimacy (or the lack thereof), you might be thinking, "But what about the experience of sitting at a bar, drinking a beer, and just 'BS-ing'? At the end of the evening, you shake hands and head out. Isn't that closeness?" Granted, those can be close, good times, but do these experiences actually create intimacy in a friendship? One study found that men believed their friendships with other men to be just as intimate as other forms of friendships. These men felt just as close, supported, and satisfied in their male friendships as women did in their female friendships (Botschner, 1996).

Communication researchers Wood and Inman (1993) explored some characteristics traditionally associated with intimacy in relationships, such as conversations of a deeply personal nature and displays of emotion. What they determined is that these traits may better describe female friendship than male; pronouncements of what "counts" as intimacy in a relationship may be indicative of a feminine bias. In their research, male subjects regarded practical help, mutual assistance, and companionship as marks of caring and closeness. In a subsequent study, Inman (1996) discovered that men characterize their friendships with other men as being steeped in "continuity, perceived support and dependability, shared understandings, and perceived compatibility" and as being based on "self-revelation and self-discovery, having fun together, intermingled lives, and assumed significance" (p. 100). Men may base their friendships on unspoken assumptions, rather than actual conversations about the relationship. Thus we may conclude, regarding male-male intimacy in friendship, that men often gain intimacy by sharing activities and experiences, rather than through the more traditional displays of intimacy described in relationship and self-help literature (Floyd & Parks, 1995; Greif, 2008; Yager, 1999).

SELF-DISCLOSURE IN MALE–MALE FRIENDSHIP   In addition to differences in the way same-sex friends achieve intimacy, differences also exist in the amount and type of self-disclosure exchanged between same-sex friends. Researchers generally conclude that men are less self-disclosing than women (Baxter, Dun, & Sahlstein, 2001; Dindia & Allen, 1992; Giordano, Longmore, & Manning, 2006). In terms of the three possibilities for relationships (male–male, female–female, and female–male), male–male friendships have been found to contain the least amount of disclosure (Derlega, Winstead, Wong, & Hunter, 1985).

What might be some reasons for these trends regarding disclosure within male friendships? One theory for men's lesser disclosure relates to topics men tend to discuss.

You may think this sounds like a stereotype, but many people recognize it as reality: Men tend to talk more about *what,* meaning what they do in their jobs, what happened, and so on, while women tend to talk more about *who,* who they work with, who's doing what, and how the whos are feeling.

Some research suggests that preference, not ability, is responsible for the differing tendencies for same-sex friendship disclosure. Reisman's (1990) male college students described their same-sex friendships as being as high in disclosure as female subjects described theirs. In addition, he found that male subjects believed they have the capability of disclosing as much as women. Perhaps men *prefer* not to disclose as much with their male friends as they do with their female friends, dating partners, or spouses.

Some men equate disclosure with vulnerability—the belief that if a man discloses his thoughts and feelings to women or to other men, he has put himself in a powerless position. Since powerlessness is undesirable, actions linked to powerlessness are to be avoided, even at the cost of closeness in friendship (Rawlins, 2001).

It's quite possible that online male–male friendships operate differently than face-to-face friendships, in terms of self-disclosure, risk, and intimacy. Research has shown that certain features of computer-mediated communication (such as anonymity, decreased likelihood of future interaction, less emphasis on physical appearance, and diminished shyness and nervousness) enhance the frequency and depth of self-disclosure and accelerate the rate at which many relationships develop (Bargh, McKenna, & Fitzsimons, 2002; McKenna, Green, & Gleason, 2002; Ward & Tracey, 2004). Perhaps male friends feel less vulnerable disclosing their more intimate thoughts, feelings, and fears in an online format than in face-to-face settings, where they might run the risk of ridicule by individuals or groups of male friends.

So, we are left with two conflicting lines of thought regarding intimacy and disclosure. On the one hand, some sources indicate that male–male friendships are deficient owing to a lack of intimacy that can be derived only through personal disclosure. On the other hand, some people argue that the type of closeness men achieve through shared activities and experiences is just as legitimate and beneficial as any other type of closeness. Perhaps we could suggest a combination of perspectives. Intimacy in male–male friendships requires common activities and experiences, but it may be enhanced by disclosure of personal information and displays of emotion.

Female–Female Friendship: Functions and Characteristics

Many women can attest to the fact that since the earliest days they can remember as girls, same-sex friendships have been sustaining, highly significant forces in their lives. However, until only recently, little research specific to female friendship was available. In fact, sociologist Lionel Tiger (1969) argued that women were not genetically programmed to bond with one another! Gender scholar Fern Johnson (1996) suggests that female–female friendship has been an underresearched area because of stereotypes that women are too competitive, catty, and jealous to have meaningful friendships. More academic and popular attention has been paid to female friendships over the last decade (Bane, Cornish, Erspamer, & Kampman, 2010; Bleske-Rechek & Lighthall, 2010; Castaneda & Burns-Glover, 2008; Galupo, 2007; Goodman & O'Brien, 2000; Greif & Sharpe, 2010; Rose, 2007)

THE VALUE OF WOMEN'S FRIENDSHIPS   Just as men's friendships have changed throughout history, women's friendships have also evolved. Given the social restrictions on male–female interactions in earlier centuries, coupled with the fact that women historically inhabited a world primarily made up of other women and children, close friendships between women became an accepted form of social interaction, albeit one generally discounted by men (O'Connor, 1992). The women's movement ascribed more status to friendships between women and emphasized their value and significance in women's lives (Eichenbaum & Orbach, 1988). Research suggests that women are, in general, more likely than men to form very close same-sex friendships and to value those friendships highly (Rose, 2007; Wright, 1998).

The best time to make friends is before you need them.
—Ethel Barrymore, actress, member of an acting dynasty

Women also appear to develop friendships that function on multiple levels, as opposed to male friendships that tend to operate around one activity, issue, or function (Barth & Kinder, 1988). Gender development theorist Carol Gilligan (1982) characterizes female friendships as developing an intertwined series of obligations and responsibilities, which draws the participants into a friendship that bonds at multiple levels. Women focus on the individuals involved in the friendship and the pattern of interconnectedness between them. This pattern encourages mutual support, emotional sharing, and increased acceptance (Rawlins, 1992, 2009). Earlier, we briefly discussed the role of rituals in men's friendships. Bruess and Pearson (1997) found that women's friendship rituals were markedly different from men's, in that women's rituals involved conversation, emotional expression, and shared support, while men's rituals revolved around shared activities.

INTIMACY IN FEMALE–FEMALE FRIENDSHIP   At present, two schools of thought exist on intimacy in women's friendships versus men's. One body of information claims that women's friendships are generally more intimate and close than men's (Brehm, 2001; Eichenbaum & Orbach, 1988; Sherrod, 1989; Wright, 1982). Friendship researcher William Rawlins (1993) suggests that women have a greater intimacy competence than men, which stems from women's tendency to embrace the intimacy challenge and to learn how to communicate closeness with female friends quickly.

Authors of *Girlfriends: Invisible Bonds, Enduring Ties*, Carmen Renee Berry and Tamara Traeder (1995) contrast women's friendships with men and women's friendships with women. Women's conversations with male friends tend to focus more on ideas or

Hot Button Issue

"My Gay"

A research assistant for this book prompted a discussion in this chapter of the topic of hetero-sexual women and gay male friends because she believes it's a unique and wonderful relationship that many people experience, especially people of college age. She and her fiancé were talking about doing some activity together when he remarked, "Oh that's right—you can't because you're having a night out with your gay." The student explained that she often called her best friend, an openly gay man, "her gay" or "my gay" as a form of affectionate shorthand, and that her gay male friend didn't take offense; in fact, he viewed it as a term of endearment. Granted, some people might take offense, mainly to possessive pronouns like "her" or "my" that could connote ownership or dominance, whereas others might be affronted by use of the noun *gay* to stand for a whole person, almost as a substitute name or nickname.

No matter your view of the language in the example, we want to briefly discuss this unique form of friendship, because we do see evidence of heterosexual women who prize their relation-ships with self-identified gay men. What attracts straight women and gay men into friendship, many times with stronger bonds than same-sex friendships? The research on similarity we mentioned earlier in this chapter offers one explanation, in that straight women and gay men are both attracted to men as sexual partners, so having that kind of commonality can create a bond. Another possible explanation or contributing factor is the fact that gay men and straight men have their biological sex in common, no matter the differences in their sexual orientations, thus gay men may be perceived as being able to offer insight into straight men. Some people suggest that such common interests as fashion, design, and the arts may contribute to the prevalence of the straight female–gay male friendship, but this explanation evokes unfortunate gay male stereotypes.

Research has begun to explore this form of relationship in more depth (Gaiba, 2008; Tillmann-Healy, 2001). One study conducted by a group of Canadian scholars examined women's body self-esteem, confidence, and attention received from friends (Bartlett, Patterson, Vander-Laan, & Vasey, 2009). In specific, these researchers explored the stereotype that suggests that straight women who hang out with gay men tend to be physically unattractive and lacking in attention from straight men, thus they form friendships with gay men who don't reject them or make them feel bad about themselves. In their study, the stereotype had some basis in reality: Heterosexual women in the study reported enhanced self-esteem and confidence in terms of their own attractiveness when they spent time with and received attention from their gay male friends. Perhaps to avoid feeling a loss of self-esteem or rejection by straight men, some heterosexual women are drawn to gay men because they perceive that they won't judge them on their looks, but will instead form connections with them because of their other, more important qualities. Maybe these women feel freer to be who they are in the company of gay male friends, without fear of judgment or indifference.

We invite you to discuss this with groups of your friends or classmates, perhaps in a class discussion. Do you find that many women who self-identify as heterosexual have close friends who are gay men? From your perspective and experience, do heterosexual men have close lesbian friends with equal frequency as heterosexual women have close gay male friends? If you'd like to read more about this topic, we refer you to Lisa Tillmann-Healy's (2001) book, *Between Gay and Straight: Understanding Friendship across Sexual Orientation,* as well as Robert Hopcke and Laura Raferty's (1999) work, *A Couple of Friends: The Remarkable Friendship between Straight Women and Gay Men.*

problem solving than on shared feelings; if they want advice, suggestions, or a "fix-it" approach, women are likely to receive that from male friends. However, women most often seek out other women for a listening, sympathetic ear or for empathy in regard for what they're going through or feeling. This doesn't mean that women friends don't discuss ideas or help each other problem solve, but female–female friendships may develop stronger bonds of intimacy because a greater range of responses can be obtained; shared feelings, not just information, can lead to a greater closeness between women friends. Another element that makes women's friendships with other women different than their friendships with men is men's tendencies to withhold personal information. Even though evidence previously reviewed in this book shows that men are more likely to self-disclose to women than to other men, men tend to disclose less, in general, and to keep things "close to the vest." This tendency can pose a challenge to intimacy between friends (as well as in romantic relationships).

However, another school of thought contends that the differences in intimacy levels in male–male versus female–female friendships is not so great as previous research suggests, in fact there are minimal differences (Duck & Wright, 1993). Scholar Paul Wright (1998, 2006) reexamined earlier findings and concluded that men's and women's friendships are more similar than different. Specifically, Wright argues that the "women talk, men do" characterizations of friendship is an overgeneralization. On closer inspection of studies that discerned a tendency for women's intimate friendships to develop through communication whereas men's develop through shared activities, Wright found that female subjects also reported shared activities as a mainstay of their friendships with other women. Male subjects reported that they did, in fact, view talk as a central characteristic of their friendships with other men. Wright concludes that "the body of work on the talk-activity issue, as a whole, leaves me convinced that both women and men friends talk a lot and do a lot. Probably they most often talk while doing. However, when reflecting on their friendships, as in responses to interview questions and self-report items, women more often talk about talking and men more often talk about doing" (p. 50).

Again, an assessment of intimacy within a female–female or male–male friendship depends on how you operationalize or define intimacy. If you believe, as many communication scholars do, that genuine intimacy must be achieved and sustained primarily through communication—the sharing of ideas, secrets, fears, and emotions—then you will most likely view women's friendships as epitomizing intimacy and men's friendships as important and satisfying, but superficial. However, an expanded definition of intimacy—one that includes experiencing, not just talking—might lead you to a judgment that men's and women's friendships can be equally intimate, but that intimacy may emerge or reveal itself in different ways.

SELF-DISCLOSURE IN FEMALE–FEMALE FRIENDSHIP   Goodman and O'Brien (2000) explain, regarding their longtime friendship, "We were friends; we had to talk. It was the single most important—and most obvious—connection. Talk is at the very heart of women's friendships, the core of the way women connect. It's the given, the absolute assumption of friendship" (pp. 34–35).

How important is self-disclosure to same-sex friendships? People of both sexes agree that self-disclosure is the primary source of intimacy in friendships, with shared activity second (Derlega, Winstead, & Greene, 2008; Fehr, 2004, 2008). According to

Laugh and the world laughs with you. Cry and you cry with your girlfriends.
—*Laurie Kuslansky, author*

Berry and Traeder (1995), "Frequently a woman lets another woman know that she is her most trusted friend by sharing an aspect of herself that she has kept secret from the rest of the world" (p. 71). Reisman (1990) points out that individuals of both sexes who rate their friendships low in disclosure also tend to rate them low in closeness and satisfaction. One study of college students examined the relationship between reported levels of self-disclosure and satisfaction with same-sex friendships; findings showed that college women participating in the study reported higher levels of self-disclosure and satisfaction with their same-sex friendships than did men (Jones, 1991).

Research shows, in general, that women are more self-disclosing in their same-sex friendships than men (Clark & Reis, 1988; Dindia & Allen, 1992; Martin, 1997; Rawlins, 2001, 2009; Reis, 1998). However, O'Connor (1992) cautions against using disclosure of personal information and open expression of emotions as defining characteristics of female friendships. The danger, as she describes it, is that if we define women's friendships as operating primarily at a feeling level and "exclude any discussion of ideas or involvement with the world, they [women] abdicate any attempt in changing that world" (p. 31). The concern is that relegating women's friendships to the realm of the emotional reinforces stereotypes of women as purely emotional, with little ability to think rationally or rely on their sense of logic.

Just as we suggested that online male–male friendships may operate differently than face-to-face friendships, in terms of self-disclosure, risk, and intimacy, research has begun to explore this possibility for female–female friendship. Bane, Cornish, Erspamer and Kampman (2010) studied over 300 female bloggers' perceptions of "real-life" same-sex friendships versus online friendships, in terms of self-disclosure, perceptions of intimacy, and relationship satisfaction. Online self-disclosure (revealing information in one's blog, as well as reading others' disclosures via blogs) was correlated with relationship satisfaction, meaning that women who offered and received online friends' disclosures were highly positive about these relationships. However, although these same participants in this study reported having close online friends, they also believed that their "real-life" friendships were more intimate and that face-to-face friendships offered more potential for developing intimacy through shared disclosure than online relationships afforded.

Same-sex friendships for both men and women offer unique problems and possibilities. In this section, we have introduced you to the major functions and characteristics in each type of same-sex friendship and explored the role of communication in these relationships. Same-sex friendships are very important to us all, but so are cross-sex friendships. Let's turn our attention to the issues surrounding these sometimes troubling but often fulfilling friendships.

CROSS-SEX FRIENDSHIP: IS IT POSSIBLE TO BE "JUST FRIENDS"?

For some people, "friends of the opposite sex" is an oxymoron (like "death benefits"). Just a few decades ago, young men and women only socialized together as dates—rarely if ever as friends. Perhaps young women and men are leading a social change related to cross-sex friendships, because friendships between the sexes have become much more prevalent (Guerrero & Chavez, 2005; Rawlins, 2009).

Net Notes

Friendship Force International (FFI) is a nonprofit international cultural exchange organization, headquartered in Atlanta, Georgia. The organization's mission is "to create an environment in which personal friendships are established across the barriers that separate people." FFI has active chapters in over sixty countries, and its members seek to promote goodwill through homestay exchange programs. For those of you who think you'd might like to travel abroad and have friendly faces of people to stay with, visit the FFI site, located at **www.friendshipforce.org**.

As with other aspects of friendship we've discussed, society continues to change its expectations and notions about the appropriateness of cross-sex friendship. Whereas research from the 1970s suggested that both women and men preferred and actually had more same-sex friendships than cross-sex friendships, the experiences of today's friends are quite different (Booth & Hess, 1974; Canary & Emmers-Sommer, 1997; Guerrero & Chavez, 2005; Kalmijn, 2002; Monsour, 2002; Rawlins, 2009; Reeder, 2000; Weger & Emmett, 2009; Werking, 1997a, 1997b). Anecdotal evidence from students suggests that both sexes are seeking friendships with members of the opposite sex. As more and more women continue to enter various walks of life (e.g., business, politics, education), friendships between women and men are increasingly necessary and probable.

As is the case for other topics, the sex-versus-gender distinction is relevant to a discussion of cross-sex friendship. Psychologist Heidi Reeder (2003) found that that psychological gender affects the frequency of cross-sex friendship. In her study, feminine men had a significantly greater number of cross-sex friendships than did masculine men; masculine women had a significantly greater number of cross-sex friendships than did feminine women. Many participants in this study indicated that they did not prefer one sex or the other for friendship.

What Gets in the Way of Cross-Sex Friendships?

Many of us have experienced the joys that cross-sex friendships can provide, but we also know that these friendships come with their own unique complexities. Let's examine a few issues that typically pose challenges to cross-sex friendships.

THE PURPOSE OF CROSS-SEX FRIENDSHIP   One challenge to a successful cross-sex friendship exists in the minds of the friends before they ever meet and decide to become friends. We describe here the differing perceptions of what cross-sex friendship means, or what purpose it serves. Studies over four decades reveal that many heterosexual men, in contrast to heterosexual women, consistently report difficulty developing cross-sex friendships that are free of romantic implications and sexual activity, and that men may actually be motivated to form friendships with women because they believe these relationships will lead to "something else" (Bell, 1981; Halatsis & Christakis, 2009; Lipman-Blumen, 1976; Rose, 1985; Rubin, Peplau, & Hill, 1980). Rawlins (2001) explains:

> Typically, males sharply distinguish between same-sex and opposite-sex relationships but view their associations with women rather uniformly.

> Cross-sex bonds offer more disclosure, intimacy, and emotional involvement, which many males have difficulty interpreting as something other than precursors to romance. Informed by the socially conditioned alternatives of either friendship or romance, they often enact their cross-sex friendships as "not friendship," that is, as possible romances. By contrast, females differentiate less markedly between same-sex and opposite-sex relationships, but make distinctions among their male partners. They are able to form close relationships with females and males. And they clearly distinguish between the males they consider friends and those they regard romantically. Accordingly, their cross-sex friendships are typically enacted as "not romance," that is, as possible friendships. (p. 102)

You can see the potential for conflict and disappointment here, in that the two friends may have very different visions of what the relationship is and where it is heading. Even if the male friend agrees that the relationship is strictly a friendship and nonromantic, research suggests that he is more likely than the female friend to hold, perhaps in the back of his mind, the hope or expectation that the friendship will lead to romance. While some men are certainly capable of a truly platonic friendship with a woman and some women have romantic inclinations toward men whom they swear are "just friends," the research consistently shows the first pattern we described (Messman, Canary, & Hause, 2000).

AN UNDERCURRENT OF SEXUALITY AND SOCIAL PRESSURE   Some research suggests that underlying heterosexual, cross-sex friendships is a pervasive current of attraction and sexuality (Egland, Spitzberg, & Zormeier, 1996; Halatsis & Christakis, 2009; Hughes, Morrison, & Asada, 2005; Monsour, 2006; Sapadin, 1988). Earlier, we explored the challenge of differing views of the purpose of a cross-sex friendship—the tendency for heterosexual men more often than heterosexual women to view friendships with members of the opposite sex as precursors to romantic relationships. In one of the studies that support this finding, female subjects reported that their suspicion of men's sexual motives made them distrustful of male friendship overtures and less willing to establish friendships with men (Rose, 1985). This suspicion may be at least partially justified. Psychologists Bleske and Buss (2000) found that men are much more likely than women to view cross-sex friendships as an opportunity to gain sexual access. In some ways, these findings reflect a remnant attitude of past generations—that relationships with women are for one thing, and that one thing is not friendship. Research on sexual practices of cross-sex friends bears this out. In one study of college students, half of the participants admitted that they had sex with at least one platonic friend (Afifi & Faulkner, 2000).

Although American society is becoming more used to and accepting of cross-sex friendships, people in those friendships tire of the badgering they get from family, coworkers, and other friends about the true nature of their friendship, the hints people drop about becoming a "couple." People frequently use the word *platonic* to describe a friendship they suspect is something else altogether. Rawlins (2001) explains that society creates static for cross-sex friendships because a "romantic involvement between a man and a woman is much more celebrated than cross-sex friendships in American culture" (p. 95). (Think about how many plots of movies and television shows depict male–female friends versus male–female romantic partners.) Another barrier to cross-sex friendship development is the fact that, although this form of friendship is more prevalent now than ever before, we still don't have that many role models or prototypes of cross-sex friendships; the partners in each friendship seem to make up their own rules as they go. As we observe cross-sex friendships and perhaps experience our own such couplings, it's a safe bet that the people who maintain successful cross-sex friendships have worked to create and communicate to others their own definition of success.

Friends often have no sexual attraction or romantic interest when they start hanging out; it can be a real relief to enjoy someone *without* any sexual tension (i.e., no "benefits") or romantic expectations. (Refer a few pages back to the Hot Button Issue box about the special friendship many straight women enjoy with gay men.) But over time and with repeated input from others, the pressure can increase and erode the friendship, or it can cause the friends to reassess their relationship, perhaps looking for it to "lead to something" (Guerrero & Mongeau, 2008). Some friendships do successfully change definitions and evolve into romantic relationships because many people believe that the seed or root of a successful intimate relationship is friendship (Hendrick & Hendrick, 2000; Mongeau, Serewicz, Henningsen, & Davis, 2006).

But what happens if one friend starts giving into societal pressure or if romantic feelings start to develop on one side of the friendship, but not the other? (Homosexual women and men in friendships with straight men and women sometimes face this challenge too.) Sometimes one friend feels an attraction brewing and may have romantic intent toward a friend, but those feelings go unexpressed and time passes; then the other person in the friendship starts to develop feelings and perhaps attraction, but the other friend doesn't. As the saying goes, timing is everything. These are tough situations to figure out how to handle. Sometimes wonderful friendships come crashing down simply because feelings changed and communication stopped or became tense.

Relationship expert Michael Motley and colleagues have studied the fate of friendships after one friend discloses romantic interest toward the other friend, but the romantic overture isn't reciprocated (sometimes called "unrequited romance"; Motley, Faulkner, & Reeder, 2008, p. 27). Motley, Faulkner, and Reeder (2008) contend that "it is extremely common for people, by age 20 or so, to have experienced one or more episodes of unrequited romantic attraction within a friendship" (p. 46). In multiple studies of this situation, these researchers found that unrequited romantic disclosure was awkward for the friends, at best, and completely disruptive to the friendship, at worst.

This research provides helpful suggestions for friends who might find themselves in this situation, but who want to maintain a friendship and get past the awkwardness, embarrassment, and potential hurt feelings. Motley and colleagues suggest the following:

1. Friends should continue to pursue their friendship and use clear communication to indicate that maintaining a connection is important to both people.
2. It's wise to reestablish a pattern of contact, meaning do things together that you normally did as friends.
3. Even if it's awkward to talk about, friends should acknowledge that one person felt romantic feelings but the other didn't, and that the resulting imbalance of feelings exists and will take time to become balanced once again.

4. Friends shouldn't prolong the embarrassment or have repeated conversations about the situation, but instead drop the matter.

5. Flirting, teasing, or making jokes about what happened aren't helpful and can make the rejected friend feel worse.

6. One of the toughest challenges can be for the rejected friend to accept, and even encourage, her or his friend's romantic interest in other people, but this acceptance is necessary if the friendship is expected to continue (Motley, Reeder, & Faulkner, 2008).

INTERPERSONAL COMMUNICATION PATTERNS   Another source of difficulty in cross-sex friendships arises from interpersonal communication patterns that may relate to gender. For example, how is conflict managed in a cross-sex friendship? Is it handled any differently than two female or two male friends might handle disagreement in their friendship? Does one friend consistently exert more influence or power over the other? Is one friend more often the discloser and the other the recipient of disclosure? Could that become a problem?

Research shows that many men seek friendships with women as an emotional outlet and so that they will have someone (other than their romantic partners) who will listen to their disclosures, particularly about personal problems, and respond with empathy (Aries, 2006; Burleson, 2003; Dindia, 2002). As we discussed in an earlier section of this chapter, men typically avoid emotional expression and intimacy with other men; thus, they often seek it with women. In contrast, many women feel that they cannot have their emotional needs met only through their relationships (romantic and otherwise) with men, so they seek relationships with other women to fulfill this purpose. Can you see the potential for difficulty here? If men tend to seek emotional support from women, and women tend to seek emotional support from women, that can create a sort of imbalance of friendship. This may also pose a challenge to the cross-sex friendship: If the male friend views the friendship as an outlet for meeting his emotional needs, but the female friend sees it as unable to do so for her, the relationship might be headed for problems. The purposes and parameters of the friendship may need to be discussed directly.

One interpersonal pattern that warrants discussion isn't research based, but stems from experience, corroborated by numerous students' accounts. A unique form of communication emerges primarily between men—a form that tends to backfire when men use it with women. In a gender communication class a few semesters back, this phenomenon received the label "jocular sparring." Here's how it typically works: A guy will see one of his buddies and greet him by saying, "Man, you look *terrible* today; where'd you get that shirt, off somebody who died?! And your hair, geez—put a hat on." This harmless teasing between male friends can be directly translated into "I like you; you're my buddy." It's an unthreatening way for men to communicate liking and affection for one another. We realize that the following statement is generalizing a bit, but women don't typically talk this way with their female friends. If a woman greeted a female friend by saying, "Hey, you look like death warmed over today—what happened?! That outfit looks like it's been through the wringer and your hair looks like the cat's been chewing on it," the female friend would probably feel hurt, get angry, or wonder what in the world had gotten into her friend.

So what happens when a guy teases a female friend, assuming that she'll react the way his male friends do? For example, consider what's likely to happen if a guy greets a female friend by saying, "Not getting enough sleep lately? Your eyes look like you've been on a four-day drunk. And that outfit—did you get dressed in the dark?!" More often than not, the woman will not take the teasing lightly. She might act as though she is tossing off the comments, but in fact the teasing may cause her discomfort because it introduces an element of uncertainty into the relationship.

This doesn't mean that women don't have a sense of humor or that they're fragile creatures who can't take teasing among friends. In fact, after a friendship foundation has been established and with greater understanding of one another's communication styles, women can often take jocular sparring (and dish it right back) in the friendly spirit intended. It's not that women can't or don't engage in teasing with both their male and female friends, but they tend not to prefer it as a form of showing closeness or affection. When women do engage in teasing, they tend to communicate it differently and with a different effect than when men spar this way. Jocular sparring has the potential either to hurt or engender a sense of playfulness and closeness in a relationship; if you desire the positive outcome, it's wise for friends to talk about the use of this kind of communication.

What Enhances Cross-Sex Friendships?

Each of us needs friends, and one of the benefits of the changes over past decades is the increased potential for satisfying friendships between men and women. While many students are aware of some of the problems we just discussed, they also report a desire for more and better friendships with members of the opposite sex. In this final section of the chapter, let's explore some strategies one might follow to increase the chance that a cross-sex friendship will develop successfully.

I have always detested the belief that sex is the chief bond between man and woman. Friendship is far more human.
—Agnes Smedley, journalist and author

CROSS-SEX FRIENDS AS ROMANCE ADVISORS   One of the benefits of cross-sex friendship is getting firsthand information and insight into members of the opposite sex. How many of us have asked an opposite-sex friend to explain that sex and their behavior to us? How many of us have compared a date's behavior to that of our opposite-sex friend, and then found the date wanting? Our curiosity about the opposite sex is a natural, fun part of life, but when it turns into perplexity because one relational partner cannot understand the other, then we feel we need help. Who better to turn to than an opposite-sex friend?

It's common for men to ask their female friends to help them understand women or just to seek support, empathy, or sympathy. This applies to the guy who is frustrated over his lack of success in the dating market, to the man who wants female insight into his dating relationships, or to the married man who seeks advice about his relationship with his wife, possibly from one of her friends. At times, women remain a mystery to men, so they often feel that a female friend can help them understand women more so than a male friend can. As some research we reviewed in the male–male friendship section indicates, men may not want to disclose their problems, insecurities, or concerns to other men for fear of appearing weak or vulnerable. Thus men often find female friends to be valuable confidantes. Likewise, women who are puzzled or troubled by some situation involving romantic entanglements with men (or the lack thereof) can find their male friends a source of support, strength, and insight.

Of course, like anything else, this advice-giving, lend-an-ear function of cross-sex friendships has its abuses as well as its benefits. For example, if your sole purpose for having an opposite-sex friend is to seek counsel on your romantic relationships, your friend may quickly tire of that. Cross-sex friendships need special kinds of maintenance. Using someone merely as a source of support, a guidance counselor, a spokesperson for all men or all women, or a captive audience for your relational problems could be considered a selfish, abusive way to conduct a friendship. What if your friend needs your ear sometime? What if your friend becomes unwilling to be there for you, simply because the friendship ended up being too one-sided? These important issues warrant sensitive discussion and negotiation between cross-sex friends. If you don't talk about possible abuses of the friendship—or of any relationship for that matter—you might wind up with one less friend.

FRIENDS WITH BENEFITS (FWBRs)   Thus far in this chapter, we've been operating under the assumption that cross-sex friendships are platonic, that is, they don't include sexual activity. Some cross-sex friendships do include sexual tension, as we've discussed. This tension may be positive (making you enjoy the person's company more because the friendship involves an element of flirtation or attraction) or negative (adding a dimension that isn't expected or reciprocated, or that impedes the relationship). Increasingly nowadays, friends become sexual partners with no effect on the friendship or expectation of romantic involvement. Among college-aged people "friends with benefits relationships" (FWBRs), sometimes called (in PG-13 language) "f-buddies," are more common now than they were even a few short years ago. One study of college students found that over half reported being in an FWBR, more men than women (Puentes, Knox, & Zusman, 2008); in other college student surveys, the figure was 60 percent (Bisson & Levine, 2009; McGinty, Knox, & Zusman, 2007). In fact, a movie released in 2011 starring Justin Timberlake and Mila Kunis, aptly titled *Friends With Benefits*, explored this complicated form of friendship.

Communication scholars Hughes, Morrison, and Asada (2005) define the FWBR as a relationship that emerges from a preexisting friendship but that evolves to include sexual activity. The sexual contact doesn't change the friendship into a romantic relationship or imply a commitment; in fact, people in successful FWBRs don't want anything more from their partners than what they have. Hughes et al. (2005) explain that "these types of relationships are distinct in that they combine both the benefits of friendship with the benefits of a sexual relationship, yet avoid the responsibilities and commitment that romantic relationships typically entail" (p. 50).

Although some of us wouldn't dream of having FWBRs because it goes against our moral code, religious beliefs, or simply our preferences for keeping sexual activity only with romantic partners, you probably know people at your college or university who enjoy the occasional (or frequent) "booty call." This phenomenon begs a few questions: Is a physical/sexual relationship a logical extension of the intimacy that two friends can develop? If a strong friendship includes deep sharing at psychological, emotional, and possibly spiritual levels, what about the physical level? If both friends are sexually active (or believe sexual activity outside of marriage or committed partnership is acceptable) and both have sexual desires, is it necessarily wrong or inappropriate to turn to one's friend for mutual sexual gratification? If the "booty call" gets answered, is the relationship still a friendship or is it something else? What if sex happens because two friends get drunk or high and their inhibitions lessen—is the friendship now an FWBR or is it just an "oops" situation, a mistake? We ask these questions to get you thinking about cross-sex friendships and what they should or shouldn't include. Same-sex gay and lesbian friends often have the same issues to contend with.

Researchers continue to explore the nature of FWBRs, how men and women negotiate them, and the communication involved in the maintenance of such friendships (Epstein, Calzo, Smiler, & Ward, 2009; Goodboy & Myers, 2008; Paik, 2010). In one of the studies in which 60 percent of college students reported either currently experiencing or having experienced an FWBR, researchers found that women and men differed in their basic conception of the friendship (McGinty, Knox, & Zusman, 2007). Women in the study emphasized the "friends" aspect, viewing the FWBR as more involved and emotional, whereas men viewed the relationship as more casual and emphasized the sexual aspect or "benefits" of the connection. From the women's point of view, the fear or concern is that women in FWBRs who view the relationship in a different light than men will have their feelings hurt or experience conflict when the difference emerges. From the men's point of view, differing perspectives on an FWBR might lead to pressure to change the relationship into something the woman wants or make it a deeper friendship than the man desires.

Hughes et al. (2005) explain that FWBRs can function effectively, provided both friends follow these rules:

1. Friends with benefits must maintain their original friendship, meaning that sexual activity doesn't change the friendship and the participants continue to do things together that they typically did as friends.
2. Emotions don't become involved, or the friendship will be at risk.
3. The friends with benefits relationship is maintained in secret, even if this means that their romantic or sexual partners don't know about it.
4. The relationship may be renegotiated, with either participant opting out at any time.

Is it possible to go back to being just friends after being FWBRs? Earlier in this chapter we reviewed some research on how friends recover after an unrequited romantic attempt—one friend's desire to change the friendship into something more intimate is rejected. Although not specific to FWBRs, the research findings apply. If one person in an FWBR begins to develop romantic feelings and a desire to move the friendship into a romantic realm, but the other person doesn't, negotiating the situation can be awkward. Many times, communication becomes tense or nonexistent and the FWBR simply doesn't continue. Some people find they can "notch back" the FWBR into just a good friendship, but for others, this isn't easy or even imaginable. Navigating this relatively new form of friendship takes effort and clear, open communication if the friends are to view the relationship equitably.

The Future for Cross-Sex Friendship

Friendship between men and women has changed and will continue to evolve. We wonder where these changes will lead, and so we close this chapter with one thought on the direction and future of friendship between the sexes. Buhrke and Fuqua (1987) concluded the following from their research:

> Given that [our research found] women wanted more contact with men, wanted to be closer to men, and wanted more balance in their relationships

> with men . . . , one could conclude that women more highly value their rela-
> tionships with men and wish to better those relationships. However, women
> were already more satisfied with the frequency of contact, closeness, and
> balance in their relationships with women. Thus it seems women want more
> from their relationships with men and make efforts to improve the quality of
> those relationships so that they are more similar to their relationships with
> women. (p. 349)

This is an interesting thought—that women want better relationships with men,
but want them to become more like their friendships with other women. Perhaps men
would like their cross-sex friendships to become more like their same-sex friendships.
We suggest that neither goal is complete. It may not be a good idea to force cross-sex
friendships into the mold of the familiar same-sex friendship. Indeed, the terms *cross-sex*
and *same-sex* friendships tend to dichotomize the two types and exaggerate their differences while minimizing their similarities (Arnold, 1995; Werking, 1994). If we classify
relationships into same-sex and cross-sex, we may restrict our understanding of communicative practices and experience. Men and women can develop more effective cross-sex
friendships by learning to incorporate the patterns of the opposite sex into their communication repertoire and by treating each friendship as a unique entity, not as having
come from another planet. The process takes thought, sensitivity, and a willingness to
learn and change.

 ## Conclusion

This chapter began with the suggestion that
the nature of and value placed on same-
sex and cross-sex friendships are changing.
Research supports that suggestion and provides great insight into friendships and the
kind of communication that sustains them.
We first explored in this chapter how we
learn, as children, what friendship means;
we examined gender-related friendship patterns that begin in childhood and change as
we progress into adolescence and adulthood. Friendship between the sexes is something we learn to do, because structures in
society generally do not teach us how to
embrace members of the opposite sex as
friends.

We then explored the unique functions
and characteristics of male–male friendships,
as compared with female–female friendships. While these relationships are more
similar than different, some aspects such as

the purpose of the friendship, the approaches
to and need for developing intimacy, and the
role of self-disclosure in the relationship do
differ.

Finally, we examined cross-sex friendship, in terms of factors that impede the
development and satisfaction of this kind of
friendship, as well as factors that enhance
friendship. Specifically, such factors as varying purposes or expectations for the friendship, the undercurrent of sexuality, societal
pressure, and interpersonal communication
patterns—such as who more often discloses
versus who more often receives the other's
disclosure—may actually impede the success
of a cross-friendship. We also offered some
suggestions for cross-sex friendship enhancement, such as communicating to develop
a clear definition of the relationship and
being careful not to overuse one's opposite-
sex friend as a romantic advisor. Finally, we

discussed the murky waters of sexual activity between cross-sex friends, in terms of the effects on a friendship.

Each type of friendship has unique communication issues and unique potential, but one thing is clear: Friendships are among our most important relationships in life. We have all probably suffered the consequences of assuming that friends will always be there for us, that we don't have to exert much energy to keep them. Such assumptions will soon leave us friendless. So, just like other important relationships—with family, coworkers, or romantic partners—friendships need communication, as well as shared experiences, to develop and grow.

 ## Discussion Starters

1. In your experience, how do most male friendships seem to form? What brings the friends together? Are the circumstances different than those that bring female friends together?
2. Some researchers propose that the intimacy men achieve through doing things together is of the same quality as the intimacy achieved by women through conversation. Do you believe men and women are equally capable of forming intimate relationships? Intimate same-sex friendships? Intimate cross-sex friendships? How are women and men different in terms of accomplishing intimacy in their relationships? How are they similar?

3. Think about the issue of sexual activity in heterosexual, cross-sex friendships, meaning the "friends with benefits" arrangement. How is the issue dealt with in most of the cross-sex friendships you know? In your own cross-sex friendships? Is the issue discussed openly, hinted at, or avoided?
4. What do you think are the biggest obstacles to effective cross-sex friendships? What do you think it will take to improve friendships between women and men? Which sex will have to change the most and why? What will the ideal cross-sex friendship look like?

 ## References

Afifi, W. A., & Faulkner, S. L. (2000). On being "just friends": The frequency and impact of sexual activity in cross-sex friendships. *Journal of Social and Personal Relationships, 17*, 205–222.

Aries, E. (2006). Sex differences in interaction: A re-examination. In K. Dindia & D. J. Canary (Eds.), *Sex differences and similarities in communication* (2nd ed., pp. 21–37). Mahwah, NJ: Erlbaum.

Arnold, L. B. (1995). Through the narrow pass: Experiencing same-sex friendship in heterosexual(ist) settings. *Communication Studies, 46*, 234–244.

Bane, C. M. H., Cornish, M., Erspamer, N., & Kampman, L. (2010). Self-disclosure through weblogs and perceptions of online and "real-life" friendships among female bloggers. *Cyberpsychology, Behavior, and Social Networking, 13*, 131–139.

Bank, B. J., & Hansford, S. L. (2000). Gender and friendships: Why are men's best same-sex friendships less intimate and supportive? *Personal Relationships, 7*, 63–78.

Bargh, J. A., McKenna, K. Y. A., & Fitzsimons, G. M. (2002). Can you see the real me? Activation and expression of the "true self" on the Internet. *Journal of Social Issues, 58*, 33–48.

Barth, R. J., & Kinder, B. N. (1988). A theoretical analysis of sex differences in same-sex friendships. *Sex Roles, 19*, 349–363.

Bartlett, N. H., Patterson, H. M., VanderLaan, D. P., & Vasey, P. L. (2009). The relation between women's body esteem and friendships with gay men. *Body Image, 6*, 235–241.

Bate, B., & Bowker, J. (1997). *Communication and the sexes* (2nd ed.). Prospect Heights, IL: Waveland.

Baxter, L. A., Dun, T., & Sahlstein, E. (2001). Rules for relating communicated among social network members. *Journal of Social & Personal Relationships, 18*, 173–199.

Beck, M. (2006, August). The relationship two-step. *O: The Oprah Winfrey Magazine, 47*.

Beck, M. (2007, June). Lover's leap. *O: The Oprah Winfrey Magazine, 51*.

Bell, R. R. (1981). *Worlds of friendship*. Beverly Hills, CA: Sage.

Bentall, D. C. (2004). *The company you keep: The transforming power of male friendship.* Minneapolis: Augsburg Fortress Publishing.

Berry, C. R., & Traeder, T. (1995). *Girlfriends: Invisible bonds, enduring ties.* Berkeley, CA: Wildcat Canyon Press.

Bisson, M. A., & Levine, T. R. (2009). Negotiating a friends with benefits relationship. *Archives of Sexual Behavior, 38*, 66–73.

Bleske, A. L., & Buss, D. M. (2000). Can men and women be just friends? *Personal Relationships, 7*, 131–151.

Bleske-Rechek, A., & Lighthall, M. (2010). Attractiveness and rivalry in women's friendships with women. *Human Nature, 21*, 82–97.

Booth, A., & Hess, E. (1974, February). Cross-sex friendship. *Journal of Marriage and the Family*, 38–47.

Botschner, J. V. (1996). Reconsidering male friendships: A social-developmental perspective. In C. W. Tolman & F. Cherry (Eds.), *Problems in theoretical psychology.* North York, Ontario: Captus.

Brehm, S. S. (2001). *Intimate relationships* (3rd ed.). New York: McGraw-Hill.

Bruess, C. J. S., & Pearson, J. C. (1997). Interpersonal rituals in marriage and adult friendship. *Communication Monographs, 64*, 25–46.

Buhrke, R. A., & Fuqua, D. R. (1987). Sex differences in same- and cross-sex supportive relationships. *Sex Roles, 17*, 339–351.

Burleson, B. R. (2003). The experience and effects of emotional support: What the study of cultural and gender differences can tell us about close relationships, emotion, and interpersonal communication. *Personal Relationships, 10*, 1–23.

Burleson, B. R., & Samter, W. (1996). Similarity in communication skills of young adults: Foundations of attraction, friendship, and relationship satisfaction. *Communication Reports, 9*, 127–139.

Canary, D. J., & Emmers-Sommer, T. M. (1997). *Sex and gender differences in personal relationships.* New York: Guilford.

Castaneda, D., & Burns-Glover, A. L. (2008). Women's friendships and romantic relationships. In F. L. Denmark & M. A. Paludi (Eds.), *Psychology of women: A handbook of issues and theories* (2nd ed., pp. 332–350). Westport, CT: Praeger.

Clark, M., & Reis, H. T. (1988). Interpersonal processes in close relationships. *Annual Review of Psychology, 39*, 609–672.

Crawford, M., & Unger, R. (2004). *Women and gender: A feminist psychology* (4th ed.). New York: McGraw-Hill.

Derlega, V. J., Winstead, B. A., & Greene, K. (2008). Self-disclosure and starting a close relationship. In S. Sprecher, A. Wenzel, & J. Harvey (Eds.), *Handbook of relationship initiation* (pp. 153–174). New York: Psychology Press.

Derlega, V. J., Winstead, B. A., Wong, P., & Hunter, S. (1985). Gender effects in initial encounters: A case where men exceed women in disclosure. *Journal of Social & Personal Relationships, 2*, 25–44.

Dindia, K. (2002). Self-disclosure research: Knowledge through meta-analysis. In M. Allen, R. W. Preiss, B. M. Gayle, & N. A. Burrell (Eds.), *Interpersonal communication research: Advances through meta-analysis* (pp. 169–185). Mahwah, NJ: Erlbaum.

Dindia, K., & Allen, M. (1992). Sex differences in self-disclosure: A meta-analysis. *Psychological Bulletin, 112*, 106–124.

Duck, S., & Wright, P. (1993). Reexamining gender differences in friendships: A close look at two kinds of data. *Sex Roles, 28*, 709–727.

Egland, K. L., Spitzberg, B., & Zormeier, M. (1996). Flirtation and conversational competence in cross-sex platonic and romantic relationships. *Communication Reports, 9*, 106–117.

Eichenbaum, L., & Orbach, S. (1988). *Between women: Love, envy, and competition in women's friendships.* New York: Viking.

Epstein, M., Calzo, J. P., Smiler, A. P., & Ward, L. M. (2009). "Anything from making out to having sex": Men's negotiations of hooking up and friends with benefits scripts. *Journal of Sex Research, 46*, 414–424.

Fehr, B. (2004). Intimacy expectations in same-sex friendships: A prototype interaction-pattern model. *Journal of Personality and Social Psychology, 86,* 265–284.

Fehr, B. (2008). Friendship formation. In S. Sprecher, A. Wenzel, & J. Harvey (Eds.), *Handbook of relationship initiation* (pp. 29–54). New York: Psychology Press.

Fine, J. (2001, October). Intimacy. *O: The Oprah Winfrey Magazine, 225.*

Fisher, H. (2009, October). Intimacy: His & hers. *O: The Oprah Winfrey Magazine,* 138.

Floyd, K., & Morman, M. T. (1997). Affectionate communication in nonromantic relationships: Influences of communicator, relational, and contextual factors. *Western Journal of Communication, 61,* 279–298.

Floyd, K., & Parks, M. (1995). Manifesting closeness in the interactions of peers: A look at siblings and friends. *Communication Reports, 8,* 69–76.

Foster, G. (2005). Making friends: A nonexperimental analysis of social pair formation. *Human Relations, 58,* 1443–1465.

Gaiba, F. (2008). Straight women and gay men friends: A qualitative study. *Dissertation Abstracts International: Section A. Humanities and Social Sciences, 69* (1-A), 262.

Galupo, M. P. (2007). Women's close friendships across sexual orientation: A comparative analysis of lesbian-heterosexual and bisexual-heterosexual women's friendships. *Sex Roles, 56,* 473–482.

Galupo, M. P. (2009). Cross-category friendship patterns: Comparison of heterosexual and sexual minority adults. *Journal of Social & Personal Relationships, 26,* 811–831.

Gifford-Smith, M. E., & Brownell, C. A. (2003). Childhood peer relationships: Social acceptance, friendships, and peer networks. *Journal of School Psychology, 41,* 235–284.

Gilligan, C. (1982). *In a different voice.* Cambridge, MA: Harvard University Press.

Giordano, P. C., Longmore, M. A., & Manning, W. D. (2006). Gender and the meanings of adolescent romantic relationships: A focus on boys. *American Sociological Review, 71,* 260–287.

Goodboy, A. K., & Myers, S. A. (2008). Relational maintenance behaviors of friends with benefits: Investigating equity and relational characteristics. *Human Communication, 11,* 71–85.

Goodman, E., & O'Brien, P. (2000). *I know just what you mean: The power of friendship in women's lives.* New York: Simon & Schuster.

Greif, G. L. (2008). *Buddy system: Understanding men's friendships.* New York: Oxford University Press.

Greif, G. L., & Sharpe, T. L. (2010). The friendships of women: Are there differences between African-Americans and whites? *Journal of Human Behavior in the Social Environment, 20,* 791–807.

Guerrero, L. K., & Chavez, A. M. (2005). Relational maintenance in cross-sex friendships characterized by different types of romantic intent: An exploratory study. *Western Journal of Communication, 69,* 339–358.

Guerrero, L. K., & Mongeau, P. A. (2008). On becoming "more than friends": The transition from friendship to romantic relationship. In S. Sprecher, A. Wenzel, & J. Harvey (Eds.), *Handbook of relationship initiation* (pp. 175–194). New York: Psychology Press.

Halatsis, P., & Christakis, N. (2009). The challenge of sexual attraction within heterosexuals' cross-sex friendships. *Journal of Social & Personal Relationships, 26,* 919–937.

Hendrick, S. S., & Hendrick, C. (2000). Romantic love. In C. Hendrick & S. S. Hendrick (Eds.), *Close relationships: A sourcebook* (pp. 203–215). Thousand Oaks, CA: Sage.

Hopcke, R., & Raferty, L. (1999). *A couple of friends: The remarkable friendship between straight women and gay men.* Berkeley, CA: Wildcat Canyon Press.

Hughes, M., Morrison, K., & Asada, K. J. K. (2005). What's love got to do with it? Exploring the impact of maintenance rules, love attitudes, and network support on friends with benefits relationships. *Western Journal of Communication, 69,* 49–66.

Inman, C. (1996). Friendships among men: Closeness in the doing. In J. T. Wood (Ed.), *Gendered relationships* (pp. 95–110). Mountain View, CA: Mayfield.

Johnson, F. L. (1996). Friendships among women: Closeness in dialogue. In J. T. Wood (Ed.), *Gendered relationships* (pp. 79–94). Mountain View, CA: Mayfield.

Jones, D.C. (1991). Friendship satisfaction and gender: An examination of sex differences in contributors to friendship satisfaction. *Journal of Social & Personal Relationships, 8,* 167–185.

Kalmijn, M. (2002). Sex segregation of friendship networks: Individual and structural determinants of having cross-sex friends. *European Sociological Review, 18,* 101–117.

Lipman-Blumen, J. (1976). Toward a homosocial theory of sex roles: An explanation of the sex segregation of social institutions. In M. M. Blaxall & B. Reagan (Eds.), *Women and the workplace* (pp. 15–22). Chicago: University of Chicago Press.

Maccoby, E. E. (1998). *The two sexes: Growing up apart, coming together.* Cambridge, MA: Harvard University Press.

Martin, R. (1997). "Girls don't talk about garages!" Perceptions of conversations in same- and cross-sex friendships. *Personal Relationships, 4,* 115–130.

McGinty, K., Knox, D., & Zusman, M. E. (2007). Friends with benefits: Women want "friends," men want "benefits." *College Student Journal, 41,* 1128–1131.

McKenna, K. Y. A., Green, A. S., & Gleason, M. E. J. (2002). Relationship formation on the Internet: What's the big attraction? *Journal of Social Issues, 58,* 9–31.

Messman, S. J., Canary, D. J., & Hause, K. S. (2000). Motives to remain platonic, equity, and the use of maintenance strategies in opposite-sex friendships. *Journal of Social & Personal Relationships, 17,* 67–94.

Mongeau, P. A., Serewicz, M. C. M., Henningsen, M. L. M., & Davis, K. L. (2006). Sex differences in the transition to a heterosexual romantic relationship. In K. Dindia & D. J. Canary (Eds.), *Sex differences and similarities in communication* (2nd ed., pp. 337–358). Mahwah, NJ: Erlbaum.

Monsour, M. (2002). *Women and men as friends: Relationships across the life span in the 21st century.* Mahwah, NJ: Erlbaum.

Monsour, M. (2006). Communication and gender among adult friends. In B. J. Dow & J. T. Wood (Eds.), *The Sage handbook of gender and communication* (pp. 57–69). Thousand Oaks, CA: Sage.

Motley, M. T., Faulkner, L. J., & Reeder, H. (2008). Conditions that determine the fate of friendships after unrequited romantic disclosures. In M. Motley (Ed.), *Studies in applied interpersonal communication* (pp. 27–50). Thousand Oaks, CA: Sage.

Motley, M. T., Reeder, H., & Faulkner, L. J. (2008). Behaviors that determine the fate of friendships after unrequited romantic disclosures. In M. Motley (Ed.), *Studies in applied interpersonal communication* (pp. 71–93). Thousand Oaks, CA: Sage.

Nardi, P. M. (1992). *Men's friendships.* Newbury Park, CA: Sage.

O'Connor, P. (1992). *Friendships between women: A critical review.* New York: Guilford.

Paik, A. (2010). "Hookups," dating, and relationship quality: Does the type of sexual involvement matter? *Social Science Research, 39,* 739–753.

Perry, L. A. M., Turner, L. H., & Sterk, H. M. (Eds.) (1992). *Constructing and reconstructing gender: The links among communication, language, and gender.* Albany: State University of New York Press.

Pinel, E. C., Long, A. E., Landau, M. J., Alexander, K., & Pyszczynski, T. (2006). Seeing I to I: A pathway to interpersonal connectedness. *Journal of Personality and Social Psychology, 90,* 243–257.

Puentes, J., Knox, D., & Zusman, M. E. (2008). Participants in "friends with benefits" relationships. *College Student Journal, 42,* 176–180.

Rawlins, W. K. (1992). *Friendship matters: Communication, dialectics, and the life course.* Hawthorne, NY: Aldine de Gruyter.

Rawlins, W. K. (1993). Communication in cross-sex friendships. In L. P. Arliss & D. T. Borisoff (Eds.), *Women and men communicating: Challenges and changes* (pp. 51–70). Fort Worth, TX: Harcourt, Brace, & Jovanovich.

Rawlins, W. K. (2001). Times, places, and social spaces for cross-sex friendship. In L. P. Arliss & D. E. Borisoff (Eds.), *Women and men communicating: Challenges and changes* (2nd ed., pp. 93–114). Prospect Heights, IL: Waveland.

Rawlins, W. K. (2009). *The compass of friendship: Narratives, identities, and dialogues.* Los Angeles: Sage.

Reeder, H. M. (2000). "I like you . . . as a friend": The role of attraction in cross-sex friendship. *Journal of Social & Personal Relationships, 17,* 329–348.

Reeder, H. M. (2003). The effect of gender role orientation on same- and cross-sex friendship formation. *Sex Roles, 49,* 143–152.

Reis, H. T. (1998). Gender differences in intimacy and related behaviors: Context and process. In D. J. Canary & K. Dindia (Eds.), *Sex differences and similarities in communication* (pp. 203–231). Mahwah, NJ: Erlbaum.

Reisman, J. J. (1990). Intimacy in same-sex friendships. *Sex Roles, 23,* 65–82.

Romaine, S. (1999). *Communicating gender*. Mahwah, NJ: Erlbaum.

Rose, S. M. (1985). Same- and cross-sex friendships and the psychology of homosociality. *Sex Roles, 12*, 63–74.

Rose, S. M. (2007). Enjoying the returns: Women's friendships after 50. In V. Muhlbauer & J. C. Chrisler (Eds.), *Women over 50: Psychological perspectives* (pp. 112–130). New York: Springer Science + Business Media.

Rubin, Z., Peplau, L. A., & Hill, C. T. (1980). Loving and leaving: Sex differences in romantic attachments. *Sex Roles, 6*, 821–835.

Rushton, J. P., & Bons, T. A. (2005). Mate choice and friendship in twins: Evidence for genetic similarity. *Psychological Science, 16*, 555–559.

Sanderson, C. A., Keiter, E. J., Miles, M. G., & Yopyk, D. J. A. (2007). The association between intimacy goals and plans for initiating dating relationships. *Personal Relationships, 14*, 225–243.

Sapadin, L. A. (1988). Friendship and gender: Perspectives of professional men and women. *Journal of Social & Personal Relationships, 5*, 387–403.

Sherrod, D. (1989). The influences of gender on same-sex friendships. In C. Hendrick (Ed.), *Close relationships* (pp. 164–186). Newbury Park, CA: Sage.

Spain, D. (1992). The spatial foundations of men's friendships and men's power. In P. M. Nardi (Ed.), *Men's friendships* (pp. 59–73). Newbury Park, CA: Sage.

Strikwerda, R. A., & May, L. (1992). Male friendship and intimacy. *Hypatia, 7*, 110–125.

Thorne, B. (1994). *Gender play: Girls and boys in school*. New Brunswick, NJ: Rutgers University Press.

Tiger, L. (1969). *Men in groups*. New York: Random House.

Tillman-Healy, L. M. (2001). *Between gay and straight: Understanding friendship across sexual orientation*. Walnut Creek, CA: AltaMira Press.

Veniegas, R. C., & Peplau, L. A. (1997). Power and the quality of same-sex friendships. *Psychology of Women Quarterly, 21*, 279–297.

Ward, C. C., & Tracey, T. J. G. (2004). Relation of shyness with aspects of online relationship involvement. *Journal of Social & Personal Relationships, 21*, 611–623.

Way, N. (2011). *Deep secrets: Boys' friendships and the crisis of connection*. Cambridge, MA: Harvard University Press.

Weger, H., & Emmett, M. C. (2009). Romantic intent, relationship uncertainty, and relationship maintenance in young adults' cross-sex friendships. *Journal of Social & Personal Relationships, 26*, 964–988.

Werking, K. J. (1994, May). *Barriers to the formation of cross-sex friendship*. Paper presented at the meeting of International Network for Personal Relationships, Iowa City, IA.

Werking, K. J. (1997a). Cross-sex friendship research as ideological practice. In S. Duck (Ed.), *Handbook of personal relationships: Theory, research, and interventions* (2nd ed., pp. 391–410). Chichester, UK: Wiley.

Werking, K. J. (1997b). *We're just good friends: Women and men in nonromantic relationships*. New York: Guilford.

Wood, J. T., & Inman, C. C. (1993). In a different mode: Masculine styles of communicating closeness. *Journal of Applied Communication Research, 21*, 279–295.

Wright, P. (1982). Men's friendships, women's friendships, and the alleged inferiority of the latter. *Sex Roles, 8*, 1–19.

Wright, P. (1998). Toward an expanded orientation to the study of sex differences in friendships. In D. J. Canary & K. Dindia (Eds.), *Sex differences and similarities in communication* (pp. 41–63). Mahwah, NJ: Erlbaum.

Wright, P. (2006). Toward an expanded orientation to comparative study of women's and men's same-sex friendships. In K. Dindia & D. J. Canary (Eds.), *Sex differences and similarities in communication* (2nd ed., pp. 41–63). Mahwah, NJ: Erlbaum.

Yager, J. (1999). *Friendshifts: The power of friendship and how it shapes our lives* (2nd ed.). Stamford, CT: Hannacroix Creek Books.

HOT TOPICS

- The language of romance
- The pressure to establish romantic relationships
- How stereotypical notions of romance impede relational success
- Tensions in romantic relationships, including autonomy versus connection, power versus empowerment, acceptance versus change, developing comparable views of intimacy, expressing love, and making a commitment

- The role of relational talk and metacommunication in the development of couple communication patterns
- Conflict management in romantic relationships
- The effects of gender and the role of communication in relationship termination
- Attitudes and communication about sexual activity in a romantic relationship

Beyond Friendship
Gender Communication in Romantic Relationships

CHAPTER 7

Case Study

Persistent Traditions in the Realm of Romance

"You know one thing that still really bothers me? Guys are still the ones who have to ask girls out. With all this liberation we're supposed to have had, why do we still have to put ourselves on the line all the time?" This was Cliff's complaint in class one day about something he doesn't see changing—the continued responsibility a man feels to put his ego on the line and ask a woman for a date. Bonnie countered with, "Wait a second, you don't know what it's like to wait or hope you'll be asked out. That's really hard, too." This led Nicole to chime in, "Hey, if you don't like waiting for a guy to ask you out, ask *him* out. I know lots of women who ask guys out on dates. Just send a text." At this point, an informal class poll showed that the traditional model, despite changing times, was still very much in evidence. Few men get asked out by women (even though they'd *like* to); few women actually ask men out (even though they know they *can*). Men feel the responsibility to do the asking, and while some women do take the initiative, most are uncomfortable with it.

As the class discussion continued, Bonnie asked, "Why haven't things changed much? The way it used to be still seems to be the way it is." Jawarren responded, "I think you're right. A couple of friends of mine got married this summer, and even though they had a pretty balanced relationship in college, when they graduated, got married, and he got a job, all of a sudden he's the breadwinner and she's taking care of the house. They're behaving just like their parents!" Bonnie answered, "Yeah, I know what you mean. It seems like there are lots of opportunities to change, but when it comes right down to it, there's a lot of pressure to keep things they way they've been."

In this chapter, we discuss some things that have changed and some things that haven't in the realm of romantic relationships. It seems that despite changes in many areas of relationships, romantic partnerings often cling to old patterns. Do you think things have changed, in terms of roles in dating and romantic relationships? Does the traditional model still make its presence felt? Changing our patterns, expectations, and communication within romantic relationships takes conscious effort and an awareness of options.

AH, LOVE AND ROMANCE (AND GENDER)

Hollywood movies would have us believe that romantic relationships happen almost by magic, as though we all know what it takes to make them happen and how to keep them going. Movies throughout the years have also shown us various faces of pain when romantic relationships have gone awry. Given the idealized, overdrawn images in our heads, it may sometimes come as a shock to find a different reality when we embark on romantic relationships of our own. Romantic relationships bring their own unique communication and challenges to men and women who venture into them. But even when we are in the midst of a breakup, when a relationship seems doomed and we wonder why we ever wandered into such uncharted territory, we'd probably say we'd do it all over again if given the chance. Humans are innately romantic creatures, and for many of us, the opportunity for romance and love is one of life's greatest experiences. Because romantic relationships tap such strong emotions and because our culture has such a strong interest in them, communication within them is critical and complex.

A guy knows he's in love when he wants to grow old with a woman. When he wants to stay with her in the morning. When he starts calling sex "making love" and afterward wants a great big hug. When he loses interest in the car for a couple of days. It's that simple, I swear.

—Tim Allen, actor

The Language of Romance

Romantic relationships are complicated (an understatement). To begin, consider the terms used to describe the nature of a romantic relationship and the two people in it. For heterosexual couples, the term *girlfriend* is still the most common usage of traditionally aged male students, but use of *boyfriend* seems to be on the decline among their female counterparts. Instead, college women often say "the guy I'm dating" or, less often, "a man I'm seeing" (which may imply that he's somewhat older than the woman). Homosexual couples face the naming problem as well, if not to a more difficult degree. Most often they refer to one another as *partners,* a term that some heterosexual couples have co-opted, because it communicates the sense of equality and cooperativeness inherent in a partnership. Older adults especially cringe when they refer to a romantic involvement, given the choices of descriptors available to them: juvenile terms (as in *boyfriend* and *girlfriend*), ambiguous and nondescript terms (e.g., *my friend*), terms that are just too personal (*lovers*), or clinical, psycho-babble terms (as in *significant other,* a term widely used in the 1970s).

Occasionally, people stumble in introductions, saying such things as "I'd like you to meet my . . . uh. . . ." Sadly enough, the English language hasn't progressed much past calling these relationships "uh." (The best option in an introduction situation like this is to simply introduce the person by her or his name, leaving out the "my.") For the purposes of this chapter, the term *relational partner* is used to refer to members of romantic relationships and *marital partner* or *spouse* to refer to married partners. *Relational partner* may sound a bit clinical, but not as clinical as *significant other*. We use the term *romantic relationship* to include the range of relationships from dating relationships to longer-term, committed relationships (when the term *dating* doesn't seem to fit), and nonmarital relationships that include sexual activity. (We don't mean to insinuate that marital relationships are somehow not romantic; we're just trying to be clear.) On occasion, we use the term *monogamous relationship,* in reference to a romantic relationship in which the partners date only each other.

The Pressure to Partner

Psychologists Hendrick and Hendrick (2000), in their extensive review of romantic love, make the point that romantic love in our culture has become the overwhelming reason for people entering into long-term relationships, such as marriage or homosexual partnerings. Love, as a reason for partnering, is a relatively recent occurrence in our culture. In the early twentieth century in American history, economic and social reasons were more important than love in choosing a mate. In many parts of the world, love and romance are not significant parts of marriage; business opportunities, the furtherance of family, and tradition override love as motivations for marrying.

Many people still feel a great deal of pressure to partner or couple, as though they can't be taken seriously or haven't really arrived until they're in a committed, monogamous relationship. Even in the twenty-first century, women generally feel more pressure to marry than men, and they report a willingness to make more sacrifices in order to marry (Blakemore, Lawton, & Vartanian, 2003). Traditionally aged college students probably don't experience much of this pressure while completing their education; in fact, students say that they feel pressure in the opposite direction—they feel pressure, primarily from peers, to stay single and "play the field." If they do involve themselves in a monogamous relationship, they may actually take heat or teasing from their friends, and may even feel pressure to cheat or end the relationship and begin dating lots of people again. However, students report that they do feel increasing pressure to find the "right" person and commit to a romantic relationship the closer they get to graduation. They begin to hear well-meaning voices, like from family members, asking when they're going to get a job and settle down. If you stay single through graduation and beyond, you may really feel the pressure when you're in a career-type job, because you may not be looked upon as being as stable or as reliable a bet for the future as a married colleague. While gay and lesbian couples experience both the stereotype and the reality of pressure to play the field, the people who tend to receive the most respect and envy among members of gay and lesbian communities are those in committed, monogamous relationships (Isay, 2006).

The pressure to couple is embodied in the often-asked question, "So how come you're still single?" This attitude is hard on singles. Couples sometimes become so self-involved that they tend to forget or gravitate away from their single friends, perceiving that they'll have less in common. Some married women see single women as potential threats. Some single men may find their sexual orientation questioned, especially if they have male roommates.

Hot Button Issue

"Dating versus Frugaling"

Ever heard of the term "frugaling," as applies to an activity just short of dating but more romantic than being friends? (We hadn't either, until we stumbled on it while reading a book about college students' romantic relationships.) Donna Freitas (2010) is the author of *Sex and the Soul: Juggling Sexuality, Spirituality, Romance, and Religion on America's College Campuses.* She focuses on college students' views of sexuality and spirituality and how such views affect their formation of relationships. She conducted research primarily at evangelical Christian colleges in the United States, which is where she discovered frugaling. Freitas explains:

> Frugaling is not dating, but it's not *not* dating either. It's something in between: a boy and girl start hanging out together all the time; they are seen talking in public, just the 2 of them, regularly, but the man never declares anything. There is no DTR (determine-the-relationship) conversation. There are no PDAs (public displays of affection). There is no private intimacy either. But *everybody knows* when people are frugaling. (pp. 115–116)

The term seems to be derived from another form of frugaling, which involves thrift shopping. Think about it: Spending time together that's not officially a date is much cheaper than dating!

In conservative evangelical schools, the pressure for female students to have an engagement ring on their fingers as they near graduation is enormous, thus it affects their dating choices and behaviors (and the male students know this as well). The further along one progresses in college studies, the more intense the question becomes of whether a date can become a mate. So to avoid the mating pressure, many male students prefer frugaling over dating because the "what are we" discussions don't come up. The relationship definition stays fuzzy, that is, until one or both partners become dissatisfied or desire to move the frugaling relationship into something that implies more commitment.

Frugaling makes us ask, What year are we living in? We realize that this mostly pertains to conservative Christian schools, where students may be more inclined to partner differently than at secular universities. But from another view, this harkens back to an earlier age when the prevailing view was that all women went to college for was to get their "Mrs." degree, meaning to meet a good man to marry. What's your view? Have you experienced frugaling, but didn't know what to call it? Do you feel pressure to have some sort of committed romantic relationship established before or as you graduate with your degree? Or is that the *last* thing you're worried about or want?

Stereotypical Notions of Romance

Social psychologist Caryl Avery (1989) states that "Given one wish in life, most people would wish to be loved—to be able to reveal themselves entirely to another human being and be embraced, caressed, by that acceptance" (p. 27). The strength, depth, and pervasiveness of this wish causes our culture to be highly romantic.

As with other aspects of gender communication, women and men tend to approach romance from different points of view, dating back to early influences on their notions of

Net Notes

The number of Internet dating sites has expanded dramatically in recent years; many more people turn to online dating sites than in years past—still with mixed results. So many sites exist, with new ones springing up all the time, that we can't cover them all here. Dating sites have also become more specific, meaning that if you're Jewish, you could check out **jdate.com** or **jmatch.com**. Christian singles can go to **christianmingle.com**, a site that offers shortcuts to finding other Christians, rather than using a subset of a larger site like **match.com**. The site **girldates.com** is one of many online dating services for lesbians, and for longer-term gay relationships, gay men can use the services of **mypartner.com**.

Chances are now that you, one of your friends, family members, or coworkers have checked out Internet dating. Maybe you haven't tried this approach yet, but are contemplating such a move. If so, Erin J. Shea (2009), a contributor to Oprah Winfrey's website (**www.oprah.com**), offers Tips for Successful Online Dating, which we suggest you read if you've not tried online dating before, or if you've tried it but need to brush up on your skills.

Joe Tracy (2011), publisher of Online Dating Magazine (**www.onlinedatingmagazine.com**), rates the top five best dating sites for heterosexuals. Topping the list is **match.com**, followed by **chemistry.com**, **perfectmatch.com**, **eharmony.com**, and **spark.com**. Tracy offers a chart that helps online daters compare these sites, including entries for main features of each site, number of singles who participate, overall quality rating of one to five stars, and consumer reviews.

what romance is supposed to be. Children gain stereotypical notions about romance very early through viewing movies and hearing or reading stories of princes and princesses.

For many women, the romance novel contains the stereotypical cultural script. These novels follow a predictable formula of "woman meets a (perfect) stranger, thinks he's a rogue but wants him anyway, runs into conflicts that keep them apart, and ends up happily in his arms forever" (Brown, as in Crawford & Unger, 2000, p. 279). The man is usually cold, rejecting, even brutal at the beginning, but through the woman's love, we learn that his cold demeanor hides his true emotions and character. While the culture is changing slowly, these images still predominate. They tend to lead men to focus on sex and women to focus on being swept away in a romantic rush. Clearly, neither focus is very accurate, yet these romantic images remain a powerful force.

By the time you're an adult, you've seen and read countless stories of passionate, engulfing, magical love between, typically, very attractive people. These images and legends that you grew up with may have formed powerful, albeit unrealistic models for romantic relationships. Such images lead our culture to assert pressure on finding, winning, and keeping a desirable partner. It's particularly challenging for gays and lesbians who have grown up with, if not exclusively then primarily, images of heterosexual romance. Homosexual, bisexual, and transgender people often grow up without role models, in life and in media, of romantic couplings, with the result being that the learning curve is greater for establishing and maintaining romantic relationships than what heterosexuals typically experience. No matter one's sexual orientation, the contrast between the myth and the reality of romantic relationships can lead to a high degree of frustration, disillusionment, and even violence (Arliss, 2001).

Significant Other: Term that emerged in the 1970s to describe a relational partner

Relational Partner: Preferred term for someone involved in a romantic, nonmarried relationship

Romantic Relationship: Nonmarital relationship that may range from dating to a more long-term, committed relationship, which may or may not include sexual activity

Monogamous Relationship: Romantic relationship in which the partners only date one another and not others; may also imply a sexual relationship in which partners are only involved sexually with each other

Tensions within Romantic Relationships

In comparison to friendships, romantic relationships engender a different set of issues, perhaps more aptly described as *tensions* within a relationship. By *relationship tensions*, we don't mean to imply the negative connotation you might normally associate with the term. Romantic relationship tensions arise from the decision making a couple faces in developing and defining their relationship, not necessarily because of the individuals in the relationship (Baxter, 2010; Baxter & Erbert, 2000; Baxter & Montgomery, 1996, 2000; DeGreef, 2008; Metts, 2006; Pawlowski, 1999; Turner & West, 2011). These tensions are usually framed in questions related to "Should I (we) do this or that?" and "Should our relationship be this or that?" These tensions are not unique to romantic relationships, but they seem to intensify in a romantic context.

Communication researchers Baxter and Montgomery (2000) make the point that relationships aren't static but dynamic; relationships involve contradiction, change, and interdependence. Recognizing the presence and shifting nature of these relationship tensions, partners may talk about them, thus making resolution easier, or partners may decide that they just aren't suited for each other. The earlier couples talk about these issues, the sooner they can make a wise decision. Let's discuss some relational tensions in more detail.

AUTONOMY VERSUS CONNECTION   Philosopher Robert Nozick (1993) believes that a defining characteristic of love is the declaration of *we;* he states that the primary feature of *we* is the close *connection* of one person's well-being with that of another person. The connection has its trade-off; it comes with limits on *autonomy*. Gender scholar Letitia Peplau (1994) describes autonomy as the extent to which a person values individual pursuits apart from an intimate relationship. This particular tension arises when relational partners feel a contradictory and simultaneous need to be connected, and yet to remain independent individuals (Baxter & Montgomery, 1996, 2000; Sahlstein & Dun, 2008). The amount of autonomy partners desire within a relationship varies widely; thus, autonomy is one of the most difficult issues to confront within a relationship.

In the early stages of romance, the tendency is to spend as much time together as possible. This creates a sense that your life together almost operates in a vacuum, sheltered from the outside world. Have you ever experienced this kind of immersion in a relationship? A major event could have happened and you wouldn't know it, nor would you particularly care. After a period like this, the rest of life usually intrudes and begins to whittle time away from the people in the relationship. It is at this point that a couple may first experience the tension created by autonomy versus connection.

If this hasn't happened to you, you probably have friends who, when they first start dating or hanging out, spent every waking (and perhaps, nonwaking) moment together, so enthralled by that rush of getting to know a new person. Those first feelings of love, excitement, or sexual attraction are intoxicating, so the emotional connectedness two people feel solidifies their relationship. But then, as the saying goes, when the "dew is off the rose" and the excitement subsides or changes, the relationship encounters a point of transition. How do couples manage the transition from constant togetherness that often typifies the beginning stages of romantic relationships to a more balanced blend of togetherness and separation? How can partners enjoy a necessary autonomy while avoiding the possible hurt or rejection the other person might feel when the first clues of separateness arise?

It probably won't surprise you to learn that cell phone usage—both talking and texting—is having an impact on the autonomy–connection tension (Duran, Kelly, & Rotaru, 2011). It probably *will* surprise you to learn that cell phone use between relational partners can be a source of conflict, meaning it doesn't mediate this particular tension; it can make it worse. Research shows that mobile phones are more often used by people who already know each other than people making a first contact, so relational partners rely considerably on this form of communication as they coordinate time together and keep each other informed of what they're doing (Igarashi, Takai, & Yoshida, 2005). But conflict can arise as to *how* (calling versus texting) and *how often* partners use their phones, meaning who calls who and how often, who texts who, how quickly one partner responds to the other's texts, what a nonresponse might mean (time spent with someone else?), and so forth. Some partners experience conflict as a result, but few set ground rules on cell phone usage (Duran et al., 2011).

Back to your friends (or your own relationship): What happened when one person in the relationship planned a night away from the partner, like a night out with the guys or girls, or just announced or requested some time alone? Like we said, because each partner in a relationship may have her or his own sense of timing for such transitions, it can be awkward when one wants togetherness and one wants separation. Will it surprise you to learn that we recommend *communication* to assist with this situation?

Although it doesn't always prevent this tension from arising and causing difficulty in a relationship, this is one topic that couples should discuss (preferably face to face, not through a text message), without fear that such a discussion will wreck the romance or seem nerdy. Time spent together versus apart is a negotiation; relational partners can benefit from an honest, open, nondefensive conversation about how they want to choose to spend their time. Talking about this tension won't necessarily ensure a perfect balance or prevent the problem from arising again, but it will allow partners to know each other better and open the door for discussion.

And here's another thing to remember: Moving through various stages of a relationship is progress! Relationships tend not to stay in the "honeymoon" period; they need to grow and change, so movement through different phases should be seen as steps forward, rather than stagnation, retreat, or relational doom.

The notion that women are more likely to have problems with men's assertion of autonomy in heterosexual romantic relationships than the reverse may be more a myth than a reality. As more women pursue career goals, as they continue to explore the range of options open to them, and as they enjoy the fulfilling companionship of friendships with other women, their dependence on men and the significance they attach to relationships with men have decreased (Tichenor, 2005; A woman's nation changes everything, 2009). This doesn't mean romantic relationships aren't as important to women as they once were; it simply means there is more competition for women's attention now than in the past, as well as less emphasis on "getting and keeping a man" as a way to achieve happiness. More structures in society exist today than in the past to support women's autonomy in relationships.

POWER VERSUS EMPOWERMENT   Another source of tension that can become a factor in romantic relationships is the pattern of control or *power*. For many couples, this boils down to decision making, ranging from the simplest of things to the future of the relationship. At the root of decision making is a measure of power, control, or influence over another person.

For many people the drive for power and the will to love represent opposite poles of human existence and are great sources of human conflict.

—Anonymous

Traditional stereotypes suggest that men hold more power than women in heterosexual relationships, because of men's generally higher status in society and greater income (Kalbfleisch & Herold, 2006). To many people, financial success confers greater power and more potential to exert influence. Thus, in many couplings—particularly in marriages or cohabiting relationships in which finances are shared—the stereotype rings true and the breadwinner, typically the man, may control more of the decision making. However, in committed relationships financial accomplishment is not as much of a basis for power or control as it once was. In many modern heterosexual relationships, the person who manages the household, in terms of caring for children, handling food purchases and preparation, paying the bills, and generally keeping the household running smoothly, is the woman. She may be seen as the powerful person in the couple, because without her efforts the household and the structure of the family might fall apart (Boushey, 2009; O'Leary & Kornbluh, 2009).

In keeping with the values we described in Chapter 1, we believe that a pattern of equality of control in a relationship, particularly a committed relationship, is the most effective for both people. This type of coupling has been termed *egalitarian,* in that partners have equal power and authority and share responsibilities equally, without regard for gender roles, income levels, job demands, and so forth (Crawford & Unger, 2004; Guerrero, Andersen, & Afifi, 2001). Egalitarian relationships are characterized by *empowerment*— power *to* rather than power *over*—which involves a shared approach that capitalizes on the strengths of each relational partner (Amichai-Hamburger, McKenna, & Tal, 2008; Gill & Ganesh, 2007; Green, 2008). Interpersonal communication scholars Guerrero, Andersen, and Afifi (2001) describe egalitarian marriages as "deep and true friendships, as well as romances" and as more intimate and committed than traditional marriages (p. 309). In virtually all committed relationships, shared decision making is a benefit.

ACCEPTANCE VERSUS CHANGE   One unfortunate belief that often exists in romantic relationships is, "I can change this person. I know she or he has faults, but I can fix those faults." This is such a part of relational folklore that, even though your friends will warn you that you can't change a person, deep down inside you might be saying,

"I'll be the exception; I'll be the one to do it." Family communication experts Galvin and Bylund (2001) describe this phenomenon in relation to the early stages of marriage: "Newlywed couples frequently make allowances for behavior that isn't quite acceptable because spouses focus on what they are getting, and differences seem enhancing. Later, differences become annoying and call out for resolution" (p. 141). It may be a stereotype, but it's safe to say that more heterosexual women declare that they will change their men than the reverse. You rarely overhear two men talking about a relationship when one friend says, "My honey has her faults, but over time, I can change them."

How do you feel when you know another person wants to change you or change the relationship? The tendency is to resist the person's attempt or to view it as a power play designed to exert control over you. Consider an example: Anthony and Arthur were in the middle of the powerful, exhilarating emotions that exist early on in a romantic relationship. But the intense romantic feelings subsided a bit for Arthur before they did for Anthony. He didn't care for Anthony any less, but he wasn't as caught up in the emotional rush as he once was. Anthony was really bothered by this subtle change in Arthur; he tried several ways to restore the initial level of feeling. Arthur neither wanted nor was able to change his feelings. The more Anthony pushed to get things back to the way they were, the more Arthur resisted and began to resent Anthony's pressure. It wasn't until Anthony stopped putting on the pressure and relaxed enough to accept the change in Arthur that Arthur regained some of his positive feelings about the relationship. They didn't return to the early phase, but the relationship attained a new degree of closeness.

The importance of acceptance in a romantic relationship can hardly be overemphasized. It's a great feeling to have complete confidence in another person, and it's quite disconcerting when your belief in another person is lacking. Humanistic psychologist Carl Rogers (1970) based much of his highly successful client-centered counseling strategies on what he called "unconditional positive regard." In describing how human beings change, Rogers pointed out the paradox that real change in people seems to be possible only when a person feels completely secure and accepted in a relationship.

COMPARABLE VIEWS OF INTIMACY   In Chapter 5, we explored varying definitions of and perspectives on intimacy, but one thing most people can agree on is that intimacy—however you define it—is the goal of almost all committed romantic relationships (Andersen, Guerrero, & Jones, 2006; Beck, 2006, 2007; Burleson, 2003; Jarvis, 2009; Metts, 2006; Sanderson, Keiter, Miles, & Yopyk, 2007). Research shows that women and men often have differing views of what intimacy is and how much intimacy is desirable in a relationship (Fisher, 2009; Harvey & Weber, 2002). In fact, one partner may view a relationship as highly intimate but the other partner does not; at the root of this common problem may be a difference in the basic perception of what intimacy is (Cross, Bacon, & Morris, 2000; Gore, Cross, & Morris, 2006; Laurenceau, Barrett, & Rovine, 2005; Reis, Clark, & Holmes, 2004).

One source of basic misunderstanding arises when one partner equates intimacy with physical or sexual closeness, whereas the other believes intimacy also involves shared feelings, thoughts, and experiences (Motley, 2008a, 2008b). Research over a few decades consistently shows that women and men, whether in opposite-sex or same-sex relationships, tend to have differing views of the role of sexual activity and emotional involvement in judgments of intimacy. Women more closely link emotions with sexual activity in their perceptions of how intimate their relationships are (Bailey, Gaulin, Agyei, & Gladue, 1994; Christopher & Cate, 1984; Hill, 2002; O'Sullivan & Gaines, 1998).

To achieve an increased level of relational satisfaction, common definitions of intimacy are critical (Gottman, Katz, & Hooven, 1997). One way to agree on what constitutes intimacy is to use what communication scholars call "relational currencies"—agreed-upon ways of conveying affection, information, caring, and other relational variables (Galvin & Brommel, 1991; Wilkinson & Grill, 2011). The key is the mutual definition of the currency, because through this mutual definition couples become able to be more empathic with each other, which leads to greater clarity and shared expression of emotion in the relationship.

EXPRESSIONS OF LOVE   One of the clearest expressions of a desire to move a relationship to a more intimate level is saying the words "I love you." These words can bring a reaction of intense pleasure or of nervous questioning like, "What do you mean by that?" A consistent theme throughout this text is the need to verbalize intentions, desires, and goals with your relational partner, including the expression of love.

The statement "I love you" has many different meanings. Back in the 1950s, a communication researcher penned this truly memorable description of the range of meanings for the phrase:

Brevity may be the soul of wit, but not when someone's saying "I love you." When someone's saying "I love you," he always ought to give a lot of details. Favorable comparisons with all the other women he ever loved are also welcome. And even though he insists it would take forever to count the ways in which he loves you, let him start counting.

—Judith Viorst,
television writer

Sometimes it means: I desire you or I want you sexually. It may mean: I hope you love me or I hope that I will be able to love you. Often it means: It may be that a love relationship can develop between us or even I hate you. Often it is a wish for emotional exchange: I want your admiration in exchange for mine or I give my love in exchange for some passion or I want to feel cozy and at home with you or I admire some of your qualities. A declaration of love is mostly a request: I desire you or I want you to gratify me, or I want your protection or I want to be intimate with you or I want to exploit your loveliness. "I love you"—wish, desire, submission, conquest; it is never the word itself that tells the real meaning here. (Meerloo, 1952, pp. 83–84)

In heterosexual relationships, who is more likely to express love and under what circumstances? Contrary to romance novels, movies, and stereotypes, which tend to cast women as the first to say "I love you," research has shown otherwise (Brantley, Knox, & Zusman, 2002; Brehm, 2001; Metts, 2006). Communication scholar William Owen (1987) found that men more often initiated a declaration of love, a critical communication event in a romantic relationship. Owen offered the following four reasons for this tendency:

1. It is a way to coerce commitment from women.
2. Men are less able than women to withhold their expressions of love when they feel love.
3. Women are more capable of discriminating between love and related emotions.
4. Women wait until they hear the phrase from men because they often play a reactive rather than active (or proactive) role in a romantic relationship.

Subsequent research supports Owen's findings (Booth-Butterfield & Trotta, 1994). The stereotype that men in romantic relationships don't say "I love you" is still evident. Some men believe that actions speak louder than words ("I'm here, aren't I? I don't need to tell you that I love you."). Research, however, indicates that actually saying the words is a predictor of a positive relational future. Communication scholars Dainton, Stafford, and Canary (1994) found that saying "I love you" was among a group of activities positively associated with predicting long-term love, including assuring the other person of feelings, keeping a positive outlook, and practicing maintenance strategies such as being patient and forgiving, being cooperative during disagreements, and avoiding criticism.

If you've ever been (or are currently) in a heterosexual romantic relationship that involves love, who said the three words first—the woman or the man? Another difficult issue in all relationships concerns whether you'll hear "I love you, too" in response to a declaration of love. Not having the sentiment reciprocated may signal an imbalance of emotion or level of commitment in a relationship, which may in turn signal troubled waters.

MAKING A COMMITMENT   *Commitment* involves the decision to stay in a relationship, but it also implies a coordinated view of the future of the relationship. In many ways, being in a relationship is largely a coordination problem—a meshing of the language, gestures, and habits of daily life, primarily through attentiveness, courtesy, and a mutual desire to make the relationship work.

Commitment also represents a level of seriousness about one's relational partner (Harvey & Weber, 2002). It indicates a deeper level of regard and intimacy in a relationship. What are some factors related to the decision to commit? Sometimes a trial or crisis causes people to make the decision to commit to each other. Here's a real-life example (with altered names) taken from some friends' experience. Fred and Jacquie had been going together for about three years and were considering marriage when Fred met another woman and had a brief affair with her. This affair wasn't just about sex; it involved strong emotions. Because of Fred's feelings for Jacquie, he told her about his affair. As you might well imagine, this event precipitated a crisis in Jacquie and Fred's relationship. After hours of very emotional discussion, Fred and Jacquie decided they wanted to stay together. Fred felt that if he wasn't going to leave Jacquie for this other woman, he wasn't going to leave her for anyone. Jacquie couldn't imagine a more stressful crisis and decided that if they could get through this one, they could get through anything. The crisis resulted in a renewed commitment to each other.

Achieving a matched or equal level of commitment within romantic relationships appears to be related to how well couples handle *turning points*—critical moments in the life of a relationship that alter the relationship in some way (Baxter & Pittman, 2001; Graham, 1997; Mongeau, Serewicz, Henningsen, & Davis, 2006). Communication researchers Bullis, Clark, and Sline (1993) analyzed seventeen different factors related to various turning points in relationship development; one factor examined was *relational talk,* or conversation about the relationship itself. They found that more mature relationships with greater levels of commitment involved a higher amount of relational talk, which was used as a means of handling the turning points. Relational talk and commitment seemed to feed off each other; positive relational talk increased commitment, which increased positive relational talk, and so on. Again, relationships that follow a more equitable model more easily benefit from these conversations

(Crawford, Feng, Fischer, & Diana, 2003). In most situations and relationships, talking about the relationship actually does make it better. Particularly in the context of romance, where emotions and self-esteem issues are heightened, couples need to hold periodic conversations about the quality of their relationship, because these conversations clear the air and reinforce commitment (Sillars, Shellen, McIntosh, & Pomegranate, 1997).

The long-standing stereotype about commitment in heterosexual relationships suggests that women are more willing to commit than men. Do you think the stereotype holds true in relationships today? Are men just as likely as women to desire a committed relationship and work to maintain one? A social psychologist in the 1980s termed the general condition of being unable to commit *commitmentphobia*, which she defined as "a social disease characterized by fear of the opposite sex, inability to establish a long-term intimate relationship, and unsatisfying sexual encounters and loneliness" (Schnall, 1981, p. 37). Schnall contends that commitmentphobia was "first noticed among men in the 1970s," but has "spread to the female population" (p. 37).

The tension surrounding commitment is similar to what we described in our discussion of autonomy versus connection: More options mean greater flexibility and more complex decision making (Galvin & Bylund, 2001). Some of you reading this text for a gender class may be nontraditional students who married at a young age and are now returning to college to start or complete a degree at a later point in life. It used to be more common to marry in one's teens or twenties. College-educated men and women frequently married in the last year of college or upon graduation. Indeed, only a few decades ago, it was quite common for couples to marry upon graduation from high school. For many people, getting married around age eighteen is unthinkable today. Granted, teenagers still marry, but with nowhere near the frequency of past generations.

Talking about Communication, or Communicating about Talking

Research shows overwhelmingly that highly satisfied couples engage in significantly more communication than do less satisfied couples (Burleson & Denton, 1997; Richmond, 1995; Teichner & Farnden-Lyster, 1997). Every relationship develops its own communication patterns, even in the management of conflict (Driver, Tabares, Shapiro, Nahm, & Gottman, 2003; Koesten, 2004; Waite Miller, 2011). These patterns help lend predictability to a situation, and the predictability breeds security in the relationship (Bruess & Pearson, 1997). At times, the patterns change due to circumstances outside of the couple's relationship. The arrival of a child, change in employment, a move to a new city, and other changes will have a clear (and sometimes negative) impact on the communication patterns in a relationship (Sinclair & McCluskey, 1996). According to Galvin and Bylund (2001), communication patterns are especially critical in first marriages, because the patterns of each spouse's family of origin will be incorporated into the new marriage (sometimes causing conflict), spouses' interaction patterns reflect sex differences, and these patterns will change over developmental stages of a family, as affected by peers and culture. Most of the time, communication patterns evolve on their own, influenced by societal rules and norms and by the individuals' needs and desires. For the most part, people in relationships don't sit down together and say, "Let's work out our patterns of communication." You may have noticed, however, that we have advocated exactly that in more than one place in this text.

Bizarro © 2006 Dan Piraro/King Features Syndicate.

It's important to *talk about talking;* in communication research, the term for this activity is *metacommunication.* Various marriage researchers and therapists have researched the value of this type of conversation in marriage enrichment groups and have found significant increases in marital satisfaction for couples who talked openly about the communication patterns in their relationships (Bodermann, 1997; Hickmon, Protinsky, & Singh, 1997; Worthington, McCullough, Shortz, & Mindes, 1995). It takes courage to sit down and carefully examine the communication patterns of your relationship, especially if the patterns engender defensiveness or are ineffective (Becker, Ellevold, & Stamp, 2008).

A discussion about the kinds of communication that work well and are supportive in a relationship is critical, yet many couples avoid this kind of conversation until a disagreement or major conflict arises (Wilmot & Hocker, 2010). Some don't even talk about their communication tendencies and patterns in the event of a conflict. It's easier to just let the event play out and hope that things fix themselves or get back to normal. But many times this can breed resentment, as partners simply bury their feelings and "go along to get along," and the resentment builds.

The most obvious communication behavior to discuss is how each partner approaches and deals with conflict, which we deal with more specifically in the next section of this chapter, but other aspects of couple communication need to be discussed. For instance, married or cohabiting couples often experience tension when they are reunited at the end of the workday. Whether both persons or just one work outside the home, the period of time when partners see each other after hours apart can create tension. Typically, the tension arises when one or the other partner arrives home last, has had a tough or long day, and simply wants some time to herself or himself and some peace and quiet before starting the evening's activities. The other person wants to jump right into conversation, because she or he has had some time to decompress from the day. Rather than having a fight and hurting feelings over something like this, the better strategy is to discuss it, preferably before a potential conflict arises or as a result of the first conflict over this situation.

The stereotype is that women are typically the ones in heterosexual romantic partnerings to raise the issue of communication, to stage the discussion about communication preferences and patterns. This is related to the view that women, more often than men, take the "temperature" of a relationship, meaning that women are more likely to raise relationship issues and to ask their partners or husbands "How do you think we're doing?" However, research shows that this is more than a stereotype (Canary &

Wahba, 2006; Messman & Mikesell, 2000). Earlier we talked about power distribution in relationships and suggested that egalitarian relationships have advantages. Research suggests that relational partners of this type of relationship report greater use of maintenance conversations and behaviors (Canary & Stafford, 1992; Stafford, 2003;Vogel-Bauer, Kalbfleisch, & Beatty, 1999).

In Chapter 4, we discussed the relational and content approaches to communication. Given research that shows that women tend to approach communication in order to connect and establish or strengthen the relationship and that men tend to approach communication for the purposes of exchanging information, one can see this trend in evidence in the typical patterns within romantic relationships (Beebe, Beebe, & Ivy, 2013). Granted, there certainly are exceptions, but the tendency to "let things blow over" or avoid talking about talking isn't advisable, and it shouldn't be only up to women in heterosexual romantic relationships to seek opportunities to discuss the relationship and the communication within it.

Conflict: The Inevitable in a Relationship

Why do we say that conflict is inevitable in a relationship? We've simply never witnessed a healthy relationship free from conflict; in fact, a relationship may achieve its apparent health because partners cope with conflict in an effective way. Interpersonal scholar David Johnson (2000) compares conflicts to natural storms:

> Interpersonal storms are a natural and unavoidable aspect of life that vary in intensity from mild to severe. . . . When individuals work together to achieve shared goals, participate in a division of labor, have complementary roles, and depend on each other's resources, storms will arise. Two people in a relationship are interdependent. What each does influences what the other does. But at the same time, each person has different perspectives, goals, and needs. The combination of interdependence and differing perspectives makes it impossible for a relationship to be free from conflict. (pp. 249–250)

Conflict arises when two people cannot agree on a way to meet their needs (Beebe, Beebe, & Ivy, 2013; Wilmot & Hocker, 2010). Conflict may also arise when a transgression (breaking the spoken or unspoken rules of the relationship) is committed (Emmers-Sommer, 2003; Kelley, 2011). Needs may simply be incompatible or too few resources may exist to satisfy the needs; however, often conflict arises or intensifies because relational partners compete rather than cooperate to resolve the difference. And the more important the relationship, the greater the potential for conflict because more is at stake. To put this another way, we're less likely to disagree with people who don't matter much to us. Conflict with people who matter a great deal to us is to be expected, but it's extremely important that the conflict be handled in an effective way because of the potential to damage the relationship, as well as the potential for real growth to emerge (Avtgis & Rancer, 2010; Canary & Lakey, 2011; Segrin, Hanzal, & Domschke, 2009). The ability to discover negative conflict patterns in a relationship and to change them toward more positive ones is critical to long-term relationship success (Driver et al., 2003; Hocker & Wilmot, 2011; Stone, Patton, & Heen, 2011).

Are there sex differences in approaches to conflict? Studies are mixed on this issue. Research has shown that men and masculine people are more likely to avoid conflict than women and feminine people; when conflict can't be avoided, men are more likely to resort to competitive, unilateral (one-sided) conflict resolution strategies (Stafford, Dutton, & Haas, 2000). Women tend not to be as comfortable as men in negotiating to resolve a conflict, preferring to defer or compromise (Babcock & Laschever, 2003; Jones & Brinkert, 2008). Communication scholars Taylor and Miller (1994) believe: "Girls are socialized to value relationships and maintain harmony while boys are socialized to value status and seek victory. This is thought to translate into women taking a cooperative stance in conflict situations, whereas men are more competitive" (p. 155). However, other researchers contend that women and men do not approach and handle conflict differently, especially within marital relationships (Burggraf & Sillars, 1987; Fitzpatrick, 1988; Keashly, 1994). Across a variety of studies, male and female subjects preferred to handle conflict through the following strategies, in descending order: accommodation, avoidance, compromise, collaboration, and, least of all, competition.

Research has identified one very interesting conflict pattern in particular—the *demand–withdraw pattern* (Julien, Arellano, & Turgeon, 1997; Klinetob & Smith, 1996; Littlejohn & Domenici, 2007). This pattern involves one partner trying to discuss a problem, criticizing and blaming the other partner for the problem, and asking for or demanding a change. The other partner tries to avoid the discussion, becomes defensive against the criticism and blame, and eventually withdraws from the conflict altogether (Anderson, Umberson, & Elliott, 2004; Berns, Jacobson, & Gottman, 1999; Kelly, Fincham, & Beach, 2003). In most research on this pattern in heterosexual relationships, men are more likely to avoid conflict and women more likely to approach it. Marriage scholars Klinetob and Smith (1996) point out that "the spouse with the most to gain by maintaining the status quo is likely to withdraw, and the discontented spouse demands change. Insofar as the status quo in marriage generally tends to favor men, men will appear most frequently as withdrawers" (p. 954). Breaking out of such a negative pattern is quite difficult, especially if the status quo works well for the dominant person.

Ending a Relationship

Not all relationships can be salvaged. We realize a discussion of ending relationships can be depressing, but you're probably realistic and experienced enough to know that not all relationships make it. Although we may enter a romantic relationship with a vision of forever and ever in mind, relationships often don't work out as we first imagine. Thus it's wise to consider some effective communication strategies for ending romantic relationships.

WHO DOES THE BREAKING UP?   Breakups can cause stress and anguish for both persons involved—and that may be the understatement of the year! Who is more likely to end a heterosexual romantic relationship? The stereotype suggests that women are more interested in relationships and, thus, suffer more than men when a relationship ends; however, that stereotype is not supported by research. Research shows that men more often

> *Why do we suffer so? Why can't we just skip on with life and instantly forget the devil who has abandoned us? Because loving is the most important thing we do.*
>
> —*Helen Fisher, relationship expert, author, and anthropology professor*

Remember . . .

Relationship Tensions: Issues that arise within romantic relationships that need negotiation

Autonomy: Need for independence and time alone from one's partner

Connection: Need for affiliation and association with one's romantic partner, which often involves time spent together

Power: Power *over*, instead of power *to*, in which one partner exerts control or influence over the other

Egalitarian Relationship: Romantic relationship or marriage in which partners have equal power and authority and share responsibilities equally, without regard for sex roles, income levels, job demands, and so on

Empowerment: Power *to,* versus power *over;* mutual control or shared influence within a relationship

Commitment: Decision to stay in a relationship; a level of seriousness about one's partner

Turning Points: Critical moments in the life of a relationship that alter the relationship in some way

Relational Talk: Conversation between relational partners about the relationship itself

Commitmentphobia: Fear of long-term, intimate relationships

Metacommunication: Talking about communication; having a conversation about how one communicates, one's preferences in communicating and being communicated to, how communication functions, and so on

Conflict: Communication that arises when people cannot agree on a way to meet their needs

Demand–Withdraw Pattern: Relational conflict pattern in which one partner raises a problem, criticizes and blames the other partner for the problem, and asks for or demands a change; the other partner tries to avoid the discussion, becomes defensive against the criticism and blame, and eventually withdraws from the conflict

initiate relationships while women more often terminate them (Cullington, 2008; Davis, Shaver, & Vernon, 2003; Metts, 2006). Findings also indicate that women tend to foresee a breakup sooner than men, but men tend to be more deeply affected by relationship strain and termination, sometimes with serious consequences to their physical and mental health, as well as their self-concept or basic view of self (Koenig Kellas & Manusov, 2003; Simon & Barrett, 2010; Slotter, Gardner, & Finkel, 2010; Sutherland, 2010). Feminist psychologists Crawford and Unger (2004) suggest that men fall in love more readily than women; feel more depressed, lonely, and unhappy after a breakup; and are less likely to initiate a breakup than their female partners.

Perhaps the stereotype relates more to the difference in the ways men and women express themselves regarding relationships than to an actual value placed on relationships in general. As we discussed in our chapter on friendship, women usually deal with things and make sense of their world via talk. Men typically deal with things by distracting themselves with activities or by withdrawing and isolating themselves until the situation is resolved. When men do choose to talk out a relational issue such as a breakup, the conversation is typically not as long, in depth, detailed, and emotionally displayed as a woman's conversation on the subject.

Obviously, how you weather the end of a relationship depends on many factors, such as the nature of the relationship (e.g., long-term or serious versus a casual, short-term connection); your past experience with breakups (having experienced so many that it's no big deal or so few that it feels more devastating); your personality, upbringing, and culture; how the breakup was handled; and so forth. Let's explore that "how the breakup was handled" aspect in a bit more depth.

COMMUNICATING TO END A RELATIONSHIP   You may be wondering whether there is one personally effective way to end a romantic relationship. Romantic relationships are so situation- and person-specific that proposing an optimum termination strategy would be unwise. However, as we've said time and again, to communicate is better than not to communicate.

One study examined college students' preferred medium (delivery method) when breaking up with someone (Levine & Fitzpatrick, 2005). Of the different delivery methods students reported using, 43 percent of breakups were accomplished through a face-to-face conversation, followed by phone calls (32%), Instant Messages (10%), e-mail messages (8%), voice mail messages (3%), written letters (2%), and using a third party, like a friend, to deliver the bad news (2%). About a third of students said that they'd used two methods in combination to get the message across, whereas some students reported using up to six different mediums to deliver their bad news. (Talk about a barrage!) Surprisingly, students didn't report breaking up via text message, but some of our students have revealed that they've been broken up with via text, which made them angrier and more upset than if they'd been told to their face. Those who've gotten the "Dear John text" from someone say that the method is so rude and "chicken" that they'd never use that approach to break up with someone.

What's interesting, as well as surprising, is that the predominant breakup medium of students in this research was the good old-fashioned face-to-face conversation. With all the available technology existing to make communication faster and, many would argue, less personal, you'd think that people would rely mostly on mediated methods like texting, e-mailing and IM-ing to break up. But this study shows that students are still choosing to use their interpersonal communication skills to end a relationship, which is encouraging.

Writer Kathryn Matthews (2007) calls breakups "dreaded conversations," and she offers some helpful hints for how to manage this particularly tricky form of communication. Believing that breakups should always be done in person, she suggests that relational partners avoid breaking up on a special occasion (like a holiday, birthday, or anniversary). The conversation should be held in a public location rather than a private one, but not one that's so public it's embarrassing, with no way to make a graceful exit. The person breaking up should practice what he or she wants to say ahead of time, but not so much as to sound canned or overly rehearsed. Matthews also believes that the person forcing the breakup shouldn't think of himself or herself as "the bad guy," but as someone who doesn't want to hurt others; these conversations are tough on both parties. If the person breaking up can find a genuine way to subtly praise the person they're breaking up with, that can be helpful; then time is needed to allow the other person to react to the hurt and rejection. Finally, Matthews suggests adding a healthy dose of empathy to the situation, becoming mindful of what it feels like to be in each other's shoes.

One breakup method that can lead to hurt and disillusionment is the silent treatment. Even a screaming match, while traumatic, doesn't seem to carry the same sting as noncommunication or one-sided communication. While distancing from one's partner is typical as a relationship comes apart, expanding distance—physical and psychological—so that a person "gets the hint," without ever communicating about the breakup, is ill-advised (Knapp & Vangelisti, 2009). It's painful also to be told it's over without any explanation, any chance for negotiation, and no opportunity for the one who gets "terminated" to express her or his feelings. Many people would rather talk it out—even argue it out—than be shut out and left to wonder what went wrong, which is likely to plunge a person's self-esteem to a new low.

Just for the record, let's all agree on something, related to ending a romantic relationship: The line "I still want to be friends," extended from the "terminator" (one doing the dumping) to the "terminated" (one getting dumped), should *never* be used. If you're nodding your head in agreement, then you've probably experienced this terrible utterance—perhaps you've said it yourself as a way to soften the blow of a breakup. But never again, right? The problem is that the terminator is in the dominant position; his or her wish or will is being imposed against the other person. You don't typically hear terminators say that they want to break up, then their partners try to talk them out of it, and then the terminators agree to resume the relationship. For most of us in the position of being dumped, the last thing we want to try to do, or even conceive of, is to act like friends with our former romantic partners. A request that a relationship regress into something less intimate is understandable if you're doing the dumping, because you may genuinely want a friendship with your former romantic partner and offering friendship makes you feel as though you're easing the sting of the breakup. But it is completely self-serving and unreasonable to expect that someone will be able to shift relationship definitions as quickly as you'd like.

Research has begun to examine how people communicate to renegotiate their relationships to a different level after the romantic aspect has ended (Busboom, Collins, Givertz, & Levin, 2002; Koenig Kellas, Bean, Cunningham, & Cheng, 2008; Koenig Kellas & Manusov, 2003; Koenig Kellas & Sato, 2011; Lambert & Hughes, 2010; Lannutti & Cameron, 2002). Sure, research on divorced couples' communication has been prevalent for decades, but research is now exploring postdissolution relationships, meaning situations where romantic partners (both gay and straight) simply morph into a different kind of relationship, or actually agree to go back to being friends once the romance is gone. Some couples who break up still have to work together or may have the same circle of friends they're not willing to give up, so they must find a way to function even though they've broken up. Research has also begun to try to understand something that many students (and our contemporaries) experience—the "on-again, off-again" relationship (Dailey, Hampel, & Roberts, 2010; Dailey, Rossetto, Pfiester, & Surra, 2009). Some people "break up to make up," and the back and forth iterations of their relationship can be dizzying to track and exhausting for the people involved, and yet they keep coming back to the same person, over and over.

The tensions we've discussed in this section are by no means *all* of the issues relational partners may have to face, but they represent some of the more prominent, common, and troublesome ones examined by research. One remaining issue connected to romantic relationships surrounds the presence of sexual activity—more specifically, how gender communication plays a significant role in a relationship that becomes sexual.

GENDER ISSUES SURROUNDING SEXUAL ACTIVITY

Passionate love is one of the most intense feelings a person can experience. Anthropologists Hatfield and Rapson (1996) describe it this way: "Passionate love is a 'hot,' intense emotion, sometimes called a crush, obsessive love, lovesickness, head-over-heels in love, infatuation, or being in love" (p. 3). They go on to describe passionate love as associated with fulfillment and ecstasy generally expressed through sexual union. It is difficult to separate considerations of passionate love from considerations of sex. Freud, in fact, believed they were one and the same (as in Hendrick & Hendrick, 2000); at the very least, the two are deeply intertwined. Regarding the connection between expressions of love and the onset of sexual activity, communication researcher Sandra Metts (2004) found that when expressions of love occurred prior to sexual involvement in dating relationships, the expressions were more likely to have positive consequences for the relationship, both immediately and over time as relationships continue to develop. However, some men will say "I love you" to get sex, and some women will engage in sex to get love. These possibilities and the intricate relationship between sex and love illustrate the need for open conversations about both topics.

As we stated earlier, romantic relationships experience a number of turning points, of which sexual intimacy is one of the most significant (Mongeau, Serewicz, Henningsen, & Davis, 2006). Thus at some point in a romantic relationship, the issue of sexual activity will probably develop (Guerrero, Andersen, & Afifi, 2001). Then the questions become, "What does sex mean to us?" and "What do we do about it?" Hendrick and Hendrick (2000) point out that for some individuals, sex without love is unthinkable, while for others sex is intrinsically good and can be an end in itself. Most couples are likely to have different meanings for sex within their relationship. Regarding the "what to do about it" question, a number of answers are possible, ranging from "absolutely nothing" to "absolute passion." We're not making any assumptions about how the questions should be answered, for obvious reasons. What's more important is the communication of a clear and mutually agreed-upon decision about what course to take.

Women need a reason to have sex. Men just need a place.
—*Billy Crystal, actor/comedian*

In Chapter 8, we explore the downside of sexual activity, specifically when sex is used as a weapon or power play. But to close this chapter, we focus on the positive side of consensual sex, in an attempt to better understand varying attitudes toward sexual activity, learn more effective ways of talking about sex with a relational partner, and develop a broader repertoire of communication behavior in dealing with problematic sexual situations.

Sexual Activity: Attitudes and Options

Many factors affect our views of sex and sexuality: cultural values, upbringing (primarily in terms of lessons our parents or other family members taught us), childhood experimentation, exposure to media, peer group influences, and self-esteem. Research shows that, at early ages, when we are first thinking about ourselves as sexual creatures, and during other stages of our development, the likelihood that we will engage in sexual activity is highly influenced by whether we perceive that our peers are having sex (Diamond, 2007; Fisher, 2004; Regnerus & Uecker, 2011).

In considering your options, it may be helpful to know what some research over a couple of decades has said about the sexes' attitudes toward sexual activity. One of the most widely cited series of studies of misperceptions of sexual interest was produced by Antonia Abbey (1982, 1987, 1991). In her first study, opposite-sex dyads conversed for five minutes while hidden male and female subjects observed the interaction. Results indicated that, in comparison to female observers, male observers more often perceived female friendliness as seduction, made more judgments that female interactants were promiscuous, and frequently reported being sexually attracted to female interactants. Male observers also rated male interactants' behavior as sexual in nature, whereas female observers did not perceive as much sexuality in male subjects' behavior. From these results, Abbey (1982) concluded that "men are more likely to perceive the world in sexual terms and to make sexual judgments than women are" (p. 830).

Hot Button Issue

Risky Sex

If you had to guess which "slice" of the population was experiencing significantly increased risk, sexually speaking, who would you guess? High school teens? Tweeners? College students? All those answers would be wrong. STD and HIV rates of infection have increased dramatically over the last decade for older adults, primarily aged 45 and older (Ilea et al., 2010; Kuehn, 2008; Lekas, Scrimshaw, & Siegel, 2005). Studies conducted in different countries document that middle-aged and elderly people are having unprotected sex at a rate faster than younger folks who've been warned most of their lives about sexual risks, and they are paying the price with their health (Ball, 2010; Sharples, 2008).

Although you may not want to think about it, many people feel that the ability to be sexually active longer in life is a gift! Reasons for the trend include better health information, healthier and longer life span, Viagra and other erectile dysfunction drugs, and online dating that leads to enhanced opportunities to form relationships that become sexual (Hillman, 2007, 2008; Karlovsky, Lebed, & Mydio, 2004). However, along with the "gift" of an extended sex life may come another "gift"—a sexually transmitted disease.

Because they're no longer able to become pregnant, many older adult women don't practice safe sex, believing that they don't need protection. Older men and women alike may equate protection with birth control, not realizing that they can catch and spread STDs and HIV (Lovejoy et al., 2008; Sadeghi-Nejad, Wasserman, Weidner, Richardson, & Goldmeier, 2010). Some women also hold onto the view that they developed while growing up in a different generation that condoms were only for "dirty girls," ones who slept around. Such attitudes motivate people like Sharon Lee (2010), Executive Director of HIV Wisdom for Older Women, to get the word out about sexual safety.

One reason that it's extremely difficult for these older adults to have open and frank discussions about sexual activity stems from the era in which they grew up—a time of less openness about sexuality, less negotiation about sex, and greater condemnation for multiple sexual partners. And yet older adults, like younger ones, need to learn how to use their communication skills to discuss sexual desires, abilities, and dysfunctions with their partners, so that they can truly enjoy an extended, healthy sexual life.

Communication scholars Mongeau, Yeazell, and Hale (1994) conducted similar research on heterosexual people's interpretations of behavior on first and second dates. Men in the study tended to perceive interaction in more intimate and sexual ways than women. Thus, research suggests that men appear to be more likely to perceive sexual interest when, in fact, it may not be there.

In her review of the literature about heterosexual men and women in love, Peplau (1994) examined the cultural stereotype which suggests that men initiate increases in sexual intimacy and women set the limits and control the progress toward that intimacy. She wondered if this stereotype had changed since it was first researched in the 1950s. She concluded it had not: "Despite the sexual permissiveness of many couples, a traditional pattern of male initiation and female limit-setting was apparent. The traditional pattern provides a familiar and well-rehearsed script that enables the partners to interact comfortably" (p. 28). Researchers suggest this tendency may be based in biology (Buss, 2003; Hendrick & Hendrick, 2000). Males of many species align their reproductive strategies to maximize the number of offspring they have, while females maximize success by having the offspring grow to adulthood. This leads females to be choosier about their partners, with the net result that males compete for sexual access to females while females are the guardians of that access. We aren't suggesting this pattern *should* change, but couples shouldn't assume the stereotype will hold for them or be shocked if the roles are reversed. It's possible for women to initiate and men to set limits.

Research over several decades has produced consistent findings regarding motives for engaging in sexual activity, in that women (heterosexual and homosexual) are more likely to connect sex with emotional involvement, intimacy, and commitment, whereas men (heterosexual and homosexual) more often connect sex with lust, physical gratification, and conquest (Allen, Emmers-Sommer, D'Alessio, Timmerman, Hanzal, & Korus, 2007; Meston & Buss, 2009; Peter & Valkenburg, 2010; Tolman, 2002, 2004; Voh, Catanese, & Baumeister, 2004). This doesn't mean that women don't use sex to fulfill their lustful needs or that men don't view sex as building intimacy and closeness in a relationship, but the trend has persisted in research findings.

These research findings suggest sex differences in both the perception of sexual interest and the motivations for having and avoiding sexual activity. Do the researchers' findings match your experience or the experiences of your friends? Is it your perception that men tend to read more sexuality into things than women? Or do you think that the difference is more a stereotype than a reality? One thing seems obvious to us: Stereotypes or not, given findings that reveal potential differences in women's and men's approaches to sexual activity in their relationships, it seems to be even more critical for relational partners to communicate openly and honestly about sex—preferably *before* they engage in it.

Net Notes

Budding authors should check out **www.genders.org**, a website that publishes essays about gender and sexuality in relation to social, political, artistic, and economic concerns.

Women, Men, Communication, and Sex

Communicating directly about sexual activity represents a proactive approach to what can be a critical turning point in a relationship, although some people may see it as taking the romance out of the act or the situation. Interaction on sexuality is encouraged because research consistently finds that the quality of a couple's communication about sexuality is linked to the quality of their relationship, and an individual's skill in communicating about sexuality is central to successful relationships (Faulkner & Lannutti, 2010; Holmberg & Blair, 2009).

One of the most revealing studies of college students' dating and sexual behavior was conducted by sociologists Knox and Wilson (1981), who asked their subjects, "What do university men and women do to encourage their partners to become more sexually intimate?" (p. 257). One-third of the female and one-fourth of the male respondents said that they preferred to "be open about sexual desires and expectations" (p. 257). Other less direct methods of expressing sexual expectations included "creating an atmosphere" for sexual intimacy, "expressing love," "moving closer" to a partner, and "hinting" (p. 257). Additional research has shown that couples who can talk about sex have higher levels of sexual satisfaction, and that the inability to talk about sex leads to serious problems (Byers & Demmons, 1999; LaFrance, 2010; Litzinger & Gordon, 2005; MacNeil & Byers, 2005, Menard & Offman, 2009). These findings suggest that direct, open discussion of sexual activity isn't a first option for many people, but it's becoming a viable option as opposed to the guessing games that often cause misunderstanding. Honest communication is preferable to trying to read each other's minds (and nonverbal cues), or expecting sexual activity to be like it's portrayed on television or in the movies, or taking the plunge only to discover that one's haste was a real mistake—one that may cost a relationship.

It seems that talking about sex requires more intimacy than actually doing it.

—Jane Fonda, actor/political activist

Although an honest conversation about sex is preferable and more expected these days, most of us still find this topic hard to talk about. Just how do you approach the topic of sex with someone you're involved with or dating? When we say approach the topic of sex, we mean having a conversation about sexual activity in a relationship—no matter your views on whether sexual activity outside of marriage is wrong in general, inadvisable for you and a partner, or something that might occur in your relationship. This also involves discussing topics related to sexual activity, such as birth control, monogamy versus multiple partners, and views about protection from sexually transmitted diseases.

One of the problems in conversations about sex is the fact that our language doesn't provide much help, in fact it often works against honest, serious discussion. What language can you use in a frank discussion with a partner about sex? Here are your options:

1. Clinical, scientific language, such as "You believe that sexual intercourse and oral sex should be postponed until marriage, but heavy petting of clothed genitalia is okay?"

2. Speaking in *euphemisms* (terms that serve as more comfortable alternatives for other terms), which may sound immature or condescending, as in "When I get close to you, my 'thing' reacts."

3. Using "gutter" or "street" terms for sexual acts and body parts, examples of which you're probably well aware.

Many of us are uncomfortable using clinical terms for fear we'll come off sounding like someone's therapist or a character out of *Grey's Anatomy*. Euphemisms can bring about such embarrassment or laughter that the discussion goes off-track, plus they can be extremely ambiguous (e.g., Just what "thing" are you referring to?). Gutter terms may be acceptable (even enjoyable), but are usually more appropriate once a relationship has become sexual or is further along, rather than at the beginning of development. "Street" sexual slang can make sex sound crude and unappealing, but—like everything—it depends on the person.

The sexual-help gurus, therapists, books, workshops, and courses all warn about the importance of clear communication when it comes to sexual protection—protection from disease as well as pregnancy. We believe that schools and universities are doing a better job of confronting the realities of sexuality and educating students on sexual issues than in decades past. The media, particularly film and TV, are now more realistically portraying those moments where couples have the "do you have a condom" discussion. Creators of media products have been roundly chastised for reprehensible, nonresponsible depictions of unprotected sexual activity, so they've responded and we've learned from their responses. Quite often you see movie characters discussing protection, even if it's the quick "Do you have something?" exchange while characters grope in the heat of passion. The phrase "no glove, no love" is more prevalent now than in decades past, which shows that we're at least learning how to talk about protection, even if coarsely.

Research has explored how these conversations occur (and ought to occur), particularly with regard to condom use (Bowleg, Belgrave, & Reisen, 2000; Boyle & O'Sullivan, 2010; Hadley et al., 2009; Zukoski, Harvey, & Branch, 2009). However, we still have much work to do in this area, given research like the study conducted by psychologists Moore and Rosenthal (2006), which found that only half of 18-year-olds reported that they would buy condoms at a store, would feel comfortable carrying a condom with them, and would have a discussion with a sexual partner about condom use.

Although we, as a society, are more "on board" and aware of the importance of frank conversations about sex, that doesn't make the topic any easier to discuss, even in an age of more openness. Research on college women's communication about sex shows that heterosexual women are still highly unlikely to discuss their sexual histories, to ask a new partner about his previous sex partners (or his other partners, if the relationship isn't monogamous), to explore tough but important topics like risk and protection, and to share openly their sexual desires and preferences for activity (Moore & Davidson, 2005). Part of the problem is that a good deal of sexual activity, especially first-time sexual encounters and one-time "hookups," occurs between partners under the influence of alcohol or drugs—impediments to effective, clear communication (Caruthers, 2006; Flack et al., 2007; O'Dougherty Wright, Norton, & Matusek, 2010; Paul & Hayes, 2002; Paul, McManus, & Hayes, 2000).

Would it surprise you to know that older adults also have difficulty talking about sex? (It likely won't surprise those of you who are nontraditional college students.) Much of the research on older, sexually active adults' conversations about sex focuses on health problems, life changes (like pregnancy and menopause), and sexual dysfunction

(Badr & Carmack Taylor, 2009; Burgess, 2004; Dourado, Finamore, Barroso, Santos, & Laks, 2010; Meston & Buss, 2009). Less frequently explored is how to have healthy, open conversations about the role of sexual activity in one's relationship, how sex often changes as people age, how partners' preferences about sexual activity may have changed, and so forth. Compounding the problem, older adults may be more conservative in their upbringing and their views of sex, unused to the sexual openness that characterizes younger generations, making it harder to have a comfortable conversation about sex. And yet, if you read the Hot Button Issue box a few pages back, you understand why it's more important than ever for older, sexually active adults to have frank conversations about sex.

Given all these challenges, what do we recommend? Sorry—there's no quick, easy fix we can offer, but we have a few suggestions. First, realize that language is part of the problem; have metacommunication with your partner, meaning talk about talking about sex. If you have a good laugh over how difficult it is to talk about sex without sounding clinical, nerdy, or vague, it can open the door for further discussion. Second, technology might actually help this situation. Some people find that texting about sex is more comfortable than talking in person (Mark, 2011). We don't recommend that texting replace face-to-face conversation because many nonverbal cues helpful in such intimate conversations are missing or altered when texting, but texting may open the door to a more comfortable conversation. Don't get this advice about texting confused with *sexting*, which is when people send sexually suggestive messages or sexual pictures of themselves through their phones (Bean, 2010; Burns & Lohenry, 2010; Chaifen, 2010; Juntunen & Valiverronen, 2010). Sexting is controversial; some people believe it's a fun way to sexually communicate with a partner, more appropriate for ongoing relationships than those just getting off the ground. Others believe it's risky because of the potential for the sext message to backfire and embarrass or offend the recipient, or go beyond its intended receiver (just ask Brett Favre!).

Similar to recommendations about texting, some people find sex easier to discuss via e-mail messages or over the phone than in person; again, mediated communication is a supplement, not a substitute for face-to-face communication. Caution should be used however, because using your workplace e-mail system or phone for sexual communication is asking for trouble (Cooper, McLoughlin, & Campbell, 2004). Finally, practice doesn't make perfect when it comes to talking about sex, but it does help. We hope we've convinced readers to try (and try again) to use their knowledge and communication skills to overcome their fears, apprehensions, and discomfort because open, honest, ongoing communication will only help you enhance your sex life and relationships.

Remember . . .

Euphemisms: Terms that serve as more comfortable alternatives for other terms
Sexting: When people send sexually suggestive messages or sexual pictures of themselves through their cell phones

Conclusion

Gender communication in love, romance, and sex is complicated by a wide range of sociological, physiological, linguistic, and relational factors. Success in these relationships is never guaranteed, but the chances for success can be increased by broadening the range of communication behaviors that you bring to these contexts.

Autonomy, change, power, commitment, intimacy, conflict—these are just some of the integral issues or tensions within a romantic relationship. Although the tensions in romance aren't particularly easy to write or talk about, they're easier to talk about than to negotiate in an actual relationship. Your own experience, the experiences of your friends, and what we've described in this chapter should reemphasize the considerable complexities inherent in romantic relationships.

Patterns of communication within intimate relationships are particularly critical because effective patterns lead to success and feelings of satisfaction, whereas ineffective patterns lead to any number of destructive outcomes. It may sound simple, for example, to read about negotiating a balance between your sense of independence in a relationship versus time spent with your partner. However, when you actually confront that first discussion and witness the hurt resulting from one partner's assertion of independence,

you find that it's a much harder and more complex issue to manage. It's easy to give lip service to the sentiment, "I love you for what you are; I'll never want to change you," but what happens when you really, honestly think your way is better? Even understanding the complexity involved in these kinds of relationships, however, isn't enough to scare us away from romance and marriage. When it's going well, when it's right, there's hardly anything comparable.

Here, as in other chapters in this text, we continue to suggest that communicating is preferable to *not* communicating. Most of us function better when we have information than when we feel we've been left out of the loop, and romantic partners definitely need information. It's fairly safe to say that an expanded communication repertoire and a willingness to openly communicate with one's partner in a way that's not stereotyped by sex constitute a more successful approach to romantic relationships than a narrow repertoire and an unwillingness to communicate. This approach doesn't mean you'll be successful every time—you know there are no guarantees, especially in a romantic context. But, given the chances that your relationship success ratio could improve, it's probably well worth it to attempt to expand the range of your gender communication in this unique context.

Discussion Starters

1. Think of an example—in your own life or the life of someone close to you—that epitomizes the tension of autonomy versus connection. If you're married or in a committed romantic relationship, was it difficult when you and your partner experienced that first rift of independence? How did you both handle it? Do

   you think this issue is more easily negotiated between marital partners, as compared to people who are only steadily dating?

2. Review the information in this chapter on *commitmentphobia*. Is it your current opinion that men are generally more fearful of commitment in a heterosexual romantic relationship than

women, or the reverse, or neither? Could it be that commitmentphobia has more to do with personality variables and family background, for instance, than with gender?

3. What's the best pattern of communication you've seen in a marriage? What made it effective? Did the two people involved develop this consciously or did the pattern tend to evolve out of trial and error? Should decisions be 50–50 propositions, or should different partners take the lead on different things?

4. Do you think that negotiating the sexual waters with a relational partner is a difficult communication challenge? If so, why is it that women and men may have difficulty openly discussing sexual activity in their relationships? Do you think that same-sex partners have an easier time discussing sexual activity, since they have similar physiology? What are the barriers to a successful discussion of this kind?

 References

Abbey, A. (1982). Sex differences in attributions for friendly behavior: Do males misperceive females' friendliness? *Journal of Personality and Social Psychology, 42,* 830–838.

Abbey, A. (1987). Misperception of friendly behavior as sexual interest: A survey of naturally occurring incidents. *Psychology of Women Quarterly, 11,* 173–194.

Abbey, A. (1991). Misperception as an antecedent of acquaintance rape: A consequence of ambiguity in communication between men and women. In A. Parrot & L. Bechhofer (Eds.), *Acquaintance rape: The hidden crime* (pp. 96–111). New York: Wiley.

Allen, M., Emmers-Sommer, T. M., D'Alessio, D., Timmerman, L., Hanzal, A., & Korus, J. (2007). The connection between the physiological and psychological reactions to sexually explicit materials: A literature summary using meta-analysis. *Communication Monographs, 74,* 541–560.

Amichai-Hamburger, Y., McKenna, K. Y. A., & Tal, S.-A. (2008). E-empowerment: Empowerment by the Internet. *Computers in Human Behavior, 24,* 1776–1789.

Andersen, P. A., Guerrero, L. K., & Jones, S. M. (2006). Nonverbal behavior in intimate interactions and intimate relationships. In V. Manusov & M. L. Patterson (Eds.), *The Sage handbook of nonverbal communication* (pp. 259–277). Thousand Oaks, CA: Sage.

Anderson, K. L., Umberson, D., & Elliott, S. (2004). Violence and abuse in families. In A. L.

Vangelisti (Ed.), *Handbook of family communication* (pp. 629–646). Mahwah, NJ: Erlbaum.

Arliss, L. P. (2001). When myths endure and realities change: Communication in romantic relationships. In L. P. Arliss & D. J. Borisoff (Eds.), *Women and men communicating: Challenges and changes* (2nd ed., pp. 115–131). Fort Worth, TX: Harcourt Brace Jovanovich.

Avery, C. S. (1989, May). How do you build intimacy? *Psychology Today,* 27–31.

Avtgis, T., & Rancer, A. S. (2010). *Arguments, aggression, and conflict.* New York: Routledge.

Babcock, L., & Laschever, S. (2003). *Women don't ask: Negotiation and the gender divide.* Princeton, NJ: Princeton University Press.

Badr, H., & Carmack Taylor, C. L. (2009). Sexual dysfunction and spousal communication in couples coping with prostate cancer. *Psycho-Oncology, 18,* 735–746.

Bailey, J. M., Gaulin, S., Agyei, Y., & Gladue, B. A. (1994). Effects of gender and sexual orientation on evolutionarily relevant aspects of human mating psychology. *Journal of Personality and Social Psychology, 66,* 1081–1093.

Ball, H. (2010). Death of a spouse may be associated with increased STD diagnosis among older men. *Perspectives on Sexual and Reproductive Health, 42,* 64.

Baxter, L. A. (2010). *Voicing relationships: A dialogic perspective.* Thousand Oaks, CA: Sage.

Baxter, L. A., & Erbert, L. A. (2000). Perceptions of dialectical contradictions in turning points of development in heterosexual romantic relationships. *Journal of Social & Personal Relationships, 16,* 547–569.

Baxter, L. A., & Montgomery, B. M. (1996). *Relating: Dialogues and dialectics.* New York: Guilford.

Baxter, L. A., & Montgomery, B. M. (2000). Rethinking communication in personal relationships from a dialectical perspective. In K. Dindia & S. Duck (Eds.), *Communication and personal relationships* (pp. 31–53). New York: Wiley.

Baxter, L. A., & Pittman, G. (2001). Communicatively remembering turning points of relational development in heterosexual romantic relationships. *Communication Reports, 14,* 1–17.

Bean, M. (2010, October). Ask the guy next door. *Women's Health,* 33.

Beck, M. (2006, August). The relationship two-step. *O: The Oprah Winfrey Magazine,* 47.

Beck, M. (2007, June). Lover's leap. *O: The Oprah Winfrey Magazine,* 51–54.

Becker, J. A. H., Ellevold, B., & Stamp, G. H. (2008). The creation of defensiveness in social interaction II: A model of defensive communication among romantic couples. *Communication Monographs, 75,* 86–110.

Beebe, S. A., Beebe, S. J., & Ivy, D. K. (2013). *Communication: Principles for a lifetime* (5th ed.). Boston: Pearson/Allyn & Bacon.

Berns, S. B., Jacobson, N. S., & Gottman, J. M. (1999). Demand-withdraw interaction patterns between different types of batterers and their spouses. *Journal of Marital and Family Therapy, 25,* 337–348.

Blakemore, J. E. O., Lawton, C. A., & Vartanian, L. R. (2003). I can't wait to get married: Gender differences in drive to marry. *Sex Roles, 53,* 327–335.

Bodermann, G. (1997). Can divorce be prevented by enhancing the coping skills of couples? *Journal of Divorce & Remarriage, 27,* 177–194.

Booth-Butterfield, M., & Trotta, M. R. (1994). Attributional patterns for expressions of love. *Communication Reports, 7,* 119–129.

Boushey, H. (2009). Women breadwinners, men unemployed. In H. Boushey & A. O'Leary (Eds.), *The Shriver report: A woman's nation changes everything.* Washington, DC: Center for American Progress.

Bowleg, L., Belgrave, F. Z., & Reisen, C. A. (2000). Gender roles, power strategies, and precautionary sexual self-efficacy: Implications for Black and Latina women's HIV/AIDS protective behaviors. *Sex Roles, 42,* 613–635.

Boyle, A. M., & O'Sullivan, L. F. (2010). General and sexual communication in established relationships: An exploration of possible links to condom use among young adults. *The Canadian Journal of Human Sexuality, 19,* 53–64.

Brantley, A., Knox, D., & Zusman, M. E. (2002). When and why: Gender differences in saying "I love you" among college students. *College Student Journal, 36,* 614–615.

Brehm, S. S. (2001). *Intimate relationships* (3rd ed.). New York: McGraw-Hill.

Bruess, C. J. S., & Pearson, J. C. (1997). Interpersonal rituals in marriage and adult friendship. *Communication Monographs, 64,* 25–46.

Bullis, C., Clark, C., & Sline, R. (1993). From passion to commitment: Turning points in romantic relationships. In P. J. Kalbfleisch (Ed.), *Interpersonal communication: Evolving interpersonal relationships* (pp. 213–236). Hillsdale, NJ: Erlbaum.

Burgess, E. O. (2004). Sexuality in midlife and later life couples. In J. H. Harvey, A. Wenzel, & S. Sprecher (Eds.), *The handbook of sexuality in close relationships* (pp. 437–454). Mahwah, NJ: Erlbaum.

Burggraf, C., & Sillars, A. L. (1987). A critical examination of sex differences in marital communication. *Communication Monographs, 54,* 276–94.

Burleson, B. R. (2003). The experience and effects of emotional support: What the study of cultural and gender differences can tell us about close relationships, emotion, and interpersonal communication. *Personal Relationships, 10,* 1–23.

Burleson, B. R., & Denton, W. H. (1997). The relationship between communication skill and marital satisfaction: Some moderating effects. *Journal of Marriage & the Family, 59,* 884–902.

Burns, S. M., & Lohenry, K. (2010). Cellular phone use in class: Implications for teaching and learning: A pilot study. *College Student Journal, 44,* 805–810.

Busboom, A. L., Collins, D. M., Givertz, M. D., & Levin, L. A. (2002). Can we still be friends? Resources and romantic barriers to friendship after romantic relationship dissolution. *Personal Relationships, 9,* 215–223.

Buss, D. M. (2003). *The evolution of desire: Strategies of human mating* (Rev. ed.). New York: Basic Books.

Byers, E. S., & Demmons, S. (1999). Sexual satisfaction and sexual self-disclosure within dating relationships. *The Journal of Sex Research, 36,* 180–189.

Canary, D. J., & Lakey, S. (2011). *Strategic conflict.* New York: Routledge.

Canary, D. J., & Stafford, L. (1992). Relational maintenance strategies and equity in marriage. *Communication Monographs, 59,* 243–276.

Canary, D. J., & Wahba, J. (2006). Do women work harder than men at maintaining relationships? In K. Dindia & D. J. Canary (Eds.), *Sex differences and similarities in communication* (2nd ed., pp. 359–378). Mahwah, NJ: Erlbaum.

Caruthers, A. S. (2006). "Hookups" and "friends with benefits": Nonrelational sexual encounters as contexts of women's normative sexual development. *Dissertation Abstracts International: Section B. Science and Engineering, 66* (10-B), 5708.

Chaifen, R. (2010). Commentary sexting as adolescent social communication. *Journal of Children and Media, 4,* 350–354.

Christopher, F. S., & Cate, R. M. (1984). Factors involved in premarital sexual decision-making. *The Journal of Sex Research, 20,* 363–376.

Cooper, A., McLoughlin, I. P., & Campbell, K. M. (2004). Sexuality in cyberspace: Update for the 21st century. In M. S. Kimmel & R. F. Plante (Eds.), *Sexualities: Identities, behaviors, and society* (pp. 285–299). New York: Oxford University Press.

Crawford, D. W., Feng, D., Fischer, J. L., & Diana, L. K. (2003). The influence of love, equity, and alternatives on commitment in romantic relationships. *Family and Consumer Sciences Research Journal, 31,* 253–271.

Crawford, M., & Unger, R. (2000). *Women and gender: A feminist psychology* (3rd ed.). New York: McGraw-Hill.

Crawford, M., & Unger, R. (2004). *Women and gender: A feminist psychology* (4th ed.). New York: McGraw-Hill.

Cross, S. E., Bacon, P. L., & Morris, M. L. (2000). The relational-interdependent self-construal and relationships. *Journal of Personality and Social Psychology, 78,* 791–808.

Cullington, D. (2008). *Breaking up blues: A guide to survival.* New York: Routledge.

Dailey, R. M., Hampel, A. D., & Roberts, J. B. (2010). Relational maintenance in on-again/off-again relationships: An assessment of how relational maintenance, uncertainty, and commitment vary by relationship type and status. *Communication Monographs, 77,* 75–101.

Dailey, R. M., Rossetto, K. R., Pfiester, A., & Surra, C. A. (2009). A qualitative analysis of on-again/off-again romantic relationships: "It's up and down, all around." *Journal of Social & Personal Relationships, 26,* 443–466.

Dainton, M., Stafford, L., & Canary, D. (1994). Maintenance strategies and physical affection as predictors of love, liking, and satisfaction in marriage. *Communication Reports, 7,* 88–98.

Davis, D., Shaver, P. R., & Vernon, M. L. (2003). Physical, emotional, and behavioral reactions to breaking up: The roles of gender, age, emotional involvement, and attachment style. *Personality and Social Psychology Bulletin, 29,* 871–884.

DeGreef, B. (2008, November). *Weekend warriors: Autonomy-connection and openness-closedness relational dialectics and coping strategies of marital partners in nonresidential stepfamilies.* Paper presented at the meeting of the National Communication Association, San Diego, CA.

Diamond, L. M. (2007). "Having a girlfriend without knowing it": Intimate friendships among adolescent sexual-minority women. In K. E. Lovaas & M. M. Jenkins (Eds.), *Sexualities and communication in everyday life: A reader* (pp. 107–115). Thousand Oaks, CA: Sage.

Dourado, M., Finamore, C., Barroso, M. F., Santos, R., & Laks, J. (2010). Sexual satisfaction in dementia: Perspectives of patients and spouses. *Sexuality and Disability, 28,* 195–203.

Driver, J., Tabares, A., Shapiro, A., Nahm, E. Y., & Gottman, J. M. (2003). Interactional patterns in marital success or failure: Gottman laboratory studies. In F. Walsh (Ed.), *Normal family processes: Growing diversity and complexity* (pp. 493–513). New York: Guilford.

Duran, R. L., Kelly, L., & Rotaru, T. (2011). Mobile phones in romantic relationships and the dialectic of autonomy versus connection. *Communication Quarterly, 59,* 19–36.

Emmers-Sommer, T. M. (2003). When partners falter: Repair after a transgression. In D. J. Canary & M. Dainton (Eds.), *Maintaining relationships through communication: Relational, contextual, and cultural variations* (pp. 185–208). Mahwah, NJ: Erlbaum.

Faulkner, S. L., & Lannutti, P. J. (2010). Examining the content and outcomes of young adults' satisfying and unsatisfying conversations about sex. *Qualitative Health Research, 20,* 375–385.

Fisher, H. (2009, October). Intimacy: His & hers. *O: The Oprah Winfrey Magazine,* 138.

Fisher, T. D. (2004). Family foundations of sexuality. In J. H. Harvey, A. Wenzel, & S. Sprecher (Eds.), *The handbook of sexuality in close relationships* (pp. 385–409). Mahwah, NJ: Erlbaum.

Fitzpatrick, M. A. (1988). *Between husbands and wives: Communication in marriage.* Newbury Park, CA: Sage.

Flack, W. F., Daubman, K. A., Caron, M. L., Asadorian, J. A., D'Aureli, N. R., Gigliotti, S. N., et al. (2007). Risk factors and consequences of unwanted sex among university students: Hooking up, alcohol, and stress response. *Journal of Interpersonal Violence, 22,* 139–157.

Freitas, D. (2010). *Sex and the soul: Juggling sexuality, spirituality, romance, and religion on America's college campuses.* New York: Oxford University Press.

Galvin, K. M., & Brommel, B. J. (1991). *Family communication: Cohesion and change* (3rd ed.). New York: HarperCollins.

Galvin, K. M., & Bylund, C. (2001). First marriage families: Gender and communication. In L. P. Arliss & D. E. Borisoff (Eds.), *Women and men communicating: Challenges and changes* (2nd ed., pp. 132–148). Prospect Heights, IL: Waveland.

Gill, R., & Ganesh, S. (2007). Empowerment, constraint, and the entrepreneurial self: A study of white women entrepreneurs. *Journal of Applied Communication Research, 35,* 268–293.

Gore, J. S., Cross, S. E., & Morris, M. L. (2006). Let's be friends: Relational self-construal and the development of intimacy. *Personal Relationships, 13,* 83–102.

Gottman, J. M. K., Katz, L. F., & Hooven, C. (1997). *Meta-emotion: How families communicate emotionally.* Mahwah, NJ: Erlbaum.

Graham, E. E. (1997). Turning points and commitment in post-divorce relationships. *Communication Monographs, 64,* 350–368.

Green, J. H. (2008). Measuring women's empowerment: Development of a model. *International Journal of Media and Cultural Politics, 4,* 369–389.

Guerrero, L. K., Andersen, P. A., & Afifi, W. A. (2001). *Close encounters: Communicating in relationships.* Mountain View, CA: Mayfield.

Hadley, W., Brown, L. K., Lescano, C. M., Kell, H., Spalding, K., DiClemente, R., Donenberg, G., & Project STYLE Study Group. (2009). Parent-adolescent sexual communication: Associations of condom use with condom discussions. *AIDS and Behavior, 13,* 997–1004.

Harvey, J. H., & Weber, A. L. (2002). *Odyssey of the heart: Close relationships in the 21st century* (2nd ed.). Mahwah, NJ: Erlbaum.

Hatfield, E., & Rapson, R. L. (1996). *Love and sex: Cross-cultural perspectives.* Boston: Allyn & Bacon.

Hendrick, S. S., & Hendrick, C. (2000). Romantic love. In C. Hendrick & S. S. Hendrick (Eds.), *Close relationships: A sourcebook* (pp. 203–215). Thousand Oaks, CA: Sage.

Hickmon, W. A., Jr., Protinsky, H. O., & Singh, K. (1997). Increasing marital intimacy: Lessons from marital enrichment. *Contemporary Family Therapy: An International Journal, 19,* 581–589.

Hill, C. A. (2002). Gender, relationship stage, and sexual behavior: The importance of partner emotional investment within specific situations. *The Journal of Sex Research, 39,* 228–240.

Hillman, J. (2007). Knowledge and attitudes about HIV/AIDS among community-living older women: Reexamining issues of age and gender. *Journal of Women and Aging, 19,* 53–67.

Hillman, J. (2008). Sexual issues and aging within the context of work with older adult patients. *Professional Psychology: Research and Practice, 39,* 290–297.

Hocker, J. L., & Wilmot, W. W. (2011). Collaborative negotiation. In K. M. Galvin (Ed.), *Making connections: Readings in relational communication* (5th ed., pp. 215–222). New York: Oxford University Press.

Holmberg, D., & Blair, K. L. (2009). Sexual desire, communication, satisfaction, and preferences of men and women in same-sex versus mixed-sex relationships. *The Journal of Sex Research, 46,* 57–66.

Igarashi, T., Takai, J., & Yoshida, T. (2005). Gender differences in social network development via mobile phone text messages: A longitudinal study. *Journal of Social & Personal Relationships, 22,* 691–713.

Ilea, L., Echenique, M., Jean, G. S., Bustamente-Avellaneda, V., Metsch, L., Mendez-Mulet, L., Eisdorfer, C., & Sanchez-Martinez, M. (2010). Project Roadmap: Reeducating older adults in maintaining AIDS prevention: A secondary intervention for older HIV-positive adults. *AIDS Education and Prevention, 22,* 138–147.

Isay, R. A. (2006). *Commitment and healing: Gay men and the need for romantic love.* New York: Wiley.

Jarvis, T. (2009, January). Bridging the intimacy gap. *O: The Oprah Winfrey Magazine,* 107–108.

Johnson, D. W. (2000). *Reaching out: Interpersonal effectiveness and self-actualization.* Boston: Allyn & Bacon.

Jones, T. S., & Brinkert, R. (2008). *Conflict coaching: Conflict management strategies and skills for the individual.* Los Angeles: Sage.

Julien, D., Arellano, C., & Turgeon, L. (1997). Gender issues in heterosexual, gay and lesbian couples. In W. K. Halford, H. J. Markman, & H. J. K. Halford (Eds.), *Clinical handbook of marriage and couples' interventions* (pp. 107–127). Chichester, UK: Wiley.

Juntunen, L., & Valiverronen, E. (2010). Politics of sexting: Re-negotiating the boundaries of private and public in political journalism. *Journalism Studies, 11,* 817–831.

Kalbfleisch, P. J., & Herold, A. L. (2006). Sex, power, and communication. In K. Dindia & D. J. Canary (Eds.), *Sex differences and similarities in communication* (2nd ed., pp. 299–318). Mahwah, NJ: Erlbaum.

Karlovsky, M., Lebed, B., & Mydio, J. H. (2004). Increasing incidence and importance of HIV/AIDS and gonorrhea among men aged over 50 years in the U.S. in the era of erectile dysfunction. *Scandinavian Journal of Urology and Nephrology, 38,* 247–252.

Keashly, L. (1994). Gender and conflict: What does psychological research tell us? In A. Taylor & J. Beinstein Miller (Eds.), *Conflict and gender* (pp. 168–190). Cresskill, NJ: Hampton.

Kelley, D. L. (2011). Communicating forgiveness. In K. M. Galvin (Ed.), *Making connections: Readings in relational communication* (5th ed., pp. 200–211). New York: Oxford University Press.

Kelly, A. B., Fincham, F. D., & Beach, S. R. H. (2003). Communication skills in couples: A review and discussion of emerging perspectives. In J. O. Greene & B. R. Burleson (Eds.), *Handbook of communication and social interaction skills* (pp. 723–752). Mahwah, NJ: Erlbaum.

Klinetob, N. A., & Smith, D. A. (1996). Demand-withdraw communication in marital interaction: Tests of interpersonal contingency and gender role hypotheses. *Journal of Marriage & the Family, 58,* 945–957.

Knapp, M. L., & Vangelisti, A. L. (2009). *Interpersonal communication and human relationships* (6th ed.). Boston: Pearson/Allyn & Bacon.

Knox, D., & Wilson, K. (1981). Dating behaviors of university students. *Family Relations, 30,* 255–258.

Koenig Kellas, J., Bean, D., Cunningham, C., & Cheng, K. Y (2008). The ex-files: Trajectories, turning points, and adjustment in the development of post-dissolutional relationships. *Journal of Social & Personal Relationships, 25,* 23–50.

Koenig Kellas, J., & Manusov, V. (2003). What's in a story? The relationship between narrative completeness and adjustment to relationship dissolution. *Journal of Social & Personal Relationships, 20,* 285–307.

Koenig Kellas, J., & Sato, S. (2011). "The worst part is, we don't even talk anymore": Post-dissolutional communication in break-up stories. In K. M. Galvin (Ed.), *Making connections: Readings in relational communication* (5th ed., pp. 297–309). New York: Oxford University Press.

Koesten, J. (2004). Family communication patterns, sex of subject, and communication competence. *Communication Monographs, 71,* 226–244.

Kuehn, B. M. (2008). Time for "the talk"—again: Seniors need information on sexual health. *Journal of the American Medical Association, 300,* 1285–1287.

LaFrance, B. H. (2010). Predicting sexual satisfaction in interpersonal relationships. *Southern Communication Journal, 75,* 195–214.

Lambert, A. N., & Hughes, P. C. (2010). The influence of goodwill, secure attachment, and positively toned disengagement strategy on reports of communication satisfaction in non-marital post-dissolution relationships. *Communication Research Reports, 27,* 171–183.

Lannutti, P. J., & Cameron, K. A. (2002). Beyond the breakup: Heterosexual and homosexual post-dissolutional relationships. *Communication Quarterly, 50,* 153–170.

Laurenceau, J.-P., Barrett, L. F., & Rovine, M. J. (2005). The interpersonal process model of intimacy in marriage: A daily-diary and multilevel modeling approach. *Journal of Family Psychology, 19,* 314–323.

Lee, S. (2010). HIV wisdom for older women. Retrieved March 5, 2011, from http://www.hivwisdom.org.

Lekas, H.-M., Scrimshaw, E., & Siegel, K. (2005). Pathways to HIV testing among adults aged fifty and older with HIV/AIDS. *AIDS Care, 17,* 674–682.

Levine, T., & Fitzpatrick, S. L. (2005, May). *You know why, the question is how? Relationships between reasons and methods in romantic breakups.*

Paper presented at the meeting of the International Communication Association, New York City, NY.

Littlejohn, S. W., & Domenici, K. (2007). *Communication, conflict and the management of difference.* Long Grove, IL: Waveland.

Litzinger, S., & Gordon, K. C. (2005). Exploring relationships among communication, sexual satisfaction, and marital satisfaction. *Journal of Sex and Marital Therapy, 31,* 409–424.

Lovejoy, T. I., Heckman, T. G., Sikkema, K. J., Hansen, N. B., Kochman, A., Suhr, J. A., Garske, J. P., & Johnson, C. J. (2008). Patterns and correlates of sexual activity and condom use behavior in persons 50-plus years of age living with HIV/AIDS. *AIDS and Behavior, 12,* 943–956.

MacNeil, S., & Byers, E. S. (2005). Dyadic assessment of sexual self-disclosure and sexual satisfaction in heterosexual dating couples. *Journal of Social & Personal Relationships, 22,* 169–181.

Mark, K. (2011, February 28). How to talk about sex. Retrieved March 5, 2011, from http://www.goodinbed.com.

Matthews, K. (2007, August). The Dear John talk and other dreaded conversations. *O: The Oprah Winfrey Magazine,* 144–146.

Meerloo, J. A. (1952). *Conversation and communication.* New York: International Universities Press.

Menard, A. D., & Offman, A. (2009). The interrelationships between sexual self-esteem, sexual assertiveness, and sexual satisfaction. *The Canadian Journal of Human Sexuality, 18,* 35–45.

Messman, S. J., & Mikesell, R. L. (2000). Competition and interpersonal conflict in dating relationships. *Communication Reports, 13,* 21–34.

Meston, C. M., & Buss, D. M. (2009). *Why women have sex: Understanding sexual motivations—from adventure to revenge (and everything in between).* New York: Times Books/Henry Holt and Company.

Metts, S. (2004). First sexual involvement in romantic relationships: An empirical investigation of communicative framing, romantic beliefs and attachment orientation in the passion turning point. In J. H. Harvey, A. Wenzel, & S. Sprecher (Eds.), *The handbook of sexuality in close relationships* (pp. 135–158). Mahwah, NJ: Erlbaum.

Metts, S. (2006). Gendered communication in dating relationships. In B. J. Dow & J. T. Wood (Eds.), *The Sage handbook of gender and communication* (pp. 25–40). Thousand Oaks, CA: Sage.

Mongeau, P. A., Serewicz, M. C. M., Henningsen, M. L. M., & Davis, K. L. (2006). Sex differences in the transition to heterosexual romantic relationship. In K. Dindia & D. J. Canary (Eds.), *Sex differences and similarities in communication* (2nd ed., pp. 337–358). Mahwah, NJ: Erlbaum.

Mongeau, P. A., Yeazell, M., & Hale, J. (1994). Sex differences in relational message interpretations on male- and female-initiated first dates. *Journal of Social Behavior and Personality, 9,* 731–742.

Moore, N. B., & Davidson, J. K., Sr. (2005). Communicating with new sex partners: College women and questions that make a differences. In J. K. Davidson, Sr., & N. B. Moore (Eds.), *Speaking of sexuality: Interdisciplinary readings* (2nd ed., pp. 117–123). Los Angeles: Roxbury.

Moore, S., & Rosenthal, D. (2006). *Sexuality in adolescence: Current trends.* New York: Routledge.

Motley, M. T. (2008a). Unwanted escalation of sexual intimacy: Pursuing a miscommunication explanation. In M. T. Motley (Ed.), *Studies in applied interpersonal communication* (pp. 121–143). Los Angeles, CA: Sage.

Motley, M. T. (2008b). Verbal coercion to unwanted sexual intimacy: How coercion messages operate. In M. T. Motley (Ed.), *Studies in applied interpersonal communication* (pp. 185–203). Los Angeles, CA: Sage.

Nozick, R. (1993). Love's bond. In A. Minas (Ed.), *Gender basics: Feminist perspectives on women and men* (pp. 152–159). Belmont, CA: Wadsworth.

O'Doughtery Wright, M., Norton, D. L., & Matusek, J. A. (2010). Predicting verbal coercion following sexual refusal during a hookup: Diverging gender patterns. *Sex Roles, 62,* 647–660.

O'Leary, A., & Kornbluh, K. (2009). Family friendly for all families. In H. Boushey & A. O'Leary (Eds.), *The Shriver report: A woman's nation changes everything.* Washington, DC: Center for American Progress.

O'Sullivan, L. F., & Gaines, M. E. (1998). Decision-making in college students' heterosexual dating relationships: Ambivalence about engaging in sexual activity. *Journal of Social & Personal Relationships, 15,* 347–363.

Owen, W. F. (1987). The verbal expression of love by women and men as a critical communication event in personal relationships. *Women's Studies in Communication, 10,* 15–24.

Paul, E. L., & Hayes, K. A. (2002). The casualties of "casual" sex: A qualitative exploration of the phenomenology of college students' hookups. *Journal of Social & Personal Relationships, 19,* 639–661.

Paul, E. L., McManus, B., & Hayes, K. A. (2000). "Hookups": Characteristics and correlates of college students' spontaneous and anonymous sexual experiences. *The Journal of Sex Research, 37,* 76–88.

Pawlowski, D. (1999). Rubber bands and sectioned oranges: Dialectical tensions and metaphors used to describe interpersonal relationships. *North Dakota Journal of Speech and Theatre, 12,* 13–30.

Peplau, L. A. (1994). Men and women in love. In D. L. Sollie & L. A. Leslie (Eds.), *Gender, families, and close relationships* (pp. 19–49). Newbury Park, CA: Sage.

Peter, J., & Valkenburg, P. M. (2010). Adolescents' use of sexually explicit Internet material and sexual uncertainty: The role of involvement and gender. *Communication Monographs, 77,* 357–375.

Regnerus, M., & Uecker, J. (2011). *Premarital sex in America: How young Americans meet, mate, and think about marrying.* New York: Oxford University Press.

Reis, H. T., Clark, M. S., & Holmes, J. G. (2004). Perceived partner responsiveness as an organizing construct in the study of intimacy and closeness. In D. J. Mashek & A. Aron (Eds.), *Handbook of closeness and intimacy* (pp. 201–225). Mahwah, NJ: Erlbaum.

Richmond, V. P. (1995). Amount of communication in marital dyads as a function of dyad and individual marital satisfaction. *Communication Research Reports, 12,* 152–159.

Rogers, C. (1970). *On becoming a person.* Boston: Houghton Mifflin.

Sadeghi-Nejad, H., Wasserman, M., Weidner, W., Richardson, D., & Goldmeier, D. (2010). Sexually transmitted diseases and sexual function. *Journal of Sexual Medicine, 7,* 389–413.

Sahlstein, E., & Dun, T. (2008). "I wanted time to myself and he wanted to be together all the time": Constructing breakups as managing autonomy-connection. *Qualitative Research Reports in Communication, 9,* 37–45.

Sanderson, C. A., Keiter, E. J., Miles, M. G., & Yopyk, D. J. A. (2007). The association between intimacy goals and plans for initiating dating relationships. *Personal Relationships, 14,* 225–243.

Schnall, M. (1981, May). Commitmentphobia. *Savvy,* 37–41.

Segrin, C., Hanzal, A., & Domschke, T. J. (2009). Accuracy and bias in newlywed couples' perceptions of conflict styles and the association with marital satisfaction. *Communication Monographs, 76,* 207–233.

Sharples, T. (2008, July 2). More midlife (and older) STDs. Retrieved March 5, 2011, from http://www.time.com.

Shea, E. J. (2009, September 28). Tips for successful online dating. Retrieved February 27, 2011, from http://www.oprah.com/relationships.

Sillars, A., Shellen, W., McIntosh, A., & Pomegranate, M. (1997). Relational characteristics of language: Elaboration and differentiation in marital conversations. *Western Journal of Communication, 61,* 403–422.

Simon, R. W., & Barrett, A. E. (2010). Nonmarital romantic relationships and mental health in early adulthood: Does the association differ for women and men? *Journal of Health and Social Behavior, 51,* 168–182.

Sinclair, I., & McCluskey, U. (1996). Invasive partners: An exploration of attachment, communication and family patterns. *Journal of Family Therapy, 18,* 61–78.

Slotter, E. B., Gardner, W. L., & Finkel, E. J. (2010). Who am I without you? The influence of romantic breakups on the self-concept. *Personality and Social Psychology Bulletin, 36,* 147–160.

Stafford, L. (2003). Maintaining romantic relationships: A summary and analysis of one research program. In D. J. Canary & M. Dainton (Eds.), *Maintaining relationships through communication: Relational, contextual, and cultural variation* (pp. 51–77). Mahwah, NJ: Erlbaum.

Stafford, L., Dutton, M., & Haas, S. (2000). Measuring routine maintenance: Scale revision, sex versus gender roles, and the prediction of relational characteristics. *Communication Monographs, 67,* 306–323.

Stone, D., Patton, B., & Heen, S. (2011). Difficult conversations: How to discuss what matters most. In K. M. Galvin (Ed.), *Making connections: Readings in relational communication* (5th ed., pp. 223–231). New York: Oxford University Press.

Sutherland, A. (2010, April). The science of heartbreak. *Women's Health,* 70.

Taylor, A., & Miller, J. B. (Eds.). (1994). *Conflict and gender.* Cresskill, NJ: Hampton.

Teichner, G., & Farnden-Lyster, R. (1997). Recently married couples' length of relationship marital communication, relational style, and marital satisfaction. *Psychological Reports, 80,* 490.

Tichenor, V. (2005). Maintaining men's dominance: Negotiating identity and power when she earns more. *Sex Roles, 53,* 191–205.

Tolman, D. L. (2002). *Dilemmas of desire: Teenage girls talk about sexuality.* Cambridge, MA: Harvard University Press.

Tolman, D. L. (2004). Doing desire: Adolescent girls' struggles for/with sexuality. In M. S. Kimmel & R. F. Plante (Eds.), *Sexualities: Identities, behaviors, and society* (pp. 87–99). New York: Oxford University Press.

Tracy, J. (2011). 5 best dating sites of 2011. Retrieved February 27, 2011, from http://www.onlinedatingmagazine.com.

Turner, L. H., & West, R. (2011). Theories of relational communication. In K. M. Galvin (Ed.), *Making connections: Readings in relational communication* (5th ed., pp. 30–45). New York: Oxford University Press.

Vogel-Bauer, S., Kalbfleisch, P. J., & Beatty, M. J. (1999). Perceived equity, satisfaction, and relational maintenance strategies in parent-adolescent dyads. *Journal of Youth and Adolescence, 287,* 27–49.

Voh, K. D., Catanese, K. R., & Baumeister, R. F. (2004). Sex in "his" versus "her" relationships. In J. H. Harvey, A. Wenzel, & S. Sprecher (Eds.), *The handbook of sexuality in close relationships* (pp. 455–474). Mahwah, NJ: Erlbaum.

Waite Miller, C. (2011). Irresolvable interpersonal conflicts: Students' perceptions of common topics, possible reasons for persistence, and communication patterns. In K. M. Galvin (Ed.), *Making connections: Readings in relational communication* (5th ed., pp. 240–247). New York: Oxford University Press.

Wilkinson, C. A., & Grill, L. H. (2011). Expressing affection: A vocabulary of loving messages. In K. M. Galvin (Ed.), *Making connections: Readings in relational communication* (5th ed., pp. 164–173). New York: Oxford University Press.

Wilmot, W. W., & Hocker, J. L. (2010). *Interpersonal conflict* (8th ed.). New York: McGraw-Hill.

A woman's nation changes everything. (2009). *The Shriver report.* Washington, DC: Center for American Progress. Retrieved October 28, 2009, from http://awomansnation.com/about.php.

Worthington, E. L., McCullough, M. E., Shortz, J. L., & Mindes, E. J. (1995). Can couples' assessment and feedback improve relationships? Assessment as a brief relationship enrichment procedure. *Journal of Counseling Psychology, 42,* 466–475.

Zukoski, A. P., Harvey, S. M., & Branch, M. (2009). Condom use: Exploring verbal and nonverbal communication strategies among Latino and African American men and women. *AIDS Care, 21,* 1042–1049.

NOT-SO-HOT TOPICS

▶ The role of power and communication in abusive situations

▶ Forms of rape and the language of survivors

▶ The prevalence of date rape and date rape drugs in American society

▶ Myths about rape and sexual aggression

▶ Advice for men and women about sexual activity

▶ The language of partner violence

▶ Statistics, types, and myths about partner violence, including gay and lesbian partner abuse

▶ Battered woman syndrome, one explanation of why victims stay with abusers

Power Abuses in Human Relationships

CHAPTER 8

A NON-CASE STUDY

The information in this chapter is difficult to write about, and it's going to be difficult to read. Certainly it isn't the first time you've read or heard about sexual assault and partner violence. But it may be the most concentrated presentation of these topics you've been assigned in college. This chapter focuses on power abuses in human relationships, the downside of interacting with others, and how communication creates options for those situations.

It doesn't seem appropriate to start this chapter like the others—with a case study to engage your thinking and energize you for the pages to come. Many cases could be included because many people suffer abuse in relationships. But we prefer to tell some of those stories in context, along with the information on each topic. Here's why: It's very hard to focus on how people abuse one another; it takes us out of our comfort zones to think or talk about it. Even when we do decide to think or talk about it, we still tend to distance ourselves from it—to view it as a social problem, a bunch of statistics, or something that happens to someone else. These are understandable ways to protect ourselves from having to confront the tough issues. But you don't really understand a problem until you put a face on it. That's what the cases in the chapter are designed to do—to make these issues real by putting human faces on them. You may be able to put the face of a relative, friend, or coworker into the situations we describe. While that's painful, we encourage you to do just that, because it will enable you to more fully understand these problems and what can be done about them.

We also realize that some of you reading this material *are* those human faces—your case could be substituted for one here. The abuses we discuss don't just happen to someone else; they happen to *us*. We hope that none of you has experienced what we examine in this chapter, but it's very likely that some of you have. If you've lived through power abuses in the past, reading this chapter will no doubt bring up unpleasant reminders for you. But perhaps you will gain a deeper understanding of what you went through or a comparison for how you coped with your situation. If you're currently in an abusive situation, our sincere hope is that this information will help you realize that you do not deserve or cause the abuse, and that you have options.

AT THE CENTER OF ABUSIVE SITUATIONS: COMMUNICATING POWER

What do sexual assault and partner (domestic) violence have in common? Neither is primarily about sex, but instead they are about power (Berryman-Fink, 1993). Whereas the gender or sexuality of the target of abuse may be an issue or play a role in the offense, an abuser's behavior is more often related to an attempt to control, influence, and dominate the other person (Angier, 2000). Rapists and batterers all have varying degrees of anger and needs for power that they inflict on their targets in the worst way, by preying on their sexuality, physicality, or insecurities.

Once, power was considered a masculine attribute. In fact, power has no sex.
—*Katherine Graham, author*/**Washington Post** *publisher*

Another common thread throughout these issues is that they involve communication. Acquaintance sexual assault or rape and partner violence usually involve a context of communication that precedes the assault, as well as follows it. Most important, full recovery from these abuses must involve communication. Not talking about an experience doesn't make it go away or allow the survivor to get past it. One of the worst things a survivor can do, but something that happens frequently, is to hide in shame and guilt and not tell anyone what happened. Communication makes an experience real, which is frightening but necessary for recovery. So these abuses are things that communication people—especially people with an interest in gender communication—should study.

PERSONAL RIGHTS AND SEXUALITY

Although significant strides have been made in recent years toward gender equity in sexual matters, the goal is not yet reached. Teachers see vestiges of these attitudes in some students who express in overt or subtle ways an expectation that men have a right to assert their sexual needs. Recall our discussion in Chapter 2 about biology becoming a cop-out from focusing on sociocultural factors to explain gender communication. The belief that some men commit sexual assault because their physical urges overtake their reason, that "men just have to have it," is a similar cop-out. This is blaming biology, taken to the extreme. In this section of the chapter, we explore the difficult topic of sexual assault and rape and the critical role of communication in sexual encounters.

Power at the Core

We've said that the abuses explored in this chapter are primarily about power, not about sex. Of the two offenses we're studying, rape is more closely associated with sex. As Pulitzer Prize–winning author Natalie Angier (2000) explains, "rape is about sex and power and a thousand other things as well . . . rape is not a monolithic constant but varies in incidence and meaning from culture to culture and epoch to epoch" (p. 81). The role of power is obvious in stranger rape, because a stranger must render a target powerless in order to assault. Here's how power emerges when the assaulter is someone the target knows: When sexual expectations and interests in a romantic or social situation differ, when one person's sexual intentions or desires don't match another's, then the sexual motive becomes a power motive, a case of someone getting his or her way no matter the cost or the wishes of the other person. One person engages in sexual conduct against the will of another person; someone's personal rights are violated.

Case Study

An Evening Out with Annie and Kris

Besides being a professor of communication, the author of your text (whom we'll simply refer to as "the professor") served as the director of the Women's Center at her university. In that capacity, she frequently made presentations on gender-related topics on campus and in her community. One campus event will stay in her memory because it so clearly illustrates our discussion of socialization and sexuality. The professor was asked by a dorm resident assistant (RA) to speak to a group of her residents about gender communication. The event drew about twenty or so students on a weeknight, with more women than men in attendance. The discussion started generally, but as usual in addressing gender communication in an informal setting, it fairly quickly turned to topics of sex. At one point, the RA said that a friend of hers (whom we'll call Annie) was studying and couldn't attend the gathering, but had an important question she was going to call in.

Annie did phone in and her question was about "blue balls" (pardon the bluntness and use of this term). She said that at the end of a date, she'd been making out with her boyfriend (whom we'll call Kris) in his car and the activity went a bit further than usual, at which point she resisted. She told Kris, "You know I'm not into that; I'm not ready to do it with you yet." He got flustered, as she said was typical of him, but this time he became angry as well. Kris said Annie was responsible for him having a "permanent case of blue balls" and that she had to have sex with him or it would hurt his health. His claim was that being sexually aroused but ungratified caused an uncomfortable and unhealthy condition for men. He said Annie owed it to him not to tease him, and he knew she really wanted sex as much as he did.

As best she could, not being a physician (or a man), the professor explained Kris's condition. A state of pressure, swelling, and discomfort can develop in men as a result of arousal that doesn't consummate in ejaculation, and, over time, it can actually cause the testicles to take on a pale blueish tint. But the condition isn't permanent, as Kris claimed. It goes away shortly, as the buildup of fluid due to arousal retreats, is absorbed, or is ejaculated via masturbation. But here's the main point the professor tried to get across to Annie: The physical state termed "blue balls" is in no way a justification for sexual coercion or aggression. Kris had no right to make Annie feel guilty for arousing him by kissing and then not giving in to his insistence on sex because of the threat of some debilitating condition. On hearing this, Annie started to cry over the phone.

There was more to the story. Annie said she felt bad about making Kris angry, she cared about him, and she didn't want to do something that would hurt him physically because she really didn't know anything about "blue balls." She'd had sex before in a prior relationship, but wasn't ready to have sex with Kris. But it turned out that Annie did have intercourse with Kris that night in the car. In Annie's perception, she didn't really say yes, she didn't say no—she just didn't resist when Kris started in again. But she kept saying no all the time in her head. She didn't enjoy the experience because she wasn't ready to go that far with Kris and she was

(continued)

Case Study *(continued)*

worried someone would see them in the car. It wasn't until later that she started to question what had happened.

Was this a case of consensual sex or date rape? One could argue that this was a classic case of date rape because Annie felt coerced into sex; although she complied with Kris's desires, she didn't really consent because she kept saying no in her head. He should have stopped when she first said she didn't want to have sex. But what about Kris's point of view? What if he thought he was just being honest with Annie by telling her that he was frustrated and needed to have sex? He first got a "no" to sex, but later Annie didn't resist or say no, so things continued. Kris may have thought that he was just fulfilling his male role—that it's up to the guy to make the first move and the woman to resist. Then when the man keeps pressing, the woman gives in and gets what she really wanted all along. Whose interpretation is the right one? Is there a right one?

Answers to these questions reveal the complexity of the issue. A court dealing with a situation like this might find merit in both Annie's and Kris's interpretations. On Annie's side, the incident could be considered date rape because she initially said no to Kris's advances and later said no in her head as Kris continued. She may have felt powerless to stop Kris, since they had argued and he had gotten angry. However, a court might find merit in Kris's interpretation by believing that Annie was inconsistent—at first saying no, but when physical activity continued, she made no attempt to push Kris away or say no again. If she was saying no in her head, Kris couldn't read her mind. At the core of this example, and so many like it, is the issue of consent. Communication—and the lack of it—is also at the core of the problem.

One lesson among many emerges from this story: A sexual situation like this involves power, but that power isn't always easy to detect or counter. In this situation, Kris used the power of persuasion by talking about a male condition he knew Annie probably wouldn't understand and by making it sound like dire consequences would result if she didn't comply. This is a classic "men have to have it" example in which one person controls events by declaring a "need," then claiming that the other person is at fault if she doesn't meet his needs. The result is that someone felt she had to do something she really didn't want to do. In Kris's mind, the incident was just sex, certainly not rape. Annie knew what had happened was wrong, but she had a hard time calling it rape. She couldn't fathom charging Kris with rape, but she ended their relationship right after this experience. It was clear that the event would stay with Annie a long time.

Changing Language as We Learn More

Naming or labeling something takes it out of the shadows and gives us a way to talk about experiences, especially traumatic experiences, so understanding the language surrounding sexual violence is important (Gay, 2007; Harned, 2004; Young & Maguire, 2003). The law recognizes different types of rape. Forcible rape, as defined by the Federal Bureau of Investigation, is "the carnal knowledge of a female forcibly and against her will" (FBI, 2009). According to the FBI's *Uniform Crime Report* (2008, 2009), incidences of violent crime (the category that includes rape) have trended downward in recent years; however, it is still the case that one forcible rape occurs in the United States every 5 minutes. The FBI's conservative stance on rape has been roundly criticized because it narrowly views rape as vaginal intercourse without consent. Because of that narrowness, we prefer the definition provided by the Bureau of Justice, in their *Statistical Tables Index* (2010); *rape* is defined as follows:

> Forced sexual intercourse including both psychological coercion as well as physical force. Forced sexual intercourse means vaginal, anal, or oral penetration by the offender(s). This category includes incidents when the penetration is from a foreign object. Includes attempted rapes, male as well as female victimization, and both heterosexual and homosexual rape. Attempted rape includes verbal threats of rape.

A very broad definition of rape is "taking possession of another's sexuality" (Moore, 2000, p. 25). A complicating factor in discussions and research, as well as laws about rape, is disagreement on a definition.

Stranger rape is just what the term says—rape by a person unknown to the victim. While people used to associate the general term *rape* primarily with stranger rape, this form of rape occurs with far less frequency than rape by a person known to the victim. *Date rape* (also termed *acquaintance rape*) occurs in the context of people who know each other, even if they have just met. Researchers Jean Hughes and Bernice Sandler (1987) define date rape as "forced, unwanted intercourse with a person you know. It is a violation of your body and your trust" (p. 1). After decades of being ignored, attention is now being paid to the very serious societal problem of acquaintance rape. We spend a good deal of time in this chapter on this form, because it's the most common sexual offense college students experience. While cases of same-sex date rape continue to be documented, few targets of date rape are male; the vast majority of targets are female (National Institute of Justice, 2008b; Tewksbury, 2010). Thus, most of the literature refers to the rapist as "he" and the person raped as "she."

The word *rape* is the historical term for this crime, but that term can be a *trigger word* for people who've experienced it. By *trigger word*, we mean that simply hearing the term can remind targets of the trauma they went through, sometimes making them feel victimized again. This is one of the primary reasons you hear the term *sexual assault* instead of *rape*. The impact of trigger words for our readers who have survived rape is a concern, but part of the healing process may be to call an act what it is rather than using a euphemism that can dilute or trivialize the experience. Women who have experienced sexual violence tend to avoid static labels when talking about their experiences, which reveals the challenges the language presents (Young & Maguire, 2003).

Another factor in word choice is the fact that in some information on the topic, *sexual assault* is a broad term that applies to a range of offenses. Some definitions include unwanted sexual intercourse; others describe a range of sexual activities, but don't include intercourse. To clarify, again we turn to the Bureau of Justice (2010) which defines sexual assault as follows:

> A wide range of victimizations, separate from rape or attempted rape. These crimes include attacks or attempted attacks generally involving unwanted sexual conduct between victims and offenders. Sexual assaults may or may

not involve force and include such things as grabbing or fondling. Sexual assault also includes verbal threats.

Note that for both the definitions of rape and sexual assault, mention is made of "threats," meaning that communicating a threat of committing rape or sexual assault is also viewed as criminal.

The preferred term for people who've lived through the ordeal of rape and sexual assault is *survivors*, which is a great term because it signals respect and hope (Young & Maguire, 2003). Rape also occurs among marital or committed partners (together or separated) and between people who used to be married or legally committed. At long last, all fifty states (and federal lands) have laws on the books addressing this form of rape (*Wife Rape*, 2004). Other terms include *marital rape, spousal rape*, and *wife rape*, defined as "sexual acts committed without a person's consent and/or against a person's will, when the perpetrator (attacker) is the woman's husband or ex-husband" (*Wife Rape*, 2004, p. 1). We prefer the term *partner rape*, because homosexual partners and people who are cohabitating can be raped just as people who are legally married, separated, or divorced.

Underestimates of an Underreported Problem

Although we provide statistics to illustrate the extent of the problem, realize that numbers don't tell even half of the story when it comes to rape and sexual assault. FBI crime statistics for 2009 indicate that rates of violent crimes (murders, robberies, and rapes) declined nationwide from the previous year (FBI, 2009). Forcible rape rates showed a decrease of 1.6 percent in this period. But remember: Rape rates reflect *reported* cases. The crime least likely to be reported and least likely to result in a conviction in the United States is rape (Crawford & Unger, 2004; Koss, as in Dusky, 2003). Determining rates of sexual assaults among college students is a difficult task, again because of under-reporting (Burnett et al., 2009; Karjane, Fisher, & Cullen, 2010; Lipka, 2009). According to National Institute of Justice (2008b) statistics, studies of self-reported sexual assaults (not crime reports) indicate that about 3 percent of college women are sexually assaulted in any given nine-month academic year. That may not seem like a large figure, but on a campus with 10,000 female students, 3 percent equals 300 assaults.

Remember . . .

Rape: Forced sexual intercourse, including vaginal, anal, or oral penetration

Stranger Rape: Rape by a person unknown to the target

Date/Acquaintance Rape: Rape by a person who is known by the target, even if they have just met

Trigger Word: Use of a term that can remind a target of past trauma, sometimes making her or him feel victimized again

Sexual Assault: Wide range of victimizations, including attacks or attempted attacks involving unwanted sexual conduct

Research estimates that 14 percent of married women will be raped by their husbands (Martin, Taft, & Resick, 2007). Underreporting is particularly the case for partner rape because some women do not consider sexual assaults by their husbands, ex-husbands, or cohabiting partners to be rape (*Wife Rape*, 2004).

FACTS ABOUT DATE RAPE   It's a devastating fact that most women are raped by people they know; only one in five rapes are committed by strangers (FBI, 2009). The effects of date rape on younger women are enormous, especially in the damage done to their ability to trust or form intimate relationships.

Once in cabinet we had to deal with the fact that there had been an outbreak of assaults on women at night. One minister suggested a curfew: women should stay home after dark. I said, "But it's the men who are attacking the women. If there's to be a curfew, let the men stay home, not the women."
—Golda Meir, former Israeli prime minister

Date rape situations are extremely difficult for survivors to understand and grapple with, because many people who are victimized by someone they know are especially reluctant to call what happened rape. They often call it a "bad date." Sexual assault survivors often blame themselves for getting into the situation in the first place, not seeing it coming, using substances that altered their judgment or impaired their ability to resist, and being generally unable to prevent the assault. Research over three decades consistently shows that alcohol and/or drugs are involved in most date rape situations (Abbey, Ross, McDuffie, & McAuslan, 1996; Lannutti & Monahan, 2004; Muehlenhard & Linton, 1987). The most common factors that increase the risk of sexual assault for female college students include alcohol use, sorority membership, numerous sexual partners, days of the week (more assaults occur on weekends than weekdays), and attendance at off-campus parties (National Institute of Justice, 2008a). In addition, being in one's first or second year of college increases the risk; the first few months of the academic year are the highest risk periods.

SLIP 'EM A MICKEY   Some of you are too young to know what "slipping a Mickey" means, but it's a reference to a Mickey Finn, a substance used to involuntarily sedate someone for the purpose of assaulting or taking advantage of her or him. The old phrase "get her drunk and take advantage of her" has a twenty-first-century incarnation in the form of date rape drugs.

You may have heard or read about date rape drugs, because many colleges and universities are offering programs to educate students about the problem. The practice of placing substances in people's drinks without their knowledge is increasing at an alarming rate. According to information found on the Women's Health (2008) website, the most commonly used, easily obtained drugs are as follows (street names included): Rohypnol (Circles, Roofies, Roachies, La Rocha, the Forget Pill); Gamma Hydroxybutyrate or GHB (Grievous Bodily Harm, Easy Lay); and Ketamine (Black Hole, Special K). The most well-known of these, Rohypnol, is a medication prescribed internationally for people with severe and debilitating sleep disorders. It's illegal in the United States, but continues to be smuggled in and sold as a street drug. The Swiss-based company that manufactures Rohypnol has reformulated the drug so that it releases a blue dye when dissolved in a liquid. While this is a step in the right direction, the problem is that the blue dye is difficult to detect in dark drinks and dark settings, such as bars and clubs. Various groups, including

Hot Button Issue

"Avatar Rape?"

On the website **insidehighered.com**, journalism professor Michael Bugeja (2010) posted an interesting (if not disturbing) article about the popular 3-D virtual world known as *Second Life,* which many students enjoy. Bugeja explained how different forms of abuse are frequently reported to Linden Lab, creator of *Second Life;* at the end of 2006, the lab received close to 2,000 abuse reports per day.

As sexual assaults and rapes are becoming more of a problem in the *Second Life* world, Bugeja suggests that research is needed on three points: (1) how avatar rape happens in virtual worlds; (2) what concepts and theories apply when the act is neither physical nor geographical; and (3) why the discussion is even necessary. How is virtual rape even possible, you ask? Bugeja explains that, "typically, users encounter the act through three scenarios: You can lure others or be lured into it yourself. You can purchase or role-play it. You can 'grief' it—a term that means *to cause grief*—or suffer it because of a griefer." Bugeja provides examples of sexual assaults he's been made aware of in the *Second Life* world, such as a situation when one avatar invited another to go skinny-dipping, and then the interaction turned into an assault. In the situation the target rebuffed her attacker, dressed her avatar, and exited *Second Life,* but later explained that she felt taken advantage of and violated.

Bugeja cites research from 1997, an online publication entitled "Virtual Rape" by Richard MacKinnon. In the article, MacKinnon states, "The concept of rape is currently being addressed by participants in virtual reality and adapted so that the virtual act of rape is recognizable as such and condemnable within their virtual society." It appears that the "concept of rape" either wasn't adequately addressed in the 1990s and early 2000s, or the threat such virtual worlds pose in terms of personal (avatar) abuse isn't something users are willing to work to conquer.

Sure, a virtual-world participant can just teleport away from the assault. Linden Lab recommends muting voice during verbal assaults, as if with one click the problem is solved. However, as Bugeja explains, "Walking away from hate speech on campus doesn't mean damage was circumvented or an epithet excusable or that charges cannot be filed against a person making slurs. Why should virtual reality be different when users assume liability for what happens there?"

What's your opinion? Are virtual worlds "free game" with "enter-at-your-own-risk" expectations? Or should there be some sort of monitoring and punishment for such offenses as virtual sexual assault and rape, just like what happens in the physical world?

colleges and universities, have developed and utilized innovations to enable date rape drug detection. Drink coasters and straws that turn colors on detection of Rohypnol are among the newest inventions (Labi, 2007).

When this tasteless, odorless drug is slipped into a person's drink, within twenty to thirty minutes the person will show symptoms of being sedated. Limited motion and voice production are two common effects; drugged rape survivors report feeling like they were in a daze, as though they were too heavy to move or call out. But perhaps the most devastating effect of the drug is its memory impairment. The D.C. Rape Crisis Center describes it this way: "Because survivors will have been heavily sedated, they may not have complete recall of the assault. It is likely that they will be uncertain about exactly what happened and who was involved. The unknowns may create tremendous anxiety as survivors are left to fill in the gaps with their imagination" (1998, pp. 4–5). Some people who've been drugged have no memory of the incident; they wake up, sometimes in a hospital, to learn that they've been raped, but can't remember how it happened or who raped them.

If you or a friend suspect you've been drugged because you feel dizzy or confused after drinking something, try to get to a hospital. If you believe you've been raped (and there are reported cases of men being drugged with Rohypnol and raped), crisis centers recommend that you get to a safe place and call a crisis center or 911. If you decide to report the assault to the police, be sure not to shower, bathe, douche, urinate or defecate, brush your teeth, eat, drink, change clothes, or straighten up the area where you suspect the rape took place until medical and legal evidence is collected. Then go to a hospital or other facility where you can receive treatment for injuries, tests for pregnancy and sexually transmitted diseases, a urine test, and counseling. The urine test is important because Rohypnol can be found in urine up to seventy-two hours after ingestion, depending on someone's metabolism and the dose of the drug (D.C. Rape Crisis Center, 2006). The Drug-Induced Rape Prevention and Punishment Act, passed in October 1996, punishes people who commit rape by administering a controlled substance without the target's knowledge.

Who Are the Rapists?

The normal, gentle, nice-looking guy sitting next to you in class could be a rapist. Does that sound paranoid or absurd? The point we're trying to make is that people capable of committing date or partner rape look just like all of us. Their profiles cross racial and ethnic, class, age, and religious lines. Research has isolated a number of characteristics more common among date rapists, such as the use or abuse of alcohol, athletic affiliation, fraternity affiliation, a history of family violence, and early and varied sexual experience (Crawford & Unger, 2004). But a date rapist *could be anybody.*

We don't want to make you overly suspicious, so you see potential rapists everywhere you look, but we do want you to realize that the "crazed man jumping out of the bushes" to rape is much more the exception than the rule. Most rapists are people you know: family members, friends of the family, classmates, boyfriends, teachers, coworkers, bosses, doctors, lawyers, ministers.

Common Myths about Rape

Research conducted by psychologist Martha Burt (1980) led to the discovery of a set of *rape myths,* beliefs people hold about rape that aren't based in fact. While these myths emerged twenty-five years ago, people still adhere to them in surprising numbers today. In fact, acceptance of rape myths by college students, as well as reporting procedures and responses to rape, have led some researchers to describe a "campus rape culture" (Burnett et al., 2009, p. 465). These myths include the following:

1. Women say "no" when they mean "yes" to avoid being seen as promiscuous.
2. Men must overcome women if they resist.
3. Some women deserve to be raped.
4. Some women actually enjoy rape, because it fulfills one of their sexual fantasies.

5. Some men just can't help themselves when they are aroused; they *have* to have sexual intercourse, even if they have to be aggressive to get it.

6. "Good girls" don't get raped—a myth related to prior sexual activity. A man may believe that if a woman has been sexually active, she will willingly have sex with anyone, including him. The "only virgins can be raped" myth suggests that sexually active women cannot be raped.

Two other myths can be added to the list. First, some people incorrectly believe that if a woman has had sex with a man but refuses to have sex with him again, it's not rape if he forces her (Shotland & Goldstein, 1992). Prior sexual involvement with someone doesn't preclude an act of rape. Second, it's a myth to believe that not hearing yes or no means yes to a sexual act. If someone is incapacitated (drunk, high, sick, etc.) and can't consent to sexual activity, there is no consent and any subsequent sexual action is assault. Let's put that another way, to emphasize the point:

> *If you read and retain nothing else in this entire chapter, please remember this: Being too drunk or high to give consent isn't consent—it isn't a reason to assert your will and assault someone. Not hearing no doesn't mean yes. Hearing nothing at all doesn't mean a person has consented. People must voice their consent for you to have consent.*

From this research, Burt developed a Rape Myth Acceptance Scale, an instrument that asks subjects questions about their experiences with sexual violence and determines to what level an individual accepts or believes certain myths about rape. Subsequent studies measuring rape myth acceptance find that men who perceive themselves as traditionally masculine, hold traditional attitudes about gender roles, are resistant to learning about sexual risk, and view feminism negatively are likely to believe in rape myths and to describe past or future aggression toward women (Good, Heppner, Hillenbrand-Gunn, & Wang, 1995; Meyer, 2010; Meyer & Johnson, 1999; Paul, Gray, Elhai, & Davis, 2009; Truman, Tokar, & Fischer, 1996; Yeater, Treat, Viken, & McFall, 2010). Interestingly enough, research shows that when men are asked out on dates by women—women who also pay for the date—those men have more general acceptance of rape myths than men who do the asking and paying for dates (Emmers-Sommer et al., 2010). Other research has determined a connection between a belief in rape myths and exposure to pornography, sexually violent media, and mainstream media depictions (such as in R-rated movies) of women acting aroused during rape or being objectified in degrading ways (Milburn, Mather, & Conrad, 2000; Mullin, 1995; Zillman & Bryant, 1982).

Changing sexual standards may lead some men to expect sex from women, almost as a given or a reward for having dated someone a few times. Some men believe that they are entitled to sex when they have spent money on a date—that somehow sex and money are an even exchange. While belief in rape myths still exists, research shows that educational programs on the topic of sexual violence can reduce rape myth acceptance among college men (Flores & Hartlaub, 1998).

Communication and the Abuse of Power in Sexual Assault

Of special interest to our study of gender communication is the miscommunication that occurs in situations that end up as sexual assault and date rape. Just to be clear, we aren't labeling date rape a simple situation of miscommunication. But some communication elements common to abusive episodes are worth talking about.

Remember . . .

Survivor: Term for a person who has survived sexual assault, rape, or partner violence

Marital/Spousal/Wife Rape: Sexual acts committed without a person's consent and/or against a person's will, when the rapist is the woman's husband or ex-husband

Partner Rape: Broader term for rape committed by one person in a relationship against the other; applies to homosexual and cohabitating partners as well as married, separated, or divorced people

Rape Myths: Beliefs about rape that aren't based in fact

CONSENT: THE CORE OF SEXUAL COMMUNICATION   The line between sexual activity and sexual assault is simple: *Consent is everything.* As author Rachel Kramer Bussel (2008) explains, "The issue of 'consent' encompasses the ways we ask for sex, and the ways we don't. It's about more than the letter of the law, and, like all sexual issues, at its heart is communication" (p. 43). But the issue of consent can sometimes be murky for people to understand. Again, let's be clear and direct: You must have a person's verbal consent for an activity to be consensual. If your sexual partner says "no," you do not have consent. If the person doesn't say anything at all, you may or may not have consent—you need to ask for clarification to make sure the sexual activity is desired, lest you be in a position of taking advantage of someone and later accused of assault or rape.

A complicating factor here is that, as research consistently shows, men tend to interpret sexual messages from flirtatious behavior, while women tend to distinguish between behavior that is flirtatious or playful versus sexual (Abbey; 1982; Guerrero & Floyd, 2006; Henningsen, 2004; Koeppel, Montagne, O'Hair, & Cody, 1999; Koukounas & Letch, 2001; Lee & Guerrero, 2001; Moore, 2002). We don't want to insinuate that women who are date raped are at fault for poor communication that somehow confused men. But we do allow that some women give mixed messages about sexual activity, like saying "no" when their actions say "yes." This behavior is called *token resistance*, which occurs when someone feigns resistance to a sexual overture in an effort to tease a partner, when sexual activity is actually desired (Osman, 2007; Sims, Noel, & Maisto, 2007). In such situations, men may think that a woman's "no" really doesn't mean no, but means "maybe," "try harder," or "try again." Some of our female students have been honest enough to admit that they sometimes say "no" before they actually agree to sex, just so the men they're with won't think them "slutty" or "easy." When the nonverbal cues communicate sexual interest, but a partner isn't verbalizing anything at all, the message is often one of consent (Harvey & Weber, 2002; Muehlenhard & Rodgers, 2005).

We're in some muddy nonverbal waters here, as pertains to sexual communication. But again, research helps clarify: People usually indicate their consent to sexual activity nonverbally, rather than verbally (Beres, Herold, & Maitland, 2004), *and that's the problem.* Many times nonverbal cues can be misunderstood. Verbal statements of consent are preferable in sexual situations, even if it feels nerdy or contrived to speak up, because the meaning is more clear than a touch, facial expression, murmur, or body position (Lim & Roloff, 1999). Women and men alike are learning how critical it is to be as clear as possible when it comes to sex—even though this kind of communication is tough for many people. But better to be taken for a nerd than a rapist.

Need we say it again? Sexual game playing is dangerous. Bottom line? If you say "no" with your voice, say "no" also with your body—make the message clear and consistent, so there's no misunderstanding about consent.

WHEN A MAN REJECTS "NO"   On the flip side, in some situations women say "no" and mean no, but the man chooses to reject that "no." In sexual encounters, these men may try to turn a woman's no into a yes, by continuing to physically arouse their partner or by displaying anger or frustration with the intent of making the woman feel nervous, uncomfortable, or guilty enough to give in (as in Kris's behavior). However, some men work to unlearn these responses and to interpret a woman's no as actually meaning no. The best advice is to take a woman's no at face value, assuming that no really does mean no—no questions asked nor disagreement voiced. Any actions beyond the woman's no are sexual violations, and sexual activity without agreement or consent is rape.

Everything you've learned about gender communication and personal effectiveness from this text applies with even more urgency to this situation of negotiating sexual waters with a relational partner. The principles behind the receiver orientation to communication and the value of expanding one's repertoire of communication to provide alternatives for confronting different situations are highly applicable and useful in sexual contexts.

Parting Considerations about Sexual Assault and Rape

It's obvious that members of both sexes need to become more aware of the different forms of sexual assault, how prevalent rape is in our culture, what elements embedded in our society actually condone and reinforce the problem, how communication plays a role, how devastating rape is (particularly date rape), and what all of us can do to help combat this crime.

We can't bury our heads in the sand about this problem, pretending it doesn't happen. Look around your classrooms, dorm rooms, apartments; there are rape survivors sitting there. Maybe you're one of them, but we hope not. Sexual assault isn't a woman's issue or a man's problem; it's a human problem that we all must work to overcome. As researchers Hughes and Sandler (1987) remind: "Rape is violence. It strikes at the heart of the personal relationship between a man and a woman, how they treat each other, and how they respect each other's wishes" (p. 2). We end this section of the chapter with excellent lists of advice on this issue, one for women from Hughes and Sandler, and one from the State University of New York at Buffalo's website.

ATTENTION: MEN   An excellent website, simply entitled *Sexual Assault and Rape: Advice for Men* (2005), out of the State University of New York at Buffalo offers this helpful information:

1. Think about whether you really want to have sex with someone who doesn't want to have sex with you; how will you feel afterward if your partner tells you she or he didn't want to have sex?
2. If you are getting a double message from a woman, speak up and clarify what she wants. If you find yourself in a situation with a woman who is unsure about having sex or is saying "no," back off. Suggest talking about it.

Net Notes

Thankfully, tons of information can be found to help people better understand sexual assault and rape and to assist survivors. We recommend the following websites and programs:

www.rainn.org   The website for Rape, Abuse, and Incest National Network, the nation's largest anti-sexual assault organization, with a hotline at 1-800-656-HOPE.

www.ncpc.org   The National Crime Prevention Council site offers current, easy-to-access information on the crimes of rape and sexual assault. The extensive section on date rape is especially useful for survivors, family members, and friends.

www.xris.com   This website provides helpful information to male survivors of rape and sexual assault who are often stigmatized because of societal ignorance and denial about male victimage.

www.oneinfourusa.org   This rape prevention organization educates men and women about rape, employing college men who travel and make presentations on college and university campuses across the country. The organization's goal is to "help men understand how to best help women."

www.mystrength.org   A California project, this organization's mission is to provide leadership, vision, and resources for rape crisis centers, individuals, and other entities committed to ending sexual violence.

3. Be sensitive to women who are unsure whether they want to have sex. If you put pressure on them, you might be forcing them.
4. Do not assume you both want the same degree of intimacy. She might be interested in some sexual contact other than intercourse. There may be several kinds of sexual activity you might mutually agree to share.
5. Stay in touch with your sexual desires. Ask yourself if you are really hearing what she wants. Do not let your desires control your actions.
6. Communicate your sexual desires honestly and as early as possible.
7. Do not assume her desire for affection is the same as a desire for sex.
8. A woman who turns you down for sex is not necessarily rejecting you as a person; she is expressing her decision not to participate in a single act at that time.
9. No one asks to be raped. No matter how a woman behaves, she does not deserve to have her body used in ways she does not want.
10. The fact that you were intoxicated [or high] is not legal defense to rape. You are responsible for your actions, whether you are drunk or sober.
11. Be aware that a man's size and physical presence can be intimidating to a woman. Many victims report that the fear they felt based on the man's size and presence was the reason they did not fight back or struggle. (p. 1)

ATTENTION: WOMEN   Hughes and Sandler (1987) offer useful advice that is applicable today to help minimize the potential for date rape. While their advice is aimed at women, men need to understand this information and be aware that acting on this advice may not come easily for some women.

First, Hughes and Sandler suggest that women think about their own feelings about sexual activity, meaning ponder who they are sexually and what forms or levels of activity they want to have, and feel comfortable with, in their relationships. Second, women need to set clear boundaries for their own sexual behavior, as well as limits for their sexual partners. When out on a date or engaged in any kind of social situation, it's important to decide, early on, if you think you might want to partake in sexual activity, and then communicate to your partner what you want, and don't want, to have happen. (That's one of those pieces of advice that sounds good, but may be hard for some women to follow, fearing that they'll be perceived negatively by a potential sexual partner if they communicate so proactively about sex, but as Hughes and Sandler suggest, it's better to communicate clearly and risk a negative reaction than play a guessing game about sex.)

Next, Hughes and Sandler suggest that partners don't send mixed messages about sex, meaning that your verbal and nonverbal cues need to be in sync, giving a consistent message about what you do, and don't, want to have happen sexually. They warn women to not worry about being polite in their communication about sex, preferring that women directly and firmly express themselves. Even in our "liberated" society, many women feel that they are obliged to do what their date or relational partner wants; Hughes and Sandler explain that women can be independent and aware when on dates, offering input as to where they'd like to go, what they'd like to do, and so forth. Since women are often concerned with being nice and avoiding unpleasantness, they may be reluctant to "rock the boat." But Hughes and Sandler are very direct about this, advising women that they don't have to do anything they don't want to do because of the fear of creating a scene or causing conflict. They also suggest that women monitor their feelings and be aware of situations that don't make them feel relaxed or in control. For example, if a woman goes to a party where activities are going on that make her uncomfortable, she should feel empowered to leave that situation.

Another important piece of advice is to protest loudly or ask for help, drawing attention to yourself, if you find yourself in a situation where your rights are being violated or you are being made to feel uncomfortable. Finally, Hughes and Sandler acknowledge the fact that drugs and alcohol are often present in situations that eventuate in rape and sexual assault, so they caution women to be careful about imbibing in mood-altering substances that may dull your senses and make you more susceptible to being taken advantage of or put in a compromising situation.

PARTNER VIOLENCE

A primary commonality among the two areas discussed in this chapter is that sexual assault and rape and partner violence are both extreme abuses of power. They involve one person's attempt to control, dominate, and render powerless another person. Another commonality is privacy, meaning that most abusive episodes occur behind closed doors, not in front of witnesses. Partner violence is a bit different in that it may occur within earshot or eyeshot of children or other family members. But there is a closed-doors quality to this too, in that violence in the home may be kept within the family and rarely spoken about outside the home. As we'll see from the case study that follows (see pages 289–290), this closed-doors quality is one of the main problems in situations of domestic violence.

You start thinking, "What could I possibly have said to make him hit me and do this?" I didn't talk about it to anyone. To no one. Not my friends, not my family. I didn't want people looking at me and feeling sorry for me, like "There goes the victim."

—*Rihanna, R&B singer*

Case Study

Living Happily Ever After

Leah (not her real name) was an attractive woman, mid-30s, who came back to school to get her degree after her divorce. She (wisely) chose communication as her major and (wisely) enrolled in a gender communication course. On the day when the class focused on issues of violence and abuse, the instructor encouraged some of the students who had not yet entered the discussion to speak up if they had something to say or ask. At that point the instructor made eye contact with Leah, and she started to tell her story. This was clearly one of those instances where you could put a face to a problem.

Leah told us of her "picture perfect" courtship with her now ex-husband (whom we'll call Matt), how he seemed like the perfect man, or near perfect anyway. The couple was the envy of all their friends and they certainly made their parents proud when they married. But less than a year into the marriage, when their first child was six weeks old, Leah's husband erupted during an argument. She really didn't see it coming; she had no hints that he was capable of being brutal. In all the time they'd dated and been engaged he'd never raised a hand to her. But it happened with her infant son just down the hall in their home.

Matt's anger was exacerbated by his drinking. The episodes became more frequent, as many days he would leave work early and head to a bar, drink for the rest of the afternoon, and arrive home that night in an abusive rage. A typical evening involved Matt slapping and punching Leah, yelling and calling her obscene names, and threatening to "really teach her a lesson" if she left him. She learned quickly how to cover bruises with makeup. A day or two later, Matt would show the typical batterer's remorse for "losing his temper," and Leah would try to convince herself that it wouldn't happen again. But it did happen again; she never knew what would trigger a violent episode. Her self-esteem plummeted; she constantly questioned herself about what she was doing wrong and what she could do better to stave off Matt's anger. She tiptoed through her life, but it seemed that nothing she tried worked.

Finally, Leah contacted Matt's parents and told them what was going on. At first they denied that their precious son could be capable of such horrible behavior. Then they downplayed it, calling it a "misunderstanding," "a show of temper," and "having a bad day." On several occasions they blamed Leah, saying that she must have done something to make Matt act this way. After Leah made repeated calls to Matt's parents to report yet another beating, they finally offered to help, but this is how: When Matt went out drinking or came home drunk, Leah would call his parents; they would pick him up, take him to their house, and keep him there until the next day when he sobered up. That way they could keep him from "misbehaving" or "throwing a fit."

Knowing that Leah was divorced, the instructor in the class asked how Leah finally managed to pull herself out of the relationship and get a divorce. She said, "Well, after about ten years of this, I decided—" The instructor had to interrupt because she, and no doubt the other students in the class, were thinking, "*Ten* years?" Leah said, "Yes, I put up with it for ten years, all the while thinking it would stop." It

(continued)

Case Study *(continued)*

took her another year to untangle from the relationship. She still has tremendous emotional scars from the experience, not only from Matt but from his parents as well for their role in protecting the abuser and leaving their daughter-in-law and grandchild in a life-threatening situation.

Leah experienced battered woman syndrome (discussed later in this chapter)—feelings of helplessness, terror, dependency, and rage, mixed with strange feelings of love and commitment. Those mixed emotions allowed her to tolerate for ten years what seems to us—those of us who haven't experienced battering—an intolerable situation. She received a divorce and custody of their son and began putting herself and her life back together. She told everyone in class that she'd often heard the phrase "never say never," but she wanted to reject that and say that she would never, *never* again tolerate a man who tried to control her. If she stayed single the rest of her life, if she never had another romantic relationship with a man, that was fine. She hoped she might meet someone wonderful and was open to the possibility, but she didn't feel less of a woman because she wasn't in a relationship or marriage. She knew that she'd never put up with an abuser again.

The Language of Violence

Family violence is probably the broadest term describing this form of abuse because it encompasses child, spousal, and elderly abuse (Hammons, 2004). Family violence is defined as "an act carried out by one family member against another family member that causes or is intended to cause physical or emotional pain or injury to that person" (Heffernan, Shuttlesworth, & Ambrosino, 1997, p. 364). Our focus is on abuse between adults, so terms such as *domestic violence, marital abuse, spousal abuse, battering,* and the most blatant term, *wife beating,* are more descriptive. But there are problems with these terms, too.

IT'S NOT ABOUT POLITICAL CORRECTNESS   Discussions about language don't arise out of a need to find the most politically correct term for this problem; it's important to use language that allows people to accurately, honestly communicate about the problem (Ashcraft, 2000). *Domestic violence* has been defined as "a crime of power and control committed mainly by men against women, a crime in which the perpetrator does not

Net Notes

Parents are often the last to know if their daughter or son is experiencing violence at the hands of a boyfriend or girlfriend. Dating or courtship violence is a very real problem, one that groups across the country continue to address. One helpful resource can be found at **www.breakthecycle.org**, the website for the national nonprofit organization whose mission is to "engage, educate, and empower youth to build lives and communities free from domestic violence." We recommend their *Dating Violence 101* guide which offers an easy-to-follow, step-by-step guide to understanding a pattern of violent behavior. Another helpful resource is **www.loveisnotabuse.com**, founded by Liz Claiborne, Inc. The site offers materials and tools to help fight "the epidemic of domestic violence and dating abuse."

consult the victim's wishes and from which he will not let her escape" (Jones, 1994, p. 126). But one problem is that the term *domestic* tends to sanitize the abuse. As feminist scholar bell hooks (2000) explains, "For too long the term 'domestic violence' has been used as a 'soft' term which suggests it emerges in an intimate context that is private and somehow less threatening, less brutal, than the violence that takes place outside the home" (p. 62). *Battering* is a term you hear often and one that we will use in this discussion, but it typically implies only physical abuse rather than other forms. Ann Jones (1994), author of *Next Time She'll Be Dead: Battering and How to Stop It*, describes problems with these two terms: "It makes the violence sound domesticated, like a special category of violence that is somehow different from other kinds—less serious. The more difficult term is 'battered woman,' because it suggests a woman who is more or less permanently black and blue and helpless. And of course most women who are abused and controlled by men don't think of themselves as battered women" (as in Jacobs, 1994, p. 56).

Wife beating leaves out husbands and other male partners, as well as people in homosexual relationships who are abused. While the majority of victims of abuse are female, a small percentage involves female abusers and male victims (Crary, 2001; Robinson, 1994; Schwartz, 2005). Marital or spousal abuse isn't as inclusive a term as *intimate partner violence* because people in both heterosexual and homosexual non-marital relationships (those who cohabitate, date, or are separated or divorced) also suffer abuse (Dutton & Goodman, 2005). One scholar uses the term *intimate terrorism* to describe ways that abusers use violence "in the service of gaining and holding general control over their partners" (Johnson, 2006, p. 93). Abusers are referred to as *batterers, wife beaters,* or, as we found at one interesting website, *intimate enemies* (*Women*, 1998).

Yet another form of abuse is *courtship violence*, also known as *dating violence* or *premarital violence*. This abuse involves "aggression between unmarried adolescents or young adults in dating-like relationships" (Crawford & Unger, 2004, p. 448). Because the predominance of this abuse is carried out by young men on young women, it's also been termed *boyfriend violence*. Estimates are that between 25 and 40 percent of female teens have been assaulted by dates; over 70 percent of pregnant or parenting teens are beaten by their boyfriends. Most of these assaults involve pushing, shoving, slapping, and grabbing

Remember . . .

Family Violence: Act perpetrated by one family member against another family member that causes or is intended to cause physical or emotional pain or injury

Domestic Violence: Crime of power and control in which a perpetrator does not consult a target's wishes and from which he or she will not let the target escape

Battering: Form of domestic violence that implies only physical abuse rather than other forms

Partner Violence: Broadest term, which can encompass psychological and/or physical violence occurring among married, separated, divorced, unmarried, homosexual, or cohabitating people

Courtship/Dating/Premarital Violence: Form of domestic violence that involves people who are dating or in committed romantic relationships, but who have not yet legally formalized those relationships

(Libby, 2001). Because the previous section of the chapter focused mostly on date rape, we're going to emphasize intimate partner abuse in this last section. Much of the patterns and problems inherent in intimate partner abuse apply to courtship violence as well.

TWO WAYS TO HURT YOUR LOVER   Intimate partner abuse is usually discussed in two forms: *physical* and *psychological.* Physical abuse ranges from a push or slap to a beating to the use of a weapon. Psychological abuse is a broad category that subsumes emotional and verbal abuse. Communication researchers have become interested in ways in which women and men exhibit verbal aggression, typically manifested in such things as severe criticism, intimidation, threats, humiliation (private and public), isolation, and degradation (Infante, Rancer, & Womack, 2003; Rancer & Avtgis, 2006; Vangelisti, Maguire, Alexander, & Clark, 2007). Research has determined a connection between verbal aggression and physical violence (McCloskey, Lee, Berman, Noblett, & Coccaro, 2008; Olson, 2002; Sabourin & Stamp, 1995). While psychological abuse is more harmful and long-lasting than physical abuse, in most instances, the two go hand in hand. Psychological abuse destroys self-esteem and leaves devastating emotional scars; physical abuse often leaves more than emotional scars (Crawford & Unger, 2004).

An "Epidemic"

That's what the American Medical Association called intimate partner violence—an epidemic (Peach, 1998). Estimates of intimate partner violence range from 960,000 incidents of violence per year to 3 million women being physically abused by their husbands or boyfriends annually (*Domestic Violence,* 2010). Like sexual assault, domestic violence is an underreported crime, mainly because of attitudes victims hold about this form of violence, as well as embarrassment and social pressures that can be roadblocks for victims who need help (Schneider Shevlin, 1994). Women are more likely to suffer violence from people they know than from strangers, whereas for men it is the opposite. Women are much more likely than men to be victimized by a current or former intimate partner (*National Crime Victimization Survey,* 2008). Estimates by the Department of Justice indicate that 84 percent of spouse abuse victims and 86 percent of victims of abuse at the hands of a boyfriend are female; three-fourths of the people who commit family violence are male (*Family Violence Statistics,* 2005). One survey sponsored by the Family Violence Prevention Foundation found that, among 3,500 women surveyed, 44 percent experienced intimate partner violence, with 12 percent of those having been victimized within the last five years. Fifteen percent reported being victimized by two or more partners, while roughly 9 percent had experienced violence that lasted over a twenty-year period in their lives (*New Studies,* 2006). The Centers for Disease Control report that approximately two million injuries from intimate partner violence are experienced by women each year in this country (*Adverse Health Conditions,* 2008).

Common Myths about Battering

Statistics for partner violence, like those for sexual assault and rape, are much lower than the reality because so much of it goes unreported. A high degree of shame and guilt is associated with partner violence, on both the part of the batterer and the battered. But a primary reason for underreporting this crime relates to *battering myths*—outdated, nonfactual beliefs about relationships and the violence that can occur within them.

MYTH #1: EVERYBODY DOES IT   You'll be surprised at how many people still believe that physical abuse is a normal part of marriage. Men used to joke with one another (and we fear some still do) about needing to "give the old lady a pop" or "a good thrashing," and keeping a woman in line by "smacking her around a bit." Only recently has society begun to treat partner violence as a crime and to decry those who batter their partners. Some of you are old enough to remember or have watched reruns of the greatly loved television series *The Honeymooners*. While no physical domestic violence was portrayed on that show, Jackie Gleason's character, Ralph Cramden, used to pump his fist near his wife's face and yell, "To the moon, Alice!" Lots of us thought that bit was hilarious, but would it be hilarious now? Would it even get on the air?

MYTH #2: THE VICTIM IS TO BLAME, AGAIN   Another myth about partner abuse is that the person being abused deserves it or is to blame for the abuse. This parallels blame-the-victim attitudes in sexual assault, but it is probably most often heard in relation to battering (Thapar-Bjorkert & Morgan, 2010). As sociologists Heffernan, Shuttlesworth, and Ambrosino (1997) explain, "It is much easier for the general public to become concerned about abused children than abused women. Many individuals still subscribe to the myth that women who are beaten somehow deserve it, or that they must enjoy it or they would not put up with it" (p. 365).

A few researchers have interviewed male batterers for their accounts of how domestic violence occurred in their homes. In one study, male abusers blamed the victim, in that they described their wives (or partners) as the abusers and attempted to justify, excuse, minimize, or deny their own abusive behavior (Stamp & Sabourin, 1995). These findings parallel other studies. For example, sociologists Anderson and Umberson (2001) interviewed men in court-mandated domestic violence educational programs. These men believed that they were victims of a biased judicial system and that their female partners were responsible for the violence in their relationships.

One factor that leads some people to blame victims or to suggest that they make their plight worse relates to victims' communication. Communication researchers Rudd and Burant (1995) found that battered women used two main strategies during arguments that escalated into violence: (1) submissive strategies in an attempt to smooth over a conflict, and (2) aggressive strategies to escalate the conflict. These aggressive strategies fuel the perception that women are to blame for the battering they receive. But as Rudd and Burant explain, "Battered women's use of aggressive strategies are a means for them to escalate the inevitable violence so that the conflict will end. Abused women have often reported that the fear of not knowing when the violence is going to occur is as frightening as the violent act itself" (p. 141).

MYTH #3: ONLY THE POOR ARE ABUSIVE   Some people believe that partner abuse only occurs in low-income and minority families. While more abuse does occur among lower-income families in which one or both spouses are unemployed, partner abuse extends across all social classes, races, and ethnicities (Activist dialogues, 2005; Gelles & Straus, 1988; Meighan, 2003; *Recognizing*, 2006). One need only remember the O. J. Simpson case to be reminded that partner violence can occur within the wealthiest of households and among marriages of people from different racial groups.

MYTH #4: GAY AND LESBIAN PARTNERS AREN'T ABUSIVE   Many of us adhere to the myth that partner abuse occurs only within heterosexual relationships, yet another disturbing aspect of this problem is its existence among gay and lesbian couples (Blosnich & Bossarte, 2009; Brown, 2008; Miller, Bobner, & Zarski, 2000; Rohrbaugh, 2006). Talk about your underreported crime. According to Aardvarc (An Abuse, Rape, and Domestic

Violence Aid and Resource Collection, 2006), same-sex partner abuse is vastly underreported for a variety of reasons, chief among them the threat of outing oneself or a partner whose gay, lesbian, bisexual, or transgender identity might still be closeted. Sometimes police officers who respond to same-sex domestic dispute calls are reluctant to view such incidents as domestic violence because they don't know the nature of the relationship, aren't told, don't care to know, or don't want to label the relationship. Thus, the disputes are labeled something else, distorting the statistics.

Research results and statistics vary widely on the extent of this problem (Brown, 2008; Rohrbaugh, 2006). According to the National Violence Against Women Survey, 11 percent of lesbians and 15 percent of gay men report experiencing intimate partner abuse (as in Tjaden, 2003). In addition, more people cohabitating in same-sex relationships report intimate partner violence than cohabitants in opposite-sex relationships (39 percent versus 22 percent; Tjaden & Thoennes, 2000). Other research reports upwards of 37 percent gay and lesbian partner abuse (Lie & Gentlewarrior, 1991; Lie, Schilit, Bush, Montagne, & Reyes, 1991). Some studies suggest more occurrences of gay male abuse than lesbian abuse, whereas other studies report the opposite; one study found more lesbian abuse, but the physical violence in the gay male abuse was more severe (Waterman, Dawson, & Bologna, 1989). Often the abuse reported is both psychological and physical.

Researchers Morrow and Hawxhurst (1989) provide four myths about women, in general, and lesbian relationships, in specific, that lead to secrecy surrounding lesbian abuse. First is the myth that because women are socialized to be less aggressive than men, they are incapable of brutalizing other women. While women tend to exhibit less aggression than men as a rule, they are certainly capable of being physically aggressive as a means of exerting power and control over another person. A second myth is that battering only occurs as a result of substance abuse or in clubs or bars. Substances may lead to or expedite a battering incident, but an urge to batter isn't necessarily prompted by substance abuse. The third myth is that because feminist lesbians are committed to equality in relationships, they do not batter. Don't equate homosexuality with a belief in equality in relationships (meaning not all lesbians are feminists). It is a stereotype to believe that a "nontraditional" relationship is automatically steeped in nontraditional thinking. Also, someone might believe in equality, but still be a batterer; the two aren't necessarily related because one is an ideological stance, and the other is a behavior based on an emotional and psychological state. Finally, the myth exists that because lesbians are women, they are incapable of inflicting serious physical harm. Some say that, compared to opposite-sex violence, the brutality that members of the same sex can inflict on each other is worse because they know best how to hurt each other.

The violence within gay male relationships also tends to be shrouded in secrecy. Many gay men report having had more than one relationship in which they experienced physical violence. That violence typically includes punching with fists, beating the head against a wall or floor, and brutal rape. One victim even recounted that his partner tried to run him down with his car. One of the reasons gay men batter relates to something we talked about back in Chapter 1, in our discussion of homophobia. The third definition we gave of homophobia was an in-group use of the term to mean gays' own hatred toward homosexuals and toward themselves for being homosexual. One of the causes of battering is rage that is an outgrowth of homophobia and self-hatred. Also, because gays are often ostracized or isolated in a society that's predominantly straight and because many are made to feel they must keep their sexual orientation a secret, they may turn their resulting rage onto one another.

Abused Partners: How Do They Stand It? Why Do They Stay?

Explanations of the dynamic between an abuser and a victim vary. Professionals who work in shelters know better than anyone the various reasons why people stay with their abusers. The Women's Shelter of South Texas provides the following information that offers insight into the thought processes of a battered person:

WHY PEOPLE STAY IN ABUSIVE RELATIONSHIPS

At first people stay because:

- They're told it won't happen again
- They remember the good times with the person and think things are getting better
- They're in love
- They think the person will grow up and change
- They think they can stop the beatings by doing the right thing
- The jealousy will end if only they can convince them of their love
- They think it is up to them to make the relationship work
- They are afraid of what will happen if the police are involved

Later, people stay because:

- They're in love, just a little less
- They still hope for change or that the abuser will get help
- Family and friends pressure them to stay
- They believe they are loved or needed
- They believe promises of change and the life of their dreams
- They are increasingly afraid of the abuser's violence

Finally, people stay because:

- Fear: The abuser has become tremendously powerful
- The abuser threatens to kill them, their family, or their pets
- They have developed low self-esteem
- They believe no one else can love them
- They believe they can't survive alone
- They are confused and blame themselves, and think they must have done something to deserve the abuse
- They feel helpless and hopeless (Nelson, 2008, p. 4B)

One body of literature suggests that people stay with their abusers because their self-esteem is so low, their powerlessness so pervasive, that they blame themselves for their victimization. Another line of thought suggests that abused people don't blame themselves; they blame external factors or their abusers, which causes them to stay in abusive relationships as well. Let's explore both of these explanations.

BLAMING ONESELF   It's very hard for those who haven't experienced battering to understand the dynamic between abuser and abused. Important contributions in this area have been made by Lenore Walker, whose research coined the terms *learned helplessness* and *battered woman syndrome*. Walker (1979, 1984, 1993) describes battered woman syndrome as including a feeling of helplessness when battered women realize they cannot change their partners or their relationships with them. When a violent episode is followed by the batterer's guilt and begging for forgiveness, followed by acts of kindness, followed again by more brutality, battered women feel they have no way of protecting themselves or escaping. Many also fear that their partners will kill them (and possibly their children) if they leave, have their partners arrested, or attempt to get a restraining order. This is a very real fear, because many abusive husbands threaten to kill their wives if they leave. For many women, economic pressures and commitments to children heighten the perception that they cannot leave the abusive relationship. This cycle creates a learned helplessness, which is so overpowering that some battered women see no solution but to kill their abusers or themselves.

Battered woman syndrome helps us understand why women remain in abusive relationships. Abused women often believe they are so stupid, worthless, and unlovable that they deserve the anger and violent displays their partners perpetrate on them (Enander, 2010). They tear themselves down psychologically, saying things like, "If I was just prettier (thinner, sexier, younger), he wouldn't be so disgusted with me" and "If I just say and do the right things, if I become a better housekeeper and cook and mother, he won't treat me this way." If you are thinking, "How pathetic that someone could let themselves get so low," think again. Even people with the strongest of self-concepts and most optimistic of dispositions are susceptible to power abuses from ones they love.

In abusive episodes, targets tend not to panic or fly into an uncontrolled rage, but to exhibit what's been termed "frozen fright," a hysterical, emotional state of numbness or paralysis (Graham, Rawlings, & Rimini, 1988, p. 220). The most important thing is survival. When targets realize that their abuser holds power over their very lives, and when abusers allow targets to live, the targets' response is often a strange sort of gratitude. The shell shock–type of reaction after an abusive episode affects the psyche, causing the target to realize that she or he may be physically free for the moment, but still not psychologically free. The chronic physical and psychological trauma battered women experience may lead to *posttraumatic stress disorder,* not unlike victims of catastrophe, hostage crises, or other forms of violence report.

Studies conducted with women in shelters have taught us a good deal about how difficult it is to leave an abuser, since most situations involve a series of leaving and returning episodes, before a successful and final departure can be accomplished (Heise, Ellsberg, & Gottemoeller, 2002). Sheltered women have also helped us understand how violent episodes occur, including the forms of communication present before, during, and after a violent encounter. One of the main things we've learned backs up Walker's observations: Battered women can recall almost every detail of every violent incident, including what blows landed where, how he looked when he started the beating, the terrible things he said, and how he acted afterward (Rudd, Dobos, Vogl-Bauer, & Beatty, 1997).

BLAMING THE ABUSER, NOT THE ABUSED   Another view about responses to abuse, one that differs from responses to sexual assault, is that battered partners tend *not* to blame themselves for the violence they receive. Research from this perspective shows that abused wives are much more likely to blame external factors (such as an economic downturn or their husband being unemployed or having a bad day at work) or their abuser's personality or behaviors (his feeling guilty about being a poor provider, his drinking, or his bad temper, which cause him to turn violent; Cantos, Neidig, & O'Leary, 1993; Libby, 2009; McFarland, 2009). While these are interesting responses that seem

Remember . . .

Physical Abuse: Violent behavior that ranges from a push or slap to a beating to the use of a weapon

Psychological Abuse: Broad category of behavior that includes emotional and verbal abuse

Battering Myths: Beliefs about partner violence that aren't based in fact

Learned Helplessness: Sense that one cannot escape or protect oneself from an abusive partner, which causes self-esteem to plummet and dependency on the batterer to increase

Battered Woman Syndrome: Condition that battered women often experience that makes them feel they cannot escape or protect themselves; a result of repeatedly going through a cycle of being battered by a partner, begged for forgiveness, extended acts of kindness, followed by more acts of brutality, and so on

Posttraumatic Stress Disorder: Psychological stress-related disorder, characterized by nightmares, muscle tremors, cold sweats, hallucinations, and flashbacks

better than blaming the self, don't adopt a rosy interpretation too quickly. Those same external factors or character flaws often give women reasons to stay with their abusers. If the battered partner perceives the cause as external or about the abuser rather than about oneself, the partner thinks that these things can change. Thinking like "once he gets a job, this will stop" or "if he'd stop drinking we'd be happier" causes women to persevere in dangerous, dead-end (often literally) relationships.

Parting Considerations about Partner Violence

As you now realize, partner violence is an enormous problem that crosses boundaries of sex, sexual orientation, race, class, educational level, age, and nationality. It's becoming less and less a silent destroyer of families and lives as survivors emerge, tell their stories, and give other abused people hope. From outsiders' perspectives, none of us can truly know the depth of despair this kind of victimization causes. We'll have to take the word of people who have experienced it—and there are far more of them than we'd like to think.

A magazine article had some great words of advice about bringing men into the conversation about violence against women (Edgar, 2002). The author points out that, like programs for sexual assault and rape, much of the educational efforts on partner violence are aimed at women. Public service ads tend to focus on raising women's awareness, encouraging them to get out of abusive relationships, and offering information on where to get help. While these efforts have been successful, as polls indicate that women's understanding of the problem has increased, they reinforce the belief that domestic violence is a woman's issue. As we've seen for other forms of power abuses, that belief isn't helpful. So, our challenge to readers is for us all—men and women alike—to give our attention to this issue and decide what we can do about it. If you're in an abusive relationship, perhaps the information in this chapter will give you options and maybe some hope. If you know someone who is being abused, perhaps you now know more about the problem, what to do, and how to help.

Conclusion

You're probably glad you made it through this chapter; we realize it's a drain to consider the terrible things people do to one another. It was a drain to research these topics and write about them, but we're sure you'll agree they're extremely important. We provided statistics and research findings in an effort to bring you the most relevant information possible, but we also put a face on each of these problems. Many of you were probably able to substitute a more familiar face for the people in our stories—Annie and Kris, Leah and Matt. The faces of the people who have suffered abuse are more real, more meaningful than all the statistics and research in the world.

We have to think about ways people use and abuse power in our society and across the world. Burying our heads in the sand, not wanting to believe that our fellow human beings commit such atrocities, not wanting to do anything to stop it, makes us part of the problem, not the solution. The author of this text often uses this adapted phrase, "Pick ye rebellions where ye may." Perhaps one of your own personal rebellions against injustice may be to see that sexual assault and rape and intimate partner violence never happen to you and the ones you love.

Discussion Starters

1. Imagine that you (and an organization you belong to on campus) were asked to present a date rape awareness and prevention program on campus. Knowing what you now know about this serious problem, what would you choose to highlight in such a program? Would you spend equal amounts of time teaching men not to rape as you might teaching women how to prevent their own victimization?

2. Why do you think people continue to adhere to myths about rape and battering? Are these forms of abuse just too terrible to face, so we manufacture false ideas about them? Knowing that these myths exist because somebody believes them, how can you expose and debunk them?

References

Aardvarc: An abuse, rape, and domestic violence aid and resource collection. (2006). Retrieved July 16, 2010, from http://www.aardvarc.org

Abbey, A. (1982). Sex differences in attributions for friendly behavior: Do males misperceive females' friendliness? *Journal of Personality and Social Psychology, 42,* 830–838.

Abbey, A., Ross, L. T., McDuffie, D., & McAuslan, P. (1996). Alcohol and dating risk: Factors for sexual assault among college women. *Psychology of Women Quarterly, 20,* 147–169.

Activist dialogues: How domestic violence and child welfare systems impact women of color and their communities. (2005). Family Violence

Prevention Fund. Retrieved July 15, 2010, from http://www.endabuse.org

Adverse health conditions and health risk behaviors associated with intimate partner violence, morbidity, and mortality weekly report. (2008, February). Centers for Disease Control. Retrieved July 15, 2010, from http://www.cdc.gob

Anderson, K. L., & Umberson, D. (2001). Gendering violence: Masculinity and power in men's accounts of domestic violence. *Gender & Society, 15,* 358–380.

Angier, N. (2000, June–July). Biological bull. *Ms.,* 80–82.

Ashcraft, C. (2000). Naming knowledge: A language for reconstructing domestic violence and systemic gender inequity. *Women & Language, 23,* 3–10.

Beres, M. A., Herold, E., & Maitland, S. B. (2004). Sexual consent behaviors in same-sex relationships. *Archives of Sexual Behavior, 33,* 475–486.

Berryman-Fink, C. (1993). Preventing sexual harassment through male-female communication training. In G. L. Kreps (Ed.), *Sexual harassment: Communication implications* (pp. 267–280). Cresskill, NJ: Hampton.

Blosnich, J. R., & Bossarte, R. M. (2009). Comparisons of intimate partner violence among partners in same-sex and opposite-sex relationships in the United States. *American Journal of Public Health, 99,* 2182–2184.

Brown, C. (2008). Gender-role implications on same-sex intimate partner abuse. *Journal of Family Violence, 23,* 457–462.

Bugeja, M. (2010, February 25). Avatar rape. Retrieved March 20, 2010, from http://www.insidehighered.com

Bureau of Justice. (2010). Statistical tables index. Retrieved July 13, 2010, from http://bjs.ojp.usdoj.gov

Burnett, A., Mattern, J. L., Herakova, L. L., Kahl, D. H., Jr., Tobola, C., & Bornsen, S. E. (2009). Communicating/muting date rape: A cocultural theoretical analysis of communication factors related to rape culture on a college campus. *Journal of Applied Communication Research, 37,* 465–485.

Burt, M. R. (1980). Cultural myths and supports for rape. *Journal of Personality and Social Psychology, 38,* 217–230.

Cantos, A. L., Neidig, P. H., & O'Leary, K. D. (1993). Men's and women's attributions of blame for domestic violence. *Journal of Family Violence, 8,* 289–302.

Crary, D. (2001, August 12). Male victims of domestic violence are asking for more support. Associated Press, as in *Corpus Christi Caller Times,* p. A25.

Crawford, M., & Unger, R. (2004). *Women and gender: A feminist psychology* (4th ed.). New York: McGraw-Hill.

D.C. Rape Crisis Center. (1998). *Myths about rape.* Retrieved from www.dcrcc.org.

D.C. Rape Crisis Center. (2006). Turning anger into change. Retrieved from www.dcrcc.org

Domestic violence is a serious, widespread social problem in America: The facts. (2010). Family Violence Prevention Foundation. Retrieved July 15, 2010, from http://endabuse.org

Dusky, L. (2003, Spring). Harvard stumbles over rape reporting. *Ms.,* 39–40.

Dutton, M. A., & Goodman, L. A. (2005). Coercion in intimate partner violence: Toward a new conceptualization. *Sex Roles, 52,* 743–756.

Edgar, J. (2002, Summer). Stopping violence against women: Bring men into the conversation. *Ms.,* 7.

Emmers-Sommer, T. M., Farrell, J., Gentry, A., Stevens, S., Eckstein, J., Battocletti, J., & Gardener, C. (2010). First date sexual expectations: The effects of who asked, who paid, date location, and gender. *Communication Studies, 61,* 339–355.

Enander, V. (2010). "A fool to keep staying": Battered women labeling themselves stupid as an expression of gendered shame. *Violence Against Women, 16,* 5–31.

Family violence statistics. (2005). U.S. Department of Justice, Bureau of Justice Statistics. Retrieved July 15, 2010, from http://www.ojp.usdoj.gov

Federal Bureau of Investigation. (2008). *Uniform crime report.* Retrieved July 12, 2010, from http://www.fbi.gov

Federal Bureau of Investigation. (2009). *Uniform crime report.* Retrieved July 12, 2010, from http://www.fbi.gov

Flores, S. A., & Hartlaub, M. G. (1998). Reducing rape-myth acceptance in male college students: A meta-analysis of intervention studies. *Journal of College Student Development, 39,* 438–448.

Gay, W. C. (2007). Supplanting linguistic violence. In L. L. O'Toole, J. R. Schiffman, & M. L. Kiter

Edwards (Eds.), *Gender violence: Interdisciplinary perspectives* (2nd ed., pp. 435–442). New York: New York University Press.

Gelles, R. J., & Straus, M. A. (1988). *Intimate violence.* New York: Simon & Schuster.

Good, G. E., Heppner, M. J., Hillenbrand-Gunn, T. L., & Wang, L. (1995). Sexual and psychological violence: An exploratory study of predictors in college men. *Journal of Men's Studies, 4,* 59–71.

Graham, D. L. R., Rawlings, E., & Rimini, N. (1988). Survivors of terror. In K. Yello & M. Bograd (Eds.), *Feminist perspectives on wife abuse* (pp. 217–233). Newbury Park, CA: Sage.

Guerrero, L. K., & Floyd, K. (2006). *Nonverbal communication in close relationships.* Mahwah, NJ: Erlbaum.

Hammons, S. A. (2004). "Family violence": The language of legitimacy. *Affilia, 19,* 273–288.

Harned, M. (2004). The relationship between labeling unwanted sexual experiences and distress. *Journal of Consulting and Clinical Psychology, 72,* 1090–1099.

Harvey, J. H., & Weber, A. L. (2002). *Odyssey of the heart: Close relationships in the 21st century* (2nd ed.). Mahwah, NJ: Erlbaum.

Heffernan, J., Shuttlesworth, G., & Ambrosino, R. (1997). *Social work and social welfare* (3rd ed.). New York: West.

Heise, L., Ellsberg, M., & Gottemoeller, M. (2002). Is domestic violence best treated as a gender crime? In E. L. Paul (Ed.), *Taking sides: Clashing views on controversial issues in sex and gender* (2nd ed., pp. 226–234). New York: McGraw-Hill/Dushkin.

Henningsen, D. D. (2004). Flirting with meaning: An examination of miscommunication in flirting interactions. *Sex Roles, 50,* 481–489.

hooks, b. (2000). *Feminism is for everybody: Passionate politics.* Cambridge, MA: South End.

Hughes, J. O., & Sandler, B. R. (1987). *"Friends" raping friends: Could it happen to you?* Washington, DC: Project on the Status and Education of Women, Association of American Colleges.

Infante, D. A., Rancer, A. S., & Womack, D. F. (2003). *Building communication theory* (4th ed.). Prospect Heights, IL: Waveland.

Jacobs, G. (1994, September–October). Where do we go from here? An interview with Ann Jones. *Ms.,* 56–63.

Johnson, M. P. (2006). Gendered communication and intimate partner violence. In B. J. Dow & J. T. Wood (Eds.), *The Sage handbook of gender and communication* (pp. 71–87). Thousand Oaks, CA: Sage.

Jones, A. (1994). *Next time she'll be dead.* Boston: Beacon.

Karjane, H. M., Fisher, B. S., & Cullen, F. T. (2010). Sexual assault on campus: What colleges and universities are doing about it. In B. Hutchinson (Ed.), *Annual editions: Gender 10/11* (pp. 215–221). Boston: McGraw-Hill.

Koeppel, L. B., Montagne, Y., O'Hair, D., & Cody, M. J. (1999). Friendly? Flirting? Wrong? In L. K. Guerrero, J. DeVito, & M. L. Hecht (Eds.), *The nonverbal communication reader* (pp. 290–297). Prospect Heights, IL: Waveland.

Koukounas, E., & Letch, N. M. (2001). Psychological correlates of perception of sexual intent in women. *Journal of Social Psychology, 141,* 443–456.

Kramer Bussel, R. (2008). Beyond yes or no: Consent as sexual process. In J. Friedman & J. Valenti (Eds.), *Yes means yes! Visions of female sexual power and a world without rape* (pp. 43–51). Berkeley, CA: Seal Press.

Labi, A. (2007, February 2). Date rape's last straw. *The Chronicle of Higher Education,* p. A5.

Lannutti, P. J., & Monahan, J. L. (2004). Resistance, persistence, and drinking: Examining goals of women's refusals of unwanted sexual advances. *Western Journal of Communication, 68,* 151–169.

Lee, J. W., & Guerrero, L. K. (2001). Types of touch in cross-sex relationships between co-workers: Perceptions of relational and emotional messages, inappropriateness, and sexual harassment. *Journal of Applied Communication Research, 29,* 197–220.

Libby, L. (2001, February 11). Many endure abuse to fit in and feel loved. *Corpus Christi Caller Times,* pp. H1, H3.

Libby, L. (2009, February 1). Domestic violence is on ugly upswing. *Corpus Christi Caller Times,* p. 1B.

Lie, G.-Y., & Gentlewarrior, S. (1991). Intimate violence in lesbian relationships: Discussion of survey findings and practical implications. *Journal of Social Service Research, 15,* 41–59.

Lie, G.-Y., Schilit, R., Bush, J., Montagne, M., & Reyes, L. (1991). Lesbians in currently aggressive relationships: How frequently do they report aggressive past relationships? *Violence & Victims, 6,* 121–135.

Lim, G. Y., & Roloff, M. E. (1999). Attributing sexual consent. *Journal of Applied Communication Research, 27,* 1–23.

Lipka, S. (2009, January 30). In campus-crime reports, there's little safety in the numbers. *The Chronicle of Higher Education,* pp. A1, A15–A17.

MacKinnon, R. (1997). Virtual rape. *Journal of Computer-Mediated Communication, 2* [Electronic version].

Martin, E. K., Taft, C. T., & Resick, P. A. (2006). A review of marital rape. *Aggression and Violent Behavior, 12,* 329–347.

McCloskey, S., Lee, R., Berman, M. E., Noblett, K. L., & Coccaro, E. F. (2008). The relationship between impulsive verbal aggression and intermittent explosive disorder. *Aggressive Behavior, 34,* 51–60.

McFarland, S. (2009, August 16). Economy down, family violence up. *Corpus Christi Caller Times,* pp. 1B, 2B.

Meighan, T. (2003, August 10). Unsafe at home: Domestic violence reaches frightening levels. Scripps Howard, as in *Corpus Christi Caller Times,* p. A11.

Meyer, A. (2010). "Too drunk to say no." *Feminist Media Studies, 10,* 19–34.

Meyer, M., & Johnson, R. (1999, October). *The "F-word" as a predictor of date rape myth acceptance.* Paper presented at the meeting of the Organization for the Study of Communication, Language, and Gender, Wichita, KS.

Milburn, M. A., Mather, R., & Conrad, S. D. (2000). The effects of viewing R-rated movie scenes that objectify women on perceptions of date rape. *Sex Roles, 43,* 645–664.

Miller, A., Bobner, R., & Zarski, J. (2000). Sexual identity development: A base for work with same-sex couple partner abuse. *Contemporary Family Therapy: An International Journal, 22,* 189–200.

Moore, B. M. (2000, October–November). License to rape. *Ms.,* 25.

Moore, M. M. (2002). Courtship communication and perception. *Perceptual & Motor Skills, 94,* 97–105.

Morrow, S. L., & Hawxhurst, D. M. (1989). Lesbian partner abuse: Implications for therapists. *Journal of Counseling & Development, 68,* 58–62.

Muehlenhard, C. L., & Linton, M. A. (1987). Date rape and sexual aggression in dating situations: Incidence and risk factors. *Journal of Counseling Psychology, 24,* 186–196.

Muehlenhard, C. L., & Rodgers, C. S. (2005). Token resistance to sex: New perspectives on an old stereotype. In J. K. Davidson & N. B. Moore (Eds.), *Speaking of sexuality* (2nd ed., pp. 280–289). Los Angeles: Roxbury.

Mullin, C. R. (1995). Desensitization and resensitization to violence against women: Effects of exposure to sexually violent films on judgments of domestic violence victims. *Journal of Personality and Social Psychology, 69,* 449–459.

National crime victimization survey: Criminal victimization, 2007. (2008). U.S. Department of Justice, Bureau of Justice Statistics. Retrieved July 15, 2010, from http://www.ojp.usdoj.gov

National Institute of Justice. (2008a). *Factors that increase sexual assault risk.* U.S. Department of Justice, Office of Justice Programs. Retrieved July 13, 2010, from http://www.ojp.usdoj.gov

National Institute of Justice. (2008b). *Measuring frequency.* U.S. Department of Justice, Office of Justice Programs. Retrieved July 13, 2010, from http://www.ojp.usdoj.gov

Nelson, A. (2008, June 8). Breaking the cycle: Women's shelter lends helping hand. *Corpus Christi Caller Times,* pp. 1B, 4B.

New studies document prevalence, cost of violence, inadequate response. (2006, October 16). Family Violence Prevention Foundation. Retrieved from www.endabuse.org

Olson, L. N. (2002). Exploring "common couple violence" in heterosexual romantic relationships. *Western Journal of Communication, 66,* 104–128.

Osman, S. L. (2007). Predicting perceptions of sexual harassment based on type of resistance and belief in token resistance. *Journal of Sex Research, 44,* 340–346.

Paul, L. A., Gray, M. J., Elhai, J. D., & Davis, J. L. (2009). Perceptions of peer rape myth acceptance and disclosure in a sample of college sexual assault survivors. *Psychological Trauma: Theory, Research, Practice, and Policy, 1,* 231–241.

Peach, L. J. (1998). Sex, sexism, sexual harassment, and sexual abuse: Introduction. In L. J. Peach (Ed.), *Women in culture: A women's studies anthology* (pp. 283–301). Malden, MA: Blackwell.

Rancer, A. S., & Avtgis, T. A. (2006). *Argumentative and aggressive communication: Theory, research, and application.* Thousand Oaks, CA: Sage.

Recognizing domestic partner abuse. (2006, September). *Harvard Women's Health Watch*, 6–7.

Robinson, V. (1994). Denial and patriarchy: The relationship between patriarchy and abuse of women. In A. Taylor & J. Beinstein Miller (Eds.), *Conflict and gender* (pp. 25–44). Cresskill, NJ: Hampton.

Rohrbaugh, J. (2006). Domestic violence in same-gender relationships. *Family Court Review, 44,* 287–299.

Rudd, J. E., & Burant, P. A. (1995). A study of women's compliance-gaining behaviors in violent and non-violent relationships. *Communication Research Reports, 12,* 134–144.

Rudd, J. E., Dobos, J. A., Vogl-Bauer, S., & Beatty, M. J. (1997). Women's narrative accounts of recent abusive episodes. *Women's Studies in Communication, 20,* 45–58.

Sabourin, T. C., & Stamp, G. H. (1995). Communication and the experience of dialectical tensions in family life: An examination of abusive and nonabusive families. *Communication Monographs, 62,* 213–242.

Schneider Shevlin, J. (1994). Wife abuse: Its magnitude and one jurisdiction's response. In A. Taylor & J. Beinstein Miller (Eds.), *Conflict and gender* (pp. 45–71). Cresskill, NJ: Hampton.

Schwartz, M. D. (2005). The past and future of violence against women. *Journal of Interpersonal Violence, 20,* 7–11.

Sexual assault and rape: Advice for men. (2005). Retrieved from http://ub-counseling.buffalo.edu/advice

Shotland, R. L., & Goldstein, L. (1992). Sexual precedence reduces the perceived legitimacy of sexual refusal: An examination of attributions concerning date rape and consensual sex. *Personality and Social Psychology Bulletin, 18,* 756–764.

Sims, C. M., Noel, N. E., & Maisto, S. A. (2007). Rape blame as a function of alcohol presence and resistance type. *Addictive Behaviors, 32,* 2766–2775.

Stamp, G. H., & Sabourin, T. C. (1995). Accounting for violence: An analysis of male spousal abuse narratives. *Journal of Applied Communication Research, 23,* 284–307.

Tewksbury, R. (2010). Effects of sexual assaults on men: Physical, mental, and sexual consequences. In B. Hutchinson (Ed.), *Annual editions: Gender 10/11* (pp. 230–236). Boston: McGraw-Hill.

Thapar-Bjorkert, S., & Morgan, K. J. (2010). "But sometimes I think . . . they put themselves in the situation": Exploring blame and responsibility in interpersonal violence. *Violence Against Women, 16,* 32–59.

Tjaden, P. (2003). Symposium on Integrating Responses to Domestic Violence: Extent and Nature of Intimate Partner Violence as Measured by the National Violence Against Women Survey, *47,* 41–54. Retrieved July 16, 2010, from the American Bar Association Commission on Domestic Violence, 2010, http://new.abanet.org

Tjaden, P., & Thoennes, N. (2000). *Full report of the prevalence, incidence, and consequences of violence against women.* Washington, DC: Department of Justice.

Truman, D. M., Tokar, D. M., & Fischer, A. R. (1996). Dimensions of masculinity: Relations to date rape supportive attitudes and sexual aggression in dating situations. *Journal of Counseling & Development, 74,* 555–562.

Vangelisti, A. L., Maguire, K. C., Alexander, A. L., & Clark, G. (2007). Hurtful family environments: Links with individual, relationship, and perceptual variables. *Communication Monographs, 74,* 357–385.

Walker, L. (1979). *The battered woman.* New York: Harper Colophon.

Walker, L. (1984). *The battered woman syndrome.* New York: Springer.

Walker, L. (1993). The battered woman syndrome is a psychological consequence of abuse. In R. J. Gelles & D. R. Loseke (Eds.), *Current controversies on family violence* (pp. 133–153). Newbury Park, CA: Sage.

Waterman, C., Dawson, L., & Bologna, M. (1989). Sexual coercion in gay and lesbian relationships: Predictors and implications for support services. *Journal of Sex Research, 26,* 118–124.

Wife rape information page. (2004). Retrieved from www.unh.edu

Women killed by partner/spouse. (1998). Retrieved from www.newcountrycanada.com

Women's Health. (2008). *Date rape drugs.* Retrieved July 13, 2010, from http://www.womenshealth.gov

Yeater, E. A., Treat, T. A., Viken, R. J., & McFall, R. M. (2010). Cognitive processes underlying women's risk judgments: Associations with sexual victimization history and rape myth. *Journal of Consulting and Clinical Psychology, 78,* 375–386.

Young, S. L., & Maguire, K. C. (2003). Talking about sexual violence. *Women & Language, 26,* 40–52.

Zillman, D., & Bryant, J. (1982). Pornography, sexual callousness, and the trivialization of rape. *Journal of Communication, 32,* 10–21.

HOT TOPICS

- The 50/50 workforce and the wage gap
- How stereotypes can impede the likelihood of getting hired
- How relational and content approaches to communication emerge in job interviewing
- Verbal and nonverbal indications of sex bias in job interviews
- Men's and women's advancement on the job
- The glass ceiling and the sticky floor
- Juggling family and career
- Managerial communication styles of women and men
- An update on the problem of sexual harassment in the workplace

Women and Men in the Workplace

The Challenges of Talking Shop

CHAPTER 9

Case Study

How Does 50/50 Sound?

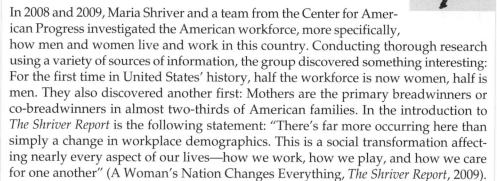

In 2008 and 2009, Maria Shriver and a team from the Center for American Progress investigated the American workforce, more specifically, how men and women live and work in this country. Conducting thorough research using a variety of sources of information, the group discovered something interesting: For the first time in United States' history, half the workforce is now women, half is men. They also discovered another first: Mothers are the primary breadwinners or co-breadwinners in almost two-thirds of American families. In the introduction to *The Shriver Report* is the following statement: "There's far more occurring here than simply a change in workplace demographics. This is a social transformation affecting nearly every aspect of our lives—how we work, how we play, and how we care for one another" (A Woman's Nation Changes Everything, *The Shriver Report*, 2009).

Then in March of 2011, the Obama administration released *Women in America: Indicators of Social and Economic Well Being*, a comprehensive report on women's status in the United States. The investigation focused on women's progress in educational, home, and professional contexts, finding out that younger women now outnumber men in colleges and universities, and that today's woman is less "June Cleaver" and more "Liz Lemon." According to the report, 61 percent of women work outside the home and make up half the American workforce, yet the pay gap with men is as strong as ever. (We address this issue more in depth a bit later in this chapter.) In accord with *The Shriver Report*, women now make up 40 percent of the breadwinners in American families. Women are also delaying marriage by five years, compared to women in the 1950s, plus they are delaying having children—all of which has ramifications for the workforce.

(continued)

Case Study (*continued*)

Many students don't think much about these new statistics—particularly the fact that men and women are equally represented (at least in numbers) in the American workforce. Many of you have no doubt come to expect a fully sex-integrated workplace; for most occupations, it's not a shock or an aberration to work for or with people of both sexes. But the 50/50 profile does represent a significant shift from how Americans worked and lived in past generations, with all kinds of implications for our current society. As you plunge into this chapter, ponder how having a 50/50 workforce might affect gender communication, both professionally and personally.

What would you say if we were to ask you, What are some challenges in the working world today? That may seem like a strange question, given that students are striving to get their degrees so that they can more successfully gain employment, enjoy active professional lives, and fulfill their goals. But more students than ever are working—many full time, many with multiple jobs. Gone are the days when college students graduated with little or no work experience because they were so focused on their studies, much as we might all be nostalgic for that kind of economic freedom. The most common profile of today's college student is combo worker/student, with the ratio of work to study dependent on one's circumstances. Because of their work responsibilities, students now tend to take lighter course loads, which means that many finish their undergraduate degrees in five years or more, rather than the four-year period common for college students in past generations. So, given your work experience, what *are* the more pressing issues related to sex, gender, and communication in the world of work? Competing for the best jobs? Acing the interview? Facing sex-based discrimination, like a glass ceiling blocking your advancement? Handling an office romance? Juggling work and home responsibilities? Finding your way as a manager or leader of an organization? Dealing with sexual harassment? These are several of the topics we explore as we examine workplace communication in this chapter.

WOMEN AND MEN WORKING TOGETHER: WALKING ON EGGSHELLS?

For many of us, our work is our livelihood, our most time-consuming activity. In fact, Americans are working longer hours, spending significantly greater amounts time on the job than three decades ago (Hochschild & Machung, 2006). In fact, as of 2010, Americans work a full week's worth of hours more per year than in the year 2000—a full week's worth of hours added in just one decade! (Work & Family Facts & Statistics, 2010). Work can be a rewarding experience or a real downer for self-esteem. Many things make a job worthwhile and rewarding. However, when asked what makes their jobs enjoyable, most employees—men and women alike—say that relationships with people they work with make the most difference between job satisfaction and dissatisfaction. At the same time that people feel coworker relationships are important, they also reveal a sense that coworker communication—especially between female and male coworkers—is complicated. Because some of the rules, roles, and boundaries continue to shift in the world of work, people often feel that they're "walking on eggshells" so as to not say the wrong thing and get themselves or someone else into trouble. We're not suggesting that gender is in the center of every ineffective communication situation at work; however, a good number of problems in the workplace that appear to be power- or status-based may really be problems between the sexes.

U.S. Census data for 2010 reveal that the U.S. workforce is 49.9 percent female, compared to 47 percent in 2000, 45 percent in 1990, and 43 percent in 1980 (U.S. Census Bureau, 2010; U.S. Department of Labor, 2010). Four in ten American mothers bring home the majority of the family's earnings, while nearly two-thirds are breadwinners or co-breadwinners in their families (Boushey, 2009). However, 2010 statistics also show that a woman working full time earns, as an average weekly wage, about 83 cents for every dollar a man earns. In the 1970s, that figure was 59 cents; in the 1980s, the gender pay gap narrowed to its greatest extent, but that was because men's wages fell, not because women's wages rose (Blau & Kahn, 1997). In the early part of the first decade of this new century, the statistic was 76 cents, so some progress has been made over the last 10 years, but many people wonder why the wage gap still exists (U.S. Census Bureau, 2010).

Other statistics paint the wage gap as being more dire than census data shows. As we alluded to in the opening case study for this chapter, in March of 2011, the Obama administration released *Women in America: Indicators of Social and Economic Well Being*, a comprehensive report on women's status in the United States. The White House's research led to the conclusion that women currently make 75 cents to the man's dollar, suggesting an even greater wage gap currently existing in the country. Most likely, the difference is that the census statistic reflects only full-time female workers, whereas the White House report factors in full-time and part-time female workers.

You've probably heard wage statistics like these before, but consider this: According to the White House report, *Women in America* (2011), the earnings gap will not disappear until the year 2056! For a woman with only a high school diploma, the pay gap will cost her $700,000 in lost income over her lifetime, according to economist and author Evelyn Murphy (as in Troy, 2009; Murphy, 2006). Murphy is president of WAGE (Women Are Getting Even), a nonprofit organization established to "end discrimination against women in the American workplace in the near future" (Women Are Getting Even, 2006). For those women who've completed college, the economic loss is closer to $1 million; for those with graduate degrees, the figure is $1.2 million. Wage discrepancies are also affected by race and ethnicity, with a general downward trend over a twenty-year period in earnings for members of minority groups (Burk, 2006; England, Garcia-Beaulieu, & Ross, 2007; Katz & Andronici, 2006; Lips, 2007; O'Neill, 2007; U.S. Department of Labor, 2010).

The truth is that women's income, on average, will always be a fraction of men's, so long as America remains free.

—Patrick Buchanan, political pundit & former presidential candidate

It is beyond the parameters of our discussion in this chapter to interpret trends in workforce statistics, nor do we want to attempt to assess the impact of a 50/50 male/female workforce. We do want to explore some possible explanations for the fact that in recent years only a minuscule increase has been achieved among the ranks of female senior management. We also examine how the increased presence of women in the workplace is affecting professional communication and the dynamics between the sexes, particularly at the management level. However, before tackling these on-the-job issues, it's a good idea to understand how one's sex may affect getting a job in the first place.

GETTING THAT ALL-IMPORTANT JOB

Sex and gender bias may impede you from getting a chance at a job. Often you don't know that this has happened; you just never get a response from an organization to your résumé. If and when you do get job interviews, bias may be operating as well.

Vestiges of Affirmative Action

Affirmative action isn't nearly the hot-button issue it once was; even as recently as a decade ago, the air waves and publications of all sorts frequently contained stories debating the pros and cons of affirmative action. Court cases are still pending regarding the controversial action, which became law between 1961 and 1973, when Presidents Kennedy, Johnson, and Nixon issued executive orders designed to eliminate discrimination (Papa, Daniels, & Spiker, 2007). The focus of the current debate seems to be more about discrimination in college and university admissions practices than employment, with more emphasis on race than sex or gender (Charles, Fischer, Mooney, & Massey, 2009; Contreras, 2008; Kahlenberg, 2010; Moses, Marin, & Yun, 2008; Ramasubramanian, 2010; Wiedeman, 2008).

However, as you embark on the process of landing a post college, career-type job, you may encounter policies about affirmative action, equal employment opportunity notices on job applications or job listing sites, or hiring approaches that have been enlightened due to the impact of affirmative action.

The debate over affirmative action has already affected you because of its impact on admission standards at colleges and universities. Looking toward the future, you will no doubt want to know how professional schools (like law schools or medical schools) and potential employers view affirmative action and if they have programs in place that enhance the diversification of their student bodies and workforces. Then you will have to weigh that information with your own stance on the issue.

Gender Issues and the Job Interview

There's no doubt about it—job interviews are extremely important. As communication scholars Kirkwood and Ralston (1999) suggest, "The employment interview is more than just a gateway to the organization. Whatever transpires between parties during interviews is part of their long-term relationship" (p. 56). Once you've landed an interview, your insight into gender communication will be helpful.

APPROACHES TO TALK: INSIGHT INTO THE INTERVIEW   What application to the job interview can you make of the information in Chapter 4 about *relational* and *content approaches* to communication? First, a caution: Don't take the relational-content instruction too far by assuming that a person's sex delineates his or her preferred approach to communication.

Research suggests a *tendency* for men to view conversation as functioning to impart content or information and women to view it as relationship maintenance or a means of connecting with others. Use this knowledge to better understand yourself and your own approach to communication and maybe to help you read clues from an interviewer.

A well-developed communication repertoire, good listening skills, an alertness to nonverbal cues, and a flexible communication style will increase the likelihood of success in the interview context (as well as other contexts for communication (Beebe, Beebe, & Ivy, 2013). It's wise to survey yourself to understand your goals for an interview and your own preferences regarding approaches to talk. Then you will be able to detect when relational or content approaches are in use and respond, if appropriate, by aligning your behavior with that of the interviewer.

BEING TAKEN SERIOUSLY   Unfortunately, a concern about being taken seriously still applies more to female than male candidates for jobs, unless a man applies for a job in a traditionally female-dominated field. Even though women now comprise half of the workforce, their presence seems to be noted in a different way than men's. The expectation still exists that men work out of necessity—*that's just what men do*. Although the corresponding stereotype for women is diminishing, some still believe that women work outside the home for mere distraction, for a secondary supplemental income, or as an interim activity before they settle down and have families (Adler & Elmhorst, 2008; Ivy & Wahl, 2009; O'Hair, Friedrich, & Dixon, 2010). Alternative explanations given for why women work are far more numerous than the simple possibility that they work for the same reasons as men.

NONVERBAL INDICATIONS OF SEX BIAS   Nonverbal communication is critical in a job interview; the nonverbal most often carries the true message, rather than the verbal communication. Some women have encountered what one author calls the "maternal wall," employers' assumption that any woman who is a mother is the primary parent, and because of that status, she will no doubt be unable to commit to her job the way a father can (Williams, as in Meers & Strober, 2009, p. 86). But just how might sex-based expectations be revealed nonverbally during a job interview?

A dead giveaway (or at least a fairly reliable nonverbal signal that a sex-based stereotype is in operation) comes in the opening greeting, especially the handshake. We make judgments about someone's personality based on the simple greeting ritual of the handshake (Kish, 2009). A team of psychologists developed what they call a *handshake index*, a determination based on strength, vigor, completeness of grip, and duration of handshake (Chaplin, Phillips, Brown, Clanton, & Stein, 2000). They studied judgments subjects made about people with high handshake indexes versus low handshake indexes. Women and men with higher handshake indexes communicated more favorable first impressions and were deemed extroverted, open to experience, and less shy. Women with high handshake indexes were also perceived to be highly agreeable, in comparison to women with weak or poor handshakes.

Often men and women alike appear awkward when shaking hands with a woman. This situation is improving, but women still get the "cupped fingers, half handshake" (the one that translates into "You sweet, fragile thing; I couldn't possibly grasp your whole hand because it'd fall right off"). A potential employer likely has no intention of conveying negative impressions regarding a female applicant's credibility; the person just has a lousy handshake or has never learned the importance of a firm one. Nonetheless, it should raise the eyebrows of a female applicant when the handshake extended to her is less firm or confidence-inducing than one extended to a male applicant or colleague. This can be a subtle indication of a sex-based value system that is tolerated and perpetuated within the organization.

Job candidates have to exercise care when they extend handshakes to company employees, especially the person doing the hiring. For women, too firm of a handshake may violate expectations, be read as masculine, too forceful, or unconfident, as though the woman is overcompensating by using an overly gripping handshake (Ralston & Kinser, 2001). Management professors Stewart, Dustin, Barrick, and Darnold (2008) explored the influence of a handshake during an interview on job suitability and recommendations to hire. They found that women, in general, received lower ratings than men for the quality of their handshake and that perceptions about hiring were more strongly affected by women's handshakes than men's. Perhaps some perception of handshaking being more of a male-expected, male-appropriate behavior still persists in both professional and social contexts in our culture, but this perception needs to change. It's important that male and female students alike work on this very important nonverbal cue, which can make or break a job interview.

Besides the handshake in an interview, bias may be subtly communicated through other nonverbal cues. Applicant physical appearance has an impact on impression-making and, in some cases, hiring decisions (Barrick, Shaffer, & DeGrassi, 2009; DeGroot & Motowidlo, 1999; Goldberg & Cohen, 2004; Hosada, Stone-Romero, & Coats, 2003). Studies show that being overweight, especially for women, negatively affects a person's chances of being perceived positively in a job interview (Pingitore, Dugoni, Tindale, & Spring, 1994; Rudolph, Wells, Weller, & Baltes, 2009).

Although an asset for male applicants, physical attractiveness is a bit trickier for female job seekers (Marlowe, Schneider, & Nelson, 1996). If a woman is highly physically attractive, her looks may be a deterrent to getting a job because of the stereotype that female beauty is accompanied by a lack of intelligence. Another suspicion is that the woman will cause more problems on the job than she is worth by "being a distraction" or inciting male interest. She may be perceived as a poor choice for a job because of her potential to "sexualize" a workplace. We contend that highly physically attractive male employees have similar potential to disrupt a workplace or change how people interact in their presence; we've seen some attractive male job candidates receive different scrutiny than others, so the potential for bias in this area can certainly work both ways. In a perfect world, one's looks shouldn't matter in a decision about who gets the job; one's qualifications should outweigh such things as appearance, but we don't live in a perfect world, do we?

Some negative nonverbal cues that may emerge in job interviews include indications of general disinterest such as a lack of eye contact, which may communicate you're not being taken seriously for the position. If the interviewer seems unprepared, if she or he rushes through the interview or shows impatience by interrupting or overlapping your answers to questions, or if he or she accepts multiple interruptions from associates, text messages, or phone calls, these actions can signal that the candidate isn't a serious contender for the job. Granted, you can't always tell whether the behavior has to do with your sex, your qualifications, some idiosyncratic reaction on the part of the interviewer, or some other variable totally unrelated to you and your interview. But it's important to take in as many nonverbal cues as possible and apply caution when interpreting what the cues mean (Beebe, Beebe, & Ivy, 2013).

VERBAL INDICATIONS OF SEX BIAS   Another way that sex-based stereotypes are evidenced in job interviews has to do with the interviewer questioning process. If a potential employer holds some doubt as to whether a person of your sex is serious about a job or is capable of handling the job, the interviewer might reveal these doubts by asking leading questions. *Leading questions* are designed to trap the interviewee into a forced response or a no-win situation. They often take the form of a posed hypothetical situation followed by a question as to what the applicant would do. For example, when men apply for jobs in a currently female-dominated field such as nursing, they may receive leading questions that translate into doubts about their nurturing abilities. Or a woman applying for a position in a male-dominated office might get a leading question such as, "What would you do if a male colleague disagreed with one of your ideas and started to argue with you in front of your coworkers? Would you be able to handle that?"

One of the more overt means of communicating gender bias in a job interview is the use of *unethical questions* to applicants. It is unethical for a potential employer to ask an applicant about his or her marital status, parental status, or sexual orientation, among other things. Most employers know this, so most of them avoid these areas. But if they want to know this information before making a hiring decision, they have to use covert means or be indirect in how they approach these subjects during a job interview. By covert means, we refer to checking out a person's background, learning information in roundabout ways from former employers, and similar tactics.

Your textbook author experienced an awkward situation some years back. During a segment of a job interview with the vice president of an organization, the subject of transition was raised. The interviewer talked about how moving from one job and one state to another was stressful, even more so if one had a spouse and children who were uprooted in the process. After making this statement, he stopped talking, made direct eye contact, and waited for her response. Even though she knew what information he was after, she wanted the job, so her reply revealed her current marital and parental status.

This example is fairly typical of the way an employer might attempt to learn information that cannot be asked directly. In this example, hindsight caused the applicant to think, "I wish I hadn't fallen into that trap; I could have simply agreed with him by saying 'Yes, transition can be quite stressful.'" There are nonconfrontational ways to communicate effectively to an employer that you know what's going on, but you're not going to play along. One option is to respond to the question with a question, as though you didn't understand what the interviewer was getting at. You may decide to use more confrontational, educative responses, but you have to weigh the risks of such tactics (such as not getting the job). The main thing to think about is whether or not you want to work for a company whose interviewers would use strategies like these. When verbal and nonverbal indications of gender bias surface in a job interview, it increases the likelihood that gender-biased behavior and attitudes will be in evidence on the job (Ralston & Kinser, 2001).

ON THE JOB AND MOVING UP

Congratulations! You got the job. You're on the job. So what gender-related variables might emerge at your job? How will you respond?

Advancement within an Organization

Refer back to the statistics cited early in this chapter—you might conclude that the workforce is equitable since women have increased their presence in the work arena. But a more careful inspection is revealing: Although women now make up half the American workforce, they do not represent half the workers in *every kind* of job. As Heather Boushey (2009), a contributor to *The Shriver Report* explains, "Continued sex segregation in employment is one of the primary factors explaining the wage gap between men and women" (p. 4). Men hold most of the blue-collar jobs in this country, while women hold the majority of what's come to be termed "pink-collar jobs," meaning primarily those involving administrative work or care services (Albelda, 2009). Of the top 20 occupations in the United States (meaning most commonly held), men are mostly employed as truck drivers, managers, and first-line supervisors, whereas the most common jobs for women are secretaries/administrative assistants, nurses, and schoolteachers. Only four of the top 20 jobs (salespersons, first-line supervisors of retail stores, managers, and cooks) employ men and women with roughly equal frequency (Boushey, 2009).

Even though sex segregation is the reality in many American workplaces, we have witnessed some progress in recent years in terms of women entering male-dominated fields such as engineering, law, and medicine, according to Boushey (2009). Women still constitute the overwhelming majority in such fields as teaching, dental hygiene, and child care; men hold the majority in construction, carpentry, and as chief executives of corporations.

Remember . . .

Affirmative Action: Governmental effort to help overcome barriers to members of under-represented groups, in terms of recruiting, hiring, and promoting

Relational Approach to Communication: View that communication functions primarily to establish and develop relationships between interactants

Content Approach to Communication: View that communication functions primarily for information exchange between interactants

Handshake Index: Perception of a handshake, based on strength, vigor, completeness of grip, and duration

Leading Question: Interviewer question that traps an interviewee into a forced or no-win response

Unethical Question: Interviewer question about personal life, such as a question about marital status, parental status, sexual orientation, religious affiliation, and so on

---

While more women are now being hired than in times past, greater numbers of men than women achieve the higher, more responsible, and more rewarding ranks (Dubeck & Dunn, 2006; Williams, 2006). Each year, *The Wall Street Journal* puts out its "50 Women to Watch" list. *Fortune* magazine continues to publish its "Fifty Most Powerful Women" lists, and, according to one *Newsweek* report, women have reached "critical mass" in leadership positions (Kantrowitz, 2005, p. 47). However, even with gains for women at higher levels and in leadership positions, significant inequity still exists in many businesses and organizations in the country (Eagly & Carli, 2009; Parloff, 2007). For example, statistics show that women represent over 40 percent of graduating classes at American law schools, a figure that is up from a mere 7 percent in 1972. These women have achieved in all aspects of the practice of law except for one: positions of power, such as partnerships and the management of law firms (Rosenberg, Perlstadt, & Phillips, 2002). What factors are connected to the trends regarding advancement?

GLASS CEILINGS AND STICKY FLOORS   We expect you've heard the *glass ceiling* term before. It stems from a larger metaphor for working women who operate in "glass houses," whose behavior is not only scrutinized by individuals on every level of the organization, but whose success or failure affects the status of employed women everywhere. Professional women who look higher, see the possibilities, yet are unable to reach them because of a transparent barrier have encountered the glass ceiling (Drago, 2007; Longo & Straehley, 2008; Miller, 2009; Ragins, Townsend, & Mattis, 2006; Zhang, Schmader, & Forbes, 2009).

> *As in other fields, women seem to break through the glass ceiling just as the air-conditioning is being turned off in the penthouse office suites.*
>
> —*Alessandra Stanley,*
> *columnist,*
> **The New York Times**

In 1991 the Federal Glass Ceiling Commission was formed, headed by Secretary of Labor Lynn Martin. This group's Glass Ceiling Initiative studied nine *Fortune* 500 companies in order to understand the barriers to advancement for women and minorities and to assist corporations in determining strategies for eliminating the barriers.

Over twenty years later, little progress has been made. Surveys of *Fortune* 1500 companies reveal that, in the decade of the 90s, 97 percent of senior managers (vice presidents and above) were men (Federal Glass Ceiling Commission, 2006). In 2009, out of the 500 companies on *Fortune*'s list, only 15 were led by female chief executive officers; among the next group of 500 companies on *Fortune*'s list, only 14 more female CEOs added to the ranks (Harrington & Ladge, 2009). These numbers constitute only 3 percent of CEO positions at America's largest companies being held by women. The percentage of women holding corporate officer positions—not CEOs, but positions of significant authority within companies—has remained stagnant over the last decade, hovering at around 15 percent.

Another phenomenon warrants brief discussion because it contributes to the overall picture of leadership and the sex and gender issues that affect advancement. The *sticky floor* phenomenon pertains to "factors that keep women in low level, non-managerial and support roles and prevent them from seeking or gaining promotion or career development" (Bnet business dictionary, 2010). Some of these factors or barriers include family commitments, attitudes, stereotyping, and organizational structures that aren't conducive to gender equity (Bjerk, 2008; Engberg, 1999; Rainbird, 2007). The sticky floor metaphor applies also to women who are loyal to their organizations and who may be promoted, but who don't receive pay increases along with the promotions.

As one group of labor researchers described it, the sticky floor is a "situation in which the gender wage gap widens at the bottom of the wage distribution" (Arulampalam, Booth, & Bryan, 2007). Women may receive symbolic rewards and may be viewed as valuable employees, but their pay doesn't match their value; thus, they feel "stuck." Rebecca Shambaugh (2007), author of *It's Not a Glass Ceiling, It's a Sticky Floor*, identifies several key factors that contribute to women's lack of advancement in the workforce. Primary among them is the need to strike a balance between work life and personal life, the "work–life balance" issue that's been around for decades, which we explore in the next section of this chapter.

Some notable strides have been made toward narrowing the wage gap for workers. In 2009, President Barack Obama's first signed piece of legislation was the Lilly Ledbetter Fair Pay Act; the bill overturned a Supreme Court ruling and made it easier for women to sue employers if they discover they're not being paid as much as their male colleagues (Andronici & Katz, 2008; The Bliss List, 2009; Brazile, 2009; Intelligence Report, 2009; Katz & Andronici, 2009; Troy, 2009; Williams, 2009). However, more work remains to be done to achieve gender equity in the workforce, both in compensation and advancement. To combat the gender differential in upper-level management, organizations must actively ensure that male and female employees' careers are developed with equal attention (Buzzanell & Lucas, 2006; Williams, 2006). Teachers, parents, and academic advisors and mentors should work with children at early ages to eliminate negative gender stereotypes *where they begin* (Correll, 2006; Mendelson Freeman, 2006). In addition, women should plan their careers well in advance and proactively seek the advancement of their careers, rather than waiting for a superior to notice and reward their accomplishments. Stewart (2001) suggests networking and developing mentor relationships as excellent strategies to help women overcome barriers in the workplace. Women who use both formal and informal channels for developing contacts, and who actively work to learn from and emulate more experienced professionals, widen their options and heighten their satisfaction and comfort levels in their jobs (Hall, 2001; Sloan & Krone, 2000).

DIFFICULT CHOICES: FAMILY, CAREER, OR BOTH?   One of the most obvious factors complicating women's professional advancement is a basic biological function—the fact that women give birth to babies. As a culture we have moved a bit forward on this front, creating more choices for families. Efforts in the 70s and 80s helped to break the constricted thinking that women would automatically choose home and family over careers. In the 1990s, women who could afford to sacrifice their paychecks to stay home and raise young children felt more free to do so without feeling that they'd violated some basic tenet of women's liberation. We've witnessed political progress through such laws as Title VII of the Civil Rights Act (1964), the Pregnancy Disability Act (1978), the EEOC's guidelines on sexual harassment (1980), and the Family and Medical Leave Act (1996; Gerstel & McGonagle, 2006; McDorman, 1998; Paul, 2002). Today, in the second decade of the twenty-first century, changes in family profile and the country's workplaces have sex and gender implications. According to Bureau of Labor Statistics (2009), only 21 percent of American families with children at home are "traditional" families in which the father is the breadwinner, while the mother is a homemaker and the primary child caretaker for the children. In 39 percent of American households, women are the major breadwinners; in nearly two-thirds of households, women are primary or co-breadwinners, bringing home the majority of the family's earnings (even though they still earn only, on average, 79 cents to the man's dollar) (Boushey, 2009). Because 79 percent of American families fit the "juggler" profile—families juggling both parents' jobs plus child rearing—the workplace has had to adjust to cope with changing demands (O'Leary & Kornbluh, 2009).

Changing workplace language indicates changing attitudes toward work and family. In the 1980s, we saw the emergence of "superwomen" who were "doing it all" and "having it all" because they raised children while maintaining their careers (Friedan, 1981). Then the term *second shift* was coined to describe the work of employed women who returned home from their jobs to hours of cleaning, cooking, and child care (Hochschild, 1989, as in Saltzman Chafetz, 1997). The 1990s brought about the *mommy track* (a variation of "fast track"), which applied to women who sought advancement in the workplace at the same time as they had child-rearing responsibilities (Hill, Martinson, Ferris, & Zenger Baker, 2006; Noonan & Corcoran, 2006).

We also saw in the 1990s greater use of *flextime*, a system some organizations adopt that allows workers to come and go early or late, or to work longer hours fewer days of the week, to better respond to home and family demands (Hochschild & Machung, 2006; Meers

> *When women make less than men for the same work, it hurts families. When a job doesn't offer family leave, that also hurts men. When there's no affordable child care, that hurts children. And when any of our citizens cannot fulfill their potential, that says something about the state of our democracy.*
>
> —*President Barack Obama*

Hot Button Issue

"Parents Who Work Outside the Home"

Do you agree that the pull between family and career exerts more pressure on women than men—even in a twenty-first century world of work? While men are assuming greater roles in child rearing than ever before, very few give up or take a break from their careers to raise children. In two-parent families that can afford to function on only one salary, the parent who stays home with the children is usually the mother. There's nothing wrong with this, but some cultural assumptions behind the practice are worth taking a look at. Granted, most men's salaries are still higher than women's in our culture, so it makes sense that the higher-salaried person would retain his or her job. A stereotype also exists, which some believe has a basis in genetic fact, that mothers are more nurturing and naturally should be the ones to tend to young children. What's your stance on this issue? Do you know any families in which the father is actually more "naturally" nurturing than the mother, and even though he makes more money, he opts to stay home with the kids while she continues her career? If a woman wants to "have it all," just like most men want to "have it all," how can our culture enable her to do that?

& Strober, 2009; Welsh, 2006). We saw an effort to create more *family-friendly* workplaces, a descriptor that emerged when *Working Mother* magazine began identifying the best places in the country for women and mothers to work (Dubeck, 2006). Organizations attempted to better accommodate workers who had family issues that could affect their job performance (Dubeck & Dunn, 2002 O'Leary & Kornbluh, 2009). However, evidence shows that family-friendly efforts aren't raising the number of women in higher ranks (Meers & Strober, 2009) and flextime opportunities aren't readily available for workers across different levels of organizations, particularly low-wage workers, even in those firms deemed at the top of the family-friendly lists (Finnegan, 2001; Holcomb, 2002). In some highly competitive workplaces, family-friendly initiatives exist as mere public relations devices; the informal internal word is that employees shouldn't actually take advantage of them (Crary, 2002; Maloney, 2008).

In reaction to the pressures of juggling home and job, some women choose *sequencing*, meaning that they temporarily drop out of the workforce so that they can more adequately raise their children. As news writer Michelle Quinn (2004) describes it, "The original concept was simple: Work hard before the children arrive. Step off the career track to be at home when the kids are young. Step back on when the children are older with work that allows flexibility" (p. D2). However, sequencing is not without its drawbacks, some of which include the inability to step back in once you've stepped out. While employers can't legally penalize women by replacing them with other workers, they can "restructure" the organization or write new job descriptions for which the employee wanting to return to work no longer qualifies. In addition, women can lose confidence in their skills during time away from work, and can experience an overwhelming feeling that too much new information and too many new skills will be required of them if they are to be successful once again on the job (Kanter, as in McGinn, 2005).

In 2003, another phenomenon—the "opt-out" trend—was discussed in an article in the *New York Times Magazine*, but the "trend" was later viewed as more media hype than reality. The article described a "talent drain" of highly trained women who "opted out" or chose not to aspire to executive positions within corporations, choosing instead to abandon their successful careers to concentrate on their families (Belkin, 2003). The problem was that the research generalized a trend based on its small, elite sample of Princeton female graduates who were privileged enough to be able to leave their careers behind to focus on family life (Mainiero & Sullivan, 2006). The ensuing media frenzy over the so-called trend suggested that large numbers of successful professional women were failing to achieve the highest career positions because they weren't willing to work as hard as men, they were too timid or passive to claim the top spots, they simply didn't want power, and the rewards of staying at home were psychologically too compelling compared to the rewards of professional life (Douglas Vavrus, 2007; Moe & Shandy, 2009). Although it certainly is the case that some women choose to opt out of their professional lives because their priorities shift, their situations demand that they refocus their energies, or they tire of hitting an advancement wall and wish to change their lives, women aren't "opting out" of careers in droves because they find work life too challenging (Williams, Manvell, & Bornstein, 2006).

Three other relatively recent and positive workplace changes warrant mention. The first is the development of on-site child care facilities and company-sponsored programs that increase employees' access to child care (Trei, 2002; Whitehurst, 2002). The second change surrounds the technological innovation of *telecommuting*, gaining steam in the twenty-first century (Hylmo, 2004; Stewart, 2001). A third development regards the growing number of self-employed parents, especially mothers, who decide that working for corporations or other businesses doesn't afford much flexibility (Levitz, 2010; Luna Brem, 2001). These women prefer to become entrepreneurs, mostly through the establishment of web-based businesses and services. The rise in their numbers has led to the coinage of the term *entrepreneurial mother*, which, according to scholar Paige Edley (2004), "means women who are mothers who own and operate their own businesses out of their homes" (p. 255).

But even with these important innovations, a nagging perception still exists in the minds of many regarding women and professionalism: Women in the workforce just can't be counted on over the long haul. They are likely to want to have children at some point in their careers, and that means maternity leaves, a greater potential for absenteeism, and the likelihood that they will vacate their positions in favor of staying home and raising their children (all of which costs organizations money). This is a stereotype—a painful one to write and read about.

Another complicating factor is the reality of the tension many women feel between their careers and obligations to bear and raise children (Gerson & Jacobs, 2006; Lorber, 2005; Stone & Lovejoy, 2006; Zaslow, 2002). We grant that the stereotype that women contribute significantly to organizational turnover because of pregnancy and child-rearing duties has some basis in reality; young children do reduce many women's employment

> *At work, you think of the children you have left at home. At home, you think of the work you've left unfinished. Such a struggle is unleashed within yourself. Your heart is rent.*
>
> *—Golda Meir, former Israeli prime minister*

(England, Garcia-Beaulieu, & Ross, 2007; O'Neill, 2007). Women struggle with multiple demands on their time and energies, particularly if they don't have a spouse or partner, or don't receive much help from one.

Women and Men in Leadership Positions

Communication researchers, organizational behavior experts, business leaders, and gender scholars alike have focused attention for decades on how the sexes approach leadership, management, conflict resolution, and decision making (Fine, 2009; Rivera, 2009; Rutherford, 2001). They have attempted to separate myth from fact in the perception that members of one sex versus the other make better managers.

HOW ARE MALE AND FEMALE MANAGERS PERCEIVED?   A meaningful discussion on this topic must be placed in the context of the changing workplace. The American workplace, as well as some international workplaces, has witnessed a shift away from traditional management approaches, typified by such stereotypical masculine attributes as aggression, competitiveness, control, and individualism. The shift is toward an interactional management approach, reflecting such stereotypical feminine attributes as flexibility, supportiveness, connectedness, and collaborative problem solving (Billing & Alvesson, 2000; Brownell, 2001).

A collaborative management style indicative of many female supervisors seems to bode well for the security of U.S. companies. In an economic downturn such as the country witnessed toward the end of the first decade of the 2000s, female-dominated professions (e.g., healthcare, education, government) and female managers weathered the recession better than their male counterparts (Cauchon, 2009; Fisher, 2009). Businesses that reacted to tough economic times by exerting more control over workers and depending more heavily on male senior managers did not fare too well. A diverse, adaptive leadership style that emphasizes participation and shared responsibility for decision making proved invaluable as businesses coped with economic challenges (Grashow, Heifetz, & Linsky, 2009).

One study of perceptions of managers found that female leaders were rated higher on people-oriented leadership skills, male leaders higher on business-oriented leadership skills (Kabacoff, 1998). Male managers were perceived as holding more of a vision toward strategic planning and organization, having a greater sense of tradition (building on knowledge gained from experience), being innovative and willing to take risks, and being more restrained and professional in terms of emotional expression. They were also seen as better delegators, more cooperative, and more persuasive than female managers. Female managers were perceived as being more empathic, more energetic and enthusiastic, better communicators (e.g., keeping people informed, providing feedback), and as possessing more people skills (e.g., sensitivity to others, likeability, listening ability, development of relationships with peers and superiors) than their male counterparts.

Michael Gurian and Barbara Annis (2008), authors of *Leadership and the Sexes*, suggest that sex-based brain differences offer an explanation for varying leadership styles. For example, women's brains contain more active emotive centers that are linked to their language skills; men's brains are more goal- and task-directed, less emotion-oriented. Thus, female managers may be more geared toward expressing emotions in words and providing empathy for employees, while male managers focus more on the task at hand and on accomplishing goals rather than processing employees' and clients' feelings. Another difference centers around hormones and brain functioning. Men's concentration of testosterone, a hormone linked to aggression, leads them to behave

Blondie 1999/King Features Syndicate.

more competitively, whereas women's concentration of oxytocin (a bonding chemical) influences them to build support systems around them. An overgeneralization is this: Men compete, women bond, and these differences tend to manifest themselves in our approaches to leadership and management.

HOW DO THEY COMMUNICATE AS MANAGERS?   Research has produced mixed results when it comes to sex and gender differences among the communication styles of leaders. Some research suggests that, as organizations have placed more emphasis on diversity, changes in communication styles have occurred, making male and female management approaches less distinguishable (Butler, Feng, & MacGeorge, 2003). Duehr and Bono (2006) found considerable evolution over the past 30 years, in terms of stereotypical views of managers. In their study, female managers were viewed as exhibiting more task-oriented leadership, once deemed a more male-expected approach to management. Perhaps as more women have assumed leadership positions in organizations, expectations about and reactions to them have changed over time.

However, other evidence shows that communication styles and perceptions of management abilities remain as firmly connected to sex and gender as in the past (Ayman & Korabik, 2010; Barsh & Cranston, 2009; Carli & Eagly, 2007; Fine, 2009; Rudman & Phelan, 2008). Some research indicates that subordinates often perceive female supervisors to be better communicators, both verbally and nonverbally, creating more family-friendly work environments than their male counterparts (Everbach, 2005; Madlock, 2009).

Generally speaking, a feminine management style involves supportive, facilitative leadership that tends to be effective in participatory, democratic work settings. In contrast, a masculine management style involves control or power over employees and a competitive tone that strives to create winners and losers—a style that may be more effective in a highly autocratic work environment. (Remember that we're talking about gender differences here, not sex differences; a man can demonstrate a feminine style of managing, just as a woman can exhibit masculine leadership behaviors.)

Communication scholar Steven May (1997) describes the "feminization of management," a result of a changing workplace and a changing worker (p. 3). He identifies three themes in managerial literature: The first is advice to managers to replace the notion of control with shared responsibility. Instead of commanding, directing, and deciding, "the new ideal is a manager who relinquishes control and shares responsibility, authority, and the limelight" (p. 10). The second theme is one of helping and developing employees, as opposed to regulating and supervising them. This theme underlies the team-building approach that is popular among modern American organizations. The third theme is the importance of building meaningful networks of relationships, both within and outside the organization.

CAN EFFECTIVE MANAGERS HAVE IT BOTH WAYS?   Research and popular literature on the subject of gender and management describe a blended style, one that draws on both masculine and feminine strengths in communication and leadership (Claes, 2006; Hayes Andrews, Herschel, & Baird, 1996). This represents a move away from the traditional, male-oriented management style, corresponding to the change to less traditional, less hierarchically based, flatter, and more decentralized organizations that face global competition.

One of the strongest and earliest proponents of the blended management approach was Alice Sargent, author of *The Androgynous Manager* (1981). *Androgynous management* involves blending linear, systematic problem solving with intuitive approaches, balancing competition and collaboration, and dealing with power as well as emotion. Sargent argues that men and women alike have suffered the consequences of a masculine management style, including stress and related health problems.

However, some cautions should be considered regarding an androgynous or blended management style. This may surprise you, since we are such advocates of androgyny and gender blending throughout this text. In some organizational settings, exhibiting behaviors stereotypically associated with members of the opposite sex can backfire (Lamude & Daniels, 1990). For example, a male manager who reacts emotionally to bad news at work may be labeled a "corporate wimp," rather than be valued for his honest reaction. A female manager who aggressively communicates her views to colleagues may be labeled a "corporate bitch." When women attempt to emulate the management behaviors of their male counterparts, they perpetuate the male-oriented system and are often devalued for this behavior. In fact, some women explain that they aren't drawn to the upper levels of management in their patriarchal organizations, because of concerns that they will be co-opted or forced into exhibiting the company's masculine value-based behavior (Sloan & Krone, 2000). Sometimes, when a female manager uses stereotypically feminine behaviors, she receives negative reactions as well (Papa, Daniels, & Spiker, 2007). Things are changing, and female managers are still finding their way in a male-dominated arena, so the decision to adopt an androgynous management style, or any management style, depends on the context within which you work.

ATTENTION? COMPLIMENTING? FLIRTING? SEXUAL HARASSMENT?

Just reading this heading may make you want to put the book down. As difficult as sexual harassment is to think about, it's important to examine this topic because many of you are nearing graduation and will be launching careers. We hope you don't encounter sexual harassment at work, but whether you experience it firsthand, you need to be current and knowledgeable on the topic if you want to function successfully on the job.

Some of you have no doubt become educated about sexual harassment because of educational programs at your college or university, or perhaps through media dramatizations. A powerful event played out in the national media about 20 years ago, as

Remember . . .

Glass Ceiling: Transparent barrier in the workplace that allows professional women to look higher and see possibilities for advancement, but prevents them from attaining higher positions

Sticky Floor: Factors that keep women in low-level, support roles in the workplace and that prevent them from seeking or gaining promotion or career development.

Second Shift: Work of employed women returning home from their jobs to hours of cleaning, cooking, and child care

Mommy Track: Term applied to women who seek advancement in the workplace at the same time as they have child-rearing responsibilities

Flextime: Organizational innovation that allows employees to work flexible hours, to accommodate home and family demands

Family-Friendly Workplace: Designation that a workplace is accommodating for employees with family responsibilities

Sequencing: Temporarily dropping out of the workforce in order to raise children, then stepping back into the workforce at an organization with flexible scheduling

Telecommuting: Ability to work at home with flexible hours through the use of technological advancements

Androgynous Management: Leadership style exhibiting a blend of masculine and feminine approaches to management

Clarence Thomas was being confirmed as a new Supreme Court justice. Those of us glued to our TV sets, seeing Anita Hill claim to the Senate Judiciary Committee that she was sexually harassed by Clarence Thomas, learned a great deal about sexual harassment, as well as American culture. The hearings had profound effects. First, they sparked a great deal of discussion and research on sexual harassment. They also empowered people who had experienced harassment to come forward and seek assistance. Businesses and educational institutions began scrambling to develop or update their policies on workplace conduct. Laws were changed after the Hill/Thomas debacle, and people became generally more aware of how they should behave and communicate professionally.

The Basics of Sexual Harassment

Several key elements related to sexual harassment warrant discussion. Before we explore them, let's make sure we're all on the same page in how we talk about and define sexual harassment.

THE POWER OF NAMING   Just exactly what *is* sexual harassment? Gloria Steinem (1983) answered that question like this: "A few years ago this was just called life" (p. 149). No term existed for this age-old problem until feminists in the 1970s coined the term *sexual harassment* (Sheffield, 2004; Wise & Stanley, 1987). There's power in naming—just ask medical people who get to assign their names to discoveries or diseases. Naming something makes it real, gives it significance, and brings it from silence to voice (Spender, 1984).

An inspection of the language surrounding sexual harassment justifies the struggle of many people to bring this problem into the open (Lee, 2001). Harassing behavior used to be described (and probably still is) in romantic language, such as "seduction," "overtures," "advances," or "passes." But as gender scholar Julia Wood (1993) suggests, "Using terminology associated with amorous contexts obscures the ugliness, unwanted-ness, violation, repugnance, and sheer darkness of sexual harassment" (p. 14).

Other ways to excuse sexual harassment besides a "boys will be boys" attitude include viewing unwanted attention as merely complimenting the target. If the target didn't view it as such, she or he wasn't being "gracious" and accepting the compliment. A prime way to blame a target of harassment and direct attention away from a harasser's behavior is the "just kidding" suggestion. If you couch communication as kidding, jok-ing, or teasing, then when it's interpreted as harassment, a harasser can blame the victim for not getting the joke or not having a sense of humor. A prime example of this blame-shifting technique is telling a target to "lighten up."

The language of sexual harassment has changed since the 1980s, so that we now have "targets" and "survivors" instead of "objects of attention," "complainers," and "whiners." "Pushy" or "forward" people are now named "harassers" and in some cases, "defen-dants." What once was an "advance" is now a "violation of individual rights" (Wood, 1992, 1993). But we've also seen a resurgence of euphemisms for sexual harassment, such as "inappropriate behavior," "disrespect," "personal misconduct," and "poor decision mak-ing," stemming from various scandals on the national scene (Ivy, 1999; Woodward, 1995).

FIRST THE NAME, THEN THE LEGAL DEFINITION   The definition of sexual harassment is fairly straightforward; however, the interpretation as to what behaviors constitute sexual harass-ment is much more complicated. Let's track back in time a bit, before a definition was avail-able. The fight against sexual harassment in the workplace was led by women of color and working-class women. The first victory came in the form of Title VII of the Civil Rights Act of 1964, which protected citizens from discrimination based on a variety of factors, one of which was sex. In essence, this law made sexual harassment illegal. Under Title VII, Con-gress gave the EEOC formal authority to investigate claims of workplace sexual harassment (Peach, 1998). Later, with the passage of Title IX in 1972, educational institutions were man-dated by law to avoid sex discrimination (Wood, 1992). Title IX defined sexual harassment as "the use of authority to emphasize the sexuality or sexual identity of students" (Peach, 1998, p. 291). But, as you can well imagine, sexual harassment continued despite the legislation.

In 1980 the EEOC produced the following set of guidelines on sexual harassment:

> Unwelcome sexual advances, requests for sexual favors, and other verbal or physical conduct of a sexual nature constitute sexual harassment when (1) submission to such conduct is made either explicitly or implicitly a term or condition of an individual's employment, (2) submission to or rejection of such conduct by an individual is used as the basis for employment decisions affecting such individual, or (3) such conduct has the intention or effect of unreasonably interfering with an individual's work performance or of creat-ing an intimidating, hostile, or offensive working environment. (EEOC, 1980)

Up to this time, most documented cases were *quid pro quo harassment*, which means "this for that" or "something for something." This is a more traditional or historical view of harassment, involving a threat by superiors that unless subordinates engage in some form of sexual behavior, they will lose their jobs, be overlooked for promotions and raises, be transferred to less-desirable units or locations, and so forth (Gerdes, 1999; Mink, 2005; Wendt & Slonaker, 2002).

The more overt, tangible nature of quid pro quo harassment is more easily recognizable by the courts as a form of illegal sex discrimination than the second form of harassment, *hostile climate harassment.* In 1986 the U.S. Supreme Court acted on the third clause of the EEOC guidelines, extending and legitimizing complaints of sexual harassment beyond quid pro quo (*Meritor Savings Bank* v. *Vinson,* as in Paetzold & O'Leary-Kelly, 1993). Hostile climate harassment is difficult to address, but it is far more prevalent than quid pro quo (Hill, 2002). To date, this form of harassment has generated the largest number of court cases, while also producing the most amount of confusion surrounding what actions could or could not be regarded as sexual harassment (Berryman-Fink & Vanover Riley, 1997; Gerdes, 1999; Jacobs & Bonavoglia, 1998).

Hostile climate harassment often taps into sexist structures, policies, and practices long ignored, overlooked, or even accepted as a part of the organizational culture, like gathering in the workroom to tell sexual or sexist jokes (or circulating these jokes through the office e-mail system), hanging sexual posters (pinups) on the walls of the workplace, or displaying sexually suggestive screen savers on computers (Carroll, 1993; Rosewarne, 2007). Other behaviors, documented by research, include posting lewd or insulting graffiti in workplace areas; distributing pornographic or sexually explicit materials; vandalism of one's personal belongings or work space; and behaviors such as making repeated phone calls; leaving frequent e-mail or voice mail messages; placing intimidating or sexist materials in an employer's mailbox; staring at, following, or stalking someone; and performing office pranks (Paetzold & O'Leary-Kelly, 1993). Quite often the intent of such actions is to put someone in an awkward, uncomfortable, or one-down position or to emphasize the harasser's status or power over other people. If the offending behavior falls short of actually threatening something tangible (someone's job, promotion, or raise), it may be viewed as hostile climate harassment because it pervades the target's work environment enough to create a hostile, sexualized situation.

One element that makes this situation so difficult and causes people to feel they are walking on eggshells is the fine line between flirting and harassment. Since the average American spends much more time at work than in decades past, more of us are likely to look to the workplace for friendship and romantic liaisons (Fine, 1996). While an office romance can make you look more forward to getting out of bed and going to work each day, it can also create huge problems. One person's friendly, teasing, or flirtatious behavior is another person's sexual harassment (Henningsen, 2004; Koeppel, Montagne, O'Hair, & Cody, 1999). While some organizations believe workplace romances are private and not causes for concern, worries about romantic workplace relationships and potential liability have led some organizations to create policies banning office romance (Bliss Kiser, Coley, Ford, & Moore, 2006; Eisenberg, Goodall, & Trethewey, 2006; Parent, 2009; Pitt, 2009; Zachary, 2007).

As if what we've outlined thus far wasn't enough, there's yet another complicating factor about workplace sexual harassment. Consistent research findings indicate that women react more strongly to inappropriate sexual behavior and view more behaviors as potential sexual harassment than men (Berryman-Fink & Vanover Riley, 1997; Dougherty, 2001; Ivy & Hamlet, 1996; LaRocca & Kromrey, 1999; Lucero, Middleton, & Allen, 2006; Middleton & Lucero, 2003; Mongeau & Blalock, 1994).

SEXUAL HARASSMENT IS POWER PLAY   Some harassers focus on a small number of targets and harass them persistently, while others appear to harass anybody and everybody at will (Lucero, Middleton, Finch, & Valentine, 2003). Sexual harassment can occur between individuals with differing statuses or power bases, and who function within clearly structured hierarchies. These relationships are termed *status-differentiated* (such as boss–employee, teacher–student, doctor–patient). A status-differentiated relationship may be distant and impersonal, so that harassment introduced into such a relationship is bewildering. But other such relationships may be well established and trusting, like a mentor relationship in which the lower-status person looks up to, believes, and confides in the higher status person (Lane, 2006; Taylor & Conrad, 1992). Harassment in these relationships is devastating. Some receivers of harassment describe a grooming process in which the harasser slowly develops a friendly relationship with the target, winning her or his trust and admiration before attempting to extend the relationship into a sexual arena. This type of power abuse damages a target's self-esteem and professional development.

Peer sexual harassment, harassment occurring between persons of equal status, occurs on the job as well. In academic settings—from elementary schools to universities—it is much more prevalent than teacher-to-student harassment (Ivy & Hamlet, 1996; Loredo,

Hot Button Issue

"Harassment at the Hospital"

When Stephen was a child, he had a serious illness for which he was hospitalized for a fairly lengthy period. During his stay, he was especially touched by the kindness and care he received from hospital nurses, so he grew up always wanting to be a nurse—not a doctor, lawyer, or firefighter—but a nurse, so that he could help people the way he was helped. When he finally achieved his dream and began working on a hospital ward with mostly female nurses, he was surprised and dismayed at the treatment he received. One of only a handful of male nurses in the whole hospital, he was treated disrespectfully by the female nurses. Some made a point to use sexual language around him, as they talked casually about their husbands or boyfriends and their sex lives. It was as though they were testing Stephen, to see if he could cut it in a female-dominated environment. They often complimented Stephen and looked at him in sexual ways, told sexual jokes, criticized men they knew for their sexual "shortcomings," and quizzed Stephen about his personal and sexual life. Was this a case of hostile work climate sexual harassment, or merely a "rite of passage" for the new kid on the hospital block?

Documented cases of sexual harassment with a female harasser and a male target do exist, although they are few in number. Do you think it's more difficult in our society for a man to admit that he's been sexually harassed by a woman or several women, as in Stephen's case? Does society assume that a man won't be offended by sexual talk, joking, or innuendo? If Stephen filed a complaint with the hospital personnel office about the behavior of his coworkers, what do you think would be the hospital's reaction? Are we more aware now of sexual harassment, in all its forms, such that Stephen's complaint would be taken seriously? Or is there a different standard for men who are targets of harassment?

Reid, & Deaux, 1995; Zirkel, 1995). Yet another form has been termed *contrapower harassment*, which involves a person of lower rank or status sexually harassing someone of higher rank or status (Benson, 1984). Sexual harassment has gone "high-tech" as well, meaning that *electronic* or *virtual harassment* has become a problem (Brail, 1996; King, 1993; Salaimo, 1997).

Most reported and researched sexual harassment involves heterosexuals, with a male-harasser, female-target profile (Markert, 1999; McKinney & Maroules, 1991; Reilly, Lott, Caldwell, & DeLuca, 1992). Female sexual harassment of men does occur, but it is reported and pursued in the courts with far less frequency than male-to-female harassment (Clair, 1998; Romaine, 1999; Wayne, Riordan, & Thomas, 2001). Incidences of same-sex harassment are being reported with increasing frequency (Bennett-Alexander, 1998; Dubois, 1998; MacKinnon, 2002).

Initial Reactions to Sexual Harassment

Research documents the serious toll sexual harassment takes on its victims—emotionally, physically, academically, professionally, and economically. The emotional harm leaves victims angry, afraid, alternatively passive and aggressive, anxious, nervous, depressed, and with extremely low self-esteem (Cochran, Frazier, & Olson, 1997; Hippensteele & Pearson, 1999; Wolf, 2004). They're more likely to abuse substances and become dysfunctional in relationships, and may develop serious health problems such as severe weight loss, stomach problems, and sleeplessness (Clair, 1998; Raver & Nishii, 2010; Taylor & Conrad, 1992). Even documented diagnoses of *posttraumatic stress disorder* have emerged, a condition characterized by nightmares, muscle tremors, cold sweats, hallucinations, and flashbacks (Castaneda, 1992). Professional impairment includes missing work, being less productive on the job, and feeling isolated and ostracized by coworkers (Hickson, Grierson, & Linder, 1991). Economic costs are mostly associated with changes in or the

Remember . . .

Sexual Harassment: Unwelcome sexual advances, requests for sexual favors, and other verbal or physical conduct of a sexual nature which is made a condition of one's employment or advancement, or which creates a hostile or intimidating working environment

Quid Pro Quo Sexual Harassment: "This for that" harassment; one's job, promotion, raise, grades, or other inducement is the trade-off for sexual favors

Hostile Climate Sexual Harassment: Sexual conduct that creates an intimidating or offensive working or learning environment

Status-Differentiated Relationships: Relationships in which there are clear-cut lines of status between people or a well-delineated hierarchy

Peer Sexual Harassment: Sexual harassment occurring between people of equal status

Contrapower Sexual Harassment: Person of lower rank or status sexually harassing someone of higher rank or status

Electronic or Virtual Sexual Harassment: Sexual harassment that occurs in virtual reality, through such channels such as text messages, e-mail, chat rooms, and Instant Messaging

loss of employment. If a grievance or lawsuit is filed, the obvious legal costs are exacerbated in many cases by the fact that the target may be out of work or on leave (many times without pay) until the situation is resolved. Even though they may grab headlines, frivolous claims of sexual harassment are few because, as you can see, the economic hardships are real.

CALLING IT WHAT IT IS   It's important to know when to call something sexual harassment, which sounds simpler than it really is. Research indicates that one of the more common reactions to sexual harassment is a reluctance to call it harassment (Cochran, Frazier, & Olson, 1997; Cortina, Swan, Fitzgerald, & Waldo, 1998; Ivy & Hamlet, 1996). This is particularly true of women, who report becoming numb to harassing behavior because they grew up with it. They adopt a "boys will be boys" attitude because they see so much harassment around them or they discount harassment and other forms of sexual abuse with a "nothing happened" response, often because they believe that they shouldn't rock the boat or "make a big deal" out of something (Kelly & Radford, 1996).

Targets of sexual harassment may doubt or deny the event occurred as they remember it. Since sexual harassment is power play, a harasser intends to cause the target doubt, discomfort, and "loss of face." When a target becomes befuddled or embarrassed over a comment or touch, for example, then the harasser's power play has had its intended effect. If you're a target of sexual harassment, realize that questioning the reality of the situation and your feelings of embarrassment or shame are common, understandable reactions. Also realize that you have an empowering right to label the behavior sexual harassment. You're not exaggerating, stirring up trouble, or making something out of nothing.

BLAMING ONESELF   Another quite common, understandable reaction is for the receiver of sexual harassment to blame herself or himself for the situation (DeJudicibus & McCabe, 2001; Valentine-French & Radtke, 1993). Targets report negative self-messages, such as, "If I'd only seen it coming" and "Did I encourage this person, or somehow give off clues that it was okay to talk to me like that?" It's not uncommon for a target to replay the event later, wondering in hindsight if another response would have been better (the old "I should have said" dilemma). The thing to remember is that sexual harassment, by its very definition, involves *unwarranted, unwelcome* behavior. If the target deserved or welcomed the behavior, if the target brought about the behavior, it wouldn't be considered harassment.

However—and this is a *big* however—certain behaviors increase the possibility that someone will become a target of sexual harassment. For example, the odds go up that a female employee will be seen as a sex object when she wears unprofessionally short skirts, extremely high heels, overdone makeup and hair, and flashy jewelry to work. A man who tolerates sexual teasing from female coworkers or who engages in sexual banter as a way to be accepted or to deflect attention may be tacitly condoning and contributing to that kind of atmosphere. Understand that this is not a *blame-the-victim* stance; we're not saying that people who dress provocatively or join in sexual joking deserve to be harassed. We're saying that people who present themselves in an unprofessional, sexual manner in the workplace or classroom are "playing with fire." They don't deserve unprofessional treatment, but their behavior increases the likelihood that they'll be taken any way but seriously.

After the Deed's Been Done: Responding to Harassment

Research has explored personal, professional, and legal responses to harassment (Adams-Roy & Barling, 1998). Keep in mind that, particularly for female targets, the prime motivation or goal is to get a harasser to leave her alone (Bingham, 1991; Payne, 1993). When counseled, most targets say, "I just want it to stop."

A RANGE OF RESPONSES   Sociologist James Gruber (1989) adapted conflict resolution strategies to develop a range of responses to sexual harassment. Ranging from least assertive to most assertive, these responses include *avoidance, defusion, negotiation,* and *confrontation.* No "best" response to sexual harassment exists. Being assertive is not necessarily wiser than avoiding a harasser; a judgment of a best response is up to the target because there are pros and cons to each.

Given targets' discomfort and feelings of powerlessness, along with perceptions of potential threats by harassers, it's understandable that the most common response is to *avoid* or ignore harassment. Most targets of harassment try to get out of the situation as quickly and gracefully as they can, putting as much distance between themselves and the harasser as possible (Becker, 2000). But the problem is that when targets passively try to "let it go," they usually suffer great personal loss of self-esteem, confidence, and comfort at work or in school. Ignoring the situation does not make it go away; on the contrary, it increases the likelihood that it will happen again to the same target, someone else, or both.

A second common strategy, one step away from avoidance, is to attempt to *defuse* or take the sting out of a situation by joking about it or trivializing it with one's peers (Clair, McGoun, & Spirek, 1993; Cochran, Frazier, & Olson, 1997). Many times targets simply laugh off a comment, act as though they don't understand what was said, or stammer out a "thank you" to a compliment that wasn't really appreciated. However, these actions may simply delay the process of confronting the problem (if not the harasser). Defusion responses often leave targets feeling dissatisfied, anxious about the future, and concerned about themselves (Maypole, 1986).

Some targets *negotiate* with a harasser, typically in the form of directly requesting that the behavior stop (Bingham, 1991). A negotiating response might be, "I think that kind of talk is inappropriate and it makes me uncomfortable, so I'd appreciate it if you would stop talking to me like that." However, for many targets, saying anything at all directly to a harasser is a tall order; the person in the less powerful position is often unable to summon enough will to comment directly to a harasser.

The final level of response is to *confront* the harasser by issuing an ultimatum such as "Keep your distance and stop asking me personal questions or else I'll have to talk to

Net Notes

For the latest information on sexual harassment laws and procedures for filing complaints or lawsuits, one source to turn to is **www.lawguru.com**. This site offers helpful advice on how to prove your case if you're being harassed, what to do if sexual harassment occurs at work, and ways to protect yourself while you're pursuing a case.

the boss about it." Assertive tactics like negotiation and confrontation are more likely to be used in closer relationships that have a longer history, one in which trust was set up and then violated, than when the harasser is an acquaintance. Confrontation is the least often reported response, but what's confusing is that this is the advice targets often get from people. People say, "Stand up for yourself. Just tell him to back off, that you're not going to put up with that crap." Those of us who have experienced sexual harassment know just how difficult it is to take that advice. Most of the time, harassment is so surprising, disgusting, and upsetting that a target has a hard time saying *anything*. Perhaps after some time passes a target might feel empowered enough to directly confront or negotiate with a harasser, but that's an individual choice. Our hope is that more and better information about sexual harassment will cause targets to feel more empowered, to believe that they can use assertive responses to stop a harasser's behavior without serious jeopardy to themselves. But we should all be careful about being quick or cavalier in our advice to receivers of harassment.

If you are sexually harassed and decide to respond by confronting your harasser, here are some strategies recommended by Marty Langelan (2005), a past president of the Washington D.C. Rape Crisis Center. First, Langelan suggests that you name the behavior, meaning that you state aloud to the harasser's face what the harasser is doing, call it sexual harassment, and then give a clear and direct command for the behavior to stop. Another strategy is to interrupt a harasser with an all-purpose statement, like "No one likes sexual harassment, so stop harassing people; show some respect." It's sometimes effective to use what Langelan calls an "A-B-C statement," in which a target of harassment says or writes to the harasser a clear statement of "When you do A, the effect is B, and I want C from now on," One strategy that will likely unnerve a harasser is to pull out a notebook and write down what the harasser says or describe what she or he does, then keep a copy in a safe place for documentation, should you need it at some point. This documentation strategy may make someone think more carefully about his or her words and actions.

Other recommendations Langelan makes include asking a Socratic question of a harasser, like "What makes you think you can tell that joke and no one will be offended?" In a sense, you're making the episode into a point of discussion, depersonalizing the situation. You can also simply become a human stop sign, putting your hands up in front of your chest, palms facing out, and saying "Stop right there" while making direct eye contact. It's also important to not get embroiled in what a harasser says, or become involved in a dispute over the meaning of what was said or done. According to Langelan, better to simply repeat your message of "stop this" and not be dragged into further conversation of what was or wasn't meant. Langelan also touts the safety-in-numbers strategy, meaning that groups of people confronting harassers may be more effective than the [one individual. While we don't advise a "group shaming," we do agree that sometimes numbers of people have a more powerful effect on shaping behavior. If you're female and your harasser is male, Langelan says it might be wise to enlist the help of some male coworkers, even if they're friends of the harasser. If you suggest that the harasser's buddies are complicit through their silence, they might decide to back you and help you get the behavior to stop. Finally, Langelan encourages people who aren't targets of harassment to become allies and speak up against the problem, expressing their boundaries and preferences for respectful communication.

THE DOWNSIDE OF SECRECY   Keeping harassment bottled up is an immediate, understandable reaction. In fact, research documents a characteristic time lag for responding

Remember . . .

Posttraumatic Stress Disorder: Psychological stress-related disorder, characterized by nightmares, muscle tremors, cold sweats, hallucinations, and flashbacks

Avoidance: Response to sexual harassment in which a target ignores harassment and avoids any form of confrontation with a harasser

Defusion: Response to sexual harassment in which a target tries to distract or "take the sting out" of a situation, through joking or changing the subject, and so on

Negotiation: Response to sexual harassment in which a target works with the harasser, harasser's boss, or other entity internal or external to an organization so as to arrive at a resolution

Confrontation: Response to sexual harassment in which a target confronts the harasser directly, usually insisting that the harassing behavior stop and possibly issuing an ultimatum

to harassment, due to the target's feelings of helplessness and shame and because it takes many people time to realize that sexual harassment has actually occurred (Clair, 1998; Taylor & Conrad, 1992). But we suggest that if you are a target of sexual harassment—even if you just *think* that you may have been harassed—*tell someone.* We're not necessarily talking about reporting the harassment here, but making it real by saying it out loud. Communication allows a target to gain back confidence and get useful perspectives from others (Witteman, 1993). It also creates documentation that can be used for possible professional and legal action in the future (Booth-Butterfield, 1986; Payne, 1993).

If you're the person a target speaks to about a sexually harassing experience, your knowledge of the issue will be a great comfort. Apply the principles of the receiver orientation and your understanding of gender communication to help you respond in a caring way, keeping in mind that the problem belongs to the target and it is her or his decision about what to do. The best thing you can do for someone who confides in you is to listen—with your eyes as well as your ears, watching for nonverbal cues about what the target is feeling and needing.

Going a Step Further: Reporting Sexual Harassment

After you've told someone about the incident, think about how you want to deal with it. For example, if the harasser is one of your professors, how will you handle being in his or her class the rest of the semester? Will you drop the class, become passive and withdrawn so as to endure the class, confront the professor and possibly risk your grade, report the harassment to the professor's department chair, or file an official grievance? If the harasser is a coworker, will you report the harassment? Ask for a transfer? Quit your job?

We don't mean to lay guilt trips here by saying that targets must report their harassment. Reporting is an individual decision because costs are always involved. But a target also has to weigh the costs of *not* reporting harassment. Unreported harassment leaves the harasser free from responsibility for her or his behavior, and free to harass again (Payne, 1993).

PREPARING TO CLAIM SEXUAL HARASSMENT   Many targets of sexual harassment initiate an internal grievance, rather than using less-familiar, higher-profile measures such as filing a complaint with the EEOC or launching a lawsuit. In such a situation, the first thing to do is ask this question: "What do I want to happen?" Knowing one's expectations or goals before starting the grievance process is critical; it can save some emotional toll down the road.

Once clear on one's goals, a victim of harassment should inventory the whole experience. Were any notes made on the harassment, meaning how often it occurred, what was said and done, and what was said and done in response? Creating a paper trail is a good idea, even if you don't expect harassment to recur and don't anticipate filing a grievance. If there aren't any notes, victims should write an account of harassing events, recalling specific dates, what was said and done, and other details with as much accuracy and information as possible. Were there any witnesses to the conversations and events considered harassing? Did anyone witness the victim telling the harasser directly that his or her behavior was unwelcome, or know about such? Notifying a harasser that the behavior is unwelcome is a key element courts look for; it's not a requirement, but again, it strengthens one's claims.

THE HUNT FOR THE HANDBOOK   Continuing with an internal grievance process, a target's next action might logically be to consult an employee handbook for a policy on sexual harassment and procedures for filing a grievance. Employees and students are often unaware that some company and university policies impose time limits for filing grievances (which are usually unreasonable, given the toll harassment takes on its victims; Geist & Townsley, 1997). Knowing what we now know about sexual harassment, having seen many more documented cases and successful prosecutions, many companies, organizations, and educational institutions now have policies on the books about sexual harassment and recourse for employees, clients, students, and so forth who believe they've been harassed.

Most policies advise targets of sexual harassment to report the situation to an immediate supervisor, as a first step in a multistep process. If the harasser is one's supervisor, the next option is to report the harassment claim up the chain of command or to a third party or entity, like a personnel or human resources office. Sometimes victims take their claims directly to the EEOC, bypassing local or internal processes, because they believe they will be taken more seriously and treated with more respect than is likely in their workplace.

OF LAWS AND LAWSUITS   Legal recourse for victims of sexual harassment action is costly and time consuming, and it offers no guarantee of a desired outcome. But as charges continue to be filed, harassment is taken more seriously, laws and policies are strengthened, and more victims are compensated. Increasingly, organizations are taking seriously the prospect of sexual harassment litigation by reviewing or creating policies and grievance procedures and by conducting training sessions (Gruber, 2006).

U.S. Supreme Court rulings and case law continue to change the way sexual harassment is viewed, victims are compensated, and liability is assessed. Some rulings are contradictory, just to make things more confusing. A law passed back in 1991 made it possible for sexually harassed individuals to sue for both punitive and compensatory damages (Clair, 1992; Wood, 1992). Prior to 1991, victims could only sue for compensation, such as lost wages and benefits; the law enabled victims to receive remuneration for the personal, psychological, and physical effects of harassment. Another area of concern is legal liability, meaning who is responsible and who must compensate for harassment. Several rulings in the 1990s determined that managers and companies could be held legally liable for harassment among their employees (Casey, Desai, & Ulrich, 1998; Laabs, 1998).

If a victim pursues an internal grievance but isn't pleased with the outcome, he or she can file a civil suit against the company, but only after weighing the risks and getting legal advice about the current status of the law and the chances of winning a case. Some people go as far as they can with their claims; others never report harassment. Let's remember that as outsiders to a situation, we aren't really in a position to judge a target's decision regarding action (or inaction) after the fact. Because so many factors depend on the circumstances of the individual situation, advising a specific response to sexual harassment is inappropriate and unhelpful. The best advice is for targets to get as much information as possible in order to make the best decision possible.

A Proactive Approach to the Problem of Workplace Sexual Harassment

How can an organization educate its employees, create respectful, harassment-free working climates, and protect the rights of its workers if and when harassment occurs? Everything we have experienced and read about sexual harassment calls for a proactive approach, meaning that organizations and workers shouldn't bury their heads in the sand as if sexual harassment didn't exist or couldn't happen to them or their businesses (Gruber, 2006). Ignoring the problem is very risky because employers are legally liable for sexual harassment in their workplaces, whether or not they knew the harassment was occurring (Casey, Desai, & Ulrich, 1998). The proactive approach we recommend for organizations involves a four-part strategy, including the development and updating of a sexual harassment policy, the institution of a training program, use of mediation services, and the establishment and maintenance of a supportive, open communication climate in the workplace.

GETTING SOMETHING ON PAPER   National attention to sexual harassment in recent decades brought about some important changes, one being the widespread development of company harassment policies. Organizations must develop clear and comprehensive policies on sexual harassment and review those policies frequently (Vijayasiri, 2008). Along with a statement of the organization's philosophical stance on workplace equality and freedom from discrimination, the policy should detail procedures for both reporting and responding to claims of sexual harassment. A thorough explanation of the range of behaviors that could constitute sexual harassment in the workplace, especially hostile climate harassment, should be provided since the policy will educate workers about sexual harassment in general and outline the organization's procedures in specific. Policies—and the managers and trainers who explain those policies—need to be as specific and blatant as possible in educating employees as to behaviors that reflect professionalism and those that do not. Gruber's (2006) research shows that the presence of a sexual harassment policy within an organization does affect men's and women's behavior; however, policies are more effective at curtailing hostile climate harassment, in such forms as denigrating sexual comments made by men about women or the presence of sexual posters or materials in workplaces. A policy alone is not effective in deterring more serious and personal forms of harassment.

Management researchers Paetzold and O'Leary-Kelly (1993) suggest two important provisions that typically do not appear in most policies, but which every policy should contain: (1) a description of the variety of ways an employee can indicate that a harasser's conduct is unwelcome and offensive, and (2) a clear statement of the consequences for harassers, enumerating steps the organization will take once a claim of harassment is made or a person's behavior is called into question. Finally, since harassment court rulings and laws continue to change, organizations should institute a procedure for a periodic review and update of the policy.

PROVIDING MEANINGFUL, USEFUL TRAINING   We put these adjectives in the heading because we've been to some training programs that seemed to be conducted for appearance' sake—token attempts at dealing with a problem that they didn't really believe was a problem, but that someone else (in a higher or influential position) *said* was a problem. Have you been to sessions like these? One of the first things that reveals the seriousness of a training session is who is involved, meaning both who puts on the training and who is expected (or required) to attend. For example, internal trainers may be more trusted and familiar, thereby increasing the potential for meaningful discussion of a difficult subject. However, external consultants may be viewed as more credible, with their fees signaling how seriously the organization views the subject. Probably the best option is a team of internal and external trainers, mixed by sex so as to diminish the potential for stereotypes.

A mandated training program sends a different message than a voluntary program; voluntary programs sometimes suffer from low attendance because of employees' fears that they'll be perceived as either targets of harassment or as harassers who were "advised" to attend. Training only human resources personnel and supervisors is commendable but incomplete (Berryman-Fink, 1993). A training program that targets lower-level employees while exempting upper levels certainly sends the wrong message. And it doesn't help an organization much, since research indicates that sexual harassment occurs at all levels within organizations, regardless of the salary, status, or power of an employee (Dougherty, 2001). Training programs that involve everyone in an organization produce the best results. This includes temporary workers, who, as research documents, are especially vulnerable to workplace sexual harassment (Henson, 1996; Rogers & Henson, 2006). Plans need to be instituted for repeating training sessions as an organization experiences turnover, with provisions for including sexual harassment information in new employee orientation sessions and personnel interviews. In an insightful chapter on effective training, communication scholar Cynthia Berryman-Fink (1993) offers this suggestion: "In addition to teaching supervisors how to recognize, detect, and deal with sexual harassment, organizations need to educate employees about professional behavior that is neither sexually intimidating nor sexually inviting" (p. 268). This is in reference to such behaviors as coworker teasing and banter, which can sometimes be sexual and may involve flirtation, but which is nonetheless unprofessional.

One factor that makes training programs a success is active participation from employees instead of delivering information in a lecture format. Since research shows that sex-based and individual differences exist in perceptions of sexual harassment, employees need to have forums where they can comfortably discuss their perspectives (Haunani Solomon & Miller Williams, 1997).

Net Notes

If you're interested in learning more about mediation services, check out **www.mediation.com**. This site offers referral services and information on how to locate a mediator or mediation service that will help you with your particular issue. For example, some mediators work specifically with divorce disputes, others handle employment disputes, and so forth. The site also provides articles on mediation, information about careers in mediation, and descriptions of and links to mediation centers across the country, many of which are on college and university campuses.

MEDIATION SERVICES   Organizations might want to consider the wisdom of developing in-house mediation services. *Mediation*, which some agencies, courts, and organizations require, is a middle step between a complaint and litigation. It calls for complaining parties to have a conversation—a highly structured conversation controlled (mediated) by an impartial third party. Many times situations can be rectified and compromises reached before they escalate into expensive and time-consuming lawsuits. Of course, in-house mediation services are more feasible for larger organizations than small because of the costs involved and the potential frequency of usage. But mediation services continue to spring up in many communities, small and large, typically offering services at no or low cost.

AN OPEN AND SUPPORTIVE COMMUNICATION CLIMATE   Finally, but probably most important, organizations must develop communication climates in which employees feel safe bringing their concerns to the attention of employers. This is neither easily nor quickly accomplished in an organization. But as Paetzold and O'Leary-Kelly (1993) appropriately suggest, "Employers bear the responsibility of communicating a desexualized and degendered culture to their employees" (p. 70). Organizational leaders must continually work with managers and employees at all levels to create and foster open lines of communication so that an organizational climate is established and maintained in which concerns can be communicated. Sexual harassment is a difficult problem to discuss; for harassment survivors it is deeply personal, emotional, and often embarrassing, which makes it even harder to talk about with anyone. An organizational climate of openness—one in which female employees, in particular, know that their problems will be taken seriously—contributes more to successful employee relations than extensive policies, great training programs, and mediation.

Parting Considerations about Sexual Harassment

Whether we want to believe it or not, sexual harassment is a reality in the workplace—not in all workplaces, but in more than you'd imagine. Sometimes it arises out of ignorance, sometimes out of sincere intentions to get acquainted or to compliment, but sometimes out of a desire to embarrass and outpower another individual.

When students ask how to avoid sexual harassment in the workplace, here's our answer: Communicate professionally—not personally or sexually—with bosses, coworkers, clients, and customers. This is not a suggestion that you "walk on eggshells," but that you exercise personally effective communication. Sexual innuendo, the dissemination of sexual material, sexist language and jokes, excessive compliments about appearance rather than professional performance, questions about private life, requests for social contact, invasive and unwelcome nonverbal behaviors—anything of this sort basically *has no place at work.* Consultants advise, "If what you're thinking even vaguely involves sex, keep it to yourself" (Cloud, 1998, p. 52).

Put your knowledge of gender communication to work to minimize the likelihood of being accused of harassment. Communicate equally and consistently at work, meaning in the same professional manner with members of the same and opposite sex. If someone reacts nonverbally with embarrassment or discomfort to something you say or do, or says that she or he doesn't appreciate your behavior, try not to get defensive. Be responsible for your own behavior and try to rectify the situation, not by explaining what you meant or trying to justify your behavior, but by apologizing and offering to make amends. If the person won't accept your apology, then *leave her or him alone.* Accept the person's interpretation of the event, rather than asserting your will into the situation. Chalk up that experience and learn some lessons from it; perhaps you'll get a chance to start anew if the person is ready at some future point.

 ## Conclusion

This chapter has presented some of the more predominant issues that challenge today's working women and men. We've explored this particular context with students in mind, considering situations and concerns that may arise when students launch, restart, or redirect their careers. We've examined affirmative action, job interviewing, on-the-job communication, advancement opportunities and barriers, and management styles. The complicated topic of sexual harassment has also been explored for its effects on work relationships and the work environment. Are you now magically equipped with a solution for every problem and a strategy for overcoming every obstacle you might encounter at work? Will you be able to confront sex bias and sex-related communication perplexities with skill and ease? The answers are "probably not" to the first question, and "we hope so" to the second one.

Again, when it comes to gender communication, to the unique and complex dynamics of communication between women and men, there are no magical formulas, no sure-fire remedies, no easy answers. But by ridding your professional communication of stereotypes and personal or sexual forms of communication that are inappropriate in the workplace and by assuming a flexible, communicative style with colleagues, bosses, and clients that is not gender specific, you will have gone a long way toward projecting a professional, successful image at work.

 ## Discussion Starters

1. Think of a time you interviewed for a job you really wanted. It could be any kind of job—paper route, babysitter, part-time waitperson, and so on. Now imagine yourself in

that interview, but as a member of the opposite sex. Would the person who interviewed you treat you any differently? If so, how so? Do you think your sex had anything to do with getting or not getting that job?

2. Think of a person who holds a position of power and authority in her or his job. This person might be one of your parents, your doctor, someone you've worked for, and so on. What is the sex of that person? If that person is male, do you think he'd have as much power and respect in his job if he were female? Would he have to change his communication style or the way he deals with coworkers, subordinates, and clients if he were female? If the person is female, what kinds of barriers or challenges has she faced as she achieved that position of respectability?

3. Think about the difference between quid pro quo and hostile climate sexual harassment. Have you ever known anyone who experienced quid pro quo harassment? Think about jobs you've had; was there anything in your workplace that someone could have interpreted as contributing to a hostile sexual climate?

 ## References

Adams-Roy, J., & Barling, J. (1998). Predicting the decision to confront or report sexual harassment. *Journal of Organizational Behavior, 19,* 329–336.

Adler, R. B., & Elmhorst, J. M. (2008). *Communicating at work* (9th ed.). New York: McGraw-Hill.

Albelda, R. (2009). Up with women in the downturn. *Ms.,* 35–37.

Andronici, J., & Katz, D. S. (2008, Spring). Stall tactics. *Ms.,* 57.

Arulampalam, W., Booth, A., & Bryan, M. (2007). Is there a glass ceiling over Europe? Exploring the gender pay gap across the wages distribution. *Independent Labor Relations Review, 60,* 163–186.

Ayman, R., & Korabik, K. (2010). Leadership: Why gender and culture matter. *American Psychologist, 65,* 157–170.

Barrick, M. R., Shaffer, J. A., & DeGrassi, S. W. (2009). What you see may not be what you get: Relationships among self-presentation tactics and ratings of interview and job performance. *Journal of Applied Psychology, 94,* 1394–1411.

Barsh, J., & Cranston, S. (2009). *How remarkable women lead.* New York: Crown.

Becker, E. (2000, May 14). Sexual harassment kept under wraps, female officers say. *New York Times* News Service, as in *Corpus Christi Caller Times,* p. A20.

Beebe, S. A., Beebe, S. J., & Ivy, D. K. (2013). *Communication: Principles for a lifetime* (5th ed.). Boston: Pearson/Allyn & Bacon.

Belkin, L. (2003, October 26). Q: Why don't more women choose to get to the top? A: They choose not to. *New York Times Magazine,* 42–47, 58, 85.

Bennett-Alexander, D. (1998). Same-gender sexual harassment: The Supreme Court allows coverage under Title VII. *Labor Law Journal, 49,* 927–948.

Benson, K. (1984). Comment on Crocker's "An analysis of university definitions of sexual harassment." *Signs, 9,* 516–519.

Berryman-Fink, C. (1993). Preventing sexual harassment through male-female communication training. In G. L. Kreps (Ed.), *Sexual harassment: Communication implications* (pp. 267–280). Cresskill, NJ: Hampton.

Berryman-Fink, C., & Vanover Riley, K. (1997). The effect of sex and feminist orientation on perceptions in sexually harassing communication. *Women's Studies in Communication, 20,* 25–44.

Billing, Y. D., & Alvesson, M. (2000). Questioning the notion of feminine leadership: A critical perspective on the gender labeling of leadership. *Gender, Work, & Organization, 7,* 144–157.

Bingham, S. G. (1991). Communication strategies for managing sexual harassment in organizations: Understanding message options and their effects. *Journal of Applied Communication, 19,* 88–115.

Bjerk, D. (2008). Glass ceilings or sticky floors? Statistical discrimination in a dynamic model of hiring and promotion. *The Economic Journal, 118,* 961–982.

Blau, F., & Kahn, L. (1997). Swimming upstream: Trends in the gender wage differential in the 1980s. *Journal of Labor Economics, 15.* Available at http://papers.ssrn.com

The Bliss list. (2009, July/August). *Women's Health,* 111.

Bliss Kiser, S., Coley, T., Ford, M., & Moore, E. (2006). Coffee, tea, or me? Romance and sexual harassment in the workplace. *Southern Business Review, 31,* 35–50.

Bnet business dictionary. (2010). Retrieved July 9, 2010, from http://www.bnet.com

Booth-Butterfield, M. (1986). Recognizing and communicating in harassment-prone organizational climates. *Women's Studies in Communication, 9,* 42–51.

Boushey, H. (2009). Women breadwinners, men unemployed. In H. Boushey & A. O'Leary (Eds.), *The Shriver report: A woman's nation changes everything.* Washington, DC: Center for American Progress.

Brail, S. (1996). The price of admission: Harassment and free speech in the wild, wild west. In L. Cherny & E. R. Weise (Eds.), *Wired women: Gender and new realities in cyberspace* (pp. 141–157). Seattle: Seal.

Brazile, D. (2009, Summer). No more penny pinching. *Ms.,* 47.

Brownell, J. (2001). Gender and communication in the hospitality industry. In L. P. Arliss & D. J. Borisoff (Eds.), *Women and men communicating: Challenges and changes* (2nd ed., pp. 289–309). Prospect Heights, IL: Waveland.

Bureau of Labor Statistics. (2009). Employment characteristics of families in 2008. Retrieved July 9, 2010, from http://www.bls.gov

Burk, M. (2006, Fall). The sin of wages. *Ms.,* 59–60.

Butler, G., Feng, B., & MacGeorge, E. (2003). Gender differences in the communication values of mature adults. *Communication Research Reports, 20,* 191–199.

Buzzanell, P. M., & Lucas, K. (2006). Gendered stories of career: Unfolding discourses of time, space, and identity. In B. J. Dow & J. T. Wood (Eds.), *The Sage handbook of gender and communication* (pp. 161–178). Thousand Oaks, CA: Sage.

Carli, L. L., & Eagly, A. H. (2007). *Through the labyrinth: The truth about how women become leaders.* Boston: Harvard Business School Press.

Carroll, C. M. (1993, Winter). Sexual harassment on campus: Enhancing awareness and promoting change. *Educational Record,* 21–26.

Casey, T., Desai, S., & Ulrich, J. (1998, Fall). Supreme Court unpredictable on harassment and sex. *National NOW Times,* pp. 6, 15.

Castaneda, C. J. (1992, August 3). Tailhook investigation "no help." *USA Today,* p. 3A.

Cauchon, D. (2009, September 3). Women gain as men lose jobs. *USA Today.* Retrieved July 9, 2010, from http://www.usatoday.com

Chaplin, W. F., Phillips, J. B., Brown, J. D., Clanton, N. R., & Stein, J. L. (2000). Handshaking, gender, personality, and first impressions. *Journal of Personality and Social Psychology, 79,* 110–117.

Charles, C. Z., Fischer, M. J., Mooney, M. A., & Massey, D. S. (2008, March 27). Affirmative-action programs for minority students: Right in theory, wrong in practice. *The Chronicle of Higher Education,* p. A29.

Claes, M. T. (2006). Women, men, and management styles. In P. J. Dubeck & D. Dunn (Eds.), *Workplace/women's place: An anthology* (3rd ed., pp. 83–87). Los Angeles: Roxbury.

Clair, R. P. (1992, November). *A critique of institutional discourse employed by the "Big Ten" universities to address sexual harassment.* Paper presented at the meeting of the Speech Communication Association, Chicago, IL.

Clair, R. P. (1998). *Organizing silence.* Albany: State University of New York Press.

Clair, R. P., McGoun, M. J., & Spirek, M. M. (1993). Sexual harassment responses of working women: An assessment of current communication-oriented typologies and perceived effectiveness of the response. In G. L. Kreps (Ed.), *Sexual harassment: Communication implications* (pp. 209–233). Cresskill, NJ: Hampton.

Cloud, J. (1998, March 23). Sex and the law. *Time,* 48–54.

Cochran, C. C., Frazier, P. A., & Olson, A. M. (1997). Predictors of responses to unwanted sexual attention. *Psychology of Women Quarterly, 21,* 207–226.

Contreras, A. (2008, September 26). The wrong fight against discrimination. *The Chronicle of Higher Education,* p. B40.

Cortina, L. M., Swan, S., Fitzgerald, L. F., & Waldo, C. (1998). Sexual harassment and assault: Chilling the climate for women in academia. *Psychology of Women Quarterly, 22,* 419–441.

Correll, S. J. (2006). Gender and the career choice process: The role of biased self-assessment. In P. J. Dubeck & D. Dunn (Eds.), *Workplace/women's place: An anthology* (3rd ed., pp. 37–51). Los Angeles: Roxbury.

Crary, D. (2002, May 12). Corporate ladder might still be more male-friendly. Associated Press Wire Service, as in *Corpus Christi Caller Times,* p. A5.

DeGroot, T., & Motowidlo, S. J. (1999). Why visual and vocal interview cues can affect interviewers' judgments and predict job performance. *Journal of Applied Psychology, 94,* 986–993.

DeJudicibus, M., & McCabe, M. P. (2001). Blaming the target of sexual harassment: Impact of gender role, sexist attitudes, and work role. *Sex Roles, 44,* 401–417.

Dougherty, D. S. (2001). Sexual harassment as [dys]functional process: A feminist standpoint analysis. *Journal of Applied Communication Research, 29,* 372–402.

Douglas Vavrus, M. (2007). Opting out moms in the news: Selling new traditionalism in the new millennium. *Feminist Media Studies, 7,* 47–63.

Drago, R. (2007, March 30). Harvard and the academic glass ceiling. *The Chronicle of Higher Education,* p. C3.

Dubeck, P. J. (2006). Are we there yet?: Reflections on work and family as an emergent social issue. In P. J. Dubeck & D. Dunn (Eds.), *Workplace/women's place: An anthology* (3rd ed., pp. 312–323). Los Angeles: Roxbury.

Dubeck, P. J., & Dunn, D. (2002). Introduction to unit four: Work and family: Seeking a balance. In P. J. Dubeck & D. Dunn (Eds.), *Workplace/women's place: An anthology* (2nd ed., pp. 141–145). Los Angeles: Roxbury.

Dubeck, P. J., & Dunn, D. (2006). Introduction to the study of women and work. In P. J. Dubeck & D. Dunn (Eds.), *Workplace/women's place: An anthology* (3rd ed., pp. 1–14). Los Angeles: Roxbury.

Dubois, C. (1998). An emotional examination of same- and other-gender sexual harassment in the workplace. *Sex Roles, 39,* 731–747.

Duehr, E. E., & Bono, J. E. (2006). Men, women, and managers: Are stereotypes finally changing? *Personnel Psychology, 59,* 815–847.

Eagly, A. H., & Carli, L. L. (2009). Women and the labyrinth of leadership. In J. W. White (Ed.), *Taking sides: Clashing views in gender* (4th ed., pp. 294–302). Boston: McGraw-Hill.

Edley, P. P. (2004). Entrepreneurial mothers' balance of work and family: Discursive constructions of time, mothering, and identity. In P. M. Buzzanell, H. Sterk, & L. H. Turner (Eds.), *Gender in applied communication contexts* (pp. 255–273). Thousand Oaks, CA: Sage.

Eisenberg, E. M., Goodall, H. L. Jr., & Trethewey, A. (2006). *Organizational communication: Balancing creativity and constraint* (5th ed.). New York: Bedford/St. Martin's.

Engberg, K. (1999). *It's not the glass ceiling, it's the sticky floor: And other things our daughters should know about marriage, work, and motherhood.* Amherst, NY: Prometheus Books.

England, P., Garcia-Beaulieu, C., & Ross, M. (2007). Women's employment among blacks, whites, and three groups of Latinas. In M. T. Segal & T. A. Martinez (Eds.), *Intersections of gender, race, and class* (pp. 368–379). Los Angeles: Roxbury.

Equal Employment Opportunity Commission. (1980). Guidelines on discrimination because of sex. *Federal Register, 45,* 74676–74677.

Everbach, T. (2005). *The feminine culture of a woman-led newspaper: An organizational study.* Paper presented at the meeting of the International Communication Association, New York, NY.

Fine, G. A. (1996). Friendships in the workplace. In K. M. Galvin & P. Cooper (Eds.), *Making connections: Readings in relational communication* (pp. 270–277). Los Angeles: Roxbury.

Fine, M. G. (2009). Women leaders' discursive constructions of leadership. *Women's Studies in Communication, 32,* 180–202.

Finnegan, A. (2001, October). The inside story: Are the 100 best as good as they say they are? *Working Mother Magazine.* Retrieved from workingmother.com

Fisher, A. (2009, July 23). Do women do better in a recession? Retrieved July 9, 2010, from http://www.CNNMoney.com

Friedan, B. (1981). *The second stage*. New York: Summit.

Geist, P., & Townsley, N. (1997, November). *"Swept under the rug" and other disappearing acts: Legitimate concerns for university's sexual harassment policy and procedures*. Paper presented at the meeting of the National Communication Association, Chicago, IL.

Gerdes, L. I. (1999). Introduction. In L. I. Gerdes (Ed.), *Sexual harassment: Current controversies* (pp. 12–14). San Diego: Greenhaven.

Gerson, K., & Jacobs, J. A. (2006). The work-home crunch. In P. J. Dubeck & D. Dunn (Eds.), *Workplace/women's place: An anthology* (3rd ed., pp. 168–175). Los Angeles: Roxbury.

Gerstel, N., & McGonagle, K. (2006). Job leaves and the limits of the Family and Medical Leave Act: The effects of gender, race, and family. In P. J. Dubeck & D. Dunn (Eds.), *Workplace/women's place: An anthology* (3rd ed., pp. 340–350). Los Angeles: Roxbury.

Goldberg, C., & Cohen, D. J. (2004). Walking the walk and talking the talk: Gender differences in the impact of interviewing skills on applicant assessments. *Group and Organizational Management, 39*, 369–384.

Grashow, A., Heifetz, R., & Linsky, M. (2009, July–August). Leadership in a (permanent) crisis. *Harvard Business Review*, 62–69.

Gruber, J. E. (1989). How women handle sexual harassment: A literature review. *Sociology and Social Research, 74*, 3–7.

Gruber, J. E. (2006). The impact of male work environments and organizational policies on women's experiences of sexual harassment. In P. J. Dubeck & D. Dunn (Eds.), *Workplace/women's place: An anthology* (3rd ed., pp. 110–117). Los Angeles: Roxbury.

Gurian, M., & Annis, B. (2008). *Leadership and the sexes: Using gender science to create success in business*. New York: Jossey-Bass.

Hall, C. (2001, February 11). Mentoring crucial for new employees. *The Dallas Morning News*, as in *Corpus Christi Caller Times*, pp. D1, D4.

Harrington, B., & Ladge, J. J. (2009). Got talent? It isn't hard to find. In H. Boushey & A. O'Leary (Eds.), *The Shriver report: A woman's nation changes everything*. Washington, DC: Center for American Progress.

Haunani Solomon, D., & Miller Williams, M. L. (1997). Perceptions of social-sexual communication at work: The effects of message, situation, and observer characteristics on judgments of sexual harassment. *Journal of Applied Communication Research, 25*, 196–216.

Hayes Andrews, P., Herschel, R. T., & Baird, J. E.,Jr. (1996). *Organizational communication: Empowerment in a technological society*. Boston: Houghton-Mifflin.

Henningsen, D. D. (2004). Flirting with meaning: An examination of miscommunication in flirting interactions. *Sex Roles, 50*, 481–489.

Henson, K. D. (1996). *Just a temp*. Philadelphia: Temple University Press.

Hickson, M., III, Grierson, R. D., & Linder, B. C. (1991). A communication perspective on sexual harassment: Affiliative nonverbal behaviors in asynchronous relationships. *Communication Quarterly, 39*, 111–118.

Hill, A. (2002, Spring). The nature of the beast: What I've learned about sexual harassment. *Ms.*, 84–85.

Hill, E. J., Martinson, V. K., Ferris, M., & Zenger Baker, R. (2006). Beyond the mommy track: The influence of new-concept part-time work for professional women on work and family. In J. W. White (Ed.), *Taking sides: Clashing views in gender* (4th ed., pp. 242–248). Boston: McGraw-Hill.

Hippensteele, S., & Pearson, T. C. (1999). Responding effectively to sexual harassment. *Change, 31*, 48–54.

Hochschild, A. R., & Machung, A. (2006). The second shift: Working parents and the revolution at home. In P. J. Dubeck & D. Dunn (Eds.), *Workplace/women's place: An anthology* (3rd ed., pp. 123–133). Los Angeles: Roxbury.

Holcomb, B. (2002, Spring). Family-friendly policies: Who benefits? *Ms.*, 102–103.

Hosada, M., Stone-Romero, E., & Coats, G. (2003). The effects of physical attractiveness on job-related outcomes: A meta-analysis of experimental studies. *Personnel Psychology, 56*, 431–462.

Hylmo, A. (2004). Women, men, and changing organizations: An organizational culture examination of gendered experiences of telecommuting. In P. M. Buzzanell, H. Sterk, & L. H. Turner (Eds.), *Gender in applied communication contexts* (pp. 47–68). Thousand Oaks, CA: Sage.

Intelligence report: A new push for equal pay. (2009, January 18). *Parade Magazine*, 8.

Ivy, D. K. (1999). *"Monica madness": A feminist look at language in the Clinton sex scandal.* Unpublished manuscript.

Ivy, D. K., & Hamlet, S. (1996). College students and sexual dynamics: Two studies of peer sexual harassment. *Communication Education, 45,* 149–166.

Ivy, D. K., & Wahl, S. T. (2009). *The nonverbal self: Communication for a lifetime.* Boston: Pearson/ Allyn & Bacon.

Jacobs, G., & Bonavoglia, A. (1998, May–June). Confused by the rules. *Ms.,* 48–55.

Kabacoff, R. I. (1998). *Gender difference in organizational leadership: A large sample study.* Paper presented at the meeting of the American Psychological Association, San Francisco, CA.

Kahlenberg, R. D. (2010, June 4). Toward a new affirmative action. *The Chronicle of Higher Education,* pp. B4–B5.

Kantrowitz, B. (2005, October 24). When women lead. *Newsweek,* 46–61.

Katz, D. S., & Andronici, J. F. (2006, Fall). No more excuses! It's time to abolish the "she-didn't-ask" defense for wage discrimination. *Ms.,* 63–64.

Katz, D. S., & Andronici, J. (2009, Winter). Equal pay and beyond. *Ms.,* 63.

Kelly, L., & Radford, J. (1996). "Nothing really happened": The invalidation of women's experiences of sexual violence. In M. Hester, L. Kelly, & J. Radford (Eds.), *Women, violence, and male power: Feminist activism, research, and practice.* Buckingham, UK: Open University Press.

King, J. (1993, September–October). Harassment on-line. *New Age Journal,* 20.

Kirkwood, W. G., & Ralston, S. M. (1999). Inviting meaningful applicant performances in employment interviews. *Journal of Business Communication, 36,* 55–76.

Kish, A. (2009, December). Ace the interview. *Women's Health,* 102–103.

Koeppel, L. B., Montagne, Y., O'Hair, D., & Cody, M. J. (1999). Friendly? Flirting? Wrong? In L. K. Guerrero, J. DeVito, & M. L. Hecht (Eds.), *The nonverbal communication reader* (pp. 290–297). Prospect Heights, IL: Waveland.

Laabs, J. (1998). Sexual harassment: New rules, higher stakes. *Workforce,* 34–42.

Lamude, K. G., & Daniels, T. D. (1990). Mutual evaluations of communication competence in superior-subordinate relationships. *Women's Studies in Communication, 13,* 39–56.

Lane, A. J. (2006, May 5). Gender, power, and sexuality: First, do no harm. *The Chronicle of Higher Education,* pp. B10–B13.

Langelan, M. (2005, Fall). Stop right there! *Ms.,* 39.

LaRocca, M. A., & Kromrey, J. D. (1999). The perception of sexual harassment in higher education: Impact of gender and attractiveness. *Sex Roles, 40,* 921–940.

Lee, D. (2001). "He didn't sexually harass me, as in harassed for sex . . . he was just horrible": Women's definitions of unwanted male sexual conduct at work. *Women's Studies International Forum, 24,* 25–38.

Levitz, J. (2010, February 13–14). Rise in home-based businesses tests neighborliness. *The Wall Street Journal,* p. A5.

Lips, H. M. (2007). The gender pay gap: Concrete indicator of women's progress toward equality. In J. W. White (Ed.), *Taking sides: Clashing views in gender* (3rd ed., pp. 213–219). New York: McGraw-Hill.

Longo, P., & Straehley, C. J. (2008). Whack! I've hit the glass ceiling! Women's efforts to gain status in surgery. *Gender Medicine, 5,* 88–100.

Lorber, J. (2005). *Gender inequality: Feminist theories and politics* (3rd ed.). Los Angeles: Roxbury.

Loredo, C., Reid, A., & Deaux, K. (1995). Judgments and definitions of sexual harassment by high school students. *Sex Roles, 32,* 29–45.

Lucero, M. A., Middleton, K. L., & Allen, R. E. (2006). *Individual severity judgments of sexual harassment incidents.* Paper presented at the meeting of the Academy of Management, Atlanta, GA.

Lucero, M. A., Middleton, K. L., Finch, W. A., & Valentine, S. R. (2003). An empirical investigation of sexual harassers: Toward a perpetrator typology. *Human Relations, 56,* 1461–1483.

Luna Brem, M. (2001). *The seven greatest truths about successful women: How you can achieve financial independence, professional freedom, and personal joy.* New York: G. P. Putnam's Sons.

MacKinnon, C. A. (2002). Should Title VII apply to sexual harassment between individuals of the same sex? In E. L. Paul (Ed.), *Taking sides: Clashing views on controversial issues in sex and gender* (2nd ed., pp. 152–163). Guilford, CT: McGraw-Hill/Dushkin.

Madlock, P. (2006). Do differences in displays of nonverbal immediacy and communicator competence between male and female supervisors affect subordinates' job satisfaction? *Ohio Communication Journal, 44*, 61–77.

Mainiero, L. A., & Sullivan, S. E. (2006). Kaleidoscope careers: An alternate explanation for the "opt-out" revolution. In P. J. Dubeck & D. Dunn (Eds.), *Workplace/women's place: An anthology* (3rd ed., pp. 324–339). Los Angeles: Roxbury.

Maloney, C. B. (2008). Rumors of our progress have been greatly exaggerated. *Ms.*, 54–56.

Markert, J. (1999). Sexual harassment and the communication conundrum. *Gender Issues, 17*, 34–52.

Marlowe, C. M., Schneider, S. L., & Nelson, C. E. (1996). Gender and attractiveness bias in hiring decisions: Are more experienced managers less biased? *Journal of Applied Psychology, 81*, 11–21.

May, S. K. (1997, November). *Silencing the feminine in managerial discourse*. Paper presented at the meeting of the National Communication Association, Chicago, IL.

Maypole, D. E. (1986, January–February). Sexual harassment of social workers at work: Injustice within? *Social Work*, 29–34.

McDorman, T. F. (1998). Uniting legal doctrine and discourse to rethink women's workplace rights. *Women's Studies in Communication, 21*, 27–54.

McGinn, D. (2005, October 24). Vote of confidence. *Newsweek*, 67.

McKinney, K., & Maroules, N. (1991). Sexual harassment. In E. Grauerholz & M. A. Koralewski (Eds.), *Sexual coercion* (pp. 29–44). Lexington, MA: Lexington.

Meers, S., & Strober, J. (2009). *Getting to 50/50: How working couples can have it all by sharing it all.* New York: Bantam Books.

Mendelson Freeman, S. J. (2006). Parental influence and women's careers. In P. J. Dubeck & D. Dunn (Eds.), *Workplace/women's place: An anthology* (3rd ed., pp. 18–27). Los Angeles: Roxbury.

Middleton, K. L., & Lucero, M. A. (2003). Why don't men get it? A comparison of male and female judgments of aggressive and sexual behaviors. *Academy of Management Proceedings*, A1–A6.

Miller, P. W. (2009). The gender pay gap in the U.S.: Does sector make a difference? *Journal of Labor Research, 30*, 52–74.

Mink, G. (2005, Fall). Stop sexual harassment now! *Ms.*, 36–37.

Moe, K., & Shandy, D. (2009). *Glass ceilings and the 100-hour couples: What the opt-out phenomenon can teach us about work and family.* Athens: University of Georgia Press.

Mongeau, P. A., & Blalock, J. (1994). Student evaluations of instructor immediacy and sexually harassing behaviors: An experimental investigation. *Journal of Applied Communication Research, 22*, 256–272.

Moses, M. S., Marin, P., & Yun, J. T. (2008, October 10). Ballot initiatives that oppose affirmative action hurt all. *The Chronicle of Higher Education*, p. A39.

Murphy, E. F. (2006). *Getting even: Why women don't get paid like men—and what to do about it.* Austin, TX: Touchstone.

Noonan, M. C., & Corcoran, M. E. (2006). The mommy track and partnership: Temporary delay or dead end? In J. W. White (Ed.), *Taking sides: Clashing views in gender* (4th ed., pp. 249–255). Boston: McGraw-Hill.

O'Hair, D., Friedrich, G. W., & Dixon, L. A. (2010). *Strategic communication in business and the professions* (7th ed.). Boston: Pearson/Allyn & Bacon.

O'Leary, A., & Kornbluh, K. (2009). Family friendly for all families. In H. Boushey & A. O'Leary (Eds.), *The Shriver report: A woman's nation changes everything.* Washington, DC: Center for American Progress.

O'Neill, J. (2007). The gender gap in wages. In J. W. White (Ed.), *Taking sides: Clashing views in gender* (3rd ed., pp. 208–212). New York: McGraw-Hill.

Paetzold, R. L., & O'Leary-Kelly, A. M. (1993). Organizational communication and the legal dimensions of hostile work environment sexual harassment. In G. L. Kreps (Ed.), *Sexual harassment: Communication implications* (pp. 63–77). Cresskill, NJ: Hampton.

Papa, M. J., Daniels, T. D., & Spiker, B. K. (2007). *Organizational communication: Perspectives and trends.* Los Angeles: Sage.

Parent, J. (2009). Taking out a contract on workplace romance: "Love contract" can protect employees and the company from discrimination claims. *New Hampshire Business Review, 31*, 27–29.

Parloff, R. (2007, October 17). The war over unconscious bias. *Fortune*, 90–102.

Paul, E. L. (2002). Introduction to Issue 8. In E. L. Paul (Ed.), *Taking sides: Clashing views on controversial issues in sex and gender* (2nd ed., pp. 150–151). Guilford, CT: McGraw-Hill/Dushkin.

Payne, K. E. (1993). The power game: Sexual harassment on the college campus. In G. L. Kreps (Ed.), *Sexual harassment: Communication implications* (pp. 133–148). Cresskill, NJ: Hampton.

Peach, L. J. (1998). Sex, sexism, sexual harassment, and sexual abuse: Introduction. In L. J. Peach (Ed.), *Women in culture: A women's studies anthology* (pp. 283–301). Malden, MA: Blackwell.

Pingitore, R., Dugoni, B. L., Tindale, R. S., & Spring, B. (1994). Bias against overweight job applicants in a simulated employment interview. *Journal of Applied Psychology, 79*, 909–917.

Pitt, D. (2009, October 11). Workplace romance: Courtship among the cubicles. *Corpus Christi Caller Times*, pp. 22A, 23A.

Quinn, M. (2004, May 9). "Sequencing" parents work, leave to care for kids, then return to work. Knight Ridder Newspapers, as in *Corpus Christi Caller Times*, p. D2.

Ragins, B. R., Townsend, B., & Mattis, M. (2006). Gender gap in the executive suite: CEOs and female executives report on breaking the glass ceiling. InP. J. Dubeck & D. Dunn (Eds.), *Workplace/women's place: An anthology* (3rd ed., pp. 95–109). Los Angeles: Roxbury.

Rainbird, H. (2007). Can training remove the glue from the "sticky floor" of low-paid work for women? *Equal Opportunities International, 26*, 555–572.

Ralston, S. M., & Kinser, A. E. (2001). Intersections of gender and employment interviewing. In L. P. Arliss & D. J. Borisoff (Eds.), *Women and men communicating: Challenges and changes* (2nd ed., pp. 185–211). Prospect Heights, IL: Waveland.

Ramasubramanian, S. (2010). Television viewing: Racial attitudes and policy preferences: Exploring the role of social identity and intergroup emotions in influencing support for affirmative action. *Communication Monographs, 77*, 102–120.

Raver, J. L., & Nishii, L. H. (2010). Once, twice, or three times as harmful? Ethnic harassment, gender harassment, and generalized workplace harassment. *Journal of Applied Psychology, 95*, 236–254.

Reilly, M. E., Lott, B., Caldwell, D., & DeLuca, L. (1992). Tolerance for sexual harassment related to self-reported sexual victimization. *Gender & Society, 6*, 122–138.

Rivera, R. (2009). *There's no crying in business: How women can succeed in male-dominated industries.* New York: Palgrave/Macmillan.

Rogers, J. K., & Henson, K. D. (2006). "Hey, why don't you wear a shorter skirt?" Structural vulnerability and the organization of sexual harassment in temporary clerical employment. In P. J. Dubeck & D. Dunn (Eds.), *Workplace/women's place: An anthology* (3rd ed., pp. 272–283). Los Angeles: Roxbury.

Romaine, S. (1999). *Communicating gender.* Mahwah, NJ: Erlbaum.

Rosenberg, J., Perlstadt, H., & Phillips, W. R. F. (2002). "Now that we are here": Discrimination, disparagement, and harassment at work and the experience of women lawyers. In P. J. Dubeck & D. Dunn (Eds.), *Workplace/women's place: An anthology* (2nd ed., pp. 242–253). Los Angeles: Roxbury.

Rosewarne, L. (2007). Pin-ups in public space: Sexist outdoor advertising as sexual harassment. *Women's Studies International Forum, 30*, 313–325.

Rudman, L. A., & Phelan, J. E. (2008). Backlash effects for disconfirming gender stereotypes in organizations. *Research in Organizational Behavior, 28*, 61–79.

Rudolph, C. W., Wells, C. L., Weller, M. D., & Baltes, B. B. (2009). A meta-analysis of empirical studies of weight-based bias in the workplace. *Journal of Vocational Behavior, 74*, 1–10.

Rutherford, S. (2001). Organizational cultures, women managers, and exclusion. *Women in Management Review, 16*, 371–382.

Salaimo, D. M. (1997). Electronic sexual harassment. In B. R. Sandler & R. J. Shoop (Eds.), *Sexual harassment on campus: A guide for administrators, faculty, and students* (pp. 85–103). Boston: Allyn & Bacon.

Saltzman Chafetz, J. (1997). "I need a (traditional) wife!" Employment–family conflicts. In D. Dunn (Ed.), *Workplace/women's place: An anthology* (pp. 116–124). Los Angeles: Roxbury.

Sargent, A. G. (1981). *The androgynous manager.* New York: AMACOM.

Shambaugh, R. (2007). *It's not a glass ceiling, it's a sticky floor: Free yourself from the hidden behaviors sabotaging your career success.* New York: McGraw-Hill.

Sheffield, C. J. (2004). Sexual terrorism. In M. S. Kimmel & R. F. Plante (Eds.), *Sexualities: Identities, behaviors, and society* (pp. 419–424). New York: Oxford University Press.

Sloan, D. K., & Krone, K. J. (2000). Women managers and gendered values. *Women's Studies in Communication, 23*, 111–130.

Spender, D. (1984). Defining reality: A powerful tool. In C. Kramarae, M. Schultz, & W. O'Barr (Eds.), *Language and power* (pp. 9–22). Beverly Hills: Sage.

Steinem, G. (1983). *Outrageous acts and everyday rebellions.* New York: Holt, Rinehart, & Winston.

Stewart, G. L., Dustin, S. L., Barrick, M. R., & Darnold, T. C. (2008). Exploring the handshake in employment interviews. *Journal of Applied Psychology, 93,* 1139–1146.

Stewart, L. P. (2001). Gender issues in corporate communication. In L. P. Arliss & D. J. Borisoff (Eds.), *Women and men communicating: Challenges and changes* (2nd ed., pp. 171–184). Prospect Heights, IL: Waveland.

Stone, P., & Lovejoy, M. (2006). Fast-track women and the "choice" to stay home. In P. J. Dubeck & D. Dunn (Eds.), *Workplace/women's place: An anthology* (3rd ed., pp. 142–156). Los Angeles: Roxbury.

Taylor, B., & Conrad, C. (1992). Narratives of sexual harassment: Organizational dimensions. *Journal of Applied Communication, 20,* 401–418.

Trei, L. (2002, April 10). A feminist economic view of work and family. *The Stanford Report.* Retrieved from www.stanford.edu/dept/news/report

Troy, K. (2009, Spring). Equal pay struggle: 46 years and still shortchanged. *National NOW Times,* p. 2.

U.S. Census Bureau. (2010). Census 2010. Retrieved January 30, 2011, from http://www.census.gov

U. S. Department of Labor. (2010). Bureau of Labor Statistics. Retrieved January 30, 2011, from http://www.data.bls.gov

Valentine-French, S., & Radtke, H. L. (1993). Attributions of responsibility for an incident of sexual harassment in a university setting. *Sex Roles, 21,* 545–555.

Vijayasiri, G. (2008). Reporting sexual harassment: The importance or organizational culture and trust. *Gender Issues, 25,* 43–61.

Wayne, J. H., Riordan, C. M., & Thomas, K. M. (2001). Is all sexual harassment viewed the same? Mock juror decisions in same- and cross-gender cases. *Journal of Applied Psychology, 86,* 179–187.

Welsh, S. (2006, May). Flex and the office. *O: The Oprah Winfrey Magazine,* 281–283.

Wendt, A. C., & Slonaker, W. M. (2002, Autumn). Sexual harassment and retaliation: A double-edged sword. *Society for the Advancement of Management (SAM) Advanced Management Journal, 49–57.*

Whitehurst, T., Jr. (2002). Child care's bottom line: Employers are learning that their participation makes dollars and sense. *Corpus Christi Caller Times,* pp. D1, D4.

Wiedeman, R. (2008, November 14). Colo. voters agree to keep affirmative action. *The Chronicle of Higher Education,* p. A1.

Williams, C. L. (2006). Gendered jobs and gendered workers. In P. J. Dubeck & D. Dunn (Eds.), *Workplace/women's place: An anthology* (3rd ed., pp. 69–72). Los Angeles: Roxbury.

Williams, J. C., Manvell, J., & Bornstein, S. (2006). *"Opt out" or pushed out? How the press covers work/family conflict: The untold story of why women leave the workforce.* San Francisco: University of California, Hastings College of the Law, Center for WorkLife Law.

Williams, N. (2009, Spring). Lilly's law: Ledbetter Act helps women's fight for fair pay. *Ms.,* 17.

Wise, S., & Stanley, L. (1987). *Georgie porgie: Sexual harassment in everyday life.* New York: Pandora.

Witteman, H. (1993). The interface between sexual harassment and organizational romance. In G. L. Kreps (Ed.), *Sexual harassment: Communication implications* (pp. 27–62). Cresskill, NJ: Hampton.

Wolf, N. (2004, March 1). The silent treatment. *New York,* 23–29.

A woman's nation changes everything. (2009). *The Shriver report.* Washington, DC: Center for American Progress. Retrieved October 28, 2009, from http://awomansnation.com/about.php

Women Are Getting Even (WAGE). (2006). Home page. Retrieved July 6, 2010, from http://www.wageproject.org

Women in America: Indicators of social and economic well-being. (2011). Retrieved March 1, 2011, from http://www.whitehouse.gov

Wood, J. T. (1992). Telling our stories: Narratives as a basis for theorizing sexual harassment. *Journal of Applied Communication, 20,* 349–362.

Wood, J. T. (1993). Naming and interpreting sexual harassment: A conceptual framework for scholarship. In G. L. Kreps (Ed.), *Sexual harassment: Communication implications* (pp. 9–26). Cresskill, NJ: Hampton.

Woodward, S. (1995, September 10). Packwood his own worst enemy: Case becomes a watershed event as rules change. *The Sunday Oregonian,* pp. A1, A16, A17.

Work and family facts and statistics. (2010). Retrieved July 5, 2010, from http://www.aflcio.org/issues/factsstats/

Zachary, M-K. (2007). Fraternization policies: Inconsistency vs. unlawfulness. *SuperVision, 68,* 22–25.

Zaslow, J. (2002, September 2). Moms are rethinking staying at home. *The Wall Street Journal,* as in *Corpus Christi Caller Times,* pp. E1, E4.

Zhang, S., Schmader, T., & Forbes, C. (2009). The effects of gender stereotypes on women's career choice: Opening the glass door. In M. Barreto, M. K. Ryan, & M. T. Schmitt (Eds.), *The glass ceiling in the 21st century: Understanding barriers to gender equality* (pp. 125–150). Washington, DC: American Psychological Association.

Zirkel, P. A. (1995). Student-to-student sexual harassment. *Phi Delta Kappan, 76,* 648–650.

HOT TOPICS

▶ Effects of children's fairy tales and nursery rhymes on gender identity and attitudes

▶ Children's textbooks and literature that contribute to their ideas about gender

▶ How gender expectations form to affect classroom interaction and student learning

▶ How textbooks and communication styles affect college classroom interaction

▶ Factors that contribute to a chilly classroom climate for women in higher education

▶ Gender-linked teacher and student classroom behaviors

▶ The problem of peer sexual harassment in educational settings

A "Class Act"
Gender Communication in Educational Settings

Case Study

Two College Experiences

Stacy just transferred to a private university that was much smaller than the state school she'd attended her first year in college. She didn't really know what to expect, other than smaller classes. What she really didn't expect was how quickly she relaxed into the class, how comfortable she felt introducing herself when the professor went around the room. She actually asked the professor a question about the syllabus—on the *first day*. As the semester progressed, Stacy continued to enjoy her classes because they seemed less competitive and pressured than ones she'd had in the past. She felt like she wasn't on display, that her comments or questions didn't seem stupid to her classmates, that what she wore to class didn't matter to anyone, and that nobody cared (or particularly noticed) when she didn't wear makeup or had a "bad hair day." She actually looked forward to going to class. Stacy was learning, thriving in higher education, and her grades soared.

Javier knew college wouldn't be anything like high school, and he looked forward to the discipline of life in a military academy. That may sound strange, but Javier knew the structure and competition would be good for him. He'd been bored and a bit of a slacker in high school, but made good enough grades and scored well enough on the SAT to get admitted to a good college. It took a few weeks, but Javier adapted to the strict environment and was accepted into the corps of cadets, quite an achievement for a first-year student. He felt less conspicuous in classes, like he didn't have to show off, be macho, or act the class clown to get attention from girls. There was competition among his classmates because everyone wanted to be right or to have the best answer for the professor, but Javier expected this. He viewed it as a challenge, one that would make him smarter and stronger. He found his subjects interesting (well, most of them anyway), and earned a decent grade point average in his first semester.

What's going on in these two scenarios? Does this only happen in professors' dreams? No; what you've read are accounts of students attending single-sex institutions of higher learning. Single-sex education, both at the public school and university level, continues to a topic of considerable controversy. Back in the mid-1990s, two military colleges, the Citadel and the Virginia Military Institute (VMI), came under fire because they maintained their all-male student status while at the same time accepting public funds (Jaschik, 1995; Lederman, 1996). You may remember the big flap that hit the media when the Citadel enrolled its first female cadet. Another institution, Texas Woman's University—the country's largest university primarily for women—is always concerned about any rising tides against single-sex education. TWU is a public university that does admit men, but, historically and currently, its student body and faculty are predominantly female. At the end of the first decade of the new century, only four all-male four-year colleges existed in the U.S. (Bartlett, 2008).

New federal guidelines have made it easier for public schools to offer same-sex education for certain subjects; in a few cases, entire schools are now segregated by sex (NBC, 2006). One proponent of same-sex education describes her position as follows: "I'm one of those people who believe that males and females should mix at parties, at sporting events and in holy matrimony, but that it's far too distracting to have a member of the opposite sex sitting in class beside you" (Flowers, 2005, p. 26). In terms of her all-female education at Bryn Mawr College, Christine Flowers says "I never once worried about whether I was going to have a date on Friday night, nor did I hesitate to contribute a comment in class because I felt intimidated by the attractive young man to my left. Bryn Mawr helped me to understand that excellence has no gender preference" (p. 26).

Do you view educational institutions as havens of equality, as places where discriminatory attitudes are left outside the ivy-covered walls? While some of us who have made education our careers like to believe that academic institutions may be more sensitive to diversity issues than other types of organizations, no institution is exempt from discrimination. In this chapter, we examine a few forms of sexism lurking in the halls of education. As you read the information, weigh it against your own experience in educational settings—from preschool to college. Consider the contributions of your education and your educators to your gender identity, attitudes, and communication with women and men.

CHILDREN'S LITERATURE AND EARLY LESSONS ABOUT GENDER

When you think back to childhood, many experiences come to mind—some good, maybe some not so good. Do your fonder memories include the stories a parent read to you before you went to sleep or stories you read with classmates when you were in grade school? Can you remember imagining yourself as one of the characters of a particular story, like Gretel, who saves her brother by pushing the witch into the oven, or the prince who kisses Snow White and awakens her from her poison-induced sleep? Maybe it seems silly to think about these things now, but it's possible that who you are as an adult—your view of self, others, relationships, and communication within those relationships—has been affected in some way by the early lessons you received from children's literature at home and at school. Those early lessons contribute to your vision of what it means to be a man or a woman, what roles the sexes should play in society, how relationships ought to work, and the quality of communication it takes to make relationships work.

Fairy Tales, Nursery Rhymes, and Gender

We know what you're thinking: "Hey, don't go getting all analytical with my favorite kids' stories." We ask you to try to suspend any doubts or disbelief for just a moment to consider the potential effects of reading or hearing a number of stories with the same basic plot: The young, beautiful, helpless or abandoned girl encounters a series of obstacles (events or people) that place her in jeopardy. Enter the young, handsome, usually wealthy prince or king who rescues and marries the girl. With minor deviations, this basic theme serves as the plot for such fairy tales as *Cinderella, Snow White and the Seven Dwarfs, Sleeping Beauty, Goldilocks and the Three Bears, Little Red Riding Hood*, and *Rapunzel*, to name only a few of the more well-known tales in American folk culture. The attributes of female leading characters in such tales include beauty, innocence, passivity, patience (since they often have to wait a long time for the rescuer to come), dependence, powerlessness, and self-sacrifice (Bottigheimer, 1986). Male characters, as rescuers, have to be handsome, independent, brave, strong, action-oriented, successful, romantic, and kindhearted (for the most part). Do the characters' descriptors reflect stereotypical male and female traits? What's the potential effect of these depictions?

ONCE UPON A TIME: FAIRY TALE STEREOTYPES   Researchers have examined the effects of stereotypical portrayals in fairy tales on boys' and girls' developing views of the sexes (Baker-Sperry & Grauerholz, 2003; Brule, 2008; Gooden & Gooden, 2001; Haase, 2004; Orenstein, 2003; Zipes, 1997, 2006). Several studies have focused special attention on Disney tales, which have been alternatively criticized for their biased depictions of gender roles and praised for their occasional themes of feminine empowerment (Chyng Feng Sun & Scharrer, 2004; Dundes, 2001; Gillam & Wooden, 2008; Sumera, 2009; Zipes, 1995). With specific regard for effects on girls, gender scholar Sharon Downey (1996) suggests: "The fairy tale's popularity in children's literature is unsurpassed. Their joint universalizing and culture-specific themes contribute to the process of 'civilizing' society's young because fairy tales encourage conformity to culturally-sanctioned roles. The 'truths' validated through folktales, however, often reinforce disparaging images of females" (p. 185).

In Chapter 3 on gender and media, we discussed cultivation theory, which suggests that media consumption "cultivates" in us a distorted perception of the world we live in, blurring the lines between reality and fantasy (Fox & Gerbner, 2000; Gerbner, Gross, Morgan, & Signorielli, 1980). Just as someone may grow up expecting relationships to work like they do in Hollywood movies or television sitcoms, children may grow up believing that life is somehow supposed to be like the stories they heard and read as a child. Concern arises about the power of these stories to affect a child's sense of self, perceptions about roles women and men should play in our culture, and expectations for relationships. As noted feminist author bell hooks (2000) contends, "Children's literature is one of the most crucial sites for feminist education for critical consciousness precisely because beliefs and identities are still being formed. And more often than not narrow-minded thinking about gender continues to be the norm on the playground" (p. 23).

Consider the story of Cinderella, the beautiful young girl who was terrorized and subjugated by her evil stepmother and two stepsisters after her father's death. She lives virtually as a slave until a benevolent fairy godmother transforms her and sends her to the prince's ball. Everyone in the land knows that the handsome and wealthy prince is searching for a wife, so all the eligible women are decked out and positioned at the ball in order to win the prince's favor. You know how the story turns out: Cinderella steals the show and loses her slipper as she exits the ball, causing the now madly-in-love prince to search for her. He gallantly searches near and far for Cinderella and is finally reunited with her because of her tiny, feminine shoe size, after which he punishes her stepfamily and triumphantly marries Cinderella.

Several gendered messages can be drawn from this prominent fairy tale and others. First, main characters must be physically attractive to be worthy of romance (Baker-Sperry & Grauerholz, 2003; Henneberg, 2010). In many of these stories, love is instantaneous—an uncontrollable reaction to rapturous, extraordinary beauty. Do children, especially young girls, get the message that one must be beautiful to be deserving of love and romance? A second theme in many tales is one of competition; the primary female character must often compete with other women for the attention and affection of the hero. This message runs counter to the female tendency to cooperate rather than compete to accomplish goals. It also suggests that winning a man is more important than having good relationships with other females. A third theme is that rewards for stereotypically gendered behavior include romance, marriage, wealth, and living happily ever after (Dundes, 2001). This reinforces in girls the notion that the ultimate goal in life is to marry a wonderful man who will protect them and make them completely happy. There's nothing necessarily wrong with this goal, but is it the only appropriate goal? Since many women (even the most postmodern of modern women) feel pressure to be in a relationship and to find a partner, it's important to examine the possible seeds of those thoughts (Brule, 2008).

Also, consider the messages such fairy tales communicate about male roles: Besides the emphasis on male physical attractiveness (less stressed than for female characters, but present nonetheless), the dashing male hero is expected to rescue the girl and turn her unbearable life into wedded bliss. That's a lot of pressure on men! This plot, seen over and over again in children's stories, sets up men to be the rescuers and women the rescued—and many men and women believe in and attempt to enact these roles as adults (Gillam & Wooden, 2008). What happens when women expect princelike qualities, when they form expectations of men that are too high and all-encompassing for any man to fulfill? What happens if the "prince" turns into a "beast"? In fairy tales, you seldom see what happens after the marriage ceremony; you read only the closing line about living "happily ever after."

CONTEMPORARY ATTEMPTS AT UNBIASED CHILDREN'S TALES Some authors have attempted to "ungenderize" children's literature and counter stereotypical images found in traditional fairy tales and nursery rhymes. For example, in the 1980s and 90s, Doug Larche, more familiarly known as Father Gander, published several books of rewritten, unbiased nursery rhymes in an effort to alter a sexist trend that disturbed him and that he thought sent the wrong message to children about gender. One of Larche's revised poems is titled *Jack and Jill Be Nimble,* and it offers encouragement for Jill to be just as athletic as Jack in their efforts to leap over a candlestick. Larche revised another well-known poem's title to become *The Old Couple Who Lived in a Shoe,* broadening the story so that the central character was no longer an old woman tasked with raising lots of children, but an older couple who parented their children together. In the poem, Larche humorously suggested that if the old couple had thought through some advanced family planning, they could have avoided the problem of not having enough food to feed their children, (Some of Larche's poems were more controversial than others.)

Larche's contributions include *Father Gander* (1985) and *Father Gander's Nursery Rhymes for the Nineteen Nineties: The Alternative Mother Goose* (1990). His books and those written by other authors with similar concerns and sentiments, such as *Fearless Girls, Wise Women, and Beloved Sisters: Heroines in Folk Tales from around the World,* Kathleen Ragan's (2000) edited volume of 100 folk tales from countries across the globe, continue to be popular among parents who choose not to perpetuate limited, discriminatory, and outdated stereotypes of men and women.

These versions of two well-known nursery rhymes represent one author's attempt to "ungenderize" traditional children's literature. Doug Larche (aka Father Gander) has published several books of rewritten, unbiased nursery rhymes in an effort to alter a sexist trend he saw in children's literature. Larche's contributions include *Father Gander* (1985) and *Father Gander's Nursery Rhymes for the Nineteen Nineties: The Alternative Mother Goose* (1990). These books and others, such as *Fearless Girls, Wise Women, and Beloved Sisters: Heroines in Folk Tales from around the World,* Kathleen Ragan's (2000) edited volume of 100 folk tales from countries across the globe, continue to be popular among parents who are concerned about perpetuating limited, discriminatory stereotypes of men and women.

One of the most prolific authors on the subject of fairy tales is Jack Zipes, whose 1986 collection of feminist fairy tales, *Don't Bet on the Prince,* opened many people's eyes to gendered and cultural messages inherent in many fairy tales. Since this book was published, Zipes has continued to illuminate readers regarding the 300-year tradition of the telling and reading of fairy tales, as well as the significance of fairy tales to a given culture (Zipes, 1994, 2002, 2006).

Gender Depiction in Textbooks and Children's Literature

Gender bias in children's textbooks and literature emerges primarily in three ways: (1) the numbers of depictions of and references to men versus women, (2) representation by female versus male authors, and (3) stereotypical role portrayals of characters. Research shows that when children use gender-balanced readers in their schooling, they view various activities as being appropriate for both sexes (Friedman, 2008; Karniol & Gal-Disegni, 2009). In other words, when both boys and girls are depicted in readers doing a variety of activities not related to sex stereotypes, children believe that such activities are appropriate, regardless of sex. Conversely, when children use gender-stereotyped readers—readers depicting sex-segregated activities (e.g., sports for boys, homemaking activities for girls)—children develop narrow sex-typed attitudes about the activities.

DEPICTIONS SPEAK LOUDER THAN WORDS   According to instructional communication scholars Simonds and Cooper (2001), male characters, figures, pictures, and references to male authors still greatly outnumber those of females in current public school textbooks. They state that "despite the adoption of nonsexist guidelines during the past decade, textbook publishers have made relatively few changes to increase the visibility of females and decrease the stereotyping of males and females" (p. 235). These authors cite the usage of elementary school textbooks in which only one or two books in an entire series contain stories about females; many times these stories are added only to the reading for a single grade level. Other meager attempts include adding gendered examples or female-centric material to the middle or end of a text, with no attempt to integrate the material into the flow of the book. History books—from the elementary to college level—are notorious for focusing on men's history, with a "nod" for women's historical contributions contained in an appendix, occasional in-chapter boxed feature, or tokenized "great women in history" chapter.

High school literature classes rely heavily on anthologies as sources of reading selections. In a study of five widely used high school English literature anthologies, gender scholar Mary Harmon (2000) found serious evidence of gender bias. First, women receive limited representation in the readings, in terms of numbers of authors and page coverage. Female authors receive brief introductions to their readings compared to those written for male-authored selections. Finally, Harmon's inspection of language in anthologies revealed sexist language, including extensive use of generic masculine terms to stand for all people and many references to adult women as girls, shrews, and nags.

DICK AND JANE: SLOW TO CHANGE   For several decades, researcher's have investigated gender stereotypes in children's literature (Cooper, 1987; Diekman & Murnen, 2004; Heintz, 1987; Nilges & Spencer, 2002; Peterson & Lach, 1990; White, 1986). In *Packaging Boyhood: Saving Our Sons from Superheroes, Slackers, and Other Media Stereotypes,* authors Sharon Lamb, Lyn Mikel Brown, and Mark Tappan (2009) discuss revelations from interviewing over 600 boys and provide specific suggestions about how labels limit boys' understanding of self and create sex-based expectations. Lamb and Brown (2006) also wrote *Packaging Girlhood: Rescuing Our Daughters from Marketers' Schemes,* in which they analyzed media stereotypes bombarding today's girls. In her research on Caldecott Award-winning children's books, communication scholar Pamela Cooper (1991) found that between the years of 1967 and 1987 (strong decades for women's liberation), a mere fourteen of ninety-seven books depicted female characters who worked outside the home. A more recent study of 200 popular children's books found the same trend of underrepresentation of female characters (Hamilton, Anderson, Broaddus, & Young, 2006).

Author and Executive Director of the National Women's Studies Association Allison Kimmich (2009) explores a series of books aimed at "tweeners," children ages 8 through 12. She and her daughter discovered Jeff Kinney's *Diary of a Wimpy Kid* books, which have sold over 15 million copies and have been on *The New York Times* bestseller lists since 2007. At first glance, the *Wimpy Books* seem to make a breakthrough in terms of stereotypical depictions of male and female characters, but Kimmich notes some problems. First, the slacker character of the lead "wimpy" boy is troublesome, in that he oftens belittles emotions (deeming them feminine), fantasizes about unattainable girls (who are often objectified), and declares himself to be an alpha male, although he's labeled a wimp by other boys and is often bullied. Second, almost in opposition to the wimpiness of central male characters in the books, female characters are few and often reduced to limited stereotypes, such as "complaining, super-studious

Net Notes

Have you heard about Emily the Strange? If you have young female siblings or your own daughters, you may have been introduced to this female character that is all the rage among young teenage girls. Emily is a pop cultural icon invented on the Internet, but she is much more—a voice for individualism and self-awareness, and an alter ego for many girls. Check out Emily the Strange at **www.emilystrange.com**.

goody-goodies" (Lamb, as in Kimmich, 2009, p. 51). Kimmich calls for more gender-neutral or unbiased attempts at tweener literature, suggesting that "when such blatant stereotypes and sexism go unmentioned in the broader cultural response to *Diary of a Wimpy Kid* and its counterparts, it's time for feminists to join the conversation" (p. 51).

Alternative reading materials continue to be produced to widen the range of experience for schoolchildren (Orenstein, 2006). Contributors to *Ms.* magazine suggest the following tween lit titles that avoid sexist stereotypes and that offer even-handed depictions of female and male characters: *The View from Saturday*, by E. L. Konigsburg; *The Penderwicks: A Summer Tale of Four Sisters, Two Rabbits, and a Very Interesting Boy*, by Jeanne Birdsall; and *Rapunzel's Revenge*, by Shannon Hale, Dean Hale, and Nathan Hale.

Magazine publisher and author Michelle Humphrey (2005) conducted an online search and found some 500 titles related to the story *Peter Pan*. In her analysis of the evolution of this story, she describes how many female authors over the past decade have revisited the story, generating nonracist, nonsexist versions that offer a wider range of roles and accomplishments for female and nonwhite characters.

Other popular alternatives to gender-restrictive children's books include *My Daddy Is a Nurse*, a supplemental reader for elementary grades that depicts nontraditional career paths and roles for men and women; *The Serpent Slayer and Other Stories of Strong Women*, a mother–daughter authored book of feminist folktales that feature strong female heroines who vanquish their adversaries; *Dear America*, a series of diary readings portraying women's historical contributions; *Mothers Can Do Anything*, a book that describes mothers in traditional and nontraditional jobs; *Winning Kicker*, the story of a girl who joins a boys' football team; and *Philip Hall Likes Me, I Reckon Maybe*, a story about an enduring friendship between a girl and a boy (Jetter, 2001; Steineger, 1993; Vinnedge, 1996).

Hot Button Issue

"Teaching Kids about Social Realities: LGBT in Kids' Lit"

The reading material children are exposed to in school tends to be a hot button issue, especially concerning depictions of gay, lesbian, bisexual, and transgender individuals. Most people believe that parents should be primarily responsible for teaching children about such social realities as sexual identity, but what if parents aren't holding up their end of the deal? Should students learn some basic facts in school about "Dick and Jim" or "Doris and Jane," not just "Dick and Jane"?

Books continue to be published to help children understand family diversity, including when a child has parents of the same sex. Some recent titles include *Mommy, Mama, and Me* (Newman & Thompson, 2009) and its counterpart *Daddy, Papa, and Me* (Newman, 2009); Todd Parr's (2003) *The Family Book;* and *A Tale of Two Daddies* (Oelschlager, 2010). Children's books such as these that depict or attempt to explain adult situations are often deemed too controversial for adoption by a school district. What's your opinion? Should the decision to expose children to such reading material and enlighten them on forms of diversity in American culture best be made by schools or left to parents' discretion?

Some of you may have school-aged children, and you have no doubt confronted issues surrounding sex and gender. How do you or have you used reading material to educate your children about their own gender identities and the roles of the sexes in society? For students yet to raise children, how do you think you will approach this issue if and when you have kids? It's important to consider the kinds of subtle messages you may pass on to future generations, either by what you allow your children to read or how you react to what they read in school. We're not insinuating that there's a "correct" message, but it's important to be aware that children get some kind of message from books, stories, fairy tales, and nursery rhymes—just as they do from the programs they watch on television.

EDUCATIONAL EXPECTATIONS AND GENDER BIAS IN THE CLASSROOM

No one begins an education with a clean slate; teachers and students come to the educational setting with their own sets of beliefs, values, and opinions, and with imprints of their experiences, some of which are related to gender. When we allow these imprints to lead us to rigid expectations about the aptitude and appropriate behavior of the sexes, bias may be the result.

Expectations about Academic Achievement: The Early Years

You may remember the controversy that hit the press a few years ago, when the then-president of Harvard College offered, in a very public way, his opinion that women lacked the aptitude of men in science and math. The statement led to a firestorm of controversy, a vote of no confidence in the president by his faculty, and, ultimately, to the president's resignation (A Chilly Climate, 2005). While this topic continues to stir debate, girls and boys do not have differing learning potential. With effective instruction, equal opportunities to acquire quality education, unbiased expectations from teachers, parents, and administrators, and encouragement free from gender stereotypes, both boys and girls can achieve extraordinary things.

For several decades, research has explored the academic achievement of school girls and boys (American Association of University Women, AAUW, 1998; Brophy, 1983; Cooper & Good, 1983; Warrington & Younger, 2000). (The AAUW is a long-standing organization of national repute, whose research on trends in education are widely cited.) Studies continue to examine sex differences and achievement, especially in the STEM subjects (i.e., science, technology, engineering, and mathematics). Due to a great deal of effort on the part of educators, parents, educational agencies and nonprofit groups (like the AAUW), and governmental entities, gender gaps have closed in terms of girls' and boys' interest and abilities in the STEM areas (*ABC World News*, 2008; Corbett, Hill, & St. Rose, 2008; Hill, Corbett, & St. Rose, 2010; Mortenson, 2008). However, a new gap has been exposed: Boys lag significantly behind girls in terms of reading ability. School reading material appeals more to girls, regardless of subject matter, whereas boys must already be interested in the subject matter to be motivated to read (*NBC Nightly News*, 2010).

The so-called gender gap in educational achievement now corresponds to pursuing STEM subjects beyond secondary schooling. The AAUW report released in 2010 explains:

In elementary, middle, and high school, girls and boys take math and science courses in roughly equal numbers, and about as many girls as boys leave high school prepared to pursue science and engineering majors in college. Yet fewer women than men pursue these majors. By (college) graduation, men outnumber women in nearly every science and engineering field, and in some, such as physics, engineering, and computer science, the difference is dramatic." (Hill, Corbett, & St. Rose, 2010, p. xiv)

AAUW researchers contend that social and environmental factors help explain the sex differences, meaning why girls tend not to pursue science and math fields, even though they have equal aptitude as boys in these areas. Remnants of stereotypes about "brainy girls" and views (held by the self, as well as others) that girls aren't capable of achieving in "hard subjects" contribute to the problem. Girls tend to assess their own mathematical abilities lower than boys do, so self-belief plays a role. When parents and educators tell girls that their intelligence will expand as they learn, girls improve their achievement on tests, plus they say they're more likely to pursue STEM subjects at higher levels of education and as career fields. So part of the challenge is to let girls know that they are capable, that they can achieve, and that their achievement will pay off in future endeavors, in order to sustain their interest in STEM areas.

> *I love to see a young girl go out and grab the world by the lapels. Life's a bitch. You've got to go out and kick ass.*
> —*Maya Angelou, poet*

Expectations about Academic Achievement: The College Years

The expectations communicated to us as schoolchildren have profound effects—so profound that they tend to follow us into our college years. But, just like most things in life, those early expectations become more complex and have more serious implications as one ages.

WHAT DOES THIS PROFESSOR EXPECT FROM ME?   Did you ever sit in a classroom and feel like the teacher had formed an expectation about you before you even had a chance to open your mouth? Did you sense in high school, for example, that a teacher had labeled you a "jock," "bad girl," or "nerd" and then acted toward you based on that label? Did you ever feel that a teacher thought you were a C student in a class and that no matter how hard you tried or what you said or did, you were going to get a C in that class? These things point to the impact of expectations on achievement and enjoyment in a classroom setting, and, once again, sex plays a role.

If you're a male reader, have you ever experienced treatment from a college professor that conveyed to you a specific expectation, merely because you were male? Maybe you sensed an attitude that you were more or less valued than female students in a class. For female readers, did you ever feel like a professor held expectations of how women were going to approach his or her course content and achieve in the class, in comparison to male students? Some of our female students give us examples of differential treatment in classes, such as when they are in math classes, where they aren't expected to do well, versus communication classes, where they are most often in the majority and tend to excel. These are just a few examples of how teacher expectations can affect your appreciation, involvement, and achievement in a class.

WHAT DOES THIS STUDENT EXPECT FROM ME?   Student expectations also play a role in the classroom. We often wonder what students expect of us, as profs, and whether their attitudes about sex and gender affect how they perceive us, how well they learn from us, and how positively they experience our classrooms and our teaching.

Research over several decades has produced mixed findings on this topic (Basow, 1998, 2000; Freeman, 1994; Marsh & Roche, 1997). For many years, male professors were perceived more positively than female professors on several variables, including competence, intelligence (knowledge of subject matter), educational achievement, credibility, organizational skills, level of enthusiasm, and overall effectiveness in the classroom (Anderson & Miller, 1997; Basow & Silberg, 1987; Centra & Gaubatz, 2000; Fandt & Stevens, 1991; Feldman, 1992; Hargett, 1999; Lombardo & Tocci, 1979; Miller & Chamberlin, 2000; Sandler, 1991). One study found an effect for combined sex and age; young male professors were rated significantly higher than young female professors and old male and female professors (Arbuckle & Williams, 2003).

However, other studies have found a bias in favor of female professors, both in general and on specific aspects of teaching effectiveness (Costa, Terracciano, & McCrae, 2001; Feldman, 1993). One group of researchers examined several instructional dimensions, including instructors' involvement in the teaching–learning process, student interest, classroom interaction, course demands, and organizational skills (Smith, Yoo, Farr, Salmon, & Miller, 2007). On all five dimensions, male and female students alike rated female instructors significantly higher than male instructors.

Perceptions of teachers may operate in conjunction with the sex of the student, but again research findings are mixed. Some studies offer evidence of a same-sex bias (male students rate male profs more highly, female students rate female profs more highly; Das & Das, 2001; Ferber & Huber, 1975; Menzel & Carrell, 1999). Other studies show no same-sex bias; preferences or higher evaluations of instructors are based more on individual attributes than sex (Bachen, McLoughlin, & Garcia, 1999; Basow, Phelan, & Capotosto, 2006; Kaschak, 1978; Siskind & Kearns, 1997). Clearly, more research needs to be done in this area to understand the current effects of potential sex bias on classroom instruction and perceptions of teaching effectiveness.

We know from our discussion in Chapter 1 that a person's sexual orientation is part of her or his gender, as well as biological sex, psychological attributes, and attitudes about sex roles. One study examined students' perceptions of straight and gay instructors' credibility (Russ, Simonds, & Hunt, 2002). Since prior research documents many college students' homophobia, the researchers anticipated that heterosexual teachers would be perceived as more credible than homosexual teachers. Indeed, students rated straight teachers as being more credible than gay teachers on two dimensions: competence, or having knowledge or expertise of their given subject area; and character, or the amount of trust the teacher engenders in others. In addition, students believed that they learn significantly more from straight than gay teachers. No studies to date have found a correlation between how much students actually learn from teachers of different sexual orientations; yet, the perception exists in the minds of many students that a teacher's sexual orientation affects their learning.

Many teachers are aware of potential biases students may hold toward members of their sex, and how those expectations may affect the successfulness of their courses. Gay, lesbian, bisexual, and transgender teachers are keenly aware of how students' perceptions of them may affect their teaching and, ultimately, their career success; this awareness inserts a great deal of pressure into the teaching situation.

GENDER COMMUNICATION AND THE COLLEGE CLASSROOM

The history of higher education in America reveals a predominantly male domain. For an interesting account of the struggle women faced when they "invaded" male-dominated higher education, we refer you to Chapter 2 of Sadker and Sadker's book *Failing at Fairness: How America's Schools Cheat Girls* (1994). Even only a few years ago, it was clear that the ideal of equality for men and women was not achieved in the average college classroom. Through the 1950s, 60s, and into the 70s, men and women had very different educational opportunities. For example, your textbook author overheard a male professor once say, "Women are not capable of teaching at the college level and should not be admitted to doctoral programs." Certain fields (for example, engineering and accounting) were completely male domains. Women were guided to elementary school teaching, nursing, and home economics. A standard joke of that time period (and you still hear it some today) was that "Women come to college to get their MRS [Mrs.] degree."

How much has changed in the past few decades? While some advances have been made, there is still evidence of significant gender bias in universities. For example, how many contributions by women in history are you likely to study in the typical American history course, in comparison to men's contributions? Is this because of sheer numbers, as in the assumption that there were more key men in history than women, so it's appropriate for men to be studied more than women? Were there *really* more key male figures in history than female? Perhaps it's all in how you define the term *key*. Perhaps it relates to the fact that women in American history were not allowed to vote, hold office, or make many political or business decisions, so their accomplishments are overlooked. Many times students aren't aware of women's contributions until they take a women's history course, which to some seems a token gesture that assumes all other history courses are men's history courses.

How close are we to the ideal of equality in education? As a student, do you believe that women and men have equal opportunities to communicate in the average college classroom? That they receive similar treatment from professors? That they have equal access to careers? Research reviewed next suggests that men and women do not have the same experiences in the classroom, which has a profound impact on their education.

The "Chill" in Higher Education: Classroom Communication

In the ideal college classroom, students of both sexes participate with about the same frequency, ask similar amounts and types of questions, and actively engage in their own learning. While progress has been made, research over four decades indicates that student participation continues to be far from a gendered ideal.

Research in the 1970s found that men more often dominated class discussions, while women were less verbally aggressive (Karp & Yoels, 1977; Rich, 1979; Sternglanz & Lyberger-Ficek, 1977; Thorne, 1979). Research in the 1980s found that most classrooms tended to favor a traditionally male approach to learning and devalued or disconfirmed a traditionally female approach (Belenky, Clinchy, Goldberger, & Tarule, 1986; Gilligan, 1982; Treichler & Kramarae, 1983). Studies showed that male students initiated more interactions of greater length with teachers than female students; interrupted professors and other students significantly more often than women, particularly in female-taught classes; and were more likely to control such nonverbal aspects as physical space in a classroom (Brooks, 1982; Brophy, 1985; Krupnick, 1985; Sandler & Hall, 1986).

Differences in female and male students' communication in college classrooms and the ways professors communicated with these students were so pronounced that they gave rise to the term *chilly climate* as a descriptor for academic settings (Hall & Sandler, 1982, 1984; Sandler & Hall, 1986; Sandler, Silverberg, & Hall, 1996). These studies determined that men: (1) talked more than women; (2) talked for longer periods and took more turns at speaking; (3) exerted more control over the topic of conversation; (4) interrupted women much more frequently than women interrupted men; and (5) used interruptions that often introduced trivial or inappropriately personal comments, designed to bring women's discussion to an end or to change its focus.

Studies in the 1990s reaffirmed the presence of the chilly climate on college campuses. A tradition of male dominance in the classroom persisted (Bowker & Regan Dunkin, 1992; Wood & Lenze, 1991). In a 1998 study, a majority of college faculty agreed that male students interrupt more frequently, assume leadership roles more frequently, are less likely to seek outside help, and are less open to constructive criticism than female students (Condravy, Skirboll, & Taylor, 1998). However, fewer male dominance behaviors were detected than in earlier chilly climate studies, according to researchers Kopp and Farr (1999), who found that female students had begun to perceive themselves as emerging leaders in classrooms.

So what's the story now? Do male students still dominate college classroom interaction in the first part of this new century? Although the "chill" in college classrooms may not be as blatant as it was in past generations, studies still show evidence of male dominance in college classroom communication. Current studies tend to focus on how dominance manifests itself in classrooms, with more emphasis on context and other contributing variables, like ethnicity, age, political interest, major field, and so forth (Allan, 2002; Greene & Stockard, 2010; Kramer, 2005; Morris & Daniel, 2008; O'Connor & Yanus, 2009; Salter, 2003; Schulze & Tomal, 2006; Wasburn, 2004).

Higher education scholars Allan and Madden (2006) examined perceptions of classroom communication among students in male-dominated majors, female-dominated majors, and majors that contained roughly equal numbers of female and male students. Their research advanced our understanding, in that it didn't focus on one classroom experience, but observations over one's entire field of study while in college. Through the use of large-scale surveys as well as in-depth interviews with students, Allan and Madden found a "complex picture of classroom climate," but one that was deemed "chilly" for a significant portion of participants in their study (p. 694). Out of 19 dominance behaviors, 11 were identified by 25 percent or more of the female participants as occurring often in college classes within their fields of study. The behaviors identified by female students included male students assuming leadership roles in group activities; men telling sexually suggestive stories and jokes; men taking more class time or space; women self-censoring because they felt uncomfortable speaking up in class; men making disparaging remarks about women's behaviors, roles, and career interests; women being interrupted repeatedly by men; men making sexual remarks, including discussions of sexual or personal matters; men's inappropriate nonverbal behaviors, including staring, leering, and sexual gesturing; men ignoring women's ideas and input; and women feeling pressure to avoid being seen as supportive of women's issues (not wanting to appear too feminist).

Studies on the chilly climate in higher education have also focused on teacher behaviors that contribute to the "chill" for female students. Teacher behaviors such as using sexist language, calling more on male than female students, interrupting female students, encouraging (nonverbally and verbally) and coaching male students to get correct answers to questions, and responding more extensively to male student questions and comments have been documented in studies (Sadker & Zittleman, 2007; Simonds & Cooper, 2001). However, from Allan and Madden's (2006) study, it seems that more faculty are getting the message about creating more sex-equitable classroom experiences. Only one of sixteen faculty behaviors emerged in their study as a contributor to a "chilly" or male-dominated environment: instructors paying more attention to talkative male students, as compared to less-talkative female students. In conclusion to their research, Allan and Madden (2006) explain:

> Participants in this study identified student behaviors as a substantive contributor to chilly classrooms. In order to enhance learning opportunities for all students, faculty need to know how to monitor their own behaviors that can result in creating chilly environments for female students in both classrooms and course-related activities. Likewise, faculty must also learn strategies to identify and intervene when student behaviors contribute to chilly classrooms. This is particularly challenging when many of these behaviors reflect socially accepted patterns and norms of gendered behavior and thus appear "normal." (p. 708)

One profile of classes doesn't fit the male-domination pattern at all—communication courses for majors. In many communication departments in colleges and universities across the country, women outnumber men as communication majors. Perhaps the old "safety in numbers" adage comes into play. Female students tend to speak up faster than male students and generally contribute more in both quantity and quality. Granted, communication majors are a different breed, in that most enjoy communicating and thus are highly interactive in the classroom. Is the interaction pattern in your communication courses different than that of other classes? Do you communicate in classrooms in accord with the research findings for members of your sex? Do you find that members of the opposite sex communicate as the research describes?

Don't shut yourself up in a bandbox because you are a woman, but understand what is going on, and educate yourself to take part in the world's work for it all affects you and yours.

—Louisa May Alcott, author

SEXUAL HARASSMENT IN THE HALLOWED HALLS

In Chapter 9, we explored the problem of sexual harassment in the workplace, in particular the most complicated aspect of the Equal Employment Opportunity Commission's (EEOC) sexual harassment guidelines, the *hostile climate* clause. Many academic institutions have adapted the EEOC definition to reflect their unique concerns, the *hostile learning climate*. In this chapter, we examine two forms of sexual harassment occurring in academic institutions, from grade school through college.

Peer Sexual Harassment: Classmates Will Be Classmates?

As you know from previous reading, the pattern of sexual harassment most often documented in research involves a male harasser and a female target in a *status-differentiated relationship*, such as boss–employee, doctor–patient, or professor–student (Buzzanell, 2004). But you probably didn't know that harassment is far more prevalent among peers than in status-differentiated relationships (Eckes, 2006; Loredo, Reid, & Deaux, 1995; Zirkel, 1995). The treatment you receive from your classmates directly contributes to the creation of a hostile or nonhostile learning climate.

As we've said before, sexual harassment, just like sexual assault, has much more to do with power than with sex (Berryman-Fink, 1993). However, it appears that we may need to expand our view of power. Sexual harassment between people of equal status, such as coworkers, classmates, and social acquaintances, has been termed *peer sexual harassment*.

What people are realizing is that the learning environment is greatly affected by relationships with peers, possibly even more so than relationships with teachers. Yet more attention is paid, in research and discussions about harassment, to situations involving a clearly defined, even institutionalized status or power differential. What about power abuses within relationships in which no clear power lines exist? What about power plays between classmates? Before discussing the current status of this problem, let's think about how the problem got to be a problem.

BACK TO BASICS   Think back to when you were in grade school, when you were on the playground and a boy ran up to some girl and kissed her, to the screams of her friends and the whoops and laughter of his. Maybe this never happened at your school, but it's a common occurrence when kids test the boundaries of acceptable behavior and attempt to engage the opposite sex. If the little boy's kiss was unwelcome, should his behavior be deemed sexual harassment or is this merely an example of "boys being boys"? You may think we've lost our marbles here, but just such an incident occurred in a North Carolina elementary school in 1997 and made national headlines. A six-year-old boy was suspended from school for a few days for kissing a girl on the cheek—an action that she (and her parents) viewed as unwarranted and unwelcome. When the boy's mother sued the school district over the suspension, the media picked up the story (of course). News talk shows were full of discussions of "feminism gone overboard" and outrage that a child could be accused of inappropriate "sexual" conduct. We put that term in quotes because it was a central part of the argument—that a child who was not capable of sexual activity could be accused of mischief, but certainly not sexual harassment.

A few years later, a group of sixth-grade girls in a Duluth, Minnesota, school complained to the vice principal's office that they had been subjected to "gross" and "disgusting" sexual behavior by male classmates during a lunch break; suffice it to say that the incident involved a milk bag being shaped into the form of male genitalia, with ensuing sexual comments and jokes from the boys. The vice principal's response was to reach into her sexual harassment procedure kit and pull out a harassment complaint form. The girls signed the form, and the school system harassment specialist—a position that didn't exist until only recently—was contacted to follow up on the case. The incident resulted in scolding from the principal and detention for the boys, while the girls were made to feel that their concerns were heard and taken seriously by school officials (Gorney, 1999).

One month after this incident, a Supreme Court ruling on peer sexual harassment in the schools changed the thinking on this problem. In *Davis* v. *Monroe County Board of Education*, the Supreme Court ruled that schools receiving federal money can face sex discrimination lawsuits if they show "deliberate indifference" and fail to "intervene energetically enough" in peer sexual harassment situations (Gorney, 1999, pp. A16, A18). Justice Sandra Day O'Connor, writing the majority opinion, stated that "student-on-student sex harassment" was a deeply serious matter, and that school officials who ignored "protracted and serious" harassment could be sued under Title IX, the federal law prohibiting sex discrimination in educational institutions (p. A16).

Sexual harassment doesn't just all of a sudden become a behavior of choice for some people. It doesn't just mysteriously become a problem only adults have to deal with. It starts somewhere. Maybe it should be called something else, something without the sexual implications of the term *sexual* harassment. The term implies that sexual harassment is about sex, when it's really about power.

The phrase "boys will be boys" should really be "kids will be kids" because, as the Duluth harassment specialist described, "perps, especially in the vicious mouth department, are just as likely to be girls" (Gorney, 1999, p. A18). A lot of inappropriate behavior gets dismissed as simply part of one's childhood experience, something to be expected and endured. But this is no longer the case in the Duluth school system and many others around the country. Teasing and disrespecting members of the opposite sex does not have to be a rite of passage. Educators and parents can learn from school incidents that make headlines in the papers. Turning our heads and adopting a stance of "they're just being kids" could perpetuate the problem. And the problem does worsen in middle and high school.

THE "HOSTILE HALLWAYS" OF MIDDLE AND HIGH SCHOOL   The AAUW report of 1993, *Hostile Hallways: The AAUW Survey on Sexual Harassment in America's Schools*, was the first national scientific survey of sexual harassment in public schools. From about 1,700 students in grades 8–11 across 79 schools, 85 percent of girls and 76 percent of boys reported experiencing sexual harassment. While boys and girls are both affected, the research showed a sex difference in terms of frequency of harassment, with girls reporting many more instances of harassment than boys. The sexual harassment also takes a greater toll on girls than boys, according to the study. Harassed girls reported being more afraid in school and feeling less confident about themselves than boys.

An AAUW follow-up study entitled *Hostile Hallways: Bullying, Teasing, and Harassment in School* (2001) found that little had changed since the 1993 study. Four of five students in eighth through eleventh grades reported experiencing sexual harassment, with girls experiencing it slightly more frequently than boys. Besides the loss of self-esteem and the fear associated with sexual harassment, the most common outcome of the experience is not wanting to attend school. Harassment leads to absenteeism and truancy, which contribute to the dropout rate. A second outcome of harassment is a silencing effect, meaning that targets don't want to talk as much in class.

Research has continued to investigate the problem at the public school level, with less-than-positive results to report (Fineran & Bolen, 2006; Grube & Lens, 2003; Harrington, 2004; Stein, 2007; Stone & Couch, 2004; Terrance, Logan, & Peters, 2004). Studies have shown that upwards of 80 percent of public school students report experiencing peer sexual harassment, despite many efforts to educate students, parents, educators, and administrators about sexual harassment (Eckes, 2006; Ormerod, Collinsworth, & Perry, 2008). More school policies are in place than in decades past, more training programs exist, more instructional materials are in print, and more serious consequences for harassers are exacted, but the problem continues.

So what can be done about this problem? One positive trend is that more schools now have a sexual harassment policy than in the past. How many of those policies specifically address peer sexual harassment is unclear. But despite the school programs and policies on the problem, harassment continues, and students rarely tell adults when it happens, especially when it's an incident of same-sex harassment (AAUW, 2001). More information exists on how to combat the problem of peer sexual harassment than in years past; one such source is a practical guide authored by Bernice Sandler (2005), which identifies specific and helpful strategies.

PEER SEXUAL HARASSMENT: ANOTHER "CHILLING" EFFECT IN COLLEGE   One of the first discussions of the problem of peer sexual harassment on college campuses was coauthored by Hughes and Sandler (1988) of the Association of American Colleges. At that time, only a few colleges and universities had examined the problem. A Cornell University survey indicated that 78 percent of female students had received sexist comments and 68 percent had received unwelcome sexual attention from their male peers. At MIT, 92 percent of women and 57 percent of men reported having been targets of at least one form of sexual harassment. The range of behaviors Hughes and Sandler included in their description of peer harassment started at "teasing, sexual innuendoes, and bullying of a sexist nature, both physical and verbal" and ended with "sexual aggression" (p. 1).

What we are learning about harassment requires recognizing this beast when we encounter it. We are learning that laws against harassment on the books is not enough. The law, as it was conceived, was to provide a shield of protection for us. Yet that shield is failing us. The law needs to be more responsive to the reality of our experiences.

—Anita Hill, author/law professor

Studies continue to reveal a persistent problem with sexual harassment on college campuses (Geist & Townsley, 1997; Krolokke, 1998; Sandler, 1997; Seals, 1997). In 2006, the AAUW examined sexual harassment at the college level using a national sample of diverse male and female college students. Once again, researchers found evidence of a widespread problem of harassment on college campuses; 62 percent of participants in the study reported being harassed in some form. Harassing behaviors included being forced into a form of unwanted physical or sexual contact, being the target of a sexual rumor, being spied on, receiving unwanted sexual gestures and other nonverbal cues, being called gay or other homophobic terms, and being the object of sexual jokes and comments. The problem is even more pronounced at the nation's military and naval academies ("Hostile Environment," 2005). The rates of reported peer sexual harassment are dramatically high, but that's just the *reported* cases. The *actual* rate of occurrence is likely to be significantly higher.

Net Notes

For sexual harassment occurring in educational settings, **www.ed.gov**, a website from the U.S. Department of Education and Office of Civil Rights, offers information about sexual harassment that occurs at all educational levels—from elementary to university. The site explains Title IX protections, overviews current laws governing academic harassment, and provides answers to frequently asked questions about harassment.

To better understand how peer sexual harassment affects college students' lives, your textbook author conducted two studies at a large university (Ivy & Hamlet, 1996). A sample of 824 undergraduates, evenly divided by sex, were surveyed about experiences with peer sexual harassment. Almost half of the students reported being targets of peer sexual harassment, with 68 percent of women reporting multiple instances of verbal and nonverbal harassment from male peers. Twenty-five percent of men had experienced peer harassment primarily from women, but with more incidences of same-sex harassment than reported by women. When asked if they perceived peer sexual harassment to be a problem on college campuses, consistent with previous research, more women (81 percent) than men (64 percent) identified a problem.

The main type of verbal harassment aimed at women was sexual innuendo or lewd comments from classmates, like "guys know what it takes for girls to get an 'A' in this class" and remarks about body parts or physical appearance. Other verbal harassment involved sexual jokes, sexual notes or drawings left on desktops, repeated invitations for dates or sex (after having said no), being asked intimate details about personal or sexual life, and descriptions of dreams or fantasies harassers had about targets. Verbal harassment of men also involved repeatedly being asked out and comments about physical appearance and body parts, as well as descriptions of desired sexual activity and offers of sexual favors in exchange for help on assignments or exams. One repeated comment from the men, but not the women, described female classmates talking in sexual ways about their own body parts, which the men said made them uncomfortable.

Nonverbal harassment mainly involved unwanted and repeated touching. Other common forms included invading one's personal space and continual staring from a classmate, especially "staring up and down," the kind that makes someone feel unclothed. Some women reported situations in which harassment turned uglier, such as stalking in the parking lot and one tragic account of a beating and date rape in a male student's dorm room. In multiple instances, sexual harassment escalated into date rape.

Many students in our study were unwilling to label their experiences sexual harassment, a tendency described by one female student as "becoming numb to it." This involves becoming so used to bad behavior—being whistled at; hearing rude, often disgusting, comments about appearance and sexuality from male onlookers; being the "butt" of sexual jokes; expecting men's sexual urges to get mildly out of hand—that one is reluctant to call it something as strong as sexual harassment. Research supports this tendency of targets' reluctance to label their abuse sexual harassment (AAUW, 2006; Fitzgerald, Swan, & Magley, 1997; Ranney, 2004). But what we're finding out is that assigning the label to the behavior is empowering. It vindicates the target in some ways to know that what happened has a name, with all the legitimacy that comes with naming. It's empowering to know that the behavior is illegal, other people have experienced it, and, in almost all instances, it's not the target's fault.

Students participating in the study felt that a major complicating factor was a lack of agreement between men and women as to what behaviors constituted harassment. Thus, in a follow-up study, we developed a questionnaire to assess students' perceptions of whether fifteen behaviors were peer sexual harassment and the severity of each. Students were asked to assume that the behaviors were committed toward themselves by an opposite-sex casual acquaintance whom they considered a peer. The results showed that only one of the fifteen behaviors (humor and jokes) was *not* perceived as sexual harassment by the majority of subjects. Twelve behaviors received high agreement, meaning most students considered those behaviors sexual harassment.

For two items on the questionnaire—implied or overt sexual threats and attempted or actual kissing—women assigned much higher levels of severity than men. For nine of the fifteen behaviors, women assigned somewhat higher levels of severity. This finding is consistent with other research showing that women take a harsher view of harassment than men (Dougherty, 2001; LaRocca & Kromrey, 1999; McKinney, 1990b; Mongeau & Blalock, 1994; Scarduzio & Geist-Martin, 2008). It's an understatement to say that sexual harassment on college campuses has a chilling effect, especially for women; it contributes significantly to negative perceptions of an academic climate and to the sexual safety of all who work and study within its environs.

IT'S HAPPENING, BUT WHAT CAN WE DO?   Classrooms are not exempt locales when it comes to peer sexual harassment. No simple solutions exist, except maybe for one: Treat classmates and coworkers—your peers—as individuals worthy of respect. Keep personal and sexual verbal and nonverbal communication out of your interactions until you're *completely* sure that your actions or words will be received in a positive manner (and even then it's risky). Beyond advice to the individual, we offer some suggestions for universities. First, naiveté or denial of the problem, reflected in statements such as "This doesn't happen in my classes," makes students and teachers part of the problem. Even the most well-organized, professionally run, and academically scintillating class contains students who have grown up in a society that socializes them in some negative ways. Even in this day and age many students simply do not know what harassment is and that their behavior might be construed as harassing.

Colleges and universities, for the most part, have become much more aware of the detrimental effect and legal liability associated with sexual harassment. They've instituted policies and procedures for reporting and responding to claims of sexual harassment, and many conduct educational programs for faculty and other campus personnel (Franke, 2008; June, 2009; Wilson, 2009). Programs sponsored by such campus organizations as women's centers and offices of student activities, and classes like first-year seminars (how-to-survive-college type of classes) are working to educate students about sexual harassment. But, a word of caution is appropriate: Just like public schools, many, if not most, university policies and programs are more attuned to harassment in status-differentiated relationships than among peers. It's important to develop programs that take a comprehensive approach to the problem.

After reading this material, you may want to do your own "campus inventory." First, note whether your professors include a sexual harassment policy statement in their course syllabi. Do they create and foster a classroom climate of mutual respect, one that allows for safe reporting of harassment should it occur? Next, it might be worthwhile to locate and read your institution's sexual harassment policy. Does it contain any provisions for peer harassment? If a student is harassed by another student, whom can she or he go to for comfort and advice? Are campus counselors available and knowledgeable on this issue so they can help someone suffering the very real pains of sexual harassment? If your campus has student housing and resident advisors, are those RAs trained on this topic? They may have received some training on sexual harassment, but did it cover peer harassment? Where does a target take a complaint? If you find that your campus is lacking in awareness of the peer sexual harassment issue, that may signal it's time for you to get involved and find an avenue for volunteering your considerable knowledge on this topic.

Paying It Upward: When Students Harass Faculty

We've said in this chapter and elsewhere in this book that sexual harassment is about power, not about sex. Typically, "power plays" occur when people of higher status or greater resources behave in ways that make others feel powerless or less dominant. Sexual harassment in the workplace most commonly occurs in status-differentiated relationships, but, as we've learned from the last section of material, power plays in the form of sexual harassment can be extended from peer-to-peer too. Peer sexual harassment is the more common form occurring within educational institutions. A third form of sexual harassment exists and needs to be discussed. Its dynamics are less understood, why it occurs and how it plays out are underresearched, and it occurs with less frequency than other forms of sexual harassment, yet it can be devastating to targets.

The behavior we're alluding to is termed *contrapower sexual harassment,* first identified by Benson in 1984. It refers to those instances in which a person of lesser status or power harasses a person of higher status or power within an organization. In educational settings, contrapower sexual harassment has been studied primarily as behavior enacted by college students toward faculty, but it also occurs between other people of different statuses or power positions, such as staff members toward bosses, administrators, or faculty; students toward staff; and so forth (Attwood, 2009; Mohipp & Senn, 2008).

A few studies have been conducted on this problem, one of the earliest being a study of female faculty at Purdue University in the 1980s (Grauerholz, 1989). In this research, nearly half the faculty women participating reported experiencing at least one situation that could be considered sexual harassment from a student; most behaviors took the form of sexual or sexist comments, undue sexual attention, or suggestive nonverbal cues. In a more recent study conducted by DeSouza and Fansler (2003), more than half the faculty respondents (male and female) described at least one student behavior in the past two years that they deemed sexually harassing. Other studies examined sex differences in student-to-faculty sexual harassment, finding mixed results. Matchen and DeSouza (2000) found that female faculty were more upset by unwanted attention from students and more likely to report harassment than male faculty. However, in other studies, male faculty more readily reported student harassment than female faculty, including such behaviors as uninvited sexual comments, suggestive or invasive nonverbal cues (e.g., staring, suggestive looks, inappropriate touch, intrusions into personal space), requests for dates, offers of sexual favors, sexual propositions, and physical advances (Carroll & Ellis, 1989; McKinney, 1990a).

One of the elements that complicates this issue is the fact that, as we've explained before and documented with research, men and women often view sexual behaviors and sexual harassment differently—sometimes *quite* differently. Some workplace behaviors that women deem uncomfortable or threatening may be viewed by men as harmless flirtation, flattery, or friendly banter. Translated into the educational setting, female faculty may experience student behavior that they perceive as hostile, sexist, or aggressive, but male faculty aren't necessarily upset by that same behavior, nor do they find it harassing. Many college and university faculties are male dominated; thus, one theory is that male faculty may feel more structurally secure in their positions, whereas female faculty view contrapower sexual harassment as more of a threat to their credibility or legitimacy in their faculty role. Some female instructors also fear that a complaint they might lodge against a student's behavior won't be taken seriously or that their institution will have no mechanism in place to deal with this kind of problem. Another complicating factor is the tendency for men to feel harassed but to believe that reporting the harassment or taking a situation into complaint status is "unmanly," particularly if the harasser is a young female student (Rospenda, Richman, & Nawyn, 1998). If the harassment is same-sex, further fears of embarrassment or negative sanctions may keep this form of harassment from ever being reported. This sort of machismo motivation, in addition to homophobia, may operate to keep contrapower sexual harassment underground.

In more recent research, psychologists Lampman, Phelps, Bancroft, and Beneke (2009) surveyed 400 university professors to better understand a wide range of student behavior under the general heading of contrapower harassment (minus the word "sexual"), which included incivility, bullying, and sexual attention toward faculty. Incivility was operationalized as rude or discourteous actions that demonstrated a lack of regard for others; bullying referred to physical or verbal aggressive behavior that could potentially harm someone, either physically or psychologically. Lampman et al. (2009) found that male faculty reported receiving more sexual attention from students than female faculty, but comparable levels of incivility and bullying. However, female faculty found the harassment significantly more upsetting and as having a greater impact on their health and work lives than their male colleagues. Female faculty were more likely to take action to report the student behavior than male faculty.

It's important to remember that power and status aren't the same thing. A person may hold lesser status along formally recognized lines, but may feel emboldened or hostile enough to enact a power play to make a higher-status person feel embarrassed or uncomfortable, to attempt to "level the playing field" in some way, so as to make themselves seem more dominant or in control. Much as we'd all like to believe that our hallowed halls are somehow exempt from such injustice, that's simply not the reality in a lot of places. Now that you have a better understanding of this form of sexual harassment, maybe it's time to think back to any classroom experiences you've had where a student harassed a teacher—maybe at the time you just didn't know what to call it. Contrapower sexual harassment is real and just as illegal as other forms of sexual harassment; it can be proven and is actionable legally.

Remember . . .

Hostile Climate Sexual Harassment: Sexual conduct that has the intention or effect of interfering with an individual's work performance or creating an intimidating or offensive working environment

Hostile Learning Climate: Sexual conduct that has the intention or effect of interfering with an individual's learning or creating an intimidating or offensive learning environment

Status-Differentiated Relationship: Relationship in which the lines of status are clearly drawn; one person holds higher status than the other

Peer Sexual Harassment: Sexual harassment between persons of equal status, such as coworkers, classmates, and social acquaintances

Contrapower Sexual Harassment: Harassment directed from someone of lower status to someone of higher status

Conclusion

This wraps up this final part of the text on gender communication in specific kinds of relationships and certain contexts. Intuitively, you know that the exact same thing said among family members will be taken differently by a friend, a romantic partner, a classmate, or a coworker. But intuition or what some people like to call common sense isn't common to everyone, as Benjamin Franklin once said. Some people don't realize the power of context to affect a message. We expect that, after reading these chapters, you won't be among these people. We expect that the last several pages of this text have reinforced the importance of context in gender communication.

Learning all you can about communication in educational settings, as well as about how gender communication operates in other contexts and in various types of relationships, will take you a long way toward personal effectiveness as a communicator. Practicing what you've learned, talking with women and men about what you know, making mistakes but being wise enough to stare down those mistakes, learn from them, and avoid repeating them all put you even closer to the personal effectiveness goal. Becoming an effective communicator in a world complicated by gender, for starters, is an incredible challenge. We think you're up to it.

Discussion Starters

1. Think about your favorite children's fairy tale, maybe a Disney story or a favorite story a parent read to you when you were young. Analyze the main characters. Is the female main character the center of the story? How would you describe her character, both physically and in personality? Does her character represent a feminine stereotype? How would you describe the main male character in the story? Is he stereotypically drawn? What interpretations did you make of the story as a child? Do you have different interpretations now, as an adult?

2. This chapter discussed some of the effects of teacher expectations on students' learning and academic achievement. Can you think of a time, either in school or college, when you became acutely aware that one of your teachers held certain expectations of you? Were the expectations positive or negative, such as an instructor expecting you to excel or to fail? Were the expectations in any way related to your sex? How did the realization that those expectations were operating make you feel and affect your learning?

3. Think about the problem of peer sexual harassment on your home campus. Have you encountered any harassing experiences in college classrooms or at social events? Do you know people who believe they've been sexually harassed by a peer? Have friends told you of experiences with sexual harassment, but been reluctant to attach the label to the behavior? Knowing what you now know about the problem, will you respond to peer sexual harassment—either directed at you or at a friend—any differently?

References

ABC World News. (2008, July 24). Television broadcast.

Allan, E. J. (2002). Classroom climates in post-secondary education. In M. A. Aleman & K. A. Renn (Eds.), *Women in higher education: An encyclopedia* (pp. 282–287). Santa Barbara, CA: ABC-CLIO.

Allan, E. J., & Madden, M. (2006). Chilly classrooms for female undergraduate students: A question of method? *Journal of Higher Education, 77,* 684–711.

American Association of University Women. (1993). *Hostile hallways: The AAUW survey on sexual harassment in America's schools.* Washington, DC: AAUW Educational Foundation.

American Association of University Women. (1998). *Separated by sex: A critical look at single-sex education for girls.* Washington, DC: AAUW Educational Foundation.

American Association of University Women. (2001, Summer). *AAUW in action: American Association of University Women national leadership publication.* Washington, DC: Author.

American Association of University Women. (2006). *Drawing the line: Sexual harassment on campus.* Washington, DC: Author.

Anderson, K., & Miller, E. D. (1997). Gender and student evaluations of teaching. *PS: Political Sciences and Politics, 30,* 216–219.

Arbuckle, J., & Williams, B. D. (2003). Students' perceptions of expressiveness: Age and gender effects on teacher evaluations. *Sex Roles, 49,* 507–516.

Attwood, R. (2009, June 18–24). Lecturers talk of students' "shocking" abuse. *Times Higher Education,* pp. 10–11.

Bachen, C. M., McLoughlin, M. M., & Garcia, S. S. (1999). Assessing the role of gender in college students' evaluations of faculty. *Communication Education, 48,* 193–210.

Baker-Sperry, L., & Grauerholz, I. (2003). The pervasiveness and persistence of the feminine beauty ideal in children's fairy tales. *Gender and Society, 17,* 711–726.

Bartlett, T. (2008, May 9). The manliest campus in America. *The Chronicle of Higher Education,* pp. A1, A7.

Basow, S. A. (1998). Student evaluations: The role of gender bias and teaching styles. In L. H. Collins, J. C. Chrisler, & K. Quina (Eds.), *Arming Athena: Career strategies for women in academe* (pp. 135–156). Thousand Oaks, CA: Sage.

Basow, S. A. (2000). Best and worst professors: Gender patterns in students' choices. *Sex Roles, 43,* 407–417.

Basow, S. A., Phelan, J., & Capotosto, L. (2006). Gender patterns in college students' choices of their best and worst professors. *Psychology of Women Quarterly, 30,* 25–35.

Basow, S. A., & Silberg, N. T. (1987). Student evaluations of college professors: Are female and male professors rated differently? *Journal of Educational Psychology, 29,* 308–314.

Belenky, M., Clinchy, B., Goldberger, N., & Tarule, J. (1986). *Women's ways of knowing.* New York: Basic.

Benson, K. (1984). Comment on Crocker's "An analysis of university definitions of sexual harassment." *Signs, 9,* 516–519.

Berryman-Fink, C. (1993). Preventing sexual harassment through male-female communication training. In G. L. Kreps (Ed.), *Sexual harassment: Communication implications.* (pp. 267–280). Cresskill, NJ: Hampton.

Bottigheimer, R. B. (1986). Silenced women in the Grimms' tales: The "fit" between fairy tales and society in their historical context. In R. B. Bottigheimer (Ed.), *Fairy tales and society: Illusion, allusion, and paradigm* (pp. 115–132). Philadelphia: University of Pennsylvania Press.

Bowker, J. K., & Regan Dunkin, P. (1992). Enacting feminism in the teaching of communication. In L. A. M. Perry, L. H. Turner, & H. M. Sterk (Eds.), *Constructing and reconstructing gender: The links among communication, language, and gender* (pp. 261–268). Albany: State University of New York Press.

Brooks, V. (1982). Sex differences in student dominance behavior in female and male professors' classrooms. *Sex Roles, 8,* 683–690.

Brophy, J. E. (1983). Research on the self-fulfilling prophecy and teacher expectations. *Journal of Educational Psychology, 75,* 631–661.

Brophy, J. E. (1985). Interactions of male and female students with male and female teachers. In L. C. Wilkinson & C. B. Marrett (Eds.), *Gender influence in classroom interaction* (pp. 115–142). Orlando, FL: Academic.

Brule, N. L. (2008). *"Sleeping Beauty* gets a makeover": Using the retelling of fairytales to create an awareness of hegemonic norms and the social construction of value. *Communication Teacher, 22,* 71–75.

Buzzanell, P. M. (2004). Revisiting sexual harassment in academe. In P. M. Buzzanell, H. Sterk, & L. H. Turner (Eds.), *Gender in applied communication contexts* (pp. 25–46). Thousand Oaks, CA: Sage.

Carroll, L., & Ellis, K. (1989). Faculty attitudes toward sexual harassment: Survey results, survey process. *Initiatives, 52,* 35–41.

Centra, J. A., & Gaubatz, N. B. (2000). Is there gender bias in student evaluations of teaching? *Journal of Higher Education, 71,* 17.

A chilly climate on the campuses: A forum. (2005, September 9). *The Chronicle of Higher Education,* pp. B7–B13.

Chyng Feng Sun, K., & Scharrer, E. (2004). Staying true to Disney: College students' resistance to criticism of *The Little Mermaid. Communication Review, 7,* 35–55.

Condravy, J., Skirboll, E., & Taylor, R. (1998). Faculty perceptions of classroom gender dynamics. *Women & Language, 21,* 18–27.

Cooper, P. J. (1987). Sex role stereotypes of stepparents in children's literature. In L. P. Stewart & S. Ting-Toomey (Eds.), *Communication, gender, and sex roles in diverse interaction contexts* (pp. 61–82). Norwood, NJ: Ablex.

Cooper, P. J. (1991). *Women and power in the Caldecott and Newbery Winners.* Paper presented at the meeting of the Central States Communication Association, Chicago, IL.

Cooper, H., & Good, T. (1983). *Pygmalion grows up: Studies in the expectation communication process.* New York: Longman.

Corbett, C., Hill, C., & St. Rose, A. (2008). *Where the girls are: The facts about gender equity in education.* Washington, DC: American Association of University Women.

Costa, P., Jr., Terracciano, A., & McCrae, R. R. (2001). Gender differences in personality traits across cultures: Robust and surprising findings. *Journal of Personality and Cognition, 81,* 322–331.

Das, M., & Das, H. (2001). Business students' perceptions of best university professors: Does gender role matter? *Sex Roles, 45,* 665–676.

DeSouza, E., & Fansler, A. G. (2003). Contrapower sexual harassment: A survey of students and faculty members. *Sex Roles, 48,* 529–542.

Diekman, A. B., & Murnen, S. K. (2004). Learning to be little women and little men: The inequitable gender equality of nonsexist children's literature. *Sex Roles, 50,* 373–386.

Dougherty, D. S. (2001). Sexual harassment as [dys]functional process: A feminist standpoint analysis. *Journal of Applied Communication Research, 29,* 372–402.

Downey, S. D. (1996). Feminine empowerment in Disney's *Beauty and the Beast. Women's Studies in Communication, 19,* 185–212.

Dundes, L. (2001). Disney's modern heroine Pocahontas: Revealing age-old gender stereotypes and role discontinuity under a facade of liberation. *The Social Sciences Journal, 38,* 353–365.

Eckes, S. (2006). Reducing peer sexual harassment in schools. *The Educational Digest, 71,* 36–40.

Fandt, P. M., & Stevens, G. E. (1991). Evaluation bias in the business classroom: Evidence relating to the effects of previous experiences. *Journal of Psychology, 125,* 469–477.

Feldman, K. A. (1992). College students' views of male and female college teachers: Part I. Evidence from the social laboratory and experiments. *Research in Higher Education, 33,* 317–375.

Feldman, K. A. (1993). College students' views of male and female college teachers: Part II. Evidence from students' evaluations of their classroom teachers. *Research in Higher Education, 34,* 151–191.

Ferber, M. A., & Huber, J. A. (1975). Sex of student and instructor: A study of student bias. *American Journal of Sociology, 80,* 949–963.

Fineran, S., & Bolen, R. M. (2006). Risk factors for peer sexual harassment in schools. *Journal of Interpersonal Violence, 21,* 1169–1190.

Fitzgerald, L. F., Swan, S., & Magley, V. J. (1997). But was it really sexual harassment? Legal, behavioral, and psychological definitions of the workplace victimization of women. In W. O'Donohue (Ed.), *Sexual harassment: Theory, research, and treatment* (pp. 5–28). Boston: Allyn & Bacon.

Fox, R. F., & Gerbner, G. (2000). *Harvesting minds: How TV commercials control kids.* New York: Praeger.

Franke, A. H. (2008, November 28). New lessons in dealing with sexual harassment. *The Chronicle of Higher Education,* p. A80.

Freeman, H. (1994). Student evaluations of college instructors: Effects of type of course taught, instructor gender and gender role, and student gender. *Journal of Educational Psychology, 86,* 627–630.

Friedman, E. G. (2008, Fall). Out-of-the-box education. *Ms.,* 59.

Geist, P., & Townsley, N. (1997, November). *"Swept under the rug" and other disappearing acts: Legitimate concerns for university's sexual harassment policy and procedures.* Paper presented at the meeting of the National Communication Association, Chicago, IL.

Gerbner, G., Gross, L., Morgan, M., & Signorielli, N. (1980). The "mainstreaming" of America: Violence profile no. 11. *Journal of Communication, 30,* 10–29.

Gillam, K., & Wooden, S. R. (2008). Post-princess models of gender: The new man in Disney/Pixar. *Journal of Popular Film and Television, 36,* 2–8.

Gilligan, C. (1982). *In a different voice.* Cambridge: Harvard University Press.

Gooden, A. M., & Gooden, M. A. (2001). Gender representation in notable children's picture books: 1955–1999. *Sex Roles, 45,* 89–101.

Gorney, C. (1999, July 4). Sex patrol: Fighting harassment in schools. The *New York Times Magazine,* as in *Corpus Christi Caller Times,* pp. A15, A16, A17, A18.

Grauerholz, E. (1989). Sexual harassment of women professors by students: Exploring the dynamics of power, authority, and gender in a university setting. *Sex Roles, 21,* 789–801.

Greene, J., & Stockard, J. (2010). Is the academic climate chilly? The views of women academic chemists. *Journal of Chemical Education, 87,* 381–385.

Grube, B., & Lens, V. (2003). Student-to-student harassment: The impact of *Davis* v. *Monroe. Children and Schools, 25,* 173–185.

Hall, R., & Sandler, B. (1982). *The classroom climate: A chilly one for women?* Washington, DC: Project on the Status and Education of Women, Association of American Colleges.

Hall, R. M., & Sandler, B. R. (1984). *Out of the classroom: A chilly campus climate for women?*

Washington, DC: Project on the Status and Education of Women, Association of American Colleges.

Haase, D. (Ed.). (2004). *Fairy tales and feminism: New approaches.* Detroit, MI: Wayne State University Press.

Hamilton, M. C., Anderson, D., Broaddus, M., & Young, K. (2006). Gender stereotyping and under-representation of female characters in 200 popular children's picture books: A twenty-first century update. *Sex Roles, 55,* 557–565.

Hargett, J. (1999). Students' perceptions of male and female instructors' level of immediacy and teacher credibility. *Women & Language, 22,* 46.

Harmon, M. R. (2000). Gender/language subtexts as found in literature anthologies: Mixed messages, stereotypes, silence, erasure. In M. J. Hardman & A. Taylor (Eds.), *Hearing many voices* (pp. 75–85). Cresskill, NJ: Hampton.

Harrington, L. (2004). Peer sexual harassment: Protect your students and yourself. *The Delta Kappa Gamma Bulletin, 71,* 31–35.

Heintz, K. E. (1987). An examination of sex and occupational-role presentations of female characters in children's picture books. *Women's Studies in Communication, 11,* 67–78.

Henneberg, S. (2010). Moms do badly, but grandmas do worse: The nexus of sexism and ageism in children's classics. *Journal of Aging Studies, 24,* 125–134.

Hill, C., Corbett, C., & St. Rose, A. (2010). *Why so few? Women in science, technology, engineering, and mathematics: Executive summary.* Washington, DC: American Association of University Women.

hooks, b. (2000). *Feminism is for everybody.* Cambridge, MA: South End.

"Hostile environment" is found at academies. (2005, September 9). *The Chronicle of Higher Education,* p. A36.

Hughes, J. O., & Sandler, B. R. (1988). *Peer harassment: Hassles for women on campus.* Washington, DC: Project on the Status and Education of Women, Association of American Colleges.

Humphrey, M. (2005, Fall). Outside Neverland: Female writers reinvent *Peter Pan. Bitch,* 76–81.

Ivy, D. K., & Hamlet, S. (1996). College students and sexual dynamics: Two studies of peer sexual harassment. *Communication Education, 45,* 149–166.

Jaschik, S. (1995, April 21). Court orders Citadel to admit woman, but provides escape clause. *The Chronicle of Higher Education,* p. A37.

Jetter, A. (2001, March). The feminists Grimm. *Ms.*, 81–83.

June, A. W. (2009, February 20). Online programs to stop sexual harassment: Easy to use but not always enough. *The Chronicle of Higher Education*, pp. A10–A13.

Karniol, R. R., & Gal-Disegni, M. (2009). The impact of gender-fair versus gender-stereotyped basal readers on 1st-grade children's gender stereotypes: A natural experiment. *Journal of Research in Childhood Education, 23*, 411–420.

Karp, D. A., & Yoels, W. C. (1977). The college classroom: Some observations on the meanings of student participation. *Sociology & Social Research, 60*, 421–439.

Kaschak, E. (1978). Sex bias in student evaluations of college professors. *Psychology of Women Quarterly, 2*, 235–243.

Kimmich, A. (2009, Fall). The kid wimps out. *Ms.*, 50–51.

Kopp, L. K., & Farr, T. (1999, October 15). *Is the chilly classroom climate still a factor for women as we close the 20th century?* Paper presented at the meeting of the Organization for the Study of Communication, Language, and Gender, Wichita, KS.

Kramer, L. (2005). *The sociology of gender: A brief introduction* (2nd ed.). Los Angeles: Roxbury.

Krolokke, C. (1998). Women professors' assertive-empathic and non-assertive communication in sexual harassment situations. *Women's Studies in Communication, 21*, 91–103.

Krupnick, C. (1985). Women and men in the classroom: Inequality and its remedies. *Teaching & Learning: Journal of the Harvard Danforth Center, 1*, 18–25.

Lamb, S., & Brown, L. M. (2006). *Packaging girlhood: Rescuing our daughters from marketers' schemes.* New York: St. Martin's Press.

Lamb, S., Brown, L. M., & Tappan, M. (2009). *Packaging boyhood: Saving our sons from superheroes, slackers, and other media stereotypes.* New York: St. Martin's Press.

Lampman, C., Phelps, A., Bancroft, S., & Beneke, M. (2009). Contrapower harassment in academia: A survey of faculty experience with student incivility, bullying, and sexual attention. *Sex Roles, 60*, 331–346.

Larche, D. (1985). *Father Gander.* New York: Methuen.

Larche, D. (1990). *Father Gander's nursery rhymes for the nineteen nineties: The alternative Mother Goose.* Cambridge, UK: Oleander.

LaRocca, M. A., & Kromrey, J. D. (1999). The perception of sexual harassment in higher education: Impact of gender and attractiveness. *Sex Roles, 40*, 921–940.

Lederman, D. (1996, January 26). Supreme Court hears arguments on VMI admissions policy. *The Chronicle of Higher Education*, p. A28.

Lombardo, J. P., & Tocci, M. E. (1979). Attribution of positive and negative characteristics of instructors as a function of attractiveness, sex of instructor, and sex of subject. *Perceptual and Motor Skills, 48*, 491–494.

Loredo, C., Reid, A., & Deaux, K. (1995). Judgments and definitions of sexual harassment by high school students. *Sex Roles, 32*, 29–45.

Marsh, H. W., & Roche, L. A. (1997). Making students' evaluations of teaching effectiveness effective: The critical issues of validity, bias, and utility. *American Psychologist, 52*, 1187–1197.

Matchen, J., & DeSouza, E. (2000). The sexual harassment of faculty members by students. *Sex Roles, 41*, 295–306.

McKinney, K. (1990a). Sexual harassment of university faculty by colleagues and students. *Sex Roles, 23*, 421–438.

McKinney, K. (1990b). Attitudes toward sexual harassment and perceptions of blame: Views of male and female graduate students. *Free Inquiry in Creative Sociology, 18*, 73–76.

Menzel, K., & Carrell, L. (1999). The impact of gender and immediacy on willingness to talk and perceived learning. *Communication Education, 48*, 31–40.

Miller, J., & Chamberlin, M. (2000). Women are teachers, men are professors: A study of student perceptions. *Teaching Sociology, 28*, 283–298.

Mohipp, C., & Senn, C. Y. (2008). Graduate students' perceptions of contrapower sexual harassment. *Journal of Interpersonal Violence, 73*, 1258–1276.

Mongeau, P. A., & Blalock, J. (1994). Student evaluations of instructor immediacy and sexually harassing behaviors: An experimental investigation. *Journal of Applied Communication Research, 22*, 256–272.

Morris, L. K., & Daniel, L. G. (2008). Perceptions of a chilly climate: Differences in traditional and non-traditional majors for women. *Research in Higher Education, 49*, 256–273.

Mortenson, T. G. (2008, June 6). Where the boys were: Women outnumber them in colleges and the work force, and too many men are failing to keep up. *The Chronicle of Higher Education*, p. A31.

NBC Nightly News. (2006, October 25). Television broadcast.

NBC Nightly News. (2010, March 17). Television broadcast.

Newman, L. (2009). *Daddy, papa, and me.* New York: Tricycle Press.

Newman, L., & Thompson, C. (2009). *Mommy, mama, and me.* New York: Tricycle Press.

Nilges, L. M., & Spencer, A. F. (2002). The pictorial representation of gender and physical activity level in Caldecott Medal winning children's literature (1940–1999). *Sports, Education, & Society, 7,* 135–150.

O'Connor, K., & Yanus, A. B. (2009). The chilly climate continues: Defrosting the gender divide in political science and politics. *Journal of Political Science Education, 5,* 108–118.

Oelschlager, V. (2010). *A tale of two daddies.* Akron, OH: Vanita Books.

Orenstein, C. (2003). *Little Red Riding Hood uncloaked: Sex, morality, and the evolution of a fairy tale.* New York: Basic.

Orenstein, P. (2006). Shortchanging girls: Gender socialization in schools. In P. J. Dubeck & D. Dunn (Ed.), *Workplace/women's place* (3rd ed., pp. 28–36). Los Angeles: Roxbury.

Ormerod, A. J., Collinsworth, L. L., & Perry, L. A. (2008). Critical climate: Relations among sexual harassment, climate, and outcomes for high school girls and boys. *Psychology of Women Quarterly, 32,* 113–125.

Parr, T. (2003). *The family book.* New York: Little, Brown Books for Young Readers.

Peterson, S., & Lach, M. (1990). Gender stereotypes in children's books: Their prevalence and influence on cognitive and affective development. *Gender & Education, 2,* 185–197.

Ragan, K. (Ed.). (2000). *Fearless girls, wise women, and beloved sisters: Heroines in folk tales from around the world.* New York: W. W. Norton & Co.

Ranney, F. J. (2004). Assigning responsibility for workplace behavior: Sexual harassment as a form of organizational communication. In P. M. Backlund & M. R. Williams (Eds.)., *Readings in gender communication* (pp. 268–279). Belmont, CA: Thomson/Wadsworth.

Rich, A. (1979). *On lies, secrets, and silence: Selected prose 1966–1978.* New York: Norton.

Rospenda, K. M., Richman, J. A., & Nawyn, A. J. (1998). Doing power: The confluence of gender, race, and class in contrapower sexual harassment. *Gender and Society, 12,* 40–60.

Russ, T. L., Simonds, C. J., & Hunt, S. K. (2002). Coming out in the classroom . . . an occupational hazard?: The influence of sexual orientation on teacher credibility and perceived student learning. *Communication Education, 51,* 311–324.

Sadker, M., & Sadker, D. (1994). *Failing at fairness: How America's schools cheat girls.* New York: Charles Scribner's Sons.

Sadker, D. M., & Zittleman, K. (2007). Practical strategies for detecting and correcting gender bias in your classroom. In D. M. Sadker & E. S. Silber (Eds.), *Gender in the classroom: Foundations, skills, methods, and strategies across the curriculum* (pp. 259–275). Mahwah, NJ: Erlbaum.

Salter, D. W. (2003). Exploring the "chilly classroom" phenomenon as interactions between psychological and environmental types. *Journal of College Student Development, 44,* 110–121.

Sandler, B. R. (1991). Women faculty at work in the classroom, or why it still hurts to be a woman in labor. *Communication Education, 40,* 6–15.

Sandler, B. R. (1997). Student-to-student sexual harassment. In B. R. Sandler & R. J. Shoop (Eds.), *Sexual harassment on campus: A guide for administrators, faculty, and students* (pp. 50–65). Boston: Allyn & Bacon.

Sandler, B. R. (2005). *Student-to-student sexual harassment K–12: Strategies and solutions for educators to use in the classroom, school, and community.* New York: Rowman & Littlefield.

Sandler, B. R., & Hall, R. M. (1986). *The campus climate revisited: Chilly for women faculty, administrators, and graduate students.* Washington, DC: Project on the Status and Education of Women, Association of American Colleges.

Sandler, B. R., Silverberg, L. A., & Hall, R. M. (1996). *The chilly classroom climate: A guide to improve the education of women.* Washington, DC: National Association of Women in Education.

Scarduzio, J. A., & Geist-Martin, P. (2008). Making sense of fractured identities: Male professors' narratives of sexual harassment. *Communication Monographs, 75,* 369–395.

Schulze, E., & Tomal, A. (2006). The chilly classroom: Beyond gender. *College Teaching, 54,* 263–269.

Seals, B. (1997). Faculty-to-faculty sexual harassment. In B. R. Sandler & R. J. Shoop (Eds.), *Sexual harassment on campus: A guide for administrators, faculty, and students* (pp. 66–84). Boston: Allyn & Bacon.

Simonds, C. J., & Cooper, P. J. (2001). Communication and gender in the classroom. In L. P. Arliss & D. J. Borisoff (Eds.), *Women and men communicating: Challenges and changes* (2nd ed., pp. 232–253). Prospect Heights, IL: Waveland.

Siskind, T., & Kearns, S. (1997). Gender bias in the evaluation of female faculty at The Citadel: A qualitative analysis. *Sex Roles, 37,* 495–525.

Smith, S. W., Yoo, J. H., Farr, A. C., Salmon, C. T., & Miller, V. D. (2007). The influence of student sex and instructor sex on student ratings of instructors: Results from a college of communication. *Women's Studies in Communication, 30,* 64–77.

Stein, N. (2007). Bullying, harassment, and violence among students. *Radical Teacher, 80,* 30–35.

Steineger, M. (1993, September). Gender bias persists in texts and literature. *Northwest report: The challenge of sex equity.* Portland, OR: Northwest Regional Educational Laboratory.

Sternglanz, S. H., & Lyberger-Ficek, S. (1977). Sex differences in student-teacher interactions in the college classroom. *Sex Roles, 3,* 345–352.

Stone, M., & Couch, S. (2004). Peer sexual harassment among high school students: Teachers' attitudes, perceptions, and responses. *The High School Journal, 88,* 1–13.

Sumera, L. (2009). The mask of beauty: Masquerade theory and Disney's *Beauty and the Beast. Quarterly Review of Film and Video, 26,* 40–46.

Terrance, C., Logan, A., & Peters, D. (2004). Perceptions of peer sexual harassment among high school students. *Sex Roles, 51,* 479–490.

Thorne, B. (1979). *Claiming verbal space: Women, speech, and language in college classrooms.* Paper presented at the Conference on Educational Environments and the Undergraduate Woman, Wellesley College, Wellesley, MA.

Treichler, P. A., & Kramarae, C. (1983). Women's talk in the ivory tower. *Communication Quarterly, 31,* 118–132.

Vinnedge, M. (1996, December 29). Historical novel series aimed at girl readers. *Corpus Christi Caller Times,* p. G13.

Warrington, M., & Younger, M. (2000). The other side of the gender gap. *Gender & Education, 12,* 493–508.

Wasburn, M. H. (2004). Is your classroom woman-friendly? *College Teaching, 52,* 156–158.

White, H. (1986). Damsels in distress: Dependency themes in fiction for children and adolescents. *Adolescence, 21,* 251–256.

Wilson, R. (2009, February 20). Notoriety yields to tragedy in Iowa sexual-harassment cases. *The Chronicle of Higher Education,* pp. A1, A8.

Wood, J. T., & Lenze, L. F. (1991). Strategies to enhance gender sensitivity in communication education. *Communication Education, 40,* 16–21.

Zipes, J. (1994). *Fairy tale as myth/myth as fairy tale.* Lexington: University Press of Kentucky.

Zipes, J. (1995). Breaking the Disney spell. In E. Bell, L. Haas, & L. Sells (Eds.), *From mouse to mermaid: The politics of film, gender, and culture* (pp. 21–42). Bloomington: Indiana University Press.

Zipes, J. (1997). *Happily ever after: Fairy tales, children, and the culture industry.* New York: Routledge.

Zipes, J. (2002). *Breaking the magic spell: Radical theories of folk and fairy tales.* Lexington: University Press of Kentucky.

Zipes, J. (2006). *Why fairy tales stick: The evolution and relevance of a genre.* New York: Routledge.

Zirkel, P. A. (1995). Student-to-student sexual harassment. *Phi Delta Kappan, 76,* 648–650.

AUTHOR INDEX

SUBJECT INDEX